OPERATION AND MODELING
OF THE MOS TRANSISTOR

McGraw-Hill Series in Electrical Engineering

Consulting Editor
Stephen W. Director, *Carnegie-Mellon University*

CIRCUITS AND SYSTEMS
COMMUNICATIONS AND SIGNAL PROCESSING
CONTROL THEORY
ELECTRONICS AND ELECTRONIC CIRCUITS
POWER AND ENERGY
ELECTROMAGNETICS
COMPUTER ENGINEERING
INTRODUCTORY
RADAR AND ANTENNAS
VLSI

Previous Consulting Editors
Ronald N. Bracewell, Colin Cherry, James F. Gibbons, Willis W. Harman,
Hubert Heffner, Edward W. Herold, John G. Linvill, Simon Ramo,
Ronald A. Rohrer, Anthony E. Siegman, Charles Susskind,
Frederick E. Terman, John G. Truxal, Ernst Weber, and John R. Whinnery

OPERATION
AND MODELING
OF THE
MOS TRANSISTOR

Yannis P. Tsividis

Department of Electrical Engineering
Columbia University

McGraw-Hill Book Company

New York   St. Louis   San Francisco   Auckland   Bogotá   Hamburg
Johannesburg   London   Madrid   Mexico   Milan   Montreal   New Delhi
Panama   Paris   São Paulo   Singapore   Sydney   Tokyo   Toronto

This book was set in Times Roman by Intercontinental Photocomposition Limited.
The editor was Sanjeev Rao;
the production supervisor was Leroy A. Young;
the cover was designed by Fern Logan.
Project supervision was done by The Total Book.
R.R. Donnelley & Sons Company was printer and binder.

OPERATION AND MODELING OF THE MOS TRANSISTOR

234567890 DOCDOC 89210987

ISBN 0-07-065381-X

Library of Congress Cataloging-in-Publication Data

Tsividis, Yannis.
    Operation and modeling of the MOS transistor.

    (McGraw-Hill series in electrical engineering.
VLSI, electronics, and electronic circuits)
    Includes bibliographies.
    I. Metal oxide semiconductors--Mathematical models.
I. Title.   II. Series.
TK7871.99.M44T77 1987   621.3815′22   86 − 27389
ISBN 0-07-065381-X

A mi Puchunga

CONTENTS

PREFACE

The MOS transistor was conceived in the thirties, was developed for practical use in the sixties, and has invaded our daily lives in the seventies and eighties. Much of what is referred to as "high tech" today would not be possible if it were not for this device. The aim in writing this book was to provide a unified treatment of many phenomena responsible for the operation of the MOS transistor, and to show how such phenomena can be modeled analytically. The author believes that the following are important features of the book:

- The book starts with basic concepts. Readers should be able to follow even if they had no prior exposure to the device. The discussions of these concepts are often from a perspective different from the one usually taken, thus making them interesting reading even to those with prior exposure.
- Every effort has been made to give the subject a careful treatment. The reader may at times get the feeling that the author is "splitting hairs." The author would rather be accused of this than fudge. The MOS transistor is a device so complex that, once one has decided to fudge, things grow out of hand very quickly, and one ends up with a hodgepodge of careless derivations, conflicting models, and a lot of patchwork. This has been avoided at all costs. Also, the reason for hair-splitting at some points can only be appreciated further along in the book, where those "too fine" details can be seen to make a lot of difference. The use of one name for several quantities, common in some of the literature, is carefully avoided. For example, at least four distinct quantities encountered in MOS transistor work are described by using the single name "threshold voltage." Although the reader is amply warned of this practice, the practice itself is avoided in this book.
- The emphasis is on principles. At the same time, to illustrate these principles, relevant models are extensively derived and discussed. Thus, physics and modeling are discussed in parallel throughout the book.
- Analytical results are derived in a logical manner after carefully stating the assumptions made. Empirical modeling is avoided as much as possible.

However, there are phenomena for which the only analytical results available are empirical or semiempirical. Such results are presented for completeness after pointing out the necessary hand-waving behind them.

- A great deal of emphasis is placed on providing intuition for the various phenomena discussed. It is rather hopeless to attempt working with a device as complex as the MOS transistor relying only on analytical relations. The emphasis on intuition has made lengthy discussions necessary.

- The pace is unhurried. The author believes that this actually makes it possible to study the material faster. Thus, whereas the treatment of a given topic may be long in terms of number of pages, it actually should take less time to comprehend it, both because of the detailed derivations and the intuitive discussions. At times, the reader may get the feeling of *déja vu*, since some points are repeated more than once to make sure they are not missed, especially if the reading of the topics is done out of sequence. In general, the book is written in the style in which the author would like to have any new subject presented to him. He would very much like to see the new subject "beaten to death," presented with several points of view to increase perspective and with a significant amount of repetition. The author has been in the past grateful for treatments of this type and never felt offended by this style. If the reader happens to be "faster" than the author in this respect, he or she can easily skip some of the discussions.

- The units used are those that make most sense for discussing the MOS transistor. This breaks with common practice and will certainly be questioned. However, it was felt that there exist several advantages in a convenient and consistent system of units. For example, length is given in this book only in μm, in contrast to using μm for gate lengths and Å or nm for oxide thickness. The unit of length is kept as μm even when length is encountered in the dimensions of other quantities; for example, volume is given in μm^3 and electric field in V/μm. Apart from consistency, there is here another advantage, i.e., use of appropriate units can help in providing a better "feeling" for the device. Thus, for example, when one reads that velocity saturation is reached, say, at about 3 V/μm, one can relate immediately to this number in terms of commonly used channel lengths and voltages. It automatically registers in the mind that a modern, 1-μm-long transistor with a drain-source voltage of 3 V will show signs of velocity saturation. If one reads that the substrate doping concentration is, say, $1,000$ μm^{-3}, then one can almost "see" $1,000$ atoms in a 1-μm-deep region below a 1-μm $\times$ 1-μm gate of a modern device. Repeated exposure to such numbers can help one to get a quantitative feeling without one even realizing it. On the other hand, this would be more difficult if, say, the above numbers were given as 2×10^4 V/cm and 10^{14} cm^{-3}, since one is not likely to stop reading every once in a while to think about these numbers. Readers accustomed to commonly used units will hopefully, after some reading, agree with the author on this point. For quick conversions between units, a conversion table is provided on the inside cover.

● This book is *not* a survey. In fact, a conscious effort has been made to avoid making it one. A well-connected set of topics has been chosen, and most of these are discussed in significant detail. Emphasis is placed on phenomena encountered in well designed devices operating within their normal voltage ranges. Undesirable phenomena such as breakdown, punch-through, and hot-electron effects are only briefly described. Except for special applications, the modeling of such phenomena is mostly important in order to know how to avoid them at the device design level, an endeavor which is not addressed in this book. In addition, such phenomena are not easy to treat analytically, and a fair treatment of them would require a survey of a large number of numerical or semiempirical approaches. For similar reasons, numerical techniques and two- or three-dimensional analyses are not covered (apart from the pseudo-two-dimensional approaches used in modeling short- and narrow-channel effects). However, the references provided on both the subjects that are covered in detail and those that are not are extensive. These references have been selected because of one or more of the following attributes:

1. They are technically important.
2. They are widely referenced in the literature.
3. They have historical significance.
4. They are part of controversy that has not yet been resolved.

● Most of the homework problems fall in one of the following categories:

1. They sketch additional modeling ideas not in the main text and encourage the reader to try them out.
2. They compare several models introduced in the text.
3. They ask for computations and plots to help provide a quantitative feeling and investigate various properties.
4. They ask for detailed derivations which were sketched in the main text, but which were not shown in detail in order to avoid distraction from the main points.

The book is written for use in a senior or first-year graduate course and is well-suited for self-study by practicing engineers. It is felt that electrical engineering students have much to gain from a course devoted to the subject. The MOS transistor is the dominant VLSI device. A course devoted to it is, of course, invaluable to those planning a career in device physics and modeling. For such people, the standard courses on semiconductor devices usually cover too many different devices to do justice to any one of them, and do not present the intricacies and tradeoffs involved in a detailed modeling effort. The value of a course devoted to the MOS transistor is also very high for those who want to use the device to design state-of-the-art circuits. Integrated-circuit designers have the opportunity to suit devices to circuit needs, and they can do this most intelligently if they really understand the workings of the devices. One can, of course, design systems by using predesigned circuit building blocks, or "standard cells," as black boxes if truly high performance is not important. But when state-of-the-art performance is a must, which it often is in this competitive field, one has to consider device details.

The material provided in this book should enable one to develop better models than some of those currently found in popular circuit simulator programs. Many circuit designers in the industry spend endless hours trying to "interpret" strange circuit simulation results which are largely due to modeling inadequacies. This problem has persisted in part because of lack of a common language between circuit designers and device-modeling people, which would allow the former to communicate better their needs to the latter. It is hoped that this book will contribute to bridging this gap, and that it will even allow circuit designers to improve the models they use.

A list of chapters, and the features in each one of them, is given below.

Chapter 1: Semiconductors, Contacts, and the PN Junction

All preliminary material necessary for the understanding of MOS structures is given here. This material is important to the newcomer, but part of it should also make interesting reading for those with some previous exposure to basics. This includes the material on contact potentials, which is used to advantage in the following chapter.

Chapter 2: The Two-Terminal MOS Structure

Here the reader will find a treatment of the MOS structure with gate and substrate terminals only. Concepts not directly related to the presence of the source and drain in the MOS transistor are treated here. The regions of weak, moderate, and strong inversion are all introduced in this chapter. Potentials are used throughout rather than energy bands. This is not only common in current literature but also helps provide rigorous straightforward derivations. Consider, for example, the well-known term ϕ_{MS} appearing in the expression for the flat-band voltage. In energy band treatments it is often not clear where in the MOS structure this potential actually resides. In this book, it is made evident that ϕ_{MS} is nothing but a contact potential, and the place(s) where it resides are made obvious. Also, its presence in the flat-band voltage expression is rigorously justified through Kirchhoff's voltage law.

Chapter 3: The Three-Terminal MOS Structure

Here one more terminal is added to the structure of Chap. 2, to connect the inversion layer to the external world. MOS transistor concepts that are not directly related to current flow are presented in this chapter. This includes the important "substrate effect," which is amply treated.

Chapter 4: The Four-Terminal MOS Transistor

The four-terminal MOS transistor is obtained in this chapter by adding one terminal to the structure of Chap. 3. This device is now very easy to understand, based on the concepts already presented for the two- and three-terminal structures. This is the central chapter in the book. Four models are presented in detail:

1. A general charge sheet model, including drift and diffusion currents, valid in all regions of operation. Thanks to a simplified derivation, this material is brief but thorough.
2. The classical accurate strong-inversion model.
3. The simple, computationally efficient augmented quadratic model.
4. A weak-inversion model.

The models are extensively related to and/or compared to each other. Topics like effective mobility reduction, temperature effects, etc., are also included. The tradeoffs between accuracy and simplicity are pointed out throughout the chapter.

Chapter 5: Short-Channel and Narrow-Channel Effects

Here channel length modulation, velocity saturation, and effective threshold voltage are discussed for short-channel devices, and this is followed by a discussion of narrow-channel effects. An example of a model incorporating several of these effects is presented. Other "small-geometry" effects are considered and the topic of "scaling" is presented.

Chapter 6: MOS Transistors with Ion-Implanted Channels

In this chapter, implanted devices of two types are considered—those with implant of the same type as the substrate and those with implant of the opposite type. Several modes of operation are identified, and useful models for them are derived.

Chapter 7: The MOS Transistor in Dynamic Operation—Large-Signal Modeling

This chapter is largely devoted to charge modeling. The concept of quasi-static operation is carefully introduced, and general techniques for charge evaluation are presented, illustrated by charge computations for one representative model. Nonquasi-static analysis is then introduced.

Chapter 8: Small-Signal Modeling for Low and Medium Frequencies

The principles behind small-signal modeling are presented. The discussion is limited to quasi-static behavior. A useful small-signal model is developed for operation at low and medium frequencies. The subject of noise is introduced in the last section.

Chapter 9: High-Frequency Small-Signal models

In this chapter, two kinds of small-signal models are developed. First, complete quasi-static models are introduced, which differ from the models of Chap. 8 in that they include transcapacitors. The nature of these controversial elements is carefully discussed. Techniques are given for the rigorous development of equivalent-circuit topologies from a complete quasi-static description. Then, nonquasi-static models are introduced through a careful development of the transistor's "transmission line" equations, and a useful y-parameter model is derived for high-frequency applications. Chapters 8 and 9 put together concepts customarily discussed separately. It is shown that each level of modeling reduces to the next lower one if the frequency is sufficiently reduced.

Chapter 10: MOS Transistor Fabrication

This chapter treats the fabrication of MOS transistors in the context of integrated circuits. It has been written by an expert in the field, Dimitri Antoniadis of MIT. The chapter presents the basic fabrication steps, shows the structures resulting after each step, and discusses the aims of today's process engineering as well as the problems encountered on the way. The complex features of real devices can be appreciated in the detailed drawings provided.

The book concludes with 13 appendixes containing an introduction to energy band concepts, the basic laws of electrostatics as well as several general but complicated results which, it was felt, would distract if put in the main text. For the same reason, some material was put in fine print or in footnotes or, as already mentioned, was described in the statements of some homework problems. Such material includes certain fine details, alternate points of view, etc. To avoid distraction, it is probably best to ignore fine print footnotes, and appendixes during a first reading; the main text is self-contained. This material can always be consulted at a later time because its connection with specific points in the text is obvious. It should prove valuable for those interested in more details on certain topics, and for providing continuity with the technical literature.

For a one-semester course, a large number of possibilities exist in regard to the topics selected for coverage. Thus, for example, a course emphasizing general principles would cover Chaps. 1 through 3, Chap. 4 including a careful coverage of the general charge sheet model, Chaps. 7 through 9, and selected coverage of the general charge sheet model, Chaps. 7 through 9, and selected topics from other chapters, depending on interest and time available. On the other hand, a course with emphasis on practical models for digital circuit applications would cover Chaps. 1 through 4 (de-emphasizing the general charge sheet model and the weak-inversion region), Chaps. 5 through 7, Sec. 8.4, and Chap. 10. For parts that are to be de-emphasized, a quick qualitative coverage is possible, based mostly on the figures. The author will be happy to consider individual teaching needs and suggest specific course outlines to instructors who contact him.

The subject of this book is definitely among those that are best digested by doing. The homework problems should help to give a feeling for the kind of work involved in modeling. (Actually, some of the modeling ideas suggested in the homework problems are new and previously unpublished.) Students can be encouraged to write subroutines for the calculation of various quantities as they go along and to save them for later use. In this way, they will gradually build a library of useful subroutines that can be helpful not only in new homework assignments but also in a final project if one is assigned. It has been the author's experience that project work is invaluable, and the more extensive the project, the greater the benefits. The project can take the form of the implementation of models on the computer. Here it is not enough to just copy a model from the book into a computer program. One must worry about choosing the right models, appropriately combining them to form general models, ensuring continuity of calculated quantities with respect to all given parameters, etc. Some examples of projects follow.

- Write a computer program to evaluate the drain current of a device on a uniform substrate, including short- and narrow-channel effects. The current should be continuous with respect to any input parameter (voltage, geometric dimensions, etc.), and so should be the derivatives of the current with respect to each terminal voltage.
- Develop a computationally efficient technique for the evaluation of drain current in a long-channel device, valid in weak, moderate, and strong inversion. This will necessitate the development of efficient numerical techniques, because the general charge sheet approach, if unmodified, will lead to complex computations. Again, continuity of the current and its derivatives with respect to all parameters should be ensured.
- Develop a program for modeling ion-implanted devices in strong inversion, again ensuring continuity.
- Develop a program for the modeling of low- and medium-frequency small-signal parameters in strong inversion, paying special attention to the small-signal drain conductance in the saturation region. All small-signal parameters should be continuous with respect to all input parameters.
- Develop a program for the evaluation of all charges and small-signal capacitances. All these quantities should be continuous with respect to any input parameter.

• Develop a program for the extraction of parameter values to be used with a given model. The input to this program is assumed to consist of measured quantities.

In addition, certain long homework problems can easily be expanded to projects. In all cases, the value of the project, and the challenge in it, can be enhanced if the results are compared to measurements, obtained either in the lab or from the technical literature (the references provided should be very helpful in the latter case). Depending on the magnitude of effort foreseen, students can work separately or in teams.

The material in this book has been used at Columbia University by the author and by E. S. Yang in graduate courses devoted to MOS devices. It has also been used by D. Antoniadis for the MOS part of a graduate device course taught at MIT and in an intensive course on MOS transistors taught at DEC. The author has used parts of this material for the device portion of MOS circuits courses at Columbia University and at MIT as well as in short courses given at AT&T Bell Laboratories.

The author would like to acknowledge the contribution of many individuals in the shaping of this book. Many thanks are owed to Dimitri Antoniadis of MIT, a friend and collaborator, for writing the chapter on fabrication and for useful, lengthy discussions; to Mehran Bagheri of Bell Communications Research, some of whose results have been included in this book, and who read and commented on versions of the manuscript; to John Brews of AT&T Bell Laboratories and to Guido Masetti of the University of Bologna, for their extremely detailed comments on the manuscript; to Howard Card of the University of Manitoba, Renuka Jindal and Ed Nicolian of AT&T Bell Laboratories, Paul Diament and Ed Yang of Columbia University, Ping-Keung Ko of the University of California at Berkeley, Charlie Sodini of MIT, Don Ward of TMA, Andy Lish of Standard Microsystems, and Ranjit Mand of Toshiba for their comments on various chapters; and to the many students at Columbia University who found "bugs" in the manuscript and pointed them out to the author. Thanks are also owed to Jim Day, Gloria Gibson, Andy Russo, John Palasz, and David Vallancourt for text processing and for their patience through endless revisions.

Yannis P. Tsividis

CHAPTER

1

SEMICONDUCTORS, CONTACTS, AND THE *PN* JUNCTION

1.1 INTRODUCTION

The discussion of MOS devices in this book will be based on an understanding of a few basic concepts. These concepts have been collected in this chapter. We begin with an introduction to semiconductors and the evaluation of mobile carrier concentrations in them. We then consider the mechanisms of current transport in semiconductors. We continue with a discussion of contacts between different materials and the electrostatic potentials established in such contacts. One special contact, the *pn* junction, is the last topic of this chapter.

The material here is meant primarily as a review, but has been written in such a way that it can be understood even with no prior exposure to semiconductor electronics. A more detailed treatment can be found in several textbooks.[1-12]

1.2 SEMICONDUCTORS

Semiconductors derive their name from the fact that they can conduct current better than insulators, but not as well as conductors. The most widely used semiconductor material currently is silicon. The following discussion is focused on this material, but the qualitative arguments used are valid for other

1

semiconductors as well. Throughout this book we assume that no illumination, no radiation, no mechanical stress, and no magnetic fields are present, and that all points of the semiconductor are at the same temperature (understood to be room temperature unless indicated otherwise). Until further notice we also assume that the semiconductor material under discussion is self-contained, with no externally applied voltage or current, and that the electric field is zero in its environment (the assumption of zero electric field will be relaxed later on in this section). Finally, we will assume that all the above have been satisfied for a long time, so that conditions within the semiconductor have settled. The semiconductor is then said to be in equilibrium.

A pure (intrinsic) silicon crystal consists of an orderly three-dimensional array of atoms. This array is called the *crystal lattice* and contains 5×10^{10} atoms/μm^3.† The atoms of the lattice are held together by cooperating electrons, called *valence* electrons, which form *bonds* between the atoms. At absolute zero temperature, all such electrons are firmly held in place, and the total negative charge of the electrons in each atom is canceled by an opposite positive charge contained in the atom's nucleus. At higher temperatures, the lattice vibrates due to thermal energy; this "thermal motion" manages to set some of the electrons loose from the parent atom. These become *free electrons*, in the sense that they are now free to move about the crystal; the name "free electrons" is used to distinguish them from the rest of the electrons that are still part of the bonds between atoms and are not free to wander away. If the motion of free electrons is coordinated, it can cause the flow of current. Since the atoms from which these electrons broke loose were electrically neutral originally, they are now left with a net positive charge.

Consider now two neighboring atoms, A and B, and assume that an electron was set free from A; now there is an electron vacancy in A, so A is overall positive. A valence electron associated with atom B can move and fill this vacancy, thus creating now a vacancy in B. Notice that this electron moved from one bond to another, i.e., did not become free. The result of this valence electron transfer is that now A is neutral, whereas B has acquired a net positive charge. A valence electron from an atom C near B can now move, fill the vacancy in B, thus making B neutral and C positive, etc. We see that this mechanism transports a positive charge from A to B to C. Thus, we encounter *two* mechanisms for carrying charge around the semiconductor: (1) The motion of free electrons about the crystal lattice, each such electron carrying a negative charge; and (2) the motion of valence electrons from bond to bond, corresponding to a motion of "vacancies" (and associated positive charges) in the opposite direction. This second phenomenon can be described by modeling

---

† Commonly given as 5×10^{22} atoms/cm^3. A conversion table between units used in this book and commonly used units is provided in the inside cover. The reason for our choice of units in this book is discussed in the preface.

it as a motion of fictitious free particles, called *holes*, which carry a positive charge; each hole can be associated with one vacancy. If the charge of one electron is denoted by $-q$, then the charge of one hole is $+q$. As they wander around the lattice, a hole and a free electron can meet and annihilate each other; this is called "recombination." The picture of holes and free electrons provided here is sufficient for our purposes. It should be noted, however, that this picture is only a simple *model* for what is actually a combination of very complex physical phenomena.

In the pure semiconductor we are discussing, since each hole is created by the breaking loose of one electron which becomes free, there is an equal number of holes and free electrons. Thus, let the volume concentration of electrons and holes in the intrinsic material be denoted by n_i and p_i respectively. We will have

$$p_i = n_i \qquad (1.2.1)$$

The symbol n_i is often used to denote either concentration, and is referred to simply as the *intrinsic carrier concentration*. Its value corresponds to the equilibrium case where the rates of generation and recombination of electron-hole pairs are equal. At 300 K (degrees Kelvin) the value of n_i for silicon is approximately $0.0145 \, \mu m^{-3}$, meaning that roughly 15 electron-hole pairs are to be found in $1000 \, \mu m^3$ of the material. Since there are 5×10^{10} silicon atoms/μm^3, only three out of every 10^{13} of these atoms contribute one electron-hole pair! As might be expected from our previous discussion, n_i increases at higher temperatures.†

It is possible to make the number of free electrons different from that of the holes by introducing foreign atoms in the silicon crystal. Such atoms are called *impurities*, and the process of introducing them is called *doping*; doped semiconductors are referred to as *extrinsic semiconductors*. If it is desired to enhance the free-electron population, these foreign *dopant* atoms are chosen so as to have available for bonding one electron *more* than the number needed for perfect bonding in the silicon structure. Thus, these atoms form bonds with neighboring silicon atoms by using up all their valence electrons except one. The latter is very loosely held to the parent atom, and at room temperature the thermal vibration of the crystal lattice is enough to set it free. In contrast to the case of the intrinsic (pure) semiconductor, the departure of this electron leaves all valence bonds intact; hence it does not cause a vacancy in them, and thus it does not leave behind a hole. However, since the dopant atom was originally neutral, it is now left with a net positive charge, and is said to be *uncovered* or *ionized*. What we have described is shown in Fig. 1.1a. Each $-$ sign represents one free electron. Each circled $+$ sign represents a dopant atom which has lost

---

† An approximate formula for n_i in silicon as a function of the absolute temperature T is[1] $n_i = A_1 T^{3/2} \exp\dfrac{-A_2}{T}$, where $A_1 = 38{,}700 \, \text{K}^{-3/2} \, \mu m^{-3}$ and $A_2 = 7000 \, \text{K}$.

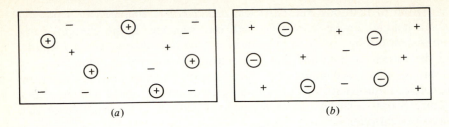

FIGURE 1.1
Free electrons, holes, and ionized dopant atoms in extrinsic silicon. (*a*) *n* type; (*b*) *p* type.

one electron, and thus is left with a net positive charge. The circle is used to indicate that this atom, being part of the crystal lattice, is *immobile* and therefore is not itself available for conduction. At room temperature practically all dopant atoms are ionized, and thus the number of free electrons created by such ionization is practically equal to the number of these atoms. As already mentioned, each such atom contributes one free electron without creating a hole. However, a few hole-electron pairs are created by the silicon atoms due to mechanisms already described for the intrinsic (pure) case; two such pairs are included in Fig. 1.1*a*.

Since the dopant atoms were chosen such at to "donate" one free electron to the silicon crystal, they are called *donors*. Donor materials commonly used to dope silicon are phosphorus, arsenic, and antimony. The donor atoms are introduced into the silicon in very minute amounts, but their concentration is usually chosen several orders of magnitude higher than n_i. For example, a donor atom concentration of 500 per μm^3 (written μm^{-3}) corresponds to one donor atom in every 10^8 silicon atoms. Nevertheless, this concentration is more than four orders of magnitude larger than the intrinsic carrier concentration at room temperature. The donor concentration will be assumed uniform unless stated otherwise. If all donor atoms are ionized, the number of free electrons they contribute is much higher than those contributed by the "intrinsic" mechanism discussed previously; hence, the concentration of free electrons, denoted by n_o, is approximately equal to the donor concentration, denoted by N_D:

$$n_o \approx N_D \tag{1.2.2}$$

With so many free electrons moving around the lattice, the chance of their encountering a hole in their way and filling it, or "recombining" with it, is significant; thus the concentration of holes, denoted by p_o, decreases compared to that in the intrinsic case. In fact, this chance of recombination is approximately proportional to n_o, and thus p_o decreases by the same factor that n_o has increased (compared to the intrinsic case). Hence, the product $n_o p_o$ remains the same as in the intrinsic case,[1] i.e., it is equal to n_i^2 as seen from (1.2.1). From this fact and (1.2.2) it follows that

$$p_o \approx \frac{n_i^2}{N_D} \tag{1.2.3}$$

If the doping concentration is very high (higher than about $10^6 \ \mu m^{-3}$), the above will not hold.[1, 5, 10] Semiconductors with very high doping concentration are called *degenerate*. Also, the above two relations will not hold at very low temperatures, where the dopant atoms will not all be ionized, or at very high temperatures, where n_i rises to the point that the assumption $N_D \gg n_i$ is not valid. Whenever the above relations are used, it will be implied that none of these extreme situations is in effect.

Because in a donor-doped semiconductor n is larger than p, the free electrons are called the *majority carriers* and the holes the *minority carriers*. Since the majority carriers carry a *negative* charge, a semiconductor doped with donor impurities is said to be *n type*.

Instead of increasing the electron population as described above, it is possible to increase the *hole* population by introducing into pure silicon impurity atoms which have one valence electron *less* than the number needed for complete bonding with neighboring silicon atoms. Thus, when each such atom attempts to form bonds, it will be short of one valence electron. It can then "steal" such an electron from a neighboring silicon atom, a process which has two effects. First, since the impurity atom was electrically neutral originally, now that is has acquired an extra electron, it will have a net negative charge; this charge is associated with one specific atom, and is thus immobile in the sense that it is not available for current conduction. Second, this stealing away one electron from a neighboring silicon atom left a valence electron vacancy in the latter, and thus created a hole; this hole can move around as it did in the case of the intrinsic (pure) crystal. Notice, however, that in contrast to the intrinsic case, the hole was created *without*, at the same time creating a free electron. Since the impurity atoms have stolen or "accepted" one valence electron from the silicon lattice, they are called *acceptors*; typical acceptor materials used to dope silicon are boron, gallium, and indium. Figure 1.1*b* illustrates the charges in a semiconductor doped with acceptor atoms. The + signs denote holes, the circled − signs denote ionized acceptor atoms (which are immobile), and the uncircled − signs denote free electrons (as in the case of donor-doped silicon, a few hole-free electron pairs are still created by silicon atoms due to the mechanisms described for the intrinsic case above). The total charge in Fig. 1.1*b* adds up to zero, indicating that the semiconductor is macroscopically neutral. Let the acceptor concentration (assumed uniform) be denoted by N_A, and assume that $N_A \gg n_i$ (a typical value of N_A is $10^3 \ \mu m^{-3}$). Assuming that practically all acceptor atoms are ionized, we will have, since each atom contributes one hole,

$$p_o \approx N_A \tag{1.2.4}$$

As in the case of donor-doped material, the product $n_o p_o$ remains equal to n_i^2; hence, we have

$$n_o \approx \frac{n_i^2}{N_A} \tag{1.2.5}$$

The above approximations will fail at extremely low or high temperatures or if the doping concentration is extremely high, as explained for the case of donor doping. In an acceptor-doped semiconductor, the holes are the "majority carriers," and the electrons the minority carriers. Since majority carriers carry a *positive* charge, semiconductors doped with acceptor impurities are said to be *p type*.

The above discussion has assumed zero electric field.† If the electric field within the semiconductor is not zero, the relations presented above will not be valid in general. Nevertheless, in certain of these cases the semiconductor is still said to be in equilibrium.[1, 6] We will encounter cases that fall in this category, which will be characterized by the lack of net energy exchange between the semiconductor and the external world and no net current flow; for example, this will be the case for a short-circuited *pn* junction, discussed in Sec. 1.5. In such cases, the following will continue to be true as before[1, 6] (with *n* and *p* denoting the electron and hole concentrations, respectively),

$$np = n_i^2 \tag{1.2.6}$$

whether the semiconductor is extrinsic or intrinsic. Note that in general the individual values of n and p will be *different* from the values of n_o and p_o found in the absence of electric field. Thus, consider a region of semiconductor material (intrinsic, *n* type, or *p* type) in equilibrium. Assume that an electrostatic potential difference ψ_{12} exists between two points 1 and 2, as shown in Fig. 1.2.‡ Then it can be shown by using "energy band" concepts (Appendix A) that the electron concentrations n_1 and n_2 at points 1 and 2, respectively, are related to ψ_{12} by

$$\frac{n_1}{n_2} = e^{\psi_{12}/\phi_t} \tag{1.2.7}$$

where the quantity ϕ_t is simply

$$\phi_t = \frac{kT}{q} \tag{1.2.8}$$

with k the Boltzmann constant, q the magnitude of the electron charge, and T

---

† The term *electric field* is reserved here for macroscopic electric fields. Of course fields will always be present at the atomic level, e.g., between electrons and the nucleus in a given atom.

‡ In this book, the potential of a point with respect to another will be indicated by an arrow pointing from the former point to the latter. If the potential is internal to a device, the arrow will be drawn with a broken line. Potentials between a device's external terminals will be indicated by solid-line arrows.

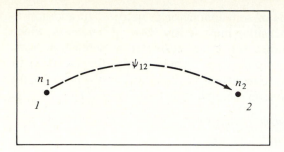

FIGURE 1.2
A piece of semiconductor material with different electron concentration at two points.

the absolute temperature. The values for the constants k and q are

$$k = 1.3809 \times 10^{-8} \, \frac{fC \cdot V}{K} \tag{1.2.9}$$

$$q = 1.602 \times 10^{-4} fC \tag{1.2.10}$$

From the above three equations, the value of ϕ_t at room temperature (300 K) is 0.0259 V.

The relation corresponding to (1.2.7) for holes is (again, assuming equilibrium; Appendix A),

$$\frac{p_1}{p_2} = e^{\psi_{21}/\phi_t} . \tag{1.2.11}$$

Note that (1.2.7) and (1.2.11) together imply $n_1 p_1 = n_2 p_2$, just as would be the case in the absence of any potential difference in equilibrium.

Let us now consider the charge density (charge concentration per unit volume) in a semiconductor. In the general case, four entities can be responsible for its value: (1) Holes, which contribute a charge density of $(+q)p$; (2) free electrons, with contribution $(-q)n$; (3) ionized donor atoms, with contribution $(+q)N_D$; and (4) ionized acceptor atoms, with contribution $(-q)N_A$. The total charge density, denoted by ρ, will be the sum of the individual contributions:

$$\rho = q(p - n + N_D - N_A) . \tag{1.2.12}$$

Of course, in the cases already discussed, we will have $N_A = 0$ if only donor atoms are present, or $N_D = 0$ if only acceptors are present. There are cases, however, where both N_D and N_A can be nonzero. For example, if it is desired to convert part of a p-type region into an n-type region, one can introduce donor atoms at a concentration higher than the concentration of acceptor atoms. The region then becomes effectively n type, with an "effective" donor concentration of $N_D - N_A$. This process is encountered often in the fabrication of semiconductor devices (Chap. 10).

In the presence of electric fields, the charge density ρ can vary from point to point. Assuming equilibrium, n and p in (1.2.12) must be such that, for any two points, they are related to the electrostatic potential by (1.2.7) and

(1.2.11), which are consequences of semiconductor properties. In addition to these relations, the *total* charge density ρ must satisfy *Poisson's equation*, which is a general relation in electrostatics and is not restricted to semiconductors. Let us consider the "one dimensional case" where ρ and the electrostatic potential ψ (taken with respect to some arbitrary reference) vary only vertically (along the y direction);† then Poisson's equation is (Appendix B)

$$\frac{d^2\psi}{dy^2} = -\frac{\rho(y)}{\epsilon_s} \tag{1.2.13}$$

where ϵ_s is the "permittivity" of the material, given by

$$\epsilon_s = k_s \epsilon_0 \tag{1.2.14}$$

with ϵ_0 the permittivity of free space (8.854×10^{-3} fF/μm) and k_s the dielectric constant of the material. For silicon we have approximately $k_s = 11.8$, corresponding to $\epsilon_s = 0.104$ fF/μm.

Our analysis of semiconductor devices in equilibrium will be based on the simple relations we have provided in this section. Several examples of the application of these relations will be found throughout this book. For the nonequilibrium cases of interest to us, a simple modification will be necessary, as will be seen.

1.3   CONDUCTION

1.3.1   Transit Time

The notion of "transit time" will be used in our discussion of MOS transistors in subsequent chapters. This notion is general and independent of the mechanisms via which current conduction takes place. Thus, it is introduced first before such mechanisms are discussed.

Consider the piece of material shown between the shaded regions in Fig. 1.3. Assume a steady flow of current in one direction, wholly due to free electrons, has been established. Also, assume that *no* recombination of electrons with holes takes place. Electrons are constantly being supplied from the left side and taken out from the right side at the same fixed rate. At any given instant, then, the magnitude of the total electron charge that happens to be inside the piece is fixed; let $|Q|$ denote its value. We will make the simplifying assumption that it takes each electron the same amount of time to travel the length of the piece; this time will be called the *transit time* and will be denoted by τ.

Let us consider the free electrons found inside the piece at a given instant and follow their motion. After the lapse of one transit time τ even those

---

† This direction is chosen in anticipation of analyses to follow later.

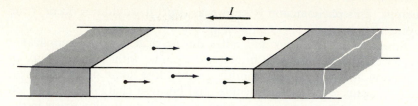

FIGURE 1.3
A piece of material with electrons flowing toward the right.

initially at the far left will have exited through the right end. Therefore all the electrons inside the piece at the initial instant of observation will have exited through the right-hand end also, and will have been replaced by new electrons coming from the left. Thus, a *negative* charge of magnitude $|Q|$ exits from the right-hand end in time τ; this corresponds to a current I in the direction shown, given by

$$I = \frac{|Q|}{\tau} \tag{1.3.1}$$

Note that in the argument leading to (1.3.1) we did not make any assumption as to the detailed mechanisms through which the current is conducted, the distribution of charge inside the material, the presence or absence of electric fields, or the constancy of electron velocity along the current path. Thus, (1.3.1) is quite general.

In the above discussion, we made the convenient assumption that all electrons spend the same amount of time τ in traveling the length of the material. However, it is customary to relax this assumption and use

$$\tau = \frac{|Q|}{I} \tag{1.3.2}$$

as the *definition* of transit time, with $|Q|$ and I as defined above. An obviously similar definition can be given in the case of conduction caused by holes. Expressions for τ will be found for each of two mechanisms of current conduction, which are considered in the next two subsections.

1.3.2 Drift

Let us consider a piece of semiconductor with no external field applied to it. A random "thermal" motion is exhibited by the holes and electrons in all directions; however, on the average these random charge movements cancel out and there is no net current produced. If an electric field is now applied (for example, by connecting the semiconductor piece across the terminals of a battery), it will exert forces on the charged particles. Thus there will be a net movement along the field lines which can be observed macroscopically as an electric current. This phenomenon is known as *drift*; it would not occur if the particles were not charged.

The movement of electrons and holes during drift is quite complicated since they accelerate in opposite directions, collide with lattice atoms in thermal vibration and with ionized impurity atoms, lose some of their energy, then accelerate again, etc. Because of this, and because charge is transported by these carriers in discrete amounts, a minute "noise" fluctuation exists in the externally observed current. For the present such fluctuations will be ignored and attention will be focused on the average current value I, which is nonzero because of the net movement caused by the nonzero electric field. The quantity I can be calculated from the carrier's *average* velocity, called *drift velocity* and denoted by v_d; in this book, v_d will be measured in μm/ns. For a given electric field, v_d depends on the type of semiconductor, the type and concentration of doping, the temperature, and the type of carrier.[5] For silicon, the magnitude of the drift velocity depends on the magnitude of the electric field $\mathscr{E}$, as shown qualitatively in Fig. 1.4. For high electric fields, the loss of energy of the carriers to the lattice becomes more effective and eventually *velocity saturation* is reached as shown. The maximum velocity value is essentially independent of doping concentration, and for silicon at room temperature is of the order of 100 μm/ns for both electrons and holes. It is reached at fields roughly above 3 V/μm for electrons and 10 V/μm for holes.

We now consider a uniformly doped n-type semiconductor bar with dimensions a, b, c as shown in Fig. 1.5, and a voltage V applied across it. In the following we will neglect the contribution of hole movement to the electric current since the holes, being the minority carriers in this case, are much fewer than the electrons. Electrons move in a complicated fashion with an *average* velocity of v_d, as discussed above. We can calculate the resulting current by considering a simpler, hypothetical picture in which the velocity of all electrons is constant and equal to v_d. The time it takes for an electron to travel the length of the bar is

$$\tau = \frac{a}{|v_d|} \tag{1.3.3}$$

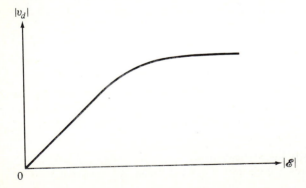

FIGURE 1.4
Magnitude of drift velocity vs. magnitude of electric field intensity.

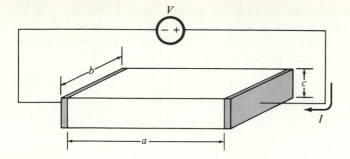

FIGURE 1.5
An *n*-type semiconductor bar with uniform electron concentration under external bias.

The magnitude $|Q|$ of the total free electron charge found inside the bar at a given time instant is given by the charge of a single electron q times the total number of electrons; the latter is given by the volume of the bar times the free electron concentration per unit volume, n. Thus

$$|Q| = nq(abc) \qquad (1.3.4)$$

Using this with (1.3.1) and (1.3.3) gives

$$I = \frac{nq(abc)}{\tau} \qquad (1.3.5a)$$

$$= nq(bc)|v_d| \qquad (1.3.5b)$$

This will now be put in a different form that will prove useful later in the discussion of transistors. The area of the bar's top surface in Fig. 1.5 is (ab). Thus $|Q|/(ab)$ is the *magnitude of the charge per unit area*.† This quantity will be denoted by $|Q'|$. Using (1.3.4) we have

$$|Q'| = \frac{|Q|}{ab} = nqc \qquad (1.3.6)$$

Substituting this in (1.3.5b) gives

$$I = b|Q'||v_d| \qquad (1.3.7)$$

THE CASE OF LOW ELECTRIC FIELDS. The above relations assume special, very useful forms in the case of low electric fields. For silicon, "low" means roughly less than 0.3 V/μm for electrons, and less than 0.6 V/μm for holes. For such fields, $|v_d|$ is proportional to $|\mathscr{E}|$, as suggested by the bottom part of the

---

† The use of this quotient is adequate because the charge is uniformly distributed horizontally; otherwise, the charge per unit area would have to be defined differentially.

curve in Fig. 1.4. The constant of proportionality is called *mobility* and is denoted by μ_B. The subscript B is used to emphasize that this mobility characterizes the "bulk" of the semiconductor. This is needed to distinguish it from a "surface" mobility which will be introduced in Chap. 4. We thus have

$$|v_d| = \mu_B |\mathscr{E}| \tag{1.3.8}$$

Electron and hole mobilities for silicon at room temperature are shown in Fig. 1.6 vs. doping concentration.[13] Mobilities decrease with temperature under common conditions.[5, 13]

The magnitude of the electric field in Fig. 1.5 is given by:

$$|\mathscr{E}| = \frac{V}{a} \tag{1.3.9}$$

With the use of this in (1.3.8) and the result in (1.3.3) we obtain, for the low-field transit time,

$$\tau = \frac{a^2}{\mu_B V} \tag{1.3.10}$$

The presence of the a^2 term reflects the fact that, for fixed μ_B and V, increasing the bar's length increases the transit time for two reasons: (1) The distance the electrons must travel becomes larger; and (2) the magnitude of the electric field becomes smaller, which slows the electrons down.

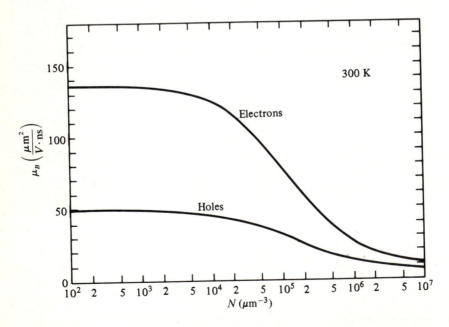

FIGURE 1.6
Electron and hole bulk mobility in silicon at 300 K vs. doping concentration.[13]

Using the above equation in (1.3.5a) we obtain:

$$I = \mu_B nq \frac{bc}{a} V \qquad (1.3.11)$$

which is nothing but Ohm's law.† This equation can be written in the form $I = GV$, where G is called the conductance and is given by

$$G = \sigma \frac{bc}{a} \qquad (1.3.12)$$

where σ is the *conductivity* given by

$$\sigma = \mu_B nq \qquad (1.3.13)$$

The *inverse* of the conductivity, called the *resistivity*, is also used.

Using the above two equations and (1.3.6), we can express the conductance as follows:

$$G = \mu_B |Q'| \frac{b}{a} \qquad (1.3.14)$$

The *I-V* relation is thus

$$I = \mu_B |Q'| \frac{b}{a} V \qquad (1.3.15)$$

As seen in the above two equations, the thickness c of the bar does not enter directly; all that counts is the value of the mobile charge concentration per unit area, and the dimensions b and a. In fact it is easy to show that *the above two results are valid even if the electron concentration is nonuniform in the vertical direction, as long as there is uniformity horizontally.*‡

The resistance of the bar $R = 1/G$ is, from (1.3.14),

$$R = R_s \frac{a}{b} \qquad (1.3.16)$$

---

† We have assumed a uniform n throughout the bar. However, we will encounter some cases where this assumption is not valid. If n varies along the x axis, one must instead consider a vertical "slice" of length Δx centered at x. Let $\Delta \psi$ be the electrostatic potential drop across the slice, defined from its right side to its left side; letting Δx approach zero, we obtain an equation in which the role of V/a in (1.3.11) is played by $d\psi/dx$:

$$I = \mu_B n(x) qbc \frac{d\psi}{dx} \qquad (1.3.11a)$$

‡ Consider the bar as consisting of thin, parallel horizontal slices within each of which n is constant. Let ΔG and $\Delta Q'$ be the conductance and charge per unit area, respectively, for one slice. Then, from the above results $\Delta G = \mu_B |\Delta Q'|(b/a)$. Note that for the combination of all slices in parallel the total G and Q' are the sum of the conductances and the charges per unit area, respectively, for each slice. Letting ΔG and $\Delta Q'$ become differentials and, integrating the resulting equation, we obtain (1.3.14) again. Equation (1.3.15) can be derived in a similar manner.

where $R_s = (\mu |Q'|)^{-1}$ is called the *sheet resistance*. When $a = b$, i.e., when the bar as seen from the *top* is square, $R = R_s$. Thus R_s is simply the bar's "resistance per square"; R will be given by R_s times the number of squares in the path of the current. This is illustrated in Fig. 1.7. Both bars are assumed to be made out of the same material, and with the same Q'. Since both have a total of $a/b = 3$ squares in the path of the current, they have the same resistance, equal to $3R_s$. Sheet resistance is often expressed in "ohms per square."

Results analogous to the ones in this section can be given in the case of hole conduction. If holes were present in Fig. 1.5, they would move in a direction opposite to that of electrons (i.e., from right to left in the semiconductor). Since the charge associated with holes is positive, the resulting contribution to the total current would be in the direction shown, i.e., in the *same* direction as that for the current owing to electrons. One could then define a conductivity σ for use in (1.3.12), which would be the *sum* of the electron and hole conductives.

1.3.3   Diffusion

Drift is only one of two mechanisms responsible for the flow of electric current in semiconductors. The other mechanism, known as *diffusion*, occurs whenever particles are not distributed uniformly over space, i.e., when there exist "concentration gradients;" then the random motion of the particles tends to make them spread out from regions of high concentration to regions of low concentration. Notice that this phenomenon is not due to electric fields, and can thus occur independently of whether or not the particles are charged; for example, particles of smoke exhibit such diffusion. However if the particles *are* charged, as are electrons and holes, diffusion gives rise to movement of charge and thus to electric current.

We consider the origin of diffusion with the help of Fig. 1.8a. Here a piece of semiconductor of rectangular cross section with width b and thickness

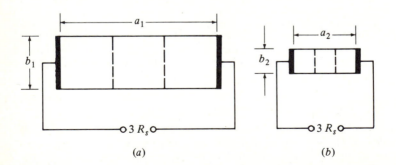

(a)   (b)

FIGURE 1.7
Top view of two bars, each with three "squares" in the path of the current.

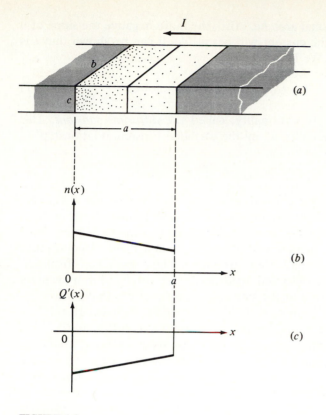

FIGURE 1.8
(*a*) A semiconductor bar with nonuniform electron concentration along its length; (*b*) the electron concentration in (*a*) for a special case of interest; (*c*) charge per unit area corresponding to (*b*).

c is assumed to contain electrons distributed uniformly across any vertical plane (such as the one shown), but *nonuniformly* along the length. No holes are assumed to be present for now. We assume that the semiconductor communicates with the external world from left and right, so that a fixed electron distribution can be maintained. This distribution can be represented by a fixed plot of *n* vs. *x*. Until further notice, we will assume this plot to be a straight line as shown in Fig. 1.8*b*.

Electrons are found on both sides of the plane shown and exhibit a random thermal motion; however, in a parallelpiped of very small length Δx immediately to the left of the plane, more electrons are to be found than those contained in an identical parallelpiped immediately to the right of the plane. Hence one can expect that in a given time interval more electrons will cross the plane moving from left to right, rather than from right to left. This corresponds to a net flow of electrons from left to right. Since each carries a negative charge, the current defined in the direction shown in the figure will be positive. This current is proportional to the magnitude *q* of the charge carried by each electron and the cross-sectional area bc. Also, the more negative the slope of n with x, the more positive the current will be; in fact it can be shown that I is proportional to $(-dn/dx)$. We have[1-11]

$$I = Dq(bc)\left(-\frac{dn}{dx}\right) \qquad (1.3.17)$$

where D is a constant of proportionality, called the *diffusion constant*. This constant is related to the mobility μ_B by the so-called Einstein relationship[1-11] (Prob. 1.11):

$$D = \mu_B \phi_t \qquad (1.3.18)$$

where ϕ_t is the thermal voltage given by (1.2.8). Analogous relations hold for the diffusion of holes; of course the values for the diffusion constants of holes and electrons are different, corresponding to their different mobilities. Note that if the particles shown in Fig. 1.8a were holes, and their concentrations were decreasing towards the right, there would be a hole movement from left to right. Since the charge associated with holes is positive, this movement would correspond to a current in the opposite direction from that shown.

   If the plot of n vs. x is not a straight line, dn/dx will vary with position and so will the diffusion current. The latter must now be written as $I(x)$, and will still be given by the right-hand side of (1.3.17). Since, in steady state, the *total* current must be the same at any point x, there must exist in this case a drift current component, varying with position in such a way that the total current (which, as can be shown, will be given by the superposition of diffusion plus drift) is independent of x. In general, current flow in semiconductors is the result of both drift and diffusion; for example, both mechanisms are encountered in a *pn* junction. Often, one of the two mechanisms dominates. In the rest of this section, we assume for simplicity that only diffusion current is present, and thus the plot of n vs. x is a straight line.

   Consider a thin vertical slice of the material in Fig. 1.8a of volume $bc \, \Delta x$ centered around a point at x. The charge in this slice is $(-q)n(x)bc \, \Delta x$, where the $-$ sign corresponds to the negative electron charge. Dividing the slice charge by the area of the slice $b \, \Delta x$ as seen from the top, and letting Δx go to zero, we obtain the *charge per unit area*, which here is a function of x:

$$Q'(x) = (-q)cn(x) \qquad (1.3.19)$$

   This quantity is shown vs. x in Fig. 1.8c. Using (1.3.19) and (1.3.18) in (1.3.17), we obtain

$$I = \mu_B \phi_t b \, \frac{dQ'(x)}{dx} \qquad (1.3.20)$$

   Consider now a more general case in which we allow the electron concentration to be *nonuniform in the vertical direction*. Assume that on a horizontal plane at any given depth, the plot of n vs. x is still a straight line (we still assume that n is uniform in the direction perpendicular to the plane of the paper in Fig. 1.8). Since n is now nonuniform vertically, electrons would have a tendency to diffuse in the vertical direction, but we will assume that an appropriate externally applied vertical electric field prevents them from doing so. In other words, we assume that the electrons still move parallel to the x direction, so that *laminar flow is maintained*. Then one can easily show that *(1.3.20) will still be valid.*†

Since the plot of $Q'(x)$ vs. x is a straight line, its slope will be

$$\frac{dQ'}{dx} = \frac{Q'(a) - Q'(0)}{a} \tag{1.3.21}$$

Use of this in (1.3.20) gives:

$$I = \mu_B \phi_t \frac{b}{a} [Q'(a) - Q'(0)] \tag{1.3.22}$$

Since (1.3.20) is valid even if n is a function of both x and the vertical dimension under the assumptions following (1.3.20), so will (1.3.22).

The transit time τ can now be easily calculated. It is easy to show that the total charge of the electrons found at any instant inside the bar will be (Prob. 1.3)

$$Q = ab \frac{Q'(a) + Q'(0)}{2} \tag{1.3.23}$$

Thus the transit time will be, from (1.3.2),

$$\tau = \frac{a^2}{\mu(2\phi_t)} \frac{Q'(0) + Q'(a)}{Q'(0) - Q'(a)} \tag{1.3.24}$$

In this book we will often be interested in the case where a "perfect sink" exists at $x = a$, reducing the electron concentration to 0 there; this means

$$Q'(a) = 0 \tag{1.3.25}$$

For this special case (1.3.24) becomes

$$\tau = \frac{a^2}{\mu_B(2\phi_t)} \tag{1.3.26}$$

Note that this form is very similar to (1.3.10).

---

† Consider the material as consisting of thin, parallel horizontal slices within each of which n does not vary vertically. If ΔI and $\Delta Q'(x)$ are the current and charge per unit area for one such slice, we will have $\Delta I = \mu \phi_t b d[\Delta Q'(x)]/dx$. The total current I will be the sum of the individual ΔI, and in this summation the $\Delta Q'(x)$ can be grouped together to give the total charge per unit area of the material at x, $Q'(x)$. More precisely, letting ΔI and $\Delta Q'(x)$ become differentials and integrating, we obtain (1.3.20) again (Prob. 1.4).

1.4   CONTACT POTENTIALS

Consider the junction of two different materials J_1 and J_2 with no external bias, as shown in Fig. 1.9a; either material can be a semiconductor or a metal. When the two materials are brought together, at first carriers move from one to the other because the energy of these carriers is in general different in J_1 and J_2, and no opposing field exists in the initially neutral materials. However, as each charged carrier crosses the junction, it leaves behind a net charge of the opposite polarity, and an electric field is thus established in the vicinity of the junction, which tends to inhibit the movement of carriers. For example, if an electron crosses from J_1 to J_2, it leaves a positive charge in J_1; the contribution of this charge to the electric field is in such a direction as to attract the electron back into J_1. Eventually, the field intensity increases to the point that it counteracts the tendency of carriers to cross the junction, and a balance is achieved at which there is no more net carrier movement. An electrostatic potential change is then encountered when going from one material, through the junction, to the other material. If $\psi(x)$ is the potential at position x, it can be of the form shown in Fig. 1.9b (arbitrary references are assumed for both ψ

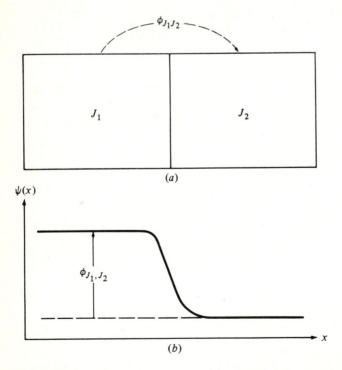

(a)

(b)

FIGURE 1.9
(*a*) Two different materials in contact (either can be a metal or a semiconductor); (*b*) potential vs. distance for (*a*).

and *x*). Depending on the two materials, the potential change can occur on both sides of the junction, as in the case shown, or mostly on one of them. The total potential drop in going from J_1 to J_2 is called the *contact potential of material* J_1 *to material* J_2, and will be denoted by ϕ_{J_1,J_2}. The concept of contact potentials will be instrumental in deriving the basic equations of MOS devices, without having to introduce the use of energy bands; hence, the use of contact potentials is discussed in considerable detail in this section. Readers interested in a treatment using energy bands are referred to Appendix A.

As an example consider the junction of a material *J* to intrinsic silicon, as in Fig. 1.10. Let ϕ_J denote the contact potential of material *J* to intrinsic silicon as shown. Depending on the material *J*, the value of ϕ_J will vary. For various materials it can be indirectly evaluated[5] and is tabulated in Table 1.1.

If *J* is a metal, the contact potential ϕ_J has a specific value as shown in the table. However, if *J* is a semiconductor, ϕ_J will depend not only on which semiconductor it is but also on its impurity type (donor or acceptor) and concentration. We will now focus on the case in which *J* is extrinsic silicon; the value of ϕ_J in this case is given by the *negative* of a quantity denoted by ϕ_F, as seen in the table. ϕ_F is a very important quantity characterizing the semiconductor which will be defined, for our purposes, as follows:†

The *Fermi potential* ϕ_F of extrinsic silicon is the contact potential that would be developed between intrinsic silicon and the extrinsic silicon if the two were brought in contact and thermal equilibrium were established. This contact potential is defined as that *of* intrinsic *to* extrinsic silicon;‡ see Fig. 1.11.

As one travels from the intrinsic side to the extrinsic side in Fig. 1.11*b*, there will be a transition region near the junction where the electrostatic potential will be changing, and the total change will be ϕ_F. At points clearly outside this transition region, the electron and hole concentrations remain at the values they had before contact was made, i.e., they are as in Fig. 1.11*a*. Let 1 and 2 denote two such points in Fig. 1.11*b*, one in each side of the junction. We assume that there is no external bias and the system is in equilibrium. We can then use (1.2.7) and (1.2.11) to obtain

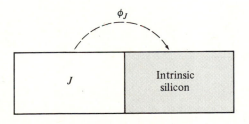

FIGURE 1.10
Junction of a material *J* and intrinsic silicon; definition of the characteristic potential ϕ_J.

---

† A formal definition of ϕ_F using energy band concepts is given in Appendix A.

‡ Analogous definitions can be given for any semiconductor.

TABLE 1.1

Approximate contact potential of materials to intrinsic silicon (V)†

Material	ϕ_J
Ag	−0.4
Au	−0.3
Cu	0.0
Ni	+0.15
Al	+0.6
Mg	+1.35
Extrinsic Si	$-\phi_F$
Intrinsic Si	0

† The values given are only approximate. Accurate values are difficult to obtain, and, in fact, different measuring techniques can yield values which differ by a large fraction of 1 V.

$$\phi_F = \phi_t \ln \frac{n_i}{n_o} \qquad (1.4.1a)$$

$$\phi_F = \phi_t \ln \frac{p_o}{n_i} \qquad (1.4.1b)$$

Let us now consider qualitatively the Fermi potential of p-type silicon. When it is joined to intrinsic silicon, one expects that a net number of electrons will diffuse from the intrinsic silicon to p-type silicon as electrons are in a larger

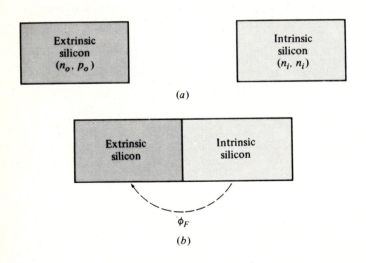

(a)

(b)

FIGURE 1.11

(a) Extrinsic and intrinsic silicon (symbols in parentheses indicate electron and hole concentrations); (b) the materials in (a) in contact with each other, and the corresponding contact potential.

supply in the former, and holes will diffuse from the *p*-type side to the intrinsic side. Therefore, there will be a net positive charge on the intrinsic side and a net negative charge on the *p*-type side; the potential will be higher on the intrinsic side. Hence ϕ_F, which is the contact potential of the intrinsic side to the *p*-type side, will be positive. Now the higher the impurity concentration N_A on the *p* side, the more the holes and the larger the tendency to diffuse. Thus a larger field needs to be established to inhibit their movement at balance. This causes ϕ_F to be higher for higher N_A. Using (1.2.4) in (1.4.1*b*), we obtain

$$\phi_F \approx +\phi_t \ln \frac{N_A}{n_i} \qquad p\text{-type material} \qquad (1.4.2)$$

Similar qualitative considerations for *n*-type silicon lead to the conclusion that ϕ_F should be negative in that case, and that $|\phi_F|$ should increase with the donor concentration N_D. We can use (1.2.2) in (1.4.1*a*) to obtain

$$\phi_F \approx -\phi_t \ln \frac{N_D}{n_i} \qquad n\text{-type material} \qquad (1.4.3)$$

It should be mentioned here that, although we have discussed ϕ_F in terms of a contact potential, it is a quality which characterizes the material by itself. Even if the material is self-contained (not in contact with anything else), to its *n* (or *p*) there corresponds uniquely a value of ϕ_F at a given temperature. This value is given by (1.4.1) or, under the assumptions made in Sec. 1.2, by (1.4.2) or (1.4.3). Thus, for example, one can talk of a certain *p*-type silicon with $N_A = 10^3 \ \mu\text{m}^{-3}$ or, equivalently, of *p*-type silicon with $\phi_F = 0.289$ V at 300 K. Values for ϕ_F obtained from (1.4.2) and (1.4.3) at 300 K are plotted vs. doping

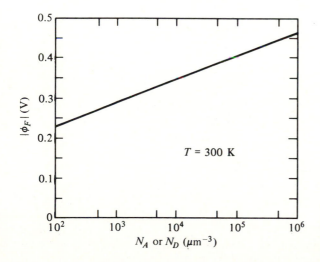

FIGURE 1.12
Magnitude of Fermi potential vs. substrate doping concentration for silicon at room temperature.

concentration in Fig. 1.12. For degenerate materials, ϕ_F is difficult to evaluate. A common approximation is 0.56 V for p-type Si, and -0.56 V for n-type Si, at 300 K (Appendix A).

We will now show that Table 1.1 is useful not only for calculating potentials in contacts with intrinsic silicon but also for calculating contact potentials for any two materials in that table, e.g., the contact potential of Au to Al. To see this, consider again the junction of two arbitrary materials J_1 and J_2, as in Fig. 1.9a. The value of the contact potential, ϕ_{J_1,J_2} is, of course, independent of intrinsic silicon, since the latter appears nowhere in the figure. However, it is very easy to express the unknown ϕ_{J_1,J_2} in terms of ϕ_{J_1} and ϕ_{J_2}, which are known and tabulated in Table 1.1. To see this, suppose that we place the system of Fig. 1.9a in a loop with intrinsic silicon, as shown in Fig. 1.13. By equating the sum of the potential drops around the loop to zero, we get:

$$\phi_{J_1,J_2} = \phi_{J_1} - \phi_{J_2} \qquad (1.4.4)$$

Therefore, intrinsic silicon is for us a *reference* material since by knowing its contact potential to other materials, we can get the contact potential between any two materials as well. It is clear that we could have chosen any other material as our reference in Fig. 1.10. We could have then constructed a table for that material similar to Table 1.1, and (1.4.4) would be valid again for ϕ_{J_1} and ϕ_{J_2} obtained from the new table. Because we will be working with

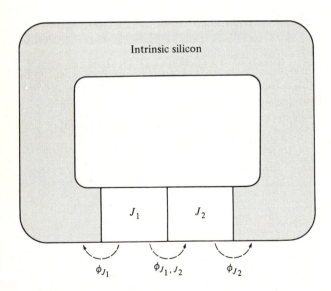

FIGURE 1.13
Two materials in a loop with intrinsic silicon.

silicon devices, our earlier choice of intrinsic silicon as a reference will prove convenient.†

> **Example 1.4.1.** Calculate the contact potential of aluminum to p-type silicon, with $N_A = 10^3 \ \mu\text{m}^{-3}$, at $T = 300 \ \text{K}$. From Table 1.1 and (1.4.2), and if P_1 denotes the above p-type material, we have
>
> $$\phi_{P_1} = -0.0259 \ \text{V} \ln \frac{10^3}{0.0145} = -0.29 \ \text{V}$$
>
> From Table 1.1, $\phi_{Al} = +0.6 \ \text{V}$. Therefore, using (1.4.4),
>
> $$\phi_{Al,P_1} = 0.6 \ \text{V} - (-0.29 \ \text{V}) = 0.89 \ \text{V}$$

> **Example 1.4.2.** Calculate the contact potential ϕ_{P_2,N_2} of p-type silicon with $N_A = 10^2 \ \mu\text{m}^{-3}$ (denoted by P_2), to n-type silicon with $N_D = 10^4 \ \mu\text{m}^{-3}$ (denoted by N_2), at $T = 300 \ \text{K}$.
>
> From Table 1.1 and (1.4.2), $\phi_{P_2} = -0.229 \ \text{V}$. From Table 1.1 and (1.4.3), $\phi_{N_2} = +0.348 \ \text{V}$. Therefore, using (1.4.4),
>
> $$\phi_{P_2,N_2} = -0.229 \ \text{V} - (+0.348 \ \text{V}) = -0.577 \ \text{V}$$

SEVERAL MATERIALS IN SERIES. We can now make an interesting observation concerning several materials in series, as in Fig. 1.14a; as before, all materials are assumed to be at the same temperature. If we express the potentials ψ_{KL} in terms of contact potentials in the loop, we have

$$\psi_{KL} = \phi_{J_1,J_2} + \phi_{J_2,J_3} + \cdots + \phi_{J_{n-1},J_n} \tag{1.4.5}$$

and, using (1.4.4) repeatedly in the above equation, we get:

$$\psi_{KL} = (\phi_{J_1} - \phi_{J_2}) + (\phi_{J_2} - \phi_{J_3}) + \cdots + (\phi_{J_{n-1}} - \phi_{J_n}) \tag{1.4.6}$$

It is clear that, with the exception of ϕ_{J_1} and ϕ_{J_n}, each ϕ_{J_i} appears twice in the sum—once with a plus and once with a minus sign. Therefore

$$\psi_{KL} = \phi_{J_1} - \phi_{J_n} \tag{1.4.7}$$

A question arises: Can we measure potential ψ_{KL} with a common voltmeter? The answer is *no*, even if the voltmeter is assumed ideal (i.e., does

---

† In energy band treatments, contact potentials are often expressed in terms of the "work functions" of the two materials, work function W_J being a quantity characterizing material J and related to the energy required to remove an electron from the material to the vacuum. According to such treatments, ϕ_{J_1,J_2} in Fig. 1.9a is $(W_{J_2} - W_{J_1})/q$, where q is the magnitude of the electron charge (Appendix A). Work functions are not easy to measure accurately, and, in fact, have to be "modified" for use in MOS device modeling. We have avoided complications in our discussion by changing our reference from "vacuum," which has little to do with the devices we will be dealing with, to something more relevant. If the reader prefers to use work functions, no confusion should arise; the difference in Eq. (1.4.4) is still correct if the symbol ϕ_J is defined to be $-W_J/q$.

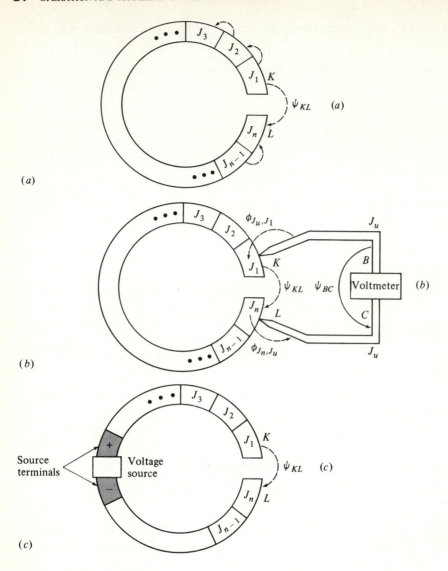

FIGURE 1.14
(a) Several materials in series; (b) the structure of (a) with a voltmeter attached; (c) the structure of (a) with a voltage source placed in series.

not draw any current from the circuit under measurement). This can be seen in Fig. 1.14b. Assume that the voltmeter leads are made by some material J_u. The potential difference ψ_{BC} between the two leads (which is what the voltmeter "sees") is

$$\psi_{BC} = \phi_{J_u,J_1} + \psi_{KL} + \phi_{J_n,J_u} \tag{1.4.8}$$

Using (1.4.4) in the above equation,

$$\psi_{BC} = (\phi_{J_u} - \phi_{J_1}) + \psi_{KL} + (\phi_{J_n} - \phi_{J_u}) \tag{1.4.9}$$

and, using (1.4.7) in (1.4.9), we get

$$\psi_{BC} = 0 \tag{1.4.10}$$

In summary then, no matter how many materials are in the loop, the electrostatic potential difference between its two ends depends *only* on the first and the last material and cannot be measured by a common voltmeter.† For such measurements, special techniques must be used.[14]

What now if a voltage source is inserted in the loop? This situation is illustrated in Fig. 1.14c. The source leads are assumed to be made of the same material. By going around the loop we have

$$\psi_{KL} = V_{source} + (\phi_{J_1} - \phi_{J_n}) \tag{1.4.11}$$

which should be compared with (1.4.7).‡

What would an ideal voltmeter like that of Fig. 1.14b measure if attached to points K and L in Fig. 1.14c? With ψ_{KL} as given by (1.4.11), (1.4.9) is still valid and we have

$$\psi_{BC} = V_{source} \tag{1.4.12}$$

which should be compared to (1.4.10).

It is now clear why contact potentials never seem to enter the picture when one works with circuits, provided all contacts are at the same temperature. As seen in the example leading to (1.4.12), such potentials cancel out, cannot be measured by common voltmeters, and do not enter in *circuit* equations. However, in investigating the physics of electronic devices, contact potentials must be taken into account; otherwise, unless a fortuitous cancellation takes place, neglecting contact potentials can lead to errors.

1.5 THE *pn* JUNCTION

The selective doping of silicon with *n*-type impurities in one region and with *p*-type impurities in an adjacent one produces what is known as a *pn junction*.

---

† The leads of a voltmeter are invariably made of the same material. The "academic" case where the leads are made of two different materials can be handled if one considers the various contact potentials within the voltmeter circuit (see Prob. 1.7).

‡ Leads of voltage sources, like the leads of a voltmeter, are assumed to be made of the same material. The case of a source with leads made of different materials is easily handled by defining V_{source} as the voltage measured by our ideal voltmeter when attached to the terminals of the source. Then (1.4.11) and (1.4.12) will remain valid (see Prob. 1.8).

Such a junction is shown in Fig. 1.15. In this figure, we have assumed that the doping changes abruptly from *n*-type to *p*-type at a boundary, and that the doping concentration is uniform on either side of the boundary; such a junction is referred to as an *abrupt*, or *step*, junction. In drawing Fig. 1.15, we have also assumed that the *n* region is more heavily doped than the *p* region. The two caps on the top and the bottom are made of a metal chosen so as to make

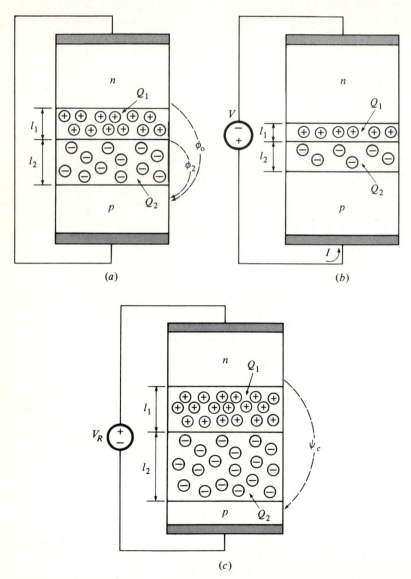

FIGURE 1.15
A *pn* junction with (*a*) zero bias, (*b*) forward bias; (*c*) reverse bias.

"ohmic contacts" (contacts that conduct well in both directions†) with the semiconductor.

Let us first consider the case in Fig. 1.15*a* where the externally applied bias is zero. Free electrons are in high concentration in the *n* side and in low concentration in the *p* side. Thus, they tend to diffuse across the boundary between the two sides (downward in the figure), leaving behind positively charged immobile donor atoms as shown. Similarly, holes tend to diffuse from the *p* side, where they are in abundance, upward to the *n* side, leaving behind negatively charged immobile acceptor atoms. For simplicity it is often assumed that the above phenomena result in complete depletion of carriers over a region with sharply defined edges, as shown in the figure. This is called the *depletion approximation*, and the region is referred to as the *depletion region*. The more the uncovered donor atoms on the *n* side, the more their total charge; therefore, the stronger the electric field they produce, and the stronger the attractive force they exert on electrons attempting to diffuse downward. Similarly, the more the uncovered acceptor atoms on the *p* side, the more they will attract holes which are attempting to diffuse upward. Eventually in this process, enough impurity atoms are uncovered on both sides that the strong fields exerted by them inhibit a further net movement of carriers. The depletion region width is then fixed, and the current in the external wire is zero. It is interesting to note that the situation inside the structure will not change if the external wire is cut. In fact, in this case it is easy to see from (1.4.6) and the associated discussion that the three contact potentials in the structure cancel each other out, and no electrostatic potential exists across the two open terminals.

In the absence of external bias, the potential across the depletion region (from deep in the *n* side to deep in the *p* side) will simply be the contact potential of the *n*-type material to the *p*-material. This potential is referred to as the *built-in potential* of the junction, and will be denoted by ϕ_o. From Table 1.1 and (1.4.4), ϕ_o is given by

$$\phi_o = \phi_{Fp} - \phi_{Fn} \qquad (1.5.1)$$

where ϕ_{Fp} and ϕ_{Fn} are the Fermi potentials of the *p*-side and the *n*-side, respectively. We will be interested in cases where one of the two regions is very heavily doped. We remind the reader that in such cases of a "degenerate" semiconductor, (1.4.2) or (1.4.3) cannot be applied; see the comment following these equations. In practice, the value of ϕ_o is sometimes chosen to provide best matching of expressions in which it appears to experimental results.

Let the depths of the depletion region at the two sides of the junction be

---

† How well current is conducted in either direction is something that cannot be deduced from the contact potential value. The theories for conduction in a metal-semiconductor contact are relatively involved and are the subject of controversy.[5, 16]

l_1 and l_2, as shown. If the cross-sectional area of the junction (as seen from above) is A, the part of the depletion region in the n side has a volume equal to $(l_1 A)$, and therefore a total number of ionized atoms equal to $(l_1 A)N_D$. Since each of these atoms carries a charge $+q$, the total charge there, denoted by Q_1, is

$$Q_1 = +q(l_1 A)N_D \qquad (1.5.2)$$

Similarly, the total charge in the p side of the depletion region (which is due to ionized acceptor atoms) is

$$Q_2 = -q(l_2 A)N_A \qquad (1.5.3)$$

For overall charge neutrality, we must have

$$Q_1 = -Q_2 \qquad (1.5.4)$$

Let us now restrict our attention to the case of a "one-sided" step junction of the type n^+p, i.e., a step junction for which $N_D \gg N_A$; this last relation, along with (1.5.2) to (1.5.4) implies

$$l_1 \ll l_2 \qquad (1.5.5)$$

which means that practically all the depletion region extends into the p side.

One can now apply Poisson's equation (1.2.13) in the depletion region, assuming all charge there is due to ionized impurity atoms (Appendix C). One finds that, in the case of $N_D \gg N_A$ considered here, practically all of the potential ϕ_o across the junction will be dropped on the p side. Denoting by ϕ_2 the potential drop across the p side, we have:

$$\phi_2 \approx \phi_o \qquad (1.5.6)$$

Also, one finds that the distance l_2, over which the acceptor atoms must be uncovered to support the potential drop $\phi_2 \approx \phi_o$, is given by (Appendix C and Prob. 1.13):

$$l_2 = \sqrt{\frac{2\epsilon_s}{qN_A}} \sqrt{\phi_o} \qquad (1.5.7)$$

with ϵ_s given by (1.2.14).

Let us now define the charge *per unit area* on the p side, Q_2', as follows:[†]

$$Q_2' = \frac{Q_2}{A} \qquad (1.5.8)$$

From (1.5.3), (1.5.7), and (1.5.8) we obtain

$$Q_2' = -F\sqrt{N_A}\sqrt{\phi_o} \qquad (1.5.9)$$

---

† The results derived here will later be extended to cases where l_2 changes with horizontal position; in such cases, one must define Q_2' at each horizontal position differentially as dQ_2'/dA.

where

$$F \equiv \sqrt{2q\epsilon_s} \qquad (1.5.10)$$

Using (1.2.10) and (1.2.14), F has a value of $0.00579 \, \text{fC} \cdot \mu\text{m}^{-1/2} \cdot \text{V}^{-1/2}$ for silicon.

We now consider the application of a *forward* bias voltage $V > 0$, as shown in Fig. 1.15b. Equilibrium is now destroyed. The polarity of the voltage tends to produce a field opposite from that produced by the uncovered impurity atoms. Assuming that the contact potential of the *ohmic* contacts is not affected, the electrostatic potential across the depletion region will be reduced from ϕ_o to $\phi_o - V$, so that the sum of the electrostatic potentials around the loop remains zero. Thus, the total electric field is reduced at each point, and carriers find it easier to diffuse across the boundary. Electrons from the n side, being majority carriers there and therefore in large supply, diffuse downward; holes from the p side, which are majority carriers there and therefore again in large supply diffuse upward. The result of both of these movements is a positive current upward, as shown. For this to make sense, of course, one should recall that the assumption that *all* mobile carriers have left the depletion region used previously was just a convenient simplification; mobile carriers actually do exist in the "depletion" region, and can support the flow of current. Assuming the current is not too large, and that the ohmic drop in the semiconductor outside the depletion region is negligible, it can be shown that the magnitude of the current will be given by[2-10, 12]

$$I = I_0(e^{V/\phi_t} - 1) \qquad (1.5.11)$$

where I_O is a quantity dependent on the details of construction and is an increasing function of temperature, and ϕ_t is the thermal voltage given by (1.2.8).

The polarity of the source in Fig. 1.15b, is such as to supply additional electrons to the n side, which "cover" some of the previously uncovered ionized donor atoms; hence the region where such ionized atoms are contained becomes narrower. From charge neutrality it is expected that some of the uncovered acceptor atoms on the other side will be covered as well. Hence the depletion region width is smaller than in Fig. 1.15a, which is consistent with our claim that the electric field at each point is less intense.

Consider now the case shown in Fig. 1.15c, where a *reverse* bias $V_R > 0$ is applied from the n-side terminal to the p-side terminal. Again, the structure will be in nonequilibrium. Now, the polarity of the applied voltage is such as to increase the electric field intensity at each point, compared to that in Fig. 1.15a. This polarity tends to move electrons upward away from the upper edge of the depletion region and holes downward away from the lower edge of that region. Thus the width of the depletion region will increase as shown. The larger the value of V_R, the wider the depletion region will become. If the n region is most heavily doped, overall charge neutrality dictates that such increases in width will take place mostly on the p side. From this it can also be shown that the p-side depletion region will support most of the voltage drop.

We see that the direction of the field is now such that it no longer aids the flow of majority carriers from each side toward the junction boundary, as it did in the case of forward bias. Instead, some of the few holes (minority carriers) near the depletion region edge in the n side are swept downward by the field; similarly, some of the few electrons near the depletion region edge in the p side are swept by the field upward. This flow of minority carriers from each side causes a net external current in the opposite direction of that in Fig. 1.15b; and, since minority carriers are in short supply, this current is very small. Equation (1.5.11) remains valid for the reverse-bias case, with $V = -V_R$. For V_R larger than a few ϕ_t, the exponential becomes negligible and the current is seen to "saturate" at the value $-I_O$. For this reason, I_O is often referred to as the *saturation current*. In practice, various "nonidealities" contribute to make the actual reverse-current magnitude larger than I_O, and indeed somewhat dependent on V_R. The reverse-current magnitude is strongly dependent on temperature, doubling for every 10°C or even less of a temperature change. If V_R exceeds a certain value V_{RX}, the theory[4-9,12] used to derive (1.5.11) fails. The junction conducts a large current from the n to the p side, and is said to be in "reverse breakdown." V_{RX} is called the *reverse-breakdown voltage* and, for the junctions encountered on MOS integrated circuits, is typically from 10 to 100 V, depending on fabrication details. A complete *I-V* characteristic of a *pn* junction, including breakdown, is shown in Fig. 1.16. Most *pn* junctions on MOS integrated circuits are reverse-biased with $V_R < V_{RX}$. Their reverse current can be neglected unless the application is extremely critical or unless

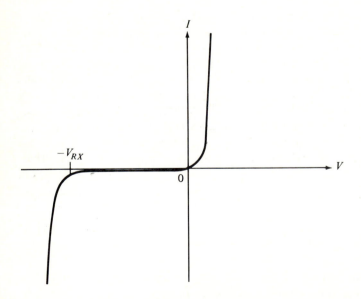

FIGURE 1.16
Current vs. voltage for a *pn* junction.

the temperature is very high. Note, however, that the reverse current in Fig. 1.15c is a manifestation of nonequilibrium. This current, no matter how small, provides communication between the junction and the external battery, which drastically alters the conditions that were present at equilibrium under zero bias. Thus, for example, relations that were valid in equilibrium, such as (1.2.6) or (1.2.7), will not be valid under nonzero bias in general.

Under the reverse bias V_R, the electrostatic potential across the depletion region (ψ_c in Fig. 1.15c) will increase by V_R, so that the potential drops around the loop add up to zero again (the contact potentials at the ohmic contacts are considered unchanged). Thus

$$\psi_c = \phi_o + V_R \qquad (1.5.12)$$

The new depletion region width will be given by (1.5.7) if the new potential ψ_c is used instead of ϕ_o (Appendix C):

$$l_2 = \sqrt{\frac{2\epsilon_s}{qN_A}} \sqrt{\psi_c} \qquad (1.5.13)$$

Similarly, the new depletion region charge per unit area on the p side will be given by the following equation instead of (1.5.9):

$$Q_2' = -F\sqrt{N_A}\sqrt{\psi_c} \qquad (1.5.14)$$

We now consider the concept of the small-signal capacitance of the reverse-biased pn junction. If the reverse bias is increased by a small amount ΔV_R, the depletion region width must increase on both sides. The charge that must be moved for this to happen must flow through the external circuit. Specifically, additional donor atoms will be uncovered in the n side, increasing the total charge there. For this to happen, electrons must be removed by the external circuit from near the depletion region's top edge. Thus, a negative charge, say $-\Delta Q$, leaves the junction from the top terminal. This can equivalently be described by saying that an opposite *positive* charge $+\Delta Q$ flows *into* the junction through the top terminal. Similarly, since the reverse bias has increased, additional acceptor atoms must be uncovered in the p side. For this to happen, the external circuit must cause positively charged holes to be removed from near the depletion region's bottom edge. This implies a positive charge $+\Delta Q$ flowing out of the bottom terminal or, equivalently, a *negative* charge $-\Delta Q$ flowing *into* the bottom terminal. Thus the changes of the charges Q_1 and Q_2 in Fig. 1.15c will be:

$$\Delta Q_1 = +\Delta Q \qquad (1.5.15)$$

$$\Delta Q_2 = -\Delta Q \qquad (1.5.16)$$

Assume now that a voltage source of value equal to the *change* of the reverse bias ΔV_R is connected across a capacitor as in Fig. 1.17, and that its capacitance value is chosen so that the charges on the two plates are $+\Delta Q$ and $-\Delta Q$, i.e., equal to the charges that entered the junction through the top and

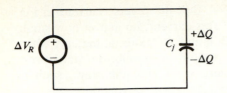

FIGURE 1.17
Small-signal equivalent circuit of a reverse-biased *pn* junction driven by a voltage source.

the bottom terminal, respectively, when the reverse bias was changed from V_R to $V_R + \Delta V_R$. Then this capacitance represents the *small-signal capacitance* of the reverse-biased *pn* junction. If this capacitance is denoted by C_j, we have

$$C_j = \frac{\Delta Q}{\Delta V_R} \qquad (1.5.17)$$

Using (1.5.16), and refining the definition of C_j by letting the finite differences become differentials, we have

$$C_j = -\frac{dQ_2}{dV_R} \qquad (1.5.18)$$

Finally, dividing both sides by the cross-sectional area A, we obtain the *small-signal capacitance per unit area* C_j/A, denoted by C_j':

$$C_j' = -\frac{dQ_2'}{dV_R} \qquad (1.5.19)$$

Using now (1.5.12) and (1.5.14) in the above gives

$$C_j' = \frac{F\sqrt{N_A}}{2\sqrt{V_R + \phi_o}} \qquad (1.5.20a)$$

which, using (1.5.12) and (1.5.13), can also be written as

$$C_j' = \frac{\epsilon_s}{l_2} \qquad (1.5.20b)$$

This equation is plotted in Fig. 1.18, where approximate values for ϕ_o are given[5] assuming the heavily doped side is degenerate. If C_{j0}' denotes the value of C_j' for $V_R = 0$, (1.5.20a) can be easily converted to the following:

$$C_j' = \frac{C_{j0}'}{\sqrt{(V_R/\phi_o) + 1}} \qquad (1.5.21)$$

Again it is emphasized that the above results have been derived for a one-sided, abrupt junction. For more complex doping transitions from the *n* to the *p* side, it can be shown that C_j' can be approximated by:

$$C_j' = \frac{C_{j0}'}{[(V_R/\phi_o) + 1]^{\alpha_j}} \qquad (1.5.22)$$

where the expression for C_{j0}' will depend on the details of the transition from *n*

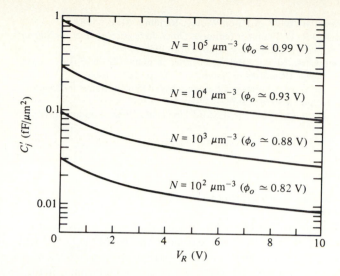

FIGURE 1.18
One-sided step-junction small-signal capacitance per unit area vs. reverse-bias voltage, with doping concentration of the lightly doped side as a parameter. The heavily doped side is assumed degenerate; corresponding approximate values of built-in voltage are indicated.[5] $T = 300$ K.

type to p type (these details form the so-called *profile* of the junction). The value of α_j is 1/2 for the one-sided abrupt junction we have discussed, and 1/3 for the linearly graded junction (one in which the net impurity concentration varies linearly with vertical position, being zero at the boundary between the two sides). For practical profiles (which are neither exactly abrupt nor exactly linearly graded) one often chooses the parameters α_j, C'_{j0}, and ϕ_o so as to obtain best matching between (1.5.22) and measurements.

REFERENCES

1. R. B. Adler, A. C. Smith, and R. L. Longini, *Introduction to Semiconductor Physics*, SEEC Series, Vol. 1, John Wiley, New York, 1964.
2. P. E. Gray, D. DeWitt, A. R. Boothroyd, and J. F. Gibbons, *Physical Electronics and Circuit Models of Transistors*, SEEC Series, Vol. 2, John Wiley, New York, 1964.
3. P. E. Gray and C. L. Searle, *Electronic Principles: Physics, Models, and Circuits*, John Wiley, New York, 1969.
4. A. S. Grove, *Physics and Technology of Semiconductor Devices*, John Wiley, New York, 1967.
5. S. M. Sze, *Physics of Semiconductor Devices*, John Wiley, New York, 1981.
6. R. S. Muller and T. Kamins, *Device Electronics for Integrated Circuits*, John Wiley, New York, 1977.
7. D. H. Navon, *Electronic Materials and Devices*, Houghton Mifflin, Boston, 1975.
8. B. G. Streetman, *Solid State Electronic Devices*, Prentice-Hall, Englewood Cliffs, N.J., 1981.
9. E. S. Yang, *Fundamentals of Semiconductor Devices*, McGraw-Hill, New York, 1978.
10. J. L. Moll, *Physics of Semiconductors*, McGraw-Hill, New York, 1964.
11. R. F. Pierret, *Semiconductor Fundamentals*, Addison-Wesley, Reading, Mass., 1983.

12. G. W. Neudeck, *The PN Junction Diode*, Addison-Wesley, Reading, Mass., 1983.
13. W. E. Beadle, J. C. C. Tsai, and R. D. Plummer (editors), *Quick Reference Manual for Silicon Integrated Circuit Technology*, Wiley-Interscience, New York, 1985.
14. B. E. Deal, E. H. Snow, and C. A. Mead, "Barrier energies in metal-silicon dioxide-silicon structures," *Journal of Physics and Chemistry of Solids*, vol. 27, p. 1873, 1966.
15. S. Kar, "Determination of Si-metal work function differences by MOS capacitance technique," *Solid-State Electronics*, vol. 18, pp. 169–181, 1975.
16. E. H. Rhoderick, *Metal-Semiconductor Contacts*, Oxford University Press, London, 1978.

PROBLEMS

1.1. Calculate the electron and hole concentrations in *p*-type Si with $N_A = 1000 \ \mu m^{-3}$ at $T = 280$ K, 300 K, and 330 K.

1.2. This problem is intended to give an idea of the order of magnitude involved for the various quantities discussed in Sec. 1.3. Consider the bar of Fig. 1.5 with $a = 100 \ \mu m$, $b = 10 \ \mu m$, $c = 2 \ \mu m$, and *n*-type doping with concentration of $10^3 \ \mu m^{-3}$; $V = 1$ V. Find the value of the conductivity, the mobility, the conductance, the sheet resistance, the total mobile charge, the mobile charge per unit area, the field intensity, the drift velocity, the transit time, and the current.

1.3. Prove that (1.3.23) is valid for the case of Fig. 1.8*b*.

1.4. (*a*) Prove mathematically that (1.3.14) and (1.3.15) are valid even if the electron concentration varies with depth as long as it is uniform horizontally.
    (*b*) Prove mathematically that (1.3.20) and (1.3.22) are valid for the conditions stated in the paragraph following (1.3.20).

1.5. Verify (1.4.1).

1.6. Calculate the contact potential of Au to *n*-type Si with $N_D = 10^4 \ \mu m^{-3}$ at 300 K.

1.7. A voltmeter with both of its leads made out of a metal X, measures a voltage V across a battery. Show that if one of the voltmeter's leads is replaced by a different material Y, the reading will not be affected.

1.8. Assume that the two terminals of a voltage source are made out of different material. Show that (1.4.11) and (1.4.12) are valid if V_{source} is defined as the voltage measured by an ideal voltmeter when it is attached to the terminals of the source.

1.9. For a two-sided step *pn* junction with neither of its sides degenerate, prove that the built-in potential ϕ_o is given by $\phi_t \ln (N_A N_D / n_i^2)$.

1.10. Plot the junction capacitance vs. reverse-bias voltage (from 0 to 5 V) for a silicon n^+p junction of area $200 \ \mu m^2$ with $N_A = 5 \times 10^3 \ \mu m^{-3}$. Assume $\phi_{Fn} = -0.56$ V.

1.11. Consider a semiconductor in equilibrium. Express the fact that the *total* current (drift plus diffusion components) must be zero, by using (1.3.11*a*) and (1.3.17). Using (1.2.7), show that the Einstein relation (1.3.18) results.

1.12. Study the material on basic laws of electrostatics in Appendix B and provide detailed derivations for results (B.4) to (B.6) given there.

1.13. Study the material on *pn* junctions in Appendix C, and provide detailed derivations for the results given there with the help of the basic electrostatics laws from Appendix B. From these results find the charge per unit area on each side of the junction. Prove (1.5.7) for the case $N_D \gg N_A$.

CHAPTER
2

THE TWO-TERMINAL MOS STRUCTURE

2.1 INTRODUCTION

In our gradual development towards the MOS transistor, we consider in this chapter the two-terminal MOS structure. This structure is often referred to as "MOS capacitor" and is shown in Fig. 2.1. Fabrication of this structure starts with a *p*- or *n*-type semiconductor material, called *substrate* or *body*, and assumed to be silicon from now on; common doping concentrations are 10^2 to $10^4 \, \mu m^{-3}$ (only uniformly doped substrates will be considered until we get to Chap. 6). An insulating layer is formed on top of the substrate. This layer is often silicon dioxide (SiO_2), simply referred to as "oxide," and its thickness is usually 0.01 to 0.1 μm. A third layer, called the *gate* is then formed on top of the insulator. The gate is made either of metal (usually aluminum) or of polycrystalline silicon. The latter refers to silicon material which is not a single crystal. Rather, it consists of many regions within which there is a regular array of atoms, and the regularity is broken at the boundaries between adjacent regions. This material is usually heavily doped *p* or *n* type (e.g., $10^8 \, \mu m^{-3}$); for brevity, it is referred to as polysilicon or simply poly. The fabrication of MOS structures is discussed in detail in Chap. 10.

The three-layer structure described above is often referred to by the acronym MOS, standing for "Metal-Oxide-Semiconductor," independently of whether the gate is actually made of metal or whether the insulator is silicon

35

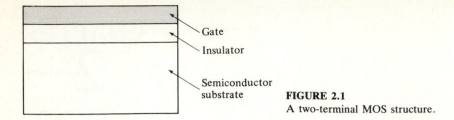

FIGURE 2.1
A two-terminal MOS structure.

dioxide. A more proper acronym, also in use, is MIS, standing for "Metal-Insulator-Semiconductor." In the days when gates were only made of metal, it became common to use the term "semiconductor" to refer unambiguously to the substrate material. Such usage continues today, even though the gate may be made of polysilicon.

The two-terminal MOS structure has been the subject of extensive studies over many years. Such studies have resulted in a detailed understanding of the structure and identified the sources of a number of undesirable effects that plagued early work. This led to the development of better fabrication methods which greatly reduced such effects and which made possible MOS transistors with high performance. A detailed study of the two-terminal MOS structure and a related history can be found elsewhere.[1] Here we will only discuss those aspects directly relevant to the objective of this book. We will consider the various potentials and charges developed in the two-terminal MOS structure (assumed made with a modern fabrication process) when a voltage is applied between gate and substrate. We will also consider the capacitance properties of the structure. The results we will obtain are put to extensive use in our later discussion of the (more complex) MOS transistor.

2.2   THE FLAT-BAND VOLTAGE

We begin our discussion with an "academic" case, shown in Fig. 2.2a. Here we assume that the gate is made of the same crystalline material as the substrate (in this case p-type silicon), with the same doping concentration. We also assume that somehow the same material is used to connect the gate to the substrate, in a sense making one an extension of the other. No charges are shown in the silicon, since to each positively charged hole of the p-type material there corresponds a negatively charged acceptor atom, from which the hole has originated, and there is no reason for the holes to pile up in any particular region. The charges, therefore, cancel and the material is shown as electrically neutral everywhere. The structure of Fig. 2.2a is basically symmetrical; assuming no parasitic charges have been introduced during fabrication, no field can exist in the insulator, and there is no reason for carriers to be attracted toward the insulator-substrate interface.

Consider now a realistic case, as shown in Fig. 2.2b. The gate is made out of a certain material, not necessarily the same as the substrate material. A

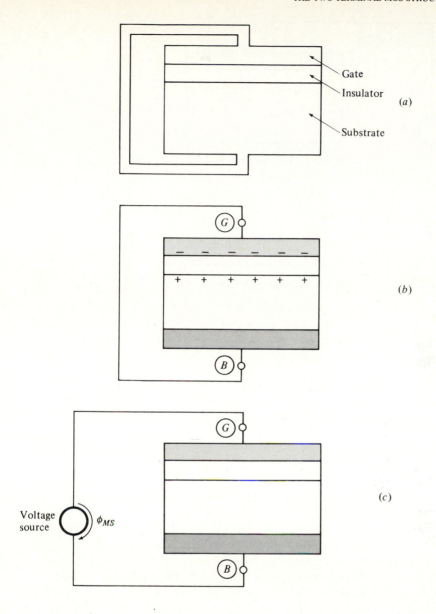

FIGURE 2.2
(*a*) A two-terminal MOS structure with gate, substrate, and short-circuiting external connection all made out of the same semiconductor material; (*b*) a MOS two-terminal structure (with gate and substrate made of different materials) with zero effective interface charge and with gate terminal short-circuited to the substrate terminal; (*c*) the structure of (*b*) with a voltage source placed in the loop, so that the surface charge becomes zero; (*d*) effect of effective interface charge Q_o; (*e*) the structure in (*d*) with additional external bias so that the surface charge becomes zero.

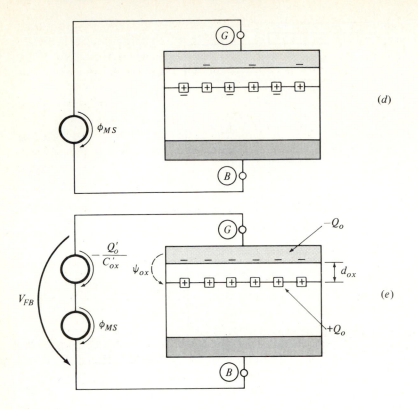

FIGURE 2.2 (continued).

metal is used to contact the gate material and form the *gate terminal G* as shown. In the following, the subscript *G* will be used to indicate the *gate terminal* rather than the gate itself. The body (substrate) is contacted through a back metal plate as shown. This plate is, in turn, contacted through some metal, which thus forms the *body terminal B*. Again, the subscript *B* will be used to denote the *body terminal*, as shown, rather than the body itself.

Let us now short-circuit the gate terminal to the body terminal by using a wire as shown. Consider going from the gate material through the external connection to the bulk. In doing so we encounter several contact potentials. However, from our discussion in Sec. 1.4 we know that their sum will only depend on the first and the last material, being independent of any material in between. Applying (1.4.7) we have

$$\begin{matrix} \text{Sum of all contact potentials} \\ \text{from gate, through external} \\ \text{connection, to bulk} \end{matrix} = \phi_{\text{gate material}} - \phi_{\text{bulk material}} \tag{2.2.1}$$

where each quantity in the right-hand side is characteristic of the corresponding material, as discussed in Sec. 1.4. The existence of a nonzero potential between the gate material and the bulk causes net charges to appear on both sides of the oxide. If, e.g., this potential is negative, the polarity of the charges will be as shown in Fig. 2.2*b*.

Consider now the following question: Can an external voltage be applied in such a way that the net charges disappear? This case is shown in Fig. 2.2*c*. To make the total potential from the gate material through the external connection to the bulk equal to zero, the voltage of the external source must precisely cancel the sum of the contact potentials. From (2.2.1) we see that it must have a value given by

$$\phi_{MS} \equiv \phi_{\text{bulk material}} - \phi_{\text{gate material}} \qquad (2.2.2)$$

where ϕ_{MS} is a widely used symbol; the value of ϕ_{MS} can be calculated from the above equation and Table 1.1.†

The effect of contact potentials is not the only one that can cause a net concentration of charges in the substrate in the absence of external bias. Another cause is a "parasitic" charge that exists within the oxide as well as at the oxide-semiconductor interface. This charge consists of four parts:[1]

1. An *oxide fixed charge* exists very close to the oxide-semiconductor interface due to the mechanisms of oxide formation at the time such formation is completed. This charge is found to be rather independent of oxide thickness, doping type (*n* or *p*), and doping concentration.
2. A so-called *oxide trapped charge* can exist throughout the oxide, but usually close to either of its interfaces to the substrate or the gate. This charge can be acquired through radiation, photoemission, or the injection of high-energy carriers from the substrate (Sec. 5.6).
3. A *mobile ionic charge* can exist within the oxide due to contamination by alkali ions (often sodium) introduced by the environment. This charge can move within the oxide under the presence of an electric field.
4. An *interface trap charge* (also called *fast surface-state charge*) exists at the oxide-semiconductor interface. It is caused by defects at that interface, which give rise to charge "traps"; these can exchange mobile carriers with the semiconductor, acting as donors or acceptors.

The above charges initially inhibited the development of high-performance MOS devices because their nature was not well understood and they were

---

† As expected from the footnote following (1.4.4), readers preferring to use "work functions" can write the right-hand side of (2.2.2) as $(1/q)(W_M - W_S)$, where W denotes work function and the subscripts M and S refer to the gate and semiconductor materials, respectively. Such usage is the origin of the subscripts MS in ϕ_{MS}.

difficult to control. In the early days, for example, the mobile ionic charge mentioned above was large and drifted about the oxide, depending on the externally applied voltage and the temperature. This charge, often transmitted to the oxide during fabrication through the hands of the people handling the device, resulted in very uncontrollable characteristics. Today, after years of work, the above four types of charge have been greatly reduced through modern fabrication techniques.[1] Throughout this book we assume that the devices we are dealing with have been fabricated by using such techniques. Until further notice, we will assume that all parasitic charge is located *at* the oxide-semiconductor interface and that its value, denoted by Q_o, is fixed.† Devices in which immobile charge exists *within* the oxide (uniformly distributed along the horizontal dimension in Fig. 2.2) can be modeled by assuming no such charge exists and by adjusting Q_o accordingly (Prob. 2.18); thus Q_o can be taken to be the *effective interface charge*. This charge is almost always positive for both *p*- and *n*-type substrates. In modern devices, the effective interface ion density is about 200 to 1000 ions/μm^2, corresponding to an effective interface charge density of 0.032 to 0.16 fC/μm^2.

The effective interface charge Q_o is shown inside the little squares in Fig. 2.2*d*. A battery of value ϕ_{MS} is used in this figure to cancel the effect of the contact potentials discussed previously, so that we can study the effect of Q_o by itself. The charge Q_o will cause a total charge $-Q_o$ to appear in the system as demanded by charge neutrality. As shown in Fig. 2.2*d*, part of that charge will appear at the gate and part in the semiconductor. If it is desired to eliminate these charges, one can note that, if all the required balancing charge $-Q_o$ were provided on the gate, no charge would be induced in the semiconductor. To provide a charge $-Q_o$ on the gate, a battery can be connected in series with the external circuit, with the $(-)$ terminal toward the gate. The following is now clear from basic electrostatics (Appendix B): Since at the gate and substrate ends of the oxide we must have charge $-Q_o$ and Q_o, respectively, the potential drop across the oxide, ψ_{ox}, defined from the gate through the oxide to the substrate, must be equal to $-Q_o/C_{ox}$, where C_{ox} is the total capacitance between the two ends of the oxide. This is exactly the voltage that must be provided by the battery, as shown in Fig. 2.2*e*.

In terms of quantities per unit area Q_o' and C_{ox}', we have, for ψ_{ox} in Fig. 2.2*e*

$$\psi_{ox} = -\frac{Q_o'}{C_{ox}'} \qquad (2.2.3)$$

The oxide capacitance per unit area is given by (Appendix B)

---

† The case of devices in which a significant fraction of Q_o is not fixed but depends instead on the externally applied potential (due to the interface traps mentioned above) will be considered later.

$$C'_{ox} = \frac{\epsilon_{ox}}{d_{ox}} \tag{2.2.4}$$

where d_{ox} is the thickness of the insulator and ϵ_{ox} is its permittivity, given by

$$\epsilon_{ox} = k_{ox}\epsilon_0 \tag{2.2.5}$$

with ϵ_0 the permittivity of free space (8.854×10^{-3} fF/μm) and k_{ox} the dielectric constant of the insulator; for SiO_2, $k_{ox} = 3.9$. Equation (2.2.4) is plotted in Fig. 2.3.

We have therefore seen that an external voltage can be used between the gate and substrate terminals to keep the semiconductor everywhere neutral by canceling the effects of the contact potentials and Q'_o. This voltage is called the *flat-band voltage*,† and is denoted by V_{FB}. From Fig. 2.2e we have the expression for the flat-band voltage:

$$V_{FB} = \phi_{MS} - \frac{Q'_o}{C'_{ox}} \tag{2.2.6}$$

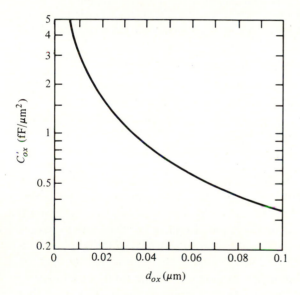

FIGURE 2.3
Capacitance per unit area vs. thickness for a silicon dioxide insulator.

---

† The name flat-band originates from the alternative description of semiconductor phenomena, which uses the concept of energy bands. It turns out that, for the uniform substrate assumed, those bands are "flat" in the semiconductor for the situation illustrated in Fig. 2.2e, and that the electric field throughout the body material is zero (Appendix D).

Example 2.1 Aluminum gate process. Calculate the flat-band voltage for a p-type substrate with $N_A = 5000 \, \mu m^{-3}$, an SiO_2 insulator with a thickness $d_{ox} = 0.042 \, \mu m$ and an aluminum gate. The equivalent interface charge Q'_o is 0.1 fC/μm^2.

The Fermi potential of the substrate is, by using (1.4.1), equal to 0.33 V. From (2.2.2) and Table 1.1, we have

$$\phi_{MS} = -0.33 \, V - 0.6 \, V = -0.93 \, V$$

From (2.2.4) $C'_{ox} = 0.822 \, fF/\mu m^2$, and therefore $-Q'_o/C'_{ox} = -0.12 \, V$. Therefore, using (2.2.6),

$$V_{FB} = -0.93 \, V - 0.12 \, V = -1.05 \, V$$

Example 2.2 Silicon gate process. Estimate the flat-band voltage if in the above process an n-type polysilicon gate with $N_D = 10^8 \, \mu m^{-3}$ is used instead of aluminum (as discussed in Chap. 10, when this material is used as the gate, the resulting "silicon gate process" offers a number of advantages).

The properties of polysilicon are not completely understood. In MOS work, it is common to use characteristic values indirectly obtained from measurements, or to assume that the gate is instead formed by crystalline silicon, and to estimate the flat-band voltage this way. Let us follow the latter approach. With the high doping concentration given, the gate material is degenerate, and its Fermi potential can be approximated by $-0.56 \, V$ (see Sec. 1.4). All other values to be used in our calculation remain the same as in the preceding example. Thus, from (2.2.2) we have

$$\phi_{MS} = -0.33 \, V - 0.56 \, V = -0.89 \, V$$

and, using (2.2.6),

$$V_{FB} = -0.89 \, V - 0.12 \, V = -1.01 \, V$$

2.3 POTENTIAL BALANCE AND CHARGE BALANCE

We will now discuss how the substrate is affected when the externally applied voltage V_{GB} assumes values different from the flat-band voltage V_{FB}. The general case is shown in Fig. 2.4. An arbitrary value of V_{GB} will in general cause charges to appear in the semiconductor. Practically all of these charges will be contained within a region adjacent to the top surface of the semiconductor, which is shown shaded in Fig. 2.4a. Outside this region the substrate is practically neutral. We define the *surface potential* ψ_s as the total potential drop across the region, defined from the *surface* to a point in the *bulk* outside that region.† We will be more specific about the width of the region later on.

---

† The top surface of the semiconductor is commonly referred to simply as "the surface" in MOS literature. The term *surface potential* is widely used as above.[2-4] However, in some treatments, this term is used for a quantity which differs from our ψ_s by the Fermi potential ϕ_F.

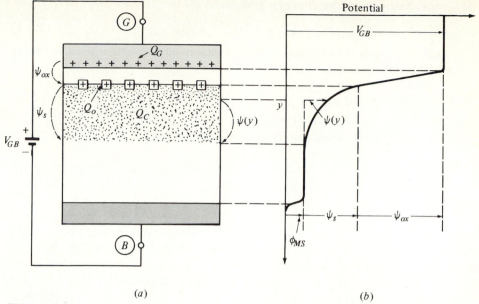

(a) (b)

FIGURE 2.4

(a) A p-substrate two-terminal MOS structure under general gate-substrate bias; (b) potential distribution assuming the gate, the substrate cap, and the external wires are all made of the same material (the special case of $\psi_s > 0$ has been assumed in drawing this plot).

Four kinds of potential drops are encountered in the loop, as seen in Fig. 2.4:

1. The voltage of the external source V_{GB}.
2. The potential drop across the oxide ψ_{ox}.
3. The surface potential ψ_s.
4. Several contact potentials. Their sum, when going clockwise, is ϕ_{MS}, as seen from (2.2.1) and (2.2.2).

Going around the loop, we can write:

$$V_{GB} = \psi_{ox} + \psi_s + \phi_{MS} \tag{2.3.1}$$

The "potential balance" expressed by the above equation is illustrated in Fig. 2.4b for the simple case in which the gate, the substrate contact, and the wires are all assumed made of the same material (e.g., Al); then, the only contact potential involved is between the substrate and its metal cap. If more than one contact is involved, (2.3.1) still holds, but a potential plot should then include all contact potentials, adding up to the value given by (2.2.2).

Note that in (2.3.1) ϕ_{MS} is a known constant; therefore, any changes in

V_{GB} must be balanced by changes in ψ_{ox} and ψ_s:

$$\Delta V_{GB} = \Delta \psi_{ox} + \Delta \psi_s \qquad (2.3.2)$$

Consider now the charges in the system. In Fig. 2.4 we encounter three kinds of charges:

1. The charge on the gate Q_G.
2. The effective interface charge Q_o.
3. The charge in the semiconductor under the oxide Q_C.

These charges must balance one another for overall charge neutrality in the system. Using charges per unit area,

$$Q'_G + Q'_o + Q'_C = 0 \qquad (2.3.3)$$

From now on, we will be using *charges per unit area* rather than charges most of the time. For brevity, though, we will often omit the words "per unit area"; these will be implied in the context.

Notice that if Q'_G is changed, the balance required by the foregoing equation will be achieved through a change in Q'_C, since the equivalent interface charge Q'_o is for the present assumed fixed:

$$\Delta Q'_G + \Delta Q'_C = 0 \qquad (2.3.4)$$

The potential balance equation (2.3.1) and the charge balance equation (2.3.3) have been deduced from general fundamental physical laws. As we will see, particular properties of the MOS system will impose additional relations between the quantities appearing in the above equations.

2.4 EFFECT OF GATE-SUBSTRATE VOLTAGE ON SURFACE CONDITION

Let us now consider the effect of V_{GB} on the condition of the region containing Q_C in Fig. 2.4. A p-type substrate is assumed. Depending on whether V_{GB} is equal to, less than, or greater than the flat-band voltage V_{FB}, we distinguished three cases discussed below.

2.4.1 Flat-Band Condition

This case has already been discussed in detail in Sec. 2.2, and is illustrated in Fig. 2.2e. From the associated discussion we have

$$V_{GB} = V_{FB} \qquad (2.4.1)$$

$$Q'_C = 0 \qquad (2.4.2)$$

$$\psi_s = 0 \qquad (2.4.3)$$

2.4.2 Accumulation

Consider the case in which V_{GB} decreases below V_{FB} (e.g., for the device of Example 2.1, this means that V_{GB} is *more negative* than -1.05 V). The negative change of V_{GB} (relative to flat band) will cause a negative change in Q'_G which, according to (2.3.4), must be balanced by a positive change in Q'_C above the value given by (2.4.2). Thus, holes will accumulate at the surface. This condition is called *accumulation*, and is illustrated in Fig. 2.5a. The negative change in V_{GB} will be shared by negative changes in ψ_{ox} and ψ_s, and (2.3.1) will remain valid. In accumulation, therefore, we have

$$V_{GB} < V_{FB} \tag{2.4.4}$$

$$Q'_C > 0 \tag{2.4.5}$$

$$\psi_s < 0 \tag{2.4.6}$$

2.4.3 Depletion and Inversion

Assume now the case in which V_{GB} increases above V_{FB}. The total charge on the gate Q_G will become more positive than the value in flat band (that value is $-Q_o$ in Fig. 2.2e). An example is shown in Fig. 2.5b, where it is assumed that the resulting Q'_G is positive. The positive change in Q'_G (relative to flat band) must be balanced by a negative change in Q'_C so that (2.3.3) remains valid. Also, the positive change in V_{GB} will be shared among ψ_{ox} and ψ_s, while (2.3.1) remains valid. Accordingly, we have:

$$V_{GB} > V_{FB} \tag{2.4.7}$$

$$Q'_C < 0 \tag{2.4.8}$$

$$\psi_s > 0 \tag{2.4.9}$$

Let us now consider the nature of the negative charge Q'_C. If V_{GB} is not much higher than V_{FB}, the positive potential at the surface with respect to the bulk will simply drive holes away from the surface, leaving it depleted. This condition is called *depletion* and it is illustrated in Fig. 2.5b. More precisely, as V_{GB} is raised above V_{FB}, the hole density will keep decreasing well below the doping concentration value N_A. For practical purposes, then, the charge Q_C is due to the uncovered acceptor atoms, each of which contributes a charge $-q$, and we can assume the presence of a "depletion region" as in the p side of the pn junction in Sec. 1.5.

As V_{GB} is increased further, more acceptor atoms are uncovered, and ψ_s becomes sufficiently positive to attract a significant number of free electrons to the surface; each of these electrons will also contribute a charge $-q$ to Q_C. Note that in the two-terminal MOS structure we are considering, these electrons come from the relatively slow process of electron-hole generation in the depletion region, caused by the thermal vibration of the lattice (assuming no radiation is present). Eventually, with a sufficiently high V_{GB} the density

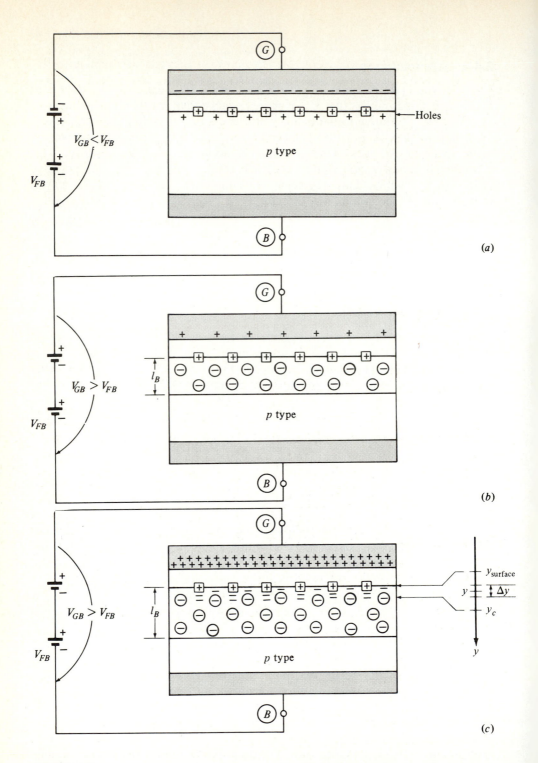

FIGURE 2.5
A MOS two-terminal structure in (*a*) accumulation; (*b*) depletion; and (*c*) inversion.

of electrons will exceed that of holes at the surface. This is a situation opposite from that normally expected in a *p*-type material; we now have surface *inversion*. The situation is illustrated in Fig. 2.5c.†

At this point we should warn the reader that the term *region* is often used with two different meanings in MOS work. Thus, for example, depletion region could refer to the physical region containing the ionized acceptor atoms in Fig. 2.5b; or it could refer to the region of V_{GB} (or ψ_s) values in which we have depletion as defined above. Which of the two meanings is employed will usually be clear from the context.

The oxide blocks the flow of current and equilibrium is maintained in the substrate. Deep in the neutral bulk outside the depletion region, the values of the hole and electron concentrations will be p_o and n_o, as given by (1.2.4) and (1.2.5). We can relate the electron concentration at the surface to that in the bulk by using (1.2.7):

$$n_{\text{surface}} = n_o e^{\psi_s/\phi_t} \tag{2.4.10}$$

Using (1.4.1a) and (1.4.1b), the above can be written as follows:

$$n_{\text{surface}} = n_i e^{(\psi_s - \phi_F)/\phi_t} \tag{2.4.11a}$$

$$= p_o e^{(\psi_s - 2\phi_F)/\phi_t} \tag{2.4.11b}$$

and, since $p_0 \approx N_A$ from (1.2.4), we have

$$n_{\text{surface}} \approx N_A e^{(\psi_s - 2\phi_F)/\phi_t} \tag{2.4.12}$$

The surface electron concentration has been plotted vs. the surface potential in Fig. 2.6. Some interesting points are shown in the figure. At $\psi_s = \phi_F$, n_{surface} becomes equal to the intrinsic concentration as seen from (2.4.11a); from (1.2.6) then, $n_{\text{surface}} = p_{\text{surface}}$. This is defined as the limit point between the depletion and inversion regions, as indicated in the figure. Of course, as seen from (2.4.11a), n_{surface} will be nonzero even in depletion, but will be much smaller than n_i, even for ψ_s smaller than ϕ_F by only a few ϕ_t. With increasing ψ_s above ϕ_F, n_{surface} increases drastically, and at $\psi_s = 2\phi_F$ we have $n_{\text{surface}} = p_o \approx N_A$, as seen from (2.4.11a) and (2.4.12).

If the substrate is made of *n*-type material, the above picture should be modified in a rather obvious manner. The inversion layer in this case will consist of holes, which will be attracted to the surface if V_{GB} is sufficiently negative. The immobile charge in the depletion region will consist of positively charged ionized donor atoms. With V_{GB} sufficiently positive, electrons will pile up at the surface and we will have accumulation. Since the case of *n*-type substrates is complementary to that of *p*-type substrates, it will not be discussed separately.

---

† The application of the basic laws of electrostatics to produce plots of charge density, electric field, and potential for this case is illustrated in Appendix E.

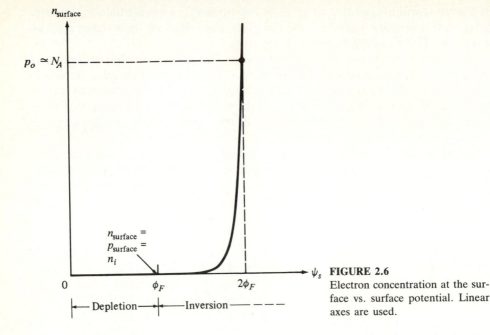

FIGURE 2.6
Electron concentration at the surface vs. surface potential. Linear axes are used.

2.4.4 General analysis

Of the three operation regions defined above, inversion is by far the most important one for the purposes of this book. This region is treated in detail in the following section. It should be noted at this point, though, that a general analysis is possible through which one can determine ψ_s and Q_C' for any value of V_{GB}, be it in accumulation, depletion, or inversion. Although such general analysis will not be of much use in this book, we will summarize the principles behind it for completeness. The mathematical details will be left for Appendix F. Consider a point or ordinate y in the substrate (Fig. 2.4), and let $\psi(y)$ be the potential there with respect to the bulk. From (1.2.7) we will have, for the electron concentration at y,

$$n(y) = n_o e^{\psi(y)/\phi_t} \tag{2.4.13}$$

which reduces to (2.4.10) at the surface. Similarly, for the hole concentration at y we will have, according to (1.2.11),

$$p(y) = p_o e^{-\psi(y)/\phi_t} \tag{2.4.14}$$

In the general case, one must allow for the presence of both electrons and holes below the oxide. Thus the charge density from (1.2.12) is

$$\rho(y) = q[p(y) - n(y) - N_A] \tag{2.4.15}$$

Substituting in this (2.4.13) and (2.4.14), we can write Poisson's equation

(1.2.13) as follows:

$$\frac{d^2\psi}{dy^2} = \frac{-q}{\epsilon_s}\left(p_o e^{-\psi(y)/\phi_t} - n_o e^{\psi(y)/\phi_t} - N_A\right) \tag{2.4.16}$$

With the help of this equation and the three above it, and for a given ψ_s, one can determine $\psi(y)$, $n(y)$, $p(y)$, and $\rho(y)$, and the corresponding total charge per unit area below the oxide, Q'_C (Appendix F). Unfortunately, only Q'_C can be derived in closed form, the other quantities requiring a numerical evaluation. As shown in Appendix F, we obtain

$$Q'_C = \mp(F\sqrt{N_A})\sqrt{\phi_t e^{-\psi_s/\phi_t} + \psi_s - \phi_t + e^{-2\phi_F/\phi_t}(\phi_t e^{\psi_s/\phi_t} - \psi_s - \phi_t)} \tag{2.4.17}$$

where $F = \sqrt{2q\epsilon_s}$ is the same constant defined in (1.5.10) ($F = 0.00579\ \text{fC}\cdot\mu\text{m}^{-1/2}\cdot\text{V}^{-1/2}$), and where the $-$ sign in front of F must be used with $\psi_s > 0$ (depletion or inversion), and the $+$ sign with $\psi_s < 0$ (accumulation).

To complete our set of basic equations, note that the charge per unit area above the oxide, Q'_G, can be simply related to the potential across the oxide, ψ_{ox}, and the oxide capacitance per unit area, C'_{ox}, by (Prob. 2.13):

$$Q'_G = C'_{ox}\psi_{ox} \tag{2.4.18}$$

We have now derived four equations that completely characterize the MOS structure under our assumptions. These equations are (2.3.1), (2.3.3), (2.4.17), and (2.4.18), and contain four unknowns: ψ_{ox}, ψ_s, Q'_C, and Q'_G. This system of equations can be solved (numerically, as it turns out) to provide the values of the above quantities for a given MOS structure (i.e., given ϕ_{MS} and N_A) and given externally applied voltage V_{GB}. With ψ_s known from this solution, one can determine $\psi(y)$, $n(y)$, $p(y)$, and $\rho(y)$, as already discussed.

The above analysis is complicated. The complexity is, in part, due to the fact that complete generality was sought, i.e., validity in accumulation, depletion, and inversion. In this book, properties in accumulation and depletion are only needed for evaluating some parasitic effects associated with turned-off MOS transistors (Chap. 7). In contrast, inversion is responsible for current conduction in MOS transistors and is much more important to us. By focusing on this region, certain approximations become possible which simplify the analysis of the MOS structure, as will be seen in the following section.

2.5 INVERSION

2.5.1 General Relations for Inversion

For substrate doping concentrations usually encountered in MOS transistor work (10^2 to $10^5\ \mu\text{m}^{-3}$), the Fermi potential ϕ_F can have values approximately between $9\phi_t$ and $16\phi_t$; thus, the quantity $2\phi_F$ in (2.4.17) lies between $18\phi_t$ and $32\phi_t$. It is easy to see that in inversion (Fig. 2.5c), where $\psi_s \geq \phi_F$, (2.4.17) can be approximated by the following:†

$$Q'_C = -(F\sqrt{N_A})\sqrt{\psi_s + \phi_t e^{(\psi_s - 2\phi_F)\phi_t}} \tag{2.5.1}$$

The total charge (per unit area) below the oxide is the sum of the charge due to the electrons in the inversion layer Q'_I and the charge due to the ionized acceptor atoms in the depletion region Q'_B:

$$Q'_C = Q'_I + Q'_B \tag{2.5.2}$$

We now undertake the evaluation of Q'_I and Q'_B. Consider first the electrons in the inversion layer. At any point of ordinate y in Fig. 2.5c, the electron concentration $n(y)$ will be given by (2.4.13). As one goes away from the surface, $\psi(y)$ decreases from ψ_s toward zero, and $n(y)$ dies out rapidly owing to its exponential dependence on $\psi(y)$. Hence, one can choose a point $y = y_c$ below which the electron concentration will be negligible. Practically all of the free electrons are then contained in a layer between $y = y_{surface}$ and $y = y_c$ (Fig. 2.5c). The number of electrons contained in a thin layer of thickness Δy, parallel to the surface and centered around y, will be $n(y)(A \Delta y)$, where A is the cross-sectional area as seen from the top. The total charge due to these electrons will be $(-q)n(y)(A \Delta y)$. We can then express the charge due to all electrons in the inversion layer, denoted by Q_I, as follows:

$$Q_I = \int_{y_{surface}}^{y_c} (-q)n(y)(A \, dy) \tag{2.5.3}$$

Therefore, the inversion layer charge per unit area Q'_I, will be given by

$$Q'_I = -q \int_{y_{surface}}^{y_c} n(y) \, dy \tag{2.5.4}$$

Evaluating Q'_I in this manner is a lengthy process and can be done through numerical integration (Appendix F). We will instead follow a widely used simplifying approach: We will determine a sufficiently accurate expression for Q'_B and then return to evaluate Q'_I from (2.5.2) and (2.5.1). Let us then concentrate on the depletion region. As in the case of the *pn* junction, we will consider this region as being defined by a sharp boundary at a depth l_B below the surface (Fig. 2.5c). The inversion layer is at the top of this region. Numerical calculations (Appendix F) show that most of the charge in this layer is concentrated very close to the surface (within a few hundredths of 1 μm). Since the depth l_B of the depletion region is normally much larger, we will assume that the inversion layer is a sheet of negligible thickness.[5-10] This has been called the *charge sheet* approximation,[8] and implies that practically all of

---

† Equation (2.5.1) can also be derived directly for the situation in Fig. 2.5c, starting from the assumption that no holes are present in the depletion region (Prob. 2.14). This equation is actually valid even in the upper part of depletion (i.e., for ψ_s larger than a few ϕ_t).

the depletion region is free of electrons. For a negligible thickness, the potential drop across the inversion layer will also be negligible (Prob. 2.15), and we can assume that all of the surface potential ψ_s is dropped across the depletion region in the p-type substrate. We can thus relate l_B to ψ_s, just as we did for the n^+p junction in Sec. 1.5. We will assume that the mobile carrier concentrations are negligible in comparison to the acceptor concentration inside the depletion region; this has been called the *depletion approximation* in Sec. 1.5. Solving Poisson's equation (1.2.13) under this assumption results in an equation analogous to (1.5.13) (Appendix E and Prob. 2.16):

$$l_B = \sqrt{\frac{2\epsilon_s}{qN_A}} \sqrt{\psi_s} \qquad (2.5.5)$$

Let Q'_B be the charge per unit area due to the uncovered acceptor atoms in the depletion region. Corresponding to (1.5.14) we have:

$$Q'_B = -F\sqrt{N_A}\sqrt{\psi_s} \qquad (2.5.6)$$

Using now the above equation and (2.5.1) in (2.5.2), we obtain the inversion layer charge per unit area:†

$$Q'_I = -F\sqrt{N_A}(\sqrt{\psi_s + \phi_t e^{(\psi_s - 2\phi_F)/\phi_t}} - \sqrt{\psi_s}) \qquad (2.5.7)$$

We have plotted $|Q'_B|$ and $|Q'_I|$ vs. ψ_s in Fig. 2.7 by using (2.5.6) and (2.5.7); their sum $|Q'_C|$ is also shown.

It is convenient to divide the inversion region into three subregions: These are marked *weak*, *moderate*, and *strong* inversion in Fig. 2.7. To be consistent with the definition of inversion in Fig. 2.6, one can define the onset of weak inversion in Fig. 2.7 as

$$\phi_{L0} = \phi_F \qquad (2.5.8)$$

The upper limit of weak inversion is defined in much of the literature as

$$\phi_{M0} = 2\phi_F \qquad (2.5.9)$$

It is seen that for surface potentials less than about this value, practically all the surface charge is due to the charge in the depletion region. The corresponding inversion layer charge is too small to be shown in the scale of the figure, but can nevertheless cause nonnegligible conduction when the MOS structure is part of a transistor. As ψ_s is raised above $2\phi_F$, $|Q'_I|$ starts to become significant because of the exponential in (2.5.7). For ψ_s exceeding $2\phi_F$ by a few ϕ_t, Q'_I becomes a very strong function of ψ_s. This should come as no surprise. From

---

† It can be shown that more accurate expressions for Q'_C, Q'_B, and Q'_I include the term $-\phi_t$ under *each* square-root sign in (2.5.1), (2.5.6), and (2.5.7) (Appendix F). The error involved in omitting this term is small for the values of ψ_s assumed in inversion. In fact, the above expressions can be used successfully *even* in the upper part of depletion.

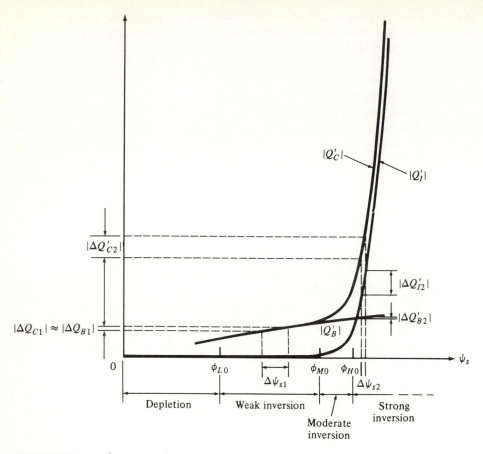

FIGURE 2.7
Magnitude of inversion layer charge, depletion region charge, and their sum (all per unit area) vs.
surface potential.

Fig. 2.6 we see that at $\psi_s = 2\phi_F$ the surface electron concentration is already as
high as the concentration of acceptor atoms. An increase of ψ_s above $2\phi_F$ by
several ϕ_t would be enough to provide very large n_{surface} because of the
exponential dependence of the latter on ψ_s (2.4.12). The concentration $n(y)$ at
points very close to the surface would also increase drastically, and Q_I' as seen
from (2.5.4) would begin "taking off." A point around which this is happening
can be defined as the onset of strong inversion, denoted by ϕ_{H0} in Fig. 2.7. We
will have

$$\phi_{H0} = 2\phi_F + \phi_{Z0} \tag{2.5.10}$$

where ϕ_{Z0} will be several ϕ_t. It is possible to make the definition "sharper" and
be more specific about the value of ϕ_{Z0}; the interested reader is referred to
Sec. 2.7.

In addition to the relative contributions of Q_I' and Q_B' to Q_C', it is very important to consider the relative contributions to *changes* $\Delta Q_C'$, associated with changes $\Delta \psi_s$ in the surface potential. Such charge changes are provided partly by a change in the inversion layer charge and partly by a change in the depletion region charge; that is, as seen from (2.5.2), we have

$$\Delta Q_C' = \Delta Q_I' + \Delta Q_B' \qquad (2.5.11)$$

Let us first consider the case where V_{GB} is low, so that ψ_s and $|Q_C'|$ are also low. Assume a change ΔV_{GB1} of V_{GB} results in a change $\Delta Q_{C1}'$ as shown in Fig. 2.7. From the figure it is clear that practically all of this change is provided by a change $\Delta Q_{B1}'$ in the depletion region charge. Furthermore, the change $\Delta \psi_{s1}$ of the surface potential, required to accommodate these charge changes, is quite significant. It is clear that what has just been described is characteristic of most of what has been marked "weak inversion" in Fig. 2.7, with the possible exception of points very close to its upper limit.

Assume now that V_{GB} is larger, causing a large ψ_s and a large $|Q_C'|$. Assume a change ΔV_{GB2} causes a change $\Delta Q_{C2}'$, as shown in Fig. 2.7. Things are now different. Practically all $\Delta Q_C'$ is provided by a change $\Delta Q_{I2}'$ of the inversion layer charge, $\Delta Q_B'$ being negligible, and the surface potential change $\Delta \psi_{s2}$ required to accommodate these changes is very small. This behavior is evident throughout what has been marked "strong inversion" in Fig. 2.7.

Let us stop for a moment and summarize the most important results in our development. We have derived enough equations to characterize the MOS system in inversion; these are:

1. *Potential balance.* Equation (2.3.1), repeated here for convenience, requires

$$V_{GB} = \psi_{ox} + \psi_s + \phi_{MS} \qquad (2.5.12)$$

2. *Charge balance.* From (2.3.3) and (2.5.2) we have

$$Q_G' + Q_o' + Q_I' + Q_B' = 0 \qquad (2.5.13)$$

3. *Relations of charges to potentials.* The final three equations relate each charge variable to the potential associated with it. In particular, the charge above the oxide is related to the potential across the oxide by (2.4.18), repeated below:

$$Q_G' = C_{ox}' \psi_{ox} \qquad (2.5.14)$$

The inversion layer charge is related to the surface potential by (2.5.7), which is of the form

$$Q_I' = Q_I'(\psi_s) \qquad (2.5.15)$$

Finally, the depletion region charge is related to the potential across that region by (2.5.6), which is of the form

$$Q_B' = Q_B'(\psi_s) \qquad (2.5.16)$$

The five equations (2.5.12) through (2.5.16) contain six variables, three of which are potentials (V_{GB}, ψ_{ox}, ψ_s) and three of which are charges per unit area (Q_G', Q_I', Q_B'). Among the five equations we can eliminate four of the variables and end up with a relationship between the other two. For example, let us develop a relation between V_{GB} and ψ_s. Eliminating the other variables, we obtain (Prob. 2.3)

$$V_{GB} = V_{FB} + \psi_s - \frac{Q'_B(\psi_s) + Q'_I(\psi_s)}{C'_{ox}} \qquad (2.5.17)$$

or, using (2.5.2) and (2.5.1),

$$V_{GB} = V_{FB} + \psi_s + \gamma\sqrt{\psi_s + \phi_t e^{(\psi_s - 2\phi_F)/\phi_t}} \qquad (2.5.18)$$

where

$$\gamma \equiv \frac{F\sqrt{N_A}}{C'_{ox}} \qquad (2.5.19)$$

The values of the parameter γ are shown in Fig. 2.8 for a variety of process

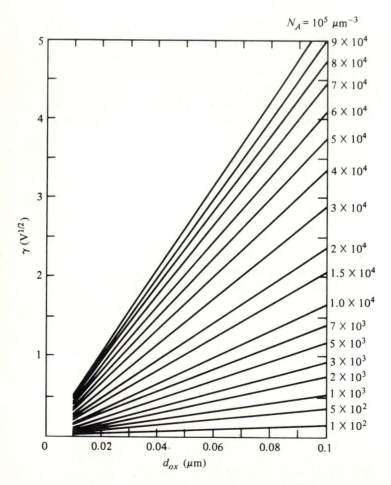

FIGURE 2.8
Body effect coefficient vs. oxide thickness for several values of substrate doping.

parameters. This parameter is called the *body effect coefficient*, for reasons that will become apparent in Chap. 3. Equation (2.5.18) is plotted in Fig. 2.9, where it is shown as ψ_s vs. V_{GB} (although the equation cannot be solved explicitly for ψ_s). Notice that for low points on the curve, significant changes $\Delta\psi_s$ are required to accommodate the charge required by ΔV_{GB} (relate also to Fig. 2.7). For points high on the curve, a slight $\Delta\psi_s$ is sufficient to accommodate these charge changes, which is in part owing to the steepness of the curves in Fig. 2.7. The weak-inversion region is characterized by significant and nearly constant slope $d\psi_s/dV_{GB}$; in strong inversion, this slope drops to small values.

In terms of V_{GB}, the onsets of weak, moderate, and strong inversion will be denoted by V_{L0}, V_{M0}, and V_{H0}, as shown in Fig. 2.9. V_{L0} and V_{M0} can be found from (2.5.18) by using in it, respectively, $\psi_s = \phi_{L0}$ from (2.5.8) and $\psi_s = \phi_{M0}$ from (2.5.9). Neglecting the resulting small exponential terms gives

$$V_{L0} = V_{FB} + \phi_F + \gamma\sqrt{\phi_F} \qquad (2.5.20)$$

$$V_{M0} = V_{FB} + 2\phi_F + \gamma\sqrt{2\phi_F} \qquad (2.5.21)$$

To find V_{H0}, one can use $\psi_s = \phi_{H0}$ in (2.5.18) *only if* ϕ_{H0} is known *accurately*. Note that here the exponential will not be negligible, since ϕ_{H0} is above $2\phi_F$ by several ϕ_t, as suggested by (2.5.10). Hence, even a small error in

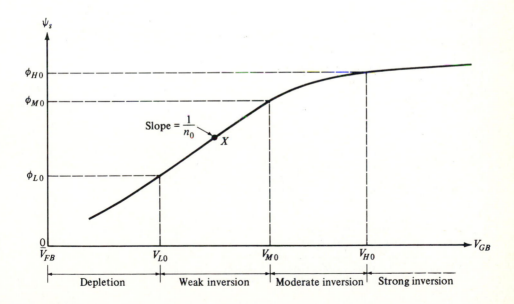

FIGURE 2.9
Surface potential vs. gate-substrate voltage.

ϕ_{H0} can result in a large error in the exponential, and thus a large error in V_{H0}. In general, one finds

$$V_{H0} = V_{M0} + V_{Z0} \tag{2.5.22}$$

where V_{Z0} is several tenths of 1 V (typically 0.6 V for practical devices at room temperature). (See Sec. 2.5.2 for a further discussion of the value of V_{Z0}.)

It is desirable in the present development to find a relation of the form

$$Q_I' = Q_I'(V_{GB}) \tag{2.5.23}$$

Unfortunately, if one attempts to derive such a relation from (2.5.12) through (2.5.16), it is found that an implicit expression results; that is, Q_I' cannot be expressed in closed form as a function of V_{GB}. The solution of the resulting complicated equation has to be obtained numerically if a value for V_{GB} is given and the value for Q_I' is desired. For our purposes, instead of (2.5.23) we can consider its parametric representation, which consists of (2.5.7) and (2.5.18). If values are assumed for ψ_s, the corresponding Q_I' and V_{GB} can be found from these equations. Q_I' can then be plotted vs. V_{GB} as in Fig. 2.10.

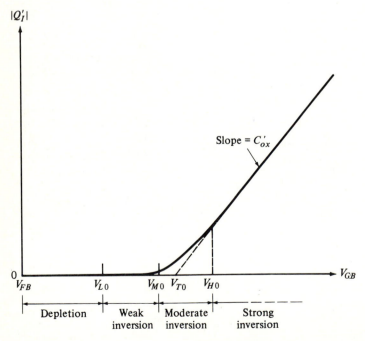

FIGURE 2.10
Magnitude of inversion layer charge per unit area vs. gate-substrate voltage.

Let us also develop an alternate expression for Q_I' for later use. If Q_G' and ψ_{ox} are eliminated among (2.5.12) to (2.5.14), and if (2.5.6) and (2.2.6) are used in the result, we obtain

$$Q_I' = -C_{ox}'(V_{GB} - V_{FB} - \psi_s - \gamma\sqrt{\psi_s}) \tag{2.5.24}$$

One can thus regard (2.5.24) and (2.5.18) as an alternative parametric representation of the relation between Q_I' and V_{GB}.

We will now consider each region of inversion (weak, moderate, and strong) separately. We will identify the dominant phenomena in each region and show certain approximations that can be made in each case. We will seek to develop explicit expressions of the form of (2.5.23), based on such approximations. This will be desirable not only for ease of computation but also because the functional form of the resulting approximate expressions will help make evident the dominant phenomena in the regions under consideration. Also, such expressions will be needed for developing simple models for the MOS transistor in subsequent chapters.

2.5.2 Strong Inversion

As seen in Fig. 2.9, in strong inversion large changes in V_{GB} result in very small changes in ψ_s. A very common assumption is that in strong inversion ψ_s is practically "pinned" to a constant value:

$$\psi_s = \phi_B \tag{2.5.25}$$

The value of ϕ_B is close to ϕ_{H0} but is difficult to define exactly. Obviously, if one is interested in operating points limited only to high V_{GB}, the value chosen for ϕ_B would be somewhat larger than that needed for low-voltage operation.† Often a single value is chosen for ϕ_B as a compromise. Since ϕ_B appears also in MOS transistor equations (Chap. 4), it is often chosen empirically to make such equations match measurements as much as possible. If measurements are not available, a rough estimate of $2\phi_F + 6\phi_t$ can be used, which is an average for a variety of process parameters and voltage values. In the literature, the value of $\phi_B = 2\phi_F$ is widely used. It is obvious from the above discussion that this value is not very accurate since ϕ_B is above ϕ_{H0} and ϕ_{H0} is already above $2\phi_F$ by several ϕ_t, as indicated by (2.5.10).‡

Equation (2.5.25) implies that the depletion region width l_B is assumed to reach a maximum value l_{Bm}, and not to increase with V_{GB} anymore. From (2.5.5) and (2.5.25),

---

† The situation is analogous to assuming a constant value for the base-emitter voltage for bipolar transistors. The value chosen depends on the context and the application, and can be expected to be higher in power circuit work than in micropower circuit work.

‡ Note that this discussion about the value of ϕ_B assumes a *uniform* substrate.

$$l_{Bm} = \sqrt{\frac{2\epsilon_s}{qN_A}} \sqrt{\phi_B} \tag{2.5.26}$$

Similarly, the depletion region charge is assumed to have reached a maximum value given by (2.5.6) and (2.5.25):

$$Q_B' = -F\sqrt{N_A}\sqrt{\phi_B} \tag{2.5.27}$$

Using (2.5.12) to (2.5.14) and (2.5.25), we obtain

$$Q_I' = -C_{ox}'(V_{GB} - V_{T0}) \tag{2.5.28}$$

where

$$V_{T0} = \phi_{MS} - \frac{Q_0'}{C_{ox}} + \phi_B - \frac{Q_B'}{C_{ox}'} \tag{2.5.29}$$

and, using (2.2.6), (2.5.27) and (2.5.19) in the above equations,

$$V_{T0} = V_{FB} + \phi_B + \gamma\sqrt{\phi_B} \tag{2.5.30}$$

Equations (2.5.28) and (2.5.30) could also have been obtained directly from (2.5.24) and (2.5.25).† Equation (2.5.28) is compared to the exact $Q_I'(V_{GB})$ in Fig. 2.10. The quantity V_{T0} is called the *extrapolated threshold voltage* of the MOS junction, for obvious reasons. The fact that the plot of $Q_I'(V_{GB})$ is practically a straight line in strong inversion will prove to be crucial in shaping the properties of the structure in this region.

Example 2.3. Estimate V_{T0} for the process of Example 2.2.
    In Example 2.2 we found $V_{FB} = -1.01$ V. Using the data of that example in (2.5.19), we find $\gamma = 0.50$ V$^{1/2}$. Let us use $\phi_B = 2\phi_F + 6\phi_t = 0.82$ V. Then (2.5.30) gives

$$V_{T0} = -1.01 \text{ V} + 0.82 \text{ V} + 0.50\sqrt{0.82} \text{ V} = 0.26 \text{ V}$$

We can now return to the discussion of the onset of strong inversion. As seen in Fig. 2.10, the transition of the exact Q_I' plot toward the straight-line behavior described by (2.5.28) is *very* gradual. No critical point can be identified that could conveniently be taken as the onset of strong inversion. Thus, a possible definition of this onset can be the minimum V_{GB} value for which (2.5.28) predicts Q_I' within an acceptable error. The value one ends up with depends, of course, on what is meant by acceptable error. For some applications, a 10 percent error in the value of Q_I' may be tolerated. Then the onset of strong inversion can be taken relatively close to V_{T0}. If only a 2 percent error can be tolerated, one should take the onset at a somewhat larger V_{GB} value. Finally, for some applications, accuracy is desirable not only for the

---

† We provide more than one way to obtain a result in an attempt to give a better "feeling" for the many new equations presented in this chapter. This will be repeated in the material to follow.

plot of Q'_I vs. V_{GB} but also for the *slope* of this plot. Then the onset of strong inversion should be defined accordingly. As is evident from the figure, at points where the slope is accurately predicted by the straight line, Q'_I itself is accurately predicted by it. Thus, definitions in terms of the slope are conservative, and "to be on the safe side," we will adopt them in this book. If a slope error of about 10 percent can be tolerated, it turns out that the onset of strong inversion V_{HO} should be taken about 0.6 V above V_{MO} at room temperature and for practical fabrication processes. There are ways to define and calculate V_{HO} precisely, if desired. These are somewhat elaborate, and are given in Sec. 2.7 for the interested reader. That section can be skipped without loss of continuity.

In some of the literature, the onset of strong inversion or (even of inversion in general) is taken at what we have defined as the onset of moderate inversion. In fact, often no distinction is made between V_{MO}, V_{TO}, and V_{HO} in the literature. All three are taken to be one and the same point, called *threshold*, and assumed to be given by (2.5.21). No moderate inversion is defined in such cases, and the strong-inversion region is taken to be adjacent to weak inversion. This practice originates in the early days of MOS work, when large V_{GB} values were common. If, for example, the actual values of V_{MO}, V_{TO}, and V_{HO} happen to be 1.0, 1.2, and 1.6 V, respectively, and the V_{GB} values of interest are 20 to 30 V, then using 1.0 or 1.6 V in lieu of V_{TO} in (2.5.28) will not result in excessive error. Today, however, with V_{GB} values limited to about 5 V for many practical cases, and with a constant drive to even lower voltages, a careful distinction between the three voltages is necessary.

2.5.3 Weak Inversion

In weak inversion $Q'_I(V_{GB})$ will be shown to assume a simple form, albeit very different from that in strong inversion. To start, consider (2.5.7) and let

$$\xi = \phi_t e^{(\psi_s - 2\phi_F)/\phi_t} \tag{2.5.31}$$

Consider the term $\sqrt{\psi_s + \xi}$ in (2.5.7). In weak inversion, ψ_s is smaller than ϕ_{MO}, which is taken equal to $2\phi_F$, as seen in (2.5.9). Thus $\xi \ll \psi_s$. The function $\sqrt{\psi_s + \xi}$ can be approximated by the first two terms of its Taylor expansion around $\xi = 0$:

$$\sqrt{\psi_s + \xi} \approx \sqrt{\psi_s} + \frac{1}{2\sqrt{\psi_s}} \xi \tag{2.5.32}$$

Using (2.5.31) and (2.5.32) in (2.5.7) we obtain

$$Q'_I \approx -\frac{F\sqrt{N_A}}{2\sqrt{\psi_s}} \phi_t e^{(\psi_s - 2\phi_F)/\phi_t} \tag{2.5.33}$$

To obtain a relation between Q'_I and the external bias V_{GB}, we need to relate ψ_s in the above equation to V_{GB}. This can be done very easily by noting that the general $V_{GB}(\psi_s)$ relation, (2.5.17), can be simplified to

$$V_{GB} \approx V_{FB} + \psi_s - \frac{Q_B'(\psi_s)}{C_{ox}'} \tag{2.5.34}$$

because in weak inversion $|Q_I'| \ll |Q_B'|$. Using (2.5.6) and (2.5.19), this becomes

$$V_{GB} \approx V_{FB} + \psi_s + \gamma\sqrt{\psi_s} \tag{2.5.35}$$

which could also have been obtained from (2.5.18) by noting that the exponential in the equation is negligible. Solving (2.5.35) we have

$$\psi_s \approx \left(-\frac{\gamma}{2} + \sqrt{\frac{\gamma^2}{4} + V_{GB} - V_{FB}}\right)^2 \tag{2.5.36}$$

Therefore, in weak inversion $Q_I'(V_{GB})$ is given explicitly by (2.5.33) if ψ_s is replaced with the right-hand side of (2.5.36).

A simpler result, which makes apparent the form of the functional dependence of Q_I' on V_{GB} can be obtained as follows. First, note that the variation of $\sqrt{\psi_s}$ in (2.5.33) is negligible when compared to the drastic variation of the exponential term in that equation; thus we can assume that $\sqrt{\psi_s}$ is practically fixed and we can replace that term by $\sqrt{1.5\phi_F}$, since $1.5\phi_F$ is the average value of ψ_s over the weak-inversion region [see (2.5.8) and (2.5.9)]. Thus,

$$Q_I' = -\frac{F\sqrt{N_A}}{2\sqrt{1.5\phi_F}} \phi_t e^{(\psi_s - 2\phi_F)/\phi_t} \tag{2.5.37}$$

This equation can be further simplified by noting that, as seen in Fig. 2.9, the slope of ψ_s vs. V_{GB} is practically constant in the weak-inversion region. Thus, for changes ΔV_{GB}, causing changes $\Delta\psi_s$ in weak inversion, we can write

$$\Delta\psi_s = \frac{\Delta V_{GB}}{n_0} \tag{2.5.38}$$

where n_0 is the inverse of the slope of the plot in Fig. 2.9, evaluated at the middle of the weak-inversion region, $\psi_s = 1.5\phi_F$.[11] Since ΔV_{GB} appears partly as $\Delta\psi_s$ and partly as $\Delta\psi_{ox}$ (see Eq. 2.3.2), it follows that $n_0 > 1$. The value of n_0 can be found by differentiating (2.3.35):

$$n_0 \equiv \left.\frac{dV_{GB}}{d\psi_s}\right|_{\psi_s = 1.5\phi_F} \tag{2.5.39}$$

or

$$n_0 = 1 + \frac{\gamma}{2\sqrt{1.5\phi_F}}\dagger \tag{2.5.40}$$

---

† If the interface trap charge (Sec. 2.2) varies with the surface potential, an extra term will be needed in this equation. This is shown at the end of Sec. 2.6.

The value of V_{GB} corresponding to the middle of the weak-inversion region will be denoted by V_{X0}. This value can be found by using $\psi_s = 1.5\phi_F$ in (2.5.35):

$$V_{X0} = V_{FB} + 1.5\phi_F + \gamma\sqrt{1.5\phi_F} \qquad (2.5.41)$$

Taking the changes in (2.5.38) with respect to the middle of weak inversion, we have

$$\psi_s - 1.5\phi_F = \frac{V_{GB} - V_{X0}}{n_0} \qquad (2.5.42)$$

Using this in (2.5.37), we obtain

$$Q_I' \approx Q_{IX0}' e^{(V_{GB} - V_{X0})/(n_0\phi_t)} \qquad (2.5.43)$$

with

$$Q_{IX0}' = -\frac{F\sqrt{N_A}}{2\sqrt{1.5\phi_F}} \phi_t e^{-0.5\phi_F/\phi_t} \qquad (2.5.44)$$

As is easily seen from (2.5.37), Q_{IX0}' above is the value of Q_I' at the middle of the weak-inversion region.

To check the exponential behavior of $Q_I'(V_{GB})$ predicted by (2.5.43), we have plotted $\ln|Q_I'|$ vs. V_{GB} in Fig. 2.11. The solid line represents the accurate equations (2.5.7) and (2.5.18), and describes the structure correctly for all regions of inversion. Also shown is the result of using (2.5.43). Over the weak-inversion region, the agreement is seen to be very good except at points very close to the upper limit of the region. Equation (2.5.43) will also tend to underestimate Q_I' near the bottom of the region (not shown in Fig. 2.11), but this is of little consequence since there Q_I' is too small to be of much practical importance.

2.5.4 Moderate Inversion

In moderate inversion, none of the simplifications discussed above is valid. The plot of $Q_I'(V_{GB})$ here is neither a straight line nor an exponential. If accurate results are needed in this region, the complete equations (2.5.7) and (2.5.18) can be used. Empirical equations (e.g., polynomial approximations) are also possible.

As has already been noted, in many treatments no moderate-inversion region is defined. Sometimes this region is considered the bottom part of strong inversion. In some treatments a point is defined, falling somewhere in our moderate-inversion region, and $Q_I'(V_{GB})$ is assumed to be exponential directly below and a straight line directly above that point. Such models can lead to large errors. This is shown in Fig. 2.11, where Q_I' as calculated from (2.5.7) and (2.5.18) is compared to the approximate equations (2.5.43) and (2.5.28). Neither of these two equations provides satisfactory accuracy in moderate inversion.

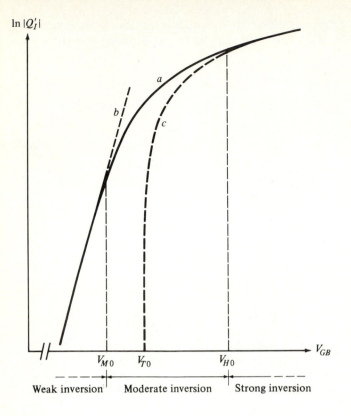

FIGURE 2.11
Logarithm of inversion layer charge magnitude per unit area vs. gate-substrate voltage. (*a*)
Equations (2.5.7) and (2.5.18); (*b*) (2.5.43); (*c*) (2.5.28).

2.6   SMALL-SIGNAL CAPACITANCE

If V_{GB} is increased by a small amount ΔV_{GB} in Fig. 2.4*a*, a positive charge $\Delta Q_G'$
will flow into the gate terminal. For overall charge neutrality, a charge of equal
value must flow out of the substrate terminal or, equivalently, a charge of value
$-\Delta Q_G'$ must flow *into* the substrate terminal. An incremental (small-signal)
capacitance per unit area, C_{gb}', can thus be defined to relate charge to voltage
changes. This is illustrated in Fig. 2.12. We define

$$C_{gb}' \equiv \frac{dQ_G'}{dV_{GB}} \tag{2.6.1}$$

The charge $-\Delta Q_G'$ flowing into the substrate goes to change the charge
Q_C' by an amount $\Delta Q_C'$:

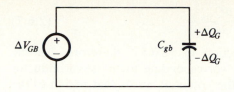

FIGURE 2.12
Small-signal equivalent circuit for a two-terminal MOS structure driven by a voltage source.

$$\Delta Q'_C = -\Delta Q'_G \tag{2.6.2}$$

The gate-to-substrate voltage change will be distributed partly across the oxide (as $\Delta\psi_{ox}$) and partly across the semiconductor (as a change $\Delta\psi_s$ in the surface potential). Equation (2.3.2) is repeated here for convenience:

$$\Delta V_{GB} = \Delta\psi_{ox} + \Delta\psi_s \tag{2.6.3}$$

Inverting (2.6.1) and using (2.6.3) in the result (with small changes replaced by differentials), we have

$$\frac{1}{C'_{gb}} = \frac{d\psi_{ox}}{dQ'_G} + \frac{d\psi_s}{dQ'_G} \tag{2.6.4}$$

The above equation can be written, by using (2.6.2), as

$$\frac{1}{C'_{gb}} = \frac{1}{dQ'_G/d\psi_{ox}} + \frac{1}{-dQ'_C/d\psi_s} \tag{2.6.5}$$

To interpret this equation, note first that from (2.5.14) we have

$$\frac{dQ'_G}{d\psi_{ox}} = C'_{ox} \tag{2.6.6}$$

The quantity $-dQ'_C/d\psi_s$ in (2.6.5) can be interpreted with the help of Fig. 2.4a as follows. If the potential across the semiconductor is changed by $\Delta\psi_s$, the charge in that region will change by $\Delta Q'_C$. This additional charge must enter the region through its *bottom*, coming from the substrate terminal. If now a capacitor had across it a voltage $\Delta\psi_s$, and the value of its capacitance were adjusted so that a charge $\Delta Q'_C$ had to flow into its *bottom* plate, the situation illustrated in Fig. 2.13 would result. From this figure we clearly have

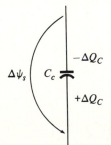

FIGURE 2.13
Illustrating the concept of semiconductor charge region small-signal capacitance.

$$C'_c \equiv -\frac{dQ'_C}{d\psi_s} \qquad (2.6.7)$$

The denominator of the last fraction in (2.6.5), therefore, can be interpreted as a small-signal capacitance corresponding to the semiconductor charge region. It relates the changes of the potential across that region to the corresponding changes in its charge.

Using now (2.6.6) and (2.6.7) in (2.6.5), we get

$$\frac{1}{C'_{gb}} = \frac{1}{C'_{ox}} + \frac{1}{C'_c} \qquad (2.6.8)$$

Therefore the small-signal capacitance C_{gb} is the same as that exhibited by two capacitors of values C_{ox} and C_c, connected in series as in Fig. 2.14. C'_{gb} can be evaluated from (2.6.8), (2.6.7), and (2.4.17) (the general expression for C'_c is given in Appendix F).

Let us consider the special case of accumulation. If ψ_s is negative and its absolute value is at least a few ϕ_t, Q'_C in (2.4.17) is a very sensitive function of ψ_s, and C'_c from (2.6.7) is very large. Then the total capacitance C'_{gb} is reduced to approximately C'_{ox}, as seen from (2.6.8). Intuitively, this should make sense. In accumulation there is an abundance of holes which can provide a conducting path from the substrate bottom through the semiconductor to the surface. For V_{GB} sufficiently smaller than V_{FB}, the resulting negative surface potential attracts huge numbers of holes immediately below the oxide, in a sense forming the bottom "plate" of the oxide capacitor. As a result, the total incremental capacitance seen between the two terminals of the MOS junction is basically that of the oxide, C'_{ox}.

Consider now the case of ψ_s positive and larger than a few ϕ_t (say, larger than $3\phi_t$; this includes the upper part of depletion, as well as the inversion region). Now there are practically no holes at the surface, and Q'_C is given by (2.5.1). Using this equation in (2.6.7), we obtain

$$C'_c = F\sqrt{N_A}\,\frac{1 + e^{(\psi_s - 2\phi_F)/\phi_t}}{2\sqrt{\psi_s + \phi_t e^{(\psi_s - 2\phi_F)/\phi_t}}}\ , \qquad \psi_s > 3\phi_t \qquad (2.6.9)$$

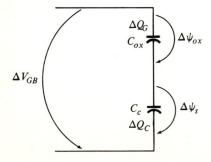

FIGURE 2.14
Circuit representation of (2.6.8).

A plot of C_c' vs. ψ_s is shown in Fig. 2.15. The rest of the plots in the figure will be discussed later in this section.

It is interesting to consider the individual contributions of the depletion region and inversion layer charges to C_c'. Equation (2.5.11) is repeated below:

$$\Delta Q_C' = \Delta Q_B' + \Delta Q_I' \qquad (2.6.10)$$

Using this equation in (2.6.7) we obtain

$$C_c' = \frac{-dQ_B'}{d\psi_s} + \frac{-dQ_I'}{d\psi_s} \qquad (2.6.11)$$

We have then separated the total semiconductor capacitance C_c' into two components, one owing to the depletion region charge and one owing to the inversion layer charge. With a reasoning analogous to that preceding (2.6.7), we can define a depletion region incremental capacitance per unit area:

$$C_b' \equiv -\frac{dQ_B'}{d\psi_s} \qquad (2.6.12)$$

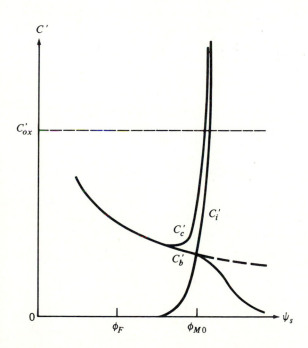

FIGURE 2.15
Small-signal capacitances per unit area vs. surface potential. C_i' is the inversion layer capacitance; C_b' is the depletion region capacitance (solid line is exact; broken line is as predicted by the charge sheet model); C_c' is the semiconductor charge region capacitance; C_{ox}' is the oxide capacitance.

This capacitance relates changes of the potential across the depletion region to the associated changes of the charge in it.

Let us also define a capacitance per unit area associated with the inversion layer. This capacitance should relate changes in the charge of that layer to the associated potential changes. In analogy with (2.6.12),

$$C_i' \equiv - \frac{dQ_I'}{d\psi_s} \tag{2.6.13}$$

From the above definitions it is seen that C_b' and C_i' are the slopes of plots $|Q_B'|$ vs. ψ_s and $|Q_I'|$ vs. ψ_s, respectively. However, to evaluate C_b' and C_i' one would have to use *very* accurate expressions for Q_B' and Q_I', since a negligible error in predicting a certain function can cause a severe error in predicting its derivative. For example, consider $|Q_B'|$ as predicted by the charge sheet model in (2.5.6) and plotted in Fig. 2.7. The corresponding C_b' is shown by the broken line in Fig. 2.15. A more exact model would be based on the general analysis outlined in Sec. 2.4, which allows for the spreading of the inversion layer into the depletion region and for the presence of holes there. Such a model gives a $|Q_B'|$ plot which, in moderate and strong inversion, is flatter than that shown in Fig. 2.7, becoming practically horizontal in very strong inversion. The corresponding error in the approximate $|Q_B'|$ is very small; yet, the slope of the exact and approximate plots are *very* different (solid line for C_b' in Fig. 2.15). The resulting exact C_b' and C_i' are given by (Appendix F)

$$C_b' = F\sqrt{N_A} \; \frac{1}{2\sqrt{\psi_s + \phi_t e^{(\psi_s - 2\phi_F)/\phi_t}}} \tag{2.6.14}$$

$$C_i' = F\sqrt{N_A} \; \frac{e^{(\psi_s - 2\phi_F)/\phi_t}}{2\sqrt{\psi_s + \phi_t e^{(\psi_s - 2\phi_F)/\phi_t}}} \tag{2.6.15}$$

It is easy to see that, using Q_B' as predicted by the charge sheet model in (2.5.6), we would have obtained (2.6.14) without the exponential term; that term, however, becomes dominant in strong inversion. Note that using the accurate formulas above we obtain $C_i' = C_b'$ at $\psi_s = 2\phi_F$.

Using (2.6.12) and (2.6.13) in (2.6.11) we obtain

$$C_c' = C_b' + C_i' \tag{2.6.16}$$

and (2.6.8) becomes

$$\frac{1}{C_{gb}'} = \frac{1}{C_{ox}'} + \frac{1}{C_b' + C_i'} \tag{2.6.17}$$

which can be represented by the circuit of Fig. 2.16. It should be kept in mind that this is a *small-signal equivalent* circuit, relating small *changes* of potentials and charges around a bias point. It does *not* relate total values of potentials and charges.

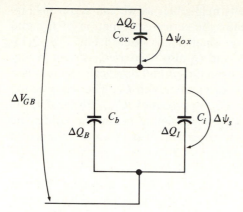

FIGURE 2.16
Small-signal equivalent circuit for the two-terminal MOS structure, showing individual capacitances.

Our ultimate goal in this development is to plot the total capacitance seen externally (C'_{gb}) vs. the totally externally applied bias (V_{GB}). This can be done as follows. For a given ψ_s, C'_c is determined; then C'_{gb} is found from (2.6.8). The result is shown by the solid curve in Fig. 2.17. We see that deep in accumulation, C'_{gb} approaches C'_{ox}, as we intuitively predicted above. For V_{GB} in the weak-inversion region (except for points close to the upper limit of the

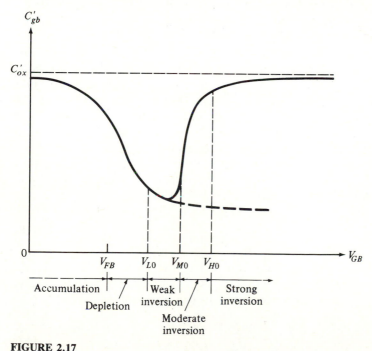

FIGURE 2.17
Total gate-substrate capacitance per unit area vs. gate-substrate bias. Solid line: "static" behavior; broken line: high-frequency behavior.

region), the inversion layer capacitance is negligible, as we can see from Fig. 2.15. From (2.6.17), then, C'_{gb} is basically the series combination of C'_{ox} and C'_b. As V_{GB} is increased, C'_b becomes smaller, as seen from Fig. 2.15. Therefore, the series combination of C'_{ox} and C'_b also decreases, as seen in Fig. 2.17. Above weak inversion, C'_i becomes significant and drastically increases if V_{GB} is raised further. This capacitance is in parallel with C'_b. The last fraction in (2.6.17) decreases drastically, and C'_{gb} approaches C'_{ox}. Physically, an abundance of electrons exists at high V_{GB} immediately below the oxide and provides the bottom "plate" of the oxide capacitor, just as an abundance of holes provided that plate in the case of accumulation.

The above discussion has been in terms of "static" changes, i.e., it is assumed that after V_{GB} is changed by a small amount ΔV_{GB}, it remains fixed at its new value. We then wait long enough for a new equilibrium to be reached, and we record the changes in the various potentials and charges. If ΔV_{GB} is a sinusoidal voltage, the steady-state charge changes will also be sinusoidal. They will correspond to equilibrium values *if* the frequency is low enough (e.g., 1 Hz). However, if the frequency is high (e.g., 10 kHz), things will be different, as shown by the broken line in Fig. 2.17. The inversion layer charge now cannot keep up with the fast changing ΔV_{GB}, and the required charge changes must be provided by covering or uncovering acceptor atoms at the bottom of the depletion region, just as in the case of depletion operation. The reason the inversion layer charge cannot follow fast enough, is that it is in a sense isolated from the outside world by the oxide on top and the depletion region below. Therefore, the electron concentration there can only be changed by the mechanisms of thermal generation and recombination, which in this case are very slow (no external irradiation is assumed). If, instead, communication with the outside world were possible, in the sense that inversion layer charge could be provided or removed externally, then the behavior exhibited by the solid curve in strong inversion would persist for much higher frequencies. This communication with the outside world will be provided by the source and drain regions in a MOS transistor, as discussed in subsequent chapters.

The incremental capacitances defined in this section can be used to provide convenient expressions for the slopes of various plots in Sec. 2.5. Thus, using (2.5.17), (2.6.12), and (2.6.13) we have

$$\frac{d\psi_s}{dV_{GB}} = \frac{C'_{ox}}{C'_{ox} + C'_b + C'_i} \tag{2.6.18}$$

which could also have been obtained from the equivalent circuit in Fig. 2.16. This relation gives simply the slope of the ψ_s vs. V_{GB} plot of Fig. 2.9. Similarly, the slope of the $|Q'_I|$ vs. V_{GB} plot in Fig. 2.10 can be found as follows:

$$\frac{d|Q'_I|}{dV_{GB}} = \frac{d|Q'_I|}{d\psi_s} \frac{d\psi_s}{dV_{GB}} \tag{2.6.19}$$

and using (2.6.13) and (2.6.18),

$$\frac{d|Q_I'|}{dV_{GB}} = \frac{C_{ox}' C_i'}{C_{ox}' + C_b' + C_i'} \qquad (2.6.20)$$

Finally, the slope of the $\ln |Q_I'|$ vs. V_{GB} plot in Fig. 2.11 can be found by using (2.6.20):

$$\frac{d \ln |Q_I'|}{dV_{GB}} = \frac{C_{ox}'}{C_{ox}' + C_b' + C_i'} \frac{C_i'}{|Q_I'|} \qquad (2.6.21)$$

The above results will be used in the next section.

Deep in weak inversion C_i' can be neglected in (2.6.18) (Fig. 2.15). The inverse of the quantity $\Delta \psi_s / \Delta V_{GB}$ evaluated at $\psi_s = 1.5\phi_F$ has been denoted by n_0 in (2.5.39); thus, from (2.6.18),

$$n_0 = 1 + \left. \frac{C_b'}{C_{ox}'} \right|_{\psi_s = 1.5\phi_F} \qquad (2.6.22)$$

which can be easily shown to reduce to (2.5.40).

It should be noted here that throughout our discussion so far we have assumed that the equivalent interface charge Q_o' is fixed and independent of voltage. This may not be accurate in some devices (especially those fabricated with the use of older techniques) in which a significant density of interface traps may exist (Sec. 2.2). These traps, located at the oxide-silicon interface, can exchange carriers with the substrate. The charge trapped in them depends on the value of the surface potential ψ_s. Thus, let Q_{it}' represent the fraction of Q_o' associated with interface traps. Then, in going from (2.3.3) to (2.3.4), one should include the term $\Delta Q_{it}'$ in the latter. If this term is also included in (2.6.2) and in the development following that equation, it can be easily seen that we can take the variation of Q_{it}' with ψ_s into account in the same way that we took into account the variation of Q_B' and Q_I' with ψ_s; that is, we can define an incremental capacitance corresponding to the interface traps in analogy with (2.6.12) and (2.6.13). This capacitance will then be

$$C_{it}' \equiv -\frac{dQ_{it}'}{d\psi_s} \qquad (2.6.23)$$

C_{it} will appear in parallel with C_b and C_i in Fig. 2.16. If it is significant, the various formulas should be modified to include it. For example, (2.6.22) would be modified as follows:

$$n_0 = 1 + \left. \frac{C_b' + C_{it}'}{C_{ox}'} \right|_{\psi_s = 1.5\phi_F} \qquad (2.6.24)$$

Measurements performed on MOS transistors have shown that, with modern fabrication processes, C_{it} is often much smaller than C_b' and may be neglected.[13]

2.7 CAREFUL DEFINITIONS FOR THE LIMITS OF MODERATE INVERSION†

In Sec. 2.5, the lower limit of the moderate-inversion region was taken to coincide with the upper limit of weak inversion. The latter is traditionally defined at $\psi_s = 2\phi_F$. At this point, the surface electron concentration becomes equal to the bulk doping concentration N_A, as seen from (2.4.11b). Also, at this point $C_i' = C_b'$, as seen from (2.6.14) and (2.6.15). These two facts hold independently of the value of C_{ox}'. However, neither of these facts says anything about the validity of common "weak-inversion approximations" [such as $Q_I'(V_{GB})$ being an exponential] at this point. This is because the validity of such approximations cannot be discussed carefully without evoking the value of C_{ox}'. It would thus make practical sense to take C_{ox}' into account, and redefine the onset of moderate inversion at some point beyond which common weak-inversion approximations become unacceptable. In weak inversion, and at points where C_i' is negligible (Fig. 2.15), C_b' varies little; thus, $d\psi_s/dV_{GB}$ in (2.6.18) will be approximately constant. That is necessary for an exponential dependence of Q_I' on V_{GB}, as can be seen from the development leading from (2.5.37) to (2.5.43). Significant departure from such behavior will be observed if C_i' starts becoming significant in comparison to $C_{ox}' + C_b'$ in (2.6.18). Thus, let us define the onset of moderate inversion as follows:[14]

ϕ_{M0}, V_{M0} are the values of ψ_s and V_{GB}, respectively, at which

$$\frac{C_i'}{C_{ox}' + C_b'} = 0.1 \qquad (2.7.1)$$

Keeping in mind that C_b' varies slowly, it is easy to see that at this point the slope $d\psi_s/dV_{GB}$ in Fig. 2.9 drops to about 91 percent of its value deep in weak inversion. The same is true for the slope of $\ln |Q_I'|$ vs. V_{GB} (Fig. 2.11), this slope being a measure of the "exponentiality" of $Q_I'(V_{GB})$ (Prob. 2.11).

Accurate evaluation of ϕ_{M0} requires using (2.6.14) and (2.6.15) in (2.7.1), and solving iteratively for ψ_s; the corresponding V_{M0} can then be found from (2.5.18). The result depends on oxide thickness and substrate doping. It can be shown that, for practical values of these parameters, the value of ϕ_{M0} as defined above will not differ by more than about $1\phi_t$ from the value of $2\phi_F$ given by (2.5.9). The corresponding value of V_{M0} will differ from that given in (2.5.21) by at most a few tens of millivolts. For most practical cases, we can continue using (2.5.9) and (2.5.21) for simplicity.

We now turn to the upper limit of moderate inversion. It makes practical sense to define this at a point below which common strong-inversion approximations, such as (2.5.28), become unacceptable. Let us look at the slope of the $Q_I'(V_{GB})$ plot, given by (2.6.20). Deep in strong inversion, C_i' is very large and (2.6.20) reduces to $d|Q_I'|/dV_{GB} \approx C_{ox}'$; this agrees of course with (2.5.28). If C_i' is not much larger than $C_{ox}' + C_b'$, $d|Q_I'|/dV_{GB}$ will be less than C_{ox}' and (2.5.28) will not hold. Thus, let us define the upper limit of moderate inversion as follows:[14]

ϕ_{H0}, V_{H0} are the values of ψ_s and V_{GB}, respectively, at which

$$\frac{C_i'}{C_{ox}' + C_b'} = 10 \qquad (2.7.2)$$

---

† This section can be skipped without loss of continuity, and is therefore set in smaller type.

From (2.6.20) it is easy to see that at this point the slope in the plot of $|Q'_I|$ vs. V_{GB} (Fig. 2.10) is reduced to about 91 percent of its theoretical maximum value of C'_{ox} (Prob. 2.11), and, from (2.6.18) it can be seen that the slope of the $\psi_s(V_{GB})$ plot (Fig. 2.9) drops to about 9 percent of its maximum value (Prob. 2.11).

To find ϕ_{H0} one must use (2.6.14) and (2.6.15) in (2.7.2) and solve for ψ_s iteratively. One finds that ϕ_{H0} is several ϕ_t above ϕ_{M0} (about $6\phi_t$), the exact value being dependent on oxide thickness and substrate doping. If ϕ_{H0} is *accurately* known, it can be used in (2.5.18) to find V_{H0}. (Note that a small error in ϕ_{H0} will result in a large error in V_{H0} because of the exponential term in that equation; that term is now large.)

The value of $V_{H0} - V_{M0}$ is given by the solid lines in Fig. 2.18 for a variety of process parameters. For this calculation, we have use the definitions (2.7.1) and (2.7.2) along with the accurate capacitance equations (2.6.14) and (2.6.15). The charge sheet model predicts a larger $V_{H0} - V_{M0}$, as shown by the broken lines. This is owing to the model's failure to predict C'_b accurately (Fig. 2.15). The width of the moderate-inversion region can be seen in Fig. 2.18 to vary significantly with process parameters. However, not all combinations of oxide thickness and substrate doping are practical. For example, in MOS transistor fabrication large doping concentrations are usually combined with thin oxides. For practical cases, then, the width of the moderate inversion does not differ much; an average value is about 0.6 V at room temperature.

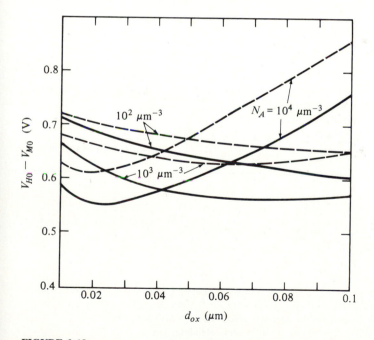

FIGURE 2.18

Width of moderate-inversion region [calculated from definitions (2.7.1) and (2.7.2.)] vs. oxide thickness, for three values of substrate doping concentration at room temperature ($T = 300$ K). Solid lines: accurate calculation based on (2.6.14) and (2.6.15); broken lines: charge sheet model.

2.8 SUMMARY OF PROPERTIES OF THE REGIONS OF INVERSION

From the relations given in this chapter, and from the associated discussions, we can summarize certain important properties for each region of inversion as shown in Table 2.1.

TABLE 2.1

Regions of inversion and properties

	Weak inversion	Moderate inversion	Strong inversion
Definition in terms of surface potential ψ_s	$\phi_{L0} \lesssim \psi_s < \phi_{M0}$	$\phi_{M0} \lesssim \psi_s < \phi_{H0}$	$\phi_{H0} \lesssim \psi_s$
Definition in terms of gate-substrate voltage V_{GB}	$V_{L0} \lesssim V_{GB} < V_{M0}$	$V_{M0} \lesssim V_{GB} < V_{H0}$	$V_{H0} \lesssim V_{GB}$
$\dfrac{|Q_I'|}{|Q_B'|}$	$\ll 1$	Varies	$\gg 1$ deep in strong inversion; not necessarily so near the bottom of the region
$\dfrac{C_i'}{C_b'}$	$\ll 1$ deep in weak inversion; not necessarily so near the top of the region	Varies	$\gg 1$
$\dfrac{d\psi_s}{dV_{GB}}$	Approximately constant; attains its maximum value in this region	Varies	Small
Dependence of Q_I' on V_{GB}	Exponential	—	First-degree polynomial

REFERENCES

1. E. H. Nicollian and J. R. Brews, *MOS Physics and Technology*, John Wiley, New York, 1982.
2. A. S. Grove, *Physics and Technology of Semiconductor Devices*, John Wiley, New York, 1967.
3. S. M. Sze, *Physics of Semiconductor Devices*, John Wiley, New York, 1981.
4. R. F. Pierret, *Field Effect Devices*, Addison-Wesley, Reading, 1983.
5. I. R. M. Mansour, "On the modeling of MOS devices," *Proceedings of the Third International Symposium on Network Theory*, Yugoslavia, pp. 705–713, 1975.
6. I. R. M. Mansour, "Improved modeling of MOS devices," *Proceedings of the European Conference on Circuit Theory and Design*, Italy, 1976.

7. G. Baccarani, M. Rudan, and G. Spadini, "Analytical i.g.f.e.t. model including drift and diffusion currents," *IEE Journal on Solid-State and Electron Devices*, vol. 2, pp. 62–68, March 1978.

8. J. R. Brews, "A charge-sheet model of the MOSFET," *Solid-State Electronics*, vol. 21, pp. 345–355, 1978.

9. F. Van de Wiele, "A long-channel MOSFET model," *Solid-State Electronics*, vol. 22, pp. 991–997, 1979.

10. J. R. Brews, "Physics of the MOS transistor," chapter 1 in *Silicon Integrated Circuits, Part A*, D. Kahng (editor), Applied Solid State Science Series, Academic Press, New York, 1981.

11. R. J. Van Overstraeten, G. J. Declerk, and P. A. Nuls, "Theory of the MOS transistor in weak inversion—new method to determine the number of surface states," *IEEE Transactions on Electron Devices*, vol. ED-22, pp. 282–288, May 1975.

12. B. E. Deal, "Standardized terminology for oxide charges associated with thermally oxidized silicon," *IEEE Transactions on Electron Devices*, vol. ED-27, pp. 606–608, March 1980.

13. E. Vittoz and J. Fellrath, "CMOS analog integrated circuits based on weak inversion operation," *IEEE Journal of Solid-State Circuits*, vol. SC-12, pp. 224–231, June 1977.

14. Y. Tsividis, "Moderate inversion in MOS devices," *Solid-State Electronics*, vol. 25, pp. 1099–1104, 1982; see also Erratum, *ibid.*, vol. 26, p. 823, 1983.

PROBLEMS

2.1. Show that, independently of how many different materials are used in the external path in Fig. 2.2c, the value of V_{GB} needed to make the charges disappear is given by (2.2.2).

2.2. (a) Calculate the flat-band voltage for an n-type substrate with $N_D = 10^4 \, \mu m^{-3}$, an SiO_2 insulator with $d_{ox} = 0.04 \, \mu m$ and an aluminum gate, and $Q'_o = 0.05 \, fC/\mu m^2$.

(b) Repeat for a polysilicon gate doped n-type with $N_D = 10^8 \, \mu m^{-3}$.

2.3. Prove (2.5.17) and (2.5.18).

2.4. In Sec. 2.5.2 we have shown that, if ψ_s is assumed to be "pinned" to a constant, the plot of Q'_I vs. V_{GB} will be a straight line. Show that a pinned ψ_s is not a necessary condition for a straight-line plot (although it is sufficient); find the correct necessary condition.

2.5. Plot $V_{T0} - V_{FB}$ vs. oxide thickness d_{ox}, from $d_{ox} = 0.01 \, \mu m$ to $d_{ox} = 0.1 \, \mu m$, for $N_A = 10^2, 10^3$, and $10^4 \, \mu m^{-3}$.

2.6. Prove that an approximate expression for $Q'_I(V_{GB})$ in weak inversion is

$$Q'_I = Q'_{IM0}e^{(V_{GB}-V_{M0})/(n_o\phi_t)}$$

where Q'_{IM0} is the value of Q'_I at the upper limit of weak inversion.

2.7. For a device with $N_A = 10^3 \, \mu m^{-3}$, $d_{ox} = 0.05 \, \mu m$, and $V_{FB} = 0 \, V$, plot $\ln|Q'_I|$ vs. V_{GB} in weak inversion, using (a) (2.5.7) with (2.5.18); (b) (2.5.33) with (2.5.36); (c) (2.5.43); and (d) the equation in Prob. 2.6. Comment on the accuracy of the last three approaches.

2.8. For $N_A = 10^3 \, \mu m^{-3}$, $d_{ox} = 0.05 \, \mu m$, and $V_{FB} = 0 \, V$, plot $Q'_I(V_{GB})$ using: (a) (2.5.7) with (2.5.18); (b) (2.5.28), from $V_{GB} = V_{M0} + 0.6 \, V$ to $V_{GB} = 5 \, V$. Comment on the accuracy of (2.5.28). Assume initially $\phi_B = 2\phi_F + 6\phi_t$, and modify this value if necessary to decrease the error.

2.9. Rewrite the equations of this chapter for the case of n-type substrates.

2.10. Show that in depletion (with ψ_s larger than a few ϕ_t) and in weak inversion C'_{gb} is approximately given by:

$$C'_{gb} = \frac{C'_{ox}}{\sqrt{1 + \frac{4}{\gamma^2}(V_{GB} - V_{FB})}}$$

2.11. (a) Using the definitions in Sec. 2.7 and the fact that C'_b varies little with ψ_s in weak inversion, show that the slopes of $\psi_s(V_{GB})$ and of $\ln|Q'_I|$ vs. V_{GB} at $\psi_s = \phi_{M0}$ are at about 91 percent of their maximum value.

(b) Show that at $\psi_s = \phi_{H0}$ the slope of $\psi_s(V_{GB})$ is at 9.1 percent of its maximum value, and the slope of $|Q'_I|$ vs. V_{GB} is at 91 percent of its maximum value.

2.12. Determine the value of the surface potential and the gate-substrate voltage at the onset of moderate inversion (ϕ_{M0}, V_{M0}) and at the onset of strong inversion (ϕ_{H0}, V_{H0}), as well as the extrapolated threshold (V_{T0}) for the process of Example 2.1.

2.13. Use (B.5) in Appendix B to prove (2.4.18). Note that the result is independent of the thickness of the shaded area containing Q_C in Fig. 2.4.

2.14. Equation (2.5.1) was derived as a special case of the general $Q'_C(\psi_s)$ relation in (2.4.17). Show that (2.5.1) can also be proved directly, using the several hints that follow. For $\psi(y)$ larger than a few ϕ_t, the hole charge is negligible, and $\rho(y) = -q[N_A + n(y)]$, with $n(y)$ related to $\psi(y)$ by $n(y) = N_A e^{(\psi - 2\phi_F)/\phi_t}$ in analogy with (2.4.14). Thus Poisson's equation (1.2.13) will be:

$$\frac{d^2\psi}{dy^2} = \frac{qN_A}{\epsilon_s}(1 + e^{(\psi - 2\phi_F)/\phi_t})$$

Multiply the above equation by $2(d\psi/dy)$, and recognize the resulting left-hand side as $(d/dy)(d\psi/dy)^2$. Integrate both sides from a point y_{bulk} outside the depletion region to a point $y_{surface}$ at the surface; note that in the bulk, $\psi = 0$ and $d\psi/dy = 0$. Solve for $d\psi/dy$ at the surface, and then relate that quantity to Q'_C (see Appendix B). Solve for Q'_C and show that the result is practically the same as (2.5.1) for ψ_s larger than a few ϕ_t.[10]

2.15. Show that, independently of the charge in the inversion layer, if the thickness of this layer is assumed to be zero, the potential across the layer will also be zero (use the material in Appendix B).

2.16. Use (B.6) in Appendix B to prove (2.5.5), assuming the "depletion approximation" (Sec. 1.5).

2.17. Plots of charge density, electric field, and potential vs. distance for the two-terminal MOS structure are given in Appendix E. Verify these plots by using the basic laws of electrostatics of Appendix B and give values for critical points on the plots.

2.18. (a) Show that, if a fixed charge sheet of charge per unit area Q' is located in the oxide at a distance d from the gate, its contribution to the flat-band voltage will be $-(1/C'_{ox})[(d/d_{ox})Q']$ (use material from Appendix B).

(b) Show that, if a charge is distributed within the oxide uniformly along the horizontal dimension in Fig. 2.2, as described by a charge density per unit volume $\rho(y)$, its contribution to the flat-band voltage will be $-(1/C'_{ox})\int_{y_g}^{y_s}(y/d_{ox})q\rho(y)\,dy$, where y_g is y at the gate-oxide interface and y_s is y at the oxide-substrate interface.

CHAPTER
3

THE THREE-TERMINAL MOS STRUCTURE

3.1 INTRODUCTION

A complete MOS transistor is formed by adding two more terminals to the basic MOS structure of Chap. 2 to contact two opposite ends of the inversion layer. Through these terminals a potential difference can be applied across the inversion layer and a current can be caused to flow in it. A number of phenomena can then be observed, some directly associated with the current flow, some not. It is not convenient to introduce all these phenomena when they are present simultaneously. Some of these, specifically the ones not directly associated with the above current flow, can best be isolated and studied by themselves by means of a structure simpler than the MOS transistor, which we call a *three-terminal MOS structure*. This structure is formed by contacting the inversion layer of the basic MOS structure at only one end. We will study the changes that take place in the charges and the potential distribution of the three-terminal structure, because of the application of an external voltage between this new terminal and the substrate. By the end of this short chapter, we will have all the facts necessary for a careful and convenient look at the MOS transistor, which will be the subject of all succeeding chapters.

3.2   CONTACTING THE INVERSION LAYER

Assume that an n^+ region is added to the basic MOS two-terminal structure, so that the structure shown in Fig. 3.1a is obtained; a constant V_{GB} will be assumed until further notice. Consider the n^+p junction formed by this region and the substrate. The depletion region on the p side contains ionized acceptor atoms as shown. The narrow depletion region part in the n^+ material containing ionized donor atoms (Fig. 1.15) is not shown for simplicity. As indicated in Sec. 1.5, one can short-circuit the n^+ region terminal to the substrate terminal without altering the picture, as shown in Fig. 3.1b. For this connection the part of the structure to the right of the n^+ region is still governed by the basic equations we have developed for the two-terminal structure, except for points too close to the n^+ region. Such points can be affected directly by the two-dimensional field distribution around this region. However, we will assume for the present that the gate is long and wide, so that edge effects can be neglected over practically all the gate's length and width.

Let us now assume that V_{GB} is fixed at some value, producing a surface potential ψ_s underneath the oxide. From (2.5.7) and the associated discussion of the various regions of operation, we recall that ψ_s is "fighting against" $2\phi_F$. For example, if ψ_s is less than about $2\phi_F$, the exponential can be neglected in that equation and we are in weak inversion or in depletion. On the other hand, if ψ_s is greater than $2\phi_F$, the exponential term becomes important and we are in moderate or strong inversion.

We will now place a voltage source of value V_{CB} between the n^+ region and the substrate terminal, as shown in Fig. 3.1c. The value of V_{CB} will be assumed *nonnegative* to ensure that the n^+p junction is *not* forward-biased. This will correspond to the practical cases of interest when the three-terminal structure will become part of an MOS transistor in Chap. 4. If V_{CB} is not zero, communication of the inversion layer with the external voltage source (through the n^+ region) can drastically change the situation in comparison with the equilibrium case discussed in Chap. 2. The structure is now in *nonequilibrium*, and extra care should be exercised when attempting to apply relations from that chapter. As we will see, most such relations will have to be modified before they can apply to the present case.

Assume initially $V_{CB} = 0$, which makes the situation identical to that in Fig. 3.1b. Let us fix V_{GB} so that the surface potential is fixed at some value ψ_x, bringing the surface to some level of inversion.† Consider now a sudden increase in V_{CB}. The n^+ region will become more positive than before by V_{CB}.

---

† Note that, since the potential of the surface is ψ_x with respect to the bulk, whereas that of the n^+ region is ϕ_o (the built-in potential of the junction), there will be a region along the surface around the n^+p junction boundary where the potential changes from ϕ_o to ψ_x. Our results in this section will be valid to the right of this region.

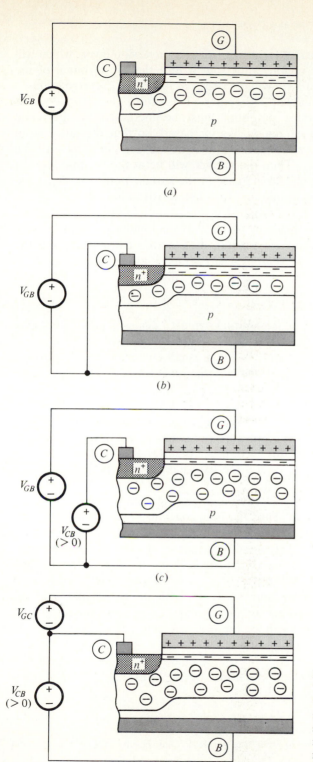

FIGURE 3.1

Three-terminal MOS structure, with n^+ region (a) left open; (b) short-circuited to p-type substrate; (c) biased at V_{CB} (>0) with respect to the substrate; (d) connection equivalent to (c) with voltages referred to terminal C.

The positive potential will attract electrons from the inversion layer, which will start flowing toward the n^+ region, and from it into the top terminal of the voltage source. The inversion level will decrease; in fact, if V_{CB} is large enough, the inversion layer can disappear altogether. To restore the surface to its previous condition, the surface potential must be increased by the same amount the potential of the n^+ region has increased, so that the latter is no longer more attractive for the electrons. Thus, the surface potential must be increased from ψ_x to $\psi_x + V_{CB}$. Then the surface will be at the original level of inversion again. To achieve such an increase in the surface potential, V_{GB} must be increased by an appropriate amount. In other words, what determines the "attractiveness" of the surface for the electrons is not how large ψ_s is, but rather how large ψ_s is in comparison to V_{CB}. What counts is the *difference* $\psi_s - V_{CB}$. As long as that difference is fixed, the electron concentration at the surface is also fixed. The role of ψ_s in (2.4.12) is then played here by $\psi_s - V_{CB}$, and we have.[1,2]†

$$n_{\text{surface}} = N_A e^{[\psi_s - (2\phi_F + V_{CB})]/\phi_t} \qquad (3.2.1)$$

Thus, just as in (2.4.12) ψ_s is "fighting against" $2\phi_F$ to increase the level of inversion at the surface, here ψ_s is instead fighting against $2\phi_F + V_{CB}$.

It should be noted that, with $V_{CB} > 0$, a small current will flow through the battery. This current is due partly to the junction reverse-bias current flowing from the n^+ region to the substrate (Sec. 1.5) and partly to a similar current flowing from the inversion layer to the substrate. The magnitude of the current is very small except at very high temperatures, and we will neglect both its electron and hole components in much of our work. It is important, though, to acknowledge its presence, as this current is a manifestation of the communication between the inversion layer and the external battery, and the resulting nonequilibrium condition.

The arguments leading to (3.2.1) cannot be extended to holes, as the n^+ region is not attractive for them. Thus the hole concentration will still be given by the same relations used for the two-terminal structure in Sec. 2.4. A general analysis including the effect of holes and electrons, and valid in accumulation, depletion, and inversion, is possible. It proceeds along the lines of the analysis in Sec. 2.4.4, only including the effect of V_{CB} on n. Readers interested in such an analysis are referred to Appendix H. In the rest of this chapter we will concentrate on *inversion*, for which relatively simple results become possible. The considerations here parallel those for the two-terminal structure, so our discussion will be kept relatively brief.

The MOS system in inversion will still be characterized by five equations (as discussed for the two-terminal structure starting with 2.5.12). Of the five

---

† In energy band parlance, V_{CB} serves to "split" the so-called "quasi-Fermi levels" of electrons and holes (Appendix G).

equations, four are identical to those for the two-terminal structure, and are repeated here for convenience:

$$V_{GB} = \psi_{ox} + \psi_s + \phi_{MS} \tag{3.2.2}$$

$$Q'_G + Q'_o + Q'_I + Q'_B = 0 \tag{3.2.3}$$

$$Q'_G = C'_{ox}\psi_{ox} \tag{3.2.4}$$

$$Q'_B = -F\sqrt{N_A}\sqrt{\psi_s} \tag{3.2.5a}$$

$$= -\gamma C'_{ox}\sqrt{\psi_s} \tag{3.2.5b}$$

where F is defined in (1.5.10) and γ has been defined in (2.5.19). As in Chap. 2, the charge sheet[3-8] and depletion approximations are implied in writing the above equation for Q'_B [see explanation above (2.5.5)].

To arrive at a complet set of equations, from which the behavior of the system can be determined, one more equation is needed, giving Q'_I as a function of ψ_s. However, (2.5.7) will not be valid as is, since it does not take into account the presence of V_{CB}. As might be expected from our discussion above, the correct relation for $Q'_I(\psi_s)$ is obtained simply by replacing $2\phi_F$ by $2\phi_F + V_{CB}$ in that equation (Appendix H or Prob. 3.11):[3-8]

$$Q'_I = -F\sqrt{N_A}(\sqrt{\psi_s + \phi_t e^{[\psi_s - (2\phi_F + V_{CB})]/\phi_t}} - \sqrt{\psi_s}) \tag{3.2.6}$$

From the above five equations everything else can be developed in the same way as for the two-terminal structure; thus, from (3.2.2) to (3.2.4) we have,

$$V_{GB} = V_{FB} + \psi_s - \frac{Q'_B(\psi_s) + Q'_I(\psi_s)}{C'_{ox}} \tag{3.2.7a}$$

where V_{FB} is the flat-band voltage defined in (2.2.6). Using (3.2.5b) and (3.2.6) in (3.2.7a), V_{GB} can be written as follows:

$$V_{GB} = V_{FB} + \psi_s + \gamma\sqrt{\psi_s + \phi_t e^{[\psi_s - (2\phi_F + V_{CB})]/\phi_t}} \tag{3.2.7b}$$

This equation cannot be solved explicitly for ψ_s. If V_{GB} and V_{CB} are given and ψ_s is desired, the equation can be solved numerically by using a computer or a calculator with an equation-solving capability.

The equation for Q'_I above uses ψ_s and V_{CB} as independent variables. For future use it will be useful to express Q'_I also as a function of V_{GB} and ψ_s. This can be most easily done by using (3.2.2) to (3.2.5):

$$Q'_I = -C'_{ox}\left(V_{GB} - V_{FB} - \psi_s + \frac{Q'_B}{C'_{ox}}\right) \tag{3.2.8a}$$

$$= -C'_{ox}(V_{GB} - V_{FB} - \psi_s - \gamma\sqrt{\psi_s}) \tag{3.2.8b}$$

Similarly, for the gate charge per unit area we obtain, from (3.2.2) and (3.2.4),

$$Q'_G = C'_{ox}(V_{GB} - V_{FB} - \psi_s) - Q'_o \qquad (3.2.9)$$

Refer now to Fig. 3.1c, and assume that V_{CB} *is held constant*. We can then define a per-unit-area small-signal capacitance of the gate to the rest of the structure, $C'_g = dQ_G/dV_{GB}$, and capacitances C'_b and C'_i as for the two-terminal structure. Reasoning as in Sec. 2.6, we obtain:

$$\frac{1}{C'_g} = \frac{1}{C'_{ox}} + \frac{1}{C'_c} = \frac{1}{C'_{ox}} + \frac{1}{C'_b + C'_i} \qquad (3.2.10)$$

where the expressions for C'_c, C'_b, and C'_i look like those in Sec. 2.6, except that $2\phi_F$ is replaced by $2\phi_F + V_{CB}$ (Appendix H):

$$C'_c = F\sqrt{N_A} \; \frac{1 + e^{[\psi_s - (2\phi_F + V_{CB})]/\phi_t}}{2\sqrt{\psi_s + \phi_t e^{[\psi_s - (2\phi_F + V_{CB})]/\phi_t}}} \qquad (3.2.11)$$

$$C'_b = F\sqrt{N_A} \; \frac{1}{2\sqrt{\psi_s + \phi_t e^{[\psi_s - (2\phi_F + V_{CB})]/\phi_t}}} \qquad (3.2.12)$$

$$C'_i = F\sqrt{N_A} \; \frac{e^{[\psi_s - (2\phi_F + V_{CB})]/\phi_t}}{2\sqrt{\psi_s + \phi_t e^{[\psi_s - (2\phi_F + V_{CB})]/\phi_t}}} \qquad (3.2.13)$$

As in Chap. 2, the expressions we give for C'_b and C'_i are more accurate than those that would be obtained by differentiating our expressions for Q'_B and Q'_I. We do this because (3.2.5) and (3.2.6), although adequate for calculating Q'_B and Q'_I, are not accurate enough to provide a correct derivative with respect to ψ_s [see the discussion preceding (2.6.14) for details]. It is easy to note from (3.2.12) and (3.2.13) that $C'_i = C'_b$ at the point $\psi_s = 2\phi_F + V_{CB}$.

Plots of ψ_s, C'_g, $\ln|Q'_I|$, and $|Q'_I|$ vs. V_{GB} are shown in Fig. 3.2; the V_{GC} axis at the bottom will be considered later. The plots shown by the broken lines are for the case of Fig. 3.1b. These plots are the same as for a corresponding two-terminal structure, with one important expection for the C'_g plot. Let us compare this plot to Fig. 2.17. In the latter, the broken line represents C'_{gb} for the two-terminal structure at high frequencies of operation. This behavior was claimed to be different from that observed at low frequencies (solid line). The reason was traced to the fact that in the two-terminal structure the inversion layer is practically "isolated from the outside world." However, in the structure of Fig. 3.1b or Fig. 3.1c communication with the outside world is possible through the n^+ region. Thus, in strong inversion plenty of electrons are available just below the oxide, and their total charge "tracks" variations in V_{GB} even if these variations are of rather high frequency. Low-frequency and high-frequency behaviors then coincide, and only one curve is observed, as shown by the broken line in Fig. 3.2b. However, if an extremely high frequency is used (e.g., in the gigahertz range), the supply of charge to the inversion layer might once again be unable to keep up; a behavior as shown by the broken line in Fig. 2.17 could then be observed.

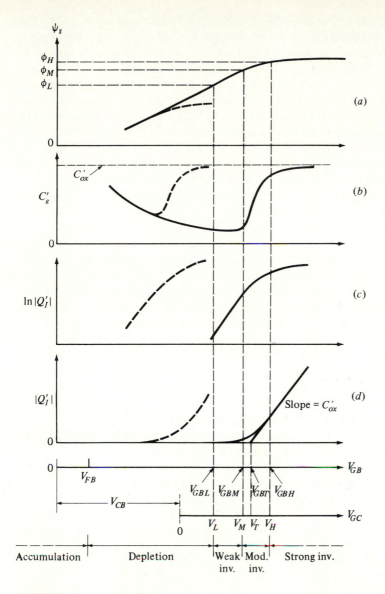

FIGURE 3.2

Various quantities characterizing the structure of Fig. 3.1c plotted vs. V_{GB} and V_{GC}. (a) Surface potential; (b) gate capacitance to the rest of the structure per unit area; (c) logarithm of inversion layer charge magnitude per unit area; (d) inversion layer charge magnitude per unit area. For the broken lines $V_{CB} = 0$; the solid lines are for a V_{CB} of a given positive value.

The plots given by the solid lines in Fig. 3.2 are for a given $V_{CB} > 0$. The behavior seen is qualitatively similar to that for $V_{CB} = 0$. Since the latter case is related to the two-terminal structure of Chap. 2, we can carry over several of the concepts and definitions discussed there to the general case of $V_{CB} > 0$. Thus, weak-, moderate-, and strong-inversion regions are again defined, as indicated at the bottom of the figure. The lower limits of these regions in terms of V_{GB} are denoted correspondingly by V_{GBL}, V_{GBM}, and V_{GBH} as shown. The corresponding surface potential values are denoted by ϕ_L, ϕ_M, and ϕ_H, as indicated in Fig. 3.2a. Precise definitions for each region and values for the above quantities will be given later on. For now, it suffices to say that the regions are defined in such a way that in weak inversion the plot of $|Q'_I|$ vs. ψ_s is essentially exponential; in strong inversion, it is essentially a straight line; and in moderate inversion, it is neither.

Note that the plots in Fig. 3.2 are for a given V_{CB} value. If V_{CB} is increased above that value, the plots will be qualitatively similar but will be shifted to the right, as predicted by the corresponding equations. To gain some further intuition about this effect, let us assume that in Fig. 3.1c V_{CB} is fixed at some value. Assume that V_{GB} is so low that not only the inversion layer is absent but also the depletion region width is smaller than shown. Let us now increase V_{GB}. Doing so will not change V_{CB}, the reverse bias of the n^+p junction on the left. Hence the depletion region under the n^+ region will not be affected. However, more positive charge will now be placed on the gate, which must be balanced by more negative charge under the oxide. An increase in the depletion region width accomplishes this balance. If V_{GB} is increased far enough, a point will eventually be reached where the depletion region under the oxide will be nearly as wide as that under the n^+ region; the value of V_{GB} needed for this to happen depends on the value of V_{CB}. When this happens, the potential across the depletion regions under the oxide and under the n^+ region will be about the same. Thus, a point at the surface is at about the same potential (with respect to the substrate deep in the bulk) as is a point in the n^+ region. Now the surface is about at "attractive" for electrons as is the n^+ region. Electrons are attracted most to regions with the most positive potential, and they have now no reason to prefer only the n^+ region as opposed to the "surface" on its right.† An inversion layer is thus formed. If now V_{CB} is raised

---

† To be more quantitative than this, one must recall that the potential at the surface is ψ_s, whereas that of the n^+ region is $\phi_o + V_{CB}$, with ϕ_o the built-in potential of the n^+p junction (Sec. 1.5). It can be verified by using (3.2.1) that, to make the electron concentration at the surface equal to that in the n^+ region, requires $\psi_s = \phi_o + V_{CB}$. For other values of ψ_s the surface concentration will be different, as determined by (3.2.1), and there will be a transition region along the surface around the n^+p junction boundary, over which the potential changes from $\phi_o + V_{CB}$ to ψ_s. As already mentioned, we are focusing on the part of the structure to the right of this transition region. As one goes from weak toward strong inversion, the potential across the transition region diminishes.

further, the depletion region under the n^+ region will become again wider than under the inversion layer. The electrons will tend again to favor the n^+ region rather than the surface, and the inversion layer will tend to disappear. If it is desired to restore the level of inversion previously achieved, V_{GB} will have to be raised further to make the depletion region width under the gate approximately the same as that under the n^+ region once again. Then the potential at the surface will again be about the same as the potential of the n^+ region (both with respect to the bulk), and electrons can once more be attracted to the surface. From the above picture, the competing roles of V_{CB} and V_{GB} are clear. Increasing V_{CB} tends to make the level of inversion lighter, increasing V_{GB} tends to make that level heavier.

It is interesting to investigate the effect of these phenomena on the surface potential. In Fig. 3.3 we show ψ_s vs. V_{GB}, as it results from (3.2.7b), for different values of V_{CB}. The regions of inversion indicated can be interpreted in terms of the corresponding Q_I' plots (which are not shown, but are nevertheless exponential in weak, straight lines in strong, and neither in moderate inversion). Note that increasing V_{CB} "postpones" the tendency of ψ_s to "flatten out" until larger V_{GB} values. This is because it "postpones" the formation of an inversion layer, as already explained. Assume now that, for a

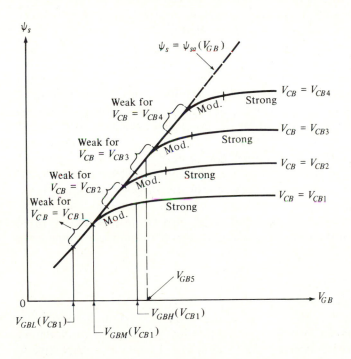

FIGURE 3.3
Surface potential vs. gate-substrate voltage with V_{CB} as a parameter. For each V_{CB} the regions of inversion are indicated on the corresponding curve.

given V_{CB}, the value of V_{GB} is so low that the inversion layer charge is negligible (e.g., in depletion); denote the corresponding value of ψ_s by ψ_{sa}. Then (3.2.7a) gives

$$V_{GB} \approx V_{FB} + \psi_{sa} - \frac{Q_B'(\psi_{sa})}{C_{ox}'} \tag{3.2.14}$$

which, using (3.2.5b), becomes:

$$V_{GB} \approx V_{FB} + \psi_{sa} + \gamma\sqrt{\psi_{sa}} \tag{3.2.15}$$

Solving this, we obtain ψ_{sa} as a function of V_{GB}:

$$\psi_{sa}(V_{GB}) \approx \left(-\frac{\gamma}{2} + \sqrt{\frac{\gamma^2}{4} + V_{GB} - V_{FB}}\right)^2 \tag{3.2.16}$$

This function is shown by the broken curve in Fig. 3.3. For any V_{CB}, as long as $\psi_s \approx \psi_{sa}(V_{GB})$ the effect of V_{CB} on ψ_s is negligible. Physically, this is because there is practically no inversion layer charge. Most electric field lines coming from the gate "pass right through" the practically absent inversion layer and terminate on ionized acceptor atoms on the substrate. Thus Q_I' has "no handle" on the overall balance of the system represented by (3.2.3), and, while varying V_{CB} will vary drastically the negligible $|Q_I'|$ in a relative sense, the rest of the system simply "does not notice." Note that $|Q_I'|$ will be negligible as long as the exponential in (3.2.6) is negligible. In fact, the same exponential appears in the general $V_{GB}(\psi_s)$ relation (3.2.7b). When the exponential there is negligible, this equation reduces to (3.2.15). Things will begin thus changing significantly when the exponential starts becoming important, which will happen at about $\psi_s \approx 2\phi_F + V_{CB}$. Then the complete (3.2.7b) must be used to find ψ_s, and the plot for the latter will begin to flatten out, as seen in Fig. 3.3.

Now let V_{GB} be *constant* and equal to the value V_{GB5} indicated on Fig. 3.3 (the subscript 5 is used in connection with a forthcoming discussion). As V_{CB} is raised, the level of inversion becomes lighter. For the values $V_{CB} = V_{CB1}$, V_{CB2}, and V_{CB3} the structure is correspondingly in strong, moderate, and weak inversion. Further increases in V_{CB} will leave the surface potential value practically unaffected at the value $\psi_{sa}(V_{GB5})$, as seen for example in going from V_{CB3} to V_{CB4}.

These observations can clearly be displayed by plotting ψ_s vs. V_{CB}, keeping V_{GB} as a parameter, and using (3.2.7b). This is shown in Fig. 3.4. The behavior discussed above for $V_{GB} = V_{GB5}$ is shown by the top curve. The quantities $V_{CBH}(V_{GB5})$, $V_{CBM}(V_{GB5})$, and $V_{CBL}(V_{GB5})$ marked on the horizontal axis give the limits between strong and moderate inversion, between moderate and weak inversion, and between weak inversion and depletion, respectively, in terms of V_{CB}. The limit between moderate and weak inversion is seen to occur when ψ_s becomes about $2\phi_F + V_{CB}$, as expected from our earlier discussion. Similarly, the limit between weak inversion and depletion occurs at

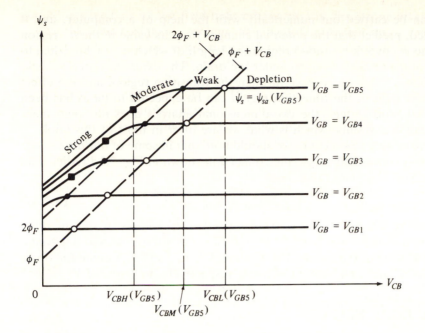

FIGURE 3.4
Surface potential vs. V_{CB} with gate-substrate voltage as a parameter. For each curve a full square denotes the limit between strong and moderate inversion; a full circle, the limit between moderate and weak inversion; and an open circle, the limit between weak inversion and depletion.

$\phi_F + V_{CB}$. The two curves below the top one behave in a similar manner, only now V_{GB} is smaller ($V_{GB3} < V_{GB4} < V_{GB5}$ is assumed), and thus smaller values of V_{CB} are needed to reduce the level of inversion to a given point. The value $V_{GB2}(<V_{GB3})$ happens to be low, so even with $V_{CB} = 0$, the surface is only in moderate inversion. Increasing V_{CB} above zero can then only drive the structure into weak inversion and eventually into depletion. Finally, $V_{GB1}(<V_{GB2})$ is so low that the device is only in weak inversion when $V_{CB} = 0$. Increasing V_{CB} above 0 then will eventually drive the device into depletion.

Note that $V_{GBL} < V_{GBM} < V_{GBH}$ (Fig. 3.3), whereas $V_{CBH} < V_{CBM} < V_{CBL}$ (Fig. 3.4). This reflects the opposing roles of V_{GB} and V_{CB} on the level of inversion.

Our analysis would seem to predict that ψ_s just to the right of the n^+ region in Fig. 3.1 could be very different from the potential on the n^+ region itself, depending on V_{CB} (Fig. 3.4). This would seem to indicate a discontinuity in the electrostatic potential as the n^+p boundary is crossed. This apparent problem is, of course, caused by our neglecting the "transition" region extending on both sides of the boundary. In this transition region the electric field is not vertical, and a two-dimensional analysis becomes necessary. Such

Example 3.2. For the device of Example 3.1 find V_{GBL}, V_{GBM}, and V_{GBH} and define the regions of inversion in terms of V_{GB}.

From (3.4.4) to (3.4.6), with $V_{CB} = 3$ V, and using the above results,

$$V_{GBL} = 4.21 \text{ V}$$

$$V_{GBM} = 4.59 \text{ V}$$

$$V_{GBH} = 5.14 \text{ V}$$

Thus, for $V_{CB} = 3$ V we have:

For 4.21 V $\leq V_{GB} <$ 4.59 V: weak inversion
For 4.59 V $\leq V_{GB} <$ 5.14 V: moderate inversion
For 5.14 V $\leq V_{GB}$:   strong inversion

Plots of V_L, V_M, and V_H vs. V_{CB} for a given fabrication process look as shown in Fig. 3.5 (also shown is the plot for V_T, for which an expression will be derived in Sec. 3.4.2). The values of these quantities at $V_{CB} = 0$ are denoted by adding the subscript 0 as shown in the figure. These values are the same as for the two-terminal MOS structure, for reasons already discussed. The fact that the curves in Fig. 3.5 are rising is a manifestation of the body effect discussed in Sec. 3.3. As is obvious from (3.4.8) to (3.4.10), how much V_L, V_M, and V_H will increase for a given increase in V_{CB} is determined by the value of the coefficient γ; hence, the name *body effect coefficient* for this quantity. We remind the reader that γ was defined in (2.5.19), which is repeated below:

$$\gamma = \frac{F\sqrt{N_A}}{C'_{ox}} \tag{3.4.11}$$

This parameter has been plotted in Fig. 2.8. It is seen that our intuitive predictions of Sec. 3.3 (that the body effect is stronger for heavier substrate dopings and/or thicker oxides) are verified.

We have so far determined the limits of the regions of inversion in terms

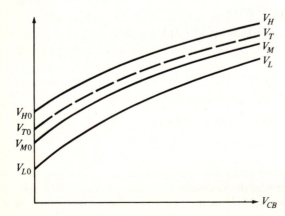

FIGURE 3.5
Onset of strong inversion V_H, extrapolated threshold V_T, onset of moderate inversion V_M, and onset of weak inversion V_L vs. V_{CB} for the three-terminal MOS structure of Fig. 3.1*d*.

of V_{GC} or V_{GB} for a given V_{CB}. It will be useful later on in this book to be also able to determine limits in terms of V_{CB} for a given V_{GB} (e.g., for the top curve of Fig. 3.4). To determine V_{CBL} for a given V_{GB}, we note that this quantity is the value of V_{CB} that brings the structure to the limit point between weak inversion and depletion. This point is characterized by $V_{GB} = V_{GBL}$. With a constant, given V_{GB} then, V_{CBL} is simply the value of V_{CB} that makes V_{GBL} in (3.4.4) equal to the given V_{GB}. Setting $V_{GBL} = V_{GB}$ in (3.4.4), using (3.4.8), and solving for $V_{CB} = V_{CBL}$, we find

$$V_{CBL} = \left(-\frac{\gamma}{2} + \sqrt{\frac{\gamma^2}{4} + V_{GB} - V_{FB}}\right)^2 - \phi_F \qquad (3.4.12)$$

Similarly, working with (3.4.5) and (3.4.9) as above, we find

$$V_{CBM} = \left(-\frac{\gamma}{2} + \sqrt{\frac{\gamma^2}{4} + V_{GB} - V_{FB}}\right)^2 - 2\phi_F \qquad (3.4.13a)$$

$$= V_{CBL} - \phi_F \qquad (3.4.13b)$$

Finally, setting $V_{GBH} = V_{GB}$ in (3.4.6), using (3.4.10) and (3.4.9) in the resulting equation, and solving for $V_{CB} = V_{CBH}$, we find

$$V_{CBH} = \left(-\frac{\gamma}{2} + \sqrt{\frac{\gamma^2}{4} + V_{GB} - V_{FB} - V_Z}\right)^2 - 2\phi_F \qquad (3.4.14)$$

From these formulas, it is easy to verify that $V_{CBH} < V_{CBM} < V_{CBL}$, as expected from our discussion.

Example 3.3. Consider the device of Example 3.1 with $V_{GB} = 5$ V. Find V_{CBL}, V_{CBM}, and V_{CBH} and define the three regions of inversion in terms of V_{CB}.
From (3.4.12) we have

$$V_{CBL} = \left[-\frac{0.59}{2} + \sqrt{\frac{0.59^2}{4} + 5 - (-0.2)}\right]^2 \text{V} - 0.33 \text{ V} = 3.69 \text{ V}$$

From (3.4.13b) we have

$$V_{CBM} = 3.69 \text{ V} - 0.33 \text{ V} = 3.36 \text{ V}$$

From (3.4.14), using $V_Z = 0.55$ V as an estimate,

$$V_{CBH} = \left[-\frac{0.59}{2} + \sqrt{\frac{0.59^2}{4} + 5 - (-0.2) - 0.55}\right]^2 \text{V} - 0.66 \text{ V} = 2.88 \text{ V}$$

Thus, we have, for the given case of $V_{GB} = 5$ V:

For $\qquad V_{CB} \le 2.88$ V: $\qquad$ strong inversion
For 2.88 V $< V_{CB} \le 3.36$ V: $\qquad$ moderate inversion
For 3.36 V $< V_{CB} \le 3.69$ V: $\qquad$ weak inversion

Thus, the given V_{GB} value of 5 V is sufficient to allow strong inversion, provided V_{CB} remains below 2.88 V. As V_{CB} is raised above this value, the moderate-inversion region is entered, followed by weak inversion and, eventually, depletion (for $V_{CB} > 3.69$ V).

Example 3.4. Repeat the above for $V_{GB} = 0.8$ V.
For this value of V_{GB}, we find

$$V_{CBL} = 0.23 \text{ V}$$

$$V_{CBM} = -0.10 \text{ V}$$

$$V_{CBH} = -0.47 \text{ V}$$

As already mentioned in Sec. 3.2, only nonnegative V_{CB} values are allowed, to ensure that the n^+p junction in Fig. 3.1c is not forward biased. The fact that V_{CBM} and V_{CBH} came out negative above simply means that neither strong nor moderate inversion is possible for the given low value of V_{GB}. That is, even with $V_{CB} = 0$, the structure is only in weak inversion; and with V_{CB} raised to just 0.23 V, even weak inversion is prevented and we enter depletion. This low value of V_{GB} can correspond, for example, to the bottom curve in Fig. 3.4.

The definitions of the regions of inversion in terms of ψ_s, V_{GB}, V_{GC}, and V_{CB} are summarized in Table 3.1. The properties listed correspond to the ones for the two-terminal MOS structure, which were summarized in Table 2.1. Some of these properties will be discussed in the following sections, in which we look separately at each region of inversion. Since the considerations in each region are similar to those for the two-terminal structure of Chap. 2, we will be relatively brief to avoid boredom.

3.4.2 Strong Inversion

As seen from Fig. 3.2, for a given V_{CB} strong inversion is defined by

$$V_{GB} \geq V_{GBH}(V_{CB}) \tag{3.4.15}$$

Exact calculations show that, although deep in strong inversion $|Q_I'| \gg |Q_B'|$, for values of V_{GB} close to V_{GBH} we can have Q_I' larger or smaller than Q_B', depending on substrate doping concentration and oxide thickness. What really makes the structure in the strong inversion behave as it does is not the relative magnitude of $|Q_I'|$ and $|Q_B'|$ but rather that of their slopes with respect to ψ_s; these slopes are simply C_i' and C_b'. One finds that, in strong inversion,

$$C_i' \gg C_b' \tag{3.4.16}$$

As seen in Fig. 3.2a, ψ_s changes only slightly with V_{GB} in strong inversion and can be assumed "pinned" to a value a little higher than ϕ_H. With $V_{CB} = 0$, that value is the same as the corresponding one for the two-terminal structure, which was denoted by ϕ_B in (2.5.25). Since the pinned value is close to ϕ_H, it roughly follows the dependence of the latter on V_{CB}. From (3.4.3), then, the value of the pinned surface potential in strong inversion can be estimated by

$$\psi_s \approx \phi_B + V_{CB} \tag{3.4.17}$$

The depletion region width can then also be assumed pinned at a value l_{Bm} which, corresponding to (2.5.26), is given by

TABLE 3.1

Regions of inversion and properties (three-terminal MOS structure)

	Weak inversion	Moderate inversion	Strong inversion
Definition in terms of surface potential ψ_s (see Fig. 3.2a)	$\phi_L \leq \psi_s < \phi_M$	$\phi_M \leq \psi_s < \phi_H$	$\phi_H \leq \psi_s$
Definition in terms of V_{GB} for a given V_{CB} (see Figs. 3.1c and 3.2)	$V_{GBL} \leq V_{GB} < V_{GBM}$	$V_{GBM} \leq V_{GB} < V_{GBH}$	$V_{GBH} \leq V_{GB}$
Definition in terms of V_{GC} for a given V_{CB} (see Figs. 3.1d and 3.2)	$V_L \leq V_{GC} < V_M$	$V_M \leq V_{GC} < V_H$	$V_H \leq V_{GC}$
Definition in terms of V_{CB} for a given V_{GB} (see Figs. 3.1c and 3.4)†	$V_{CBM} < V_{CB} \leq V_{CBL}$	$V_{CBH} < V_{CB} \leq V_{CBM}$	$V_{CB} \leq V_{CBH}$
$\dfrac{\lvert Q_I' \rvert}{\lvert Q_B' \rvert}$	$\ll 1$	Varies	$\gg 1$ deep in strong inversion; not necessarily so near the bottom of the region
$\dfrac{C_i'}{C_b'}$	$\ll 1$ deep in weak inversion; not necessarily so near the top of the region	Varies	$\gg 1$
$\dfrac{d\psi_s}{dV_{GB}}$	Approximately constant; attains its maximum value in this region	Varies	Small
Dependence of Q_I' on V_{GB} or V_{GC} for V_{CB} constant	Exponential	—	First-degree polynomial

†It is assumed here that V_{GB} is sufficiently large, so that V_{CBH}, V_{CBM}, and V_{CBL} come out non-negative; see Example 3.4 for the interpretation of negative values for these quantities.

$$l_{Bm} = \sqrt{\frac{2\epsilon_s}{qN_A}} \sqrt{\phi_B + V_{CB}} \tag{3.4.18}$$

and the depletion region charge, from (3.2.5) and (3.4.17), is pinned at the value

$$Q_B' = -F\sqrt{N_A}\sqrt{\phi_B + V_{CB}} \tag{3.4.19a}$$

$$= -\gamma C_{ox}'\sqrt{\phi_B + V_{CB}} \tag{3.4.19b}$$

As already explained in Sec. 3.3, *for the case of strong inversion only,* V_{CB} can be interpreted as the effective reverse bias of the inversion-layer–substrate field-induced junction. Changes in the potential between terminals C and B in Fig. 3.1c cause nearly equal changes in the potential ψ_s between the inversion layer and the bulk, as long as strong inversion is maintained. This is why in strong inversion $d\psi_s/dV_{CB} \approx 1$, as follows from (3.4.17), and as can also be seen in the strong-inversion part of the curves in Fig. 3.4.

The inversion layer charge can be obtained from (3.2.2) to (3.2.4) and (3.4.17):

$$Q_I' = -C_{ox}'(V_{GB} - \phi_{MS} - \phi_B - V_{CB}) - Q_o' - Q_B' \qquad (3.4.20a)$$

$$= -C_{ox}'[V_{GB} - V_{GBT}(V_{CB})] \qquad (3.4.20b)$$

where

$$V_{GBT}(V_{CB}) = \phi_{MS} - \frac{Q_o'}{C_{ox}'} + \phi_B + V_{CB} - \frac{Q_B'}{C_{ox}'} \qquad (3.4.21a)$$

$$= V_{FB} + \phi_B + V_{CB} - \frac{Q_B'}{C_{ox}'} \qquad (3.4.21b)$$

$$= V_{FB} + \phi_B + V_{CB} + \gamma\sqrt{\phi_B + V_{CB}} \qquad (3.4.21c)$$

The quantity $V_{GBT}(V_{CB})$ is the *G-B (gate-substrate) extrapolated threshold voltage*; its meaning is illustrated in Fig. 3.2d. This quantity is related to the *G-C extrapolated threshold voltage*† V_T (illustrated in the same figure) by (3.4.7). Accordingly, we have

$$V_T = V_{FB} + \phi_B - \frac{Q_B'}{C_{ox}'} \qquad (3.4.22a)$$

$$= V_{FB} + \phi_B + \gamma\sqrt{V_{CB} + \phi_B} \qquad (3.4.22b)$$

which can be written as

$$V_T = V_{T0} + \gamma(\sqrt{V_{CB} + \phi_B} - \sqrt{\phi_B}) \qquad (3.4.22c)$$

where V_{T0} is the value of V_T at $V_{CB} = 0$, given by

$$V_{T0} = V_{FB} + \phi_B + \gamma\sqrt{\phi_B} \qquad (3.4.23)$$

which is, of course, the same quantity as that encountered for the two-terminal structure in (2.5.30).

The plot of V_T vs. V_{CB} has been included in Fig. 3.5. The threshold increase $V_T - V_{T0}$ due to the body effect is shown vs. V_{CB} for various values of γ in Fig. 3.6‡

---

† C refers to terminal C in Fig. 3.1d.
‡ Plots of $V_L - V_{L0}$, $V_M - V_{M0}$, and $V_H - V_{H0}$ have similar shapes.

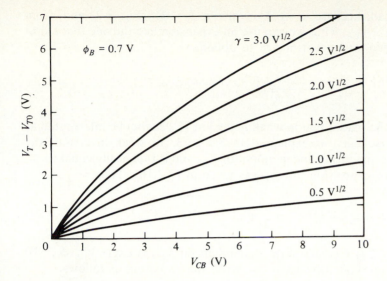

FIGURE 3.6
Increase of the extrapolated threshold voltage V_T above its value at $V_{CB} = 0$, shown vs. V_{CB} for various values of the body effect coefficient γ. A single value of $\phi_B = 0.7\,\text{V}$ is assumed.

Using $V_{GB} = V_{GC} + V_{CB}$ and $V_{GBT} = V_T + V_{CB}$ in (3.4.20b), we obtain

$$Q_I' = -C_{ox}'(V_{GC} - V_T) \qquad (3.4.24)$$

This corresponds to the straight-line part of the plot in Fig. 3.2d.

3.4.3 Moderate Inversion

As seen in Fig. 3.2, moderate inversion is defined for a given V_{CB} by[9]

$$V_{GBM}(V_{CB}) \le V_{GB} < V_{GBH}(V_{CB}) \qquad (3.4.25)$$

As was the case for the two-terminal structure, no convenient simplifications have been developed for the moderate-inversion region, and so the exact equations should be used. For a given value of ψ_s, the quantities Q_I' and V_{GB} can be found from (3.2.6) and (3.2.7b), and thus $Q_I'(V_{GB})$ can be plotted.

3.4.4 Weak Inversion

For a given V_{CB}, we define the weak-inversion region by (Fig. 3.2)

$$V_{GBL}(V_{CB}) \le V_{GB} < V_{GBM}(V_{CB}) \qquad (3.4.26)$$

In this region, we have

$$Q_I' \ll Q_B' \qquad (3.4.27)$$

Consider now (3.2.6). The magnitude of the second term under the first square root is small, because in weak inversion $\psi_s < \phi_M$ (Fig. 3.2) and, from (3.4.2), $\phi_M = 2\phi_F + V_{CB}$. Thus we can use an expansion like the one that led to (2.5.33) for the two-terminal structure to obtain

$$Q_I' = - \frac{F\sqrt{N_A}}{2\sqrt{\psi_s}}\, \phi_t e^{[\psi_s - (2\phi_F + V_{CB})]/\phi_t} \tag{3.4.28}$$

We remind the reader that in weak inversion V_{CB} *cannot* be interpreted as an effective reverse bias, as explained in Sec. 3.3. In weak inversion, the surface potential is practically independent of V_{CB} and is practically equal to ψ_{sa} (see Fig. 3.3). The expression for ψ_{sa} was given in (3.2.16). Thus:

$$\psi_s \approx \psi_{sa}(V_{GB}) = \left(-\frac{\gamma}{2} + \sqrt{\frac{\gamma^2}{4} + V_{GB} - V_{FB}}\right)^2 \tag{3.4.29}$$

Therefore, in (3.4.28) the only term dependent on V_{CB} is $\exp(-V_{CB}/\phi_t)$. To emphasize this important conclusion, we write that equation as follows:

$$Q_I' = - \underbrace{\frac{F\sqrt{N_A}}{2\sqrt{\psi_{sa}(V_{GB})}}\, \phi_t e^{[\psi_{sa}(V_{GB}) - 2\phi_F]/\phi_t}}_{\substack{\text{dependent} \\ \text{only on } V_{GB}}} \cdot \underbrace{e^{-V_{CB}/\phi_t}}_{\substack{\text{dependent} \\ \text{only on } V_{CB}}} \tag{3.4.30}$$

For any value of V_{GB} in weak inversion, ψ_{sa} can be determined from (3.4.29) and substituted in (3.4.30) to find Q_I'. For a fixed V_{CB}, $Q_I'(V_{GB})$ turns out to be an exponential. To see this, we now develop an expression for Q_I' which does not contain ψ_{sa}, as we did for the two-terminal structure. In Fig. 3.7, we have repeated one of the curves of Fig. 3.3. Let V_{CB}' denote the constant value of V_{CB} for which this curve is obtained. In the figure we show the weak-inversion limits on the surface potential from (3.4.1) and (3.4.2). As seen, the width of the region in terms of ψ_s is only ϕ_F. As V_{GB} changes over the region, the corresponding variation of the term $\sqrt{\psi_s}$ in (3.4.28) is very small compared to the drastic variation of the exponential in that equation. Thus we can assume that $\sqrt{\psi_s}$ is practically fixed at $\sqrt{1.5\phi_F + V_{CB}'}$, with $1.5\phi_F + V_{CB}'$ being the value of ψ_s at the middle of the weak-inversion region, as shown by point X in Fig. 3.7.[10] Thus (3.4.28) becomes

$$Q_I' = - \frac{F\sqrt{N_A}}{2\sqrt{1.5\phi_F + V_{CB}'}}\, \phi_t e^{[\psi_s - (2\phi_F + V_{CB}')]/\phi_t} \tag{3.4.31}$$

The slope of the plot in Fig. 3.7 is nearly constant in weak inversion, and can be approximated by the value of the slope at the middle of the region. From (3.4.29), the *inverse* of the slope at this point (commonly denoted by n, which is not to be confused with the electron concentration) is

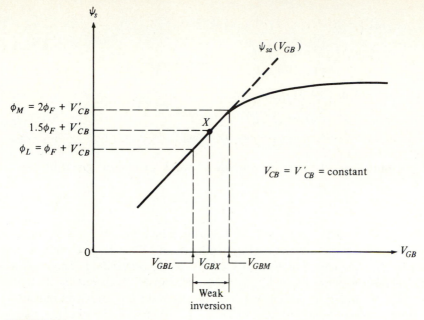

FIGURE 3.7
Surface potential vs. gate-substrate voltage for a given value V'_{CB} of V_{CB}. The point X indicates the middle of the weak-inversion region.

$$n = \frac{dV_{GB}}{d\psi_s}\bigg|_{\psi_s = V'_{CB} + 1.5\phi_F} \tag{3.4.32a}$$

$$= 1 + \frac{\gamma}{2\sqrt{1.5\phi_F + V'_{CB}}} \,\dagger \tag{3.4.32b}$$

Thus, for changes ΔV_{GB} causing changes $\Delta \psi_s$ in weak inversion, we have $\Delta \psi_s = \Delta V_{GB}/n$. We will take these changes with respect to the middle of weak inversion, where $\psi_s = 1.5\phi_F + V'_{CB}$. The corresponding value of V_{GB} at this point (X in Fig. 3.7) is, from (3.4.29),

$$V_{GBX} = V_{FB} + 1.5\phi_F + V'_{CB} + \gamma\sqrt{1.5\phi_F + V'_{CB}} \tag{3.4.33}$$

Thus, the equation $\Delta \psi_s = \Delta V_{GB}/n$ can be written as follows:

$$\psi_s - (1.5\phi_F + V'_{CB}) = \frac{V_{GB} - V_{GBX}}{n} \tag{3.4.34a}$$

$$= \frac{V_{GC} - V_X}{n} \tag{3.4.34b}$$

---

† If there is significant variation of the interface state charge (Sec. 2.2) with the surface potential, an extra term should be added in this equation; see the discussion toward the end of Sec. 2.6.

where

$$V_X = V_{GBX} - V'_{CB} \qquad (3.4.35a)$$

$$= V_{FB} + 1.5\phi_F + \gamma\sqrt{1.5\phi_F + V'_{CB}} \qquad (3.4.35b)$$

Substituting (3.4.34) in (3.4.31), we obtain

$$Q'_I = Q'_{IX}e^{(V_{GB}-V_{GBX})/(n\phi_t)} \qquad (3.4.36a)$$

$$= Q'_{IX}e^{(V_{GC}-V_X)/(n\phi_t)} \qquad (3.4.36b)$$

where Q'_{IX} is the value of Q'_I at the middle of weak inversion, given by

$$Q'_{IX} = -\frac{F\sqrt{N_A}}{2\sqrt{1.5\phi_F + V'_{CB}}}\,\phi_t e^{-0.5\phi_F/\phi_t} \qquad (3.4.37)$$

If V_{CB} is fixed and V_{GB} is varied, (3.4.36a) can be a very helpful equation since it makes explicit the exponential dependence of Q'_I on V_{GB}. However, *if V_{GB} is fixed and V_{CB} is varied instread*, (3.4.36a) *can be misleading*. The reason is that the dependence of Q'_I on V_{CB} is very awkwardly predicted by it. It is hidden in Q'_{IX}, n, and V_{GBX}, each of which depends on V_{CB} in a complicated manner. On the other hand, (3.4.30) is ideal for such cases, since it makes explicit the exponential dependence of Q'_I on V_{CB} in a very simple manner.

3.5 CAREFUL DEFINITIONS FOR THE LIMITS OF MODERATE INVERSION†

In cases where accuracy is important, the limits of moderate inversion can be defined more carefully than was done in Sec. 3.2. The reasoning leading to such definitions is the same as that for the two-terminal structure in Sec. 2.7, and need not be repeated here. Basically, such careful definitions place the onset of moderate inversion at a point above which the slope of the plot in Fig. 3.2c starts varying appreciably. Similarly, the upper limit of moderate inversion is placed at a point below which the slope of the plot in Fig. 3.2d starts varying appreciably. The corresponding limit values of the surface potential, ϕ_M and ϕ_H, can be defined in a manner analogous to that in Sec. 2.7 by

$$\frac{C'_i}{C'_{ox} + C'_b}\bigg|_{\psi_s = \phi_M} = 0.1 \qquad (3.5.1)$$

$$\frac{C'_i}{C'_{ox} + C'_b}\bigg|_{\psi_s = \phi_H} = 10 \qquad (3.5.2)$$

For a given V_{CB}, one can use (3.2.12) and (3.2.13) in the above definitions and solve iteratively for ϕ_M and ϕ_H. The values of ϕ_M for practical devices turn out to be within about $1\phi_t$ of $2\phi_F$. Those of ϕ_H are above this by about $5\phi_t$ to $6\phi_t$. The corresponding V_{GB} values, V_{GBM} and V_{GBH}, can be found from (3.2.7b) by using

---

† This section can be skipped without loss of continuity, and is therefore set in smaller type.

$\psi_s = \phi_M$ and $\psi_s = \phi_H$, respectively; an *accurate* value of ϕ_H is needed for this [see comments preceding and following (3.4.10)]. V_{GBM} turns out to be very close to the value given by (3.4.5) and (3.4.9) (within a few tens of millivolts). The value of V_{GBH} is above V_{GBM} by several tenths of 1 V. Figure 3.8 shows the width of the moderate inversion, $V_H - V_M = V_{GBH} - V_{GBM}$, for $V_{CB} = 5$ V. This figure should be compared to Fig. 2.18, which is for the case of $V_{CB} = 0$. As is evident from this comparison, the increase in V_{CB} has decreased the width of the region somewhat. For practical devices (large N_A combined with small d_{ox} and vice versa), the width of the region in Fig. 3.8 is roughly 0.5 V.

At $V_{GB} = V_{GBM}$, the slopes of the plots in Figs. 3.2*a* and 3.2*c* drop to about 91 percent of their maximum value. At $V_{GB} = V_{GBH}$, the slope of the plot in Fig. 3.2*a* drops to about 9 percent of its maximum value; the slope of the plot in Fig. 3.2*d* is about 91 percent of the theoretical maximum value of C'_{ox}.

Rather than finding ϕ_M and ϕ_H for a given V_{CB}, as suggested above, one can find these limits for a given V_{GB}. One can use (3.2.12) and (3.2.13) in the definitions (3.5.1) and (3.5.2), and then utilize (3.2.7*b*) to eliminate the exponential terms. The resulting equations can be solved *explicitly* for ϕ_M and ϕ_H. These values can then be substituted back in (3.2.7*b*) to find explicitly the corresponding V_{CB} values, V_{CBM} and V_{CBH}, respectively, for the given V_{GB} (Prob. 3.9).

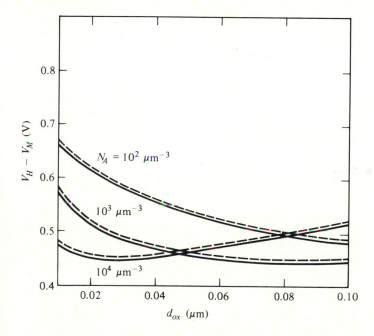

FIGURE 3.8
Width of moderate-inversion region, [calculated from definitions (3.5.1) and (3.5.2)] for the structure of Fig. 3.1*c* and *d* vs. oxide thickness, for three values of substrate doping concentration at room temperature, with $V_{CB} = 5$ V. Solid lines: accurate calculation based on (3.2.12) and (3.2.13); broken lines: charge sheet model.

REFERENCES

1. H. C. Pao and C. T. Sah, "Effects of diffusion current on characteristics of metal-oxide (insulator) semiconductor transistors," *Solid-State Electronics*, vol. 9, pp. 927–937, 1966.
2. S. M. Sze, *Physics of Semiconductor Devices*, John Wiley, New York, 1981.
3. I. R. M. Mansour, "On the modeling of MOS devices," *Proceedings of the Third International Symposium on Network Theory*, Yugoslavia, pp. 705–713, 1975.
4. I. R. M. Mansour, "Improved modeling of MOS devices," *Proceedings of the European Conference on Circuit Theory and Design*, Italy, 1976.
5. G. Baccarani, M. Rudan, and G. Spadini, "Analytical i.g.f.e.t. model including drift and diffusion currents," *IEE Journal on Solid-State and Electron Devices*, vol. 2, pp. 62–68, March 1978.
6. J. R. Brews, "A charge-sheet model of the MOSFET," *Solid-State Electronics*, vol. 21, pp. 345–355, 1978.
7. F. Van de Wiele, "A long-channel MOSFET model," *Solid-State Electronics*, vol. 22, pp. 991–997, 1979.
8. J. R. Brews, "Physics of the MOS transistor," chapter 1 in *Silicon Integrated Circuits, Part A*, D. Kahng (editor), Applied Solid State Science Series, Academic Press, New York, 1981.
9. Y. Tsividis, "Moderate inversion in MOS devices," *Solid-State Electronics*, vol. 25, pp. 1099–1104, 1982; see also Erratum, *ibid.*, vol. 26, p. 823, 1983.
10. R. J. Van Overstraeten, G. J. Declerk, and P. A. Nuls, "Theory of the MOS transistor in weak inversion–new method to determine the number of surface states," *IEEE Transactions on Electron Devices*, vol. ED-22, pp. 282–288, May 1975.

PROBLEMS

3.1. (a) For a device with $N_A = 10^3 \ \mu\text{m}^{-3}$, $d_{ox} = 0.04 \ \mu\text{m}$, and $V_{FB} = 0$, plot ψ_s vs. V_{GB}, with V_{GB} between 0.5 and 10 V and for $V_{CB} = 1, 2, 4, 6,$ and 8 V. Show approximately the three regions of inversion on each curve. Assume that $V_{GBH} \approx V_{GBM} + 0.55 \text{ V}$.

(b) For the same device plot ψ_s vs. V_{CB}, with V_{CB} between 0 and 10 V and for $V_{GB} = 1, 2, 4, 6,$ and 8 V. Show approximately the regions of inversion on each curve.

3.2. Show how the V_{CB}-V_{GB} plane can be separated into five regions, corresponding to accumulation, depletion, weak inversion, moderate inversion, and strong inversion. (*Hint*: In accumulation, take into account the fact that the concentration of holes is practically unaffected by V_{CB}.)

3.3. For the device of Prob. 3.1:

(a) Find V_{GBL}, V_{GBM}, and V_{GBH} for $V_{CB} = 0 \text{ V}$; assume $V_{GBH} \approx V_{GBM} + 0.55 \text{ V}$.

(b) Plot $|Q_I'|$ vs. V_{GB} for V_{GB} between V_{GBL} and $V_{GBH} + 5 \text{ V}$. Use (3.2.6) and (3.2.7b). Give the corresponding plot vs. V_{GC}.

(c) Repeat using a logarithmic axis for $|Q_I'|$.

(d) On each of the above plots, plot $|Q_I'|$ as given by (3.4.20b) in strong inversion and as given by (3.4.36b) in weak inversion. Comment on the accuracy obtainable.

(e) Repeat (a) through (d) for $V_{CB} = 5 \text{ V}$.

charge.[10-19] Our list of ref
complete, and many more
helped spread the knowled
industry applied the newly
digital IC's, and the nee
design.[21-37] At the same tim
considerable attention.[38-52]
to produce models valid f
including drift and diffusion
early attempts.[10] The above
our discussion in this chapte
along the way. Extensive
channel devices, ion-implan
tances, high-frequency opera
given as such topics are disc

The basic features of a
details of the structure will k
and especially in Chap. 10 in
n^+ regions (typically a few te
and the inversion layer is ofte
Fig. 4.1 consists of electrons,
or NMOS transistor. If the s
source and drain of p-type ma
or PMOS transistor. We will
4.11. Common acronyms for t
Semiconductor Transistor), M
IGFET (for Insulated-Gate F
nated to distinguish the devi

3.4. It is often assumed that there is a point below which $Q'_I(V_{GB})$ is an exponential and above which it is a straight line. Attempt to find such a point on the plots of Prob. 3.3. Is this possible? How large an error is involved in such an approximation?

3.5. It has been seen in Sec. 3.4.2 that if ψ_s is pinned to a fixed value, Q'_I plots as a straight line vs. V_{GB}. Is such pinning a *necessary* condition for obtaining such a straight line? If not, find the necessary condition for such a behavior of ψ_s.

3.6. Show that a better approximation than (3.4.17) for the surface potential in *strong* inversion is:

$$\psi_{s,\,strong} \approx 2\phi_F + V_{CB} + \phi_t \ln\left\{\frac{1}{\phi_t}\left[\frac{1}{\gamma^2}(V_{GB} - V_{FB} - V_{CB} - \phi_B)^2 - \phi_B - V_{CB}\right]\right\}$$

[*Hint*: Use (3.4.17) as an initial guess and perform one iteration using (3.2.7b).] Compare the above expression to (3.4.17) and to (3.2.7b). What happens if we attempt to use the above expressions in moderate and weak inversion?

3.7. Prove that an approximate expression for $Q'_I(V_{GB})$ in weak inversion is

$$Q'_I = Q'_{IM}e^{(V_{GC}-V_M)/(n\phi_t)}$$

where Q'_{IM} is the value of Q'_I at the upper limit of weak inversion.

3.8. Show that for the structure of Fig. 3.1c, $C'_i < 0.1C'_b$ if the surface potential $\psi_s < 2\phi_f + V_{CB} - 2.3\phi_t$.

3.9. For a given V_{GB}, find *explicit* expressions for ϕ_M, ϕ_H, V_{CBM}, and V_{CBH} using the procedure outlined at the end of Sec. 3.5.

3.10. Mark the accurate limits of the regions of inversion on the curves of Prob. 3.3 using the definitions of Sec. 3.5.

3.11. Prove (3.2.6). [*Hint*: Find the total semiconductor charge $Q'_C = Q'_I + Q'_B$ using basic electrostatics (Appendix B) by following a procedure similar to that of Prob. 2.14. From that find Q'_I by subtracting (3.2.5a).]

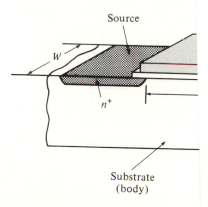

Source

W

n^+

Substrate
(body)

FIGURE 4.1
Simplified structure of an n-channel MO

$\Delta Q_I / \Delta A$, as ΔA approaches 0; similarly for Q'_B and Q'_G. In other words, we define:

$$Q'_I = \frac{dQ_I}{dA} \tag{4.1.3}$$

$$Q'_B = \frac{dQ_B}{dA} \tag{4.1.4}$$

$$Q'_G = \frac{dQ_G}{dA} \tag{4.1.5}$$

4.2 TRANSISTOR REGIONS OF OPERATION

Typical sets of dc current-voltage characteristics for an NMOS transistor are shown in Fig. 4.3a and b, corresponding to Fig. 4.2a and b, respectively. The details in these plots will be discussed later. In general, drain current I_D depends on the terminal voltages, in a complicated manner. However, for certain combinations of terminal voltages, simplifications become possible and relatively simple expressions can be developed for the current. Anticipating this, we will define transistor regions of operation as shown in Table 4.1. These definitions are consistent with long-established practice, and the rationale behind them will be seen in subsequent sections. As a mnemonic aid it should be noted that *the name of a transistor region coincides with the level of inversion at the most heavily inverted channel end.* For convenience in drawing certain figures (like Fig. 4.2) or providing certain plots, we will be assuming that the most heavily inverted channel end is the one next to the *source*, unless noted otherwise. This does not restrict generality, since the source and drain terminals in Fig. 4.1 are equivalent.

4.3 A GENERAL CHARGE SHEET MODEL

In this section, we derive an expression for the drain current, valid in all regions of operation. The term *general* in the title refers to this universal validity. The term *charge sheet* refers to the basic assumption in it, i.e., that the inversion layer is of infinitesimal thickness.† We note that we have already made this assumption in Chaps. 2 and 3. We will use expressions from those chapters in our present development. The model we will present has been derived in several references,[53, 54, 56–59] but our derivation will be simpler.

A key to the generality of the results we are about to develop is the recognition of the fact that the current in the channel can be caused by both

---

† Note, nevertheless, that when drawing a figure it is convenient to use a finite thickness for the inversion layer.

4.1 INTRODUCTI

The MOS transistor is of Chap. 3, so that th applying a voltage bet layer. Since the numb gate potential, the latt layer (i.e., turn the modulate its conductio

The basic idea on old; working independ the thirties.[1, 2] Laborat device remained essenti the early sixties the MC working devices by Kal today, and the establish review of early work, i ment of practical fabric treatments on the MOS investigations of the r

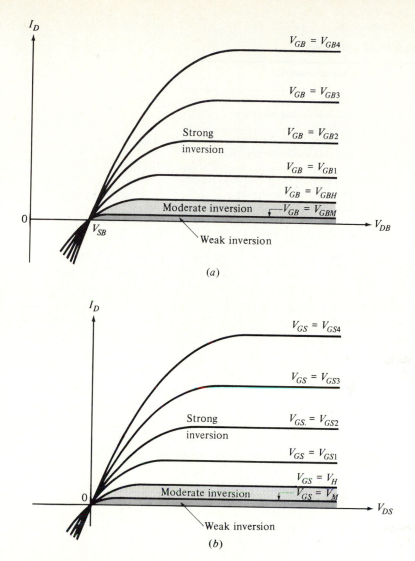

FIGURE 4.3
Current-voltage characteristics corresponding to Fig. 4.2a and b. In both cases V_{SB} is assumed fixed, and $V_{GBi} = V_{GSi} + V_{SB}$.

drift and diffusion (Sec. 1.3). Thus, let x be the horizontal position in the channel, measured from the source end. If the inversion layer current at x is denoted by $I(x)$, we will have

$$I(x) = I_{\text{drift}}(x) + I_{\text{diff}}(x) \qquad (4.3.1)$$

To write an expression for the drift component, consider a small element

TABLE 4.1

Transistor regions of operation

Region	Channel condition
Strong inversion	The most heavily† inverted channel end is in strong inversion
Moderate inversion	The most heavily† inverted channel end is in moderate inversion
Weak inversion	The most heavily† inverted channel end is in weak inversion

† If both ends are equally inverted, either end can be considered.

in the inversion layer between x and $x + \Delta x$ in Fig. 4.2a, as shown magnified in Fig. 4.4. The potential difference across this element is $\Delta \psi_s(x) = \psi_s(x + \Delta x) - \psi_s(x)$. Comparing this figure to Fig. 1.5 [and assuming that the electron velocity is proportional to the small horizontal electric field, analogous to (1.3.8)], it is obvious that we can use (1.3.15) with V replaced by $\Delta \psi_s(x)$, a replaced by Δx, b by W, and $|Q'|$ by $-Q'_I$, where Q'_I is the (negative) inversion layer charge per unit area at x. Also, μ_B must be replaced with a *smaller* mobility value because electrons move with difficulty parallel to the surface (the semiconductor-oxide interface), being pulled toward it by the vertical

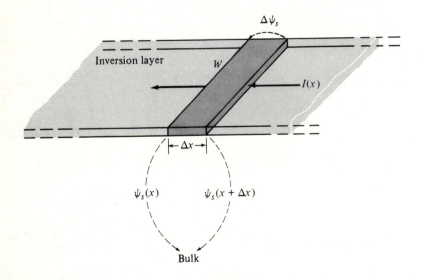

FIGURE 4.4
Small element of the inversion layer in the device of Fig. 4.2.

field. The corresponding mobility will be called the *surface mobility* and will be denoted by μ. (This quantity will be considered in more detail in Sec. 4.8; for now it can be assumed that it has roughly half the value of μ_B.) We will thus have

$$I_{\text{drift}}(x) = \mu(-Q_I')\frac{W}{\Delta x}\,\Delta\psi_s(x) \tag{4.3.2}$$

which, allowing Δx to approach zero, becomes

$$I_{\text{drift}}(x) = \mu W(-Q_I')\frac{d\psi_s}{dx} \tag{4.3.3}$$

The diffusion current component can be obtained as in (1.3.20):

$$I_{\text{diff}}(x) = \mu W\phi_t\frac{dQ_I'}{dx} \tag{4.3.4}$$

We should note here that, if the inversion layer were assumed to be of finite thickness and the electron concentration in it varied with depth, (4.3.3) and (4.3.4) would still be valid, assuming a "laminar" electron flow. This is owing to the generality of (1.3.15) and (1.3.20), discussed in the corresponding footnotes in Sec. 1.3. However, this point is not of much importance here, where it will be assumed that all inversion layer charge is concentrated within an infinitesimal depth from the "surface."

In dc steady state, which is the only case discussed in this chapter, the total current in the channel must be the same for all x and equal to the drain current. Using this fact and (4.3.3) to (4.3.4) in (4.3.1), we obtain

$$I_D = \mu W(-Q_I')\frac{d\psi_s}{dx} + \mu W\phi_t\frac{dQ_I'}{dx} \tag{4.3.5}$$

Let the surface potential at the source end of the channel ($x = 0$) be denoted by ψ_{s0}, and Q_I' there by $Q_{I,\text{source}}'$. Let the corresponding quantities at the drain end of the channel ($x = L$) be denoted by ψ_{sL} and $Q_{I,\text{drain}}'$. Integrating (4.3.5) from $x = 0$ to $x = L$ we obtain

$$\int_0^L I_D\,dx = W\int_{\psi_{s0}}^{\psi_{sL}} \mu(-Q_I')\,d\psi_s + W\phi_t\int_{Q_{I,\text{source}}'}^{Q_{I,\text{drain}}'} \mu\,dQ_I' \tag{4.3.6}$$

Since I_D is independent of x it can be moved outside the integral. Thus the left-hand side is equal to $I_D L$, and we have

$$I_D = \frac{W}{L}\left[\int_{\psi_{s0}}^{\psi_{sL}} \mu(-Q_I')\,d\psi_s + \phi_t\int_{Q_{I,\text{source}}'}^{Q_{I,\text{drain}}'} \mu\,dQ_I'\right] \tag{4.3.7}$$

Thus we can view I_D as consisting of two components I_{D1} and I_{D2}:[52, 63]

$$I_D = I_{D1} + I_{D2} \tag{4.3.8}$$

where I_{D1} is due to the presence of drift:

$$I_{D1} = \frac{W}{L} \int_{\psi_{s0}}^{\psi_{sL}} \mu(-Q_I') \, d\psi_s \tag{4.3.9}$$

and I_{D2} is due to the presence of diffusion:

$$I_{D2} = \frac{W}{L} \phi_t \int_{Q_{I,\text{source}}'}^{Q_{I,\text{drain}}'} \mu \, dQ_I' \tag{4.3.10}$$

The interpretation of I_{D1} and I_{D2} requires some caution. Note that, in general, there may not be single values of a drift current and a diffusion current in the channel, since $I_{\text{drift}}(x)$ in (4.3.2) and $I_{\text{diff}}(x)$ in (4.3.3) are functions of position.[65] Nevertheless, the development leading to (4.3.7) makes it clear that I_{D1} is there because drift was assumed to be present in the channel; were there no drift, there would be no I_{D1}. Similarly, I_{D2} is there because it was assumed that diffusion was present in the channel.

We now make the assumption that μ is constant along the channel (the more general case will be discussed in Sec. 4.8). Then μ can be moved outside the integral in (4.3.9) and (4.3.10), and we have

$$I_{D1} = \frac{W}{L} \mu \int_{\psi_{s0}}^{\psi_{sL}} (-Q_I') \, d\psi_s \tag{4.3.11}$$

$$I_{D2} = \frac{W}{L} \mu\phi_t(Q_{I,\text{drain}}' - Q_{I,\text{source}}') \tag{4.3.12}$$

To evaluate now I_{D1} and I_{D2}, we need Q_I' as a function of ψ_s. An appropriate expression has been derived in (3.2.8a) and is repeated below. (The expression is, of course, assumed valid here because of the "gradual channel approximation" made in the beginning of this section.)

$$Q_I' = -C_{ox}'\left(V_{GB} - V_{FB} - \psi_s + \frac{Q_B'}{C_{ox}'}\right) \tag{4.3.13}$$

where Q_B' is, from (3.2.5b)

$$Q_B' = -\gamma C_{ox}'\sqrt{\psi_s} \tag{4.3.14}$$

Thus Q_I' becomes

$$Q_I' = -C_{ox}'(V_{GB} - V_{FB} - \psi_s - \gamma\sqrt{\psi_s}) \tag{4.3.15}$$

Using this in (4.3.11) gives the drain current component due to the presence of drift:

$$I_{D1} = \frac{W}{L} \mu C_{ox}'[(V_{GB} - V_{FB})(\psi_{sL} - \psi_{s0}) - \tfrac{1}{2}(\psi_{sL}^2 - \psi_{s0}^2) - \tfrac{2}{3}\gamma(\psi_{sL}^{3/2} - \psi_{s0}^{3/2})] \tag{4.3.16}$$

Using (4.3.15) in (4.3.12) gives the drain current component due to diffusion:

$$I_{D2} = \frac{W}{L} \mu C'_{ox} [\phi_t(\psi_{sL} - \psi_{s0}) + \phi_t \gamma(\psi_{sL}^{1/2} - \psi_{s0}^{1/2})]\dagger \qquad (4.3.17)$$

The only step remaining is the evaluation of ψ_{s0} and ψ_{sL} from the externally applied voltages in Fig. 4.2a. Comparing this figure with Fig. 3.1c, we note the expressions developed for the latter can be used at the source end of the channel by replacing V_{CB} by V_{SB}. Similarly, such expressions can be used at the drain end of the channel by replacing V_{CB} by V_{DB}. Thus, writing (3.2.7b) for the source end and the drain end of the channel, we obtain[53-59]

$$\psi_{s0} = V_{GB} - V_{FB} - \gamma \sqrt{\psi_{s0} + \phi_t \, e^{(\psi_{s0} - 2\phi_F - V_{SB})/\phi_t}} \qquad (4.3.18a)$$

$$\psi_{sL} = V_{GB} - V_{FB} - \gamma \sqrt{\psi_{sL} + \phi_t \, e^{(\psi_{sL} - 2\phi_F - V_{DB})/\phi_t}} \qquad (4.3.18b)$$

These equations can be solved for ψ_{s0} and ψ_{sL} by iteration. This can easily be done with a computer or a calculator with an equation-solving capability.‡ A plot of ψ_{sL} vs. V_{DB} (or of ψ_{s0} vs. V_{SB}) is shown in Fig. 4.5. The symbols used on the figure are defined in Chap. 3. The numbered points are in relation to an upcoming discussion.

Note that by neglecting the edge effects near the drain we have ended up with a potential ψ_{sL} at the drain end of the channel which will, in general, be different from the potential in the n^+ region. Thus it would seem that a potential discontinuity would exist at the n^+ region boundary. As expected from the associated discussion near the end of Sec. 3.2, a more detailed picture would include a transition region containing the boundary, over which the potential would change continuously and, eventually, would become equal to the potential in the n^+ region. The length of this transition region may be expected to be roughly the same as the depth of the depletion region under the drain. In this region, one cannot assume that the electric field is practically vertical. Similar comments apply to the source end of the channel. Based on such a picture, one could interpret L in the above analysis as representing the length of the channel, excluding the source and the drain transition regions, and ψ_{s0} and ψ_{sL} as the surface potentials to the right and left of these regions, respectively. Then (4.3.18) would again be used, assuming the effect of V_{SB} and V_{DB} at the two points remained essentially the same.§ However, for the long channels assumed in this chapter we can continue viewing L as the total

---

† The reader is warned that this equation, although theoretically sound, can cause numerical difficulties in weak inversion. This is explained later in this section. An improvement is suggested in Prob. 4.2.

‡ It has been suggested[67] that the solution can be speeded up by using the so-called Schroder series.[68]

§ Readers familiar with quasi-Fermi levels (see Appendixes A and G) will recognize this assumption as equivalent to assuming that the electron quasi-Fermi levels remain essentially constant over the transition regions; a corresponding assumption is often made in pn junction theory.[18, 66]

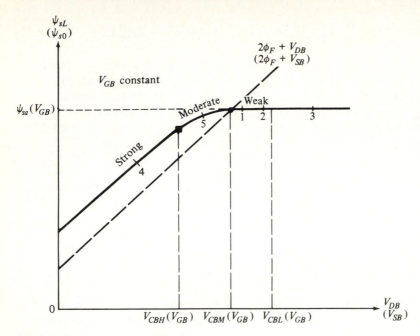

FIGURE 4.5
Surface potential at the drain (source) end of the channel vs. drain-substrate (source-substrate)
voltage for a given gate-substrate voltage.

source-drain spacing. Note that in our analysis we are forced to neglect the
above effects since they cannot be handled by the "gradual channel approximation," which we have adopted to be able to obtain simple analytical results. A
careful investigation of the above effects would have made necessary the use of
two-dimensional analysis requiring a numerical solution.

We now fix V_{SB}, keep V_{GB} as a parameter, and vary V_{DB}. We find the
corresponding ψ_{s0} and ψ_{sL} from (4.3.18) and substitute them in (4.3.16) and
(4.3.17). Adding I_{D1} and I_{D2} produces I_D as in (4.3.8), and gives the plots of
Fig. 4.3a, where the current is shown for $V_{DB} > V_{SB}$, with V_{GB} as a parameter.
These plots can be converted to the ones in Fig. 4.3b, where we show the
current vs. $V_{DS} = V_{DB} - V_{SB}$, with $V_{GS} = V_{GB} - V_{SB}$ as a parameter. On the two
figures, the regions of operation are marked according to Table 4.1, with the
limit values on V_{GB} or V_{GS} denoted by symbols defined in Chap. 3. These
values are not of interest at this point. What is important is to note that the
single expression (4.3.8) predicts the current in all these regions. Experiments
agree very well with such predictions.[56–59]

Note that all curves eventually saturate for large V_{DB}. This can be
understood by relating the drain current for one of the V_{GB} values (say, V_{GB4})
to the corresponding surface potential ψ_{sL} at the drain. This is shown in Fig.
4.6. As seen, increasing V_{DB} eventually drives the drain end of the channel into
weak inversion, where ψ_{sL} becomes practically constant at a value dependent

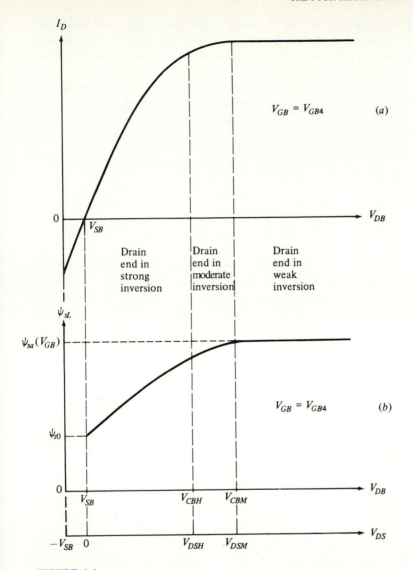

FIGURE 4.6
(*a*) Drain current for a transistor operating in strong inversion vs. drain-substrate voltage for fixed source-substrate and gate-substrate voltages; (*b*) surface potential at the drain end of the channel, corresponding to (*a*). A drain-source voltage axis is shown at the bottom of the figure.

on $V_{GB} = V_{GB4}$ only, for reasons explained in Chap. 3. Increasing V_{DB} further cannot affect ψ_{sL}. Thus I_{D1} and I_{D2} in (4.3.16) and (4.3.17) also become independent of V_{DB}. It is seen then that, although the source end of the channel can be, say, strongly inverted with a large $|Q_I'|$ and with ψ_{s0} strongly dependent on V_{SB}, the drain end of the channel can be weakly inverted with a small $|Q_I'|$ and with ψ_{sL} practically independent of V_{DB}. However, the current at the two ends (and throughout the channel) is the same. This should not be surprising since, as follows from (4.3.5), the current at any point in the channel is not determined only by Q_I' at that point. This will be discussed further later on.

Consider now a value of V_{DB} corresponding to the "flat" part of the curves in Fig. 4.3a. If I_D and its components are plotted for that value vs. V_{GB}, we obtain the curves of Fig. 4.7.[63] To include a large range of currents, a logarithmic vertical axis is used. The regions of inversion across the horizontal axis have been marked according to the definitions of Table 4.1. Here V_{DB} is larger than V_{SB}, so that the most heavily inverted channel end is the one next to the source. The region of inversion at that end can be determined as in Chap. 3. We note here that in transistor literature the weak inversion is often not bounded from below, i.e., everything below moderate inversion is called weak inversion, as long as the current does not become so low as to be masked by leakage currents (Sec. 4.6).

It is seen in Fig. 4.7 that in strong inversion $I_D \approx I_{D1}$, so that the current is mainly due to the presence of drift. In weak inversion, the current is mainly due to the presence of diffusion, since $I_D \approx I_{D2}$. However, in moderate inversion *both* I_{D1} and I_{D2} are important; both drift and diffusion play an

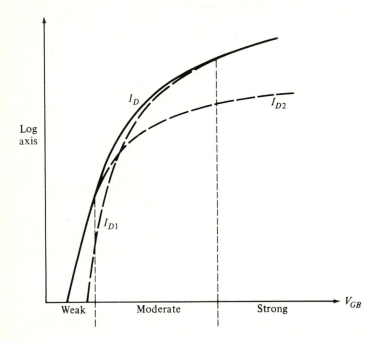

FIGURE 4.7
Drain current I_D, its component due to drift I_{D1}, and its component due to diffusion I_{D2} vs. gate-substrate voltage for a large drain-substrate voltage corresponding to the "flat" part of the characteristics in Fig. 4.3a.[63] A logarithmic axis is used for the current.

important role in this region. Similar conclusions can be reached for other V_{DB} values.

We now come to a numerical problem associated with (4.3.17) in weak inversion, where $I_D \approx I_{D2}$. Consider a transistor operating in this region with, say, V_{SB} corresponding to point 1 and V_{DB} corresponding to point 2 in Fig. 4.5. As seen, ψ_{sL} is then nearly equal to ψ_{s0} (no difference can be seen in the figure). Thus, even a very small error in the values of ψ_{sL} and ψ_{s0} can mean a large relative error in the difference $\psi_{sL} - \psi_{s0}$, on which (4.3.17) relies; thus, the resulting relative error in the current can also be large. One can then hope to get I_D from (4.3.17) *only* if ψ_{sL} and ψ_{s0} are known extremely accurately, which requires several iterations when solving (4.3.18). Approximate explicit expressions for ψ_s will not work with (4.3.17) in weak inversion. A way to circumvent this drawback is suggested in Prob. 4.2.

It is clear from (4.3.8), (4.3.16), and (4.3.17) that I_D can be written in the form

$$I_D = \frac{W}{L}[f(\psi_{sL}) - f(\psi_{s0})] \tag{4.3.19}$$

where

$$f(\psi_s) = \mu C'_{ox}[(V_{GB} - V_{FB} + \phi_t)\psi_s - \tfrac{1}{2}\psi_s^2 - \tfrac{2}{3}\gamma\psi_s^{3/2} + \phi_t\gamma\psi_s^{1/2}]$$
$$\tag{4.3.20}$$

Equation (4.3.19) is in a form which emphasizes the symmetry of the transistor. If the potentials at the source and drain are interchanged, the only difference will be that I_D will change sign. That I_D must be in the form of (4.3.19) can also be deduced directly from (4.3.7). In fact, this form, with $f(\psi_s)$ an appropriate function, will be valid *even if* μ depends on ψ_s in that equation.

The general charge sheet model we have presented is often developed in the literature by using the concept of quasi-Fermi potentials (Appendix I). This results in a more complex derivation[53, 54, 56–59] than the one we have presented. It is also possible to calculate the current without making the charge sheet approximation, allowing for the spreading of the inversion layer below the surface, and even allowing for the presence of holes in the depletion region; this was done quite early by Pao and Sah[10] (Appendix I). Although their analysis is recognized to be very general and accurate, it includes the numerical evaluation of a double integral and is, thus, computationally inefficient. It has recently been shown that the double-integral formulation can be reduced to an equivalent single-integral one,[62] but numerical integration is still required. The charge sheet model we have presented is known to be in excellent agreement with these general formulations[62] and does not require numerical integration.

SURFACE POTENTIAL AND INVERSION LAYER CHARGE VERSUS POSITION. For visualizing transistor operation and for calculating certain quantities, it will be useful to relate the surface potential ψ_s to the position along the channel x. The part of the device in Fig. 4.2a between point x and the source can be viewed as a transistor by itself, with point x playing the role of the drain and $\psi_s(x)$ playing the role of the surface potential of the drain end; the channel length of this transistor will be x. Thus, in lieu of (4.3.19), we will have for this transistor

$$I_D = \frac{W}{x}[f(\psi_s(x)) - f(\psi_{s0})] \tag{4.3.21}$$

where, of course, the current is the same as in the complete device owing to current continuity in the channel. Eliminating I_D between the above equation and (4.3.19), we obtain

$$\frac{x}{L} = \frac{f(\psi_s(x)) - f(\psi_{s0})}{f(\psi_{sL}) - f(\psi_{s0})} \tag{4.3.22}$$

This equation gives the relation between x and $\psi_s(x)$. The easy way to get results from it is to give values to $\psi_s(x)$ between ψ_{s0} and ψ_{sL}, and determine x. In strong inversion, plots obtained in this way have the form shown in Fig. 4.8. In moderate inversion, the variation of ψ_s with x for $V_{DB} > V_{SB}$ would be less pronounced. In weak inversion, the two curves would practically coincide since, in that region, the variations of the surface potential along the channel is negligible even when $V_{DB} > V_{SB}$.

The variation of charges with position in the channel can now be determined. One can, for example, consider (4.3.15) and (4.3.22) as a parametric representation of Q_I' vs. x. For each value of $\psi_s(x)$ (between ψ_{s0} and ψ_{sL}) given to (4.3.22) and (4.3.15), a point (x, Q_I') is obtained. Thus one can plot Q_I' vs. x. For the case illustrated by the upper curve of Fig. 4.8, one finds

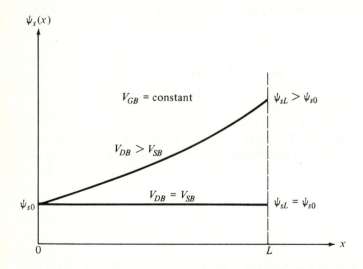

FIGURE 4.8
Surface potential vs. distance from the source for given V_{GB} and V_{SB}, for two values of V_{DB} (strong inversion is assumed).

from (4.3.15) that $|Q_I'|$ as predicted by the charge sheet model decreases monotonically along the channel as we go from the source toward the drain.

One can similarly evaluate $d\psi_s/dx$ and dQ_I'/dx as a function of position x, and substitute them into (4.3.3) and (4.3.4). It is found that $I_{\text{drift}}(x)$ decreases with x, whereas $I_{\text{diff}}(x)$ increases.[65] The values of these two current components at every x are such that their sum is constant and equal to I_D.

In the next three sections, we will discuss each region of inversion separately, looking for possible simplified expressions for the drain current. Such simplification is sought for several reasons. An obvious one is computational speed. Having to solve (4.3.18) numerically makes the general charge sheet model unsuitable for hand calculations and inefficient for computer simulation of large circuits. Another reason for seeking simplifications is that, by concentrating on the dominant phenomena in each region of inversion and by making certain approximations, the resulting form of the drain current expression can "display" these phenomena in an obvious manner in some cases. Certain easily identifiable or measurable parameters can be made to appear in the expression. Finally, if the form of the functional dependence of the drain current on the terminal voltages is made apparent in a simple, explicit expression, a circuit designer may be able to take advantage of this form in creating new circuits.

4.4 STRONG INVERSION

From Table 4.1, it follows that a transistor will be said to "operate in strong inversion" if at least one end of the channel is strongly inverted. Let us assume arbitrarily that the drain end is no more strongly inverted than the source end, i.e.,†

$$V_{DB} \geq V_{SB} \tag{4.4.1}$$

This assumption can be written equivalently in terms of $V_{DS} = V_{DB} - V_{SB}$ as follows

$$V_{DS} \geq 0 \tag{4.4.2}$$

Then we can give the conditions for strong-inversion transistor operation in terms of the inversion level at the *source*. We can use appropriate conditions developed in Chap. 3 for the structure of Fig. 3.1c or Fig. 3.1d simply by replacing terminal C by the source terminal S. Thus, from Table 3.1 the

---

† We make this convenient assumption just in order to be able to draw some figures and give some equations in a specific way. This does not really restrict the generality of our discussion. If $V_{DB} < V_{SB}$ ($V_{DS} < 0$), the role of the source and drain are interchanged; then simply replace V_{DB} by V_{SB} and vice versa, and V_{DS} by V_{SD}, in all equations that follow. See Prob. 4.5 for other ways to define regions of operation.

condition for strong inversion can be written as follows:

$$V_{GB} \geq V_{GBH} \tag{4.4.3}$$

or, in terms of $V_{GS} = V_{GB} - V_{SB}$ in Fig. 4.2b

$$V_{GS} \geq V_H \tag{4.4.4}$$

where

$$V_{GBH} = V_H + V_{SB} \tag{4.4.5}$$

and

$$V_H \approx V_{FB} + 2\phi_F + \gamma\sqrt{2\phi_F + V_{SB}} + V_Z \tag{4.4.6}$$

with the value of V_Z being several tenths of 1 V (0.5 to 0.6 V at room temperature for practical devices; V_Z decreases slightly with increasing V_{SB}).

4.4.1 An Accurate Strong-Inversion Model

With strong inversion guaranteed at the source end of the channel, if $V_{DB} = V_{SB}$ ($V_{DS} = 0$), the drain end will also be strongly inverted. If now the drain potential is raised, the level of inversion there will decrease and, eventually, strong inversion at that point will cease. For the present, we assume that the drain potential is sufficiently low so that this does not occur. With both channel ends strongly inverted, the corresponding surface potentials at these ends will be from (3.4.17), using $V_{CB} = V_{SB}$ and $V_{CB} = V_{DB}$, respectively,

$$\psi_{s0} \approx \phi_B + V_{SB} \tag{4.4.7a}$$

$$\psi_{sL} \approx \phi_B + V_{DB} \tag{4.4.7b}$$

The most commonly used value for ϕ_B is $2\phi_F$. However, this is not accurate, for reasons discussed in the beginning of Sec. 2.5.2. For the uniform substrates we are considering here, $2\phi_F + 6\phi_t$ is a good compromise value for ϕ_B, for common ranges of substrate doping concentration and oxide thickness.

Strong inversion at both ends ensures strong inversion throughout the channel since the surface potential varies monotonically from ψ_{s0} at the source to ψ_{sL} at the drain (Fig. 4.8). As established in Sec. 4.3, in strong inversion the current is almost totally due to drift. Thus, we use (4.3.16) to predict it, with ψ_{s0} and ψ_{sL} as above. Denoting by I_{DN} the current in the case we are presently considering (both channel ends strongly inverted), we have

$$I_{DN} = \frac{W}{L}\, \mu C'_{ox}\{(V_{GB} - V_{FB})(V_{DB} - V_{SB}) - \tfrac{1}{2}[(V_{DB} + \phi_B)^2 - (V_{SB} + \phi_B)^2]$$
$$- \tfrac{2}{3}\gamma[(\phi_B + V_{DB})^{3/2} - (\phi_B + V_{SB})^{3/2}]\} \tag{4.4.8a}$$

or, after some manipulations,

$$I_{DN} = \frac{W}{L}\, \mu C'_{ox}\{(V_{GB} - V_{FB} - \phi_B)(V_{DB} - V_{SB}) - \tfrac{1}{2}(V_{DB}^2 - V_{SB}^2)$$
$$- \tfrac{2}{3}\gamma[(\phi_B + V_{DB})^{3/2} - (\phi_B + V_{SB})^{3/2}]\} \tag{4.4.8b}$$

Thus, the drain current becomes an *explicit* function of the terminal voltages, a very desirable result, which is to be contrasted with the general model of Sec. 4.3. Note also that I_{DN} is of the form[23]

$$I_{DN} = \frac{W}{L}[g(V_{GB}, V_{DB}) - g(V_{GB}, V_{SB})] \tag{4.4.9}$$

which shows the symmetry of source and drain. Other forms of (4.4.8) are considered in Prob. 4.6.

In classical treatments, (4.4.8) is derived directly[7, 14] (rather than from the general case of Sec. 4.3), as follows. For any point x in the channel, where the surface potential is $\psi_s(x)$, a quantity $V_{CB}(x)$ is defined such that

$$\psi_s(x) = \phi_B + V_{CB}(x) \tag{4.4.10}$$

Thus, using (4.4.7),

$$V_{CB}(0) = V_{SB} \tag{4.4.11a}$$

$$V_{CB}(L) = V_{DB} \tag{4.4.11b}$$

Recalling now the view of the *strong*-inversion layer as an n^+ region, which along with the substrate forms a field-induced n^+p junction (see Sec. 3.3), an easy interpretation becomes possible for $V_{CB}(x)$. It can be viewed as the "effective reverse bias" between the inversion layer at point x and the substrate, changing from V_{SB} at the source to V_{DB} at the drain. We have used the symbol V_{CB} so that the equations of Sec. 3.4 become directly applicable here.

Since ϕ_B is assumed constant, from (4.4.10) we have $d\psi_s(x)/dx = dV_{CB}(x)/dx$. Thus, the drain current, assuming it is only due to drift, can be written from (4.3.3) as follows:†

$$I_{DN} = \mu W(-Q_I') \frac{dV_{CB}}{dx} \tag{4.4.12}$$

---

† With V_{CB} defined as in (4.4.10), Eq. (4.4.12) gives only the drift current and is thus not valid in weak or moderate inversion. However a more general quantity V can be defined such that, when replaced for V_{CB} in (4.4.12), that equation gives the total current (drift plus diffusion)[10] and thus becomes valid in all three regions of inversion. The quantity V is in general different from V_{CB} as defined in (4.4.10), and only tends to the latter in strong inversion (in an energy band context, V is the potential corresponding to the difference between the electron quasi-Fermi level in the inversion layer and the hole quasi-Fermi level in the bulk). This approach is common in the literature.[10, 53–59] Its details will be left for Appendix I, since we have already been able to derive general expressions including both drift and diffusion without having to employ this approach, in the simple manner presented in Sec. 4.3.

Integrating from $x = 0$ (where $V_{CB} = V_{SB}$) to $x = L$ (where $V_{CB} = V_{DB}$) produces†

$$I_{DN} = \frac{W}{L} \int_{V_{SB}}^{V_{DB}} \mu(-Q'_I) \, dV_{CB} \qquad (4.4.13)$$

The expression for Q'_I can be obtained by using (4.4.10) in (4.3.13):

$$Q'_I = -C'_{ox}\left(V_{GB} - V_{FB} - \phi_B - V_{CB} + \frac{Q'_B}{C'_{ox}}\right) \qquad (4.4.14)$$

where Q'_B is, from (4.3.14) and (4.4.10),

$$Q'_B = -\gamma C'_{ox}\sqrt{\phi_B + V_{CB}} \qquad (4.4.15)$$

Using this in (4.4.14) gives

$$Q'_I = -C'_{ox}(V_{GB} - V_{FB} - \phi_B - V_{CB} - \gamma\sqrt{\phi_B + V_{CB}}) \qquad (4.4.16a)$$

$$= -C'_{ox}[V_{GB} - V_{GBT}(V_{CB})] \qquad (4.4.16b)$$

where $V_{GBT}(V_{CB})$ is the gate-substrate extrapolated threshold voltage for an effective reverse bias V_{CB}, as given by (3.4.21c). Using (4.4.16a) in (4.4.13) and integrating gives exactly (4.4.8) again, assuming μ is constant along the channel. (The more general case where μ varies along the channel is discussed in Sec. 4.8.)

An alternative, useful form of (4.4.8) can be derived by using in it $V_{GB} = V_{GS} + V_{SB}$ and $V_{DB} = V_{DS} + V_{SB}$. After some algebra we obtain‡ (Prob. 4.6)

$$I_{DN} = \frac{W}{L} \mu C'_{ox}\{(V_{GS} - V_{FB} - \phi_B)V_{DS} - \tfrac{1}{2}V_{DS}^2$$

$$- \tfrac{2}{3}\gamma[(\phi_B + V_{SB} + V_{DS})^{3/2} - (\phi_B + V_{SB})^{3/2}]\} \qquad (4.4.17)$$

This equation is plotted in Fig. 4.9 for the same V_{SB} and V_{GS} as Fig. 4.6. We have extended the plot to negative values of V_{DS}, despite our convenient

---

†In some treatments a variable $V_{CS}(x) = V_{CB}(x) - V_{SB}$ is defined. It is easily seen that $V_{CS}(x)$ is equal to the potential at point x in the inversion layer with respect to the source end of the channel. Then (4.4.12) and (4.4.13) become

$$I_{DN} = \mu W(-Q'_I)\frac{dV_{CS}}{dx} \qquad (4.4.12a)$$

$$I_{DN} = \frac{W}{L}\int_0^{V_{DS}} \mu(-Q'_I)\, dV_{CS} \qquad (4.4.13a)$$

‡Alternatively, (4.4.17) can be obtained directly from (4.4.13a), using (4.4.16a) with $V_{CB} = V_{CS} + V_{SB}$.

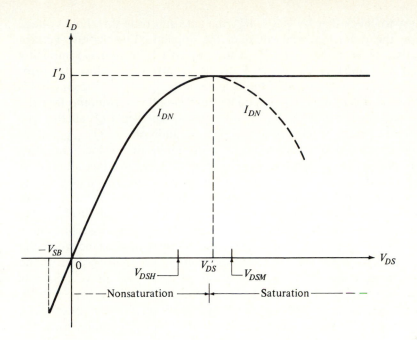

FIGURE 4.9
I_{DN} as computed from (4.4.17), and extension of its maximum value to the range $V_{DS} > V'_{DS}$. The solid curves taken together represent the complete strong inversion model (4.4.20).

assumption in (4.4.2), to show that the current equation is valid for such values. In fact, the more negative the value of V_{DS}, the smaller the value of V_{DB} and the stronger the level of inversion at the drain end. Thus, the channel remains strongly inverted everywhere for such values, and our development remains valid. Note that V_{DS} is not used below $-V_{SB}$, as then V_{DB} would be negative and the drain-substrate junction would become forward-biased.

Consider now increasing values of V_{DS}. On the horizontal axis in Fig. 4.9, we show the values of V_{DSH} and V_{DSM} from Fig. 4.6. Strictly speaking, (4.4.17) is valid *only* for $V_{DS} < V_{DSH}$. Above V_{DSH} the channel is not in strong inversion near the drain, and thus (4.4.7b) is not valid. It is customary, nevertheless, to use (4.4.17) up to the point $V_{DS} = V'_{DS}$ where the slope of the curve becomes zero; the resulting error is small for many applications. The value of V'_{DS} can be found by setting $dI_D/dV_{DS} = 0$ from (4.4.17) and solving for $V_{DS} = V'_{DS}$:

$$V'_{DS} = V_{GS} - \phi_B - V_{FB} + \frac{\gamma^2}{2} - \gamma\sqrt{V_{GS} - V_{FB} + V_{SB} + \frac{\gamma^2}{4}} \qquad (4.4.18)$$

The value of the drain current predicted by (4.4.17) with $V_{DS} = V'_{DS}$ is denoted by I'_D, as shown in Fig. 4.9. Thus,

$$I'_D = I_{DN}|_{V_{DS}=V'_{DS}} \qquad (4.4.19)$$

It is easy to check that for $V_{DS} = V'_{DS}$ the gate-substrate threshold voltage $V_{GBT}(V_{DB})$ at the drain becomes equal to the applied gate-substrate voltage V_{GB}. It can then be seen that using V_{DS} values up to V'_{DS} in (4.4.17) implicitly assumes that (4.4.16b) is valid for $V_{GB} - V_{GBT}$ arbitrarily close to zero, predicting $Q'_I = 0$ at the drain end of the channel at $V_{DS} = V'_{DS}$. (The channel is said to be "pinched off" at that point.) This corresponds to assuming that the straight-line asymptote for Q'_I in Fig. 3.2d actually represents Q'_I all the way down to $Q'_I = 0$, which is clearly incorrect. In addition, if $Q'_{I,\text{drain}} = 0$ at $V_{DS} = V'_{DS}$ the carriers would have to travel with infinite drift velocity in order for a nonzero current to be possible, as seen from (1.3.7). (We talk about drift velocity in order to be consistent with the assumption on which the strong inversion model is based, i.e., that all current is due to drift.) To make more physical sense, we will allow for a very small, but nonzero, value of $Q'_{I,\text{drain}}$ in the following discussion; then the carrier speed must be large but finite nevertheless. For $V_{DS} > V'_{DS}$, a narrow region is taken to exist between the pinched off tip of the channel and the drain, with very small $|Q'_I|$ in it; the carriers pass through this region with very high speed. The above region is actually viewed practically as a depletion region, with the excess voltage $V_{DS} - V'_{DS}$ dropped across it. The inversion layer then need only support along its length the voltage it supported when $V_{DS} = V'_{DS}$. As V_{DS} is increased, the length of the above depletion region must increase to support the excess voltage, but its length is still assumed very small in comparison to the channel length. Thus, the inversion layer length remains practically at the value L, and, since the voltage across it is still the same as when $V_{DS} = V'_{DS}$, the current is still I'_D. The complete strong-inversion model then becomes

$$I_D = \begin{cases} I_{DN}, & V_{DS} \leq V'_{DS} & (4.4.20a) \\ I'_D, & V_{DS} > V'_{DS} & (4.4.20b) \end{cases}$$

corresponding to the solid curve in Fig. 4.9. Note that I_{DN} should not be used for $V_{DS} > V'_{DS}$, because then a completely meaningless behavior is obtained, as shown by the broken curve in the figure. The region $V_{DS} \leq V'_{DS}$ is called *nonsaturation* region and the region for $V_{DS} > V'_{DS}$ is called *saturation* region.† Note that despite the fact that in saturation the drain end of the channel is not strongly inverted, strong-inversion theory has been used in this simple model to predict I_D over the whole range covered by (4.4.20). This explains the reason for the common practice of saying that the transistor "operates in strong inversion" for the entire range.

The above explanations concerning the current around $V_{DS} = V'_{DS}$ and in saturation are obviously not very satisfying. They have to be used simply

---

† The nonsaturation region is alternately called *triode* region, because the I_D-V_{DS} characteristics in it remind one of the characteristics of a triode electron tube. Similarly, the saturation region is sometimes refered to as *pentode* region.

because of the oversimplifying assumptions inherent to the model, as already discussed. Obviously, when using this model in the transition region between V_{DSH} and V_{DSM} or above it, some error can be expected. This will be more apparent in applications where the slope dI_D/dV_{DS} in the above transition region must be known accurately.[69] Let us recall, after all, that the electric field distribution next to the drain region is two-dimensional, and the "gradual channel approximation" does not hold there in the first place. However, no simple equation exists for the transition region between V_{DSH} and V_{DSM} and (4.4.20) is extensively used. The error in this equation, especially if the value of ϕ_B is chosen well, is small for most applications. A comparison of (4.4.20) to the general model of Sec. 4.3 is considered in Prob. 4.8.

  If the horizontal depletion region length discussed above cannot be neglected in comparison to L, increasing $V_{DS} - V'_{DS}$ will decrease the "effective" channel length, resulting in nonnegligible increase in the drain current. Then (4.4.20b) will not be adequate. Such effects become important when L is not too large, and they are treated in Sec. 5.2 where a more careful look at the saturation region is taken.

4.4.2 An Approximate Strong-Inversion Model

Although the model developed above provides good accuracy, it is too complicated for hand calculations or even for very fast computer simulation of large circuits. We now develop a somewhat less accurate, but simpler, model.[26]

  The complexity of (4.4.8) [or (4.4.17)] is caused by the awkward $\frac{3}{2}$ powers in it. It is clear that the origin of these powers is the square-root term in (4.4.16a), which, in turn, is due to the expression for Q'_B in (4.4.15). Figure 4.10 shows a plot of $-Q'_B/C'_{ox}$ from that equation. Since the slope of this plot does not vary much, it is reasonable to attempt to approximate $-Q'_B/C'_{ox}$ by the first two terms of its Taylor expansion around the convenient point $V_{CB} = V_{SB}$.† This gives

$$-\frac{Q'_B}{C'_{ox}} \approx \gamma\sqrt{\phi_B + V_{SB}} + \delta_1(V_{CB} - V_{SB}) \qquad (4.4.21)$$

where δ_1 is the slope of $-Q'_B/C_{ox}$ vs. V_{CB}, evaluated at $V_{CB} = V_{SB}$; a value for this quantity will be given later. The right-hand side of (4.4.21) is shown by the uppermost broken line in Fig. 4.10. It provides the correct value and slope at $V_{CB} = V_{SB}$, but overestimates $-Q'_B/C'_{ox}$ everywhere else. A better approximation can be obtained by lowering the value of the slope to some value $\delta < \delta_1$, as shown by the middle broken line:

---

† This is equivalent to approximating the threshold voltage along the channel since, from (3.4.22a),
$V_T(V_{CB}) = V_{FB} + \phi_B - Q'_B(V_{CB})/C'_{ox}$.

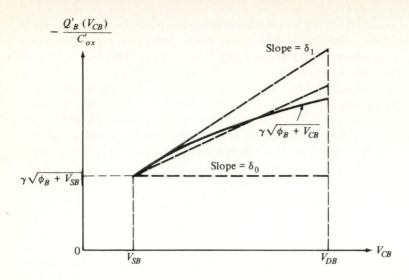

FIGURE 4.10
The quantity $-Q'_B/C'_{ox}$ in strong inversion vs. effective reverse bias in the channel. Solid line: accurate calculation; upper broken line: first-order approximation from a Taylor expansion at $V_{CB} = V_{SB}$; middle broken line: improved first-order approximation; lower broken line: zero-order approximation.

$$-\frac{Q'_B}{C'_{ox}} \approx \gamma\sqrt{\phi_B + V_{SB}} + \delta(V_{CB} - V_{SB}) \qquad (4.4.22)$$

Before considering possible values for δ, let us develop the expressions for Q'_I and I_D corresponding to this form of approximation. Using Q'_B from (4.4.22) in (4.4.14), we get

$$Q'_I(V_{CB}) = -C'_{ox}[V_{GB} - V_{SB} - V_{FB} - \phi_B - \gamma\sqrt{\phi_B + V_{SB}} - (1 + \delta)(V_{CB} - V_{SB})]$$
$$(4.4.23)$$

The drain current can be obtained by using (4.4.23) in (4.4.13) and performing the integration. Substituting $V_{DB} = V_{DS} + V_{SB}$ and $V_{GB} = V_{GS} + V_{SB}$ in the result and assuming μ is constant gives:†

$$I_{DN} = \frac{W}{L}\mu C'_{ox}[(V_{GS} - V_T|_{V_{SB}})V_{DS} - \tfrac{1}{2}(1 + \delta)V_{DS}^2] \qquad (4.4.24)$$

where $V_T|_{V_{SB}}$ is the gate-*source* extrapolated threshold voltage, obtained from (3.4.22b) with $V_{CB} = V_{SB}$. In most of the literature, the fact that the threshold voltage is taken at the source is not indicated explicitly. For simplicity, we will

---

† This can also be obtained directly from (4.4.13a), using Q_I from (4.4.23) with $V_{CB} = V_{CS} + V_{SB}$.

comply with this practice. Thus, we will write

$$I_{DN} = \frac{W}{L} \mu C'_{ox}[(V_{GS} - V_T)V_{DS} - \tfrac{1}{2}(1 + \delta)V_{DS}^2] \qquad (4.4.25)$$

where, for the rest of this book, V_T will be *defined* as the gate-source extrapolated threshold voltage given by

$$V_T = V_{FB} + \phi_B + \gamma\sqrt{\phi_B + V_{SB}} \qquad (4.4.26a)$$

$$= V_{T0} + \gamma(\sqrt{\phi_B + V_{SB}} - \sqrt{\phi_B}) \qquad (4.4.26b)$$

with

$$V_{T0} = V_{FB} + \phi_B + \gamma\sqrt{\phi_B} \qquad (4.4.27)$$

Clearly, V_T depends on V_{SB} owing to the body effect. In fact, in many treatments the term *body effect* implies only the dependence of V_T on V_{SB}. A more general point of view was provided in Sec. 3.3. The parameter ϕ_B is often taken equal to $2\phi_F$, but this is not justifiable, as has already been explained in the beginning of Sec. 2.5.2. For the *uniform* substrates considered in this chapter, a somewhat higher value should be used for ϕ_B. $2\phi_F + 6\phi_t$ is a good compromise value over common ranges of substrate concentration and oxide thickness.

A plot of (4.4.25) has the same general shape as that in Fig. 4.9. The value V'_{DS} of V_{DS} at which the maximum occurs is found from (4.4.25) by setting $dI_D/dV_{DS} = 0$ and solving for $V_{DS} = V'_{DS}$:

$$V'_{DS} = \frac{V_{GS} - V_T}{1 + \delta} \qquad (4.4.28)$$

The corresponding value of the drain current I'_D is found by using $V_{DS} = V'_{DS}$ from (4.4.28) in (4.4.25):

$$I'_D = \frac{W}{L} \mu C'_{ox} \frac{(V_{GS} - V_T)^2}{2(1 + \delta)} \qquad (4.4.29)$$

As in the accurate model, this is taken to be the value of I_D for $V_{DS} > V'_{DS}$ also. The complete model then becomes, following (4.4.20):

$$I_D = \begin{cases} \dfrac{W}{L} \mu C'_{ox}[(V_{GS} - V_T)V_{DS} - \tfrac{1}{2}(1 + \delta)V_{DS}^2], & V_{DS} \leq V'_{DS} \qquad (4.4.30a) \\[3mm] \dfrac{W}{L} \mu C'_{ox} \dfrac{(V_{GS} - V_T)^2}{2(1 + \delta)}, & V_{DS} > V'_{DS} \qquad (4.4.30b) \end{cases}$$

The model is illustrated in Fig. 4.11. The I_D-V_{DS} characteristics depend on V_{SB} through V_T in (4.4.26). This is illustrated in Fig. 4.12.

Equation (4.4.30) can be put in a very compact form by defining a convenient parameter α as follows:[70, 71]

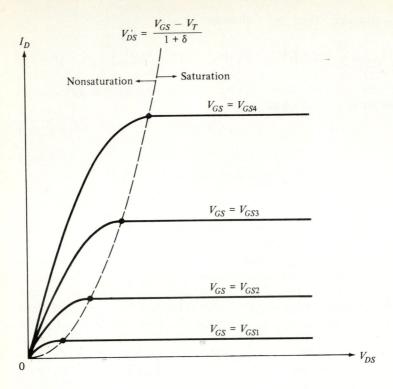

FIGURE 4.11
I_D-V_{DS} characteristics as obtained from the approximate strong-inversion model of (4.4.30).

$$\alpha = \begin{cases} 1 - \dfrac{V_{DS}}{V'_{DS}}, & V_{DS} \le V'_{DS} & (4.4.31a) \\[2ex] 0, & V_{DS} > V'_{DS} & (4.4.31b) \end{cases}$$

This parameter is plotted in Fig. 4.13. The drain current can now be expressed as follows:

$$I_D = I'_D(1 - \alpha^2), \qquad \text{both nonsaturation and saturation} \qquad (4.4.32)$$

where I'_D is given by (4.4.29).

It is easy to verify that at $V_{DS} = V'_{DS}$ (4.4.23) predicts $Q'_I = 0$ at the drain end of the channel. The reason for this unrealistic result is as discussed for the accurate strong-inversion model, and will not be repeated. Similarly, the comments made for that model concerning possible inaccuracies in the neighborhood of $V_{DS} = V'_{DS}$ apply here as well. However, such inaccuracies are consistent with the overall accuracy of the present simple model.

We now return to the problem of choosing a satisfactory value for δ in (4.4.22) and, therefore, in (4.4.30). The derivation of MOSFET characteristics

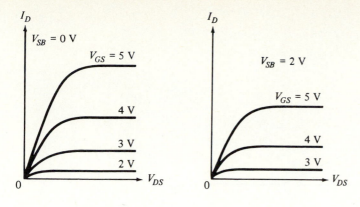

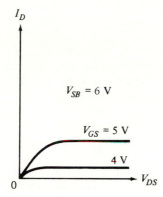

FIGURE 4.12
I_D-V_{DS} characteristics at three different V_{SB} values.

in the early days implicitly assumed the following value for δ:

$$\delta_0 = 0 \qquad (4.4.33a)$$

This corresponds to the horizontal broken line in Fig. 4.10, which is a very poor approximation to the solid line. This approximation is equivalent to assuming that the depletion region depth is the same all along the channel and equal to its actual value at the source. The result is that $|Q'_B|$ is underestimated everywhere except at the source. This, from (4.4.14) results in an overestimation of $|Q'_I|$ and a resulting overestimation of I_D. The error in I_D can be *large* for devices in which γ is not small; we will come back to this point later. Note also that, since $|Q'_I|$ is overestimated, an artificially large value of V_{DS} would be needed to reduce $|Q'_I|$ to zero at the drain. This value of V_{DS} is V'_{DS}, as already mentioned, under the simplified assumptions in the present model. The overestimation of V'_{DS} is also seen from (4.4.28), with $\delta = 0$ rather than with a more realistic positive value.

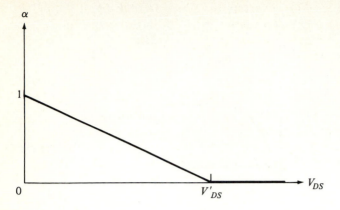

FIGURE 4.13
Parameter α vs. V_{DS}.

The next value we will consider for δ is the one that results from the Taylor expansion leading to (4.4.21).[26] This value corresponds to the slope of the solid line in Fig. 4.10 at $V_{CB} = V_{SB}$, and is given by

$$\delta_1 = \frac{\gamma}{2\sqrt{\phi_B + V_{SB}}} \quad \dagger \tag{4.4.33b}$$

It is clear from the figure that this would be a good value to use for δ only if $V_{DS} = V_{DB} - V_{SB}$ were *very* small. In the general case, though, it results in overestimating $|Q_B'|$ and, hence, underestimating $|Q_I'|$. Thus, I_D and V_{DS}' will be underestimated, i.e., the errors here are in the opposite direction from those for $\delta = \delta_0$. Clearly, one should seek values for δ between δ_0 and δ_1. Several such values have been proposed in the literature, and they usually correspond to modifications of the form of (4.4.33b) to lower its value. One such modification has the form

$$\delta_2 = d_2 \frac{\gamma}{2\sqrt{\phi_B + V_{SB}}} \tag{4.4.33c}$$

where d_2 is a correction factor. Values used[26, 30] for d_2 vary between 0.5 and 0.8. In another approach, this correction factor is allowed to depend on V_{SB} for

---

† It is interesting to note here that, as can be verified by using (4.4.26a), we have:

$$\delta_1 = \frac{dV_T}{dV_{SB}}$$

better fit,[31] and the semiempirical expression $d_2 = 1 - [k_1 + k_2(\phi_B + V_{SB})]^{-1}$ is suggested, with k_1 and k_2 being constants chosen to minimize overall error.† This, however, detracts from the simplicity of the model.

Another value suggested for δ is[37]

$$\delta_3 = \frac{\gamma}{2\sqrt{\phi_3 + \phi_B + V_{SB}}} \qquad (4.4.33d)$$

where $\phi_3 = 1$ V. This is a good empirical expression, both for its accuracy and for its simplicity, and gives satisfactory results for practical situations.

Finally, one can seek a zero-order estimate for δ for rough calculations, which is even independent of V_{SB}. One such estimate is[28]

$$\delta_4 = \frac{\gamma}{4\sqrt{\phi_B}} \qquad (4.4.33e)$$

All the above three expressions for δ have been arrived at with the goal of providing satisfactory accuracy over a reasonable range of bias voltages. One should not be very surprised if they do not work very well in extreme cases (e.g., for V_{DS} in excess of 10 V). However, they do provide satisfactory accuracy for most practical cases. In general, which expression is best to use for δ depends on the accuracy sought, the desired speed of calculations, and the range of bias voltages expected. The final criterion is how well the model predicts the drain current. One cannot judge this easily by looking at the error in predicting Q_B'. Of course the errors in Q_B' and I_D are related, but not in a very direct manner. For example, one can have a large relative error in Q_B' and still have an small error in I_D if Q_B' is small in the first place [so that $|Q_B'/C_{ox}'|$ is small in comparison to the other terms in (4.4.14)]. This will be the case for devices with thin oxides and lightly doped substrates; then γ is small, leading to a small $|Q_B'|$ from (4.4.15).

Since the final criterion of success is how well I_D is predicted by the approximate model, one could have considered deriving (4.4.25) directly from the accurate current expression in (4.4.17). This is indeed possible but amounts to little more than a mathematical exercise, not revealing the underlying physical assumptions in the approximate model. The approach is considered in Prob. 4.9.

A comparison of the various values of δ is suggested in Probs. 4.10 and 4.11. The interesting possibility of using the δ idea to simplify the general model of Sec. 4.3 is considered in Prob. 4.12.

Note that when γ is *small*, the values of δ in (4.4.33b) to (4.4.33e) are all

---

† The values of k_1 and k_2 depend on the error criterion chosen and the range of voltages over which small error is desired. Values used[31, 34, 35] include $k_1 = 1.744$ with $k_2 = 0.8364$ V^{-1}, and $k_1 = 1.41$ with $k_2 = 0.43$ V^{-1}.

small and can be approximated by 0, i.e., the value in (4.4.33a) is then reasonable. In this case, (4.4.30) becomes

$$I_D = \begin{cases} \dfrac{W}{L} \mu C'_{ox}[(V_{GS} - V_T)V_{DS} - \tfrac{1}{2}V'^2_{DS}], & V_{DS} \leq V'_{DS}, \text{ small } \gamma & (4.4.34a) \\[2em] \dfrac{W}{L} \mu C'_{ox} \dfrac{(V_{GS} - V_T)^2}{2}, & V_{DS} > V_{DS}, \text{ small } \gamma & (4.4.34b) \end{cases}$$

where $V'_{DS} = V_{GS} - V_T$. These equations have been used widely for approximate hand calculations for circuit design, and even for quick computer calculations.[21, 25] However, they are often used indiscriminately even for devices with large γ, which can result in *serious* error (e.g., 100 percent in extreme cases). This is considered further in Sec. 4.13.

For *very* crude modeling work, the strong-inversion equations are sometimes taken to be valid for V_{GS} as low as V_T, where they predict $I_D = 0$. In such cases, the moderate- and weak-inversion regions are not considered.

4.4.3 Potential versus Position

In strong inversion, one can develop a rather simple relation between the position x in the channel and the effective reverse bias $V_{CB}(x)$ at that point, extending an idea developed in Sec. 4.3. All strong-inversion expressions we have given for the nonsaturation current can be written in the form

$$I_{DN} = \frac{W}{L} h(V_{GB}, V_{SB}, V_{DB}) \tag{4.4.35}$$

with the function h depending on which model is being used. If we consider point x in the channel as the drain of a fictitious transistor with length x, we will have

$$I_{DN} = \frac{W}{x} h(V_{GB}, V_{SB}, V_{CB}(x)) \tag{4.4.36}$$

Eliminating I_{DN} among the two equations gives

$$\frac{x}{L} = \frac{h(V_{GB}, V_{SB}, V_{CB}(x))}{h(V_{GB}, V_{SB}, V_{DB})} \tag{4.4.37}$$

This equation gives the relation between x and $V_{CB}(x)$. As an example, using the approximate model developed above, gives a simple expression. Extending this expression to include the saturation region and using the parameter α in (4.4.31), we can put it in the form (Prob. 4.13)

$$V_{CB}(x) = V_{SB} + \frac{V_{GS} - V_T}{1 + \delta} \left[1 - \sqrt{1 - \frac{x}{L}(1 - \alpha^2)} \right] \tag{4.4.38}$$

This relation is plotted for various values of V_{DS} in Fig. 4.14 ($0 < V_{DS1} < V_{DS2} < V_{DS3}$). As seen, for small V_{DS} values V_{CB} is nearly proportional to x. This is because for such V_{DS} values the inversion layer is nearly

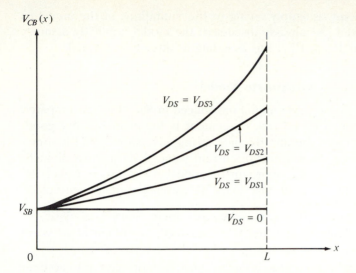

FIGURE 4.14
Channel potential with respect to the substrate vs. distance from the source for the approximate strong-inversion model and for four V_{DS} values.

uniform, so the voltage is distributed almost evenly along its length. At larger V_{DS} values, this is no longer the case. This can be explained easily. For a given V_{DS}, say $V_{DS} = V_{DS3}$, one can find from the plot the voltage drop across a chunk of the inversion layer of length Δx between two points x_1 and x_2. The drop will simply be $\Delta V_{CB} = V_{CB}(x_2) - V_{CB}(x_1)$. If another chunk of the same length Δx is taken closer to the drain, the voltage ΔV_{CB} across it will be larger, for the following reason. The second chunk contains a smaller inversion layer charge per unit area, since $|Q_I'|$ decreases as one goes from the source toward the drain [this follows, for example, from (4.4.23)]. Thus a larger voltage will be needed across the second chunk to support the same current (Sec. 1.3.2). From this argument, it is clear why the slope dV_{CB}/dx increases with increasing x. A related observation concerns the drift velocity of electrons. As follows from (1.3.7), to carry the same current the electrons must move faster at points where the inversion charge per unit area is smaller. Since the electrons are in abundance at the source end of the channel, they can carry the required charge per unit time (current) by moving slowly. As they approach the drain, they gain speed. Thus, in a given small element of length Δx near the drain, fewer electrons are to be found at any given instant than within a corresponding element near the source. If V_{DS} is large, the electrons can be traveling so fast that "velocity saturation" can occur near the drain. The effect of this on the transistor I-V characteristics can become serious in short-channel devices, and is considered in Sec. 5.3.

If $V_{CB}(x)$ were plotted for $V_{DS} = V'_{DS}$ using (4.4.38), the slope would be infinite at $x = L$. This physically impossible result, corresponding to an infinite electric field at that point, is simply owing to the limitations of the model as $V_{DS} = V'_{DS}$ is approached. As already discussed, the model implicitly assumes $Q'_I = 0$ at the drain for $V_{DS} = V'_{DS}$; this is wrong as already explained.

4.4.4 Accurate Versus Approximate Model

In strong inversion, if the accurate model introduced in Sec. 4.4.1 is compared to the general model of Sec. 4.3, the agreement is found to be very good. Compared to these models, the approximate strong-inversion model is somewhat in error (e.g., 5 percent in terms of current values). In practice, though, several factors contribute to the approximate model being favored over the accurate one in a variety of situations. These factors are summarized below:

1. The approximate strong inversion model is simple. This is a desirable feature when very large circuits must be analyzed by computer or when quick hand calculations are needed.

2. Practical devices exhibit high-order effects which are not taken into account by either model; for example, the substrate is never exactly uniform, owing to fabrication details (Chap. 10). This tends to make the difference of the two models less dramatic, in terms of accuracy.

3. The assumptions behind each model will be seen later to lead to corresponding expressions for the total charges (Chap. 7) and the capacitances (Chap. 8) of the device. In the case of the approximate strong-inversion model, the expressions for these quantities are simple. In contrast to this, the expressions for some of these quantities, as derived for the accurate strong-inversion model, are so complicated as to be totally impractical. In addition, the assumptions behind the approximate model are known to lead to simple models suitable for very high-frequency operation (Chap. 9); this is not known to be possible for the accurate model.

4. The approximate model contains explicitly the threshold voltage V_T. This is an important parameter that is widely discussed, used, and measured.† In fact, even for short-channel and/or narrow-channel devices, use is made of the approximate model with V_T replaced by an effective threshold (Chap. 5). A large amount of work has been done on how to estimate and measure this quantity in such cases. In contrast, the accurate model does not contain the threshold explicitly, and it is more difficult to adopt it for use with short- and/or narrow-channel devices.

Note that it is not desirable to keep switching between models depending on the value of some parameters (e.g., channel length, or frequency of

---

† In this book, the term *threshold voltage* will always imply *extrapolated* threshold voltage. Unfortunately, in the literature on MOS devices the term "threshold voltage" is used with several different meanings. This is discussed in Sec. 4.13.

operation), as this can cause severe problems in the computer simulation of circuits. Thus, the more versatile approximate model is favored for general use, since it is known to give simple results in a variety of situations where the accurate model fails to do so. For this reason, in the rest of this book significant attention will be paid to the approximate model, and, in fact, this model will be emphasized in some instances. Another reason for this is that it is easier to demonstrate the various principles introduced by using simple formulas. If desired, the reader can apply the same principles to the accurate model, provided complexity is not an issue.

4.4.5   A Fluid Dynamical Analog

We now present a fluid dynamical analog which helps to increase intuition about transistor operation.[72] For simplicity, this analog will be presented for a device with negligible Q'_o, ϕ_{MS}, and N_A. It is easy to check that for such a device $V_{FB} \approx 0$, $\phi_F \approx 0$, $\gamma \approx 0$, and $V_T \approx 0$. We will neglect the current in weak inversion, and we will assume that the device conducts only when $V_{GS} > V_T = 0$.

The analogy is as follows. Electrons correspond to a fluid; electric current flow corresponds to net flow of that fluid. The source and drain correspond to two very large tanks, filled with this fluid up to a certain level each. Since the tanks are assumed very large, moving fluid from one to the other will not change the levels in the tanks appreciably during a reasonable time of observation. This corresponds to the potentials at the source and drain of a transistor being held constant despite current flow. The two tanks are separated by a piston corresponding to the gate. This is shown in Fig. 4.15a. The substrate potential corresponds to the "reference level" shown. Potentials are measured from the reference level *downward*.† The source, gate, and drain potentials with respect to the substrate correspond to the distances $\hat{V}_{SB}$, $\hat{V}_{GB}$, and $\hat{V}_{DB}$ shown, taken as positive numbers. In Fig. 4.15a, $\hat{V}_{GS} = \hat{V}_{GB} - \hat{V}_{SB}$ is negative (corresponding to $V_{GS} < 0 = V_T$ in the transistor). The "channel" is cut off, and no communication exists between source and drain. Now $\hat{V}_{GB}$ is increased, as shown in Fig. 4.15b, so that $\hat{V}_{GS} = \hat{V}_{GB} - \hat{V}_{SB}$ becomes positive (corresponding to $V_{GS} > V_T = 0$ for the transistor). The channel is now filled with the fluid. Communication between source and drain is now possible, but no flow exists in the case of Fig. 4.15b, since $\hat{V}_{DB} = \hat{V}_{SB}$ and, thus, $\hat{V}_{DS} = \hat{V}_{DB} - \hat{V}_{SB} = 0$. The depth $\hat{\psi}_s$ corresponds to the surface potential in the transistor. As would be the corresponding case for the simplified transistor we are considering [with $\phi_B \approx 0$ in (4.47)], $\hat{\psi}_s$ assumes the common level of $\hat{V}_{SB}$ and $\hat{V}_{DB}$. The amount of fluid in the channel is proportional to the distance

---

† The level of the fluid's surface can be taken to correspond to electron potential energy.

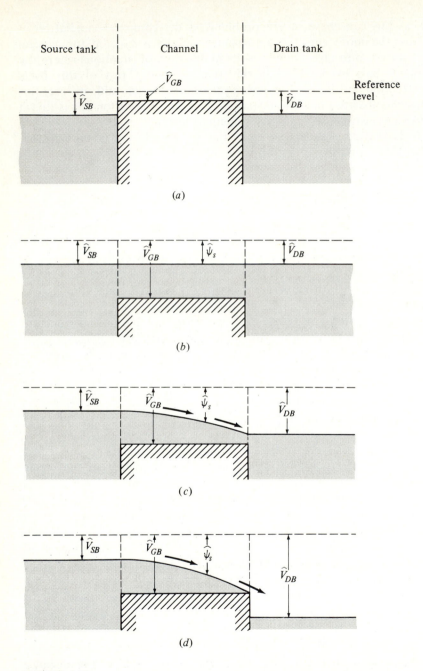

FIGURE 4.15
A fluid dynamical analog for MOS transistor operation.[72] The depths $\hat{V}_{SB}$, $\hat{V}_{GB}$, and $\hat{V}_{DB}$ correspond to the voltages V_{SB}, V_{GB}, and V_{DB} in a transistor with $V_T \approx 0$. (a) Analogy to depletion; (b) analogy to strong inversion with $V_{DS} = 0$; (c) analogy to nonsaturation; (d) analogy to saturation.

$\hat{V}_{GB} - \hat{\psi}_s$. For the simplified transistor we are considering, (4.3.13) easily gives $|Q'_I| = C'_{ox}(V_{GB} - \psi_s)$, maintaining the analogy.

Now $\hat{V}_{DB}$ is increased as shown in Fig. 4.15c, so that $\hat{V}_{DS} = \hat{V}_{DB} - \hat{V}_{SB}$ becomes positive. Flow is observed as shown. The distance $\hat{\psi}_s$ changes monotonically from $\hat{V}_{SB}$ to $\hat{V}_{DB}$. The flow increases as $\hat{V}_{DB}$ is increased further, until $\hat{V}_{DB}$ becomes larger than $\hat{V}_{GB}$, so that $\hat{V}_{DS} > \hat{V}_{GS}$ as shown in Fig. 4.15d. This corresponds to $V_{DS} > V_{GS} - V_T = V_{GS} - 0 = V'_{DS}$ for the transistor. Then further increases of $\hat{V}_{DS}$ do not affect the flow, and the flow exhibits "saturation." Note that the fluid enters slowly from the source and, as it approaches the drain, it moves faster in order to maintain a fixed flow despite the fact that the amount of fluid per unit area is less near the drain. Again, an analogy exists here to the simplified picture of transistor operation in saturation.

We will find further use for this fluid dynamical analog in providing intuition for the motion of charges, which is discussed in Chap. 7.

4.5 MODERATE INVERSION

As defined in Table 4.1, a MOS transistor will be said to "operate in moderate inversion"[73] if its most heavily inverted channel end is moderately inverted. Following our previous convention [see footnote to (4.4.1)], we will assume that this end is the one next to the *source*. This implies

$$V_{DB} \geq V_{SB} \qquad (4.5.1)$$

or

$$V_{DS} \geq 0 \qquad (4.5.2)$$

Then from Table 3.1, with C replaced by S, we obtain the required condition on V_{GB} for a given V_{SB}:

$$V_{GBM} \leq V_{GB} < V_{GBH} \qquad (4.5.3)$$

or, in terms of V_{GS},

$$V_M \leq V_{GS} < V_H \qquad (4.5.4)$$

where V_{GBH} and V_H are given by (4.4.5) to (4.4.6) and, from (3.4.5) and (3.4.9) with C replaced by S, we have

$$V_{GBM} = V_M + V_{SB} \qquad (4.5.5)$$

$$V_M \approx V_{FB} + 2\phi_F + \gamma\sqrt{2\phi_F + V_{SB}} \qquad (4.5.6)$$

The I_D-V_{DS} characteristics of the transistor in this region have a shape roughly similar to that in strong inversion (Fig. 4.3) but are not described accurately by strong inversion equations since, as shown in Sec. 4.3, in moderate inversion both drift *and* diffusion contribute significantly to the value of the drain current. Convenient simplifications are not known for this region.

One can use the general model of Sec. 4.3, which is valid in all regions, or use semiempirical models.[60, 61]

The moderate-inversion region is often completely ignored in the literature. This region is instead assumed to be the bottom of the strong-inversion region, and the strong-inversion equations of Sec. 4.4 are used in it. However, not even a single point in the channel is strongly inverted in this region; hence, equations such as (4.4.7) will be in error, and so will the models based on them. In an attempt to "stretch" the validity of the strong-inversion equations, sometimes the parameters in them are made functions of the gate voltage, for example, ϕ_B in (4.4.7) or V_T in (4.4.26).[46]

4.6 WEAK INVERSION

As seen from the last entry of Table 4.1, for a transistor operating in weak inversion[38-52] *no* part of the channel is moderately or strongly inverted. Let us conveniently assume as usual,

$$V_{DB} \geq V_{SB} \tag{4.6.1}$$

or, equivalently,

$$V_{DS} \geq 0 \tag{4.6.2}$$

so that the drain end of the channel is no more heavily inverted than the source end. Then from Table 3.1, with C replaced by S, we obtain the following condition:

$$V_{GBL} \leq V_{GB} < V_{GBM} \tag{4.6.3}$$

or, equivalently

$$V_L \leq V_{GS} < V_M \tag{4.6.4}$$

where V_{GBM} and V_M were given in (4.5.5) and (4.5.6), and, from (3.4.4) and (3.4.8),

$$V_{GBL} = V_L + V_{SB} \tag{4.6.5}$$

$$V_L = V_{FB} + \phi_F + \gamma\sqrt{\phi_F + V_{SB}} \tag{4.6.6}$$

However, when dealing with a complete transistor, the *lower* limit in (4.6.3) and (4.6.4) is rather academic, for two reasons: (1) Nothing really special happens at that limit. As seen in Fig. 3.2, the various plots are smooth, and their shape does not change drastically below $V_{GB} = V_{GBL}$. For this reason, some of the equations we will develop in this section can hold even below that limit. (2) In a real MOS transistor, the observable (and usable) drain current is the sum of the real drain current and a reverse-junction leakage current (which can include the leakage of the drain-substrate n^+p junction as well as leakage across the depletion region under the channel). Thus, a "pragmatic" lower limit for weak-inversion operation can be taken to be at a point where the leakage current can be neglected, requiring

$$I_D \gg I_j \tag{4.6.7}$$

where I_j is the leakage current. This current is difficult to predict; it depends on fabrication details and increases rapidly with increasing temperature. Often, at room temperatures and above, (4.6.7) will restrict the weak-inversion region width to a value smaller than that calculated from (4.6.3) or (4.6.4).

The general model developed in Sec. 4.3 can be used to produce a simplified equation for I_D in the weak-inversion region. This will be discussed later. For the present, we prefer to show the classical approach for obtaining such an equation to provide some independent intuition about this region of operation.

As follows from the material in Sec. 3.4.4, for a weakly inverted point in the channel, the surface potential satisfies

$$\psi_s \approx \psi_{sa}(V_{GB}) \tag{4.6.8}$$

where

$$\psi_{sa}(V_{GB}) = \left(-\frac{\gamma}{2} + \sqrt{\frac{\gamma^2}{4} + V_{GB} - V_{FB}} \right)^2 \tag{4.6.9}$$

Let us assume for the sake of simplicity that ψ_s is *exactly* equal to $\psi_{sa}(V_{GB})$; this will not affect the forthcoming analysis. Since the surface potential depends only on V_{GB}, it is independent of the position along the channel. This implies two important facts:

1. Q'_B will be independent of position along the channel, as seen from (4.3.14). This means that the depletion region depth does not change along the channel.
2. Since all points at the surface are assumed at the same potential with respect to the substrate, the potential difference between such points is zero. Therefore, the electric field has a zero horizontal component. If there is current through the channel, it cannot be caused by drift; thus, all current must be caused by *diffusion*.

It follows then from the material in Sec. 1.3.3 that the plot of Q'_I vs. x must be a straight line (Fig. 4.16). Thus, (1.3.22) gives, with $Q' = Q'_I$, $b = W$, and $a = L$:

$$I_D = -\frac{W}{L} \mu\phi_t(Q'_{I, \text{source}} - Q'_{I, \text{drain}}) \tag{4.6.10}$$

The above two values of Q'_I can be found from (3.4.30), which is valid in weak inversion and even in depletion. We have, using also (3.4.11),

$$Q'_{I, \text{source}} = -\frac{\gamma C'_{ox}}{2\sqrt{\psi_{sa}(V_{GB})}} \phi_t\, e^{[\psi_{sa}(V_{GB}) - 2\phi_F]/\phi_t}\, e^{-V_{SB}/\phi_t} \tag{4.6.11}$$

$$Q'_{I, \text{drain}} = -\frac{\gamma C'_{ox}}{2\sqrt{\psi_{sa}(V_{GB})}} \phi_t\, e^{[\psi_{sa}(V_{GB}) - 2\phi_F]/\phi_t}\, e^{-V_{DB}/\phi_t} \tag{4.6.12}$$

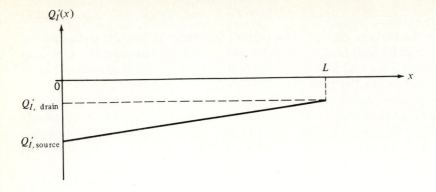

FIGURE 4.16
Inversion layer charge per unit area vs. distance from the source in weak inversion.

Using these in (4.6.10) we obtain

$$I_D = \frac{W}{L} \hat{I}(V_{GB})(e^{-V_{SB}/\phi_t} - e^{-V_{DB}/\phi_t}) \qquad (4.6.13a)$$

where

$$\hat{I}(V_{GB}) = \frac{\mu C'_{ox} \gamma \phi_t^2}{2\sqrt{\psi_{sa}(V_{GB})}} e^{[\psi_{sa}(V_{GB}) - 2\phi_F]/\phi_t} \qquad (4.6.13b)$$

Readers familiar with bipolar transistors will recognize the similarity of (4.6.13a) to the "Ebers-Moll equations."[66] This should not be surprising, as similar mechanisms are responsible for current flow in the bipolar transistor (under common assumptions) and the weakly inverted MOS transistor.

Since (3.4.30), which was used in the above development, is valid even in depletion, (4.6.13) will be valid even if V_{DB} is so large that the drain end of the channel is less than "weakly" inverted.

A useful form for I_D can be derived by rewriting (4.6.10) as follows:

$$I_D = -\frac{W}{L} \mu\phi_t Q'_{I, \text{source}} \left(1 - \frac{Q'_{I, \text{drain}}}{Q'_{I, \text{source}}}\right) \qquad (4.6.14)$$

From (4.6.11) and (4.6.12) we have

$$\frac{Q'_{I, \text{drain}}}{Q'_{I, \text{source}}} = e^{-(V_{DB} - V_{SB})/\phi_t} = e^{-V_{DS}/\phi_t} \qquad (4.6.15)$$

Thus, I_D becomes

$$I_D = \frac{W}{L} \mu\phi_t(-Q'_{I, \text{source}})(1 - e^{-V_{DS}/\phi_t}) \qquad (4.6.16)$$

which can be evaluated by using (4.6.11). A compact expression can be developed by using the approximation in $(3.4.36b)$,[47] with C replaced by S. Using this in (4.6.16) gives

$$I_D = \frac{W}{L} I'_x e^{(V_{GS}-V_X)/(n\phi_t)}(1 - e^{-V_{DS}/\phi_t}), \quad \text{fixed } V_{SB} = V'_{SB} \quad (4.6.17)$$

where

$$V_X = V_{FB} + 1.5\phi_F + \gamma\sqrt{1.5\phi_F + V'_{SB}} \quad (4.6.18)$$

$$I'_x = \mu C'_{ox}\phi_t^2 \frac{\gamma}{2\sqrt{1.5\phi_F + V'_{SB}}} e^{-0.5\phi_F/\phi_t} \quad (4.6.19)$$

and the quantity n is given by

$$n = 1 + \frac{\gamma}{2\sqrt{1.5\phi_F + V'_{SB}}} \quad (4.6.20)$$

assuming that the effect of interface traps is negligible (see end of Sec. 2.6); otherwise, n will turn out to have a larger value, which can be determined experimentally.

Next to (4.6.17) it is emphasized that this equation is useful for studying the variation of I_D with V_{GS}, when V_{SB} is *fixed* at some value denoted by V'_{SB}. Trying to use this equation to study the variation of I_D with V_{SB} is not advisable, since several quantities in the equation (V_X, I'_x, n) depend on V_{SB} in a complicated manner. In such cases, (4.6.13) should be used. It is clear from it that I_D depends on V_{SB} *only* through the quantity exp $(-V_{SB}/\phi_t)$.

I_D is plotted vs. V_{DS} by using (4.6.17) in Fig. 4.17, with V_{GS} as a parameter, for a fixed V_{SB}. As seen, the curves become horizontal for V_{DS} larger than a few ϕ_t, since the last exponential in the equation becomes negligible compared to 1. This happens at V_{DS} values *independent* of V_{GS}, a fact which is in sharp contrast to the case of strong-inversion operation (Fig. 4.11).

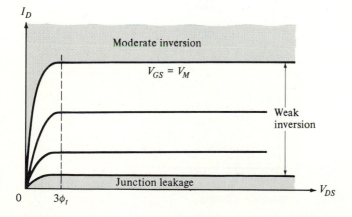

FIGURE 4.17
I_D-V_{DS} characteristics in weak inversion.

Using equal V_{GS} steps, the vertical spacing of successive curves in Fig. 4.17 for a given V_{DS} increases exponentially. This exponential behavior is brought out clearly by plotting $\log I_D$ vs. V_{GS} with V_{DS} fixed, as shown in Fig. 4.18. The result is a straight line in weak inversion. Above this region we have moderate inversion, where I_D does not vary exponentially with V_{GS}. At the bottom, I_D is so small that it is completely masked by the leakage current I_j. At room temperatures or below, where I_j is small, the weak-inversion region can span several decades of current (Sec. 4.9).

In Fig. 4.18 we also show the behavior of the strong-inversion model (Sec. 4.4) and the general model (Sec. 4.3). Concerning the latter, we can now return to the question of obtaining simplified weak-inversion expressions, starting from the general model. Since in weak inversion the current is practically caused by diffusion only, we can work with (4.3.17) and assume $I_D \approx I_{D2}$. Unfortunately, if we use (4.6.8) and substitute $\psi_{s0} = \psi_{sa}$ and $\psi_{sL} = \psi_{sa}$ in (4.3.17), we obtain $I_D = 0$! This is owing to the weak point of the *form* of this equation. In weak inversion it relies on differences of nearly equal quantities; thus, approximations such as the above are inadequate. Of course, ψ_{s0} and ψ_{sL} are *not* exactly equal; ψ_s only reaches ψ_{sa} asymptotically in Fig. 4.5. To preserve appropriately the minute difference between the two quantities, we can employ (4.3.18). The procedure is outlined in Prob. 4.17 and produces exactly (4.6.13) again.

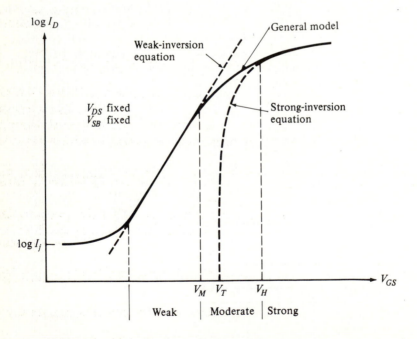

FIGURE 4.18
Log I_D vs. V_{GS} for fixed V_{DS} and V_{SB}, and comparison to weak- and strong-inversion equations.

4.7 REGIONS OF OPERATION IN TERMS OF V_{SB} AND V_{DB}

So far we have given conditions for transistor operation in the various regions in terms of V_{GB} (or V_{GS}). One can also give such conditions in terms of V_{SB} and V_{DB} for a given V_{GB}. Thus, from Fig. 4.5 it is clear that one can determine the level of inversion at the source and drain ends of the channel by comparing each of V_{SB} and V_{DB} to the quantities V_{CBH} and V_{CBM}, which were discussed in Sec. 3.4.1. For convenience, we repeat the values of these quantities below:

$$V_{CBH} \approx \left(-\frac{\gamma}{2} + \sqrt{\frac{\gamma^2}{4} + V_{GB} - V_{FB} - V_Z} \right)^2 - 2\phi_F \qquad (4.7.1)$$

$$V_{CBM} \approx \left(-\frac{\gamma}{2} + \sqrt{\frac{\gamma^2}{4} + V_{GB} - V_{FB}} \right)^2 - 2\phi_F \qquad (4.7.2)$$

where V_Z is several tenths of 1 V (0.5 to 0.6 V at room temperature for practical devices).

Thus, for example, it follows from Table 4.1 that if the conditions at the source and drain correspond respectively to points 1 and 2 in Fig. 4.5, the transistor operates in weak inversion, and the same will be true for points 1 and 3. For points 5 and 2 or 5 and 3, it operates in moderate inversion. The transistor operates in strong inversion for points 4 and 5, or 4 and 1, or 4 and 3, etc. Note that if point 3 corresponds to the source and point 4 to the drain, the transistor is *still* said to operate in strong inversion, according to Table 4.1. However, now the most heavily inverted channel end is the one next to the drain; here $V_{DB} < V_{SB}$ ($V_{DS} < 0$), which results in $I_D < 0$. This sort of operation can be termed as *reverse*, whereas *forward* operation can refer to the opposite case, for which most of our equations have been written.

Using the above observations, it is easy to see that a general way to define the regions of inversion is as shown in Fig. 4.19. As an example, a transistor with $V_{SB} < V_{CBH}$ and $V_{CBH} < V_{DB} < V_{CBM}$ can correspond to, say, point A. The transistor is then in (forward) strong inversion.

Note that in accordance with the discussion in Sec. 4.6, we prefer not to specify a limit between weak inversion and depletion. Rather, we take a transistor to operate in weak inversion if it corresponds to a point in the upper right-hand corner in Fig. 4.19 as long as the current remains well above the leakage current.

4.8 EFFECTIVE MOBILITY

In Sec. 4.3, we mentioned that the mobility of electrons in the inversion layer (called *surface mobility*) is smaller than the bulk mobility considered in Sec. 1.3.2.[19, 74] This is often made plausible by arguing that the electric field component perpendicular to the direction of current flow (referred to as

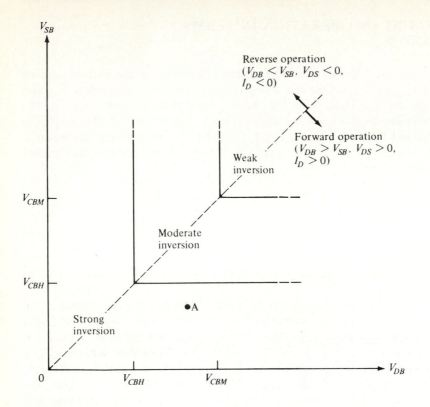

FIGURE 4.19
Definition of regions of operation for a MOS transistor in terms of source-substrate and drain-substrate voltages for a given V_{GB}.

normal, or *transverse*, component) tends to accelerate the electrons toward the semiconductor-oxide interface in Fig. 4.2, where they suffer collisions in addition to the collisions with the crystal lattice and ionized impurity atoms. This additional effect on mobility is referred to as *surface scattering*. We recall that in Secs. 4.3 and 4.4 the surface mobility μ appeared in the integrand of expressions for the drain current. For strong inversion, for example, we had (4.4.13) repeated here:

$$I_{DN} = \frac{W}{L} \int_{V_{SB}}^{V_{DB}} \mu(-Q'_I) \, dV_{CB} \qquad (4.8.1)$$

with V_{CB} as defined in (4.4.10).

Since the normal field, in general, varies along the channel, μ will also vary. If its variation is not negligible, one cannot move μ outside the integral, as was done in Sec. 4.4. One can then attempt to determine μ as a function of V_{CB} (see below) and try to include this function in the integration. This results in a very complicated expression. Another approach taken is to define an *effective* mobility μ_{eff} such that, when used in the expression

$$I_{DN} = \frac{W}{L} \mu_{\text{eff}} \int_{V_{SB}}^{V_{DB}} (-Q'_I) \, dV_{CB} \qquad (4.8.2)$$

I_{DN} is predicted correctly.† Since the electric field at each point in the channel and, thus, μ in (4.8.1) depend on the terminal voltages, one should expect that to make (4.8.2) give the same result as (4.8.1), μ_{eff} should be made a function of the terminal voltages. This function is sometimes determined empirically, but a more analytical approach can be used, as will be shown. Note that what we did in Sec. 4.4 was to assume that μ in (4.8.1) was constant and move it outside the integral. Comparing the resulting expression to (4.8.2), we see that, when the effective-mobility approach is taken, I_{DN} will be given by the same expressions found in Sec. 4.4, if in them μ is replaced by μ_{eff}:

$$I_{DN, \text{ including mobility} \atop \text{dependence on normal field}} = I_{DN, \text{ assuming constant} \atop \text{mobility (Sec.4.4)}} \Big|_{\mu = \mu_{\text{eff}}} \qquad (4.8.3)$$

Whether one wants to evaluate the integral in (4.8.1) or to determine an adequate expression for μ_{eff}, one needs to characterize the surface mobility μ first. There have been many attempts to do so, evoking surface roughness, interface traps, quantum-mechanical effects, etc.; a review of such attempts can be found elsewhere.[59, 75] It has been difficult, however, to explain rigorously what has been observed experimentally, namely, that except at very low fields, the surface mobility is practically independent of doping concentration (as long as $N_A < 10^5 \ \mu\text{m}^{-3}$) and of surface fabrication processing details. For a given temperature, the value of surface mobility is found[76] to be only a function of an average normal electric field $\bar{\mathscr{E}}_y$ in the inversion layer, defined by[26, 76]

$$\bar{\mathscr{E}}_y = \frac{\mathscr{E}_{ys} + \mathscr{E}_{yb}}{2} \qquad (4.8.4)$$

where $\mathscr{E}_{ys}$ is the value of the normal field at the surface and $\mathscr{E}_{yb}$ is its value "just below" the inversion layer; these values will be discussed shortly. These findings suggest that the large electron concentration in the inversion layer "screens" the ionized acceptor atoms there, and that surface scattering dominates bulk scattering. The experimental data appear to conform to the following relation:

---

† A formal definition of μ_{eff} can be obtained by equating the right-hand sides of (4.8.1) and (4.8.2). It is then seen that one should define $\mu_{\text{eff}} = [\int_{V_{SB}}^{V_{DB}} \mu(-Q'_I) \, dV_{CB}] / [\int_{V_{SB}}^{V_{DB}} (-Q'_I) \, dV_{CB}]$. However, this is not useful for evaluating μ_{eff} since, if one can evaluate the first integral with adequate simplicity, then μ_{eff} is not needed; one would, in this case, have found I_{DN} directly from (4.8.1).

$$\mu = \frac{\mu_0}{1 + \alpha_\theta \bar{\mathscr{E}}_y} \tag{4.8.5}$$

where μ_0 and α_θ depend on temperature and can be considered fitting parameters.† For practical conditions, μ_0 is roughly half of the bulk mobility (as evaluated for lightly doped substrates) and α_θ is roughly $0.025 \ \mu\text{m}/\text{V}$ at room temperature.

The electric field at the surface can easily be related to the total charge per unit area below the surface from basic electrostatics (Appendix B):‡

$$\mathscr{E}_{ys} = -\frac{Q_I' + Q_B'}{\epsilon_s} \tag{4.8.6}$$

where Q_I' and Q_B' are the inversion layer and depletion region charges per unit area, respectively, and ϵ_s is the permittivity of the semiconductor. Similarly, the field just below the inversion layer can be determined by assuming a very thin inversion layer, so that the total charge per unit area below the inversion layer is practically all of Q_B':

$$\mathscr{E}_{yb} = -\frac{Q_B'}{\epsilon_s} \tag{4.8.7}$$

Using the above equations in (4.8.4), we obtain

$$\bar{\mathscr{E}}_y = -\frac{Q_I' + 2Q_B'}{2\epsilon_s} \tag{4.8.8}$$

and thus (4.8.5) becomes

$$\mu = \frac{\mu_0}{1 - [\alpha_\theta/(2\epsilon_s)](Q_I' + 2Q_B')} \tag{4.8.9}$$

Expressions for Q_I' and Q_B' in strong inversion are given by (4.4.16) and (4.4.15). These can be substituted in (4.8.9), and the result in (4.8.1). The integration can then be performed, but the resulting expression is very complicated[26] and, thus, is not practical. An alternative technique will thus be used. One can substitute (4.8.9) in (4.4.12) to obtain

---

† It is interesting to note that the form of (4.8.5) is not totally empirical. It can be made plausible by starting from the so-called "Mathiessen's rule" for combining mobility contributions, which gives $1/\mu = 1/\mu_1 + 1/\mu_2$, with μ_1 the mobility due to bulk scattering and μ_2 the mobility due to surface scattering; contributions to bulk mobility are combined in a similar manner.[18, 66] If we assume that μ_2 is inversely proportional to $\bar{E}_y$ (which, in turn, can be made plausible under certain physical assumptions,[75] it is easily seen that the form of (4.8.5) results. However, the values of the parameters in that equation are difficult to justify rigorously. A semiempirical discussion is given elsewhere.[75]

‡ Due to the gradual channel approximation (Sec. 4.1), the electric field component parallel to the direction of current flow is assumed negligible compared to the normal component. Hence, a one-dimensional analysis can be used.

$$I_{DN} = \frac{\mu_0}{1 - [\alpha_\theta/(2\epsilon_s)](Q_I' + 2Q_B')} W(-Q_I') \frac{dV_{CB}}{dx} \qquad (4.8.10)$$

From this it follows that

$$I_{DN} \int_0^L \left[1 - \frac{\alpha_\theta}{2\epsilon_s}(Q_I' + 2Q_B')\right] dx = \mu_0 W \int_{V_{SB}}^{V_{DB}} (-Q_I') \, dV_{CB} \qquad (4.8.11)$$

If this is solved for I_{DN}, one obtains an expression of the form of (4.8.2), with

$$\mu_{\text{eff}} = \frac{\mu_0}{\frac{1}{L} \int_0^L \{1 - [\alpha_\theta/(2\epsilon_s)](Q_I' + 2Q_B')\} \, dx} \qquad (4.8.12)$$

Unfortunately, the calculation of this is not easy since Q_I' and Q_B' depend on x through $V_{CB}(x)$, which is, in general, given by a complicated expression; see, for example, (4.4.38). It is here that a simplification is made: For the purposes of evaluating (4.8.12), it is assumed[32] that V_{CB} is approximately linear with x. (As seen from Fig. 4.14, this assumption is mostly satisfactory for low values of V_{DS}.) Then we can write $dV_{CB}/dx \approx (V_{DB} - V_{SB})/L$. Using this to perform a change of variables in the integral of (4.8.12), we obtain

$$\mu_{\text{eff}} \approx \frac{\mu_0}{[1/(V_{DB} - V_{SB})] \int_{V_{SB}}^{V_{DB}} \{1 - [\alpha_\theta/(2\epsilon_s)](Q_I' + 2Q_B')\} \, dV_{CB}} \qquad (4.8.13)$$

The integration can be completed by using Q_I' and Q_B' from (4.4.16a) and (4.4.15) for the accurate strong-inversion model,[32] or from (4.4.23) and (4.4.22) for the approximate strong-inversion model. After some algebra, we obtain

$$\mu_{\text{eff}} = \frac{\mu_0}{1 + \theta f_\mu} \qquad (4.8.14)$$

where

$$\theta = \frac{\alpha_\theta}{2\epsilon_s} C_{ox}' \qquad (4.8.15)$$

and f_μ is given by the following expressions.
For the accurate strong-inversion model:[32]

$$f_\mu = (V_{GB} - V_{FB} - \phi_B) - \tfrac{1}{2}(V_{DB} + V_{SB}) + \tfrac{2}{3}\gamma \frac{(\phi_B + V_{DB})^{3/2} - (\phi_B + V_{SB})^{3/2}}{V_{DB} - V_{SB}} \qquad (4.8.16a)$$

$$= (V_{GS} - V_{FB} - \phi_B) - \tfrac{1}{2}V_{DS} + \tfrac{2}{3}\gamma \frac{(\phi_B + V_{SB} + V_{DS})^{3/2} - (\phi_B + V_{SB})^{3/2}}{V_{DS}} \qquad (4.8.16b)$$

For the approximate strong-inversion model:

$$f_\mu = V_{GS} - V_{FB} - \phi_B + \gamma\sqrt{\phi_B + V_{SB}} - \tfrac{1}{2}(1 - \delta)V_{DS} \qquad (4.8.17a)$$

$$= V_{GS} - V_T + 2\gamma\sqrt{\phi_B + V_{SB}} - \tfrac{1}{2}(1 - \delta)V_{DS} \qquad (4.8.17b)$$

where V_T is given by (4.4.26).

As seen, the effect of the gate voltage is dominant. For this reason, it is sometimes said that μ_{eff} "depends on the gate field." It is more correct, though, to say that μ_{eff} depends on the normal field, which, in turn, depends on all terminal voltages, as has been seen. We should note here that in the denominator of the expression for μ_{eff} another term proportional to V_{DS} is often included to model "velocity saturation" effects. This is not related to the V_{DS} terms in the above equations, and will be considered in detail in Sec. 5.3.

Using μ_{eff} from (4.8.14) and (4.8.16) in lieu of μ in the accurate strong-inversion expression (4.4.8) or (4.4.17) has been shown to result in an accurate model with excellent agreement to experiment.[32] One can also use (4.8.14) with (4.8.17) in conjunction with (4.4.25). In either case, of course, one must use the approach indicated by (4.4.20) to extend the characteristics into the saturation region. V'_{DS} in that equation is the value of V_{DS} at which $dI_{DN}/dV_{DS} = 0$. Note that, because of the presence of V_{DS} in the expression for μ_{eff}, a new differentiation is required to obtain the value of V'_{DS}. The V'_{DS} expressions of Sec. 4.4 will not be valid here, since they were obtained by assuming a constant mobility. This results in additional complications which are often avoided by neglecting the dependence of μ_{eff} on V_{DS}. For example, consider (4.8.17b). In that equation the last term is usually dropped.† In addition, the term dependent on V_{SB} is sometimes replaced by a term linear in V_{SB}. Thus the following form has been suggested for (4.8.14):[27, 37]

$$\mu_{\text{eff}} = \frac{\mu_0}{1 + \theta(V_{GS} - V_T) + \theta_B V_{SB}} \qquad (4.8.18)$$

By now several approximations have been made, and one should expect that the values of μ_0, θ, and θ_B used in the above equation may have to be chosen empirically by comparison to measurements, to minimize the error. A typical value for μ_0 is 60 $\mu\text{m}^2/(\text{V}\cdot\text{ns})$ for n-channel devices at room temperature. The parameter θ is of the form β_θ/d_{ox}, with d_{ox} the oxide thickness, and β_θ typically 0.001 to 0.004 $\mu\text{m V}^{-1}$.‡ The value of θ_B is usually small (for

---

† Often the effect of this term is absorbed into a similar term that results from "velocity saturation" effects; these are considered in Sec. 5.3.

‡ The value of θ is sometimes adjusted to help model an effect quite unrelated to the field dependence of mobility, i.e., the effective drain-source voltage reduction due to the voltage drop across the series resistance of the source and drain regions. This effect is discussed in Sec. 5.7.

example, a few hundredths of 1 V^{-1}), and often the V_{SB}-dependent term in (4.8.18) is omitted altogether. This, however, can cause problems, as then increasing V_{SB} would imply an increase in μ_{eff}, since V_T would be increasing owing to the body effect. However, μ_{eff} should actually *decrease* with increasing V_{SB}. This is most easily seen from (4.8.16b) or (4.8.17a), and is also expected intuitively. Let us refer all voltages to the source. Then increasing V_{SB} means making the voltage at the substrate terminal more negative. This would tend to increase the normal field and "push" the electrons more toward the surface, which is the same effect an increase in the gate voltage would have; thus μ_{eff} should be expected to decrease. This is verified experimentally,[32] and is found to be more evident in p-channel devices (Sec. 4.11).[37] Thus omitting the V_{SB}-dependent term in (4.8.18) can have a serious effect, especially in the small-signal modeling of analog circuits (Chaps. 8 and 9). If, in addition to omitting the V_{SB}-dependent term in (4.8.18), V_T is replaced by V_{T0} [as given by (4.4.27)],[28] μ_{eff} appears independent of V_{SB}.

The effect of mobility dependence on V_{GS} is shown in Fig. 4.20. I_D is plotted vs. V_{GS} for a fixed V_{SB} and very small V_{DS}. Then, as seen from (4.4.30), we will have $I_D \approx (W/L)\mu C'_{ox} V_{DS}(V_{GS} - V_T)$. If μ is constant, a straight line is obtained in strong inversion, as shown by the broken line (the bottom, curved part is caused by moderate inversion). If μ is replaced by μ_{eff}, which varies with V_{GS} as suggested above, the plot becomes as shown by the solid line. In some devices this effect is so strong that one never really gets to see a straight-line part in the characteristic. Note that very small V_{DS} is not a necessary condition for obtaining a straight line in *nonsaturation*. However, such plots are usually obtained for very small V_{DS} since, then, nonsaturation occurs at small V_{GS} values, at which one can hope to see the initially straight

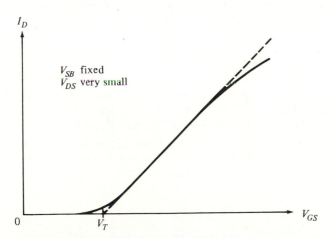

FIGURE 4.20
I_D vs. V_{GS} for fixed V_{SB} and fixed, very small V_{DS} for constant effective mobility and neglecting moderate and weak inversion (broken line), and V_{GS}-dependent effective mobility and including moderate and weak inversion (solid line).

part of the curve before mobility degradation takes over. Also, for very small V_{DS}, the intercept of an extension of the straight-line part with the horizontal axis is approximately V_T. This is a convenient method for determining the threshold voltage experimentally (Sec. 4.13).

The parameter μ_{eff} is often simply referred to as the *mobility* instead of the more complete *effective mobility*, and is denoted by μ for simplicity. For convenience, we will adopt this notation in the rest of this book. No confusion should arise because it should be understood that, every time μ is encountered in expressions that give the drain current as a function of the terminal voltages, it will be the *effective* mobility.

As already pointed out, the results obtained in this section are valid in the strong-inversion region, where the normal electric field is not very small and (4.8.5) is valid. At very low fields (e.g., corresponding to weak inversion) this equation is no longer claimed to be valid. It has been suggested that the electron density in the inversion layer at such fields is no longer large enough to "screen" the ionized acceptor atoms, and that it can show significant fluctuations due to the presence of localized charges at the oxide-semiconductor interface.[78,75] Devices have been reported to exhibit a drop in mobility when operating in weak inversion,[74, 75, 77, 78] although not all results reported in the literature show such behavior.[79] In contrast to strong inversion, not much work has been done toward developing simple expressions for the effective mobility in weak inversion.

4.9   TEMPERATURE EFFECTS

MOS transistor characteristics are strongly temperature-dependent.[20, 30, 37, 66, 80–84] One of the main parameters responsible for this is the effective mobility, which is known to decrease with temperature. An often used approximation is

$$\mu(T) = \mu(T_r)\left(\frac{T}{T_r}\right)^{-k_3} \tag{4.9.1}$$

where T is absolute temperature, T_r is room absolute temperature, and k_3 is a constant, with various values used for it[37, 66, 76] between 1.5 and 2.0.

Other temperature-dependent parameters are ϕ_B and V_{FB} [the latter is temperature-dependent through ϕ_{MS} in (2.2.6), assuming Q'_o is fixed]. These effects are manifested in the value of V_T in (4.4.26), which is found to exhibit an almost straight-line decrease with temperature[20, 80, 81, 83, 84] and can be approximated by:

$$V_T(T) = V_T(T_r) - k_4(T - T_r) \tag{4.9.2}$$

where k_4 is usually between 0.5 mV/K and 4 mV/K, with larger values in this range corresponding to heavier doped substrates, thicker oxides, and smaller values of V_{SB}.

As an example of the effect of temperature on transistor characteristics, consider a device operating in the saturation region. From (4.4.30) we have

$$\sqrt{I_D} = \sqrt{\mu(T)}\sqrt{\frac{1}{2}\frac{W}{L}\frac{C'_{ox}}{1+\delta}}\,[V_{GS} - V_T(T)] \qquad (4.9.3)$$

Thus a temperature increase should tend to increase the drain current through $V_{GS} - V_T(T)$, and to decrease it through $\mu(T)$. A measured set of $\sqrt{I_D}$ vs. V_{GS} curves is shown in Fig. 4.21. With a positive threshold voltage, the condition $V_{DS} = V_{GS}$ ensures operation in saturation, as can be seen from (4.4.30) and (4.4.28). At high currents, the decrease of $\mu(T)$ with temperature wins out; the opposite is true at low currents. In certain cases a value of V_{GS} can be found at which the current becomes practically temperature-independent over a large temperature range.[20, 80, 83] This effect is evident in the figure. The bottom, curved part of the characteristics is due to moderate and weak inversion.

As can be deduced from the above figure, in weak inversion and for a given V_{GS} the drain current increases with temperature. Plots of I_D (logarithmic scale) vs. V_{GS} are shown for various temperatures in Fig. 4.22. As seen, increasing temperature decreases the slope of the curves. Also, the junction leakage (the effect of which is shown by broken curves) drastically increases with temperature and masks the weak-inversion current, thus diminishing the range of currents over which exponential behavior is observed.

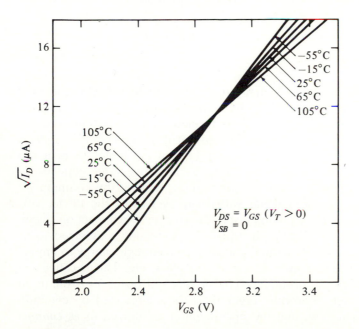

FIGURE 4.21
Measured $\sqrt{I_D}$ vs. V_{GS} for a device with $V_T > 0$, with fixed V_{SB} and $V_{DS} = V_{GS}$, for various temperatures.

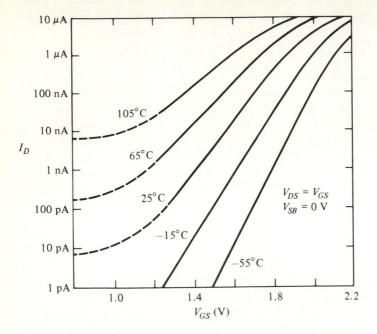

FIGURE 4.22
Measured I_D (logarithmic axis) vs. V_{GS} at low currents for various temperatures. The broken part indicates the effect of leakage.

4.10 BREAKDOWN

The value of the various voltages that can be applied to a MOS transistor should be limited to avoid several forms of breakdown.[20, 30, 66, 85] One such form is *junction breakdown*. The junctions formed by the substrate and the drain or source regions will conduct a large current if the reverse bias applied to them exceeds a certain value (because the field in the junctions near the surface is influenced by the presence of the gate, the above value depends on the gate potential and can be different from that predicted by common *pn* junction theory). Junction breakdown will occur even with the device off. When the device is on, carriers moving fast in the channel can impact on silicon atoms and ionize them, producing electron-hole pairs; this is referred to as *impact ionization*. The newly generated pairs can gain enough energy to impact on silicon atoms and produce more electron-hole pairs, etc. This is called the *avalanche* effect, and is more pronounced in the pinchoff region near the drain where fields can be high. Currents larger than those predicted by common device models will then flow, and the phenomenon is referred to as *channel breakdown*.

The above forms of breakdown are nondestructive. Once the large voltages producing them are removed, the device will function properly as long as no permanent damage caused by overheating has occurred. The effect of such breakdown on device characteristics is shown in Fig. 4.23.†

A *destructive breakdown* mechanism is *oxide breakdown*. It occurs when the electric field in the gate insulator exceeds a certain value (about 600 V/μm in silicon dioxide). The result is a permanent short circuit through the insulator. Static charge, such as that transferred to gates by handling devices with bare hands, is known to cause oxide breakdown. For this reason, protective devices are often used at those input terminals of an MOS integrated circuit that are connected to transistor gates.

4.11 THE *p*-CHANNEL MOS TRANSISTOR

If the substrate is made of *n*-type material, and the source/drain regions of p^+-type material, we have what is known as the *p-channel* MOS transistor or PMOS transistor. Figure 4.24 shows such a device. An example of *p*-channel transistor characteristics is shown in Fig. 4.25.

The operation of the *p*-channel transistor is the "dual" of *n*-channel operation. The role of electrons is played by holes, and the role of ionized acceptor atoms is played by ionized donor atoms. Statements made about *n*-channel devices can be adapted to the case of *p*-channel devices with simple modifications. For example, in Fig. 4.24, the more *negative* the gate-source voltage the heavier the concentration of *holes* near the surface. The more *negative* the drain-source voltage the heavier the flow of *holes* from source to

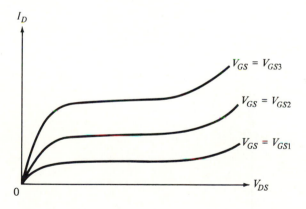

FIGURE 4.23
Effect of breakdown on I_D-V_{DS} characteristics.

---

† Our discussion here is limited to long-channel devices. An additional form of breakdown, called *punchthrough*, is encountered in short-channel devices; this effect is considered in Sec. 5.6.

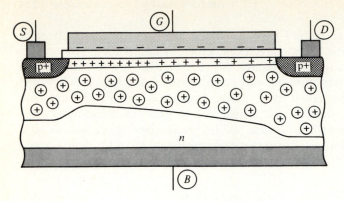

FIGURE 4.24
A *p*-channel MOS transistor.

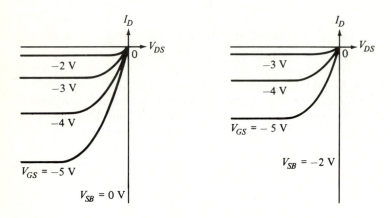

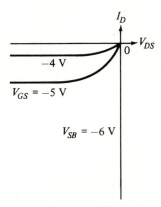

FIGURE 4.25
I_D-V_{DS} characteristics for a *p*-channel MOS transistor for three different V_{SB} values.

152

drain; hence, the more *negative* the drain current (assuming the reference direction is chosen as before, i.e., from the drain through the channel to the source). The more *negative* the source-substrate bias the larger the number of *donor* atoms that are depleted. The body effect coefficient γ is given by

$$\gamma = \frac{F\sqrt{N_D}}{C'_{ox}} \qquad (4.11.1)$$

where N_D is the concentration of donor atoms in the substrate.

In describing *p*-channel devices, there are some rather obvious sign changes in the model equations; for example, instead of (4.4.25) we will have

$$I_{DN} = -\frac{W}{L}\,\mu C'_{ox}[(V_{GS} - V_T)V_{DS} - \tfrac{1}{2}(1 + \delta)V_{DS}^2] \qquad (4.11.2)$$

and instead of (4.4.26*b*) we will have

$$V_T(V_{SB}) = V_{T0} - \gamma(\sqrt{-V_{SB} - \phi_B} - \sqrt{-\phi_B}) \qquad (4.11.3)$$

where V_{SB} and ϕ_B are negative and, instead of (4.4.27), we have

$$V_{T0} = V_{FB} + \phi_B - \gamma\sqrt{-\phi_B} \qquad (4.11.4)$$

The various equations for *p*-channel devices are considered in Prob. 4.22. The value of the effective mobility for *p*-channel devices at low gate voltages is smaller than that in *n*-channel devices by a factor of 2 to 4; a typical value is $25\ \mu\mathrm{m}^2/(\mathrm{V}\cdot\mathrm{ns})$.

4.12 ENHANCEMENT MODE AND DEPLETION MODE TRANSISTORS

Consider the simple model of (4.4.30). Depending on the sign of V_{T0}, MOS transistors are separated into two categories. The *n*-channel transistors with positive V_{T0} are called *enhancement* mode (or "normally off") devices, whereas *n*-channel transistors with negative V_{T0} are said to be *depletion* mode (or "normally on") devices. These names originated in the days when weak inversion was neglected, and the *n*-channel transistor was viewed as being on for $V_{GS} > V_{T0}$ and off for $V_{GS} < V_{T0}$ (with $V_{SB} = 0$ assumed). Thus, if V_{T0} is positive, an *n*-channel device is off at $V_{GS} = 0$, and it takes a positive V_{GS} to "enhance" the channel and turn the device on. If V_{T0} is negative, the *n*-channel device is already on with $V_{GS} = 0$, and it takes a negative V_{GS} to "deplete" the channel and turn the device off. For *p*-channel devices, a negative V_{T0} corresponds to the enhancement mode and a positive V_{T0} to the depletion mode. The I_D-V_{GS} characteristics for the four types of devices for a very small $|V_{DS}|$ are shown in Fig. 4.26.

The value of V_{T0} can, in principle, be set by a very shallow ion implantation during fabrication. In such a process, the device is bombarded with high-energy ions. If all such ions could end up at the oxide-semiconductor interface, their effect would be the same as that of Q'_o in (2.2.6). Hence, the value of V_{FB} could be adjusted, which, in turn, would adjust the value of V_{T0} in (4.4.27). In practice, however, ion implantation cannot be that shallow. The spreading of ions into the substrate can create second-order effects, and then the resulting device cannot be modeled accurately as in this chapter. Ion-implanted devices are considered in Chap. 6.

4.13   MODEL ACCURACY AND PARAMETER EXTRACTION

In the models we have developed, some parameters do not have an exact theoretical value. Such is the case with ϕ_B, which represents the supposedly "pinned" value of the surface potential in strong inversion (with $V_{SB} = 0$). Since the surface potential is never exactly pinned but instead varies with bias, the best single value to be used for ϕ_B will depend on the bias range we are interested in. The same is true for V_{T0}, which contains ϕ_B in its definition. Even parameter values which have been specified "exactly" (e.g., the body effect coefficient γ) are actually exact only for the fictitious, idealized device corresponding to the simplifying assumptions we have made (e.g., that the substrate doping is "exactly" uniform). Thus, when a model is used to represent a real device, the parameter values that will result in minimum error between model predictions and experiment are not necessarily dictated by a simple theory. For this reason, what is sometimes done is to choose the model parameters empirically to provide "best matching" between model predictions and measurements. In this process, the "theoretical" values for the parameters might simply play the role of an initial guess. Of course, what constitutes "best matching" is subject to interpretation. One might desire good matching for devices with $L = 10\ \mu\text{m}$ and V_{DS} from 2 to 5 V; or, most likely, for devices of various lengths and widely varying bias voltages. The sets of parameter values to be used in these two cases will not necessarily be the same, and the overall matching is likely to be better in the first case, assuming the same model is used. Also, if the same parameter appears in two different models (e.g., ϕ_B appears in both the accurate model and the approximate model of Sec. 4.4), different values of it might have to be used in each model for best results. For this reason direct comparison of model equations is difficult and should be taken with a grain of salt.

Let us offer an example of problems that can arise when model predictions are compared to experiment. Let us say that the weak-inversion model of (4.6.17) for given terminal voltages and process parameters predicts a current four times larger than the measured value. Is the model bad? Not necessarily. The problem may just be that the process parameters are not accurately known. This is notably true of V_{FB}, for example, which appears in the exponential term in (4.6.17) through V_X. With $n = 1.3$, just a 50-mV error in the value of V_{FB} is enough to give four times the actual current! This, of

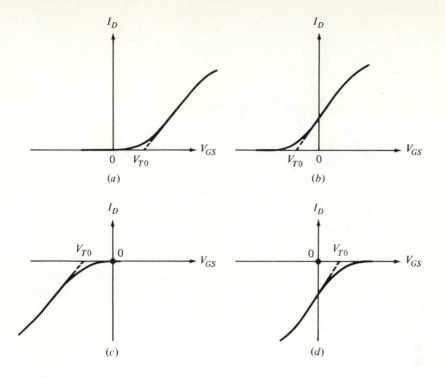

FIGURE 4.26
I_D vs. V_{GS} for $V_{SB} = 0$ and very small $|V_{DS}|$. (a) *n*-channel enhancement device; (b) *n*-channel depletion device; (c) *p*-channel enhancement device; (d) *p*-channel depletion device.

course, happens because in weak inversion the log I_D vs. V_{GS} curves (e.g., Fig. 4.22) are so steep that a slight shift horizontally corresponds to a large current change. Note that, if *I-V plots* were compared rather than numbers, the above problem with V_{FB} could have been spotted immediately. The eye would see that the curves produced by the model had the same shape as the measured ones, only they were shifted somewhat horizontally. Thus, V_{FB} would be suspected and a new value would be tried for that parameter. In general, blind number comparison can be extremely misleading.

Let us now give a simple example of "parameter extraction" for the approximate strong-inversion model of Sec. 4.4.2. To determine $\mu C'_{ox}$ and V_T empirically for a given device note that, from (4.4.30) and a *very* small V_{DS}, we obtain

$$I_D = \frac{W}{L} \mu C'_{ox} V_{DS}(V_{GS} - V_T), \quad \text{very small } V_{DS} \qquad (4.13.1)$$

Values of I_D and V_{GS}, as obtained from measurements for very small V_{DS} and for fixed values of V_{SB}, can be plotted as shown in Fig. 4.27. Straight lines are fitted through the points as shown. [The deviation from straight-line

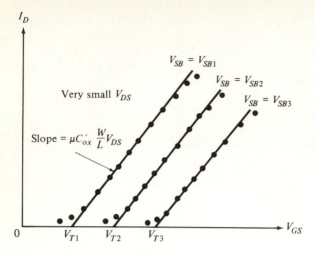

FIGURE 4.27
Graphical method for determining $\mu C'_{ox} W/L$ and V_T.

behavior at low and high V_{GS} values is due to moderate inversion and effective mobility degradation, respectively. The effective mobility is assumed to drop at high V_{GS} values, as explained in Sec. 4.8. The parameter μ in (4.13.1) will be assumed here to be the value of the effective mobility at *low* V_{GS} values before the effect of V_{GS} on the effective mobility becomes noticeable.] The straight lines are extended to the horizontal axis. The slope of these lines gives $(W/L)\mu C'_{ox} V_{DS}$ as seen from (4.13.1); from this, $\mu C'_{ox}$ is found if W/L is known. If the slope is not exactly the same for all curves, an average should be taken. The intercept of each curve gives V_T for each V_{SB} value, according to (4.13.1). If V_{DS} is not completely negligible, a small correction will be needed; see Prob. 4.23. V_T values thus obtained are plotted vs. $\sqrt{V_{SB} + \phi_B}$, as shown in Fig. 4.28, assuming a value for ϕ_B, say 0.7 V. If these points fall approximately

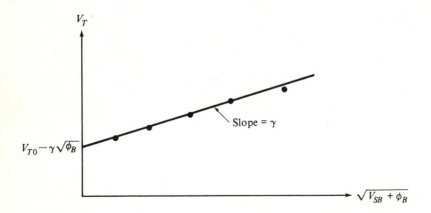

FIGURE 4.28
Graphical method for determining γ and ϕ_B; the value of ϕ_B should be chosen so that the points fall on a straight line.

on a straight line, they can be modeled by (4.4.26b); otherwise, a different value for ϕ_B should be tried until a straight-line fit is satisfactory. The slope of the straight line is then the body effect coefficient γ; the intercept is $V_{T0} - \gamma\sqrt{\phi_B}$, from which V_{T0} can be found. Notice that this value of V_{T0} might be a little off from the "exact" value that can be found from Fig. 4.27 with $V_{SB} = 0$; this is a price we might have to pay for an overall fit. The determination of δ requires the value of I_D at another value of V_{DS} (Prob. 4.24). An alternative procedure would be to plot $\sqrt{I_D}$ vs. V_{GS} in saturation as shown in Fig. 4.29. From (4.4.30b) the result should be a straight line with intercept of V_T and slope of $[\frac{1}{2}\mu C'_{ox}(W/L)/(1 + \delta)]^{1/2}$. From these and the value of $\mu C'_{ox}$, as found from Fig. 4.27, one can determine the value of δ. Note that the values of V_T determined in Fig. 4.29 are those for best fit in the saturation region; they might not be exactly the same as those found in Fig. 4.27.

We shall take the opportunity here to emphasize that in our discussion V_T is the *extrapolated* threshhold voltage, a term originating in Sec. 3.4.2 and also justified by the construction in Figs. 4.27 and 4.29. Unfortunately, the term *threshold voltage* is used in the literature with at least three other meanings. Sometimes it is taken to denote the quantity $V_{FB} + 2\phi_F + \gamma\sqrt{2\phi_F + V_{SB}}$. This quantity is actually very nearly the value of V_{GS} at the lower limit of moderate inversion, as has been seen in Sec. 4.5. It is *different* from V_T in (4.4.26a), simply because ϕ_B is different from $2\phi_F$ (Sec. 2.5.2). Elsewhere, "threshold voltage" is used to imply what is sometimes called *constant current threshold voltage*. This is the value of V_{GS} needed to reach a set value of $I_D/(W/L)$, which often happens to fall somewhere in the moderate-inversion region or even in the weak-inversion region. Finally, sometimes threshold voltage is taken to mean vaguely "the value of V_{GS} at which inversion begins," without specifying which level of inversion is meant (often strong inversion is implied). The name "threshold voltage" is often used indiscriminately for all these quantities, and sometimes during parameter extraction it is attempted to match

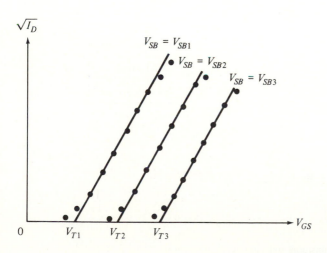

FIGURE 4.29
$\sqrt{I_D}$ vs. V_{GS} in saturation for different values of V_{SB}.

calculated values of one of these thresholds (e.g., $V_{FB} + 2\phi_F + \gamma\sqrt{2\phi_F + V_{SB}}$) to measured values of another threshold (e.g., the extrapolated threshold). All this originated in the early days, when V_{GS} values of, say, 20 V were not uncommon; compared to these, an ambiguity of, say, 0.5 V in the value of threshold was not a problem. Today, however, when the trend is clearly toward low-voltage circuit operation, a distinction of the above quantities is important. In this book "threshold voltage" will always imply *extrapolated* threshold voltage. The extrapolation can be in terms of current, as in this section, or in terms of inversion layer charge, as in Fig. 3.2*d*.

The determination of parameter values, which we have described above by means of a simple example and with the help of Figs. 4.2.7 to 4.2.9, is done in a much more sophisticated way in automatic systems devoted to data acquisition and parameter extraction. These take the general form shown in Fig. 4.30. Under the central control of a microcomputer, measurements such as *I-V* or *C-V* characteristics are performed on many devices of a certain type. The data obtained are then used as input to software which contains the algorithms for the determination of parameter values. Crucial in this process is the minimization of a certain error (e.g., mean square error) between the measured data and the values predicted by the model used. The selection of an appropriate error criterion depends on the application for which the model is intended. For example, for analog applications the error should involve small-signal parameters[69] (Chap. 8). Various systems for data acquisition and parameter extraction as well as the algorithms involved are discussed in the literature.[28, 29, 32–34, 86–89]

We have seen that by empirically "adjusting" the parameter values of a

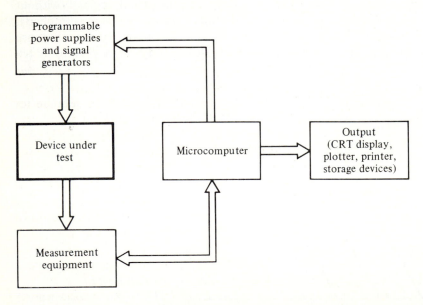

FIGURE 4.30
A system for automatic data acquisition and parameter extraction.

model one can extend its region of validity. *If the model is good, the final parameter values one ends up with in this process will be close to their theoretical values.* However, good models are usually complex since they have to take into account carefully several physical phenomena which the simpler models ignore. By the time all regions of operation are included, one can easily end up with nightmarish models with, say, 40 parameters. These can provide accuracy at the expense of complexity. Note however that satisfactory accuracy and a large number of parameters do not always mean that the physics of the device has been modeled correctly. There exist models which are based on faulty premises but which, just because they contain many parameters, can give adequate accuracy after extensive empirical adjustment. A serious drawback of such models is that they mislead the user. Consider, for example, a strong-inversion model used in what we have called moderate inversion (a practice seen often). In an attempt to "fit the unfittable," a parameter extraction system will try all kinds of variations on the parameter values, and might end up, for example, with completely fictitious values of the constants involved in an expression giving the effective mobility as a function of bias. The complete current equation now might "fit" the experimental data reasonably well, but the artificial behavior forced on mobility will mislead the user, and might even tempt him or her to develop a "theory" to explain such mobility behavior. (Our example concerning mobility may be fictitious, but similar cases are not rare.) Another major problem with models based on wrong physical assumptions is that they are likely to fail in *predicting* ahead of time what will happen if some fabrication process parameters are changed in the future. Such predictions are invaluable, yet experimental data are not available at the time the prediction is needed and curve fitting cannot be done. A good model based on correct physical assumptions is then the only resort.

At the other extreme of models with too many parameters to "fiddle with" are models which just do not have enough parameters to adjust, and which fail to match experimental results no matter what amount of curve fitting is attempted. As an example, consider (4.4.34), often used in digital circuit calculations. This equation, as was remarked above it, might be adequate for lightly doped substrates and/or thin oxides, since then δ in (4.4.30) is small, thus leading to (4.4.34). Consider, however, a device not belonging in that category, the measured characteristics of which are shown in Fig. 4.31 by curve 1. Curve 2 represents (4.4.34), with $(W/L)\mu C'_{ox}$ adjusted for good matching in saturation. The model clearly fails in nonsaturation, and it predicts a V'_{DS} which is too large. If $(W/L)\mu C'_{ox}$ is instead adjusted for a good fit in the low nonsaturation region, then the model gets out of hand in saturation, as shown by curve 3. If the model of (4.4.30) is used instead, we have the additional flexibility of choosing δ; with $\delta = 0.7$, we obtain curve 4.

Developing a model is an art involving constant tradeoffs between accuracy and simplicity. Again, we emphasize that models based on correct physical assumptions are invaluable. For such models, the parameter values one ends up with after "parameter extraction" will be close to the values predicted by theory.

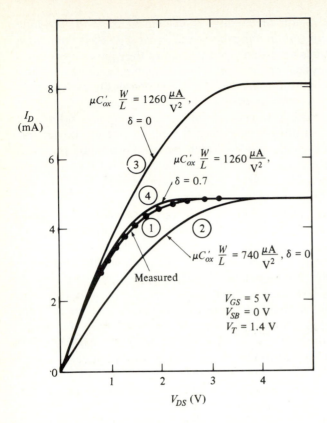

FIGURE 4.31
I_D vs. V_{DS} for fixed V_{SB} and $V_{GS} = 5$ V. Curve 1: measured characteristic of n-channel transistor on a heavily doped substrate (taken from a 14007-type CMOS inverter); curve 2: approximate model with $\delta = 0$, adjusted for good matching in the saturation region; curve 3: approximate model with $\delta = 0$, adjusted for good matching at very low V_{DS} values; curve 4: approximate model with $\delta = 0.7$, chosen for good matching at very low V_{DS} and in the saturation region.

REFERENCES

1. J. E. Lilienfeld, Canadian Patent application filed October 25; U.S. Patent 1,745,175 (1930), 1,877,140 (1932), 1,900,018 (1933).
2. O. Heil, British Patent 439,457 (filed and granted 1935).
3. W. Shockley and G. L. Pearson, "Modulation of conductance of thin films of semiconductors by surface charges," *Physical Review*, vol. 74, pp. 232–233, July 1948.
4. D. Kahng and M. M. Atalla, "Silicon-silicon dioxide field induced devices," *Solid-State Device Research Conference*, Pittsburgh, June 1960.
5. H. K. J. Ihantola, "Design theory of surface field-effect transistor," Stanford Electronics Laboratories, *Technical Report No. 1161-1*, Stanford University, California, September 1961.
6. S. R. Hofstein and F. P. Heinman, "The silicon insulated-gate field effect transistor," *Proceedings of the IEEE*, vol. 51, pp. 1190–1202, September 1963.
7. H. K. J. Ihantola and J. L. Moll, "Design theory of a surface field-effect transistor," *Solid-State Electronics*, vol. 7, pp. 423–430, June 1964.
8. C. T. Sah, "Characteristics of the metal-oxide-semiconductor transistors," *IEEE Transactions on Electron Devices*, vol. ED-11, pp. 324–345, July 1964.
9. E. H. Nicollian and J. R. Brews, *MOS Physics and Technology*, Wiley-Interscience, New York, 1982.
10. H. C. Pao and C. T. Sah, "Effects of diffusion current on characteristics of metal-oxide (insulator)-semiconductor transistors," *Solid-State Electronics*, vol. 10, p. 927–937, 1966.

11. J. T. Wallmark and H. Johnson, *Field Effect Transistors: Physics, Technology and Applications*, Prentice-Hall, Englewood Cliffs, 1966.
12. C. T. Sah and H. C. Pao, "The effects of fixed bulk charge on the characteristics of metal-oxide semiconductor transistors," *IEEE Transactions on Electron Devices*, vol. ED-13, pp. 393–409, April 1966.
13. R. S. Cobbold, "MOS transistor as a four terminal device," *Electronics Letters*, vol. 2, pp. 189–90, June 1966.
14. J. A. Van Nielen and O. W. Memelink, "The influence of the substrate upon the D.C. characteristics of silicon MOS transistors," *Philips Research Reports*, vol. 22, pp. 55–71, February 1967.
15. P. Richman, *Characteristics and Operation of MOS Field Effect Devices*, McGraw-Hill, New York, 1967.
16. R. H. Crawford, *MOSFET in Circuit Design*, McGraw-Hill, New York, 1967.
17. M. B. Das, "Dependence of the characteristics of MOS transistors on the substrate resistivity," *Solid-State Electronics*, vol. 11, pp. 305–322, 1968.
18. A. S. Grove, *Physics and Technology of Semiconductor Devices*, John Wiley, New York, 1967.
19. M. B. Das, "Physical limitation of MOS structures," *Solid-State Electronics*, vol. 12, pp. 305–336, May 1969.
20. R. S. C. Cobbold, *Theory and Applications of Field-Effect Transistors*, Wiley-Interscience, New York, 1970.
21. H. Shichman and D. A. Hodges, "Modeling and simulation of insulated-gate field-effect transistor switching circuits," *IEEE Journal of Solid-State Circuits*, vol. SC-3, pp. 285–289, September 1968.
22. D. Frohman-Bentckowsky and L. Vadasz, "Computer-aided design and characterization of digital MOS integrated circuits," *IEEE Journal of Solid-State Circuits*, vol. SC-4, pp. 57–64, April 1969.
23. J. E. Meyer, "MOS models and circuit simulations," *RCA Review*, vol. 32, pp. 42–63, March 1971.
24. W. N. Carr and J. P. Mize, *MOS/LSI Design and Applications*, McGraw-Hill, New York, 1972.
25. W. M. Penney and L. Lau (editors), *MOS Integrated Circuits*, Van Nostrand Reinhold, New York, 1972.
26. G. Merckel, J. Borel, and N. Z. Cupcea, "An accurate large-signal MOS transistor model for use in computer-aided design," *IEEE Transactions on Electron Devices*, vol. ED-19, pp. 681–690, May 1972.
27. F. M. Klaassen, "A MOS model for computer-aided design," *Philips Research Reports*, vol. 31, pp. 71–83, 1976.
28. G. Merckel, "CAD models of MOSFETS," in *Process and Device Modelling for Integrated Circuit Design*, F. Van de Wiele, W. L. Engl, and P. G. Jespers (editors), Noordhoff, Leyden, The Netherlands, 1977.
29. F. M. Klaassen, "A MOST model for CAD with automated parameter determination," in *Process and Device Modelling for Integrated Circuit Design*, F. Van de Wiele, W. L. Engl, and P. G. Jespers (editors), Noordhoff, Leyden, The Netherlands, 1977.
30. F. M. Klaassen, "Review of physical models for MOS transistors," in *Process and Device Modelling for Integrated Circuit Design*, F. Van de Wiele, W. L. Engl, and P. G. Jespers (editors), Noordhoff, Leyden, The Netherlands, 1977.
31. H. C. Poon, private communication, 1977.
32. M. H. White, F. Van de Wiele, and J. P. Lambot, "High-accuracy models for computer-aided design," *IEEE Transactions on Electron Devices*, vol. ED-27, pp. 899–906, May 1980.
33. R. E. Oakley and R. J. Hocking, "CASMOS—an accurate MOS model with geometry-dependent parameters: I," *IEE Proceedings*, vol. 128, part I, pp. 239–247, December 1981.
34. H. I. Hanafi, L. H. Camnitz, and A. J. Dally, "An accurate and simple MOSFET model for computer-aided design," *IEEE Journal of Solid-State Circuits*, vol. SC-17, pp. 882–891, October 1982.

35. S. Liu and L. W. Nagel, "Small-signal MOSFET models for analog circuit design," *IEEE Journal of Solid-State Circuits*, vol. SC-17, pp. 983–998, December 1982.

36. G. T. Wright, "Simple and continuous MOSFET models for the computer-aided design of VLSI," *IEE Proceedings*, vol. 132, part I, pp. 187–194, August 1985.

37. F. M. Klaassen, "MOS device modelling," in *Design of VLSI Circuits for Telecommunications*, Y. Tsividis and P. Antognetti (editors), Prentice-Hall, Englewood Cliffs, N.J., 1985.

38. Y. Hayashi and Y. Tarui, "Exponential current in MOST-type devices and deterioration of reverse current in p-n junctions," Technical Group on Semiconductors and Semiconductor Devices, Institute of Electronics and Communications Engineers of Japan, *Technical Report SSD 67-6*, 1967.

39. A. A. Guzev, G. L. Kuryshev, and S. P. Sinitsa, "Investigation of carrier capture on the surface of silicon in a metal-insulator-semiconductor transistor," *Soviet Physics–Semiconductors*, vol. 4, pp. 1245–1249, February 1971.

40. R. M. Swanson and J. D. Meindl, "Ion-implanted complementary MOS transistors in low-voltage circuits," *IEEE Journal of Solid-State Circuits*, vol. SC-7, pp. 146–153, April 1972.

41. M. B. Barron, "Low-level currents in insulated-gate field-effect transistors," *Solid-State Electronics*, vol. 15, pp. 293–302, 1972.

42. R. A. Stuart and W. Ecceleston, "Leakage currents of MOS devices under depletion conditions," *Electronics Letters*, vol. 8, pp. 225–227, May 1972.

43. R. R. Troutman and S. N. Chakravarti, "Subthreshold characteristics of insulated-gate field-effect transistors," *IEEE Transactions on Circuit Theory*, vol. CT-20, pp. 659–665, November 1973.

44. R. J. Van Overstraeten, G. Declerck, and G. L. Broux, "Inadequacy of the classical theory of the MOS transistor operation in weak inversion," *IEEE Transactions on Electron Devices*, vol. ED-20, pp. 1150–1153, December 1973.

45. R. R. Troutman, "Subthreshold design considerations for insulated gate field-effect transistors," *IEEE Journal of Solid-State Circuits*, vol. SC-9, pp. 55–60, April 1974.

46. T. Masuhara, J. Etoh, and M. Nagata, "A precise MOSFET model for low-voltage circuits," *IEEE Transactions on Electron Devices*, vol. ED-21, pp. 363–371, June 1974.

47. R. J. Van Overstraeten, G. J. Declerck, and P. A. Muls, "Theory of MOS transistor in weak inversion—new method to determine the number of surface states," *IEEE Transactions on Electron Devices*, vol. ED-22, pp. 282–288, May 1975.

48. R. R. Troutman, "Subthreshold slope for insulated gate field-effect transistors," *IEEE Transactions on Electron Devices*, pp. 1049–1051, November 1975.

49. E. Vittoz and J. Fellrath, "CMOS analog circuits based on weak inversion operation," *IEEE Journal of Solid-State Circuits*, vol. SC-12, pp. 224–231, June 1977.

50. G. W. Taylor, "Subthreshold conduction in MOSFETs," *IEEE Transactions on Electron Devices*, vol. ED-25, pp. 337–350, March 1978.

51. W. Fichtner and H. W. Potzl, "MOS modelling by analytical approximations. I. Subthreshold current and threshold voltage," *International Journal of Electronics*, vol. 46, pp. 33–55, 1979.

52. H. K. Lim and J. G. Fossum, "An analytic characterization of weak-inversion drift current in a long-channel MOSFET," *IEEE Transactions on Electron Devices*, vol. ED-30, pp. 713–715, June 1983.

53. I. R. M. Mansour, "On the modeling of MOS devices," *Proceedings of the Third International Symposium on Network Theory*, Yugoslavia, pp. 705–713, 1975.

54. I. R. M. Mansour, "Improved modeling of MOS devices," *Proceedings of the European Conference on Circuit Theory and Design*, Italy, 1976.

55. Y. A. El-Mansy and A. R. Boothroyd, "A new approach to the theory and modeling of insulated-gate field-effect transistors," *IEEE Transactions on Electron Devices*, vol. ED-24, pp. 241–253, March 1977. See also related comments by J. R. Brews, *ibid.*, pp. 1369–1370, December 1977, and reply by Y. A. El-Mansy and A. R. Boothroyd, *ibid.*, vol. ED-25, pp. 393–394, March 1978.

56. G. Baccarani, M. Rudan, and G. Spadini, "Analytical i.g.f.e.t. model including drift and diffusion currents," *IEE Journal on Solid-State and Electron Devices*, vol. 2. pp. 62–68, March 1978.

57. J. R. Brews, "A charge sheet model for the MOSFET," *Solid-State Electronics*, vol. 21, pp. 345–355, 1978.

58. F. Van de Wiele, "A long-channel MOSFET model," *Solid-State Electronics*, vol. 22, pp. 991–997, 1979.

59. J. R. Brews, "Physics of the MOS transistor," chapter 1 in *Silicon Integrated Circuits, Part A*, D. Kahng (editor), Applied Solid-State Science Series, Academic Press, New York, 1981.

60. H. Oguey and S. Cserveny, "Modèle du transistor MOS valable dans un grand domaine de courants," *Sonderdruck aus dem Bulletin des SEV/VSE*, vol. 73, pp. 113–116, 1982.

61. P. Antognetti, D. D. Caviglia, and E. Profumo, "CAD model for threshold and subthreshold conduction in MOSFETS," *IEEE Journal of Solid-State Circuits*, vol. SC-17, pp. 454–458, December 1982.

62. R. F. Pierret and J. A. Shields, "Simplified long-channel MOSFET theory," *Solid-State Electronics*, vol. 26, pp. 143–147, 1983.

63. C. Turchetti, "Relationships for the drift and diffusion components of the drain current in an MOS transistor," *Electronics Letters*, vol. 19, pp. 960–962, November 10, 1983.

64. C. Turchetti and G. Masetti, "A CAD-oriented analytical MOSFET model for high-accuracy applications," *IEEE Transactions on Computer-Aided Design of Integrated Circuits and Systems*, vol. CAD-3, pp. 117–122, 1984.

65. M. Bagheri and C. Turchetti, "The need for an explicit model describing MOS transistors in moderate inversion," *Electronics Letters*, vol. 21, pp. 873–874, September 12, 1985.

66. S. M. Sze, *Physics of Semiconductor Devices*, John Wiley, New York, 1981.

67. P. P. Guebels and F. Van de Wiele, "A charge sheet model for small geometry MOSFET's," *Technical Digest*, International Electron Devices Meeting, pp. 211–214, Washington, 1981.

68. A. M. Ostrowsky, *Solution of Equations and Systems of Equations*, Academic Press, New York, 1973.

69. Y. Tsividis and G. Masetti, "Problems in precision modeling of the MOS transistor for analog applications," *IEEE Transactions on Computer-Aided Design of Integrated Circuits and Systems*, vol. CAD-3, pp. 72–79, January 1983.

70. J. A. Geurst, "Calculation of high frequency characteristics of thin film transistors," *Solid-State Electronics*, vol. 8, pp. 88–90, 1965.

71. J. J. Paulos and D. A. Antoniadis, "Limitations of quasi-static capacitance models for the MOS transistor," *IEEE Electron Device Letters*, vol. EDL-4, pp. 221–224, July 1983.

72. C. H. Sequin, "A fluid model for visualizing MOS transistor behavior," in C. Mead and L. Connway, *Introduction to VLSI Systems*, Addison-Wesley, Reading, pp. 29–33, 1980.

73. Y. Tsividis, "Moderate inversion in MOS devices," *Solid-State Electronics*, vol. 25, pp. 1099–1104, 1982; see also Erratum, *ibid.*, vol. 26, p. 823, 1983.

74. P. Rossel, "Influence de la réduction de mobilité due au champ transversal sur les caractéristiques des m.o.s.t.," *Electronics Letters*, vol. 5, pp. 604–605, 1969.

75. S. A. Schwarz and S. E. Russek, "Semi-empirical equations for electron velocity in silicon— Part II: MOS inversion layer," *IEEE Transactions on Electron Devices*, vol. ED-30, pp. 1634–1639, December 1983.

76. A. G. Sabnis and J. T. Clemens, "Characterization of the electron mobility in the inverted <100> Si surface," *Technical Digest*, IEEE International Electron Devices Meeting, pp. 18–21, Washington, 1979.

77. J. T. C. Chen and R. S. Muller, "Carrier mobilities at weakly inverted silicon surfaces," *Journal of Applied Physics*, vol. 45, p. 828, 1974.

78. J. R. Brews, "Carrier-density fluctuations and the IGFET mobility near threshold," *Journal of Applied Physics*, vol. 46, p. 2193, 1975.

79. C. G. Sodini, T. Ekstedt, and J. L. Moll, "Charge accumulation and mobility in thin dielectric MOS transistors," *Solid-State Electronics*, vol. 25, pp. 833–841, September 1982.

80. G. Giralt, B. Andre, J. Simonne, and D. Esteve, "Influence de la température sur les dispositifs semiconducteurs du type M.O.S.," *Electronics Letters*, vol. 1, pp. 185–186, September 1965.

81. R. Wong, J. Dunkley, T. A. DeMassa, and J. F. Jelsma, "Threshold voltage variations with temperature in MOS transistors," *IEEE Transactions on Electron Devices*, vol. ED-18, p. 386, 1971.

82. S. K. Tewksburry, "N-channel enhancement-mode MOSFET characteristics from 10 to 300 K," *IEEE Transactions on Electron Devices*, vol. ED-28, pp. 1519–1529, December 1981.

83. F. Shoucair, W. Hwang, and P. Jain, "Electrical characteristics of large scale integration (LSI) MOSFETs at very high temperatures," *Microelectronics and Reliability*, vol. 24, part I, pp. 465–485, part II, pp. 487–510, 1984.

84. F. M. Klaassen and W. Hes, "On the temperature coefficient of the MOSFET threshold voltage," *Solid-State Electronics*, vol. 29, pp. 787–789, 1986.

85. G. Merckel, "Short channels-scaled down MOSFETs," in *Process and Device Modelling for Integrated Circuit Design*, F. van de Wiele, W. L. Engl, and P. G. Jespers (editors), Noordhoff, Leyden, The Netherlands, 1977.

86. P. Yang and P. K. Chatterjee, "An optimal parameter extraction program for MOSFET models," *IEEE Transactions on Electron Devices*, vol. ED-30, pp. 1214–1219, September 1983.

87. K. Doganis and D. L. Scharfetter, "General optimization and extraction of IC device model parameters," *IEEE Transactions on Electron Devices*, vol. ED-30, pp. 1219–1228, September, 1983.

88. P. Conway, C. Cahill, W. A. Lane, and S. U. Lidholm, "Extraction of MOSFET parameters using the Simplex direct search optimization method," *IEEE Transactions on Electron Devices*, vol. ED-32, pp. 694–698, October 1985.

89. C. F. Machala, III, P. C. Pattnaik, and Ping Yang, "An efficient algorithm for the extraction of parameters with high confidence from nonlinear models," *IEEE Electron Device Letters*, vol. EDL-7, pp. 214–218, April 1986.

90. M. Bagheri and Y. Tsividis, "A small-signal dc-to-high frequency nonquasistatic model for the four-terminal MOSFET valid in all regions of operation," *IEEE Transactions on Electron Devices*, vol. ED-32, pp. 2383–2391, November 1985.

PROBLEMS

4.1. Plot the total drain current, the component due to drift, and the component due to diffusion, using relations from Sec. 4.3, for an n-channel transistor with $N_A = 10^4 \ \mu\text{m}^{-3}$, $W = 10 \ \mu\text{m}$, $L = 10 \ \mu\text{m}$, $d_{ox} = 0.04 \ \mu\text{m}$, $\mu = 60 \ \mu\text{m}^2/(\text{V} \cdot \text{ns})$, $V_{FB} = 0 \ \text{V}$, $V_{SB} = 1 \ \text{V}$, $V_{DB} = 10 \ \text{V}$, and for V_{GB} between 2 and 10 V. Use a log current axis. Identify the three regions of inversion on the plot, and evaluate the percentages of the current due to drift and due to diffusion at the limit points between weak and moderate inversion and between moderate and strong inversion.

4.2. As explained in Sec. 4.3, in using (4.3.17) in weak inversion a small error in each of ψ_{sL} and ψ_{so} can cause a large relative error in I_{D2}, since ψ_{sL} and ψ_{so} have nearly equal values. Show that if $\psi_{sL} - \psi_{so}$ in (4.3.17) is substituted by the difference of the *right*-hand sides of (4.3.18a) and (4.3.18b), an expression much more immune to error results.[64] Explain why the new expression obtained may not be acceptable for use with (4.3.8) in strong inversion if ψ_{so} and ψ_{sL} are not known accurately (see also Prob. 4.3).

4.3. Consider the device of Prob. 4.1 with $V_{SB} = 1$ V, $V_{DB} = 4$ V, and V_{GB} corresponding to 0.2 V below the upper limit of weak inversion. Find ψ_{s0} and ψ_{sL} from (4.3.18) to very good accuracy (e.g., to eight significant digits) by using a computer or calculator with an equation-solving ability. Then, find I_{D2} from (4.3.17) and from the expression of Prob. 4.2, assuming ψ_{s0} and ψ_{sL} are known to only five, four, three, and two significant digits each. Which expression is more immune to limited accuracy? Explain the reasons by using specific numbers from the computation.

4.4. Plot the inversion layer and depletion region charges per unit area vs. distance from the source for the device of Prob. 4.1, with $V_{SB} = 1$ V, $V_{DB} = 4$ V, and $V_{GB} = 6$ V.

4.5. This problem deals with various ways of defining regions of operation.
(a) Without restricting V_{DS} to positive values, define $V = \min (V_{SB}, V_{DB})$ and give general definitions for the regions of inversion as described in Table 4.1, in terms of V and V_{GB}.
(b) Repeat, in terms of V and V_{GA}, where $V_{GA} = \max (V_{GS}, V_{GD})$.

4.6. Starting from (4.4.8a), prove (4.4.8b) and (4.4.17), as well as the following equation:

$$I_{DN} = \frac{W}{L} \mu C'_{ox} \{ \tfrac{1}{2}[(V_{GS} - V_{FB} - \phi_B)^2 - (V_{GD} - V_{FB} - \phi_B)^2]$$
$$- \tfrac{2}{3}\gamma[(V_{DB} + \phi_B)^{3/2} - (V_{SB} + \phi_B)^{3/2}]\}$$

4.7. Derive (4.4.17), starting from (4.4.13a).

4.8. For the device of Prob. 4.1 with $V_{SB} = 0$ V and $V_{GB} = 6$ V (strong inversion), plot I_D vs. V_{DS}, from $V_{DS} = 0$ to $V_{DS} = 10$ V, using (a) the general model of Sec. 4.3 and (b) the strong inversion model of (4.4.20) and (4.4.17). Discuss the effect of the value of ϕ_B in (b).

4.9. Consider the bracketed quantity containing the 3/2 powers in (4.4.17). Starting from an expansion of this quantity into a Taylor series around $V_{DS} = 0$, derive (4.4.25). Prove that the value to be used for δ should be less than δ_1 in (4.4.33b).

4.10. For the device of Prob. 4.1, compare the expression for $-Q'_B/C'_{ox}$ in (4.4.15) to the approximation in (4.4.22) for each value of δ in (4.4.33); use $d_2 = 0.8$ in (4.4.33c). Use values of $V_{CB} = V_{SB}$, $V_{SB} + 1$ V, $V_{SB} + 2$ V, $V_{SB} + 3$ V, $V_{SB} + 4$ V, and $V_{SB} + 5$ V for $V_{SB} = 0, 1, 2,$ and 4 V.

4.11. For the transistor in Prob. 4.1, assume $V_{SB} = 0$ V and plot I_D vs. V_{DS} for $V_{GS} = 3,$ 5, and 7 V using (a) (4.4.20) with (4.4.17) and (b) (4.4.30) for each of the five values of δ considered in Prob. 4.10. Comment on the accuracy obtained for each value of δ. Can this accuracy be improved if δ is allowed to be chosen at will? What value would you choose?

4.12. (a) Extend the idea behind (4.4.22) to the general model of Sec. 4.3 and prove that it leads to the following equations:

$$I_{D1} = \frac{W}{L} \mu C'_{ox}[(V_{GB} - V_N)(\psi_{sL} - \psi_{s0}) - \tfrac{1}{2}(1 + \hat{\delta})(\psi_{sL} - \psi_{s0})^2]$$

$$I_{D2} = \frac{W}{L} \mu C'_{ox} \phi_t(1 + \hat{\delta})(\psi_{sL} - \psi_{s0})$$

where $V_N \equiv V_{FB} + \psi_{s0} + \gamma\sqrt{\psi_{s0}}$ and $\hat{\delta}$ is an appropriate parameter. Comment on the value of $\hat{\delta}$ in weak inversion and strong inversion and propose an expression for it.

(b) Show that I_{D1} in (a) in nonsaturation reduces to (4.4.25).

(c) Prove that $I_D = I_{D1} + I_{D2}$, using the model derived in (a), can be written in the form[90]

$$I_D = \frac{W}{L} \mu C'_{ox} \frac{[U_C(0)]^2 - [U_C(L)]^2}{2(1 + \hat{\delta})}$$

where
$$U_C(0) = V_{GB} - V_{FB} - \psi_{s0} - \gamma\sqrt{\psi_{s0}} + (1 + \hat{\delta})\phi_t$$

$$U_C(L) = V_{GB} - V_{FB} - \psi_{s0} - \gamma\sqrt{\psi_{s0}} + (1 + \hat{\delta})\phi_t - (1 + \hat{\delta})(\psi_{sL} - \psi_{s0})$$

(d) Show that $U_C(L)$ can become slightly negative in the saturation region. Comment on the source of this problem and on the resulting effect on modeling I_D.

(e) Show that the problem in (d) is eliminated if $U_C(L)$ is redefined as

$$U_C(L) = V_{GS} - V_{FB} - \psi_{sL} - \gamma\sqrt{\psi_{sL}} + (1 + \hat{\delta})\phi_t$$

4.13. Prove (4.4.38).

4.14. For the approximate strong-inversion model and for the device of Prob. 4.1 with $\delta = \delta_3$, $V_{SB} = 1$ V, $V_{GS} = 5$ V, and $V_{DS} = V'_{DS} - 0.6$ V, plot (a) Q'_B and Q'_I as functions of V_{CB}, and (b) V_{CB}, Q'_B, and Q'_I as functions of the distance from the source.

4.15. For the device of Prob. 4.1 in weak inversion, plot (a) I_D vs. V_{DS}, with $V_{SB} = 0$, for V_{DS} between 0 and 1 V, and for V_{GS} values of $V_M - 50$ mV and $V_M - 100$ mV. Use (4.6.17); (b) log I_D vs. V_{GS} with $V_{DS} = 1$ V, for $V_{SB} = 0$ V and $V_{SB} = 2$ V.

4.16. Show that a simple approximate expression for the current in weak inversion is

$$I_D = \frac{W}{L} I'_M e^{(V_{GS} - V_M)/(n\phi_t)}(1 - e^{-V_{DS}/\phi_t})$$

where V_M is the upper V_{GS} limit of weak inversion, and

$$I'_M = \mu C'_{ox} \phi_t^2 \frac{\gamma}{2\sqrt{1.5\phi_F + V_{SB}}}$$

Comment on the accuracy of this equation.

4.17. Show that I_{D2} in (4.3.17) in weak inversion can be reduced to (4.6.13) as follows: Replace $\psi_{sL} - \psi_{s0}$ in (4.3.17) by the difference of the right-hand sides of (4.3.18b) and (4.3.18a). In this difference expand the square roots of the form $\sqrt{\psi_s + \xi}$ in a Taylor series around $\xi = 0$ and keep only the first two terms (justify this); in the resulting expression for I_{D2}, use $\psi_{s0} \approx \psi_{sL} \approx \psi_{sa}$.

4.18. For the device of Prob. 4.1, indicate the regions of inversion in the manner of Fig. 4.19, for $V_{GB} = 4$, 1.5, and 1 V.

4.19. Plot I_D in nonsaturation vs. V_{GS} with $V_{SB} = 0$, $V_{DS} = 10$ mV, and V_{GS} between 2 and 10 V, assuming $(W/L)\mu C'_{ox} = 14$ μA/V², $N_A = 10^4$ μm^{-3}, $d_{ox} = 0.04$ μm, and $V_T = 1$ V. Now repeat, assuming a mobility dependence on V_{GS} as given by (4.8.18), with $\theta = 0.05$ V^{-1}. Can V_T be obtained from the second plot by extrapolating to $I_D = 0$ from the point of maximum slope?

4.20. For the device of Prob. 4.19, plot I_D vs. V_{DS} with V_{DS} between 0 and 10 V, for $V_{GS} = 2$, 4, 6, and 8 V.
(a) Assume a constant mobility.
(b) Assume a V_{GS}-dependent mobility as given by (4.8.18) with $\theta = 0.05$ V^{-1}.

4.21. Using the data in Fig. 4.21, plot V_T and $\mu(T)/\mu(298\,\mathrm{K})$ vs. absolute temperature. Find an approximate value for k_3 in (4.9.1) and for k_4 in (4.9.2).

4.22. Rewrite the main equations in this chapter for p-channel transistors.

4.23. In Fig. 4.27, for a negligible V_{DS} the intercept is V_T, as has been discussed in Sec. 4.13. If V_{DS} is not negligible (but is still small), show that the above value must be modified by a small correction term.

4.24. In Sec. 4.13 a procedure has been described for obtaining the values of $(W/L)\mu C'_{ox}$, ϕ_B, and γ with the help of Figs. 4.27 and 4.28. Complete this procedure by suggesting a method for determining δ.

4.25. Shown in Fig. P4.25 are measured characteristics for an n-channel transistor, giving I_D vs. V_{DS} with V_{GS} a parameter; each set of curves is for a different value of V_{SB}. Choose a *single* value for each of the parameters $(W/L)\mu C'_{ox}$, V_{T0}, γ, δ, and ϕ_B, so that the approximate model equations of Sec. 4.4.2 are reasonably matched to the measurements.

4.26. For the 25°C curve in Fig. 4.22, find the values of n and $I'_M(W/L)$ used in the weak-inversion equations of Prob. 4.16. (*Hint*: Estimate the upper limit of weak inversion from the plot.)

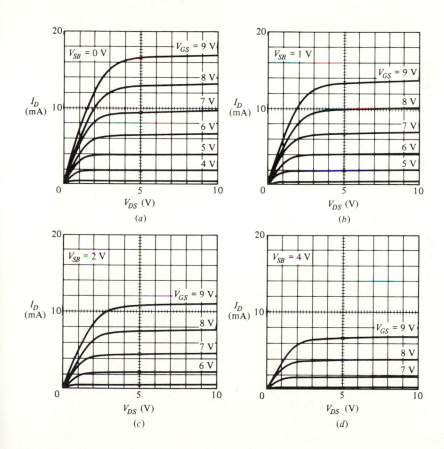

FIGURE P4.25

CHAPTER
5

SHORT-CHANNEL AND NARROW-CHANNEL EFFECTS

5.1 INTRODUCTION

In the previous chapter we assumed that the transistors under consideration had a channel sufficiently long and wide, so that "edge" effects along the four sides of the channel could be neglected. This allowed us to assume that the electric field lines were everywhere perpendicular to the surface (i.e., they had components only along the y direction), and we performed what is called a *one-dimensional* analysis by using the gradual-channel approximation. The equations we derived based on such assumptions fail to characterize adequately devices with short and/or narrow channels. If the channel is short (i.e., L is not much larger than the sum of the source and drain depletion widths), a significant part of the electric field lines will have components along both the y and the x directions, the latter being the direction along the channel's length. Thus, a *two-dimensional* analysis will be needed. If the channel is instead narrow (i.e., W is not much larger than the depletion region depth under the gate), a significant part of the field lines will have components along the y and z directions, the latter being the direction along the channel's width. Again, a two-dimensional analysis must be employed. If the channel is short *and* narrow, field lines will, in general, have components along the x, y, and z directions; now a *three-dimensional* analysis becomes necessary.

168

Two- and three-dimensional analyses can be carried out numerically with the help of a computer.[1-14] However, such analyses, albeit accurate, do not provide a simple model for efficient calculation. Thus, much has been done on the way to simplification by using empirical approximations and semiempirical approaches. In these, usually the complex two- or three-dimensional phenomena are broken down into simple, separate phenomena examined one at a time. A number of simplifying assumptions are then made, *which are sometimes difficult to justify rigorously*, and relatively simple relations are derived. Often such techniques are characterized by an attempt to maintain the general form of the *I-V* relations for the long- and wide-channel devices, and to "stretch" these relations by modifying them somewhat so that they can be used in the case of short and/or narrow channels. What is considered to justify these empirical approaches is their success in simulating the behavior observed experimentally. Although some of these approaches necessarily lack rigor and elegance, they have often been helpful when more precise work failed to give computationally efficient models. Some representative examples of the semiempirical modeling process, which has largely been limited to the strong-inversion region, will be presented in this chapter.

5.2 CHANNEL LENGTH MODULATION

As mentioned in Sec. 4.4, in the saturation region the I_D-V_{DS} characteristics are not exactly parallel to the horizontal axis but have, instead, a positive slope.[15-39] Other things being equal, this slope has been found to be larger for shorter channels, and may be easily noticeable, as shown in Fig. 5.1. Historically, this phenomenon was the first "short-channel effect" to be studied. It was not originally classified as such, partly because its investigation began well before various other short-channel effects were recognized and named that way, and partly because it can play an important role in circuit work even in devices with relatively long channels (e.g., 10 μm or longer).†

Two-dimensional analyses of the region near the drain in saturation present a very complicated picture.[19, 30] Field lines emanate from the drain n^+ region and terminate on points in the channel. Of these some are nearly horizontal, but others can start from the bottom of the n^+ region with a downward direction, curve gradually upward, and terminate on the inversion layer. In addition, the field lines from the gate to the channel and from the channel to the bulk curve in a complicated manner near the drain. The concentration of electrons decreases toward the drain, and these electrons are pushed away from the surface and into the bulk. Thus, one can think of the

---

† An example is the analog "CMOS inverter." The small-signal gain of such a circuit turns out to be inversely proportional to the sum of the I_D-V_{DS} slopes of two devices in saturation. The model of Sec. 4.4 would thus predict infinite gain!

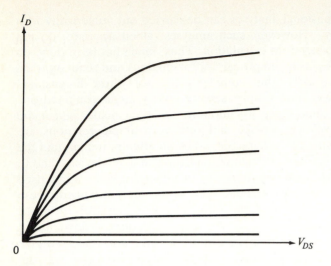

FIGURE 5.1
Transistor characteristics in the presence of channel length modulation.

channel as curving downward in the vicinity of the drain and of the current flowing in a "subsurface" path there. From such a picture one can suspect that the drain junction depth can affect the current value and, in fact, this is the case.

The above complicated picture has so far failed to provide simple analytical models. However, many semiempirical formulations have been worked out.[15-18, 20-39] Sometimes, to obtain approximate but manageable analytical results for the behavior in saturation, a greatly simplified picture is used; this will now be described. Figure 5.2a shows the semiconductor part of a transistor with $V_{DS} = V'_{DS}$, with V'_{DS} being the value at which "pinchoff" is assumed to occur at the drain end of the channel, as described in Sec. 4.4. As explained there, under this assumption $|Q'_I|$ at the drain end has a small non-

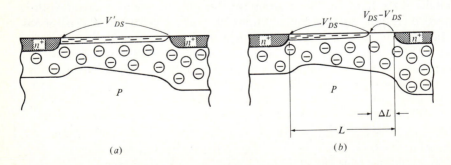

(a)   (b)

FIGURE 5.2
Channel (a) at pinchoff; (b) above pinchoff.

zero value, which is much smaller than the magnitude of the depletion region charge per unit area at that end. If now V_{DS} is increased above V'_{DS}, $|Q'_I|$ at the drain end will decrease below the above value. The pinched-off tip of the inversion layer will now move to the left, as shown in Fig. 5.2b, and the region between it and the drain n^+ region is approximated by a depletion region. In such an approximation picture, the assumption of a depletion region is only approximate and does *not* imply zero current. The reader might be familiar with *pn* junctions and bipolar transistors in which large currents can flow through depletion regions. However, since $|Q'_I|$ is small in this region, one must assume that the electrons travel at high speeds in it in order for a considerable value of I_D to be possible.

In Fig. 5.2b the channel cannot support more voltage than V'_{DS} since it becomes pinched off when the voltage across it reaches that value. The *excess* voltage $V_{DS} - V'_{DS}$ must then be dropped between the drain and the tip of the channel. Such a nonzero voltage can only exist over a region of nonzero length ΔL, as shown. If V_{DS} is raised still further, more excess voltage must be dropped across the depletion region. To support this voltage, the region must widen, and the inversion layer will shrink somewhat in length. This is referred to as *channel length modulation*. If the electron concentration in the depletion region is very small, we can assume that practically all the charge in the region is due to ionized acceptor atoms, with volume concentration N_A. Let us denote by E_1 the value of the channel field intensity in the x direction at the left end of the depletion region. Then, assuming that the field in the depletion region near the surface is approximately horizontal, it can be shown by using Poisson's equation (1.2.13) that the length ΔL of the depletion region can be related to the potential $V_{DS} - V'_{DS}$ across it by (Prob. 5.1)

$$\Delta L = \sqrt{\frac{2\epsilon_s}{qN_A}} \left[\sqrt{\phi_D + (V_{DS} - V'_{DS})} - \sqrt{\phi_D} \right] \tag{5.2.1}$$

where

$$\phi_D = \frac{\epsilon_s E_1^2}{2qN_A} \tag{5.2.2}$$

According to this simple model, the current conduction mechanism is as follows. Electrons enter the source end and travel along the channel; at the pinchoff point, they find themselves in what is practically a depletion region. As seen in Fig. 5.2b, the direction of the field in that region is such as to sweep these electrons through the depletion region to the drain. Note that the above one-dimensional model totally ignores the influence of the gate on the electric field near the drain, which can be important.[19, 21, 28, 37]

In a different formulation,[22, 23] pinchoff is taken to occur when the field near the drain becomes high enough to cause velocity saturation† (assuming a

---

† Velocity saturation was introduced in Sec. 1.3. Its effect on MOS transistor charactersitics will be considered in detail in Sec. 5.3.

simplified model for electron velocity in which velocity saturation is attained abruptly at a finite value of field intensity). For V_{DS} above the value corresponding to this point, the electrons are assumed to travel in the depletion region at maximum velocity. Such a formulation results again in (5.2.1) and (5.2.2), with E_1 taken to be a field value above which the electron velocity is assumed saturated. In some treatments, pinchoff is taken to correspond to the point at which the inversion layer "dives" below the interface, as predicted by two-dimensional simulations. This point can be defined more precisely as the point at which the surface electric field component in the vertical direction becomes zero.[30] For the orientation of the device in Fig. 5.2b, the gate field "pulls" the inversion layer toward the interface to the left of the pinchoff point and "pushes" it below the interface to the right of this point. Such a formulation can again result in (5.2.1) and (5.2.2), but with an E_1 value which must be found from a numerical solution. In practice, independently of which definition is used for pinchoff, one usually ends up adjusting the value of E_1 in (5.2.2) empirically for a best fit to experimental results. A single value of E_1 is sometimes used for simplicity, which lies between 1 and $20 \, V/\mu m$.

Let us now consider the effect of these phenomena on the drain current. At $V_{DS} = V'_{DS}$, the current I'_D is usually computed from the nonsaturation equations, which are assumed to be valid up to this point. From such computations [see, for example, (4.4.19) with (4.4.17)] we see that

$$I'_D = (\text{const}) \, \frac{1}{L} \qquad (5.2.3)$$

where the constant of proportionality (const) depends on V_{GS} and V_{SB}.

Consider now some value of V_{DS} larger than V'_{DS}, and let the corresponding current be I_D. This current can be calculated by considering the part of the channel that is *not* pinched off in Fig. 5.2b. For that part, the situation is the same as in Fig. 5.2a, save for the fact that the role of L is now played by $L - \Delta L$; thus, similar to (5.2.3), we will have

$$I_D = (\text{const}) \, \frac{1}{L - \Delta L} \qquad (5.2.4)$$

From the above two equations we obtain:

$$I_D = I'_D \, \frac{L}{L - \Delta L} \qquad (5.2.5a)$$

$$= \frac{I'_D}{1 - \Delta L/L} \qquad (5.2.5b)$$

The value of $\Delta L/L$ predicted by (5.2.1) is

$$\frac{\Delta L}{L} = \frac{B_1}{L \sqrt{N_A}} \, [\sqrt{\phi_D + (V_{DS} - V'_{DS})} - \sqrt{\phi_D}] \qquad (5.2.6)$$

where the above development predicts $B_1 = (2\epsilon_s/q)^{1/2}$. In practice, however, this constant and ϕ_D can be empirical parameters chosen for best matching between the resulting expressions for I_D and experimental data. An even more simple formulation[18] results in $\phi_D = 0$. However, such a formulation is based on the inaccurate assumption that the field E_1 at the pinched off point is zero. It has the additional problem that, as V_{DS} is reduced toward V'_{DS}, it predicts a slope dI_D/dV_{DS} which tends to infinity.

The error in the saturation current predicted by (5.2.5) and (5.2.6) is acceptable for many applications. However, it is possible for the error in I_D to be small, while at the same time the error in the *slope* dI_D/dV_{DS} is large, especially if dI_D/dV_{DS} is small in the first place. This is discussed in detail in Sec. 8.2.2. In cases where accurate prediction of dI_D/dV_{DS} is essential (e.g., in analog circuit design), the above model may not be adequate. One may have to go to more precise (and much more complicated) analyses, which include the effect of the gate on the field in the pinchoff region as well as the nonzero charge and shape of the inversion layer in that region. Such analyses can be expected to lead to expressions for ΔL of the following general form

$$\Delta L = f_{\Delta L}(L, N_A, d_{ox}, r, \phi_{MS}, Q_o, V_{DS}, V_{GS}, V_{SB}) \qquad (5.2.7)$$

where r is the drain junction depth. The derivation of results in the above form requires two-dimensional or pseudo-two-dimensional analyses and, again, the use of certain simplifications (recall that the whole idea behind ΔL is a simplification). Several such analyses have been presented in the literature,[19, 21, 26–30, 33, 39] although not all of them take every effect mentioned into account. Parameters such as V_T, V'_{DS}, maximum velocity of carriers, and even inversion layer thickness appear sometimes as parameters in the expressions for ΔL, although, in principle, these parameters are functions of the quantities shown in the right-hand side of (5.2.7). Two examples of the results of such analyses are given in Appendix J.

For digital circuit design, where dI_D/dV_{DS} in saturation is often not important *per se*, the complicated results mentioned in the preceding paragraph are avoided for reasons of computational speed. In fact, sometimes models simpler than (5.2.5) and (5.2.6) are used, predicting a first-degree dependence of I_D on V_{DS}.[20] To relate those models to the ones above, let us substitute (5.2.6) into (5.2.5), expand the resulting expression in a Taylor series around $V_{DS} = V'_{DS}$, and keep only the first two terms. The result is (Prob. 5.2)

$$I_D = I'_D\left(1 + \frac{V_{DS} - V'_{DS}}{V_A}\right) \qquad (5.2.8)$$

with

$$V_A = B_2 L \sqrt{N_A} \qquad (5.2.9)$$

where B_2 is a constant of proportionality of the order of 0.1 to 0.2 V μm$^{1/2}$. Equation (5.2.8) is plotted in Fig. 5.3*a*. The intercept with the horizontal axis is $-V_A + V'_{DS}$, and thus depends on V_{GS} through V'_{DS}. Another empirical model in use is:[31]

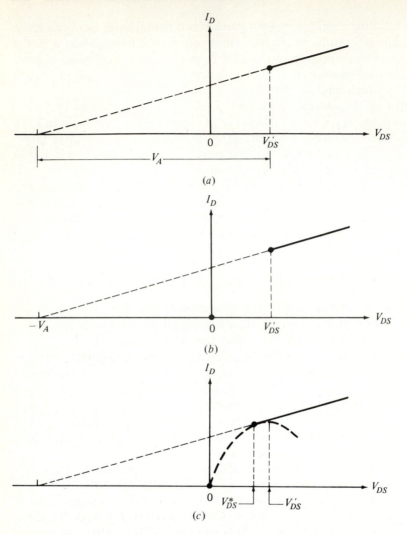

FIGURE 5.3
First-order modeling of the saturation region. (*a*) As provided by (5.2.8); (*b*) as provided by (5.2.10); (*c*) modification to ensure continuous slope at the transition point.

$$I_D = I'_D \left(1 + \frac{V_{DS} - V'_{DS}}{V_A + V'_{DS}}\right) \tag{5.2.10}$$

The plot of this equation intercepts the horizontal axis at $-V_A$, as indicated in Fig. 5.3*b*, independent of V'_{DS}. Thus, saturation curves for various V_{GS} values are all assumed to be straight lines which, if extended, cross one another at the same point on the horizontal axis. Such behavior might be approximately observed in real devices for some fabrication processes. A convenient estimate for V_A in this formulation has been suggested:[31]

$$V_A = 5 \frac{V}{\mu m} L \sqrt{\frac{N_A}{10^3 \, \mu m^{-3}}} \qquad (5.2.11)$$

which has the functional form of (5.2.9).

Note that the above saturation curves predict nonzero slope at V'_{DS}, whereas the nonsaturation equations predict zero slope at the same point. Such discontinuous slope behavior is unnatural and is also undesirable in the numerical algorithms used in the computer simulation of circuits. To avoid this problem, the saturation lines are drawn tangentially to the nonsaturation curves, as shown in Fig. 5.3c. Thus the limit between nonsaturation and saturation is defined slightly to the left of V'_{DS}; this limit is shown by V^*_{DS} in Fig. 5.3c.

Example 5.1. Let us develop a model based on the nonsaturation equation (4.4.30a) and the saturation equation (5.2.10), but using V^*_{DS} instead of V'_{DS} due to the above considerations. We will have

$$I_D = \frac{W}{L} \mu C'_{ox}[(V_{GS} - V_T)V_{DS} - \tfrac{1}{2}(1 + \delta)V_{DS}^2], \qquad V_{DS} \leq V^*_{DS} \quad (5.2.12)$$

and

$$I_D = I^*_D \left(1 + \frac{V_{DS} - V^*_{DS}}{V_A + V^*_{DS}} \right), \qquad V_{DS} > V^*_{DS} \quad (5.2.13)$$

where I^*_D is the value of current at the upper limit of validity of (5.2.12):

$$I^*_D = \frac{W}{L} \mu C'_{ox}[(V_{GS} - V_T)V^*_{DS} - \tfrac{1}{2}(1 + \delta)V^{*2}_{DS}] \qquad (5.2.14)$$

The value of V^*_{DS} required for continuous slope can now be obtained by equating dI_D/dV_{DS} as obtained from (5.2.12) and (5.2.13). The result is (Prob. 5.3)

$$V^*_{DS} = V_A \left[\sqrt{1 + \frac{2(V_{GS} - V_T)}{(1 + \delta)V_A}} - 1 \right] \qquad (5.2.15)$$

From the graphical construction in Fig. 5.3c we expect that, as V_A approaches infinity, V^*_{DS} should approach V'_{DS}. This is easily checked to be the case with (5.2.15) (Prob. 5.3): As V_A approaches infinity, V^*_{DS} approaches the value of $(V_{GS} - V_T)/(1 + \delta)$, which is, indeed, the value of V'_{DS} for the model considered in the absence of channel length modulation [see (4.4.28)].

We emphasize again that (5.2.8) and (5.2.10) are only good for approximate predictions of the drain current in saturation. In applications where accurate prediction of the *slope* dI_D/dV_{DS} is required (e.g., analog circuits), these equations are totally inadequate.

5.3 VELOCITY SATURATION

All the nonsaturation region models we have considered so far are based on an assumption stated above (4.3.2) concerning the electric field in the inversion layer. To recall that assumption, let $\mathscr{E}_x$ be the value of the *longitudinal* field component (i.e., *parallel* to the direction of current flow; also called *tangential*, or *lateral*, component). We have assumed that at all points in the inversion layer $|\mathscr{E}_x|$ is small enough so that the magnitude of the carrier velocity $|v_d|$ is proportional to $|\mathscr{E}_x|$. In devices with small-channel lengths this assumption can be violated, and the I_D-V_{DS} relations we have derived will not be valid. In this section we will show how adequate modeling can be achieved in such cases.[17, 22, 23, 26, 33, 35–46]

Figure 5.4 illustrates the behavior of $|v_d|$ with $|\mathscr{E}_x|$. As was the case for bulk conduction (Sec. 1.3), the velocity of carriers in the inversion layer tends to saturate at high $|\mathscr{E}_x|$ values.† Effects due to the lack of proportionality between $|v_d|$ and $|\mathscr{E}_x|$ on device characteristics are often referred to as *velocity saturation effects*, although the $|\mathscr{E}_x|$ values involved may be below those corresponding to a clear saturation trend in the figure.

It is convenient to define a "critical" value of $|\mathscr{E}_x|$, denoted by $\mathscr{E}_c$, at the

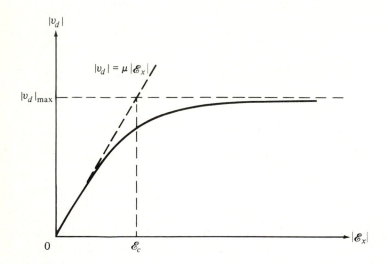

FIGURE 5.4
Magnitude of carrier velocity in the inversion layer vs. magnitude of longitudinal component of electric field.

---

† The velocity can attain values larger than $|v_d|_{max}$ over very short times or very short distances. This effect, referred to as *velocity overshoot*,[47, 48] is not considered here. The physics behind velocity saturation are complicated; readers with adequate background in quantum physics can consult Ref. 44. In general, the physics of carrier transport over very short distances is involved; even the expression of current as a drift plus a diffusion component has been questioned. For a summary of such considerations, the reader is referred elsewhere.[38] These considerations are in the realm of physics for numerical simulation and so far have not led to simple device models.

intersection of the $|v_d| = \mu|\mathcal{E}_x|$ line and an imaginary horizontal asymptote, as shown in the figure. We have

$$|v_d| \approx \mu|\mathcal{E}_x|, \qquad |\mathcal{E}_x| \ll \mathcal{E}_c \qquad (5.3.1a)$$

$$\approx |v_d|_{max}, \qquad |\mathcal{E}_x| \gg \mathcal{E}_c \qquad (5.3.1b)$$

and

$$\mathcal{E}_c = \frac{|v_d|_{max}}{\mu} \qquad (5.3.2)$$

Values used for the parameters in the above equation vary. The values for $|v_d|_{max}$ and $\mathcal{E}_c$ must, of course, be consistent with the values for μ, which can typically be about 65 μm/(V·ns) for electrons and 23 μm/(V·ns) for holes at room temperature and at low normal fields; "normal" indicates the direction perpendicular to the direction of current flow. In some treatments, the same value of $|v_d|_{max}$ is used for both electrons and holes (50 to 200 μm/ns), which results in $\mathcal{E}_c$ values of about 0.7 to 3 V/μm for electrons and 2 to 10 V/μm for holes. In other treatments $|v_d|_{max}$ is taken in the above range for electrons but somewhat lower for holes (by a factor usually close to 1, but sometimes as large as 3), in which case $\mathcal{E}_c$ for holes is reduced accordingly. The reason for these discrepancies is that these parameters are difficult to measure, and that several different theories have been developed to explain them. Also, in MOS transistor work these theories are usually applied in a simplified manner. Hence, some empirical adjustment of numerical values is performed to improve overall accuracy in the resulting device models.

Various empirical relations have been used to model the dependence of $|v_d|$ on $|\mathcal{E}_x|$. Thus, in some treatments the curve in Fig. 5.4 is replaced by a piecewise-linear plot, as suggested by the two asymptotes.[22] Another relation in use is:[40, 42]

$$|v_d| = |v_d|_{max} \frac{|\mathcal{E}_x|/\mathcal{E}_c}{1 + |\mathcal{E}_x|/\mathcal{E}_c} \qquad (5.3.3)$$

This tends to model better the region between very low and very high fields and is still in agreement with (5.3.1). Although expressions more complicated than (5.3.3) can provide more accuracy,[46] this equation is widely used because it leads to a simple transistor model as will be seen.

Consider now operation in the nonsaturation region of the I_D-V_{DS} strong-inversion characteristics and assume, as in Sec 4.4, that all current is due to drift. Let $V_{CB}(x)$ be the "effective reverse bias" of the inversion layer at point x with respect to the bulk, as in Sec. 4.4. The voltage drop across a piece of the inversion layer (say, of length Δx) is equal to the difference ΔV_{CB} between the V_{CB} values at the two ends of the piece. Letting the above finite differences become differentials, we have, for the magnitude of the field intensity at point x,

$$|\mathcal{E}_x(x)| = \frac{dV_{CB}}{dx} \qquad (5.3.4)$$

Thus the magnitude of the electron velocity at point x becomes, from (5.3.3),

$$|v_d(x)| = |v_d|_{max} \frac{(1/\mathscr{E}_c)(dV_{CB}/dx)}{1 + (1/\mathscr{E}_c)(dV_{CB}/dx)} \tag{5.3.5a}$$

or, using (5.3.2):

$$|v_d(x)| = \mu \frac{dV_{CB}/dx}{1 + (1/\mathscr{E}_c)(dV_{CB}/dx)} \tag{5.3.5b}$$

To calculate the drain current in nonsaturation I_{DN}, we cannot use (4.4.12) anymore. That equation was based on (1.3.15), which was derived by assuming $|v_d|$ was proportional to $|\mathscr{E}_x|$. Since this is not the case anymore, we will use the more general expression (1.3.7). For the MOS transistor, Q' is the inversion layer charge per unit area Q'_I, the value of which depends on $V_{CB}(x)$ and will be denoted by $Q'_I[V_{CB}(x)]$, and b is the channel width W. Thus

$$I_{DN} = W(-Q'_I)|v_d(x)| \tag{5.3.6}$$

Using (5.3.5b) in (5.3.6) we obtain

$$I_{DN}\left(1 + \frac{1}{\mathscr{E}_c} \frac{dV_{CB}}{dx}\right) = \mu W(-Q'_I) \frac{dV_{CB}}{dx} \tag{5.3.7}$$

Integrating from $x = 0$ (where $V_{CB} = V_{SB}$) to $x = L$ (where $V_{CB} = V_{DB}$), and assuming μ is independent of the transversal field as in Sec 4.4, we obtain

$$I_{DN}\left(L + \frac{V_{DB} - V_{SB}}{\mathscr{E}_c}\right) = \mu W \int_{V_{SB}}^{V_{DB}} (-Q'_I)\, dV_{CB} \tag{5.3.8}$$

Using $V_{DB} - V_{SB} = V_{DS}$, we have

$$I_{DN} = \frac{W}{L} \frac{\mu}{1 + V_{DS}/(L\mathscr{E}_c)} \int_{V_{SB}}^{V_{DB}} (-Q'_I)\, dV_{CB} \tag{5.3.9}$$

Comparing now this equation to (4.4.13), with μ assumed constant, we see that they are identical except for the multiplicative factor $1/[1 + V_{DS}/(L\mathscr{E}_c)]$ *outside* the integral. Consequently, all nonsaturation region expressions developed so far, starting from (4.4.13), can be made to be valid in the presence of velocity saturation effects by multiplying them with this factor. Thus

$$I_{DN, \text{ including velocity saturation}} = \frac{I_{DN, \text{ not counting velocity saturation}}}{1 + V_{DS}/(L\mathscr{E}_c)} \tag{5.3.10}$$

In the right-hand side of this equation one can use the accurate model of (4.4.17), the approximate model of (4.4.25), or any other model at hand, depending on the accuracy desired.

Example 5.2. Using the approximate model of (4.4.30a) in (5.3.10), we have for the current in the presence of velocity saturation effects,

$$I_D = \frac{W}{L} \frac{\mu C'_{ox}[(V_{GS} - V_T)V_{DS} - 0.5(1 + \delta)V_{DS}^2]}{1 + V_{DS}/(L\mathscr{E}_c)}, \qquad V_{DS} \leq V'_{DS} \tag{5.3.11}$$

The effect of normal field (Sec. 4.8) can also be incorporated in the above formulation. Assuming independence between mobility and saturation velocity,[44] one can replace μ in (5.3.1) and (5.3.2) by (4.8.9), and rederive I_{DN} using the approximations suggested in Sec. 4.8. One then obtains again the above expressions, only with μ replaced by the effective mobility μ_{eff} given by (4.8.14) or (4.8.18). Other approaches[26] give similar results.

The I_D expressions developed as shown above can easily be seen to attain zero slope dI_D/dV_{DS} at a V_{DS} value *smaller* than that found in the absence of velocity saturation effects. This suggests the following simplifying assumption, the validity of which will be considered shortly: the "saturation" of I_D-V_{DS} curves will be assumed to be attained purely owing to velocity saturation effects. Thus, the value V'_{DS} of V_{DS} at which saturation occurs can be found by solving $dI_D/dV_{DS} = 0$ as before.†

Example 5.3. For the model of Example 5.2 we have, setting dI_D/dV_{DS} equal to zero and solving (Prob. 5.7),

$$V'_{DS} = L\mathscr{E}_c \left[\sqrt{1 + \frac{2(V_{GS} - V_T)}{(1 + \delta)L\mathscr{E}_c}} - 1 \right] \qquad (5.3.12)$$

This value is smaller than the value of $(V_{GS} - V_T)/(1 + \delta)$ expected in the absence of velocity saturation effects. It only approaches that value as $L\mathscr{E}_c$ approaches infinity, i.e., in the absence of velocity saturation effects in the limit (Prob. 5.7).

In the saturation region $(V_{DS} > V'_{DS})$, the inclusion of channel length modulation effects is necessary. Continuing our simplifying assumptions from above, we postulate that in the channel region adjacent to the drain, where $V_{DS} - V'_{DS}$ is dropped, the electron density is small. Then the width ΔL of this region can be found as in Sec. 5.2 by using (5.2.1), and, again, we will allow ϕ_D to be an empirical parameter. Thus the drain current in saturation can be found from (5.2.5) and (5.2.6), as before, and I'_D in that formulation is the value of I_D at $V_{DS} = V'_{DS}$, where V'_{DS} is found as explained above. The value of V'_{DS} can be replaced by a slightly lower value V^*_{DS} to allow continuity of the slope dI_D/dV_{DS}, as has been already discussed in conjunction with Fig. 5.3c.

In Ref. 36, the saturation region is at first investigated without making the simplifying assumptions above. Simplifications are then sought, using two-dimensional computer simulations as a guide. The final result consists of the same form of equations as the ones we found above, and these are shown to be in satisfactory agreement with experimental results.

Velocity saturation effects can have a drastic influence on I_D-V_{DS} characteristics. Figure 5.5 compares results calculated, assuming such effects are

---

† Alternatively, one can equate (5.3.11) evaluated at $V_{DS} = V'_{DS}$, to (5.3.6) evaluated at the drain with $|v_d(L)| = |v_d|_{max}$, and solve for V'_{DS}. The result will be the same. A more exact calculation[36] aided by numerical simulation results, leads to a complicated expression for V'_{DS} which, however, results in practically the same value as the approach suggested here.

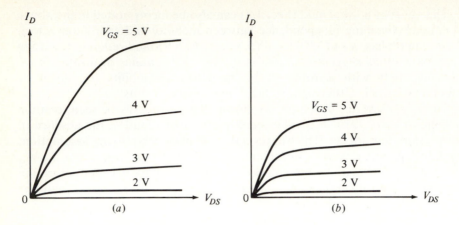

FIGURE 5.5
Device characteristics (*a*) in the absence and (*b*) in the presence of velocity saturation effects.

absent (Fig. 5.5*a*) and present (Fig. 5.5*b*). It is seen that, for the same V_{GS}, saturation is achieved at smaller values of V_{DS} when velocity saturation is included. Most importantly, in that case the spacing of the curves in the saturation region is *not* according to the "square law" of (4.4.30*b*). In fact, if the velocity saturation effects are severe, the spacing becomes nearly proportional to the V_{GS} increment, as is the case in Fig. 5.5*b*. We now have a device the saturation current of which depends almost *linearly* on $V_{GS} - V_T$! This can be seen from the equations in Examples 5.2 and 5.3. The effects of saturation velocity become stronger as L is decreased. V'_{DS} decreases with decreasing L, although not as fast as L itself. The saturation current, neglecting channel length modulation, will be given by (5.3.11) with $V_{DS} = V'_{DS}$. Under the assumption of very small L (small V'_{DS}), we can neglect the square term in the numerator of that expression and the term 1 in the denominator; thus,

$$I'_D \approx \frac{\mu C'_{ox} (W/L)(V_{GS} - V_T)V'_{DS}}{V'_{DS}/(L\mathscr{E}_c)}, \qquad \text{very small } L \qquad (5.3.13a)$$

$$\approx WC'_{ox}(V_{GS} - V_T)\mu\mathscr{E}_c, \qquad \text{very small } L \qquad (5.3.13b)$$

The linear dependence of I_D on $V_{GS} - V_T$ is apparent. We can put this relation in an alternative form by postulating that, since $V_{DS} = V'_{DS}$ is small, the channel charge will be approximately uniform and independent of x, so that we have $-Q'_I \approx C'_{ox}(V_{GS} - V_T)$ at any point x. Using this fact and using (5.3.2) in (5.3.13*b*), we have

$$I'_D \approx W(-Q'_I)|v_d|_{max} \qquad (5.3.14)$$

which could have been obtained directly from (5.3.6), assuming the carriers are traveling at maximum velocity.

The above two relations also reveal another major effect in the limit of very strong velocity saturation: *The drain current is independent of L!* A physical feeling for this effect can be obtained as follows. The transit time of carriers in the channel (the time it takes them to travel the length of the channel) is proportional to L, assuming for simplicity that they travel at constant maximum velocity. The total mobile charge in the channel is also proportional to L. Hence the current, which is the ratio of this charge to the transit time, is independent of L. To put it another way, if the distribution of mobile charge is uniform and that charge moves at constant velocity, a fixed amount of charge passes per unit time for a given W. Thus the drain current is also fixed. The length of the channel does not enter in this reasoning at all, provided, of course, that L is small enough so that the velocity saturation effect assumed is valid in the first place.

The approximations used in the preceding three paragraphs are actually oversimplified since, when the channel length is small, the two-dimensional field near the source and drain regions can have an important influence on the channel charge, as discussed in the following section. The above discussion is, nevertheless, useful for providing intuition and for relating several of the results we have presented. Note that, because $|v_d|_{max}$ has similar values for electrons and holes,[43] n-channel and p-channel devices tend to perform similarly under velocity saturation, other things being equal. This is not the case under normal operation, since then I_D is proportional to μ, the value of which for p-channel devices is one-half to one-fourth the corresponding value for n-channel devices.

5.4 BARRIER LOWERING, TWO-DIMENSIONAL CHARGE SHARING, AND THRESHOLD VOLTAGE

5.4.1 Introduction

The small-channel effects to be considered in this section are of such a nature that they can be approximately described by the equations developed so far, provided that in them the threshold voltage is replaced by another quantity, called the *effective threshold voltage*. This quantity will be seen to be dependent on channel length, channel width, source-substrate voltage, and drain-source voltage.[49-88] We will initially consider the cases of short channels and of narrow channels separately.

5.4.2 Short Channel Devices

Let us review some of our assumptions for a *long*-channel device, shown in Fig. 5.6a; for simplicity, we are assuming here $V_{DS} = 0$. Neglecting the edge effects, as we have done so far, is equivalent to assuming that the situation between source and drain is the same as one would have with the source and drain removed, as shown in Fig. 5.6b, but with the channel somehow still

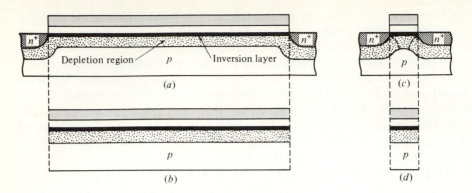

FIGURE 5.6
(a) A long-channel transistor; (b) the channel of (a) with edge effects neglected; (c) a short-channel transistor; (d) the channel of (c) with edge effects neglected.

communicating with the external world. Calculating Q'_I and then I_D by using this assumption provides accurate results as long as the value of L is large. Consider now a short-channel device, as shown in Fig. 5.6c, made with the same process and biased with the same terminal voltages as the long-channel device. Here the edge effects practically extend over all of the channel. Neglecting these effects amounts to viewing the device as shown in Fig. 5.6d, which can hardly be expected to provide credible results. Indeed, assume a very small but nonzero V_{DS}, so that drain current can flow without appreciably disturbing the picture in the channel in Fig. 5.6c. It has been found experimentally that the V_{GS} value required to produce a given I_D value is smaller than what would have been expected from the picture in Fig. 5.6d, as shown in Fig. 5.7. To get some intuitive feeling for the reasons behind this, one can use a number of viewpoints found in the literature. One of these uses the concept of

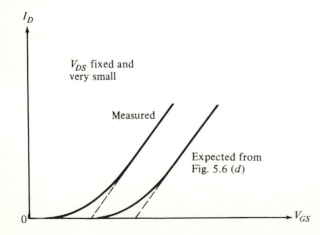

FIGURE 5.7
Drain current vs. gate-source voltage for very small, fixed drain-source voltage.

barrier lowering,[60, 66] referring to the following. The effect of decreasing L is to deplete more of the region under the inversion layer; this is easily visualized if the source and drain are imagined to approach one another as shown in Fig. 5.6c. The deeper depletion region is accompanied by a larger surface potential,† which makes the channel more attractive for electrons. Thus the device can conduct more current than what would be predicted from long-channel theory for a given V_{GS}. Since, in long-channel theory, the drain current is an increasing function of $V_{GS} - V_T$, the long-channel equations may be made to describe artificially the current increase if V_T is replaced by a smaller quantity $\hat{V}_T$, which will be called the *effective threshold*. This quantity is a decreasing function of L. For devices with channels of the order of 1 μm, $\hat{V}_T$ can be smaller than V_T by several tenths of 1 V. Notice that in the short-channel device of Fig. 5.6c the depletion region under the channel can also be widened, and the corresponding surface potential can be increased, by raising the potential of the drain; this will further increase I_D above the value expected from other considerations. Hence, the effective threshold $\hat{V}_T$ need also be made a decreasing function of V_{DS}. Unfortunately, it is not easy to come up with simple analytical results by using the barrier-lowering concept.

An alternative description goes as follows. The situation in the channel region is influenced by field lines emanating from nearby structures. Two such structures considered in the analysis of long-channel devices are, of course, the gate and the substrate ("back gate"). In short-channel devices the source and drain are so close to all points in the channel that they can affect the latter through their proximity just as the gate does. In effect, the source and drain now play something of a gate role in addition to their normal function. Now field lines emanating from all four structures (gate, bulk, source, and drain) and terminating on points in the channel must be considered for an accurate description of the device. Bringing the source and drain regions closer to all points in the channel is similar to bringing the gate closer to the channel. The corresponding increase in drain current, however, is not predicted by long-channel theory and is modeled instead by using an effective threshold, as explained above. Also, increasing the drain potential increases the inversion layer charge just as increasing the gate potential would. The above picture again leads us to expect an effective threshold which decreases with decreasing L and increasing V_{DS}.

A third related viewpoint which has provided the basis for most of the analytical/empirical models for short-channel devices uses the idea of "charge sharing."[49–53, 57–59, 61–65, 67, 70–74, 78–80, 82, 83, 85–88] We will describe this idea below. But first we should warn the reader that charge-sharing models have

---

† In an energy band formulation, an increase in surface potential corresponds to a decrease in the potential energy for electrons. The potential energy "barrier" to the entrance of electrons in the channel is lowered, hence the name *barrier lowering* is used to describe these phenomena.

been developed with the aim to obtain simple semiempirical expressions for describing very complex two-dimensional phenomena; in such development, *it has not been possible to justify rigorously all steps.* To begin, let us assume that the equivalent interface charge Q'_o is zero for simplicity. In Figs. 5.6*c* and *d*, it can be imagined that one field line emanates from each positive charge q on the gate. Such a field line terminates either on an electron in the inversion layer or on an ionized acceptor in the depletion region, neglecting the "fringing" field lines terminating on the n^+ regions. In Fig. 5.6*d*, all of the depletion region charges are "imaged" on gate charges through connecting field lines. In the more realistic picture of Fig. 5.6*c*, however, this is not the case. Some of the field lines terminating on ionized acceptor atoms near the n^+ regions can be originating from ionized donor atoms in the n^+ regions (inside a thin depletion layer there). Thus, only part of the depletion region charge is imaged on the gate charge in this case. If we can assume the gate charge in *c* and *d* is the same, some gate charges cannot be imaged on depletion charges, and more of them are available to be imaged on inversion layer charges, which must, thus, increase to accept the extra field lines. The extra I_D observed is attributed to this extra inversion layer charge, although, strictly speaking, one would have to know the spatial distribution of that charge before such a conclusion could be reached. A number of arbitrary assumptions are obviously involved in the above arguments (Prob. 5.10). Some of these assumptions are critically considered elsewhere.[75, 82]

Next, a large empirical step is taken: The short-channel device is assumed to behave as a fictitious device with a uniform depletion region, but with an effective depletion region charge $\hat{Q}_B$, which has a smaller magnitude than the corresponding quantity Q_B in Fig. 5.6*d*. Because $\hat{Q}_B$ and Q_B are defined for devices with uniform depletion regions and equal gate areas, we will have $\hat{Q}'_B/Q'_B = \hat{Q}_B/Q_B$, where the primes denote quantities per unit area. The above assumption for an effective charge $\hat{Q}_B$ then implies that, instead of the long-channel threshold given by (3.4.22),

$$V_T = V_{FB} + \phi_B - \frac{Q'_B}{C'_{ox}} \tag{5.4.1a}$$

$$= V_{FB} + \phi_B + \gamma\sqrt{\phi_B + V_{SB}} \tag{5.4.1b}$$

we will have an effective threshold given by

$$\hat{V}_T = V_{FB} + \phi_B - \frac{\hat{Q}'_B}{C'_{ox}} \tag{5.4.2a}$$

$$= V_{FB} + \phi_B + \frac{\hat{Q}_B}{Q_B}\gamma\sqrt{\phi_B + V_{SB}} \tag{5.4.2b}$$

We thus see that the above charge-sharing effect can be viewed as resulting in an effective decrease of the body effect coefficient by the factor $\hat{Q}_B/Q_B$. This may make sense intuitively since, in a short channel device, the substrate's control on the channel is reduced, as expected from Fig. 5.6c, and much of the channel is controlled by the gate, the source, and the drain. However, defining $(\hat{Q}_B/Q_B)\gamma$ as the new body effect "coefficient" is not very practical, since $(\hat{Q}_B/Q_B)$ is itself a function of V_{SB}, as we will see.

From the above equations we can write

$$\hat{V}_T = V_T - \Delta V_T \tag{5.4.3}$$

where ΔV_T is the "threshold reduction" due to the short channel effect, given by

$$\Delta V_T = \left(1 - \frac{\hat{Q}_B}{Q_B}\right)\gamma\sqrt{\phi_B + V_{SB}} \tag{5.4.4}$$

The meaning of ΔV_T is illustrated in Fig. 5.8. Note that the V_{SB} dependence of ΔV_T in (5.4.4) does not include the total effect of V_{SB} on $\hat{V}_T$. For a given V_{SB}, one must first find V_T for a long-channel device and then reduce it by the corresponding ΔV_T to arrive at the value of $\hat{V}_T$. The value of $\hat{V}_T$ obtained in this way is widely used in lieu of V_T in long-channel equations, such as (4.4.30). There is a large amount of literature on how $\hat{V}_T$ should be calculated, but practically nothing on why one has the right to use this value in long-channel equations for the drain current (derived by using the gradual-channel approximation) and expect the result to be correct for short-channel devices. The issue is not just what value of threshold voltage should be used in such equations when modeling short-channel devices, but rather why the very *form* of such equations should be valid for short channel devices in the first place. The author has not seen a convincing argument in this regard. However, satisfactory agreement with measurement has led to wide use of the aforementioned approach.

Of the many techniques proposed for determining the quantity $\hat{Q}_B/Q_B$, let us consider one as an example.[53] The n^+-region edges will be assumed cylindrical with radius r equal to the junction depth, as shown in Fig. 5.9a.

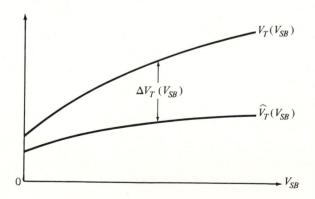

FIGURE 5.8
Threshold voltage of long-channel transistor, V_T, effective threshold voltage of short-channel transistor with a given channel length, $\hat{V}_T$, and difference between the two, ΔV_T, all as a function of V_{SB}.

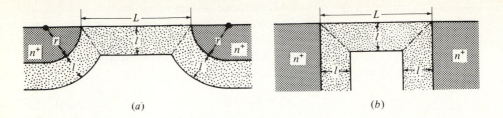

(a)   (b)

FIGURE 5.9
(a) Trapezoid approximation used for deriving the effective bulk charge; (b) the limiting case of
(a) for very deep n^+ regions.

Next, the depletion regions around each of them and below the inversion layer
are drawn as if each existed by itself (i.e., no interaction is assumed), and then
they are joined together. The width of all three regions is considered equal by
assuming that the junction built-in potential ϕ_o is equal to ϕ_B; thus, this width
is, from (3.4.18),

$$l = \zeta\sqrt{\phi_B + V_{SB}} \tag{5.4.5a}$$

with

$$\zeta = \sqrt{\frac{2\epsilon_s}{qN_A}} \tag{5.4.5b}$$

In this picture, L is assumed to be at least large enough so that a region
of trapezoidal cross section can be defined as shown in Fig. 5.9a. $\hat{Q}_B$ is taken to
be equal to the charge in that region and Q_B is assumed to be the charge
corresponding to a rectangle of the same depth and length L. Simple geometry
then gives (Prob. 5.11):

$$\frac{\hat{Q}_B}{Q_B} = 1 - \frac{r}{L}\left(\sqrt{1 + \frac{2l}{r}} - 1\right) \tag{5.4.6}$$

$\hat{V}_T$ and ΔV_T can now be found from (5.4.2b) and (5.4.4) to (5.4.6). If L is
too small, the trapezoid in Fig. 5.9a becomes a triangle; this case is considered
in Prob. 5.12.

For some practical applications the above formulation is too complicated.
It has been suggested that for approximate calculations the quantity in parenthesis in (5.4.6) can be approximated by using a Taylor expansion and
neglecting the high-order terms,[59] resulting in (Prob. 5.11):

$$\frac{\hat{Q}_B}{Q_B} = 1 - \frac{l}{L} \tag{5.4.7}$$

This expansion will be more accurate if l/r is small. Negligible l/r
corresponds to Fig. 5.9b, for which (5.4.7) can easily be obtained directly.
Since, for larger values of l/r, the expression can be in considerable error, we

will help expand its region of validity by introducing an empirical constant:

$$\frac{\hat{Q}_B}{Q_B} = 1 - \alpha_1 \frac{l}{L} \tag{5.4.8}$$

where nominally $\alpha_1 = 1$, but we will allow for adjusting this parameter to obtain best overall fit in a given region of parameter variations.† Using this equation and (5.4.5) in (5.4.2b), we obtain

$$\hat{V}_T = V_{FB} + \phi_B + \gamma\sqrt{\phi_B + V_{SB}}\left(1 - \frac{\alpha_1 \zeta}{L}\sqrt{\phi_B + V_{SB}}\right) \tag{5.4.9}$$

The factor in parentheses can be thought of as an effective reduction in the body effect coefficient. As expected, this reduction is more severe for smaller L. The behavior predicted by the above equation is illustrated in Fig. 5.10. It is seen that, for short channels and large V_{SB}, the dependence of the effective threshold on V_{SB} diminishes. This is because the factor in parentheses in (5.4.9) becomes very small. Physically, this corresponds to the fact that the lower base of the trapezoid in Fig. 5.9 diminishes in length. The bottom of the trapezoid is then practically cut off from the rest of the substrate, and, thus, the control of the substrate on the charge inside the trapezoid is small (Prob. 5.12).

A calculation of the reduction ΔV_T corresponding to the above effects is illuminating. Using (5.4.5) and (5.4.8) in (5.4.4), and recalling that $\gamma = (2q\epsilon_s N_A)^{1/2}/C'_{ox}$, with $C'_{ox} = \epsilon_{ox}/d_{ox}$, we obtain

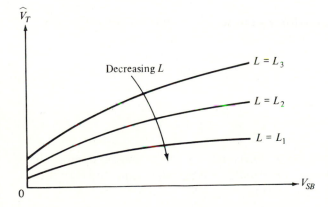

FIGURE 5.10
Effective threshold voltage as a function of source-substrate bias for various channel lengths.

---

† The same can be done with ϕ_B. Recall that the value of this parameter was somewhat ambiguous even for long-channel devices (see Secs. 2.5.2 and 4.13). Thus, although the value of $2\phi_F$ is widely used for ϕ_B, better results can be obtained if one allows ϕ_B to be chosen empirically. Given the heavily empirical nature of the charge-sharing model we are discussing, this is especially advisable.

$$\Delta V_T = 2\alpha_1 \frac{\epsilon_s}{\epsilon_{ox}} \frac{d_{ox}}{L} (\phi_B + V_{SB}) \tag{5.4.10}$$

From this equation it is clear that the channel length and the oxide thickness have a competing role. Although decreasing L tends to increase the short-channel effect, decreasing d_{ox} tends to decrease it. This is because then the gate is closer to the channel and is thus better able to keep control of the depletion region charge (as opposed to releasing this control to the other structures surrounding the channel).

Good agreement has been reported between (5.4.9) and (5.4.10) and experimental results, with $\alpha_1 = 1$.[59] However, other work has produced models equivalent to taking α_1 proportional to a negative power of L,[67] or even replacing α_1/L by a negative exponential in L.[68, 73]

EFFECT OF DRAIN-SOURCE VOLTAGE. The above results have been derived for negligible V_{DS}. For fixed V_{SB}, if V_{DS} (and thus V_{DB}) is increased, the depletion region width around the drain will widen. This, in turn, following the lines of the above arguments, will decrease $|\hat{Q}_B|$ below the values obtained so far, thus further decreasing $\hat{V}_T$. Thus, for short-channel devices, $\hat{V}_T$ becomes a decreasing function of V_{DS}! The effective charge $\hat{Q}_B$ is still calculated using a method similar to the one illustrated in Fig. 5.9a, only now the trapezoid there will become distorted. The resulting expression is considered in Prob. 5.15. If r is large and certain simplifications are made (Prob. 5.15), we can obtain

$$\frac{\hat{Q}_B}{Q_B} = 1 - \alpha_1 \frac{1}{L} \frac{l_S + l_D}{2} \tag{5.4.11}$$

where l_S and l_D are the depletion region widths of the source and the drain, respectively, and α_1 is again an empirical constant, nominally equal to 1. Note that for $V_{DS} = 0$ ($l_D = l_S = l$), the above equation reduces to (5.4.8). The quantity $(l_S + l_D)/2$ is, from (5.4.5a) and a similar equation for the drain depletion region,

$$\frac{l_S + l_D}{2} = \frac{\zeta}{2} (\sqrt{\phi_B + V_{SB}} + \sqrt{\phi_B + V_{DB}}) \tag{5.4.12}$$

We can write $V_{DB} = V_{SB} + V_{DS}$. For small V_{DS}, the second square root can be expanded in a Taylor series around $V_{DS} = 0$ and approximated by the first two terms; this results in (Prob. 5.15):

$$\frac{l_S + l_D}{2} = \zeta \left(\sqrt{\phi_B + V_{SB}} + \frac{\alpha_2 V_{DS}}{\sqrt{\phi_B + V_{SB}}} \right) \tag{5.4.13}$$

where $\alpha_2 = 0.25$ results from the expansion. To increase the region of validity of this expression, however, we will allow for empirical adjustment of α_2. Using now (5.4.13), (5.4.11), and (5.4.2b), we obtain,

$$\hat{V}_T = V_{FB} + \phi_B + \gamma\sqrt{\phi_B + V_{SB}} \left[1 - \frac{\alpha_1 \zeta}{L} \left(\sqrt{\phi_B + V_{SB}} + \frac{\alpha_2 V_{DS}}{\sqrt{\phi_B + V_{SB}}} \right) \right]$$

(5.4.14)

and thus

$$\Delta V_T = 2\alpha_1 \frac{\epsilon_s}{\epsilon_{ox}} \frac{d_{ox}}{L} [(\phi_B + V_{SB}) + \alpha_2 V_{DS}]$$

(5.4.15)

Although this expression was derived by using the charge-sharing idea, it predicts a variation V_T with V_{DS} in the same direction as considerations using the barrier-lowering concept[60, 66] discussed in the beginning of this section. (The name *drain-induced barrier lowering* is used to describe the effect of the drain on the barrier.[66]) Also, although the above expressions were obtained based on the assumption of small V_{DS}, in practice it is often found that their form happens to be valid even for relatively large V_{DS} ranges, provided an appropriate value is chosen for α_2. This value will be different for different L; in fact, for some devices it has been found that α_2 is roughly proportional to $1/L$.[36] To explain such behavior, one should consider a more detailed picture in which the field lines emanating from the drain do not only affect the channel charge near the drain but rather affect it throughout the channel length. Two-dimensional numerical simulations are needed to get quantitative results in this case.[77]

It is important to note here that the effect of the drain on the channel depletion region charge, resulting in (5.4.15), continues even beyond pinchoff. Thus, even if channel length modulation is neglected, I_D in the saturation region will not saturate. It will continue to increase as V_{DS} is increased, since $\hat{V}_T$ will keep decreasing by the amount in (5.4.15). This is discussed further in Sec. 5.5. Note, also, that a device which has been turned off by reducing V_{GS} sufficiently below V_T, may turn on just by increasing V_{DS} if $\hat{V}_T$ is lowered enough by the above mentioned effect. This can have a serious effect in some digital applications if not properly considered.

The onsets of moderate and of strong inversion, V_M and V_H, stay close to V_T and follow qualitatively a similar dependence on L, V_{SB}, and V_{DS}. To a first order, short-channel effects can then be thought of as a shift in the I_D-V_{GS} curves to lower V_{GS} values, with the shift being approximately equal to ΔV_T. Thus, ΔV_T can be estimated from measuring the shift in what is called the *constant-current threshold*, which is defined as the V_{GS} value needed to reach a fixed, agreed upon value of $I_D/(W/L)$. With such a value taken in weak inversion, measured results for constant-current threshold are shown in Fig. 5.11 for various values of L, V_{SB}, and V_{DS}.[60] These results show qualitatively the same behavior as the one predicted previously for the extrapolated threshold (Prob. 5.16). Note, though, that one should not confuse the two thresholds and expect them to have the same value. A discussion of the confusion that can arise from the indiscriminate use of the term "threshold" for various different quantities has been given in Sec. 4.13.

Let us now briefly look at the current in weak inversion. Assuming

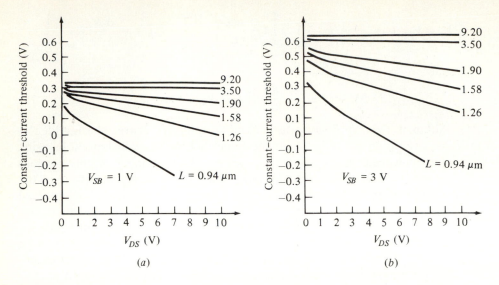

FIGURE 5.11
Measured constant-current threshold (with the constant current taken in weak inversion) vs. V_{DS}, with L as a parameter.[60] (a) $V_{SB} = 1$ V; (b) $V_{SB} = 3$ V. $N_A = 7 \times 10^3$ μm^{-3}, $d_{ox} = 0.037$ μm.

(4.6.17) holds, if V_X is shifted by ΔV_X due to short-channel effects we see that

$$I_{D, \text{ short channel}} = I_{D, \text{ long channel}}\, e^{\Delta V_X/(n\phi_t)}, \qquad \text{weak inversion} \quad (5.4.16)$$

Assuming $\Delta V_X = \Delta V_T$ and using (5.4.15), it is clear that, in short-channel devices, I_D will depend on V_{DS} for any value of the latter; in other words, no real leveling off of I_D will be observed. This is verified by experimental results.[38, 61, 64, 66] Thus, the long-channel weak-inversion theory of Sec. 4.6 has been "stretched" to hold in the case of short channels by using (5.4.16). However, if the channel becomes very short, even this relation will eventually fail. In such cases, the slope of log I_D becomes very small, and the device cannot be turned off adequately even if V_{GS} is decreased significantly.† This behavior is predicted by two-dimensional simulations (see also the discussion of the "punchthrough" effect in Sec. 5.6). Experimental results[86] are shown in Fig. 5.12a. One might expect that it should be possible to eliminate the undesirable behavior for very short channels by increasing N_A, since then the source and drain depletion region widths will decrease, as predicted by (5.4.5). Indeed, raising N_A ten times leads to the results in Fig. 5.12b. Here it is also interesting to note that for the long-channel curve (7 μm) the current does not depend on V_{DS}, just as is expected from long-channel theory for weak-

---

† A parameter used to indicate the degree of difficulty in turning a transistor off is the gate swing S, defined[38] as the change in V_{GS} needed to reduce the weak-inversion current by a factor of 10.

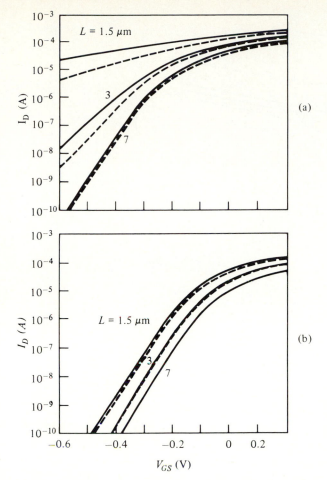

FIGURE 5.12
Measured I_D (log axis) vs. V_{GS} for various channel lengths.[86] $d_{ox} = 0.013 \ \mu\text{m}$, $V_{SB} = 0$. Solid lines: $V_{DS} = 1.0 \ \text{V}$, broken lines: $V_{DS} = 0.5 \ \text{V}$. (*a*) $N_A = 10^2 \ \mu\text{m}^{-3}$; (*b*) $N_A = 10^3 \ \mu\text{m}^{-3}$.

inversion and $V_{DS} > 3\phi_t$. However, a V_{DS} dependence is apparent for shorter channel lengths, as may be expected from (5.4.14) or (5.4.15).

With considerable computational complexity, it is possible to develop short-channel models that continuously describe the drain current in all regions of operation.[74, 80, 88]

5.4.3 Narrow-Channel Devices

A cross section of a device's channel along its *width* is shown in Fig. 5.13*a*. This figure is drawn highly idealized for simplicity. A real device may, for some fabrication processes, look as in Fig. 5.13*b*. A thick oxide becomes gradually thinner, giving rise to the characteristic shape shown, referred to as *bird's beak* (Chap. 10). As seen from either figure, the depletion region is not limited to just the area directly below the thin oxide. This is because some of the field lines emanating from the gate charges terminate on ionized acceptor atoms on

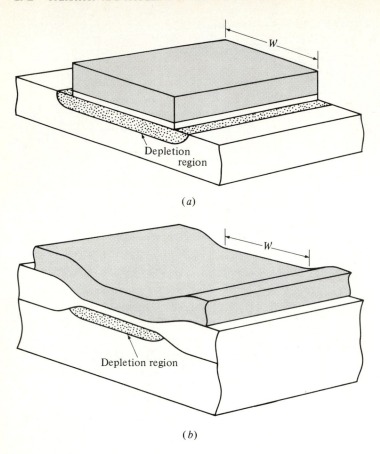

(a)

(b)

FIGURE 5.13
Effect of fringing field on spreading the depletion region sideways. (*a*) Simplified picture; (*b*) realistic picture for a device with bird's beak (Chap. 10).

the sides. These lines constitute what is called a *fringing field*. If W is large, the part of the depletion region on the sides is a small percentage of the total depletion region volume and can be neglected. However, with W values of only a few micrometers, the side parts become a large percentage of the total. In contrast to the short-channel case, now the gate is responsible for depleting a region which is *larger* than what our theory in Chap. 4 would predict[54-56, 59, 62, 70, 74, 76-81, 83, 85-87] (a long channel is assumed in this discussion). Thus, it takes a higher V_{GS} value to deplete that amount before an inversion layer can be formed, and V_M, V_H and V_T must be replaced by *larger*, "effective quantities." In addition, an increase in V_{SB}, while keeping V_{GS} constant, increases $|Q_B|$ both under the gate and in the side parts, and, thus, the body effect will be more pronounced than in the wide-channel case. Assuming again $V_{DS} = 0$ and using an empirical approach similar to that in the previous subsection, an effective depletion region charge $\hat{Q}_{B1}$ can be employed. This will result in an effective threshold $\hat{V}_T$ given by

$$\hat{V}_T = V_{FB} + \phi_B + \frac{\hat{Q}_{B1}}{Q_B} \gamma \sqrt{\phi_B + V_{SB}} \tag{5.4.17}$$

which corresponds to (5.4.2b), only here $\hat{Q}_{B1}/Q_B$ is *larger* than unity. Thus, compared to the long- and wide-channel threshold V_T given by (5.4.1b), we have here a threshold *increase*:

$$\hat{V}_T = V_T + \Delta V_{T1} \tag{5.4.18}$$

with
$$\Delta V_{T1} = \left(\frac{\hat{Q}_{B1}}{Q_B} - 1 \right) \gamma \sqrt{\phi_B + V_{SB}} \tag{5.4.19}$$

One of the ways suggested for the empirical evaluation of $\hat{Q}_B/Q_B$ uses the simplified picture of Fig. 5.13a and assumes that the side parts of the depletion region have a quarter-circle cross-section.[59] This gives, assuming negligibly small V_{DS} (Prob. 5.17),

$$\frac{\hat{Q}_B}{Q_B} = 1 + \alpha_3 \frac{\pi}{2} \frac{l}{W} \tag{5.4.20}$$

where l is the depth of the depletion region given by (5.4.5), and $\alpha_3 = 1$ nominally. As usual, α_3 has been introduced as an empirical parameter which can be adjusted for best fit. Comparing the simplified and "real" pictures in Fig. 5.13, it is rather obvious that such an empirical adjustment is necessary. Using (5.4.20) and (5.4.5) in (5.4.17) we obtain the corresponding effective threshold $\hat{V}_T$:

$$\hat{V}_T = V_{FB} + \phi_B + \gamma \sqrt{\phi_B + V_{SB}} \left(1 + \frac{\alpha_3 \zeta \pi}{2W} \sqrt{\phi_B + V_{SB}} \right) \tag{5.4.21}$$

and, using the above and (5.4.1b) in (5.4.18), with $\gamma = (2q\epsilon_s N_A)^{1/2}/C'_{ox}$ and $C'_{ox} = \epsilon_{ox}/d_{ox}$,

$$\Delta V_{T1} = \alpha_3 \pi \frac{\epsilon_s}{\epsilon_{ox}} \frac{d_{ox}}{W} (\phi_B + V_{SB}) \tag{5.4.22}$$

This equation is in agreement with our intuitive picture above. Values of several tenths of 1 V are typical for ΔV_{T1} for channel widths of the order of 1 μm. The quantity ΔV_{T1} does not include the total dependence of $\hat{V}_T$ on V_{SB}. V_T must be first found for the wide-channel case for a known V_{SB} and then augmented by ΔV_{T1}. Note that ΔV_{T1} in the *narrow*-channel device represents an *increase*, whereas the quantity ΔV_T used in the discussion of *short*-channel devices represents a *decrease*. The opposite behavior of narrow-channel and short-channel devices is illustrated in Figs. 5.14, 5.15, and 5.16. The value of V_T for devices with small W (but large L) is commonly assumed independent of V_{DS}. [The above arguments would tend to predict an increase with V_{DS} (Prob.

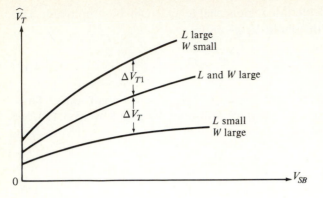

FIGURE 5.14
Effective threshold voltage vs. source-substrate bias for three combinations of channel length and width.

5.18), but no experimental verification of such an effect is known to the author.]

Depending on fabrication details, the above analysis may give satisfactory results if W is not too small. For some devices, though, it is observed that, in order to fit measured results, it is not sufficient to replace V_T by the effective threshold $\hat{V}_{T1}$ as above, and one must, in addition, replace W by an "effective channel width" $\hat{W}$. Unfortunately, to evaluate $\hat{W}$ one must resort to either measurements or to two-dimensional simulations, including the details of the so-called "channel-stop" regions (Chap. 10). Qualitatively, one observes two effects: (1) $\hat{W}$ tends to increase with increasing gate voltage, since then a wider part of the channel tends to be inverted in Fig. 5.13b. (2) $\hat{W}$ tends to decrease with V_{SB}.[87] This is because, as two-dimensional simulations show (including the channel-stop regions), the bottom of the depletion region is actually rounded, and the electric field lines in the semiconductor are perpendicular to the surface only near the center of the channel in Fig. 5.13b; toward the sides, they curve sideways. In such cases, the inversion layer on both sides of the center turns out to be lighter than expected or it practically disappears altogether there. This effect becomes stronger with increasing V_{SB}, causing a reduction in $\hat{W}$, which can be very significant for some fabrication processes.

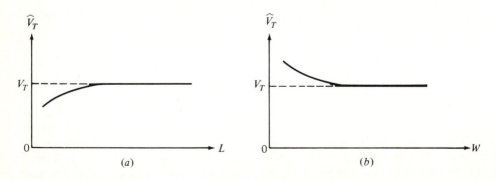

FIGURE 5.15
Effective threshold voltage vs. (a) channel length; (b) channel width.

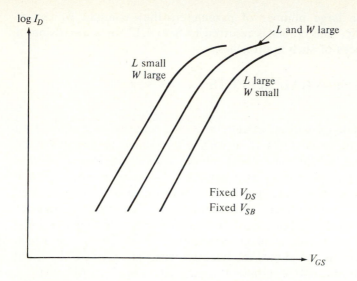

FIGURE 5.16
Log I_D vs. V_{GS} for fixed V_{DS} and V_{SB}, for three combinations of channel length and width. The straight-line part of the plots corresponds to weak inversion.

5.4.4 Summary and comments

We have seen that several factors affect the value of the effective threshold voltage. From our general expressions for long-channel devices as well as from our discussion of small-channels above, we can summarize qualitatively as follows:

The effective threshold voltage *increases* when:

1. The substrate doping *increases*.
2. The oxide thickness *increases*.
3. The channel length *increases*.
4. The channel width *decreases*.
5. The junction depth *decreases*.

The concept of effective threshold represents an attempt to maintain the form of well-known equations (derived for long- and wide-channel devices) in cases where such equations are, in principle, not valid. In this section, we have presented some representative examples of this approach taken from the literature. As explained, in this approach it has not been possible to avoid some arbitrary assumptions (or, at least, assumptions that are not carefully justified). This is typical of empirical models. Although this has often provided practical results, at times too much attention is paid to deriving elaborate models based on some arbitrary assumptions, rather than taking extra pains to consider the validity of those assumptions. The resulting models, although they may be based on inadequate assumptions, may still be able to model practical devices owing to the large number of parameters they contain, which are "adjusted" empirically. The reader is referred to Sec. 4.13 for a discussion of the potential drawbacks of such approaches.

5.5   COMBINING SEVERAL EFFECTS IN ONE MODEL

So far we have considered various effects, one at a time for simplicity. In a practical device model, however, several such effects have to be considered simultaneously. Doing so properly would require considering the *interaction* between these effects, but then, unfortunately, the expressions obtained become complicated. An empirical approach often taken, *if each effect by itself is small*, is to assume that the effects are noninteracting. For example, consider a device with a channel that is both short *and* narrow. Here three-dimensional analysis would be needed to obtain accurate results.[77] However, for rough estimates such a device is sometimes modeled by using an effective-threshold formulation, with the effective threshold $\hat{V}_T$ being given by $V_T - \Delta V_T + \Delta V_{T1}$, where V_T is the long-channel threshold, ΔV_T is the reduction assuming only short-channel effects are present, and ΔV_{T1} is the increase assuming only narrow-channel effects are present.[62] For small ΔV_T and ΔV_{T1}, this approach can be justified to some extent (Prob. 5.21).

> **Example 5.4.** As an example of a model based on the above assumption of noninteraction, let us attempt to develop drain current expressions which include the following effects:
>
> **1.** Effect of L on effective threshold
> **2.** Effect of V_{DS} on effective threshold
> **3.** Effect of W on effective threshold
> **4.** Velocity saturation effects
> **5.** Effective mobility dependence on normal field
> **6.** Channel length modulation in saturation
>
> The approach used will be a variation of one used elsewhere.[36] Effects 1, 2 and 3 will be modeled by using the following effective threshold voltage (see discussion above):
>
> $$\hat{V}_T(V_{DS}) = V_T - \Delta V_T(L, V_{DS}) + \Delta V_{T1}(W) \tag{5.5.1}$$
>
> where $\Delta V_T(L, V_{DS})$ and $\Delta V_{T1}(W)$ can be calculated as described in Sec. 5.4. Effect 4 will be modeled as in Example 5.2 (Sec. 5.3), and effect 5 will be included by using (4.8.18) [see discussion following (5.3.11)]. Thus, in the nonsaturation region we have
>
> $$I_D = \frac{\mu_0 C'_{ox} \dfrac{W}{L} \{[V_{GS} - \hat{V}_T(V_{DS})]V_{DS} - 0.5(1 + \delta)V^2_{DS}\}}{\{1 + \theta[V_{GS} - \hat{V}_T(V_{DS})] + \theta_B V_{SB}\}[1 + V_{DS}/(L\mathscr{E}_c)]} , \qquad V_{DS} \leq V'_{DS} \tag{5.5.2}$$
>
> where $\hat{V}_T(V_{DS})$ is given by (5.5.1).

The value of the pinchoff drain-source voltage V'_{DS} will be found as shown in Sec. 5.3 by setting dI_D/dV_{DS} equal to zero from (5.5.2) and neglecting the dependence of V_T on V_{DS} for this calculation. This results in (5.3.12) again. A more exact calculation results in a much more complicated expression which gives practically the same value as (5.3.12).[36]

We will now determine I_D in saturation. This requires some caution. If $\hat{V}_T$ were independent of V_{DS}, as implicitly assumed in Sec. 5.2, we could use (5.2.5), where I'_D would be given from (5.5.2) after replacing V_{DS} by V'_{DS}. In the resulting expression for I'_D, V_{DS} itself would not appear. This, of course, would be so because the channel end, being considered to be pinched off, would be assumed to be at potential V'_{DS} with respect to the source, no matter what the actual value of V_{DS}. However, here we want to include the effect of V_{DS} on $\hat{V}_T$, as explicitly indicated in (5.5.1). As already pointed out, this effect is assumed unrelated to pinchoff and is present whether V_{DS} is smaller or larger than V'_{DS}, since even for $V_{DS} > V'_{DS}$ the channel area is directly influenced by the field lines emanating from the nearby drain. Hence, even in saturation, $\hat{V}_T$ will continue to be a function of V_{DS}, *not* V'_{DS}. Accordingly, we have

$$I_D = \frac{\mu_o C'_{ox} \dfrac{W}{L} \{[V_{GS} - \hat{V}_T(V_{DS})]V'_{DS} - 0.5(1+\delta)V'^2_{DS}\}}{(1 - \Delta L/L)\{1 + \theta[V_{GS} - \hat{V}_T(V_{DS})] + \theta_B V_{SB}\}[1 + V'_{DS}/(L\mathscr{E}_c)]}$$

$$V_{DS} > V'_{DS} \qquad (5.5.3)$$

with $\Delta L/L$ given by (5.2.6). At this point one might want to argue that one should have used $L - \Delta L$ rather than L in the last factor of the denominator. However, at the present level of empirical modeling it is not worth considering this, because the difference will be small. Finally, a slight modification of the V'_{DS} value will be needed if the slope of $I_D(V_{DS})$ at $V_{DS} = V'_{DS}$ is to be continuous, as explained in Sec. 5.2 (Prob. 5.22).

The above model, with $\theta_B = 0$, has been proposed elsewhere[36] and compared to experimental results as shown in Fig. 5.17.† We prefer to allow for a nonzero θ_B for reasons discussed in Sec.4.8.

As has been seen in this section, short- and narrow-channel effects have been mostly investigated in the literature in terms of the effective threshold voltage. Thus, the usefulness of the approximate model in (4.4.30), which contains the threshold explicitly, is apparent. In contrast, the accurate model of (4.4.8) does not contain the threshold explicitly, and the results in this section cannot be used in conjunction with it in a direct manner. This has led to wide use of the approximate model for small devices.

---

† A similar model, with $\theta_B = 0$, has also been proposed in Ref. 87, but there short- and narrow-channel effects are taken into account in a cruder way: The long-channel threshold expression in (5.4.1b) is assumed, only with γ replaced by an effective body effect coefficient $\hat{\gamma}$, and an extra term representing the effect of V_{DS}:

$$V_T = V_{FB} + \phi_B + \hat{\gamma}\sqrt{\phi_B + V_{SB}} - k_D V_{DS}$$

with

$$\hat{\gamma} = \gamma - \frac{k_L}{L} + \frac{k_W}{W}$$

where k_D, k_L, and k_W are fitting parameters determined from measurements.

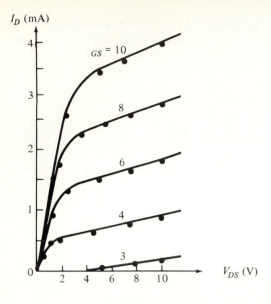

I_D (mA)

V_{DS} (V)

FIGURE 5.17
Comparison of measurements (dots) to model of Example 5.4.[36] Substrate doping concentration is between 2500 and 4300 μm^{-3}, $d_{ox} = 0.05$ μm, $W = 12$ μm, $L = 2$ μm, $V_{T0} = 1.56$ V, $V_{SB} = 5$ V.

5.6 PUNCHTHROUGH, BREAKDOWN, PARASITIC CURRENTS, AND RELATED EFFECTS

In this section we will discuss some undesirable phenomena which can disturb "normal" MOS transistor behavior.[26, 34, 38, 59, 66–69, 86, 89–115] Most of these phenomena can be predicted by two-dimensional computer simulations but do not yield themselves to simple analytical modeling. As such effects can be eliminated by proper device design (Chap. 10) and by avoiding the application of excessively large bias voltages, our discussion will be very brief. As usual, *n*-channel devices are assumed in the discussion unless stated otherwise.

The forms of breakdown discussed in Sec. 4.10 for the long-channel device (oxide breakdown, junction breakdown) occur, of course, in short-channel devices as well. However, the latter also exhibit an effect called *punchthrough*.[26, 34, 38, 59, 66–69, 86, 89–93] Punchthrough is attributed to the barrier-lowering effect we have already discussed, in which two-dimensional effects in the region between the source and drain increase the electrostatic potential there (compared to the long-channel case), thus reducing the barrier to the electrons' entering that region. A current can then flow even at gate-source voltages lower than the flat-band voltage, and, in fact, two-dimensional simulations show that this current flows in a subsurface path. [At somewhat higher gate voltages the current can flow along the surface, but then it is often considered to be part of the drain-enhanced weak-inversion current described by (5.4.16).] If the drain potential is increased, the electrostatic potential at points between source and drain will increase and, thus, the barrier to electrons will decrease, resulting in the *drain-induced barrier lowering effect*.[66] Thus the punchthrough current will increase. Experiments and two-dimensional numerical simulations show that the punchthrough current is decreased if the substrate potential is made more negative. Punchthrough effects can be decreased by reducing two-dimensional effects along the channel length. From our qualitative discussion in Sec. 5.4.2, we expect that this can be achieved with thinner oxides, larger substrate doping, shallower junctions, and, of course, longer channels [the trend is, however, to reduce constantly channel lengths to achieve higher speeds (Sec. 5.8)]. Experiments and two-dimensional simulations verify the above predictions. If one defines a *punchthrough voltage* as the drain-source voltage at which a perceptible punchthrough current is observed (e.g., 1 nA/μm of channel width), then from the above discussion it follows that the punchthrough voltage will be larger for longer channels, thinner oxides, shallower junctions, larger substrate doping, smaller gate voltage, and more negative substrate voltage. A semiempirical model has been developed to describe punchthrough, using two-dimensional numerical simulations as a guide.[93] Devices with punchthrough problems typically exhibit the behavior illustrated in Fig. 5.18. To avoid such problems, the substrate doping is increased through ion implantation below the surface (where punchthrough would normally occur), to limit the source and drain depletion regions there, thus reducing two-dimensional effects and the associated barrier lowering. The implanted region does not extend too deep, and hence the body effect and junction capacitances still correspond to the more lightly doped bulk, which is desirable. Note that the implant used for punchthrough control can be in addition to a shallow implant used to set the value of the threshold voltage (Chap. 6).

Other undesirable effects occur due to the high velocity of electrons in the presence of high longitudinal fields.[34, 38, 86, 94–115] This was already reported for long-channel devices in Sec. 4.10, but such effects can be more troublesome in short-channel devices. High-velocity electrons can generate electron-hole pairs by impact ionization and avalanche, resulting in a form of breakdown. Of

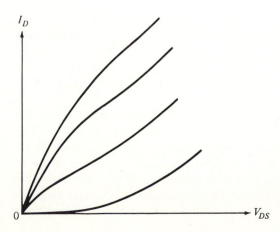

FIGURE 5.18
Typical characteristics of a device with punchthrough problems.

course, most of the electrons are normally attracted by the drain, but the holes enter the substrate and constitute part of the parasitic substrate current. This situation is further complicated by the fact that the region between source and drain can act like the base of a bipolar *npn* transistor, with the source acting as the emitter and the drain as the collector. If some of the holes mentioned above are collected by the source, and if the corresponding hole current creates a voltage drop in the substrate material of the order of 0.6 V, the substrate-source *pn* junction will conduct significantly. Electrons can then be injected from the source to the substrate, just like electrons injected from emitter to base in *npn* transistors. These electrons can, in turn, gain sufficient energy as they travel toward the drain to cause additional impact ionization and create new electron-hole pairs. This constitutes a positive feedback mechanism, which can sustain itself if the drain voltage exceeds a certain value. This is observed externally as *breakdown*, causing current values higher than normally expected. Further complications can arise from the fact that some electrons generated due to high fields can escape the drain field. These electrons can travel long distances into the substrate (hundreds of micrometers in some cases), and can affect other devices on a chip.[97, 98] Impact ionization effects are less severe in *p*-channel devices.

Yet another troublesome phenomenon, related again to high electric fields either longitudinal or normal, is caused by the fact that high-energy electrons or holes (referred to as *hot electrons* or *hot holes*) can enter the oxide where they can be trapped, resulting in "oxide charging."[97, 105–108] Sudden transients can augment this effect. Oxide charges produced in this way accumulate with time, and tend to degrade gradually the device performance (notably increase the threshold voltage and decrease the control of the gate on the drain current). Thus, for given bias conditions, the device can have a limited lifetime, after which its performance will be unacceptable for a given application. Such effects can occur in long-channel devices also, but are much less severe because electric fields in them are usually smaller and, when such fields occur, they are limited to a small part of the channel (notably the pinchoff region).

Depending on the fabrication process details, one or more of the above phenomena will limit the acceptable range of bias voltages for a given device.

5.7   EFFECT OF SOURCE AND DRAIN SERIES RESISTANCES

The MOS transistor channel is in series with two "parasitic" resistances, one associated with the source and the other associated with the drain.[116, 117] One can identify three contributions to each resistance: (1) The resistance of the metal contact to the n^+ region; (2) the resistance of the main body of the n^+ region, and (3) the resistance associated with the crowding of the current flow lines as they go from the n^+ region to the normally thinner inversion layer (the "spreading resistance" effect[118, 119]). Let R be the total resistance due to these effects in series with either channel end. Then one has the situation shown in Fig. 5.19. The effective drain-source voltage $\hat{V}_{DS}$ is reduced below the voltage V_{DS} applied at the external terminals by the voltage drops across the series resistors:

$$\hat{V}_{DS} = V_{DS} - 2RI_D \tag{5.7.1}$$

We will use (4.4.30a) to obtain the drain current, with V_{DS} replaced by $\hat{V}_{DS}$. For simplicity, we will assume that RI_D is much smaller than $V_{GS} - V_T$. Then we do not need to consider the effective reduction in the gate-source voltage. Also, we will assume that $\hat{V}_{DS}$ is much smaller than $V_{GS} - V_T$, so that we can neglect the square term in (4.4.30a). Thus we have

$$I_D \approx \frac{W}{L} \mu C'_{ox}(V_{GS} - V_T)\hat{V}_{DS} \tag{5.7.2}$$

Substituting (5.7.1) in this and solving for I_D we obtain

$$I_D = \frac{\mu C'_{ox}(W/L)}{1 + \alpha_R(V_{GS} - V_T)} (V_{GS} - V_T)V_{DS} \tag{5.7.3}$$

with

$$\alpha_R = \frac{2\mu C'_{ox}RW}{L} \tag{5.7.4}$$

In conservative fabrication processes, deep junctions, thick oxides, and large contact windows are used; then $C'_{ox}RW$ is small. In addition, L is large. Thus $\alpha_R \approx 0$ can be used in (5.7.3), which implies that the current will be about the same as what would be observed if the series resistances were replaced by short circuits. In aggressive, short-channel fabrication processes, though, α_R is not negligible (Sec. 5.8) and the series resistance effect must be taken into account. The I_D-V_{GS} characteristic obtained from (5.7.3) is of the same form as that caused by the effective mobility reduction with V_{GS}, illustrated in Fig. 4.20. If we assume that both effects are present, then we should replace μ in (5.7.2) by an effective mobility expression from Sec. 4.8. Let us use (4.8.18) with $\theta_B = 0$ for simplicity. Then it is easy to show that, if $\theta(V_{GS} - V_T)$ and

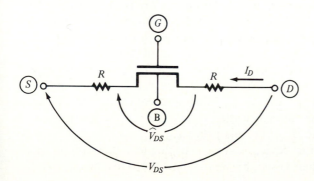

FIGURE 5.19
A MOS transistor with the associated source and drain resistances.

$\alpha_R(V_{GS} - V_T)$ are both sufficiently smaller than 1, the factor $\mu/[1 + \alpha_R(V_{GS} - V_T)]$ in (5.7.3) should be replaced by $\mu_0/[1 + (\theta + \alpha_R)(V_{GS} - V_T)]$. This has lead to the confusing usage of terms like "mobility reduction due to series resistance." Such terms do not properly describe what happens. As is clear from our analysis, the two effects are totally seperate. The fact that both happen to contribute to a term proportional to $V_{GS} - V_T$ in the denominator of the current expression is because of a mathematical coincidence.

A similar analysis can be carried out without making assumptions as to the relative magnitude of the various voltages involved. It is found, though, that even in such cases it is often sufficient to model the series resistance effect as above, i.e., by adding α_R to θ.

5.8   SCALING

Efforts are under way to make transistors as small as possible to increase speed and circuit complexity per unit of chip area. However, if the channel length is made too small, depletion regions around source and drain can meet, and punchthrough can occur, as discussed in Sec. 5.6. Thus, to make L small, the depletion region widths should be made small. This can be done by increasing the substrate doping concentration and decreasing the reverse bias. To achieve the latter under any circuit operating conditions, the power supply voltage must be decreased. Increasing now the doping concentration increases the threshold voltage and makes it more difficult to turn the device on; this can be corrected by decreasing the oxide thickness.

What has just been described, i.e., adjusting a fabrication process and the bias voltages to allow proper operation of reduced-size devices, is one of the constant pursuits of fabrication process engineering.[120-128, 117] The adjustments aim at achieving small dimensions while, at the same time, avoiding severe side effects, such as the several small-dimension effects already considered in this chapter. Depending on what aspects of a given process should be optimized for an application in mind, there are many ways such adjustments can be made. Several of these are discussed in this section.

We will first describe a set of rules aimed at reducing size in such a way that the resulting device along with its depletion region is simply a scaled version of a large device, as is shown in Fig. 5.20. Then no significant side effects should appear, and one can analyze the scaled device by using well-known large-device concepts, thus taking advantage of the significant experience gained with large devices over the years. A process proposed to achieve the reduction shown in Fig. 5.20b will now be briefly described.[120] It will be seen to result in a "scaled" device, in which internal electric field shape and maximum magnitude is the same as in the original device; hence the name *constant-field scaling* is used to describe this process.

Let us assume that a large device is scaled in all three dimensions by a factor $1/\kappa$, where κ is larger than 1 (say, between 1 and 10). This means that L,

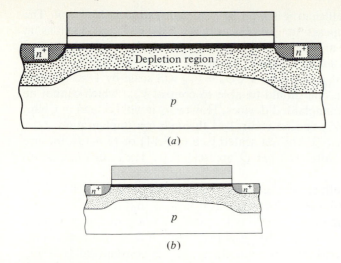

FIGURE 5.20
(a) A MOS transistor; (b) a MOS transistor obtained from (a) by scaling all geometrical dimensions by the same factor.

W, oxide thickness, and junction depth are all scaled by the same factor. Thus, areas (e.g., gate area) are scaled by $(1/\kappa)^2$. The depletion region underneath a junction has a thickness l given by [see (1.5.12) and (1.5.13)].

$$l = \sqrt{\frac{2\epsilon_s}{qN_A}} \sqrt{\phi_o + V} \qquad (5.8.1)$$

where V is the reverse bias and ϕ_o the built-in potential. The form of this equation is also valid for the depletion region underneath the inversion layer; for example, in strong inversion the equation is valid with $\phi_o = \phi_B$. We will assume ϕ_o is small compared to V.† Then we can scale l by $1/\kappa$, by scaling $\sqrt{V/N_A}$ by $1/\kappa$ in the above equation. Let us scale N_A by κ and V by $1/\kappa$. To achieve a properly scaled V throughout the channel, all operating voltages as well as the threshold voltage must be scaled by $1/\kappa$. From basic electrostatics (Appendix B) it is easy to see that under this scaling the shape and maximum magnitude of the electric field in the structure will remain the same. Thus breakdown will not occur. As seen in (1.5.20b) and (2.2.4) capacitances *per unit area* C' are inversely proportional to distances, so they are scaled by κ. However, capacitances C *per se* are given by $C'A$, where A is the area, and thus are seen to scale by $\kappa(1/\kappa^2) = 1/\kappa$.

---

† This assumption is, of course, not valid for all bias conditions; it is made for simplicity. Thus, a device scaled as described will deviate from ideal constant field scaling behavior when the reverse bias is small.

The body effect coefficient γ is seen from (2.5.19) to scale by $1/\sqrt{\kappa}$. The threshold voltage V_T appears in differences with bias voltages, such as in (4.4.30). Since the latter are scaled by $1/\kappa$, V_T should also be scaled by $1/\kappa$ as already mentioned. Consider (4.4.26a). From the above discussion, if ϕ_B is very small compared to V_{SB}, the term $\gamma\sqrt{\phi_B + V_{SB}}$ will scale by $1/\kappa$. To scale $V_{FB} + \phi_B$ in that equation one should be able to control V_{FB}, which cannot be done independently for unimplanted devices. However, it will be seen in Chap. 6, that an "equivalent" V_{FB} can be controlled through ion implantation.

Charges *per unit area* Q' are not scaled [see (1.5.14) or (3.4.19) and use the above results]. Therefore, *charges* Q are scaled by $1/\kappa^2$, since areas are scaled by this factor.

What is now the effect of the above scaling procedure on the drain current? Let us look at (4.4.30). If δ is small, it is seen that since all voltages are scaled by $1/\kappa$, the quantity in brackets is scaled by $1/\kappa^2$. At the same time C'_{ox} is scaled by κ. Thus, recalling that μ is practically independent of doping concentration (Sec. 4.8) and thus does not change under constant-field scaling, the current in (4.4.30) is scaled by $1/\kappa$.

Consider now the slope of $\ln I_D$ vs. V_{GS} in weak inversion for a constant V_{DS}. As seen from (4.6.17), that slope is proportional to $1/n$, with n given by (4.6.20). Since γ scales by $1/\sqrt{\kappa}$ and $V_{SB} + 1.5\phi_F$ by $1/\kappa$ (assuming V_{SB} is large), n remains the same, and the slope of $\ln I_D$ vs. V_{GS} does not scale. For digital circuits, this is undesirable since it makes it more difficult to turn a device off. For example, it takes as much reduction in gate voltage to reduce I_D by one decade as it does for large devices. Since the total voltage swings possible have been scaled by $1/\kappa$, the gate-voltage reduction needed to turn the device off represents a larger fraction of the total swing, and noise margins in digital circuits are reduced. The width of the moderate-inversion region[129] does not scale either (Fig. 2.18). Thus this region now becomes a larger part of the power supply voltage, and more attention must be paid to it.[129, 130]†

Since both voltages and currents are scaled by $1/\kappa$, power dissipation is scaled by $1/\kappa^2$. However, since device areas have been scaled by $1/\kappa^2$, the density of devices per unit area is scaled by κ^2; thus, the power per unit of chip area is not scaled.

Since all device currents are scaled by $1/\kappa$ and the various capacitances are scaled by the same factor, the rate of change of charging these capacitances, $dV/dt = I/C$, will not scale. However, these capacitances now only need to be charged to voltages scaled down by $1/\kappa$, and thus the time needed to charge them scales by $1/\kappa$; hence, the speed of digital circuits increases by κ. Since the power dissipation for a transistor has scaled by $1/\kappa^2$, the "power

---

† In moderate inversion the slopes of the inversion layer charge (Fig. 2.10) and of I_D for low V_{DS} (Fig. 4.20) vs. gate voltage are seen to decrease. This can be traced to the finite-inversion-layer capacitance in this region[129] [see (2.6.20)], and, for this reason, sometimes moderate-inversion effects are identified as "finite-inversion-layer capacitance effects."

delay product" (a figure of merit used for digital circuits) scales by $1/\kappa^3$. Constant-field scaling is summarized in Table 5.1.

Consider now the metal and polysilicon lines used to form the gates and interconnections. Since we now have a fabrication process capable of small dimensions, let us attempt to scale the width of these lines by $1/\kappa$. The new process may also require reducing the height of these lines, since trying to make very thin, but tall, lines can run into fabrication problems (Chap. 10); let us attempt to scale that height by $1/\kappa$ also. Then the cross-sectional area of the lines is scaled by $1/\kappa^2$. Since the current that these lines carry has been seen to scale by $1/\kappa$, the current *density* in these lines will scale by κ. This is very undesirable since the increased current density can cause what is known as electromigration, a phenomenon in which atoms are carried by the flow of current and can result in failure. For aluminum lines, the current density should not be larger than about $1\,\mathrm{mA}/\mu\mathrm{m}^2$. Another problem with scaling interconnection lines is that the resistance of the lines is proportional to length and inversely proportional to the cross-sectional area, and thus scales by κ. The parasitic capacitances of these lines to the substrate scales by $1/\kappa$, and thus the corresponding time constant does not scale. If the lines are long, this can cause a problem since it prevents us from taking advantage of the fact that the speed of transistors has scaled by κ. Also, since the resistance of these lines scales by κ and the current through them by $1/\kappa$, the voltage drop across them does not scale. Thus, a larger fraction of the total voltages available, which have been scaled by $1/\kappa$, is now wasted across interconnection lines. Because of the above problems, the height of interconnection lines is reduced less drastically.

TABLE 5.1

Constant-field scaling

Quantity	Scaling factor
Device dimensions (L, W, d_{ox}, junction depth)	$1/\kappa$
Area	$1/\kappa^2$
Packing density (devices per unit of chip area)	κ^2
Doping concentration, N_A	κ
Bias voltages and V_T	$1/\kappa$
Bias currents	$1/\kappa$
Power dissipation for a given circuit	$1/\kappa^2$
Power dissipation per unit of chip area	1
Capacitances, C	$1/\kappa$
Capacitances per unit area, C'	κ
Charges, Q	$1/\kappa^2$
Charges per unit area, Q'	1
Electric field intensity	1
Body effect coefficient, γ	$1/\sqrt{\kappa}$
Transistor transit time, τ	$1/\kappa$
Transistor power-delay product	$1/\kappa^3$

Additional problems are caused by the "contact windows," etched through the thick oxide in order to make contacts between various layers. If the area of these windows is scaled by $1/\kappa^2$, their resistances will scale by κ^2. For currents scaled by $1/\kappa$, this means that the voltage drop across the contacts will scale by κ, i.e., in the *opposite* direction from the bias voltages, which were scaled by $1/\kappa$. Another undesirable effect of scaling is an increase in the resistance per square of the source and drain n^+ regions due to the decreased junction depth and the increase in the spreading resistance. The effect of the source and drain resistances on the transistor characteristics has been considered in Sec. 5.7.

The scaling scenario discussed above presents certain problems. As already discussed, the weak-inversion region width does not scale. Hence, the voltage swings required for turning the device from off to on may be an unacceptably large fraction of the total voltage available. In addition, established chip interface requirements must often be obeyed for which voltage levels are fixed, and, hence, the voltage cannot be scaled. The rules followed in such cases, for decreasing device dimensions while keeping the voltages unchanged, are referred to as *constant-voltage scaling*. In these, W, L, and N_A are scaled as before. However, if the oxide thickness is scaled by the same factor, the resulting field can be exceedingly high since voltages are not scaled; this can cause mobility degradation (Sec. 4.8). To alleviate this problem somewhat, oxide thickness is usually scaled less drastically.[117] One column in Table 5.2 summarizes these scaling rules. The resulting effect on the various quantities (such as those entered in Table 5.1) is considered in Prob. 5.24. It is, of course, to be expected that undesirable effects associated with high electric fields can become severe under constant-voltage scaling.

To avoid the extreme cases of constant-field and constant-voltage scaling, compromise scaling rules have been proposed. For example, geometric dimensions and substrate doping are scaled as in the case of constant-field scaling,

TABLE 5.2

Scaling rules

Quantity	Constant-field scaling	Constant voltag scaling $1 < \beta < \kappa$	Quasi-constant voltage scaling $1 < \beta < \kappa$	Generalized scaling $1 < \beta < \kappa$
W, L	$1/\kappa$	$1/\kappa$	$1/\kappa$	$1/\kappa$
d_{ox}	$1/\kappa$	$1/\beta$	$1/\kappa$	$1/\kappa$
N_A	κ	κ	κ	κ^2/β
V, V_T	$1/\kappa$	1	$1/\beta$	$1/\beta$

but voltages are scaled less drastically. This has been termed *quasi-constant-voltage scaling*,[117] and is summarized in the corresponding column of Table 5.2. As is evident from (5.8.1), under this type of scaling the depletion region widths do not scale by the same factor as W, L, and d_{ox}. This is avoided if the scaling factor for N_A is modified appropriately, resulting in the *generalized scaling* rules shown in the last column of Table 5.2.[125]

A different approach concentrates on decreasing device dimensions while maintaining long-channel behavior in the weak-inversion region, such behavior being a sensitive indicator of the absence of severe short-channel effects. It has been found empirically that the minimum channel length for which such behavior is maintained fits the following relation:[122]

$$L_{min} = (\text{const})[rd_{ox}(l_S + l_D)^2]^{1/3} \qquad (5.8.2)$$

where r is the source and drain junction depth, d_{ox} the oxide thickness, l_S and l_D the depletion region widths at the source and drain, respectively, and (const) has the value of 8.8 $\mu\text{m}^{-1/3}$. The above relation portrays the various compromises involved and has proved to be a useful guide for decreasing device dimensions. The fabrication issues of device scaling are discussed in Sec. 10.5.

Before closing this section, let us speculate as to what might eventually be achieved[123, 124, 126, 131–141] by the ongoing effort to decrease physical dimensions and power supply voltages. We will try to present what might be considered an "average" view. However, predictions for the "future" concerning MOS devices have been repeatedly proved wrong in the past. Thus, one should not be surprised if the same were to happen with the predictions that follow.

The power supply voltage of an integrated circuit cannot be reduced arbitrarily because the correspondingly reduced signals become vulnerable to noise. For practical processes, also, the uncertainties of achieving a desired threshold voltage value are of the order of 0.1 V or more. In logic circuits the swings should be at least a few times that amount to ensure that all devices can be turned on and off with certainty. The last two considerations place a lower limit on the power supply voltage of 0.5 V or so, but speed considerations and driving requirements of off-chip components can make this value higher (e.g., 2 V). This places a lower limit on device dimensions, to avoid breakdown. Other limitations can be posed by the requirement to avoid overheating of the chip. Forced-air cooling allows about 2 W/cm^2 of chip area to be dissipated without overheating. Liquid cooling could increase this by an order of magnitude or even more by using special techniques.[126, 134] The degree of cooling imposes a limit on the number of transistors that can be placed in a given area if they dissipate significant power. For dynamic circuits, the need to avoid overheating has another repercussion. A circuit charging and discharging capacitor C to a voltage V, f times per second dissipates a power of fCV^2. If many such circuits are closely packed, then, in order not to exceed the maximum power dissipation per unit of chip area, the maximum allowable clock frequency f may have to be limited.

Considerations such as the above can be found in several references dealing with fundamental limits.[126, 131-141] Taking the various factors into account, predictions as to what an "ultimate" MOS technology might look like vary. Devices with channel lengths as low as 0.14 μm have been considered.[141] Maximum "packing" densities predicted[131, 134] are in the range of 10^7 to 10^8 transistors per cm^2. Minimum switching times of inverters, "packed" as allowed by thermal limitations could be about 10 ps.[134] Finally, because of delays encountered in propagating a signal over interconnection lines, clock frequency for a synchronous digital network with 10^5 gates could be limited to about 3 GHz.[134] Again, the above numbers have not been achieved in a production environment. They tend to indicate, though, what may be possible to achieve, and suggest that there is much room for improvement in VLSI.

REFERENCES

1. D. Vandorpe, J. Borel, G. Merckel, and P. Saintot, "An accurate two-dimensional numerical analysis of the MOS transistor," *Solid-State Electronics*, vol. 15, p. 547, 1972.
2. D. P. Kennedy and P. C. Murley, *IBM Journal of Research and Development*, vol. 17, p. 2, 1973.
3. M. S. Mock, "A two-dimensional mathematical model of the insulated gate field-effect transistor," *Solid-State Electronics*, vol. 16, pp. 601–609, 1973.
4. R. Kasai and T. Kimura, "Two-dimensional structure analysis of short-channel C-MOS and transient analysis of the C-MOS circuits," Technical Group, Institute of Electronics and Communications Engineers of Japan, *ED76-5*, 1976 (in Japanese).
5. J. A. Greenfield and R. W. Dutton, "Nonplanar VLSI device analysis using the solution of Poisson's equation," *IEEE Transactions on Electron Devices*, vol. ED-27, pp. 1520–1532, 1980.
6. S. Selberherr, A. Schütz, and H. W. Pötzl, "MINIMOS—A two-dimensional MOS transistor analyzer," *IEEE Transactions on Electron Devices*, vol. ED-27, pp. 1540–1549, 1980.
7. B. T. Brown and J. J. H. Miller (eds.), *Numerical Analysis of Semiconductor Devices*, Boole Press, Dublin, 1979.
8. E. M. Buturla, P. E. Cottrel, B. M. Grossman, K. A. Salzburg, M. B. Lawlor, and C. T. McMullen, "Three-dimensional finite element simulation of semiconductor devices," *Digest of Technical Papers*, IEEE International Solid-State Circuits Conference, San Francisco, pp. 76–77, 1980.
9. A. Yoshii, H. Kitazawa, M. Tomizawa, S. Horiguchi, and T. Sudo, "A three-dimensional analysis of semiconductor devices," *IEEE Transactions on Electron Devices*, vol. ED-29, pp. 184–189, 1982.
10. A. Husain and S. G. Chamberlain, "Three-dimensional simulation of VLSI MOSFET's: the three-dimensional simulation program WATMOS," *IEEE Transactions on Electron Devices*, vol. ED-29, pp. 631–638, 1982.
11. W. L. Engl, H. K. Dirks, and B. Meinerhagen, "Device modeling," *Proceedings of the IEEE*, vol. 71, pp. 10–33, January 1983.
12. C. L. Wilson, P. Roitman, and L. Blue, "High accuracy physical modeling of submicrometer MOSFET's," *IEEE Transactions on Electron Devices*, vol. ED-32, pp. 1246–1258, July 1985.
13. C. L. Wilson and J. L. Blue, "Accurate current calculations in two-dimensional MOSFET models," *IEEE Transactions on Electron Devices*, vol. ED-32, pp. 2060–2068, October 1985.
14. B. Meinerzhagen, H. K. Dirks, and W. L. Engl, "Quasi-simultaneous solution method: a new highly efficient strategy for numerical MOST simulations," *IEEE Transactions on Electron Devices*, vol. ED-32, pp. 2131–2138, October 1985.
15. S. R. Hofstein and F. P. Heinman, "The silicon insulated-gate field-effect transistor," *Proceedings of the IEEE*, vol. 51, pp. 1190–1202, September 1963.

16. C. Goldberg, "Pinch off in insulated-gate field-effect transistors," *Proceedings of the IEEE*, vol. 52, pp. 414–415, April 1964.

17. S. R. Hofstein and G. Warfield, "Carrier mobility and current saturation in the MOS transistor," *IEEE Transactions on Electron Devices*, vol. ED-12, pp. 129–138, March 1965.

18. V. K. G. Reddi and C. T. Sah, "Source to drain resistance beyond pinch-off in Metal-Oxide Semiconductor transistors (MOST)," *IEEE Transactions on Electron Devices*, vol. ED-12, pp. 139–141, March 1965.

19. J. E. Schroeder and R. S. Muller, "IGFET analysis through numerical solution of Poisson's equation," *IEEE Transactions on Electron Devices*, vol. ED-15, pp. 954–961, 1968.

20. H. Shichman and D. A. Hodges, "Modeling and simulation of insulated-gate field-effect transistor switching circuits," *IEEE Journal of Solid-State Circuits*, vol. SC-3, pp. 285–289, September 1968.

21. D. Frohman-Bentchkowsky and A. S. Grove, "Conductance of MOS transistors in saturation," *IEEE Transactions on Electron Devices*, vol. ED-16, pp. 108–113, January 1969.

22. G. Baum and H. Beneking, "Drift velocity saturation in MOS transistors," *IEEE Transactions on Electron Devices*, vol. ED-17, pp. 481–482, June 1970.

23. G. Baum, "Driftgeschwindigkeitssättigung bei MOS-Feldeffekttransistoren," *Solid-State Electronics*, vol. 13, pp. 789–798, 1970.

24. R. S. C. Cobbold, *Theory and Applications of Field-Effect Transistors*, Wiley-Interscience, New York, 1970.

25. G. A. Armstrong and J. A. Magowan, "The distribution of mobile carriers in the pinch-off region of an insulated-gate field effect transistor and its influence on device breakdown," *Solid-State Electronics*, vol. 14, pp. 723–733, 1971.

26. G. Merckel, J. Borel, and N. Z. Cupcea, "An accurate large-signal MOS transistor model for use in computer-aided design," *IEEE Transactions on Electron Devices*, vol. ED-19, pp. 681–690, May 1972.

27. D. Vandorpe, J. Borel, G. Merckel, and P. Saintot, "An accurate two-dimensional numerical analysis of the MOS transistor," *Solid-State Electronics*, vol. 15, pp. 547–557, 1972.

28. A. Popa, "An injection level dependent theory of the MOS transistor in saturation," *IEEE Transactions on Electron Devices*, vol. ED-19, pp. 774–781, 1972.

29. P. Rossel, H. Martinot, and G. Vassilieff, "Accurate two-sections model for MOS transistor in saturation," *Solid State Electronics*, vol. 19, pp. 51–56, 1976.

30. Y. A. El-Mansy and A. R. Boothroyd, "A simple two-dimensional model for IGFET operation in the saturation region," *IEEE Transactions on Electron Devices*, vol. ED-24, pp. 254–262, 1977.

31. G. Merckel, "CAD models of MOSFETS" in *Process and Device Modelling for Integrated Circuit Design*, F. Van de Wiele, W. L. Engl, and P. G. Jespers (editors), Noordhoff, Leyden, The Netherlands, 1977.

32. F. M. Klaassen, "Review of physical models for MOS transistors," in *Process and Device Modelling for Integrated Circuit Design*, F. Van de Wiele, W. L. Engl, and P. G. Jespers (editors), Noordhoff, Leyden, The Netherlands, 1977.

33. H. C. Poon, "V_{th} and beyond," presented at the Workshop on Device Modelling for VLSI, Burlingame, California, March 29, 1979; also L. Cong, Bell Laboratories, private communication.

34. B. Hofflinger, H. Sibbert, and G. Zimmer, "Model and performance of hot-electron MOS transistors for VLSI," *IEEE Transactions on Electron Devices*, vol. ED-26, pp. 513–520, April 1979.

35. M. El Nokali and H. Miranda, "A simple model for the MOS transistor in saturation," *Solid-State Electronics*, vol. 29, pp. 591–596, 1986.

36. F. M. Klaassen and W. C. J. de Groot, "Modeling of scaled-down MOS transistors," *Solid-State Electronics*, vol. 23, pp. 237–242, 1980.

37. T. Poorter and J. H. Satter, "A DC model for an MOS transistor in the saturation region," *Solid-State Electronics*, vol. 23, pp. 765–772, 1980.

38. J. R. Brews, "Physics of the MOS transistor," chapter 1 in *Silicon Integrated Circuits, Part A*, D. Kahng (editor), Applied Solid-State Science Series, Academic Press, New York, 1981.

39. S. Liu and L. W. Nagel, "Small-signal MOSFET models for analog circuit design," *IEEE Journal of Solid-State Circuits*, vol. SC-17, pp. 983–998, December 1982.
40. F. N. Trofimenkoff, "Field-dependent mobility analysis of the field-effect transistor," *Proceedings of the IEEE*, vol. 53, pp. 1765–1766, January 1965.
41. R. H. Crawford, *MOSFET in Circuit Design*, McGraw-Hill, New York, 1967.
42. B. Hoeneisen and C. A. Mead, "Current-voltage characteristics of small size MOS transistors," *IEEE Transactions on Electron Devices*, vol. ED-19, pp. 382–383, 1972.
43. P Smith, M. Inoue, and J. Frey, "Electron velocity in Si and GaAs at very high electric fields," *Applied Physics Letters*, vol. 37, pp. 797–798, 1980.
44. K. K. Thornber, "Relation of drift velocity to low-field mobility and high-field saturation velocity," *Journal of Applied Physics*, vol. 51, pp. 2127–2133, April 1980.
45. M. H. White, F. Van de Wiele, and J. P. Lambot, "High-accuracy MOS models for computer-aided design," *IEEE Transactions on Electron Devices*, vol. ED-27, pp. 899–906, May 1980.
46. C. G. Sodini, P-K. Ko, and J. L. Moll, "The effect of high fields on MOS device and circuit performance," *IEEE Transactions on Electron Devices*, vol. ED-31, pp. 1386–1393, October 1984.
47. J. G. Ruch, "Electron dynamics in short-channel field-effect transistors," *IEEE Transactions on Electron Devices*, vol. ED-19, pp. 652–654, May 1972.
48. T. Kobayashi and K. Saito, "Two-dimensional analysis of velocity overshoot effects in ultrashort-channel Si MOSFETs," *IEEE Transactions on Electron Devices*, vol. ED-32, pp. 788–792, April 1985.
49. G. T. Cheney and R. A. Kotch, "A simple theory for threshold voltage modulation in IGFETs," *Proceedings of the IEEE*, vol. 56, pp. 837–888, 1968.
50. H. S. Lee, "An analysis of the threshold voltage for short-channel IGFETs," *Solid-State Electronics*, vol. 16, pp. 1407–1414, 1973.
51. R. C. Varschney, "Simple theory for threshold voltage modulation in short-channel MOS transistor," *Electronics Letters*, vol. 9, pp. 600–602, 1973.
52. H. C. Poon, L. D. Yau, R. L. Johnston, and D. Beecham, "D.C. model for short channel IGFETs," *Technical Digest*, International Electron Devices Meeting, Washington, D.C., pp. 156–159, 1973.
53. L. D. Yau, "A simple theory to predict the threshold voltage of short-channel IGFETs," *Solid-State Electronics*, vol. 17, pp. 1059–1063, 1974.
54. K. O. Jeppson, "Influence of the channel width on the threshold voltage modulation in MOSFETs," *Electronics Letters*, vol. 11, pp. 297–299, July 1975.
55. K. E. Kroell and G. K. Ackermann, "Threshold voltage of narrow channel field effect transistors," *Solid-State Electronics*, vol. 19, pp. 77–81, 1976.
56. W. P. Noble and P. E. Cottrell, "Narrow width effects in insulated gate field effect transistors," *Technical Digest*, International Electron Devices Meeting, pp. 582–586, 1976.
57. W. R. Bandy and D. P. Kokalis, "A simple approach for accurately modeling the threshold voltage of short-channel MOST's," *Solid-State Electronics*, vol. 20, pp. 675–680, 1977.
58. D. J. Coe, H. E. Brakman, and K. H. Nicholas, "A simple approach for accurately modeling the threshold voltage of short-channel MOST's," *Solid-State Electronics*, vol. 20, p. 993, 1977.
59. G. Merckel, "Short channels—scaled down MOSFETs," in *Process and Device Modelling for Integrated Circuit Design*, F. Van de Wiele, W. L. Engl, and P. G. Jespers (editors), Noordhoff, Leyden, The Netherlands, 1977.
60. R. R. Troutman and A. G. Fortino, "Simple model for threshold voltage in short-channel IGFETs," *IEEE Transactions on Electron Devices*, vol. Ed-24, pp. 1266–1268, October 1977.
61. G. W. Taylor, "Subthreshold conduction in MOSFETs," *IEEE Transactions on Electron Devices*, vol. ED-25, pp. 337–350, March 1978.
62. P. P. Wang, "Device characteristics of short-channel and narrow width MOSFETs," *IEEE Transactions on Electron Devices*, vol. ED-25, pp. 779–786, 1978.

63. E. Sun, "Short-channel MOS modeling for CAD," *Proceedings of the Twelfth Annual Asilomar Conference on Circuits, Systems, and Computers*, Pacific Grove, CA, pp. 493–499, November 1978.

64. W. Fichter and H. W. Potzl, "MOS modeling by analytical approximations. I. Subthreshold current and threshold voltage," *International Journal of Electronics*, vol. 46, pp. 33–55, 1979.

65. L. M. Dang, "A simple current model for short-channel IGFET and its application to circuit simulation," *IEEE Journal of Solid-State Circuits*, vol. SC-14, pp. 358–367, April 1979.

66. R. R. Troutman, "VLSI limitations from drain-induced barrier lowering," *IEEE Journal of Solid-State Circuits*, vol. SC-14, pp. 383–391, April 1979.

67. G. W. Taylor, "The effects of two-dimensional charge sharing on the above-threshold characteristics of short-channel IGFETs," *Solid-State Electronics*, vol. 22, pp. 701–717, 1979.

68. T. Toyabe and S. Asai, "Analytical models of threshold voltage and breakdown voltage of short-channel MOSFET's derived from two-dimensional analysis," *IEEE Transactions on Electron Devices*, vol. ED-26, pp. 453–461, 1979.

69. H. Masuda, M. Makai, and M. Kubo, "Characteristics and limitation of scaled-down MOSFET's due to two-dimensional field effect," *IEEE Transactions on Electron Devices*, vol. ED-26, pp. 980–986, 1979.

70. G. Merckel, "A simple model of the threshold voltage of short and narrow channel IGFETs," *Solid-State Electronics*, vol. 23, pp. 1207–1213, 1980.

71. A. Vladimirescu and S. Liu, "The simulation of MOS integrated circuits using SPICE 2," *Memorandum No. UCB/ERL M80/7*, Electronics Research Laboratory, University of California, Berkeley, February 1980.

72. P. K. Chatterjee and J. E. Leiss, "An analytic charge-sharing predictor model for sub-micron MOSFETs," *Technical Digest*, IEEE International Electron Devices Meeting, Washington, D.C., pp. 28–33, 1980.

73. K. N. Ratnakumar, J. D. Meindl, and D. L. Scharfetter, "New IGFET short-channel threshold voltage model," *Technical Digest*, IEEE International Electron Devices Meeting, Washington, D.C., pp. 204–206, 1981.

74. P. P. Guebels and F. Van de Wiele, "A charge sheet model for small geometry MOSFETs," *Technical Digest*, IEEE International Electron Devices Meeting, Washington, D.C., pp. 211–214, 1981.

75. T. N. Nguyen and J. D. Plummer, "Physical mechanisms responsible for short channel effects in MOS devices," *Technical Digest*, IEEE International Electron Devices Meeting, Washington, D.C., pp. 596–599, 1981.

76. A. A. Naem and A. R. Boothroyd, "Compensation tendency of short-channel and narrow-channel effects in small-geometry IGFETs," *Electronics Letters*, vol. 18, pp. 135–136, February 4, 1982.

77. R. Kasai, K. Yokoyama, A. Yoshii, and T. Sudo, "Threshold-voltage analysis of short- and narrow-channel MOSFETs by three-dimensional computer simulation," *IEEE Transactions on Electron Devices*, vol. ED-29, pp. 870–876, March 1982.

78. L. A. Akers and C. S. Chao, "A closed-form threshold voltage expression for a small-geometry MOSFET," *IEEE Transactions on Electron Devices*, vol. ED-29, pp. 776–778, April 1982.

79. L. A. Akers and J. J. Sanchez, "Threshold voltage models of short, narrow, and small geometry MOSFET's: a review," *Solid-State Electronics*, vol. 25, pp. 621–641, 1982.

80. P. P. Guebels and F. Van de Wiele, "A small geometry MOSFET model for CAD applications," *Solid-State Electronics*, vol. 26, pp. 267–273, 1983.

81. C. R. Ji and C. T. Sah, "Analysis of the narrow gate effect in submicrometer MOSFET's," *IEEE Transactions on Electron Devices*, vol. ED-30, pp. 1672–1677, December 1983.

82. C. R. Viswanathan, B. C. Burkey, G. Lubberts, and T. J. Tredwell, "Threshold voltage in short-channel MOS devices," *IEEE Transactions on Electron Devices*, vol. ED-32, pp. 932–940, May 1985.

83. A. M. Asenov, E. N. Stefanov, B. Z. Antov, and P. K. Vitanov, "Numerical analysis of MOS transistor effective channel width," *Electronics Letters*, vol. 21, pp. 595–597, July 4, 1985.

84. T. W. Tang, Q. L. Zhang, and D. H. Navon, "Analytical model for predicting threshold voltage in submicrometer-channel MOSFETs," *IEEE Transactions on Electron Devices*, vol. ED-32, pp. 1890–1893, September 1985.

85. C. T. Wang, "A threshold voltage expression for small-size MOSFET's based on an approximate three-dimensional analysis," *IEEE Transactions on Electron Devices*, vol. ED-33, pp. 160–164, January 1986.

86. S. M. Sze, *Physics of Semiconductor Devices*, John Wiley, New York, 1981.

87. F. M. Klaassen, "MOS device modelling," in *Design of MOS VLSI Circuits for Telecommunications*, Y. Tsividis and P. Antognetti (editors), Prentice-Hall, Englewood Cliffs, 1985.

88. C. Turchetti and G. Masetti, "A charge-sheet analysis of enhancement-mode MOSFET's," *IEEE Journal of Solid-State Circuits*, vol. SC-21, pp. 267–275, April 1986.

89. P. Richman, *MOSFET's and Integrated Circuits*, John Wiley, New York, 1973.

90. R. A. Stuart and W. Eccleston, "Punchthrough currents in short channel M.O.S.T. devices," *Electronics Letters*, vol. 9, pp. 586–588, December 1973.

91. J. R. Brews, "Geometrical factors in avalanche punchthrough erase," *IEEE Transactions on Electron Devices*, vol. ED-24, pp. 1108–1116, August 1977.

92. J. J. Barnes, K. Shimohigashi, and R. W. Dutton, "Short channel MOSFETs in the punchthrough current mode," *IEEE Transactions on Electron Devices*, vol. ED-26, pp. 446–453, April 1979.

93. F. S. Hsu, R. S. Muller, C. Hu, and P-K. Ko, "A simple punchthrough model for short-channel MOSFETs," *IEEE Transactions on Electron Devices*, vol. ED-30, pp. 1354–1359, October 1983.

94. W. W. Lattin and J. L. Rutledge, "Impact ionization current in MOS devices," *Solid-State Electronics*, vol. 16, p. 1043, 1973.

95. T. Kamata, K. Tanabashi, and K. Kobayashi, "Substrate current due to impact ionization in MOSFETs," *Japanese Journal of Applied Physics*, vol. 15, p. 1127, 1976.

96. E. Sun, J. Moll, J. Berger, and B. Alders, "Breakdown mechanism in short-channel MOS transistors," *Technical Digest*, IEEE International Electron Devices Meeting, Washington, D.C., pp. 478–482, 1978.

97. J. Matsunaga, M. Konaka, S. Kohyama, and H. Iizuku, "Design limitations due to substrate currents and secondary impact ionization electrons in NMOS LSI's," *Proceedings of the Eleventh International Conference on Solid-State Devices*, Tokyo, p. 45, August 1979.

98. P. K. Chatterjee, "VLSI dynamic NMOS design constraints due to drain induced primary and secondary impact ionization," *Technical Digest*, IEEE International Electron Devices Meeting, Washington, D.C., pp. 14–17, 1979.

99. B. Eitan and D. Frohman-Bentchkowsky, "Holding time degradation in dynamic MOS RAM by injection-induced electron currents," *IEEE Transactions on Electron Devices*, vol. ED-28, pp. 1515–1519, December 1981.

100. Y. El-Mansy, "MOS device and technology constraints in VLSI," *IEEE Transactions on Electron Devices*, vol. ED-29, pp. 567–573, April 1982.

101. S. Tam, P. Ko, F. C. Hsu, C. Hu, and P. S. Muller, "Hot electron-induced excess currents in n-channel MOSFETs," Device Research Conference, Colorado State University, Fort Collins, Colo., June 1982.

102. F-C. Hsu, P-K. Ko, S. Tam, C. Hu, and R. S. Muller, "An analytical breakdown model for short-channel MOSFET's," *IEEE Transactions on Electron Devices*, vol. ED-29, pp. 1735–1740, November 1982.

103. W. Muller, L. Risch, and A. Schutz, "Short-channel MOS transistors in the avalanche-multiplication regime," *IEEE Transactions on Electron Devices*, vol. ED-29, pp. 1778–1784, November 1982.

104. R. Kuhnert, C. Werner, and A. Schutz, "A novel impact-ionization model for 1-μm MOSFET simulation," *IEEE Transactions on Electron Devices*, vol. ED-32, no. 6, pp. 1057–1063, June 1985.

105. H. Hana, Y. Okamoto, and H. Ohnuma, *Japanese Journal of Applied Physics*, vol. 9, p. 1103, 1970.

106. T. H. Ning, C. M. Osburn, and H. N. Yu, "Effect of electron trapping on IGFET characteristics," *Journal of Electronics Materials*, vol. 6, pp. 65–76, 1977.

107. T. H. Ning, P. W. Cook, R. H. Dennard, C. M. Osburn, S. E. Shuster, and H. N. Yu, "1-μm MOSFET VLSI technology: Part IV—Hot-electron design constraints," *IEEE Transactions on Electron Devices*, vol. ED-26, pp. 346–353, April 1979.

108. P. E. Cottrell, R. R. Troutman, and T. H. Ning, "Hot electron emission in n-channel IGFETs," *IEEE Transactions on Electron Devices*, vol. ED-26, pp. 520–533, April 1979.

109. R. B. Fair and R. C. Sun, "Threshold voltage instability in MOSFETs due to channel hot-hole emission," *IEEE Transactions on Electron Devices*, vol. ED-28, pp. 83–94, January 1981.

110. S. Tam, F-C. Hsu, C. Hu, R. S. Muller, and P. K. Ko, "Hot-electron currents in very short channel MOSFET's," *IEEE Electron Device Letters*, vol. EDL-4, pp. 249–251, July 1983.

111. S. Tam, P-K. Ko, and C. Hu, "Lucky-electron model of channel hot-electron injection in MOSFETs," *IEEE Transactions on Electron Devices*, vol. EDL-31, pp. 1116–1124, September 1984.

112. E. Takeda, "Hot-carrier effects in submicrometre MOS VLSI's," *IEE Proceedings*, vol. 131, part I, pp. 153–162, October 1984.

113. T. Tsuchiya and J. Frey, "Relationship between hot-electrons/holes and degradation of p- and n-channel MOSFET's," *IEEE Electron Device Letters*, vol. EDL-6, pp. 8–11, January 1985.

114. K. R. Hofmann, C. Werner, W. Weber, and G. Dorda, "Hot-electron and hole emission effects in short n-channel MOSFETs," *IEEE Transactions on Electron Devices*, vol. ED-32, pp. 691–699, March 1985.

115. K. Brennan and K. Hess, "A theory of enhanced impact ionization due to the gate field and mobility degradation in the inversion layer of MOSFETs," *IEEE Electron Device Letters*, vol. EDL-7, pp. 86–88, February 1986.

116. R. C. Foss, R. Hartland, and J. Roberts, "An MOS transistor model for a micro-mini computer based circuit analysis system," *Proceedings of the Fifth European Solid-State Circuits Conference*, 1979.

117. P. K. Chatterjee, W. R. Hunter, T. C. Holloway, and Y. T. Lin, "The impact of scaling laws on the choice of n-channel or p-channel for MOS VLSI," *IEEE Electron Device Letters*, vol. EDL-1, pp. 220–223, October 1980.

118. G. Baccarani and G. A. Sai-Halasz, "Spreading resistance in submicron MOSFETs," *IEEE Electron Device Letters*, vol. EDL-4, pp. 27–29, February 1983.

119. K. K. Ng, R. J. Bayruns, and S. C. Fang, "The spreading resistance of MOSFETs," *IEEE Electron Device Letters*, vol. EDL-6, pp. 195–198, April 1985.

120. R. H. Dennard, F. H. Gaensslen, H. N. Yu, V. L. Rideout, E. Bassous, and A. R. LeBlanc, "Design of ion-implanted MOSFETs with very small physical dimensions," *IEEE Journal of Solid-State Circuits*, vol. SC-9, pp. 256–268, 1974.

121. R. H. Dennard, F. H. Gaensslen, E. J. Walker, and P. W. Cook, "1 μm MOSFET VLSI technology: Part II—Device designs and characteristics for high-performance logic applications," *IEEE Transactions on Electron Devices*, vol. ED-26, pp. 325–333, April 1979.

122. J. R. Brews, W. Fichtner, E. H. Nicolian, and S. M. Sze, "Generalized guide for MOSFET miniaturization," *IEEE Electron Device Letters*, vol. EDL-1, pp. 2–3, January 1980.

123. Y. El-Mansy, "MOS device and technology constraints in VLSI," *IEEE Transactions on Electron Devices*, vol. ED-29, pp. 567–573, April 1982.

124. VLSI Laboratory, Texas Instruments, "Technology and design challenges of MOS VLSI," *IEEE Journal of Solid-State Circuits*, vol. SC-17, pp. 442–448, June 1982.

125. G. Baccarani, M. R. Wordeman, and R. H. Dennard, "Generalized scaling theory and its application to a 1/4 micron MOSFET design," *IEEE Transactions on Electron Devices*, vol. ED-31, pp. 452–462, April 1984.

126. A. Reisman, "Device, circuit, and technology scaling to micron and submicron dimensions," *Proceedings of the IEEE*, vol. 71, pp. 550–565, May 1983.

127. J. H. King, "A novel approach to silicon gate CMOS device scaling," *Solid-State Electronics*, vol. 26, pp. 879–891, 1983.

128. E. Sangiorgi, E. A. Hofstatter, R. K. Smith, P. F. Bechtold, and W. Fichtner, "Scaling issues related to high field phenomena in submicrometer MOSFETs," *IEEE Electron Device Letters*, vol. EDL-7, pp. 115–118, February 1986.

129. Y. Tsividis, "Moderate inversion in MOS devices," *Solid-State Electronics*, vol. 25, pp. 1099–1104, 1982; see also Erratum, *ibid.*, vol. 26, p. 823, 1983.

130. G. Baccarani and M. R. Wordeman, "Transconductance degradation in thin-oxide MOS-FET's," *IEEE Transactions on Electron Devices*, vol. ED-30, pp. 1295–1304, October 1983.

131. B. Hoeneisen and C. A. Mead, "Fundamental limitations in microelectronics—I. MOS technology," *Solid-State Electronics*, vol. 15, pp. 819–829, 1972.

132. R. M. Swanson and J. D. Meindl, "Fundamental performance limits of MOS integrated circuits," *Digest of Technical Papers*, International Solid-State Circuits Conference, Philadelphia, pp. 110–111, February 1975.

133. R. W. Keys, "Physical limits in digital electronics," *Proceedings of the IEEE*, vol. 63, pp. 740–767, May 1975.

134. O. G. Folberth and J. H. Bleher, "The fundamental limitations of digital semiconductor technology," *Microelectronics Journal*, vol. 9, pp. 33–41, 1979.

135. K. N. Ratnakumar and J. D. Meindl, "Performance limits of E/D NMOS VLSI," *Digest of Technical Papers*, International Solid-State Circuits Conference, San Francisco, pp. 72–73, February 1980.

136. J. Meindl, "Circuit scaling limits for ultra large scale integration," *Digest of Technical Papers*, International Solid-State Circuits Conference, New York, pp. 36–37, February 1981.

137. C. Svensson, "VLSI physics," *Integration*, vol. 1, pp. 3–19, 1983.

138. H. Shichijo, "A re-examination of practical performance limits of scaled n-channel and p-channel MOS devices for VLSI," *Solid-State Electronics*, vol. 26, pp. 969–986, 1983.

139. J. Pfiester, J. D. Shott, and J. D. Meindl, "Performance limits of NMOS and CMOS," *Digest of Technical Papers*, International Solid-State Circuits Conference, San Francisco, pp. 158–159, February 1984.

140. E. Takeda, G. A. C. Jones, and H. Ahmed, "Constraints on the application of 0.5 μm MOSFET's to VLSI systems," *IEEE Transactions on Electron Devices*, vol. ED-32, pp. 322–327, February 1985.

141. J. R. Pfiester, J. D. Shott, and J. D. Meindl, "Performance limits of CMOS ULSI," *IEEE Transactions on Electron Devices*, vol. ED-32, pp. 333–343, February 1985.

PROBLEMS

5.1. Derive (5.2.1) using (1.2.13) (see Appendix B).

5.2. Prove (5.2.8) and state the condition(s) for its validity.

5.3. Prove (5.2.15) and show that, in the limit of V_A approaching infinity, V_{DS}^* approaches V_{DS}'. Investigate how close V_{DS}^* is to V_{DS}' for $\delta = 0$, V_A in the range of 20 to 50 V, and $V_{GS} - V_T$ in the range of 1 to 5 V.

5.4. Consider a model consisting of (4.4.25) in nonsaturation, and (5.2.5) and (5.2.6) in saturation. Assume the two regions are adjacent at the point $V_{DS} = V_{DS}^*$. Find the value of V_{DS}^* that will guarantee continuity of $I_D(V_{DS})$ and of its slope.

5.5. Consider a transistor with $N_A = 400 \ \mu\text{m}^{-3}$, $d_{ox} = 0.04 \ \mu\text{m}$, $Q_o' = 0.05 \ \text{fC}/\mu\text{m}^2$, and $\phi_{MS} = 0$, biased at $V_{GS} = 5 \ \text{V}$, $V_{SB} = 0$. Consider channel length modulation as described by (J.1) in Appendix J. Plot ΔL vs. V_{DS} for values of V_{DS} between $V_{DS}' + 1 \ \text{V}$ and $10 \ \text{V}$. How long should the device channel be to ensure a $\Delta L / L$ of 1 percent or less for the voltage range considered?

5.6. Derive expressions corresponding to (5.3.9) and (5.3.10) assuming, instead of (5.3.3), a two-section piecewise-linear model for $v_d(\mathcal{E}_x)$ (i.e., assume that $|v_d| = \mu |\mathcal{E}_x|$ for $|\mathcal{E}_x| \le \mathcal{E}_c$, and $|v_d| = |v_d|_{\max}$ for $|\mathcal{E}_x| > \mathcal{E}_c$).

5.7. Prove (5.3.12) and show that, in the absence of velocity saturation effects ($L\mathcal{E}_c$ approaching infinity), V_{DS}' as given there reduces to $(V_{GS} - V_T)/(1 + \delta)$.

5.8. Give the complete equations for nonsaturation and saturation in the presence of velocity saturation effects, using a model based on (5.3.11), (5.2.5), and (5.2.6). The value of V_{DS}' should be slightly modified from (5.3.12) to ensure continuity of both I_D and dI_D/dV_{DS} at $V_{DS} = V_{DS}'$.

5.9. (a) Consider a device with $\mu C_{ox}' = 30 \ \mu\text{A}/\text{V}^2$, $\delta = 0.2$, $\mathcal{E}_c = 2.5 \ \text{V}/\mu\text{m}$, and $V_T = 1 \ \text{V}$. Neglect channel length modulation for simplicity. By using the model of Example 5.2, plot I_D vs. V_{DS} with V_{GS} as a parameter ($V_{GS} = 2, 3, 4, 5 \ \text{V}$), and for $W = L = 10, 5$, and $2 \ \mu\text{m}$.

(b) Repeat for the above values of L, but keep W constant at $5 \ \mu\text{m}$. Discuss the results obtained. Neglect the effect of channel length and width on the threshold voltage.

5.10. Examine carefully the arguments related to charge sharing up to (5.4.2). Identify the points where arbitrary assumptions were used.

5.11. Prove (5.4.6) and show that it reduces to (5.4.7) if l/r is small.

5.12. Equation (5.4.6) was derived for L large enough so that a trapezoidal region could be defined as shown in Fig. 5.9a. Investigate the case where L is so small that the trapezoid becomes a triangle. Derive expressions for $\hat{Q}_B/Q_B$, $\hat{V}_T$, and ΔV_T in this case. Assume punchthrough does not occur.

5.13. Compare the model of (5.4.2b), (5.4.5), and (5.4.6) to the model of (5.4.9), (adjusting α_1 if necessary for best fit) for a device with $N_A = 10^{-5} \ \mu\text{m}^{-3}$, $d_{ox} = 0.02 \ \mu\text{m}$, and $r = 0.8 \ \mu\text{m}$ by plotting $V_T - V_{FB}$ vs. V_{SB} for $L = 3, 2$, and $0.9 \ \mu\text{m}$.

5.14. Consider a transistor with $N_A = 10^4 \ \mu\text{m}^{-3}$, $d_{ox} = 0.05 \ \mu\text{m}$, $V_{FB} = 0$, and $\phi_B = 0.8 \ \text{V}$; assume $V_{DS} = 0$. Plot $\hat{V}_T$ vs. L for L between 2 and $10 \ \mu\text{m}$, and for $V_{SB} = 0, 2$, and $4 \ \text{V}$, using (5.4.9).

5.15. Proceeding along the lines of the derivation of (5.4.6), derive a similar expression for the case of a relatively small nonzero V_{DS}, assuming that the edge of the depletion region in the center part of the device is horizontal at a depth equal to the average value of the source and drain depletion regions. From this find $\hat{V}_T$ and ΔV_T. Show the details of the derivation of (5.4.11) to (5.4.15).

5.16. Assume for simplicity that the constant-current threshold plotted in Fig. 5.11 differs from the effective threshold $\hat{V}_T$ calculated in Sec. 5.4.2 by a fixed amount. What values should be used for α_1 and α_2 in (5.4.14) and (5.4.15) in order that the predicted threshold *changes* agree reasonably well with the *changes* seen in the figure ?

5.17. Prove (5.4.20).

5.18. Equation (5.4.21) was derived for $V_{DS} = 0$. Attempt to extend this result to the case of a small nonzero V_{DS}. (*Note*: the author is not aware of any experimental evidence of $\hat{V}_T$ dependence on V_{DS} for narrow-channel devices; the result obtained in this problem should be taken with a grain of salt.)

5.19. For the device of Prob. 5.14, and assuming the channel is long, plot V_T vs. W for W between 2 and 10 μm and for $V_{SB} = 0$, 2, and 4 V ($V_{DS} = 0$).

5.20. Consider a device with a long but narrow channel, in which the effects of effective threshold increase and effective channel narrowing are both evident (Sec. 5.4.3). Suggest a measuring technique that can be used to determine ΔV_{T1} and $\Delta \hat{W}$.

5.21. Define an effective depletion region charge $\hat{Q}_B$ (Sec. 5.4) in the case of channels that are *both* short *and* narrow. Give the resulting expression for $\hat{V}_T$ in terms of $\hat{Q}_B/Q_B$, and attempt to justify the approach suggested in Sec. 5.5 for combining short- and narrow-channel effects when each effect acting by itself is small.

5.22. Show the equation that must be solved for V'_{DS} in the model of Example 5.4 so that the slope of $I_D(V_{DS})$ at $V_{DS} = V'_{DS}$ is continuous.

5.23. Develop a formula for roughly estimating the value of V_{DS} at which punchthrough begins.

5.24. Extend Table 5.2, giving values for all entries in Table 5.1, for the cases of constant voltage, quasi-constant voltage, and generalized scaling.

CHAPTER 6

MOS TRANSISTORS WITH ION-IMPLANTED CHANNELS

6.1 INTRODUCTION

We have so far assumed that the transistors we are considering have a uniformly doped substrate. For modeling devices with unimplanted channels, this is a resonable assumption (although not strictly correct because of some impurity redistribution which takes place during oxide growth). In this section we will consider devices for which the substrate doping between source and drain is purposely made very nor.uniform[1] through ion implantation, a process via which the substrate is bombarded with ions during fabrication. The effective substrate doping concentration is changed in the areas where these ions land (Chap. 10). Ion implantation is also used to dope the polysilicon gates and to form the source and drain regions[2] (Chap. 10), but here we focus attention to its use in the region in between, which can drastically change the *I-V* characteristics. Since its early application to MOS transistors[1,3,4] this process has been used extensively and is currently a standard part of device fabrication.[5,6] Ion implantation is desirable for several reasons. Among these is the adjustment of the threshold voltage value V_{T0}.[1,3-6] For circuit design purposes, this quantity should have a known, convenient value. In *enhancement mode* devices it should be sufficiently positive over all tolerances of fabrication process parameters so that a transistor can be turned off by applying a zero gate-source voltage. As can be deduced from (4.4.27), a sufficiently positive value of V_{T0} can be attained by increasing the substrate doping concentration N_A. This would increase both ϕ_B and the body effect coefficient γ (Sec. 2.5). However, an increase in γ implies increased body effect, causing large variations in V_T when V_{SB} is changed (4.4.26); this can cause complications in circuit design. In addition, a large value of N_A results in a large junction capacitance (Sec. 1.5), which reduces circuit speed (Chaps. 7–9). Thus increasing N_A is not an attractive way to increase V_{T0}. What can be done instead is to implant ions very close to the surface. These act in a way analogous to that of the effective interface charge Q_o in (2.2.6), and their effect is similar to modifying V_{FB}. On the other hand, the substrate concentration is not increased at points below the implant where most of the depletion region is located. Thus the body effect coefficient and the junction capacitances are kept small. Unfortunately the location of the implant close to the surface, although optimal for threshold adjustment, is not optimal for handling a different problem encountered in short-channel devices. As discussed in Chap. 5, in such devices the depletion region lengths become a significant part of the channel length, resulting in several two-dimensional effects including punchthrough (Sec. 5.6). To prevent punchthrough, the depletion region widths should be contained at points between source and drain below the surface, where punchthrough currents can flow. This can be achieved by using ion implantation to selectively increase the substrate doping there, as is evident from (1.5.13). The substrate doping below the source and drain areas can still be kept low, thus keeping the junction capacitances small. As is obvious from the above discussion, the design of an implanted device is not an easy problem since several compromises are involved.[5,6] The use of two implants is sometimes made to allow some degree of independence in controlling the threshold voltage value and the punch-through effect.

In contrast to the usage described above, a substrate can also be implanted with ions of the opposite type (e.g., *n*-type implant on a *p*-type substrate). This technique is often used to make *depletion mode* devices which can conduct significant current even with $V_{GS} = 0$ (Sec. 4.12).

The characteristics of the devices with ion-implanted substrates have been the subject of extensive studies.[7-53] The purpose of this chapter is to present some representative models which are simple enough to provide manageable analytical results, yet are sufficient to predict most of the important effects associated with implanted substrates. Our quantitative results will be limited to drift currents in long-channel devices, this being the case for which most of the analytical results in the literature have been obtained.

An ion-implanted *n*-channel transistor is shown in Fig. 6.1*a*; the implant can be *p*- or *n*-type. As before, we will first consider a simpler three-terminal structure, as shown in Fig. 6.1*b*. The ion implant is characterized by the

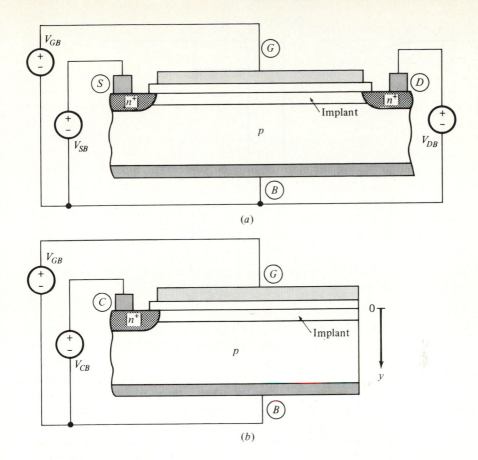

FIGURE 6.1
(a) A transistor with an ion-implanted channel, (b) three-terminal structure used to facilitate the study of (a).

"effective dose" (number of implanted ions within the semiconductor per unit area, typically 10^3 to $10^4/\mu m^2$) and by the average kinetic energy of the ions as they leave the ion implanter (10 to 300 keV), which determines how deep they enter the semiconductor. The distribution of ion concentration within the semiconductor has the general shape shown by $N(y)$ in Fig. 6.2a, where y is the depth measured from the Si-SiO$_2$ interface and N_{AB} is the doping concentration of the unimplanted substrate. The shape of $N(y)$ is initially gaussian and changes with high-temperature fabrication steps following the implantation process. Because of the complicated shape of $N(y)$, the detailed analysis of ion-implanted transistors is very involved. However, it has been found that practical and useful results can be obtained by approximating $N(y)$ as shown in Fig. 6.2b,[14] where N_I and y_I are appropriate constants chosen to make the resulting models as accurate as possible. As a starting point, y_I is sometimes

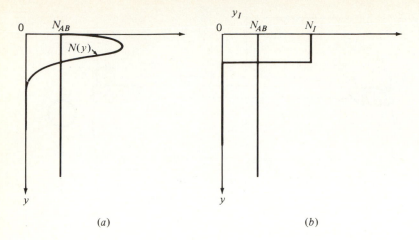

FIGURE 6.2
(a) Substrate doping concentration before implant, N_{AB} and implant concentration $N(y)$ vs. depth from surface; (b) step approximation for the implant concentration of (a).

chosen at the point where $N(y) = N_{AB}$ in Fig. 6.2a or at a depth equal to the mean plus the standard deviation of the distribution $N(y)$, assuming a gaussian shape; y_I can be, for example, 0.1 μm. N_I is then chosen so that $N_I y_I$ is equal to the total effective dose [the integral under $N(y)$ in Fig. 6.2a]. We emphasize that these choices represent only a starting point. The best values for these parameters depend on what aspects of *I-V* characteristics need be modeled and the bias range over which reasonable accuracy is desired (see below).

In this chapter we will continue using a *p*-type substrate as an example. The implanted ions can be of the same type as the substrate dopants (i.e., acceptors) or of the opposite type (donors). These two alternatives are commonly used to increase the threshold of enhancement devices or to make depletion devices, respectively.

6.2   IMPLANT AND SUBSTRATE OF THE SAME TYPE

In this section, we discuss the transistor of Fig. 6.1a with a *p*-type substrate and a *p*-type implant.[10–14, 16, 18–22, 30, 33–37, 41, 42, 44–46, 51, 53] Our objective is to derive a simple model for the drain current, which approximately predicts the important features of measured *I-V* characteristics. We will thus assume the rectangular implant distribution shape of Fig. 6.2b.[14]

6.2.1   Charges and Threshold Voltages

Consider first the corresponding three-terminal structure of Fig. 6.1b, assuming a very small V_{CB}. As V_{GB} is increased, a depletion region is formed at the surface. Its width increases with V_{GB} until a strong inversion layer is created, at which point the depletion region width becomes practically pinned to a certain value l_{Bm}. Assume that this value is smaller than the effective implant depth y_I, as shown in Fig. 6.3a.† If now V_{CB} is increased while strong inversion is maintained, the depletion region will widen and its bottom will eventually reach the bottom of the simplified implant profile. The critical value of V_{CB} at which this happens will be denoted by V_I and will be evaluated shortly. For $V_{CB} \le V_I$, we can think of the gate oxide-implanted region as a device by itself, and consider the material below it as part of the substrate contact. The effective substrate doping of this device will be, from Fig. 6.2b,

$$N_{AS} = N_{AB} + N_I \tag{6.2.1}$$

We can use then the results of Chap. 3, with N_A replaced by N_{AS}. The width of the depletion region in strong inversion will be, from (3.4.18),

$$l_{Bm} = \sqrt{\frac{2\epsilon_s}{qN_{AS}}} \sqrt{\phi_{B1} + V_{CB}} , \qquad V_{CB} \le V_I \tag{6.2.2}$$

where ϕ_{B1} will be somewhat larger than that corresponding to a substrate doping of N_{AB} (Sec. 2.5). The depletion region charge per unit area can be found as in Sec. 3.4.2:

$$Q'_B = Q'_{B1} = - \gamma_1 C'_{ox} \sqrt{\phi_{B1} + V_{CB}} , \qquad V_{CB} \le V_I \tag{6.2.3}$$

where

$$\gamma_1 = \frac{F\sqrt{N_{AS}}}{C'_{ox}} \tag{6.2.4}$$

The inversion layer charge per unit area will be, again from Sec. 3.4.2,

$$Q'_I = - C'_{ox}(V_{GB} - V_{CB} - V_{T1}) , \qquad V_{CB} \le V_I \tag{6.2.5}$$

where

$$V_{T1} = V_{FB1} + \phi_{B1} - \frac{Q'_{B1}}{C'_{ox}} \tag{6.2.6a}$$

$$= V_{FB1} + \phi_{B1} + \gamma_1 \sqrt{\phi_{B1} + V_{CB}} \tag{6.2.6b}$$

with

$$V_{FB1} \approx V_{FB} \tag{6.2.7}$$

where V_{FB} is the "flat-band" voltage corresponding to the unimplanted sub-

---

† Note that the depletion region around the n^+ region is not shown for simplicity.

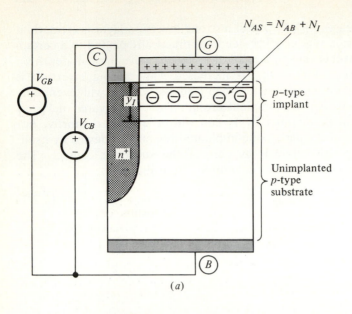

(a)

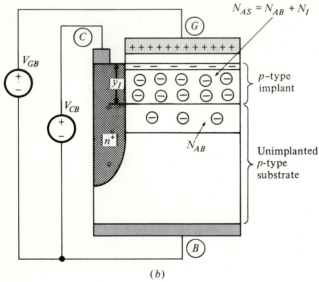

(b)

FIGURE 6.3

The structure of Fig. 6.1b, with a p-type implant on a p-type substrate in the strong-inversion region. (a) Small V_{CB} (depletion region totally within the implant); (b) large V_{CB} (depletion region extending outside the implant). The depletion region around the n^+ region is not shown for simplicity.

strate†, given by (2.2.6) and repeated below:

$$V_{FB} = \phi_{MS} - \frac{Q'_o}{C'_{ox}} \tag{6.2.8}$$

The critical value V_I of V_{CB} at which the depletion region bottom reaches the bottom of the implant can be found by setting $V_{CB} = V_I$ and $l_{Bm} = y_I$ in (6.2.2), and solving for V_I. This gives

$$V_I = \frac{qN_{AS}y_I^2}{2\epsilon_s} - \phi_{B1} \tag{6.2.9}$$

Increasing V_{CB} above V_I will move the depletion region bottom outside the implanted region, as shown in Fig. 6.3b. The results obtained above obviously do not apply in this case since they were obtained on the assumption that a single doping concentration characterizes the depletion region. In contrast, here we have a region with doping N_{AS}, followed by a region with doping N_{AB}. Let ψ_s be the surface potential, taken across *both* regions. A detailed analysis can be performed along the lines of Sec. 3.2; in fact, (3.2.2) to (3.2.4) hold unmodified. Such analysis leads to similar conclusions as in Sec. 3.2. In particular, in strong inversion we have again $\psi_s \approx \phi_B + V_{CB}$, and we will use the value $\phi_B = \phi_{B1}$ as before for simplicity. The resulting *total* depletion region charge per unit area (as contributed by *both* regions in Fig. 6.3b) can be found using basic electrostatics (Appendix B), and is given by (Prob. 6.10)

$$Q'_B = Q'_{B2} = -qM - \gamma_2 C'_{ox}\sqrt{\phi_{B1} - \frac{qMy_I}{2\epsilon_s} + V_{CB}}, \qquad V_{CB} \geq V_I \tag{6.2.10}$$

where

$$\gamma_2 = \frac{F\sqrt{N_{AB}}}{C'_{ox}} \tag{6.2.11}$$

and

$$M = N_I y_I \tag{6.2.12}$$

is the implant "dose" corresponding to the rectangular shape of the distribution in Fig. 6.2b, measured in ions per μm^2 (or in μm^{-2}). It is seen that

---

† We are neglecting here the small contact potential between the implanted region and the unimplanted substrate. This is consistent with the overall level of approximations in the present analysis. We should note here that even when V_{GB} is such that the surface is neutral, one cannot expect that the electrostatic potential will be constant in the vertical direction *throughout* the substrate, because the doping concentration varies in that direction [see (1.2.11)]. Thus the corresponding energy bands (Appendix A) will not be "flat" throughout, in contrast to the case of uniform substrates (Sec. 2.2 and Appendix D). In implanted device work the name "flatband voltage" is a carry-over from uniform substrate device discussions, and does not imply such flatness.

(6.2.10) with $M = 0$ reduces to the corresponding equation for an unimplanted device (3.4.19b).

One can find the inversion layer charge per unit area from (6.2.10), (3.2.2), (3.2.3), and (3.2.4) by eliminating among these equations the quantities Q'_G, ψ_{ox}, and Q'_B and using $\psi_s \approx \phi_{B1} + V_{CB}$ as before. This gives

$$Q'_I = -C'_{ox}(V_{GB} - V_{CB} - V_{T2}), \qquad V_{CB} \geq V_I \qquad (6.2.13)$$

with

$$V_{T2} = V_{FB} + \phi_{B1} - \frac{Q'_{B2}}{C'_{ox}} \qquad (6.2.14a)$$

$$= V_{FB} + \phi_{B1} + \frac{qM}{C'_{ox}} + \gamma_2\sqrt{\phi_{B1} - \frac{qMy_I}{2\epsilon_s} + V_{CB}} \qquad (6.2.14b)$$

It is seen that (6.2.13) is of the same form as (6.2.5). Also, (6.2.14) has the same functional dependence on V_{CB} as (6.2.6). In fact, consider a *fictitious* unimplanted device with a threshold voltage given by

$$V_{T2} = V_{FB2} + \phi_{B2} + \gamma_2\sqrt{\phi_{B2} + V_{CB}} \qquad (6.2.15)$$

Then it is easy to see that such a device will have a threshold behaving identically as (6.2.14) if we choose

$$\phi_{B2} \equiv \phi_{B1} - \frac{qMy_I}{2\epsilon_s} \qquad (6.2.16)$$

and

$$V_{FB2} \equiv V_{FB} + qM\left(\frac{1}{C'_{ox}} + \frac{y_I}{2\epsilon_s}\right) \qquad (6.2.17)$$

It is emphasized here that V_{FB2} is the flat-band voltage of the *fictitious* unimplanted device and should not be thought of as a flat-band voltage of the real one (similarly) for the quantity ϕ_{B2}. Nevertheless, we can take advantage of the convenient, familiar functional form of (6.2.15) and use it to describe the actual implanted device under consideration for $V_{CB} \geq V_I$, viewing ϕ_{B2} and V_{FB2} as mere symbols defined by (6.2.16) and (6.2.17).† Note that

$$V_{FB2} > V_{FB1} \qquad (6.2.18)$$

$$\phi_{B2} < \phi_{B1} \qquad (6.2.19)$$

$$\gamma_2 < \gamma_1 \qquad (6.2.20)$$

---

† One should not, for that matter, be surprised if for some combinations of process parameters ϕ_{B2} is found to have a negative value. This simply means that the implant is such that $qMy_I/(2\epsilon_s) > \phi_{B1}$, from (6.2.16). It is easy to check that the quantity under the square root in (6.2.15) never becomes negative in the domain of definition of that expression ($V_{CB} \geq V_I$).

In conclusion, we can write Q_I' as follows:

$$Q_I' = -C_{ox}'(V_{GB} - V_{CB} - V_T) \qquad (6.2.21)$$

with

$$V_T = \begin{cases} V_{T1}, & V_{CB} < V_I \\ V_{T2}, & V_{CB} \geq V_I \end{cases} \qquad \begin{matrix} (6.2.22a) \\ (6.2.22b) \end{matrix}$$

where

$$V_{Ti} = V_{FBi} + \phi_{Bi} + \gamma_i\sqrt{\phi_{Bi} + V_{CB}}, \qquad i = 1, 2 \qquad (6.2.23)$$

Since two regions are distinguished, and a number of approximations were made in deriving V_T for each region, it is important to check for possible anomalies at the critical point $V_{CB} = V_I$. A simple calculation shows that both $V_T(V_{CB})$ and dV_T/dV_{CB} are continuous at this point. Thus, no troublesome "kinks" will be caused in I-V characteristics by using this model for V_T (see below).

The quantity $V_T(V_{CB})$ is plotted in Fig. 6.4a. Two regions are clearly distinguishable. This behavior is verified by experiment. To obtain some intuition about this behavior,[14] consider an unimplanted device with uniform doping N_{AS} throughout the substrate. Then $V_T = V_{T1}$ for all V_{CB} values, resulting in curve a in Fig. 6.4b, characterized by γ_1. Next, consider a device with uniform substrate concentration N_{AB} (no implant). Then V_T vs. V_{CB} will look as shown by curve b in Fig. 6.4b, and will be characterized by a body effect coefficient γ_2 as given by (6.2.11). Finally, consider the substrate concentration unchanged from the value N_{AB}, and assume that the device has

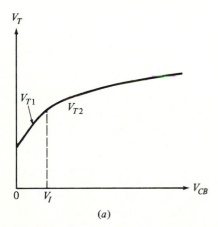

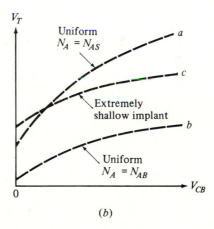

(a)   (b)

FIGURE 6.4

Threshold voltage vs. reverse bias for a p-type implant, p-substrate three-terminal MOS structure (Fig. 6.1b). (a) For a step-approximated implant; (b) for three limit cases.

been subjected to an extremely shallow implant such that all ions end up practically at the oxide-semiconductor interface; the dose is assumed to be $M = N_I y_I$, the same as for Fig. 6.2b. Now, the total charge per unit area of these ions, $(-q)M$, simply serves to modify the value of the effective interface charge Q_o'. From (6.2.8) it follows that this will only result in a positive shift in V_{FB} by an amount qM/C_{ox}'. Hence, for this case, the plot of V_T vs. V_{CB} will be as shown by curve c in Fig. 6.4b. This curve results from a vertical shift of curve b by an amount equal to the change in V_{FB}. The substrate doping is still N_{AB} and, thus, the body effect coefficient is still γ_2. The plot of V_T in Fig. 6.4a follows curve a for $V_{CB} < V_I$ and is close to curve c if V_{CB} is large. If y_I is reduced, the "transition point" in the plot will move to the left. For extremely shallow implants the curve in Fig. 6.4a will become practically the same as curve c in Fig. 6.4b. The device can then be characterized as discussed in previous chapters, with only a shift in V_{FB}. Comparing the curve in Fig. 6.4a to curve b in Fig. 6.4b (unimplanted device), it is seen that a p-type implant on a p-type substrate *increases* the extrapolated threshold voltage (for a given V_{CB}).†

The simple model we have presented is adequate for demonstrating the important threshold effects associated with the devices we are considering. (Other models are discussed elsewhere.[21]) Of course, since a number of approximations were made in the course of deriving the model, one should allow for the adjustment of parameter values, notably M and y_I, to attain satisfactory agreement with measured results. A related discussion was presented in Sec. 4.13. Since the above model will be used in deriving I-V expressions, the final values of M and y_I one ends up with will depend on what aspects of the I-V characteristics must be modeled most accurately, over what range accuracy is desired, etc.‡

6.2.2   Drain Current Model for Strong Inversion

For the connection shown in Fig. 6.1a, the drain current in the nonsaturation region can be determined from (4.4.13) which is repeated here:

$$I_{DN} = \frac{W}{L} \int_{V_{SB}}^{V_{DB}} \mu(-Q_I') \, dV_{CB} \qquad (6.2.24)$$

---

† This threshold-adjust implant is often in addition to the punchthrough control implant mentioned in Sec. 5.6. Since the latter would extend below the former, to depths where punchthrough would normally occur, the doping below the threshold-control implant considered in this chapter may not be N_{AB} as assumed, and, in fact, the picture of the depletion region there may be quite complicated. As a first-order correction, then, one may have to modify the value of N_{AB} appearing in our expressions. If N_{AB} is allowed to be chosen by a "parameter extraction" system (Sec. 4.13) for best matching to measurements, this modification would be done automatically.

‡ One can be more specific if only particular aspects of the I-V characteristics need be modeled. An exact analysis of threshold voltages due to an arbitrary profile of any shape or depth in terms of dose and centroid parameters is given elsewhere.[34]

We will assume for now that μ is constant. [The mobility dependence on the gate field can be taken into account by using an effective mobility approach (Sec. 4.8).[21, 46, 53]] With this assumption, and using Q_I' from (6.2.21), the above equation becomes

$$I_{DN} = \frac{W}{L} \mu C_{ox}' \int_{V_{SB}}^{V_{DB}} [V_{GB} - V_{CB} - V_T(V_{CB})] \, dV_{CB} \qquad (6.2.25)$$

Assuming $V_{DB} > V_{SB}$ ($V_{DS} > 0$), we distinguish three cases:[21]

1. $V_{SB} < V_{DB} \le V_I$. In this case, neglecting edge effects very close to the source and the drain, the depletion region is inside the step-approximated implant throughout the length of the channel (Fig. 6.5a). Using (6.2.22a) and (6.2.6) in (6.2.25) gives

$$I_{DN} = I_1(V_{SB}, V_{DB}) \qquad (6.2.26)$$

where, for compactness in the formulation to follow, we use the notation

$$I_i(V_K, V_N) = \frac{W}{L} \mu C_{ox}' \{ (V_{GB} - V_{FBi} - \phi_{Bi})(V_N - V_K) - \tfrac{1}{2}(V_N^2 - V_K^2)$$
$$- \tfrac{2}{3} \gamma_i [(V_N + \phi_{Bi})^{3/2} - (V_K + \phi_{Bi})^{3/2}] \} \qquad (6.2.27)$$

This equation is in the form of (4.4.8b).

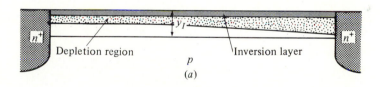

Depletion region   Inversion layer

p

(a)

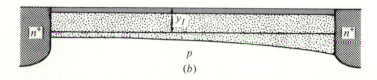

p

(b)

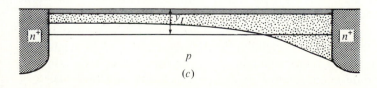

p

(c)

FIGURE 6.5
Depletion region (shaded area) in a transistor with a p substrate and a p implant. The depletion region around the n^+ region is not shown for simplicity. (a) $V_{SB} < V_{DB} < V_I$; (b) $V_I < V_{SB} < V_{DB}$; (c) $V_{SB} < V_I < V_{DB}$.

2. $V_I \leq V_{SB} < V_{DB}$. Here the depletion region edge is outside the step-approximated implant throughout the length of the channel (Fig. 6.5b). Using then (6.2.22b) and (6.2.15) in (6.2.25) we get

$$I_{DN} = I_2(V_{SB}, V_{DB}) \tag{6.2.28}$$

where I_2 is given by (6.2.27) with $i = 2$.

3. $V_{SB} < V_I < V_{DB}$. In this case, the depletion region edge is inside the implant near the source and outside near the drain (Fig. 6.5c). It is at depth y_I at a point where the reverse bias V_{CB} in the inversion layer is equal to V_I. Hence, we write (6.2.25) as follows:

$$I_{DN} = \frac{W}{L} \mu C'_{ox} \left\{ \int_{V_{SB}}^{V_I} [V_{GB} - V_{CB} - V_{T1}(V_{CB})] \, dV_{CB} \right.$$

$$\left. + \int_{V_I}^{V_{DB}} [V_{GB} - V_{CB} - V_{T2}(V_{CB})] \, dV_{CB} \right\} \tag{6.2.29}$$

Using (6.2.6) in the first integral and (6.2.15) in the second, we obtain

$$I_{DN} = I_1(V_{SB}, V_I) + I_2(V_I, V_{DB}) \tag{6.2.30}$$

where I_i, $i = 1, 2$, is given by (6.2.27).

The onset of saturation can be obtained as in Chap. 4 at the point where the slope of I_D with drain voltage becomes zero. Since we are currently using voltages with respect to the substrate, let us define for this onset $V'_{DB} = V'_{DS} + V_{SB}$. If pinchoff occurs at $V'_{DB} < V_I$, we have, by equating the slope of (6.2.26) to zero

$$V'_{DB1} = V_{GB} - V_{FB1} - \phi_{B1} + \frac{\gamma_1^2}{2} - \gamma_1 \sqrt{V_{GB} - V_{FB1} + \frac{\gamma_1^2}{4}} \tag{6.2.31}$$

If, instead, pinchoff occurs at some value of V_{DB} larger than V_I, we find, by equating the slope of either (6.2.28) or (6.2.30) to zero

$$V'_{DB2} = V_{GB} - V_{FB2} - \phi_{B2} + \frac{\gamma_2^2}{2} - \gamma_2 \sqrt{V_{GB} - V_{FB2} + \frac{\gamma_2^2}{4}} \tag{6.2.32}$$

If $V_{SB} > V_I$, it is clear that (6.2.32) must be used in determining V'_{DB}. If $V_{SB} < V_I$, (6.2.31) will be the equation to use if the value it predicts for a given V_{GB} is less than V_I. If, however, it predicts a value larger than V_I, that value should be discarded and (6.2.32) should be used instead, as in that case pinchoff occurs while the depletion region edge near the drain end of the channel is outside the implant. If channel length modulation can be neglected, the saturation current can be obtained by replacing the correct V'_{DB} value for V_{DB} in the appropriate equation among (6.2.26), (6.2.28), and (6.2.30):

$$I'_D = I_{DN}|_{V_{DB} = V'_{DB}} \tag{6.2.33}$$

and the complete model, covering both nonsaturation and saturation becomes

$$I_D = \begin{cases} I_{DN}, & V_{DB} \leq V'_{DB} & (6.2.34a) \\ I'_D, & V_{DV} > V'_{DB} & (6.2.34b) \end{cases}$$

Channel length modulation in implanted devices has not been well characterized. Frequently unimplanted device models are used (Sec. 5.2) with an empirical adjustment of their parameters.

The general shape of I_D-V_{DS} characteristics is similar to that for unimplanted devices, but some peculiarities do arise. To make a simple discussion of these possible, we first introduce a simplified model.

6.2.3 Piecewise Quadratic Model for Strong Inversion

We can simplify the current equations and develop an approximate model related to that of (4.4.30). We can obtain such a model by using an approach similar to the one that lead to (4.4.30) or even directly through an appropriate expansion of (6.2.27). However, here two different δ parameters must be used: δ_1 associated with the implanted region and δ_2 associated with the unimplanted substrate. The details are outlined in the statement of Prob. 6.2. We find that in such a model we again obtain the nonsaturation current in the form

$$I_{DN} = \begin{cases} I_1(V_{SB}, V_{DB}), & V_{SB} < V_{DB} \leq V_I & (6.2.35a) \\ I_2(V_{SB}, V_{DB}), & V_I \leq V_{SB} < V_{DB} & (6.2.35b) \\ I_1(V_{SB}, V_I) + I_2(V_I, V_{DB}), & V_{SB} < V_I < V_{DB} & (6.2.35c) \end{cases}$$

only with $I_i(V_K, V_N)$ as follows:

$$I_i(V_K, V_N) = \frac{W}{L} \mu C'_{ox}\{[V_{GB} - V_K - V_{Ti}(V_K)](V_N - V_K) - \tfrac{1}{2}(1 + \delta_i)(V_N - V_K)^2\}$$
$$(6.2.36)$$

where V_{Ti}, $i = 1, 2$, is given by (6.2.23). The parameters δ_1 and δ_2 must be carefully chosen, as the value of these parameters turns out to be crucial for guaranteeing continuity of the slope of the I_D-V_{DB} characteristics as V_{DB} goes past the critical value V_I. Slope discontinuity is undesirable because it leads to discontinuous small-signal parameters and can cause numerical problems when the model is incorporated in some computer programs for circuit analysis. This is discussed further in the statement of Prob. 6.2, where the following values are suggested for δ_1 and δ_2:

$$\delta_1 = \frac{\gamma_1(\sqrt{\phi_{B1} + V_I} - \sqrt{\phi_{B1} + V_{SB}})}{V_I - V_{SB}} \qquad (6.2.37a)$$

$$\delta_2 = \frac{\gamma_2}{2\sqrt{\phi_{B2} + V_I}} \qquad (6.2.37b)$$

Care should be exercised when using the expression for δ_1 because for values of V_{SB} very close to V_I, we will have a ratio of differences of nearly equal numbers, which can cause numerical inaccuracies. At $V_{SB} = V_I$, the expression becomes indeterminate, and can be replaced by its limit value at that point, which is $\gamma_1/(2\sqrt{\phi_B + V_I})$ (Prob. 6.2).

It is easy to show that

$$\delta_1 > \delta_2 \tag{6.2.38}$$

which may be expected, since δ_1 characterizes the heavily doped implanted region whereas δ_2 characterizes the unimplanted substrate. Unlike what was done for uniform substrates [see (4.4.33) and associated discussion], here we are not completely free to choose the δ parameters for best matching to experiment; our choices are limited by the requirements of continuity of I_D and its derivatives. One cannot expect then that the above simple model will match measurements very well in all situations. Nevertheless, we will need the simplicity of the above model to illustrate some important aspects in the *I-V* characteristics of the devices we are considering. Interested readers may want to attempt an empirical improvement of this simple model.

In the saturation region we use (6.2.33) as before, with V'_{DB} determined as the value of V_{DB} at which the nonsaturation equation gives $dI_{DN}/dV_{DB} = 0$. If $V_{SB} < V_I$ and pinchoff occurs at $V'_{DB} < V_I$, we have, working with (6.2.35a) and (6.2.36).

$$V'_{DB1} = V_{SB} + \frac{V_{GB} - V_{SB} - V_{T1}(V_{SB})}{1 + \delta_1} \tag{6.2.39}$$

However, if the above equation predicts a V'_{DB} larger than V_I, we should realize that the pinchoff point is outside the implanted region, and thus we should have worked with (6.2.35c) and (6.2.36), obtaining,

$$V'_{DB2} = V_I + \frac{V_{GB} - V_I - V_{T2}(V_I)}{1 + \delta_2} \tag{6.2.40}$$

Finally, if $V_I < V_{SB} < V_{DB}$, we work with (6.2.35b) and (6.2.36) and obtain

$$V'_{DB3} = V_{SB} + \frac{V_{GB} - V_{SB} - V_{T2}(V_{SB})}{1 + \delta_2} \tag{6.2.41}$$

The complete strong-inversion model is again given by (6.2.34), with the expressions for I_{DN} and V'_{DB} appropriately chosen as explained.

For simplicity, sometimes the unimplanted-channel approximate model of Sec. 4.4.2 is used instead of the above models.[51] In such a case, the parameters δ, V_{FB}, ϕ_B, and γ are assigned single "compromise" values. Such an approach can give satisfactory results if the dose is low. However, for high doses the results can be inaccurate. Shown in Fig. 6.6 is $\sqrt{I'_D}$ plotted vs. V_{GS} for a device with a *high* implant dose (this figure is to be contrasted with Fig. 4.27). Such behavior, which cannot be predicted by the model of Sec. 4.4.3, can be explained as follows. Assume first $V_{SB} = 0$. When V_{GS} is low, V'_{DS} is also low

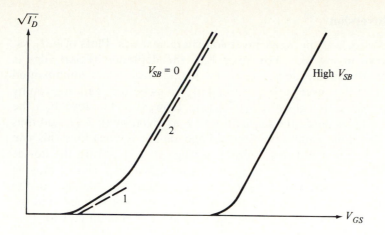

FIGURE 6.6

$\sqrt{I_D}$ as a function of V_{GS} in saturation for a p-implant, p-substrate transistor in the case of a heavy-dose deep implant, with V_{SB} as a parameter.

and $V'_{DB} < V_I$. If I'_D is the saturation current, using (6.2.33), (6.2.35a), (6.2.36), and (6.2.39), we find

$$\sqrt{I'_D} = \sqrt{\frac{(W/L)\,\mu C'_{ox}}{2(1+\delta_1)}}\,[V_{GS} - V_{T1}(0)] \qquad (6.2.42)$$

This is shown as the broken curve 1 in Fig. 6.6. Consider now very large values of V_{GB} (with V_{SB} still zero). Then V'_{DB} will be much larger than V_I and will be predicted by (6.2.40). Using this equation in (6.2.33), with I_{DN} from (6.2.35c) and (6.2.36) and neglecting I_1 in comparison to I_2, we find

$$\sqrt{I'_D} \approx \sqrt{\frac{(W/L)\,\mu C'_{ox}}{2(1+\delta_2)}}\,\{V_{GS} - [V_I + V_{T2}(V_I)]\} \qquad (6.2.43)$$

This is shown as broken curve 2 in Fig. 6.6. Note that the V_{GS} intercept in (6.2.43) is larger than that in (6.2.42), and the slope is larger since $\delta_2 < \delta_1$, as mentioned above. A plot for a real device is close to curve 1 for low V_{GS} and close to curve 2 for large V_{GS}, as shown. Finally, when $V_{SB} > V_I$, (6.2.33), (6.2.35b), (6.2.36), and (6.2.41) give

$$\sqrt{I'_D} = \sqrt{\frac{(W/L)\,\mu C'_{ox}}{2(1+\delta_2)}}\,[V_{GS} - V_{T2}(V_{SB})] \qquad (6.2.44)$$

which is shown by the straight part of the right-hand solid curve in Fig. 6.6 (the bottom curved part is due to moderate and weak inversion). In this case, a single slope is predicted (assuming, of course, a mobility independent of V_{GS}).

6.2.4 Weak Inversion

Let us now briefly look at the weak inversion characteristics. Plots of $\ln I_D$ vs. V_{GS} look as shown in Fig. 6.7. For large V_{SB}, the depletion region edge is outside the implant and the device behaves qualitatively as an unimplanted device. The slope of the curve is proportional to $1/n$ as before, with n given by (4.6.20), where $\gamma = \gamma_2$ as given by (6.2.11). However, for low V_{SB} the depletion region edge is inside the implant, $\gamma = \gamma_1$ as given by (6.2.4), and thus n is large and the slope small. For low-voltage digital applications this can create problems since it now takes a larger "swing" of V_{GS} to turn the device off. Note, also, that as V_{GS} increases the depletion region edge can be moving over a region with a widely varying concentration (from the "center" of the implant toward its "sides"). Then no simple value for n can be defined, and the slope of $\ln I_D$ with V_{GS} changes as shown; I_D is no longer exponential with V_{GS}.

6.2.5 Concluding Remarks

From the above discussion it should be clear that, if the dose is high and the implant is not shallow, several detrimental effects can occur. These include strong body effect at low V_{SB} values, degradation of $\Delta I_D/\Delta V_{GS}$ at small V_{GS} and V_{SB} values, loss of exponentiality in weak inversion, and slow turnoff. Thus, the energy of the ions being implanted is kept at a minimum (but high enough to ensure that the ions will end up in the semiconductor and not in the oxide), and high-temperature treatments are avoided to prevent spreading the implant inward. However, punchthrough considerations can dictate requirements conflicting with the above, or the use of two implants, as already discussed. It should also be noted that the implanted devices discussed in this section can show a degradation in mobility values. This is because the increased effective

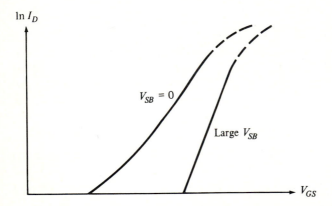

FIGURE 6.7
Weak inversion $\ln I_D$ vs. V_{GS}, with V_{SB} as a parameter, for a p-implant, p-substrate transistor.

doping causes higher electric field in the inversion layer, thus increasing surface scattering (Sec. 4.8). An effective mobility approach can be used to model the mobility degradation due to the vertical field, as in Sec. 4.8.[21, 46, 53] Short- and narrow-channel effects[46] have not been fully characterized in implanted devices. They can be qualitatively similar to those encountered in unimplanted devices, especially if the implant is shallow and the dose is small. However, deep and heavy implants have been found to result sometimes in "anomalous" short-channel effects, such as an increase in threshold voltage with decreasing channel length.[37]

6.3 IMPLANT AND SUBSTRATE OF THE OPPOSITE TYPE

We now consider a device with a p-type substrate and an n-type implant.[8, 9, 17, 21, 22–34, 38–40, 43, 47, 48–52] In the hypothetical case where all implanted ions (donors) end up at the surface, they simply change the value of the effective interface charge per unit area, Q'_o, by the value $(+q)M$, where M is the effective dose; hence, V_{T0} shifts *down* by qM/C'_{ox}.† More realistically, though, the implant profile will look again as in Fig. 6.2a. It will again be approximated as in Fig. 6.2b [here $N(y)$ and N_I represent *donor* concentrations]. With $N_I > N_{AB}$, the region between the surface and $y = y_I$ can thus be viewed as uniformly doped n-type region, with effective *donor* concentration of

$$N_{DS} = N_I - N_{AB} \tag{6.3.1}$$

We will now analyze devices with the above type of implant. The operation of such devices is rather complicated, so we must ask for the reader's patience.

6.3.1 Charges and Critical Voltages

Let us again consider the three-terminal structure of Fig. 6.1b first. For this structure we show in Fig. 6.8 the conditions in the semiconductor below the gate for a fixed V_{CB} and different V_{GB} values; the details in this figure will be explained shortly. The depletion region of the n-implant region–p-substrate junction is shown with fixed width, since V_{CB} is fixed. Note that the depletion region around the n^+ region boundary is not shown for simplicity. Since N_{DS} is not necessarily much larger than N_{AB}, we use the two-sided step junction results in Appendix C to find the magnitude of the charge per unit area on each

---

† If the resulting V_{T0} is negative, we have a depletion mode device (Sec. 4.12). A main use of such devices is as "loads" in inverters fabricated in NMOS technology.

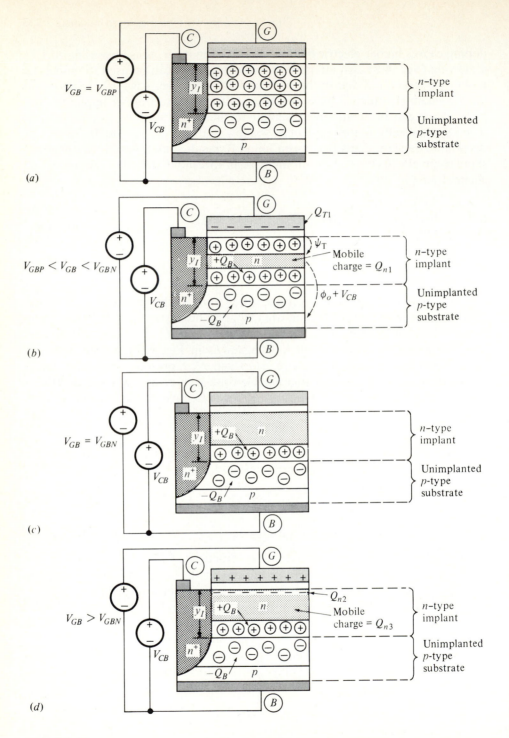

FIGURE 6.8
Condition below the oxide of an n-implant, p-substrate device for various gate-substrate voltage values. The depletion region around the n^+ region boundary is not shown for simplicity.

side of the junction. We easily obtain

$$Q'_B = F\sqrt{\frac{N_{DS}N_{AB}}{N_{DS} + N_{AB}}} \sqrt{\phi_o + V_{CB}} \qquad (6.3.2)$$

where ϕ_o is the built-in potential of the junction, and $F = (2q\epsilon_s)^{1/2}$.

We will discuss the effect of V_{GB} going *backward* in Fig. 6.8. For the moment neglect the symbols Q_{n1}, Q_{n2}, and Q_{n3} in the figure. In Fig. 6.8d, V_{GB} is assumed to be large enough to attract electrons at the surface; this is an *accumulation* condition for the *n*-type region. If V_{GB} is decreased, a point is reached where all electrons leave the surface and the latter becomes neutral, as shown in c. Reducing V_{GB} below this value makes $Q'_G - Q'_o$ negative (with Q'_G the gate and Q'_o the effective interface charges per unit area), and donor atoms must be depleted at the surface to balance this charge, as shown in b. Finally, with further reduction in V_{GB}, the top depletion region widens until it meets with that of the *pn* junction, as shown in a.

Let Q'_T be the charge per unit area in the layer below the surface (caused by either donor atoms or electrons). Charge balance requires

$$Q'_G + Q'_o + Q'_T = 0 \qquad (6.3.3)$$

Note that the charge in the bottom depletion region is $Q'_B - Q'_B = 0$, and thus Q'_B does not appear in (6.3.3). The potential balance equation is obtained by going from the gate terminal through the device to the substrate terminal:

$$V_{GB} = \psi_{ox} + \psi_T + (\phi_o + V_{CB}) + \phi_{MS} \qquad (6.3.4)$$

where ψ_T is the potential across the *top* depletion region, as shown in Fig. 6.8b, $\phi_o + V_{CB}$ is the total potential drop across the depletion regions of the implant-substrate junction, as again shown in Fig. 6.8b [see (1.5.12)], and ϕ_{MS} is the work function potential difference corresponding to the gate and the *unimplanted p*-substrate materials, as always. We also have, as in (3.2.4),

$$Q'_G = C'_{ox}\psi_{ox} \qquad (6.3.5)$$

To solve for the four unknowns (Q'_G, Q'_T, ψ_{ox}, and ψ_T) a fourth equation is needed. The form of this equation will be simple if we distinguish two cases.

1. *Surface depletion, Fig. 6.8b.* Here Q_T is due to ionized donor atoms and is positive. This is opposite from the depletion condition we have encountered in *p*-type substrates, and the potential ψ_T indicated in the figure has a *negative* sign. We can use a relation like (3.2.5a), but with appropriate sign changes:

$$Q'_T = Q'_{T1} = +F\sqrt{N_{DS}}\sqrt{-\psi_T} \qquad (6.3.6)$$

where $F = (2q\epsilon_s)^{1/2}$ has been used. Using (6.3.3) to (6.3.6):

$$Q'_{T1} = qN_{DS}\left[-\frac{\epsilon_s}{C'_{ox}} + \sqrt{\left(\frac{\epsilon_s}{C'_{ox}}\right)^2 - \frac{2\epsilon_s}{qN_{DS}} (V_{GB} - V_{FB} - \phi_o - V_{CB})} \right]$$

$$(6.3.7)$$

Consider now the region between the two depletion regions in Fig. 6.8b. This region is neutral since ionized impurity atoms are "covered" by mobile carriers of the opposite sign (Sec. 1.2). Hence, this region does not contribute to the charge balance equation (6.3.3). The region is n type, with effective donor concentration N_{DS}, as given by (6.3.1). If the structure becomes part of a transistor, the mobile electrons in this region can contribute to current conduction. For later use, then, we will evaluate here the charge per unit area Q'_{n1} of these mobile electrons. If the depletion regions were absent, the number of mobile electrons would be equal to the effective number of donor atoms. Thus Q'_{n1} would be equal to $-q\hat{M}$, where $\hat{M} = N_{DS} y_I$. However, now some donor atoms have already been depleted. Since the electron population is reduced by one electron for each depleted donor atom, the remaining mobile electron charge is

$$Q'_{n1} = -(q\hat{M} - Q'_{T1} - Q'_B) \tag{6.3.8}$$

The value V_{GBP} of V_{GB} for which the two depletion regions meet (Fig. 6.8a) can now be determined by setting $Q'_{n1} = 0$ and using (6.3.2) and (6.3.7). The expression resulting is of the form

$$V_{GBP} = V_{CB} + V_P(V_{CB}) \tag{6.3.9}$$

where V_P is the "pinchoff voltage,"† a detailed expression for which is the subject of Prob. 6.4. That expression, if we assume $N_I \gg N_{AB}$, simplifies to the following[22] (Prob. 6.4):

$$V_P(V_{CB}) = V_{P0} + \gamma_I(\sqrt{\phi_o + V_{CB}} - \sqrt{\phi_o}), \qquad N_I \gg N_{AB} \tag{6.3.10}$$

where

$$V_{P0} = V_{FB} + \phi_o - \frac{q\hat{M}}{C'_{ox}}\left(1 + \frac{y_I C'_{ox}}{2\epsilon_s}\right) + \gamma_I\sqrt{\phi_o} \tag{6.3.11}$$

with $V_{FB} = \phi_{MS} - Q'_o/C'_{ox}$ and

$$\gamma_I = \left(1 + \frac{y_I C'_{ox}}{\epsilon_s}\right)\gamma \tag{6.3.12}$$

with γ being the body effect coefficient of an *unimplanted* device on the same p-type substrate. It is thus seen from (6.3.10) that the pinchoff voltage V_P increases with V_{CB} in a way similar to the threshold voltage of unimplanted devices, only with an effective body effect coefficient γ_I larger than γ.

If V_{GB} is increased sufficiently, the surface depletion region will disappear, as shown in Fig. 6.8c. At this point, the surface will be neutral and $Q'_T = 0$, thus $\psi_T = 0$. Using these observations and (6.3.3) to (6.3.5),

---

† "Pinchoff" in the present context refers to the condition illustrated in Fig. 6.8a, rather than to the pinchoff condition encountered in our discussion of unimplanted devices.

we obtain the corresponding value of V_{GB}, denoted by V_{GBN}:

$$V_{GBN} = \phi_{MS} - \frac{Q_o'}{C_{ox}'} + \phi_o + V_{CB} \tag{6.3.13a}$$

$$= V_{FB} + \phi_o + V_{CB} \tag{6.3.13b}$$

$$= V_{FBN} + V_{CB} \tag{6.3.13c}$$

where

$$V_{FBN} = V_{FB} + \phi_o \tag{6.3.14}$$

It is easy to see that V_{FBN} is actually the flat-band voltage of the structure comprised of the gate, the insulator, and the n-type implanted region (assumed uniform).

From our analysis so far, it is seen that for V_{GB} values satisfying

$$V_{GBP} < V_{GB} < V_{GBN} \tag{6.3.15}$$

an undepleted n region will exist between two depletion regions, as in Fig. 6.8b. This undepleted region can conduct current when it is part of a transistor. Because it is located *below* the surface rather than being adjacent to it, it is referred to as *buried channel*. For later use, we will express the conditions for buried-channel formation in terms of the voltage between the gate and terminal C in Fig. 6.8b. Writing $V_{GB} = V_{GC} + V_{CB}$ in (6.3.15) and using (6.3.9) and (6.3.13c) we obtain

$$V_P(V_{CB}) < V_{GC} < V_{FBN} \tag{6.3.16}$$

Before leaving the discussion of surface depletion, we parenthetically consider a special, normally undesired case. For given N_I and V_{CB}, devices with larger y_I will require more negative ψ_T to achieve the pinchoff condition illustrated in Fig. 6.8a. If y_I is too large, then ψ_T must attain such values that, before pinchoff can be achieved, surface inversion will occur, as shown in Fig. 6.9. (Note that the implanted region is n type, so the inversion layer consists of *holes*.) Once this inversion becomes strong, the surface potential and the width of the top depletion region do not change appreciably with V_{GB}. They become pinned to some value, as in the case of unimplanted devices. It now becomes impossible to pinch off the device by making V_{GB} more negative. Pinchoff can only be achieved by increasing V_{CB}, in which case the *bottom* depletion region in the n implant will widen until it touches the pinned edge of the top depletion region. To avoid the above problems, so that the device can be pinched off even with $V_{CB} = 0$, the simultaneous use of high dose and high energy for the implant is avoided.

2. *Surface accumulation,*† *Fig. 6.8d.* For V_{GB} values satisfying

$$V_{GB} > V_{GBN} \tag{6.3.17a}$$

---

† Also referred to as *surface enhancement*.

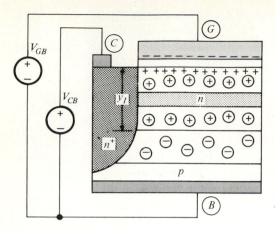

FIGURE 6.9
Illustration of the inability of the gate-substrate voltage to pinch off the channel because of a very high dose for an n-implant, p-substrate device. The depletion region around the n^+ region is not shown for simplicity.

or, in terms of V_{GC},

$$V_{GC} > V_{FBN} \tag{6.3.17b}$$

we have the situation of Fig. 6.8d. Here Q'_T is caused by the mobile electrons in the surface accumulation layer. The thickness of this layer is very small and will be assumed to be infinitesimal; hence the potential needed to support it will be negligible. This means $\psi_T = 0$, since there is no depletion region immediately below the accumulation layer to cause any additional potential drop. Thus (6.3.3) to (6.3.5) give, for this case,

$$Q'_T = Q'_{n2} = -C'_{ox}(V_{GB} - V_{FBN} - V_{CB}) \tag{6.3.18}$$

For simplicity, we will assume that this formula holds all the way down to $V_{GB} = V_{FBN} + V_{CB}$.

In addition to the above, mobile electrons also exist throughout the undepleted n-type material. Since there is now only one depletion region in the n-type region, we will have for the charge of these electrons, instead of (6.3.8),

$$Q'_{n3} = -(q\hat{M} - Q'_B) \tag{6.3.19}$$

6.3.2   Transistor Operation

We now consider a complete transistor as in Fig. 6.1a, with $V_{DB} > V_{SB}$ ($V_{DS} > 0$). We will denote the effective reverse bias between a point in the neutral part of the channel and the unimplanted substrate by V_{CB}. We will thus be able to apply directly the formulas derived above. The value of V_{CB} increases from V_{SB} at the source to V_{DB} at the drain. Thus, the depletion region of the np junction will be deeper as we go toward the drain. Depending on the relative values of the terminal voltages, we can distinguish several regions of operation, which are discussed below.

Assume first that a buried channel exists next to the source; from (6.3.16), this requires $V_P(V_{SB}) < V_{GS} < V_{FBN}$. Since V_{CB} increases toward the drain, $V_P(V_{CB})$ also increases, and tends to drive the drain end of the channel toward pinchoff. If the drain potential is not large enough actually to cause pinchoff, the channel will look as shown in Fig. 6.10a, where the shaded area represents the depletion region.[22] If the drain potential exceeds a certain value, the channel will be pinched off near the drain, as shown in Fig. 6.10b. The two regions of operation in Fig. 6.10a and b are called *nonsaturation* and *saturation*, respectively; the critical value of V_{DS} at the transition between them is denoted by V'_{DS1}. In saturation, the electrons are assumed to travel from the tip of the pinched-off channel through the depletion region to the drain, through a mechanism analogous to that for unimplanted devices in saturation. In analogy to the corresponding simplified picture for those devices, it can be argued here that, if the channel in Fig. 6.10b is long, the drain current in saturation will be practically constant and equal to the nonsaturation current obtained as V_{DS} approaches V'_{DS1}. A typical I_D-V_{DS} characteristic for this case is shown by the lower curve in Fig. 6.11. A quantitative discussion of I_D will follow later.

Assume now that V_{GB} is large enough to cause surface enhancement at the source. From (6.3.17b), this requires $V_{GS} > V_{FBN}$. If V_{DS} is small, surface enhancement can exist throughout the length of the channel, as shown in Fig. 6.10c. As the drain potential is raised, though, the depletion region widens and $|Q'_B|$ increases near the drain. From (6.3.18), with $V_{CB} = V_{DB}$, $|Q'_{n2}|$ there will be decreasing and will eventually disappear. Then the drain end of the channel will exhibit surface depletion, as shown in Fig. 6.10d. For this to happen we must have, from (6.3.16), $V_{GD} < V_{FBN}$. Writing $V_{GD} = V_{GS} - V_{DS}$, this gives the condition $V_{DS} > V_{GS} - V_{FBN}$. Finally, further increase in the drain potential can increase $V_P(V_{DB})$ to the point where the channel becomes pinched off, as shown in Fig. 6.10e. The corresponding critical value of V_{DS} is denoted by V'_{DS2}. An I_D-V_{DS} characteristic corresponding to the cases in Fig. 6.10c, d, and e is shown by the upper curve in Fig. 6.11.

We now show how the drain current can be calculated for the various regions summarized in Fig. 6.10.[21, 22] We first consider nonsaturation operation, corresponding to cases a, c, and d in Fig. 6.10. Here we cannot use (4.4.13), since there is no inversion layer involved. However, the role of Q'_I in that equation is now played by the total mobile charge per unit area Q'_n. Accordingly, we have

$$I_{DN} = \frac{W}{L} \int_{V_{SB}}^{V_{DB}} \mu [-Q'_n(V_{CB})] \, dV_{CB} \tag{6.3.20}$$

We consider each of the three nonsaturation cases (Figs. 6.10 and 6.11) separately.

1. *Surface depletion.*† In this case, shown in Fig. 6.10a, the total mobile charge

---

† This mode of operation is sometimes also referred to as the *buried-channel mode*.

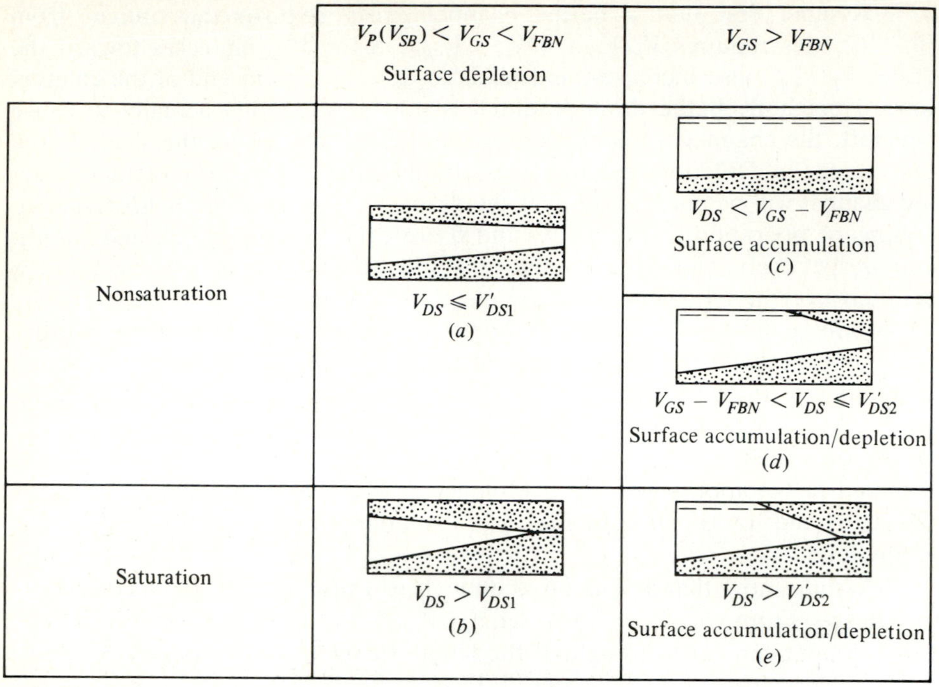

$V_P(V_{SB}) < V_{GS} < V_{FBN}$
Surface depletion
$V_{GS} > V_{FBN}$
Nonsaturation
$V_{DS} \leqslant V'_{DS1}$
(a)
$V_{DS} < V_{GS} - V_{FBN}$
Surface accumulation
(c)
$V_{GS} - V_{FBN} < V_{DS} \leqslant V'_{DS2}$
Surface accumulation/depletion
(d)
Saturation
$V_{DS} > V'_{DS1}$
(b)
$V_{DS} > V'_{DS2}$
Surface accumulation/depletion
(e)

FIGURE 6.10
Modes of operation for an n-implant, p-substrate device; shown is only the implant part.

I_D
Nonsaturation
Saturation
Surface accumulation/ depletion
Surface accumulation/ depletion
Surface accumulation
Surface depletion
0
V_{DS}

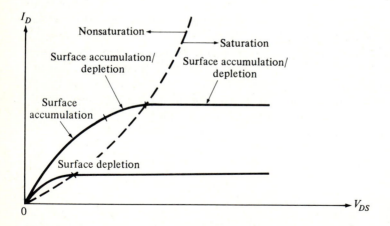

FIGURE 6.11
Relation of I-V characteristics to the modes of operation shown in Fig. 6.10.

per unit area is Q'_{n1}, given by (6.3.8). Thus (6.3.20) becomes:

$$I_{DN} = \frac{W}{L} \int_{V_{SB}}^{V_{DB}} \mu_B(-Q'_{n1}) \, dV_{CB} \qquad (6.3.21)$$

where μ_B is the value of the mobility *in the bulk* of the n region.

2. *Surface accumulation, Fig. 6.10c.* Here Q'_n consists of the surface charge Q'_{n2}, given by (6.3.18), and the charge Q'_{n3} due to the mobile electrons in the undepleted part of the n-region bulk, given by (6.3.19). Hence (6.3.20) becomes:

$$I_{DN} = \frac{W}{L} \int_{V_{SB}}^{V_{DB}} [\mu_S(-Q'_{n2}) + \mu_B(-Q'_{n3})] \, dV_{CB} \qquad (6.3.22)$$

where μ_S is the *surface* mobility. This is smaller than the bulk mobility μ_B, for reasons similar to those discussed in Sec. 4.8.

3. *Surface accumulation/depletion.* This case is shown in Fig. 6.10d. Let V_{CBI} be the value of V_{CB} corresponding to that point in the channel where, as shown, we pass from accumulation to depletion behavior. At this point, $Q'_T = 0$ and from (6.3.18) we obtain

$$V_{CBI} = V_{GB} - V_{FBN} \qquad (6.3.23)$$

We have $Q'_n = Q'_{n2} + Q'_{n3}$ to the left of this point and $Q'_n = Q'_{n1}$ to the right. Thus (6.3.20) gives

$$I_{DN} = \frac{W}{L} \int_{V_{SB}}^{V_{CBI}} [\mu_S(-Q'_{n2}) + \mu_B(-Q'_{n3})] \, dV_{CB} + \frac{W}{L} \int_{V_{CBI}}^{V_{DB}} \mu_B(-Q'_{n1}) \, dV_{CB}$$
$$(6.3.24)$$

Using the expressions developed for Q'_{n1}, Q'_{n2}, and Q'_{n3} in the above expressions provides the nonsaturation current I_{DN}. The value of V'_{DS} can be obtained as usual by setting $dI_{DN}/dV_{DS} = 0$ or by setting the total mobile charge at the drain end of the channel equal to zero. The resulting formulation is complicated but, as before, the expressions can be simplified through appropriate series expansions. Simplified formulas thus obtained are shown in Table 6.1.[22]

As before, several refinements are possible. For example, an effective *surface* mobility can be defined and made dependent on V_{GS}, in a similar way as in Sec. 4.8.[22, 31, 43]† The *bulk* mobility is often taken independent of V_{GS}.‡

---

† A simple approximate model suggested for this[22] is $\mu_{S,\text{eff}} = \mu_{S0}/[1 + \theta(V_{GS} - V_{FBN})]$.

‡ It has, however, been suggested[52] that, because the electrons move inside a thin slab of undepleted material (Fig. 6.10a), their mobility is limited to values below those for free bulk conduction. This is attributed to effects similar to those responsible for surface scattering, which become more severe as the "slab" becomes thinner. Since the thickness of the slab depends on V_{GS}, a dependence of μ_B on V_{GS} is claimed.

TABLE 6.1

Approximate strong-inversion model for n-implant–p-substrate devices[22]†

$V_P \leq V_{GS} < V_{FBN}$:

$$I_D = \frac{W}{L}\frac{\mu_B C'_{ox}}{1+\sigma}[(V_{GS}-V_P)V_{DS} - \tfrac{1}{2}(1+\delta)V_{DS}^2], \qquad V_{DS} \leq V'_{DS1}$$

$$= \frac{W}{L}\frac{\mu_B C'_{ox}}{1+\sigma}\frac{(V_{GS}-V_P)^2}{2(1+\delta)}, \qquad V_{DS} \geq V'_{DS1}$$

$$V'_{DS1} = \frac{V_{GS}-V_P}{1+\delta}$$

$V_{GS} \geq V_{FBN}$:

$$I_D = \frac{W}{L}\frac{\mu_B C'_{ox}}{1+\sigma}\{(V_{GS}-V_P)V_{DS} - \tfrac{1}{2}(1+\delta)V_{DS}^2 + (r-1)[(V_{GS}-V_{FBN})V_{DS} - \tfrac{1}{2}V_{DS}^2]\},$$
$$V_{DS} < V_{GS}-V_{FBN}$$

$$= \frac{W}{L}\frac{\mu_B C'_{ox}}{1+\sigma}[(V_{GS}-V_P)V_{DS} - \tfrac{1}{2}(1+\delta)V_{DS}^2 + \tfrac{1}{2}(r-1)(V_{GS}-V_{FBN})^2],$$
$$V_{GS}-V_{FBN} \leq V_{DS} < V'_{DS2}$$

$$= \frac{W}{L}\frac{\mu_B C'_{ox}}{1+\sigma}\left[\frac{(V_{GS}-V_P)^2}{2(1+\delta)} + \tfrac{1}{2}(r-1)(V_{GS}-V_{FBN})^2\right], \qquad V_{DS} \geq V'_{DS2}$$

$$V'_{DS2} = \frac{V_{GS}-V_P}{1+\delta}$$

where

$$V_P = V_{P0} + \gamma_t(\sqrt{\varphi_o + V_{SB}} - \sqrt{\varphi_o})$$

$$\sigma = \frac{C'_{ox}y_I}{\epsilon_s}\left(\frac{C'_{ox}y_I}{2\epsilon_s}+1\right)$$

$$r = (1+\sigma)\frac{\mu_s}{\mu_B}$$

$$\delta = (1+\sigma)\frac{\gamma}{4\sqrt{\varphi_o}}$$

† $V_{DS} \geq 0$; channel length modulation not included.

Channel length modulation can be included, with V'_{DS} values slightly modified to maintain a continuous slope in the I_D-V_{DS} curves. The saturation region for these devices has not been well characterized in the literature. The formulations of Sec. 5.2 are sometimes used with an empirical adjustment of their parameters. Finally, empirical modifications would be needed to ensure continuity for the derivatives of the current with respect to each terminal voltage at the break points.

For very small, fixed V_{DS} the plot of I_D vs. V_{GS} is as shown by the broken line in Fig. 6.12a. For buried channels ($V_P \leq V_{GS} < V_{FBN}$) the device behaves as an unimplanted device qualitatively. However, although μ_B is larger than the surface mobility, the quantity $\mu_B C'_{ox}/(1+\sigma)$, which characterizes surface depletion operation (see Table 6.1), can be smaller than the corresponding quantity $\mu C'_{ox}$ of unimplanted devices. Intuitively, this happens because, as shown in Fig. 6.10a, the channel is further away from the gate than in the case

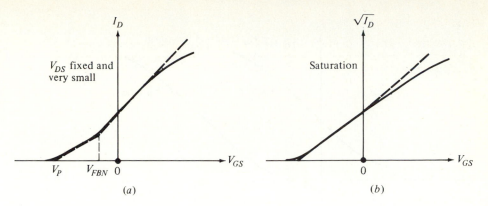

FIGURE 6.12
Characteristics of n-implant, p-substrate transistor. (a) I_D as a function of V_{GS} with very small V_{DS}; (b) saturation $\sqrt{I_D}$ vs. V_{GS}. Dotted line: model with constant mobility; solid line: real device.

of an unimplanted device, and thus the influence of the gate is somewhat reduced. Once surface accumulation occurs, however ($V_{GS} \geq V_{FBN}$), variations of the channel charge with V_{GS} occur at the surface, and, thus, the slope is determined by the surface mobility and the oxide thickness only. The solid line in Fig. 6.12a represents a real device, and no breakpoint is, of course, observed in this case. Mobility degradation at high V_{GS} (Sec. 4.8) can be seen. The deviation from straight line at very low V_{GS} is due to the presence of diffusion currents, which we have not included in the simple model we have presented. This phenomenon is reminiscent of weak inversion in unimplanted devices.[50]

For the plot of $\sqrt{I_D}$ vs. V_{GS} in saturation, the model predicts again a changing slope effect, although not so pronounced, as shown by the broken line in Fig. 6.12b. The slight upward trend of the slope, however, tends to be counteracted by the degradation of mobility with V_{GS}, and the resulting behavior is as shown by the solid line, a significant part of which is practically straight. Thus, a saturation equation like (4.4.30b) can again be used in such cases in the form

$$I_D = k(V_{GS} - V_T)^2 \qquad (6.3.25)$$

only with the constant of proportionality k somewhat reduced from that of an unimplanted device, and V_T negative for low V_{SB} (and approximately equal to V_P). For some depletion devices, the above equation has been shown to be accurate, even more so than for enhancement devices on the same substrate.[39] In fact, in some circuit analysis computer programs the complete equation (4.4.30), in both nonsaturation and saturation, is used to model implanted depletion devices, using a negative V_T. Depending on device details, however, serious errors can result from such approximations. A 3/2 power model similar to (4.4.17) has also been proposed[17] (Prob. 6.9).

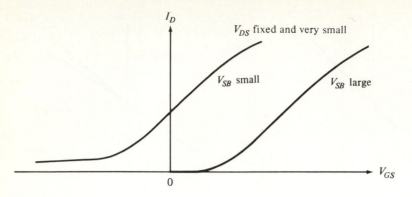

FIGURE 6.13
I_D vs. V_{GS}, with V_{SB} as a parameter, for the n-implant, p-substrate transistor with a very large implant dose of Fig. 6.9.

It should be noted that the model of Table 6.1 is not valid for devices having the problem illustrated in Fig. 6.9. In such devices, a channel will exist when V_{SB} is small, even if V_{GS} is made very negative. The behavior shown in Fig. 6.13 will then be observed. Such devices are normally avoided.

The model we have presented is not valid when the two depletion regions are about to meet. This is both because then our assumptions of "abrupt" depletion region edges are inadequate, and because diffusion currents become important. Depending on the value of V_{SB}, the "meeting point" of the two regions can occur at various depths, a fact that affects both the distance from the gate and the effective implant concentration at that point (where most of the current flows). Thus, the dependence of I_D on V_{SB} in this part of the operating range is complicated. A general model valid in all regions of operation (analogous to the charge sheet model of Sec. 4.3) has been proposed for the depletion device.[50] Short-channel effects[38] have been observed to be qualitatively similar to those for unimplanted devices.

The n-type implants on p-substrates are usually used for making depletion mode devices. However, it is possible to end up with enhancement mode devices after lowering the threshold, if one starts with a sufficiently high V_{FB}.[28, 48]

REFERENCES

1. K. G. Aubuchon, *Proceedings of the International Conference on Properties and Use of M.I.S. Structures*, Grenoble, France, p. 575, 1969.
2. R. W. Bower and H. G. Dill, *International Electron Devices Meeting*, paper 16.6 (unpublished), 1966.
3. M. R. MacPherson, "The adjustment of MOS transistor threshold voltage by ion implantation," *Applied Physics Letters*, vol. 18, pp. 502–504, 1971.

4. T. Masuhara, M. Nagata, and N. Hashimo, "A high-performance n-channel MOS LSI using depletion type load elements," *IEEE Journal of Solid-State Circuits*, vol. SC-7, pp. 224–231, June 1972.

5. T. E. Seidel, "Ion implantation," chapter 6 in *VLSI Technology*, S. M. Sze (editor), McGraw-Hill, New York, 1983.

6. L. C. Parillo, "VLSI process integration," chapter 11 in *VLSI Technology*, S. M. Sze (editor), McGraw-Hill, New York, 1983.

7. M. R. MacPherson, "Threshold shift calculation for ion implanted MOS devices," *Solid-State Electronics*, vol. 15, pp. 1319–1326, 1972.

8. J. R. Edwards and G. Mar, "Depletion-mode IGFET made by deep ion implantation," *IEEE Transactions on Electron Devices*, vol. ED-20, pp. 283–289, 1973.

9. J. S. T. Huang, "Characteristics of a depletion-mode IGFET," *IEEE Transactions on Electron Devices*, vol. ED-20, pp. 513–515, 1973.

10. P. P. Peressini and W. S. Johnson, "Threshold adjustment of n-channel enhancement mode FETs by ion implantation," *Technical Digest*, International Electron Devices Meeting, Washington, D.C., pp. 467–486, 1973.

11. R. H. Dennard, F. H. Gaensslen, H. Yu, V. L. Rideout, E. Bassons, and A. R. LeBlanc, "Design of ion-implanted MOSFET's with very small physical dimensions," *IEEE Journal of Solid-State Circuits*, vol. SC-9, pp. 256–268, 1974.

12. E. C. Douglas and A. G. F. Dingwall, "Ion implantation for threshold control in COSMOS circuits," *IEEE Transactions on Electron Devices*, vol. ED-21, pp. 324–331, 1974.

13. M. Kamoshida, "Electrical characteristics of boron-implanted n-channel MOS transistors," *Solid-State Electronics*, vol. 17, pp. 621–626, 1974.

14. V. L. Rideout, F. H. Gaensslen, and A. LeBlanc, "Device design considerations for ion-implanted n-channel MOSFETs," *IBM Journal of Research and Development*, p. 50, January 1975.

15. A. M. Mohsen and F. J. Morris, "Measurements on depletion-mode field-effect transistors and buried channel MOS capacitors for the characterization of bulk transfer charge-coupled devices," *Solid-State Electronics*, vol. 18, pp. 407–416, 1975.

16. J. R. Verjans and R. J. Van Overstraeten, "Electrical characteristics of boron-implanted n-channel MOS transistors for use in logic circuits," *IEEE Transactions on Electron Devices*, vol. ED-22, pp. 862–868, 1975.

17. J. S. T. Huang and G. W. Taylor, "Modeling of an ion-implanted silicon-gate depletion mode IGFET," *IEEE Transactions on Electron Devices*, vol. ED-22, pp. 995–1001, 1975. See also W. Marciniak and H. Madura, "Comments on the Huang and Taylor model of ion-implanted silicon-gate depletion-mode IGFET," *Solid-State Electronics*, vol. 28, pp. 313–315, 1985.

18. G. Doucet, F. Van de Wiele, and P. Jespers, "Theoretical and experimental study of MOS transistors nonuniformly doped by SILOX technique," *Solid-State Electronics*, vol. 19, pp. 191–199, 1976.

19. R. R. Troutman, "Ion-implanted threshold tailoring for insulated gate field-effect transistors," *IEEE Transactions on Electron Devices*, ED-24, p.182–192, 1977.

20. H. Feltl, "Onset of heavy inversion in MOS devices doped nonuniformly near the surface," *IEEE Transactions on Electron Devices*, vol. ED-24, pp. 288–289, 1977.

21. E. Demoulin and F. Van de Wiele, "Ion implanted MOS transistors," in *Process and Device Modelling for Integrated Circuit Design*, F. Van de Wiele, W. L. Engl, and P. G. Jespers (editors), Noordhoff, Leyden, The Netherlands, 1977.

22. G. Merckel, "Ion implanted MOS transistors—depletion mode devices," in *Process and Device Modelling for Integrated Circuit Design*, F. Van de Wiele, W. L. Engl, and P. G. Jespers (editors), Noordhoff, Leyden, The Netherlands, pp. 617–676, 1977.

23. P. E. Schmidt and M. B. Das, "D.C. and high-frequency characteristics of built-in channel MOS-FETs," *Solid-State Electronics*, vol. 21, pp. 495–505, 1978.

24. G. R. Mohan Rao, "An accurate model for a depletion mode IGFET used as a load device," *Solid-State Electronics*, vol. 21, pp. 711–714, 1978.

25. R. A. Haken, "Analysis of the deep depletion MOSFET and the use of the dc characteristics for determining bulk-channel charge coupled device parameters," *Solid-State Electronics*, vol. 21, pp. 753–761, 1978.

26. T. E. Hendrikson, "A simplified model for subpinchoff condition in depletion mode IGFET's," *IEEE Transactions on Electron Devices*, vol. ED-25, pp. 435–441, 1978.

27. Y. A. El-Mansy, "A nonlinear CAD model for the depletion-mode IGFET," *Technical Digest*, International Electron Devices Meeting, Washington, D.C., pp. 20–25, 1978.

28. K. Nishiuchi, H. Oka, T. Nakamura, H. Ishikawa, and M. Shinoda, "A normally-off type buried channel MOSFET for VLSI circuits," *Technical Digest*, International Electron Devices Meeting, Washington, D.C., p. 26, 1978.

29. F. H. Gaensslen and K. C. Jaeger, "Temperature dependent threshold behavior of depletion mode MOSFETs," *Solid-State Electronics*, vol. 22, pp. 423–430, 1979.

30. J. R. Brews, "Threshold shifts due to nonuniform doping profiles in surface channel MOS-FET's," *IEEE Transactions on Electron Devices*, vol. ED-26, p. 1696, 1979.

31. G. Baccarani, F. Landini, and B. Ricco, "Depletion-mode MOSFET model including a field-dependent surface mobility," *IEE Proceedings*, vol. 127, part I, pp. 62–66, 1980.

32. Y. A. El-Mansy, "Analysis and characterization of the depletion-mode IGFET," *IEEE Journal of Solid-State Circuits*, vol. SC-15, pp. 331–340, 1980.

33. S. M. Sze, *Physics of Semiconductor Devices*, John Wiley, New York, 1981.

34. J. R. Brews, "Physics of the MOS transistor," chapter 1 in *Silicon Integrated Circuits*, *Part A*, D. Kahng (editor), Applied Solid-State Science Series, Academic Press, New York, 1981.

35. L. M. Dang and H. Iwai, "Modeling the impurity profile of an ion-implanted IGFET for the calculation of threshold voltages," *IEEE Transactions on Electron Devices*, vol. ED-28, pp. 116–117, January 1981.

36. P. K. Chatterjee, J. E. Leiss, and G. W. Taylor, "A dynamic average model for the body effect in ion implanted short-channel ($L = 1$ μm) MOSFET's," *IEEE Transactions on Electron Devices*, vol. ED-28, pp. 606–607, May 1981.

37. M. Nishida and H. Onodera, "An anomalous increase of threshold voltages with shortening the channel lengths for deeply boron-implanted n-channel MOSFET's," *IEEE Transactions on Electron Devices*, vol. ED-28, pp. 1101–1103, September 1981.

38. N. Ballay and B. Baylac, "Analytical modelling of depletion-mode MOSFET with short- and narrow-channel effects," *IEE Proceedings*, vol. 127, part I, pp. 225–230, December 1981.

39. M. R. Wordeman and R. H. Dennard, "Threshold voltage characteristics of depletion-mode MOSFETs," *IEEE Transactions on Electron Devices*, vol. ED-28, pp. 1025–1030, 1981.

40. U. Ohno and Y. Okuto, "Electron mobility in n-channel depletion type MOS transistors," *IEEE Transactions on Electron Devices*, vol. ED-29, pp. 190–194, 1982.

41. A. M. Asenov, "Simple model for threshold voltage of a nonunifying doped short-channel MOS transistor," *Electronics Letters*, vol. 18, pp. 481–483, May 1982.

42. K-Y. Fu, "A new analysis of the threshold voltage for non-uniform ion-implanted MOS-FET's," *IEEE Transactions on Electron Devices*, vol. ED-29, pp. 1810–1813, November 1982.

43. S. Haque-Ahmed and C. A. T. Salama, "Depletion mode MOSFET modelling for CAD," *IEE Proceedings*, vol. 130, part I, pp. 281–286, 1983.

44. K. Shenai, "Analytical solutions for threshold voltage calculations in ion-implanted IGFETs," *Solid-State Electronics*, vol. 26, pp. 761–766, 1983.

45. D. A. Antoniadis, "Calculation of threshold voltage in nonuniformly doped MOSFET's," *IEEE Transactions on Electron Devices*, vol. ED-31, pp. 303–307, March 1984.

46. P. Ratnam and C. A. T. Salama, "A new approach to the modeling of nonuniformly doped short-channel MOSFET's," *IEEE Transactions on Electron Devices*, vol. ED-31, pp. 1289–1298, September 1984.

47. J. S. T. Huang, J. W. Schrankler, and J. S. Kueng, "Short-channel threshold model for buried-channel MOSFETs," *IEEE Transactions on Electron Devices*, vol. ED-31, pp. 1889–1895, December 1984.

48. F. M. Klaassen and W. Hes, "Compensated MOSFET devices," *Solid-State Electronics*, vol. 28, pp. 359–373, 1985.

49. G. J. Hu and R. H. Bruce, "Design tradeoffs between surface and buried channel FETs," *IEEE Transactions on Electron Devices*, vol. ED-32, pp. 584–588, March 1985.
50. C. Turchetti and G. Masetti, "Analysis of the depletion-mode MOSFET including diffusion and drift currents," *IEEE Transactions on Electron Devices*, vol. ED-32, pp. 773–782, April 1985.
51. F. M. Klaassen, "MOS device modelling," in *Design of VLSI Circuits for Telecommunications*, Y. Tsividis and P. Antognetti (editors), Prentice-Hall, Englewood Cliffs, 1985.
52. C-Y. Wu and K. C. Hsu, "Mobility models for the I-V characteristics of buried-channel MOSFETs," *Solid-State Electronics*, vol. 28, pp. 917–923, 1985.
53. C-Y. Wu and Y-W. Daih, "An accurate mobility model for the *I-V* characteristics of n-channel enhancement-mode MOSFETs with single-channel boron implantation," *Solid-State Electronics*, vol. 28, pp. 1271–1278, 1985.

PROBLEMS

6.1. Develop an algorithm which can be used by a computer to determine the drain current of a p-substrate–p-implant device given the model parameters and V_{GB}, V_{DB}, and V_{SB}. Assume the device is in strong inversion and neglect channel length modulation.

6.2. (*Warning*: this is a long problem.) This problem considers the development of the approximate quadratic model discussed in Sec. 6.2.3. The ideas involved are similar to the ones in Sec. 4.4.2.

(a) Show that the expressions for Q'_B, (6.2.3) and (6.2.10), can be approximated by using

$$-\frac{Q'_B}{C'_{ox}} = \gamma_1\sqrt{\phi_{B1} + V_{SB}} + \delta_1(V_{CB} - V_{SB}) \qquad V_{SB} < V_{CB} \le V_I$$

$$-\frac{Q'_B}{C'_{ox}} = \frac{qM}{C'_{ox}} + \gamma_2\sqrt{\phi_{B2} + V_{SB}} + \delta_2(V_{CB} - V_{SB}) \qquad V_I \le V_{SB} < V_{CB}$$

$$-\frac{Q'_B}{C'_{ox}} = \frac{qM}{C'_{ox}} + \gamma_2\sqrt{\phi_{B2} + V_I} + \delta_2(V_{CB} - V_I) \qquad V_{SB} < V_I < V_{CB}$$

where δ_2 is, until further notice, an empirical parameter [see part (*f*)], and δ_1 is given by (6.2.37a). Plot the exact and approximate $-Q'_B/C'_{ox}$ (in analogy to Fig. 4.10) for all cases, and show that the first and third expression for $-Q'_B/C'_{ox}$ give the same value at the boundary $V_{CB} = V_I$, and this value is exact. Comment as to why these are useful properties of the approximate expressions.

(b) Propose empirical values for δ_2 (in analogy to those for δ in Sec. 4.4.2) and show that $\delta_2 < \delta_1$. Show that for best accuracy of the equations given above, δ_2 should be made dependent on V_{SB} for $V_I \le V_{SB} < V_{CB}$ and on V_I for $V_{SB} < V_I < V_{CB}$.

(c) Show that at $V_{SB} = V_I$ the value of δ_1 given above becomes indeterminate, and can be replaced by $\gamma/(2\sqrt{\phi_B + V_I})$ at that point. Discuss the numerical problems involved in evaluating δ_1 when V_{SB} is very close to V_I, and suggest an improvement.

(d) Use the above approximations to derive the model in (6.2.35) and (6.2.36).

(e) Derive the expressions for V'_{DB} given in (6.2.39) to (6.2.41).

(f) Check the model for continuity of the current and its derivatives with respect to all bias voltages at appropriate critical points. Explain the choice of δ_2 as in (6.2.37b), for reasons of continuity of dI_D/dV_{SB} at $V_{SB} = V_I$, and comment on the ensuing effect on the accuracy of I_D.

(g) Show that, if a value different from the one suggested above is used for δ_1, dI_{DN}/dV_{DB} can be discontinuous at $V_{DB} = V_I$.

6.3. The channel of a device with $d_{ox} = 0.05 \ \mu m$ and a p substrate with $N_A = 3 \times 10^3 \ \mu m^{-3}$ is implanted with *acceptors* using an effective dose of $10^4 \ \mu m^{-2}$. The value of y_I is 0.2 μm. Assume $W/L = 10$, $\mu = 70 \ \mu m^2/(V \cdot ns)$, $V_{FB1} = 0$ V, and $\phi_{B1} = 0.7$ V. Plot (a) $V_T(V_{SB})$ vs. V_{SB}; (b) I_D vs. V_{DS} with V_{GS} as a parameter, for $V_{SB} = 0$ V; and (c) $\sqrt{I_D}$ vs. V_{GS} in saturation for $V_{SB} = 0$ V and $V_{SB} = 6$ V. Choose appropriate voltage ranges so that all pertinent effects are evident on the plots.

6.4. Find an accurate expression for $V_P(V_{CB})$ in (6.3.9). Show that for $N_I \gg N_{AB}$ it reduces to (6.3.10).

6.5. The channel of a device with $d_{ox} = 0.04 \ \mu m$ and a p substrate with $N_A = 5 \times 10^3 \ \mu m^{-3}$ is implanted with *donors* using an effective dose of $10^4 \ \mu m^{-2}$; the value of y_I is 0.1 μm. Assume $W/L = 5$, $\mu_S = 60 \ \mu m^2/(V \cdot ns)$, $\mu_B = 80 \ \mu m^2/(V \cdot ns)$, $V_{FB} = 0$ V. Using the model of Table 6.1, plot (a) I_D vs. V_{DS} with V_{GS} as a parameter, for $V_{SB} = 0$ V; (b) I_D vs. V_{GS} for $V_{DS} = 0.1$ V, for $V_{SB} = 0$ V and $V_{SB} = 5$ V. Choose appropriate bias ranges so that all pertinent effects are evident on the plots.

6.6. For the device of Prob. 6.5, what is the maximum value of y_I for which turnoff at $V_{SB} = 0$ can be guaranteed with a sufficiently negative V_{GS} (i.e., so that the problem illustrated in Fig. 6.9 does not occur)?

6.7. Find the values for V'_{DS1} and V'_{DS2} used in Fig. 6.10 by using equations from the main text. Compare the resulting expressions to the corresponding approximate relations in Table 6.1 and comment.

6.8. Consider an n-implant–p-substrate device in surface depletion operation. It has been proposed[17] to approximate Q'_{T1} (see Fig. 6.8b) by

$$Q'_{T1} \approx \bar{C}'(V_{GB} - V_{FB} - \phi_o - V_{CB})$$

where $\bar{C}'$ is an approximate parameter having the dimensions of capacitance. Show that the above relation can be derived from (6.3.7) by performing an appropriate Taylor series expansion of the square root, keeping the first two terms in it, and adjusting the coefficient of the first-order term for better accuracy. Comment on the limits of validity of such an approximation.

6.9. Using the expression in Prob. 6.8, show that the drain current for surface depletion operation can be approximated by an equation in the form of (4.4.17) if new "effective" values are defined for V_{FB} and ϕ_B.[17] Compare qualitatively the resulting expression to the model in Table 6.1.

6.10. Prove (6.2.10) using basic electrostatics (Appendix B).

CHAPTER 7

THE MOS TRANSISTOR IN DYNAMIC OPERATION— LARGE-SIGNAL MODELING

7.1 INTRODUCTION

The MOS transistor has been treated in previous chapters with the assumption that all terminal voltages are constant. However, the device is usually employed in circuits with *varying* terminal voltages. Such "dynamic" operation causes the transistor charges to vary, and the charge changes must be supplied from the outside world by extra currents flowing through the device terminals; here "extra" refers to currents not predicted by dc theory.

The subject of this chapter is the evaluation of charges and terminal currents under dynamic operation, without placing restrictions on the magnitude of the variations, i.e., we will deal with the *large-signal* dynamic operation of the MOS transistor.[1-32]† We will concentrate on the device part between source and drain, containing the inversion layer, the depletion region, the oxide, and the gate. This part is shown enclosed in a broken line in Fig. 7.1. It is called the *intrinsic* part and is mainly responsible for transistor action. The rest of the device constitutes the *extrinsic* part and is responsible for parasitic effects, which can limit overall performance. We will postpone discussion of the extrinsic device part until Chap. 8. Also, unless stated otherwise in this chapter we will assume long and wide channels, and a uniform substrate.

7.2   QUASI-STATIC OPERATION

We consider a fictitious device as shown in Fig. 7.2, with source and drain omitted to emphasize that only the intrinsic part is under consideration. The device is driven by four dc voltages, V_D, V_G, V_B, and V_S, defined with respect to some arbitrary reference point denoted by the ground symbol. Let four dc currents I_D, I_G, I_B, and I_S be defined as *entering* the device, as shown in the figure. We have seen that current flow is caused by the *transport* of electrons in the inversion layer (an *n*-channel device is assumed). Defining the *transport current* (or "conduction" current) as flowing from the drain through the channel to the source and denoting it by I_T, we have

$$I_D = I_T \qquad (7.2.1a)$$

$$I_G = 0 \qquad (7.2.1b)$$

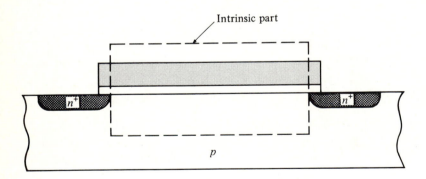

FIGURE 7.1
Indicating the intrinsic part of a transistor.

---

† The references include some papers mainly on small-signal operation, which, nevertheless, contain material pertinent to our discussion in this chapter. Chapters 8 and 9 contain an extensive discussion of small-signal operation and many more related references.

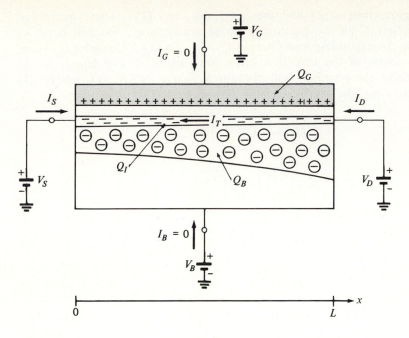

FIGURE 7.2
Definition of currents and charges under dc excitation.

$$I_B = 0 \qquad\qquad (7.2.1c)$$

$$I_S = -I_T \qquad\qquad (7.2.1d)$$

where we have neglected the extremely small leakage current through the insulator and the small leakage current through the depletion region. We have already derived several expressions for I_T, which can be written in the general form:†

$$I_T = h_T(V_D, V_G, V_B, V_S) \qquad\qquad (7.2.2)$$

where $h_T(\ )$ is an appropriate function dependent on the model used to describe the device's dc behavior. Such models have been discussed in Chap. 4.

In previous chapters we have considered the inversion layer, gate, and

---

† In most cases in previous chapters we have given the drain current as a function of voltages of the form V_{XY}, where X and Y can denote any two transistor terminals. We can write $V_{XY} = V_X - V_Y$, in which case an expression in the form of (7.2.2) is obtained. In general cases where the drain current expression includes surface potential values of the source and drain ends of the channel (Sec. 4.3), we can, in principle, use for those potentials an *approximate explicit* expression in terms of $V_{SB} = V_S - V_B$, $V_{DB} = V_D - V_B$, and $V_{GB} = V_G - V_B$; again, the result will be an explicit expression for the drain current in the form of (7.2.2).

depletion region charges per unit area (Q_I', Q_G', and Q_B'). These quantities depend, in general, on the position x along the channel. We will need to determine the corresponding *total* charges Q_I, Q_G, and Q_B. Consider Q_I as an example. A chunk of the inversion layer, with width W and length Δx at position x along the channel, will contain a charge $Q_I'(W \, \Delta x)$, where Q_I' depends on x. Thus, the total inversion layer charge will be

$$Q_I = \int_0^L Q_I'(W \, dx)$$

$$= W \int_0^L Q_I' \, dx \qquad (7.2.3a)$$

Similarly,

$$Q_G = W \int_0^L Q_G' \, dx \qquad (7.2.3b)$$

$$Q_B = W \int_0^L Q_B' \, dx \qquad (7.2.3c)$$

We will undertake the evaluation of these integrals in Sec. 7.4. For now, we only note that, as might be expected, the final results will depend on the terminal voltages

$$Q_I = f_I(V_D, V_G, V_B, V_S) \qquad (7.2.4a)$$

$$Q_G = f_G(V_D, V_G, V_B, V_S) \qquad (7.2.4b)$$

$$Q_B = f_B(V_D, V_G, V_B, V_S) \qquad (7.2.4c)$$

Q_G and Q_B can be interpreted as charges "stored" in the device; however, *the interpretation of Q_I requires more care*. Q_I is due to electrons in the inversion layer. These electrons are not really stored in the device. They enter through the source and eventually leave through the drain, being continuously replaced by new electrons entering through the source. Q_I is simply the total charge of the electrons that happen to be in the inversion layer at any given instant. This quantity is constant in Fig. 7.2 despite the fact that the "individual electrons" giving rise to it may be different at different instants.

We will now allow the terminal voltages to vary with time. Total time-varying quantities will be denoted by lower-case symbols with upper-case subscripts, as shown in Fig. 7.3. We will assume that *the variation of the terminal voltages is sufficiently slow, so that the device operates quasi-statically*.[5, 8, 10, 15, 16, 18–21, 25, 26, 28–30] This basically means the following. Let $v_D(t)$, $v_G(t)$, $v_B(t)$, and $v_S(t)$ be the varying terminal voltages; then at any position, the charges per unit area at any time t' are assumed identical to those that would be found if dc voltages were used instead, of values $V_D = v_D(t')$, $V_G = v_G(t')$, $V_B = v_B(t')$, and $V_S = v_S(t')$. Thus the total charges q_I, q_G, and q_B can still be found from (7.2.3), and will be given by

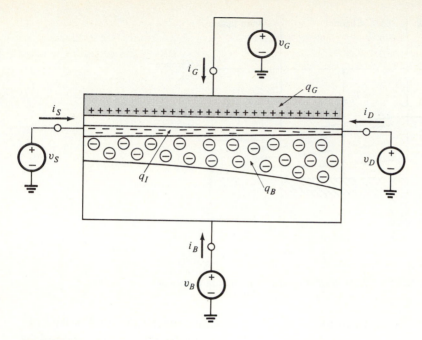

FIGURE 7.3
Definition of currents and charges in the presence of varying terminal voltages. Lowercase symbols with capital subscripts denote total time-varying quantities.

$$q_I(t) = f_I(v_D(t), v_G(t), v_B(t), v_S(t)) \ , \qquad \text{quasi-static operation}$$
$$(7.2.5a)$$

$$q_G(t) = f_G(v_D(t), v_G(t), v_B(t), v_S(t)) \ , \qquad \text{quasi-static operation}$$
$$(7.2.5b)$$

$$q_B(t) = f_B(v_D(t), v_G(t), v_B(t), v_S(t)) \ , \qquad \text{quasi-static operation}$$
$$(7.2.5c)$$

where f_I, f_G, and f_B represent the *same* functions as in (7.2.4).

It may be intuitively clear that the above assumption will fail if the terminal voltages vary too fast. For example, if a step waveform is used for one of them, the charges will exhibit some inertia and cannot be expected to readjust themselves instantaneously. Such cases are not considered in this and the next several sections. Instead, we are assuming that the terminal voltages vary sufficiently slowly for the quasi-static approximation to be valid. The limits of validity of the quasi-static approximation, and the reasons for its failing in extreme cases, will be discussed in Sec. 7.6. Nonquasi-static analysis will be discussed in Sec. 7.7.

One can obtain intuition about the quasi-static approximation by using the fluid dynamical analog introduced in Sec. 4.4.5. Consider the case shown in Fig. 7.4. Assume the piston is moving, and let $\hat{v}_{GB}(t)$ be its depth below the

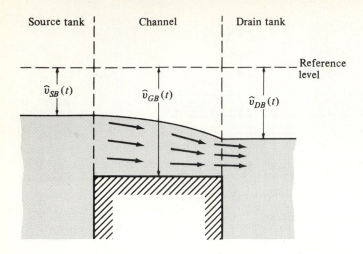

FIGURE 7.4
A fluid dynamical analog for illustrating charge motion in a transistor.

reference level. If the piston is moving sufficiently slowly, the fluid distribution at any instant t' will be practically as if $\hat{v}_{GB}(t)$ had been frozen permanently at the value $\hat{v}_{GB}(t')$. Then the quasi-static approximation holds for the fluid dynamical analog. Obviously, if $\hat{v}_{GB}(t)$ varies fast, this will no longer be the case, since the fluid is not given enough time to accommodate itself. Similar comments hold if $\hat{v}_{SB}$ or $\hat{v}_{DB}$ are varied.

7.3 TERMINAL CURRENTS IN QUASI-STATIC OPERATION

We will now evaluate the terminal currents of the *idealized* device in Fig. 7.3, assuming *quasi-static operation*. (The total terminal currents of a real device will include current components owing to extrinsic parasitic capacitances. Such capacitances are discussed in Sec. 8.4.)

Assuming there is no gate "leakage" and, therefore, no gate transport current, all gate current in Fig. 7.3 is associated with a changing gate charge:

$$i_G(t) = \frac{dq_G}{dt} \tag{7.3.1}$$

Similarly, assuming no leakage in the bulk, the transport current in the depletion region is zero. Then all bulk current is associated with carriers changing the charge in that region, by depleting or "covering" acceptor atoms there:

$$i_B(t) = \frac{dq_B}{dt} \tag{7.3.2}$$

Finally, the sum of the drain and source currents represents the total current entering the channel, which will change the inversion layer charge:[5, 8, 10, 15, 16, 18–21]

$$i_D(t) + i_S(t) = \frac{dq_I}{dt} \tag{7.3.3}$$

We need expressions for $i_D(t)$ and $i_S(t)$ separately. *The reader is cautioned that, under the assumption of quasi-static operation, conflicting ways to evaluate these quantities are suggested in the literature. This is because of conflicting interpretations of the "charges associated with the drain and with the source," quantities to be discussed below. We emphasize that just looking at equations can be very misleading in the development of relations for $i_D(t)$ and $i_S(t)$. A correct interpretation of the charges appearing in such relations is essential, and this requires making several fine points as explained below.*

We begin by noting that at dc, $i_D(t) = -i_S(t)$ [see (7.2.1)]. Hence, from (7.3.3), $dq_I/dt = 0$, that is, q_I is constant. In the general case of time-varying voltages, though, q_I will be varying too. Then $dq_I/dt \neq 0$, and $i_D(t)$ *cannot* be equal to $-i_S(t)$ in (7.3.3). To illustrate this point, assume that in Fig. 7.3 voltages v_D, v_S, and v_B are kept constant but v_G is varying as in Fig. 7.5a. We will assume that the variations of v_G are slow enough so that quasi-static operation is maintained. Then $q_I(t)$ will be given by an equation of the form (7.2.5a); its magnitude is plotted in Fig. 7.5b. The corresponding currents $i_D(t)$ and $-i_S(t)$ are shown in Fig. 7.5c. To interpret this figure, note that $i_D(t)$ is a measure of the number of *electrons leaving* the device through the drain per unit time and $-i_S(t)$ is a measure of the number of *electrons entering* the device through the source per unit time.† If "dc-like" behavior were obeyed at all times, we would have $-i_S(t) = i_D(t) = i_T(t)$. The quantity $i_T(t)$ would be given by (7.2.2) after replacing V_G in it by $v_G(t)$. This is shown by the dashed line in Fig. 7.5c. However, what we actually have is shown by the *solid* lines and can be explained as follows. When $v_G(t)$ is *increasing* $|q_I(t)|$ must increase, as shown in Fig. 7.5b. Thus the number of electrons in the channel must increase. For this to happen, the rate of supply of electrons from the source, $-i_S(t)$, must temporarily become larger than the rate of removal of electrons from the drain, $i_D(t)$. As shown later by quantitative results, this is accomplished by $-i_S(t)$ becoming temporarily larger than $i_T(t)$, and by $i_D(t)$ becoming temporarily smaller than $i_T(t)$, as in Fig. 7.5c. These comments hold for either up-going transition in the figure.

If $v_G(t)$ is *decreasing* instead, the opposite will be true. Here $|q_I(t)|$, and thus the number of electrons in the channel, must decrease. For this to happen, the rate of removal from the drain must temporarily exceed the rate of supply from the source. This is accomplished by $i_D(t)$ temporarily becoming larger

---

† Recall that negative charges moving from left to right correspond to positive current flowing from right to left.

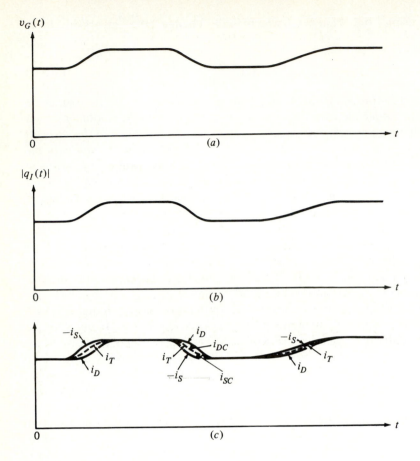

FIGURE 7.5
(a) Gate voltage waveform for the device of Fig. 7.3; all other terminal voltages are assumed fixed;
(b) corresponding inversion layer charge magnitude waveform assuming quasi-static operation; (c)
total drain current and the negative of the total source current; the transport and charging current
components are also shown.

than $i_T(t)$, and by $-i_S(t)$ temporarily becoming smaller than $i_T(t)$, as shown in
the falling part of the plots in Fig. 7.5c.

The difference between the curve for i_D and the curve for $-i_S$ in Fig. 7.5c
must be equal to the total rate of change of q_I, as follows from (7.3.3). By
integrating (7.3.3) it can be deduced that the area between the solid lines at
each transition is equal to the total change in $|q_I|$. If $|q_I(t)|$ in Fig. 7.5b goes
up, down, and up again by equal amounts, the three areas enclosed by solid
lines at each transition in Fig. 7.5c will all be equal. However, because the first
up-going transition is faster than the second up-going transition, i_D and $-i_S$
need to deviate more from i_T to accomplish the same change in q_I.

From the above arguments it follows that, in general, $i_D(t)$ and $i_S(t)$ will differ from their transport values $i_T(t)$ and $-i_T(t)$, respectively. Denoting the differences by $i_{DC}(t)$ and $i_{SC}(t)$, we can write

$$i_D(t) = i_T(t) + i_{DC}(t) \qquad (7.3.4a)$$

$$i_S(t) = -i_T(t) + i_{SC}(t) \qquad (7.3.4b)$$

From these equations and (7.3.3) we have

$$i_{DC}(t) + i_{SC}(t) = \frac{dq_I}{dt} \qquad (7.3.5)$$

Thus, we can conveniently view $i_T(t)$ as wholly responsible for the transport effect, and $i_{DC}(t)$, $i_{SC}(t)$ as wholly responsible for changing q_I. (For this reason these two currents are sometimes called "charging" currents.) Of course, it should be clear that we cannot identify particular electrons as causing transport current and others as being stored in the inversion layer. All electrons entering the source will eventually leave through the drain [see comment following (7.2.4c)]. However, since $i_D(t) \neq -i_S(t)$, the behavior an external observer sees is indistinguishable from what one *would* have *if* some of the charge went to contribute to a transport current while the rest went to change q_I, the latter often viewed as "stored" in the inversion layer at any given instant. To make this imaginary picture complete, let us associate $i_{DC}(t)$ and $i_{SC}(t)$ with two *fictitious* charges. If $i_{DC}(t)$ causes the inversion layer charge to change by an amount Δq_D in time Δt, we can write

$$i_{DC}(t) = \frac{dq_D}{dt} \qquad (7.3.6a)$$

and, if $i_{SC}(t)$ causes the inversion layer charge to change by an amount Δq_S in time Δt, we can write†

$$i_{SC}(t) = \frac{dq_S}{dt} \qquad (7.3.6b)$$

Expressions for q_D and q_S will be given shortly. The last three equations give

$$\frac{dq_I}{dt} = \frac{dq_D}{dt} + \frac{dq_S}{dt} \qquad (7.3.7)$$

Intuition about the above ideas can be increased with the help of the fluid dynamical analog in Fig. 7.4. Assume $\hat{v}_{GB}$ has been fixed for a long time, so that the fluid has attained a steady-state distribution and the total rate of flow into the channel from the source tank is equal to the rate of flow out of the

---

† The definitions of q_D and q_S here are purposely imprecise. Until further notice, q_D and q_S can be any functions the time derivatives of which predict the correct values for $i_{DC}(t)$ and $i_{SC}(t)$, respectively. The reader is urged to avoid assigning physical significance to q_D and q_S at this point. A discussion of this will follow.

channel and into the drain tank. Now assume that $\hat{v}_{GB}$ is slowly increased (the piston is slowly moved downward). The total amount of fluid in the channel must also increase, which, of course, cannot happen if the two rates of flow continue to be equal. The rate of flow from the source tank will thus temporarily become larger than what would be predicted from "dc considerations,"† while the rate of exit from the channel and into the drain tank will temporarily become smaller than what would be predicted from "dc considerations." (Note by the way that, if the movement of the piston downward is sufficiently slow, then at all times the flow of water is from left to right. Although the rate of flow is smaller at the drain end, no water is seen to flow backward from the drain tank into the channel.) If the piston is slowly raised ($\hat{v}_{GB}$ is decreasing), the total amount of fluid in the channel must decrease. The rate of flow from the source tank will become smaller while the rate of exit into the drain tank will become larger than the rate that would be predicted by "dc considerations."

Note that dq_S/dt and dq_D/dt in the above equations correspond only to the differences between the actual and the dc-like values of flow at the source and the drain; they do *not* represent total flow. For example, $dq_D/dt < 0$ should not be interpreted to imply that the drain current is negative. It only implies that the actual drain current $i_D(t)$ is less than the corresponding transport value $i_T(t)$, as can be deduced by using (7.3.6a) in (7.3.4a).

To determine $i_D(t)$ and $i_S(t)$ in (7.3.4) and (7.3.6) we need dq_D/dt and dq_S/dt. *Any functions* $q_D(t)$ *and* $q_S(t)$ *giving correct time derivatives will do for this purpose.* An obvious simple choice is to define these functions so that[16]

$$q_I(t) = q_D(t) + q_S(t) \qquad (7.3.8)$$

Because of this choice, the following interpretation is sometimes tempting, albeit *not* accurate: "The total charge stored in the inversion layer consists of two components, one that has come through the drain, and one that has come through the source." The reasons that this interpretation is not accurate are as follows. First, the view of q_I as stored charge leaves much to be desired, as explained in the paragraph following (7.2.4c). Second, as can be deduced from the comment preceding (7.3.8), q_D and q_S are not unique, so it is not justified to assign to them a unique physical significance. Third, in the general case it is not correct to identify q_D and q_S as necessarily "coming" from the drain and source respectively. For example, in the case illustrated in Fig. 7.5 in conjunction with Fig. 7.3, and provided the changes in $v_G(t)$ are sufficiently slow, electrons travel from the source through the channel to the drain at all times (just like the water in Fig. 7.4). In this picture, no electrons travel backward from the drain into the channel. Thus, all charges "come from the

---

† The "rate that would be expected from dc considerations" at time $t = t'$ is what the rate would have been if $\hat{v}_{GB}(t)$ had been frozen for a long time at the value $\hat{v}_{GB}(t')$.

source," and no charge "comes from the drain." That does not say anything about the value of q_D, which can still be nonzero and is such that its derivative, from (7.3.6a) and (7.3.4a), is equal to $i_D(t) - i_T(t)$, this difference being indicated by i_{DC} in Fig. 7.5c. It is thus better to think of q_D as the integral of this difference and not to assign a further physical significance to it. Similar comments apply to q_S. In fact, a complete development is possible dealing with i_{DC} and i_{SC} directly, without ever defining q_D and q_S. However, in conformance with the literature we will continue using these quantities, and we will assume that they are defined in such a way that (7.3.8) holds.†

Various approaches have been used in the literature for evaluating q_D and q_S, or i_{DC} and i_{SC}.[15, 16, 18–21, 24–30] Here we will adopt an approach that can be rigorously shown to be correct[21] and which has been demonstrated to agree with experiment. (More on the correctness of the approach will follow later.) We begin by assuming dc operation and define two charges Q_D and Q_S as follows:

$$Q_D = W \int_0^L \frac{x}{L} Q_I' \, dx \qquad (7.3.9a)$$

$$Q_S = W \int_0^L \left(1 - \frac{x}{L}\right) Q_I' \, dx \qquad (7.3.9b)$$

where Q_I' is the inversion layer charge per unit area. The sum of Q_D and Q_S is seen to be equal to the total inversion layer charge Q_I [from (7.2.3a)]. The evaluation of the above integrals will be considered in Sec. 7.4. For now we only mention that the results will be explicit functions of the terminal voltages:

$$Q_D = f_D(V_D, V_G, V_B, V_S) \qquad (7.3.10a)$$

$$Q_S = f_S(V_D, V_G, V_B, V_S) \qquad (7.3.10b)$$

If the terminal voltages are allowed to vary, one can evaluate the right-hand sides in (7.3.9) by using $q_I'(t)$ in lieu of Q_I'. If the variation of the terminal voltages is slow enough so that *quasi-static* operation is maintained, the results of this evaluation will be two quantities, denoted by $q_D(t)$ and $q_S(t)$, given by

$$q_D(t) = f_D(v_D(t), v_G(t), v_B(t), v_S(t)) , \qquad \text{quasi-static operation}$$
$$(7.3.11a)$$

$$q_S(t) = f_S(v_D(t), v_G(t), v_B(t), v_S(t)) , \qquad \text{quasi-static operation}$$
$$(7.3.11b)$$

where f_D and f_S represent the *same* functions as in (7.3.10). This follows from the definition of quasi-static operation given in Sec. 7.2. Thus, $q_D(t)$ and $q_S(t)$

---

† A possible definition of q_D and q_S is discussed in Appendix K.

as defined here satisfy (7.3.8). It can now be shown[21] (Appendix K) that, for the long-channel devices we are considering, the instantaneous currents $i_D(t)$ and $i_S(t)$ in quasi-static operation will be given by (7.3.4) and (7.3.6), with $q_D(t)$ and $q_S(t)$ as given by (7.3.11), and

$$i_T(t) = h_T(v_D(t), v_G(t), v_B(t), v_S(t)) \tag{7.3.12}$$

where h_T represents the *same* function as in (7.2.2). The proof relies on the "continuity equation," which is introduced in Sec. 7.7, and carefully considers the current and charge at each point in the channel. The evidence that the above approach is correct is rather overwhelming:

1. It is physically and mathematically sound. This fact can be appreciated if the quantities i_{DC}, i_{SC}, q_D, and q_S are carefully interpreted as explained earlier, and the detailed development[21] is followed (Appendix K).
2. It agrees with experiment.[21]
3. Other approaches using perturbation techniques[25] give equivalent results.[30]
4. Nonquasi-static large-scale numerical models, applied in the special case of quasi-static operation, give equivalent results.[20]
5. Small-signal models derived by using the above approach agree with nonquasi-static small-signal models in the special case of quasi-static operation (Chap. 9).

As follows from the above, the transport component can be found by using the models of Chap. 4 and will not be considered further here. To simplify our discussion, we will only consider the "charging" current components. We thus concentrate on the following equations:

$$i_{DC}(t) = \frac{dq_D}{dt} \tag{7.3.13a}$$

$$i_G(t) = \frac{dq_G}{dt} \tag{7.3.13b}$$

$$i_B(t) = \frac{dq_B}{dt} \tag{7.3.13c}$$

$$i_{SC}(t) = \frac{dq_S}{dt} \tag{7.3.13d}$$

It is interesting to note at this point that not only will Kirchhoff's current law hold for the total currents,

$$i_D(t) + i_G(t) + i_B(t) + i_S(t) = 0 \tag{7.3.14}$$

but it will also hold for the charging currents as is obvious by using (7.3.4) in the above equation:

$$i_{DC}(t) + i_G(t) + i_B(t) + i_{SC}(t) = 0 \tag{7.3.15}$$

Using (7.2.5b), (7.2.5c), and (7.3.11) in (7.3.13), and applying the chain rule of differentiation, we obtain

$$i_{DC}(t) = \frac{\partial q_D}{\partial v_D}\frac{dv_D}{dt} + \frac{\partial q_D}{\partial v_G}\frac{dv_G}{dt} + \frac{\partial q_D}{\partial v_B}\frac{dv_B}{dt} + \frac{\partial q_D}{\partial v_S}\frac{dv_S}{dt} \qquad (7.3.16a)$$

$$i_G(t) = \frac{\partial q_G}{\partial v_D}\frac{dv_D}{dt} + \frac{\partial q_G}{\partial v_G}\frac{dv_G}{dt} + \frac{\partial q_G}{\partial v_B}\frac{dv_B}{dt} + \frac{\partial q_G}{\partial v_S}\frac{dv_S}{dt} \qquad (7.3.16b)$$

$$i_B(t) = \frac{\partial q_B}{\partial v_D}\frac{dv_D}{dt} + \frac{\partial q_B}{\partial v_G}\frac{dv_G}{dt} + \frac{\partial q_B}{\partial v_B}\frac{dv_B}{dt} + \frac{\partial q_B}{\partial v_S}\frac{dv_S}{dt} \qquad (7.3.16c)$$

$$i_{SC}(t) = \frac{\partial q_S}{\partial v_D}\frac{dv_D}{dt} + \frac{\partial q_S}{\partial v_G}\frac{dv_G}{dt} + \frac{\partial q_S}{\partial v_B}\frac{dv_B}{dt} + \frac{\partial q_S}{\partial v_S}\frac{dv_S}{dt} \qquad (7.3.16d)$$

To evaluate the above currents, we need expressions for the charges as functions of the terminal voltages. Such expressions are developed in the following section.

7.4 EVALUATION OF CHARGES IN QUASI-STATIC OPERATION

7.4.1 Introduction

The charge expressions needed to complete the evaluation of the charging currents in (7.3.16) can be developed in a straightforward manner under the assumption of *quasi-static operation* (Sec. 7.2). Thus, we observe that, under this assumption, the expressions for $q_G(t)$, $q_B(t)$, $q_I(t)$, $q_D(t)$, and $q_S(t)$ in terms of $v_G(t)$, $v_B(t)$, $v_S(t)$, and $v_D(t)$ are identical to the expressions for the charges under dc conditions Q_G, Q_B, Q_I, Q_D, and Q_S in terms of the dc voltages V_G, V_B, V_S, and V_D. The latter expressions are given in the form of integrals in (7.2.3) and (7.3.9). If each region of operation is considered separately, these integrals lead to simple functions of the terminal voltages, with the exception of the moderate-inversion region. This is shown in the next several subsections. A more general evaluation is also possible, corresponding to the general charge sheet model of Sec. 4.3. This is outlined in Sec. 7.4.5.

7.4.2 Strong Inversion

GENERAL EXPRESSIONS FOR NONSATURATION. The integrations indicated in (7.2.3) and (7.3.9) cannot be carried out directly since we do not have the corresponding charges per unit area as functions of x. Accordingly, we first perform a change of variables from the position x to V_{CB}, the strong-inversion "effective reverse bias" of the inversion layer at point x, with respect to the substrate. From (4.4.12) we have

$$dx = -\frac{\mu W}{I_{DN}}Q_I'\,dV_{CB} \qquad (7.4.1)$$

Using this, the variable of integration is changed in (7.2.3b) to give

$$Q_G = W \int_{V_{SB}}^{V_{DB}} Q_G' \left(-\frac{\mu W}{I_{DN}} Q_I' \right) dV_{CB}$$

$$= -\frac{\mu W^2}{I_{DN}} \int_{V_{SB}}^{V_{DB}} Q_G' Q_I' \, dV_{CB} \qquad (7.4.2a)$$

Similarly, (7.2.3c) becomes:

$$Q_B = -\frac{\mu W^2}{I_{DN}} \int_{V_{SB}}^{V_{DB}} Q_B' Q_I' \, dV_{CB} \qquad (7.4.2b)$$

and (7.2.3a) becomes

$$Q_I = -\frac{\mu W^2}{I_{DN}} \int_{V_{SB}}^{V_{DB}} Q_I'^2 \, dV_{CB} \qquad (7.4.2c)$$

Q_D and Q_S from (7.3.9) become

$$Q_D = -\frac{\mu W^2}{I_{DN}} \int_{V_{SB}}^{V_{DB}} \frac{x}{L} Q_I'^2 \, dV_{CB} \qquad (7.4.3a)$$

$$Q_S = -\frac{\mu W^2}{I_{DN}} \int_{V_{SB}}^{V_{DB}} \left(1 - \frac{x}{L} \right) Q_I'^2 \, dV_{CB} \qquad (7.4.3b)$$

Finally, to express x in the above equations in terms of V_{CB} we integrate (7.4.1) from $x = 0$ to an arbitrary point in the channel:

$$x = -\frac{\mu W}{I_{DN}} \int_{V_{SB}}^{V_{CB}} Q_I' \, dU_{CB} \qquad (7.4.4)$$

where U_{CB} is a dummy variable of integration. A result equivalent to the above has been obtained in Sec. 4.4.3. Thus from (4.4.37) we have

$$x = L \frac{h(V_{GB}, V_{SB}, V_{CB})}{h(V_{GB}, V_{SB}, V_{DB})} \qquad (7.4.5)$$

where h represents the function multiplying W/L in the nonsaturation drain current expression:

$$I_{DN} = \frac{W}{L} h(V_{GB}, V_{SB}, V_{DB}) \qquad (7.4.6)$$

It is easy to show that (7.4.5) is equivalent to (7.4.4) (Prob. 7.1).

GENERAL EXPRESSIONS FOR SATURATION. Let the value of V_{DB} at which the transistor enters saturation be denoted by V_{DB}'. Since the channel is assumed long, if V_{DB} is raised above V_{DB}', the conditions in the channel will remain practically unaffected (Sec. 4.4). Thus, for example, let $g_I(V_{GB}, V_{SB}, V_{DB})$

represent the expression giving Q_I in nonsaturation, as it results from performing the integration in (7.4.2$\bar{c}$). We will have

$$Q_I = \begin{cases} g_I(V_{GB}, V_{SB}, V_{DB}), & V_{DB} \le V'_{DB} & (7.4.7a) \\ g_I(V_{GB}, V_{SB}, V'_{DB}), & V_{DB} > V'_{DB} & (7.4.7b) \end{cases}$$

Corresponding relations can be written for Q_G, Q_B, Q_D, and Q_S.

Using the above results, expressions of varying complexity can be found for Q_G, Q_B, Q_D, and Q_S depending on the complexity of the model used for Q'_G, Q'_B, Q'_D, Q'_S, and I_D.

APPROXIMATE MODEL. The computationally efficient approximate model derived in Sec. 4.4.2 resulted in the following expression for the drain current:

$$I_D = I'_D(1 - \alpha^2) \qquad (7.4.8)$$

where

$$I'_D = \frac{W}{L} \mu C'_{ox} \frac{(V_{GS} - V_T)^2}{2(1 + \delta)} \qquad (7.4.9)$$

and α was a parameter defined in a way that makes (7.4.8) valid in *both* nonsaturation and saturation:

$$\alpha = \begin{cases} 1 - \dfrac{V_{DS}}{V'_{DS}}, & V_{DS} \le V'_{DS} & (7.4.10a) \\ 0, & V_{DS} > V'_{DS} & (7.4.10b) \end{cases}$$

where

$$V'_{DS} = \frac{V_{GS} - V_T}{1 + \delta} \qquad (7.4.11)$$

The parameter α has been plotted in Fig. 4.13.

To develop the above model, the following expressions were used in Sec. 4.4.2 for the inversion layer and depletion region charges per unit area, in nonsaturation:

$$Q'_I = - C'_{ox}[V_{GB} - V_{SB} - V_T - (1 + \delta)(V_{CB} - V_{SB})] \qquad (7.4.12)$$

$$Q'_B = - C'_{ox}[\gamma\sqrt{\phi_B + V_{SB}} + \delta(V_{CB} - V_{SB})] \qquad (7.4.13)$$

We can thus find the corresponding nonsaturation *total* charges by using these in (7.4.2c) and (7.4.2b).[29] We can put the results in a form valid in *both* nonsaturation and saturation by using the convenient parameter α defined in (7.4.10). After some algebra, we obtain

$$Q_I = - WLC'_{ox}(V_{GS} - V_T)\frac{2}{3}\frac{1 + \alpha + \alpha^2}{1 + \alpha} \qquad (7.4.14)$$

$$Q_B = - WLC'_{ox}\left[\gamma\sqrt{\phi_B + V_{SB}} + \frac{\delta}{1 + \delta}(V_{GS} - V_T)\left(1 - \frac{2}{3}\frac{1 + \alpha + \alpha^2}{1 + \alpha}\right)\right]$$

$$(7.4.15)$$

The total gate charge can be found from (7.4.2a). However, since Q_I and Q_B have already been found, it is simpler to find Q_G by using the above results in the charge neutrality equation:

$$Q_G + Q_o + Q_I + Q_B = 0 \qquad (7.4.16)$$

where Q_o is the total equivalent interface charge. The result is

$$Q_G = WLC'_{ox} \left[\frac{V_{GS} - V_T}{1 + \delta} \left(\delta + \frac{2}{3} \frac{1 + \alpha + \alpha^2}{1 + \alpha} \right) + \gamma\sqrt{\phi_B + V_{SB}} \right] - Q_o \qquad (7.4.17)$$

To find Q_D and Q_S from (7.4.3) we need to relate x to V_{CB}. This can be done by using (7.4.4) or (7.4.5):

$$x = L \frac{(V_{GS} - V_T)(V_{CB} - V_{SB}) - \frac{1}{2}(1 + \delta)(V_{CB} - V_{SB})^2}{(V_{GS} - V_T)(V_{DB} - V_{SB}) - \frac{1}{2}(1 + \delta)(V_{DB} - V_{SB})^2} \qquad (7.4.18)$$

Using this and (7.4.12) in (7.4.3), and extending the result to cover the saturation region, we obtain

$$Q_D = -WLC'_{ox}(V_{GS} - V_T) \frac{4 + 8\alpha + 12\alpha^2 + 6\alpha^3}{15(1 + \alpha)^2} \qquad (7.4.19)$$

Similarly, Q_S can be found by using (7.4.3b). However, it is simpler here to obtain it from $Q_S + Q_D = Q_I$, using (7.4.14) and (7.4.19). The result is

$$Q_S = -WLC'_{ox}(V_{GS} - V_T) \frac{6 + 12\alpha + 8\alpha^2 + 4\alpha^3}{15(1 + \alpha)^2} \qquad (7.4.20)$$

Plots of certain quantities appearing in (7.4.14), (7.4.15), (7.4.19), and (7.4.20) are shown in Fig. 7.6. As seen, despite the rather complicated look of the expressions, the form of the plots is rather simple. The reader may want to develop simpler functions of α which would approximate these plots with good accuracy.

As a check of the above calculations, let us determine the charges at $V_{DS} = 0$ ($\alpha = 1$):

$$Q_B|_{V_{DS}=0} = -WLC'_{ox}\gamma\sqrt{\phi_B + V_{SB}} \qquad (7.4.21)$$

$$Q_I|_{V_{DS}=0} = -WLC'_{ox}(V_{GS} - V_T) \qquad (7.4.22)$$

$$Q_D|_{V_{DS}=0} = -\frac{WLC'_{ox}(V_{GS} - V_T)}{2} \qquad (7.4.23)$$

$$Q_S|_{V_{DS}=0} = -\frac{WLC'_{ox}(V_{GS} - V_T)}{2} \qquad (7.4.24)$$

$$Q_G|_{V_{DS}=0} = WLC'_{ox}[(V_{GS} - V_T) + \gamma\sqrt{\phi_B + V_{SB}}] - Q_o \qquad (7.4.25)$$

These equations make sense. Since $V_{DS} = 0$, the depletion region charge per unit area is uniform and is given by (7.4.13) with $V_{CB} = V_{SB}$. Multiplying

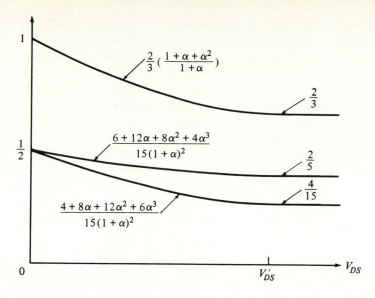

FIGURE 7.6
Quantities used in total charge expressions vs. drain-source voltage for fixed values of V_{GS} and V_{SB}.

this by the channel area WL gives (7.4.21). Similarly, (7.4.22) is simply the channel area times the uniform inversion layer charge per unit area as given from (7.4.12), with $V_{CB} = V_{SB}$. Q_D and Q_S are seen to be half of Q_I each, which makes sense because of symmetry. Finally, (7.4.25) can result from the equations above it and (7.4.16).

In the saturation region ($\alpha = 0$) we obtain

$$Q_{B,\text{sat}} = - WLC'_{ox}\left[\gamma\sqrt{\phi_B + V_{SB}} + \frac{\delta}{3(1 + \delta)}(V_{GS} - V_T)\right] \qquad (7.4.26)$$

$$Q_{I,\text{sat}} = - \tfrac{2}{3}WLC'_{ox}(V_{GS} - V_T) \qquad (7.4.27)$$

$$Q_{D,\text{sat}} = - \tfrac{4}{15}WLC'_{ox}(V_{GS} - V_T) \qquad (7.4.28)$$

$$Q_{S,\text{sat}} = - \tfrac{2}{5}WLC'_{ox}(V_{GS} - V_T) \qquad (7.4.29)$$

$$Q_{G,\text{sat}} = WLC'_{ox}\left[\frac{V_{GS} - V_T}{1 + \delta}(\tfrac{2}{3} + \delta) + \gamma\sqrt{\phi_B + V_{SB}}\right] - Q_o \qquad (7.4.30)$$

As seen, none of the above charges depends on V_{DS}. This is a manifestation of the fact that in saturation the drain can no longer have any influence on the intrinsic part of the device owing to pinchoff (excluding, of course, short-channel effects). The influence of one terminal on the charge associated with another is in general nonreciprocal. For example, assume that V_S, V_B, and V_G are fixed and that V_D is varying in the saturation region. Since (7.4.30) is independent of V_D, the gate charge will remain fixed and no transient gate current will be observed. Now, assume that instead V_S, V_B, and V_D are fixed and that V_G is varying, again in the saturation region. From (7.4.28), it is apparent that Q_D *will* vary. Thus, a nonzero "charging current" will flow through the drain terminal in addition to the conduction current. These facts are apparent from (7.3.16a) and (7.3.16b). Such nonreciprocal influence of one terminal on another, although most strongly pronounced in saturation, is also apparent in nonsaturation; it vanishes only at $V_{DS} = 0$. These effects will be considered in more detail in Chap. 9.

We note here that sometimes Q_D is assumed to be zero in the saturation region. This is justified by saying that in this region the channel is isolated from the drain. However, this isolation is only responsible for maintaining i_G independent of $v_D(t)$, as already argued. It is a fact that when $v_G(t)$ changes $i_D(t)$ will also change, and there is no reason to assume that this change will not include a charging component $i_{DC}(t)$ (Sec. 7.3). In fact, measurements and numerical simulations show that, indeed, $i_{DC}(t)$ is not zero in saturation. From (7.3.6a), then, q_D must be such as to give the correct value of $i_{DC}(t)$, which cannot happen if it is identically set to zero. So Q_D is *not* zero in saturation. There is *no* contradiction between "isolation" due to pinchoff and a nonzero value for Q_D, if Q_D is interpreted as explained in Sec. 7.3.

Plots of the total charges as a function of V_{DS}, with V_{GS} as a parameter, are shown in Fig. 7.7.

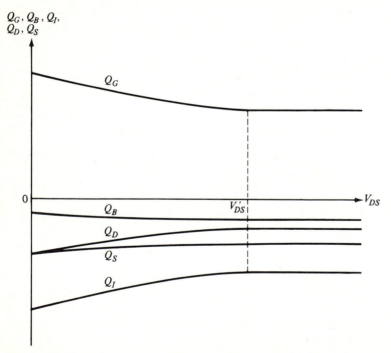

FIGURE 7.7
Total charges vs. drain-source voltage for fixed values of V_{GS} and V_{SB}.

The expressions we have given so far for the charges are adequate for most quasi-static transient response calculations.

ACCURATE MODEL. The general equations (7.4.2) and (7.4.3) can be used to develop charge expressions corresponding to the accurate model of Sec. 4.4.1. One must work in this case with the charges per unit area used in developing that model, which are given by (4.4.15) and (4.4.16). The resulting charge expressions have the attractive feature that they are completely symmetric with respect to V_{SB} and V_{DB}, just as was the case for the corresponding accurate model for the current in Sec. 4.4.1. However, these expressions are rather involved. In particular, the expressions for Q_D and Q_S are *extremely* complicated,[21] and one must resort to approximations. Since the principles have already been demonstrated, rather than hit the reader with more long formulas, we have summarized the charges for the accurate model in Appendix L.

7.4.3 Moderate Inversion

As was the case for drain current modeling, no convenient closed-form expressions have been derived for the charges in the moderate-inversion region. What is usually done for purposes of charge modeling is to neglect this region and to assume that the weak-inversion and strong-inversion expressions hold in adjacent regions of V_{GS}. The limit point between these regions is often taken to be $V_{FB} + 2\phi_F + \gamma\sqrt{2\phi_F + V_{SB}}$, which is the approximate value for what we have denoted by V_M (the bottom of the moderate-inversion region). The resulting error in the moderate-inversion charges is not large. However, if it is attempted to differentiate these charges in order to obtain capacitance expressions (Chap. 8), large errors will result as we will see.

To model better the charges in moderate inversion, one can use empirical expressions resulting in curves which connect smoothly the weak inversion curves with those for strong inversion. In doing so, it is important to maintain continuity not only of the charges at the transition points but also of the *derivatives* of those charges with respect to the terminal voltages. In this way, the charge expressions will result in continuous capacitance expressions (Chap. 8). As is true with all empirical expressions, it is also important that the parameters used in them be related to process parameters in a clear manner, so that predictions can be made in cases where experimental data are not available.

As will be seen in Sec. 7.4.5, it is possible to derive a model valid in all regions, including moderate inversion as a special case. However, as was the case with general drain current modeling, the price to be paid is complexity.

7.4.4 Weak Inversion

In weak inversion, the calculation of the charges is very easy. First, we note that the depletion region charge per unit area is given by (4.3.14), repeated here:

$$Q'_B = -\gamma C'_{ox}\sqrt{\psi_s} \tag{7.4.31}$$

As seen in Sec. 4.6, in the weak-inversion region (as well as in depletion), the surface potential ψ_s is practically independent of position, and is given by

$$\psi_s \approx \psi_{sa} = \left(-\frac{\gamma}{2} + \sqrt{\frac{\gamma^2}{4} + V_{GB} - V_{FB}}\right)^2 \tag{7.4.32}$$

Thus, Q'_B is also independent of position. The total depletion charge is thus simply WLQ'_B, which gives

$$Q_B = -WLC'_{ox}\gamma\left(-\frac{\gamma}{2} + \sqrt{\frac{\gamma^2}{4} + V_{GB} - V_{FB}}\right) \tag{7.4.33}$$

Consider now the charge neutrality equation $Q_G + Q_o + Q_I + Q_B = 0$. For the purposes of calculating Q_G, we can use the fact that in weak inversion $Q_I \ll Q_B$ (Sec. 4.6). Thus

$$Q_G = -Q_B - Q_o \tag{7.4.34}$$

To find Q_I accurately, we can use the observation in Sec. 4.6 that Q'_I varies as a straight line with position between its value at the source and its value at the drain, as shown in Fig. 4.16. Thus

$$Q'_I(x) = Q'_{I,\text{source}} + \frac{x}{L}(Q'_{I,\text{drain}} - Q'_{I,\text{source}}) \tag{7.4.35}$$

where expressions for $Q'_{I,\text{source}}$ and $Q'_{I,\text{drain}}$ have been given in Sec. 4.6. Since we have Q'_I as an explicit function of x, we can use it in (7.2.3a) directly to find Q_I. The result is (Prob. 7.7)

$$Q_I = WL\frac{Q'_{I,\text{source}} + Q'_{I,\text{drain}}}{2} \tag{7.4.36}$$

Similarly, replacing q by Q in (7.3.9) and using (7.4.35), we obtain (Prob. 7.7)

$$Q_D = WL\left(\frac{Q'_{I,\text{source}}}{6} + \frac{Q'_{I,\text{drain}}}{3}\right) \tag{7.4.37}$$

$$Q_S = WL\left(\frac{Q'_{I,\text{source}}}{3} + \frac{Q'_{I,\text{drain}}}{6}\right) \tag{7.4.38}$$

In practice, the above three charges are often neglected completely in the computation of transients for the following reason. The source and drain junction depletion regions (in the *extrinsic* part of the device, outside the channel area) contain charges which can be evaluated as in Sec. 1.5. Of those charges the ones in the n^+ material must be changed (when V_{SB} and V_{DB} are varied) by electrons supplied through the source and drain terminals. These charges and the corresponding charging currents are much larger than the ones associated with the inversion layer for typical channel lengths. Thus, in weak inversion, the source and drain charging currents are dominated by the extrinsic part of the device, and the following simplification is often used:

$$Q_I \approx Q_D \approx Q_S \approx 0 \qquad (7.4.39)$$

The accurate expressions we have developed for these charges can be found useful, nevertheless, when one considers the intrinsic dynamics of a transistor in weak inversion.

7.4.5 General Charge Sheet Model

We have seen in Secs. 7.4.2 and 7.4.4 that, if strong inversion or weak inversion is considered separately, simple expressions become possible for the charges in each of the two regions. However, it is also possible to develop a general expression for each charge which will be valid in *all* regions of inversion, just as was done for the drain current in Sec. 4.3. These expressions will even be valid in moderate inversion, a region for which no simple expression has been derived. As usual, extra complexity must be accepted to make such generality possible.

The principle on which the derivation of general charge expressions is based is simple. The general expression for the inversion layer charge per unit area, as used in Sec. 4.3, is

$$Q'_I = -C'_{ox}\left(V_{GB} - V_{FB} - \psi_s + \frac{Q'_B}{C'_{ox}}\right) \qquad (7.4.40)$$

where the corresponding general expression for the depletion region charge per unit area is

$$Q'_B = -\gamma C'_{ox}\sqrt{\psi_s} \qquad (7.4.41)$$

Equation (4.3.5) gives the drain current, assuming both drift and diffusion are present. From this equation we have

$$dx = -\frac{\mu W}{I_D} Q'_I \, d\psi_s + \frac{\mu W}{I_D} \phi_t \, dQ'_I \qquad (7.4.42)$$

Appropriate use of the above three equations in (7.2.3) and (7.3.9) results in general expressions for the total charges Q_I, Q_B, Q_G, Q_D, and Q_S.†
As an example, by using (7.4.42) in (7.2.3a), we obtain

$$Q_I = -\frac{W^2\mu}{I_D} \int_{\psi_{s0}}^{\psi_{sL}} Q'^2_I \, d\psi_s + \frac{W^2\mu}{I_D} \phi_t \int_{Q'_{I,\text{source}}}^{Q'_{I,\text{drain}}} Q'_I \, dQ'_I \qquad (7.4.43a)$$

$$= -\frac{W^2\mu}{I_D} \int_{\psi_{s0}}^{\psi_{sL}} Q'^2_I \, d\psi_s + \frac{W^2\mu}{I_D} \phi_t \frac{1}{2}\left(Q'^2_{I,\text{drain}} - Q'^2_{I,\text{source}}\right)$$

$$(7.4.43b)$$

---

† A different, more complicated procedure involves the quasi-Fermi potential in the channel.[28]

where ψ_{s0} and ψ_{sL} are the surface potentials at the source and the drain ends of the channel, respectively, and I_D is found as in Sec. 4.3. The first integral in (7.4.43b) can be evaluated after expressing Q'_I in terms of ψ_s, using (7.4.40) and (7.4.41). The result will be in terms of ψ_{s0} and ψ_{sL}, which can be determined from (4.3.18). The quantity in parenthesis in (7.4.43b) can similarly be found by expressing $Q'_{I,\mathrm{drain}}$ in terms of ψ_{sL} and $Q'_{I,\mathrm{source}}$ in terms of ψ_{s0}. Note that ψ_{sL} and ψ_{s0} must be *very* accurately known, as discussed in Sec. 4.3.

As a check of (7.4.43b) consider the special case of strong inversion in which only drift current is assumed. Then, only the first term will be present in the right-hand side of (7.4.42) (Sec. 4.3). Thus, only the term containing the integral will be present in (7.4.43b). By using in it (4.4.7) and (4.4.10), this term is seen to reduce to (7.4.2c), which was developed specifically for strong inversion. If now weak-inversion operation is considered instead, the current is practically all due to diffusion and only the second term will be present in (7.4.42). Thus, only the second term will appear in (7.4.43b). By using in it I_D from (4.6.10), this term is seen to reduce to (7.4.36), which was developed specifically for weak inversion. In moderate inversion, both terms in (7.4.43b) will be significant.

The rest of the charges can be similarly found, and can be expressed in terms of ψ_{s0} and ψ_{sL}. The procedure is rather long but mathematically straightforward and involves changes of variables and integration (Prob. 7.8). Some simplification is possible if (7.4.41) is replaced by a first-degree polynomial expression of Q'_B in terms of ψ_s (Prob. 7.9).

7.4.6 Depletion

In digital circuits, transistors are switched between conduction and cutoff. Therefore, the charges in the latter state are of importance in calculating the transient response of such circuits. The cutoff region consists of two regions—depletion and accumulation (Fig. 3.2). We consider these regions here and in the following subsection. In the depletion region, the inversion layer charge is totally negligible (Chap. 2):

$$Q_I = 0 \tag{7.4.44}$$

Because of this, the development of expressions for Q_B and Q_G is identical to that used for weak inversion in Sec. 7.4.4 and results in the same equations, repeated here for convenience:

$$Q_B = -WLC'_{ox}\gamma\left(-\frac{\gamma}{2} + \sqrt{\frac{\gamma^2}{4} + V_{GB} - V_{FB}}\right) \tag{7.4.45}$$

$$Q_G = -Q_B - Q_o \tag{7.4.46}$$

7.4.7 Accumulation

As explained in Chap. 2, when V_{GB} is sufficiently less than V_{FB}, holes in the p substrate (where they are in abundance) accumulate immediately below the oxide and form a very thin, highly conductive sheet there. The surface potential needed to support these holes is negative but of very small magnitude because the sheet of holes is so thin (this can be verified using the general analysis in Appendix H). Hence, ψ_s can be neglected in the potential balance equation (2.3.1), which results in an oxide potential $\psi_{ox} = V_{GB} - \phi_{MS}$. The gate charge per unit area $Q'_G = C'_{ox} \psi_{ox}$ is thus known, and multiplied by the gate area gives

$$Q_G = WLC'_{ox}(V_{GB} - \phi_{MS}) \tag{7.4.47}$$

The charge of the holes in the bulk, denoted by Q_C, can now be found from the charge balance equation $Q_G + Q_C + Q_o = 0$ [see (2.3.3)]. Thus

$$Q_C = -Q_G - Q_o \tag{7.4.48}$$

In the literature, the presence of Q_o in (7.4.48) is sometimes overlooked. The corresponding equation for Q_G in such cases uses V_{FB} rather than the correct ϕ_{MS} as above.

The accuracy of (7.4.47) decreases somewhat if V_{GB} is very close to V_{FB}, since then the accumulation is not heavy and the arguments used above do not really hold. If extreme accuracy is desired, one can use the material of Appendix H.

7.4.8 Plots of Charges vs. V_{GS}

In Fig. 7.7, we have seen the charges plotted as a function of V_{DS}, for a fixed V_{GS} in strong inversion. To show the behavior of the charges in all regions of operation, the opposite is often done. For a fixed V_{DS}, charges are plotted vs. V_{GS}. This corresponds to moving up a vertical line in the I_D-V_{DS} characteristics, as shown in Fig. 7.8. The regions encountered as V_{GS} is increased are accumulation, depletion, weak inversion, moderate inversion, saturation, and nonsaturation, in that order. Recall that, for the approximate strong-inversion model, nonsaturation is defined by

$$V_{DS} \le \frac{V_{GS} - V_T}{1 + \delta} \tag{7.4.49}$$

which, solved for V_{GS}, gives

$$V_{GS} \ge (1 + \delta)V_{DS} + V_T \tag{7.4.50}$$

The critical value in the right-hand side of this equation is marked in Fig. 7.8. The charges vs. V_{GS} for the fixed value of $V_{DS} = V_{DS1}$ shown in Fig. 7.8 are plotted in Fig. 7.9. (The middle plot gives the depletion region charge Q_B in inversion and depletion, and the charge of holes Q_C in accumulation.) If V_{DS} were chosen at a value $V_{DS2} > V_{DS1}$ (Fig. 7.8), we would obtain the broken lines instead. Note that V_{DS} makes a difference only in nonsaturation in these plots. This is because, as seen in the charge expressions developed in this section, in accumulation and in depletion V_{DS} does not appear at all in them,

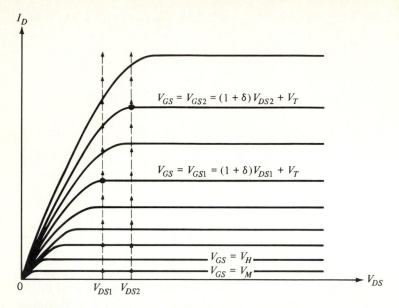

FIGURE 7.8
Drain current vs. drain-source voltage, with gate-source voltage as a parameter. V_{DS1} and V_{DS2} are two drain-source voltage values for which the plots of Fig. 7.9 are obtained.

and in weak inversion, moderate inversion, and saturation we are in the flat part of the characteristics in Fig. 7.8 where the drain cannot control the channel.

7.4.9 Use of Charges in Evaluating the Terminal Currents

The expressions we have developed above for the charges in individual regions of operation can be written as functions of V_D, V_G, V_B, and V_S by substituting in them $V_{GS} = V_G - V_S$, $V_{DS} = V_D - V_S$, and $V_{SB} = V_S - V_B$. As follows from the comments in Sec. 7.4.1, if the terminal voltages vary slowly enough so that quasi-static operation is maintained, the same expressions can be used to determine the time-varying charges. Thus the partial derivatives in (7.3.16) can be determined. In other words, we have

$$\frac{\partial q_X}{\partial v_Y} = \frac{\partial Q_X}{\partial V_Y}, \qquad \text{quasi-static operation} \qquad (7.4.51)$$

where each of X and Y can stand for D, G, B, or S. Thus, if the variation of terminal voltages with time is known, the terminal currents can be found from (7.3.16), (7.4.51), (7.3.4), and (7.3.12).

A similar approach can be taken if the general charge sheet model is used (Sec. 7.4.5), since the surface potentials ψ_{s0} and ψ_{sL} can be related to V_{SB} and V_{DB}, respectively, through (4.3.18). The algebra, however, is considerably more complicated.

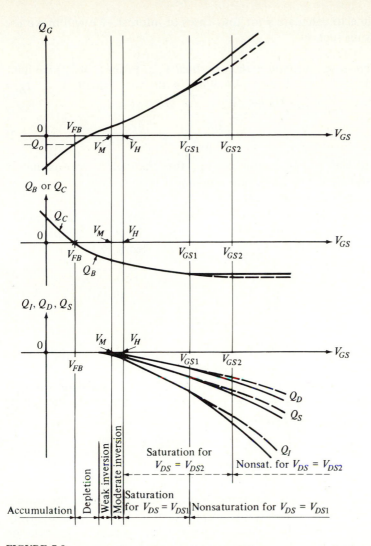

FIGURE 7.9
Total charges vs. gate-source voltage for two values of V_{DS}. Solid line: $V_{DS} = V_{DS1}$; broken line: $V_{DS} = V_{DS2}$, $V_{DS2} > V_{DS1}$ (see Fig. 7.8).

7.5 TRANSIT TIME UNDER dc CONDITIONS

The transit time (Sec. 1.3.1) associated with dc operation in a transistor is the average time it takes for an electron to travel the length of the channel:

$$\tau = \frac{|Q_I|}{I_D} \tag{7.5.1}$$

Having evaluated the inversion layer charge in the previous section, this is a convenient time to calculate τ for four cases of interest. We will make use of τ in the following section.

1. *Strong inversion–nonsaturation with very small V_{DS}.* From (7.4.22) we have $|Q_I| \approx C'_{ox}WL(V_{GS} - V_T)$. From (4.4.30a), with very small V_{DS}, $I_D = \mu C'_{ox}(W/L)(V_{GS} - V_T)V_{DS}$. Hence, from (7.5.1),

$$\tau \approx \frac{L^2}{\mu V_{DS}} \tag{7.5.2}$$

   Note that, since with negligible V_{DS} the channel is approximately uniform and the drift velocity approximately fixed, we could have used (1.3.10) to obtain the above result.

2. *Strong inversion–saturation.* Assume no velocity saturation takes place. From (7.4.27), $|Q_I| = \frac{2}{3}WLC'_{ox}(V_{GS} - V_T)$, and from (4.4.30b), $I_D = \frac{1}{2}\mu C'_{ox}(W/L)(V_{GS} - V_T)^2/(1 + \delta)$. We thus obtain, from (7.5.1),

$$\tau = \frac{4}{3}\tau_o \tag{7.5.3}$$

   where

$$\tau_o = (1 + \delta)\frac{L^2}{\mu(V_{GS} - V_T)} \tag{7.5.4}$$

   For a device with $\mu = 64 \ \mu\text{m}^2/(\text{V} \cdot \text{ns})$ and $L = 4 \ \mu\text{m}$, operated so that $(V_{GS} - V_T)/(1 + \delta) = 4$ V, the value of τ is 0.083 ns.

3. *Weak inversion with $V_{DS} > 5\phi_t$.* Here, from Sec. 4.6 we easily see that $Q'_{I,\text{drain}} \approx 0$, and from (7.4.36), $|Q_I| = \frac{1}{2}|Q'_{I,\text{source}}|WL$. From (4.6.16), $I_D = \mu(W/L) \ \phi_t \ |Q'_{I,\text{source}}|$. Hence,

$$\tau = \frac{L^2}{\mu(2\phi_t)} \tag{7.5.5}$$

   Note that in all three cases, the transit time is proportional to the *square* of L. This, of course, is so because Q_I is proportional to L, *and* I_D is inversely proportional to L. To see this effect another way, consider the case of nonsaturation with very small V_{DS}. The channel is nearly uniform and the field is everywhere approximately equal to V_{DS}/L. The drift velocity of the electrons is proportional to this field. Increasing L, say, m times decreases the drift velocity m times and these electrons now have to travel m times the distance. So the time it takes them to travel the length of the channel will increase m^2 times. Applying the simple model of Sec. 1.3.3 to weak inversion, a similar argument holds, only there the "driving force" is not the field but rather the gradient of the charge in the channel, $|Q'_{I,\text{source}}|/L$.

4. *Velocity saturation.* If velocity saturation is present over part of the channel, the above arguments break down. Although the value of the transit time in this case can be calculated by using material from Sec. 5.3, we will limit our

discussion to a simple estimate. We note that τ will be larger than what one would have if the electrons were moving at maximum speed over *all* of the channel. Thus,

$$\tau > \frac{L}{|v_d|_{max}} \tag{7.5.6}$$

Figure 7.10 shows the transit time of a device operating in the "flat" part of the I_D-V_{DS} characteristics as a function of V_{GS} (solid line). As V_{GS} is increased, V_{DS} must be raised if the device is to be kept in the saturation region. The increase in V_{DS} is accompanied by an increased electric field and, thus, if L is small, velocity saturation sets in over much of the channel. Thus, τ cannot be decreased at will by increasing V_{GS}, as one could have concluded by carelessly applying (7.5.3) and (7.5.4).

7.6 LIMITATIONS OF THE QUASI-STATIC MODEL

From our discussion so far, we expect that the quasi-static model will be valid if the terminal voltages vary sufficiently slowly so that the charge distribution in the channel can follow with negligible inertia. A quantitative definition of the term "sufficiently slowly" is difficult to come by. Whether results obtained from using the quasi-static model are trustworthy or not depend on the type of voltage waveforms applied to the terminals, on the regions of operation

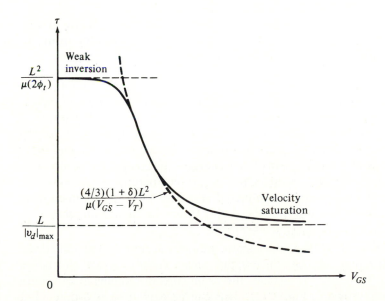

FIGURE 7.10
Transit time vs. gate-source voltage for operation in the "flat" part of the I_D-V_{DS} characteristics.

involved, on the type of result desired (e.g., current waveform shape, delay, risetime, etc.), on the accuracy sought, etc. In practice, some rules of thumb have been developed semiempirically, by using a simple basic case shown in Fig. 7.11a. Here only v_G is varying, as shown in Fig. 7.11b. We will only consider the intrinsic device effects. The drain current contains a conductive part $i_T(t)$ and a charging part $i_{DC}(t)$, as in (7.3.4a):

$$i_D(t) = i_T(t) + i_{DC}(t) \tag{7.6.1}$$

For approximate calculations in digital circuit applications, it is often assumed that a transistor is in the off state if $v_{GS} < V_T$ and in strong inversion if $v_{GS} > V_T$. Using this simplification here implies that the device goes abruptly from off to saturation operation at $t = t_1$. We will also assume that V_{DD} is large enough so that the device never goes into nonsaturation. The conductive part of the current can be found from any dc model, and is shown in Fig. 7.11c. The charging current $i_{DC}(t)$ can be found from (7.3.16a). Since v_D, v_S, and v_B are constant, this equation gives

$$i_{DC}(t) = \frac{\partial q_D}{\partial v_G} \frac{dv_G}{dt} \tag{7.6.2}$$

In saturation, the value of q_D in quasi-static operation $Q_{D,\text{sat}}$ is given by (7.4.28). Thus, $\partial q_D / \partial v_G$ is $-\frac{4}{15} WLC'_{ox}$, a negative constant independent of v_G. (In a more general case, though, one can expect the partial derivatives $\partial q_i / \partial v_j$ to be functions of the terminal voltages.) Since dv_G / dt is constant for the rising part of v_G, $i_{DC}(t)$ is of the form shown in Fig. 7.11d. Adding the two drain current components then produces $i_D(t)$, as shown in Fig. 7.11e.

Measurements of $i_D(t)$ reveal a waveform of the type shown in Fig. 7.11f assuming negligible extrinsic effects.[19-21] This is seen to differ from our "quasi-static" result of Fig. 7.11e, notably in two respects:

1. At $t = t_3$, $i_D(t)$ in Fig. 7.11e is predicted to jump to its dc steady-state value instantaneously. This is a consequence of the assumption that the charge adjusts itself with no inertia. In reality this is not the case, as illustrated in Fig. 7.11f. Nevertheless, a little "kink" *is* seen in Fig. 7.11f at $t = t_3$, for the following reason. Before $t = t_3$, the increasing v_G demanded more and more $|q'_i|$ in the channel, so only part of the charge supplied by the source was available to flow out the drain. Once v_G stops increasing, though, the channel-filling process has been completed and all new charge supplied from the source is available to flow out the drain. Hence the significant change in the slope of the plot for $i_D(t)$ at $t = t_3$.
2. For some time after t_1, the quasi-static model predicts a negative drain current, which is not observed in practice once extrinsic device effects are subtracted out (Prob. 7.11). Instead, the drain current remains at zero until some time t_2, as shown in Fig. 7.11f. This can be explained as follows. For $t < t_1$, the channel is empty. At $t = t_1$, the conditions in the channel become favorable for electrons; the latter enter the channel through the source and

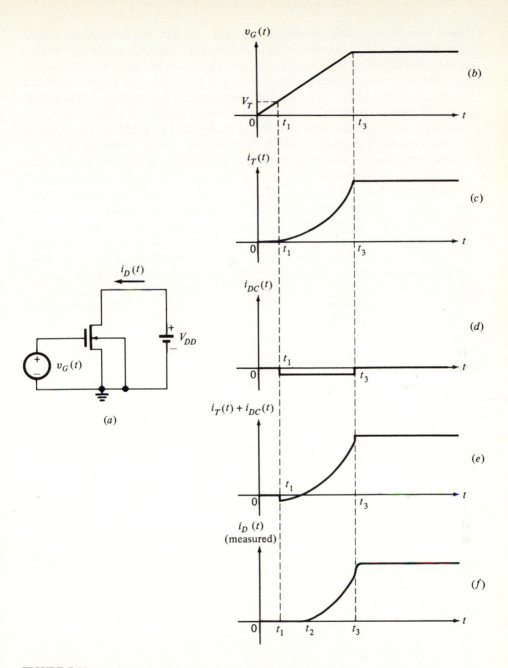

FIGURE 7.11
(a) A transistor with varying excitation; (b) gate-source voltage; (c) transport current calculated from a dc model; (d) drain charging current calculated by assuming quasi-static operation; (e) sum of (c) and (d); (f) form of actual $i_D(t)$ observed in practice. A sufficiently large V_{DD} is assumed, so that even the maximum value of v_G corresponds to operation in the saturation region. Extrinsic effects are assumed negligible.

277

move toward the drain. However, no drain current will be observed until the electrons *reach* the drain. This happens at time t_2, as shown in Fig. 7.11f. In contrast to this picture, the quasi-static model assumes that at *any* time t' after t_1 the channel contains electrons *throughout* its length, as would be the case if v_G had been frozen for a long time at the value $v_G(t')$, i.e., the nonzero time it takes for the electrons to reach the drain is not considered. A comparison with the fluid dynamical analog of Fig. 4.15d (corresponding to the saturation region) would be useful here. Assume that initially the piston is high enough so that communication between the two tanks is cut off and that there is no fluid in the channel. The piston is now moved downward fast ($\hat{v}_{GB}$ increases), and at $t = t_1$, $\hat{v}_{GB}$ moves past the fixed value of $\hat{v}_{SB}$ (recall that this analog was chosen to correspond to a transistor with $V_T \approx 0$). The piston eventually stops at the position shown in the figure. At $t = t_1$, fluid starts moving into the channel from the source tank, but it will be some time before this fluid reaches the right end of the channel and spills over to the drain tank. The quasi-static model instead corresponds to the fluid existing throughout the channel at any instant $t' > t_1$, with a distribution corresponding to a fixed piston position $\hat{v}_{GB}(t')$.† This phenomenon will be considered again in Sec. 7.7.

The quasi-static model is thus seen to fail when it comes to predicting the fine details of the drain current waveform. However, for many applications this is of no great consequence, since the fine waveform details are often of little interest. This is, for example, the case in much of digital circuit design, where quantities of interest are initial values, final values, output rise or fall times, delays between output and input, etc. Comparisons to measurements and to nonquasi-static numerical results have been used to suggest that, for much of digital circuit work, the quasi-static model can be used with acceptable results if the rise time t_R of the waveforms‡ involved satisfies the condition[20, 21]

$$t_R > 20\tau_o \tag{7.6.3}$$

where τ_o is given by (7.5.4) by using the maximum value of V_{GS} from Fig. 7.11b. It is emphasized that the above is only a *rough* rule of thumb.§ For example, depending on the application, the factor of 20 could instead be 15 or

---

† If V_{DD} were smaller, so that the maximum value of v_G corresponded to the *nonsaturation* region, we would have a situation analogous that that in Fig. 4.15c. Here, as the piston moved downward fast and stopped at the position shown, fluid would initially flow into the "channel" not only from the source but also from the drain. This would correspond to a *negative* drain current. After things settled, of course, a regular flow toward the right would have to be established, so the drain current would go through zero and then would become positive. These predictions are, indeed, verified by actual measurements on transistors.

‡ Defined for this purpose as $t_3 - t_1$ in Fig. 7.11b.

§ The origin of this result will be understood after nonquasi-static analysis is described in Sec. 7.7.

25. As a numerical example of the order of magnitude involved here, consider a device with $\mu = 64 \ \mu\text{m}^2/(\text{V}\cdot\text{ns})$, $V_T = 1 \ \text{V}$, $L = 4 \ \mu\text{m}$, $\delta \approx 0$, and $V_{GS,\text{max}} = 5 \ \text{V}$. Then (7.6.3) requires $t_R > 1.25$ ns.

In common, "bulk" fabrication technologies (Chap. 10), in which the transistor exhibits significant extrinsic parasitic capacitances, the above limit is not restrictive. The speed of operation is slowed down in these technologies because of such "stray" capacitances, and internal waveforms on a chip will often have rise times larger than this limit. On top of this, even if occasionally a gate voltage waveform has a rise time somewhat below this limit, the total transient currents and delays due to the stray capacitance of the device being driven can be significant and can mask the errors due to intrinsic effects predicted by quasi-static models. The above is not true with technologies which achieve very low stray capacitance values, such as silicon on sapphire or dielectric isolation technologies. In such cases, as well as in cases where pushing the speed limit is attempted by using bulk technologies, results obtained using quasi-static models should be looked at with suspicion.

One way to model a transistor at speeds where its quasi-static model breaks down is to view it as consisting of several sections, each section being short enough to be modeled quasi-statically. This idea is shown in Fig. 7.12. In

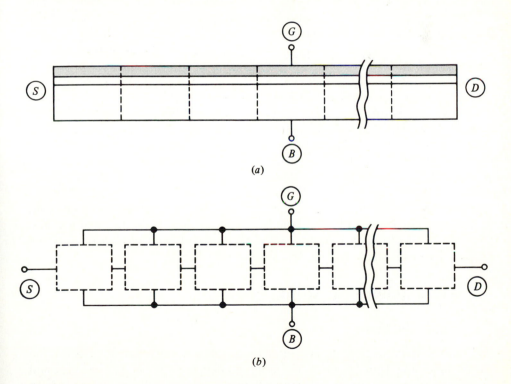

(a)

(b)

FIGURE 7.12
(a) A long-channel transistor separated into several sections; (b) model for (a); each box represents a quasi-static model corresponding to one section in (a).

b, each box is assumed to be a "subtransistor," with its own imaginary source and drain *points*. Of course, with the exception of the left and right extremes, these subtransistors are assumed to consist only of intrinsic parts. In other words, no extrinsic source and drain *regions* at intermediate points are assumed to exist.

Note that in our discussion above we have not considered short-channel effects. The latter can greatly complicate the picture. Among the phenomena observed in them, but not in truly long-channel devices, are a *transient transport* current[21] (in addition to the transient charging current) and, of course, velocity saturation which renders (7.4.1) and the relations based on it invalid. Two-dimensional numerical simulation is a valuable tool in this case.[19, 20] Finally, there is another phenomenon, not related to short-channel effects, that we have not considered in our modeling. This phenomenon is observed during the falling part of a gate voltage waveform. As $v_G(t)$ is decreased, the inversion layer charge must be reduced. To this end, electrons exit through the drain and source terminals. The dynamics of this removal process show that there is a finite removal capability associated with it.[7] If v_G is decreased too fast, the ensuing "bottlenecks" at either end of the channel result in some electrons being temporarily "trapped" in the channel. The field-induced junction consisting of the inversion layer and the substrate can then become momentarily forward-biased and the electrons can cross into the bulk. There they recombine with holes and cause a substrate current to flow. This phenomenon is called *charge pumping*. It is more pronounced for shorter falling times of the gate voltage waveform, as might be expected intuitively. It is estimated that 1 percent of the total inversion layer charge will exit through the substrate if the fall time is 0.04 ns for a 3-μm-long device, or about 1 ns for a 10-μm-long device.[20]

We conclude this section by reminding the reader that parasitic elements associated with the *extrinsic* part of the device can significantly alter the behavior of the transistor, compared to that predicted here. Such elements include the gate-source and gate-drain overlap capacitances, and the substrate-source and substrate-drain junction capacitances. In addition, the fact that the substrate is not a perfect conductor can become important. The significant resistance associated with the latter, in conjunction with the intrinsic and extrinsic substrate capacitances, can affect the dynamic performance of the device. Extrinsic elements will be considered in Sec. 8.4.

7.7 NONQUASI-STATIC MODELING

7.7.1   Introduction

In the previous section it was seen that, for a given channel length, the quasi-static model breaks down if the input changes too fast. It was suggested that one way to extend the validity of quasi-static models in that case is to consider the device as a connection of several shorter devices (Fig. 7.12) and to model each section quasi-statically. Note that, for each section, the current entering one end is, in general, different from the current leaving the other end. This accounts for possible inversion layer charge buildup within each section, just as different magnitudes of drain and source current are encountered because of charge buildup in the single-section quasi-static model. The faster the change of the input, the shorter each section must be, and the larger the number of sections. In the limit, one can let the section length approach zero, thus making the total number of sections approach infinity. The resulting model would then not be subjected to the speed limitations of quasi-static models. We will develop this idea formally in this section.[1-4, 6, 9, 12, 13, 17, 19, 20, 22, 32] Note that, following the argument above concerning currents, we should allow for the current to be a function of position x along the channel as well as, of course, time:

$$i = i(x, t) \tag{7.7.1}$$

Similarly, the inversion layer charge per unit area will be a function of position and time:

$$q'_I = q'_I(x, t) \tag{7.7.2}$$

7.7.2 The Continuity Equation

Consider a section of the inversion layer of length Δx, as shown in Fig. 7.13. Let the current entering on the right be in general different from that leaving from the left by an amount Δi, as shown. The total charge entering on the right in time Δt is $(i + \Delta i)\,\Delta t$; the total charge leaving from the left in the same amount of time is $i\,\Delta t$. Thus, in the interval Δt, the charge inside the chunk must be increasing by $(i + \Delta i)\,\Delta t - i\,\Delta t = \Delta i\,\Delta t$. The corresponding increase $\Delta q'_I$ in the inversion charge *per unit area*, will simply be the total charge increase divided by the chunk's area, as seen from above. Thus,

$$\Delta q'_I = \frac{\Delta i\,\Delta t}{W\,\Delta x} \tag{7.7.3}$$

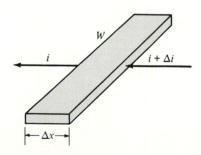

FIGURE 7.13
A chunk of the inversion layer of small length Δx.

which can also be written as

$$\frac{\Delta i}{\Delta x} = W \frac{\Delta q_I'}{\Delta t} \qquad (7.7.4)$$

We now let the finite differences approach 0. The left-hand side then becomes the partial derivative of $i(x, t)$ with respect to x. Similarly, the fraction on the right becomes the partial derivative of $q_I'(x, t)$ with respect to t. Thus,

$$\frac{\partial i(x, t)}{\partial x} = W \frac{\partial q_I'(x, t)}{\partial t} \qquad (7.7.5)$$

This equation is referred to as the *continuity* equation.† It is simply a way to express charge conservation for a chunk of infinitesimal length. Note that if q_I' does not change with time ($\partial q_I'/\partial t = 0$), the above equation gives $\partial i/\partial x = 0$, that is, i then has a constant value independent of position x. That is the case under dc conditions. In fact, the constancy of i was instrumental in developing the dc I_D equations in Chap. 4.

7.7.3 Nonquasi-static Analysis

Nonquasi-static analysis of the MOS transistor is a difficult mathematical exercise.[2, 6, 12, 13, 17, 22, 32] We will illustrate it for the special case in which all points in the channel are in *strong inversion*, which simplifies matters considerably. We can relate $q_I'(x, t)$ to the external terminal voltages and the internal effective reverse bias $V_{CB}(x, t)$ by the time-varying version of (4.4.16a):

$$q_I'(x, t) = -C'_{ox}[v_{GB}(t) - V_{FB} - \phi_B - v_{CB}(x, t) - \gamma\sqrt{\phi_B + v_{CB}(x, t)}] \qquad (7.7.6a)$$

The variation of $v_{CB}(x, t)$ with x is the "driving force" for the current flow. This is expressed from (4.4.12) with, of course, I_D replaced by $i(x, t)$:

$$i(x, t) = -\mu W q_I'(x, t) \frac{\partial v_{CB}(x, t)}{\partial x} \qquad (7.7.6b)$$

Finally, the continuity equation developed in the previous subsection is

$$\frac{\partial i(x, t)}{\partial x} = W \frac{\partial q_I'(x, t)}{\partial t} \qquad (7.7.6c)$$

Equations (7.7.6) constitute a system of three equations in three unknowns: $q_I'(x, t)$, $i(x, t)$, and $v_{CB}(x, t)$. The last two equations express basic facts about current flow. They have both been developed by considering a

---

† The reader may have encountered this equation with i defined in the opposite direction from that in Fig. 7.13, in which case a minus sign would appear in one side of the equation. The above form of the continuity equation is appropriate for our purposes. Note also that, while in the case we are considering only electrons are assumed to be present as usual, in more general cases the continuity equation remains valid if the current and charge in it are taken to include the effect of both electrons and holes. If separate equations are written for each carrier, additional terms must be included to account for carrier generation and recombination.[33]

chunk of material with mobile electrons in it. Apart from the convenient symbols used and the assumption of only drift current in (7.7.6b),† the development was independent of whether the material is part of an MOS structure. The MOS transistor physics only enters in the first equation.

The solution of (7.7.6) requires a set of *initial and boundary conditions*. These will depend on the terminal voltages. As an example, consider the circuit of Fig. 7.14a with the step input shown in Fig. 7.14b.[6] The device is assumed to have settled in the off condition before the positive step is applied. The value of the step V and of V_{DD} are such that, after a transient period, the

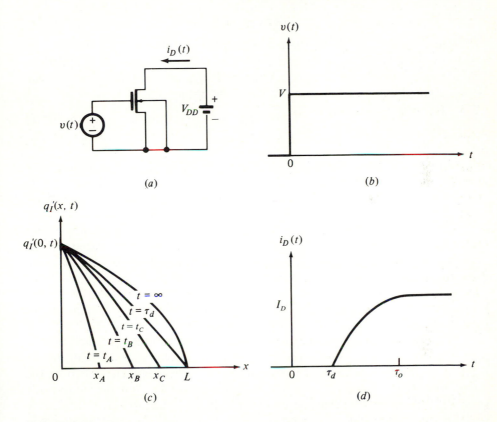

FIGURE 7.14
(a) A transistor with a step excitation; (b) gate-source voltage; (c) inversion layer charge per unit area as a function of position along the channel with time as a parameter; (d) drain current as a function of time. A sufficiently large V_{DD} is assumed, so that even the maximum value of v corresponds to operation in the saturation region.

---

† In fact, if v_{CB} is interpreted as the "quasi-Fermi potential" difference, this equation will include diffusion effects (Appendix I).

device settles in the saturation region. Since the device is initially off, q'_I will be zero at $t = 0$ everywhere in the channel:

$$q'_I(x, 0) = 0 \tag{7.7.7a}$$

With the large value $v_{GB}(t) = V$ applied at $t = 0$, the source end of the channel $(x = 0)$ is assumed to reach strong inversion immediately after $t = 0$. Since at that end $v_{CB} = v_{SB} = 0$, (7.7.6a) gives, for all positive time

$$q'_I(0, t) = -C'_{ox}(V - V_{FB} - \phi_B - \gamma\sqrt{\phi_B}) \tag{7.7.7b}$$

Finally, at the drain end $(x = L)$, q'_I is zero whether the device is off or in saturation ("pinchoff" assumption). Thus

$$q'_I(L, t) = 0 \tag{7.7.7c}$$

The system (7.7.6) with the conditions (7.7.7) can now, in principle, be solved by using partial differential equation techniques to provide the distribution of i, v_{CB}, and q'_I with position and time. The drain and source currents can be determined from the solution for $i(x, t)$ by noting that

$$i_D(t) = i(L, t) \tag{7.7.8}$$

$$i_S(t) = -i(0, t) \tag{7.7.9}$$

From the solution for $v_{CB}(x, t)$ one can determine $q'_B(x, t)$ and integrate it with respect to position to find the total instantaneous depletion region charge as in (7.2.3c). The substrate transient current can then be determined as in (7.3.2). The gate transient current can be found in a similar manner.

Unfortunately, the actual details of the solution outlined above are complicated. Results have been presented in the literature based on an approximate form of (7.7.6a) [corresponding to (4.4.23) with $\delta = 0$], but even then numerical techniques were used with the help of a computer. We will not present this long procedure here,[6, 12, 19, 20] but will only summarize the most important results. Solution of (7.7.6) for the circuit of Fig. 7.14a results in $q'_I(x, t)$, as shown in Fig. 7.14c. At $t = 0$, the channel is empty. At $t = t_A$, the electrons coming from the source have reached up to point $x = x_A$; hence, q'_I is zero beyond this point. The wave front of electrons continues moving to the right as shown, and reaches the drain at $t = \tau_d$; τ_d will be referred to as the *delay time*. At the instant $t = \tau_d$, the channel charge has not reached steady state yet. Steady state is reached asymptotically and corresponds to the curve marked $t = \infty$. Note that a quasi-static model implicitly assumes instead that this distribution is reached instantly at $t = 0^+$.

The drain current as a function of time is shown in Fig. 7.14d. It is zero up to $t = \tau_d$, at which time the electrons reach the drain. Current then begins to flow and, eventually, builds up to the value I_D, which is the value calculated from dc equations. [In contrast to the drain current, the source current starts flowing immediately at $t = 0^+$, since electrons start filling the channel from the source end as soon as $v(t)$ goes high, as expected by the fluid analog in Fig. 4.15d.]

Assuming q'_I corresponds to the approximate model of Sec. 4.4.2 with $\delta = 0$, a numerical solution of the above problem gives for the delay time[6]

$$\tau_d \approx 0.38\tau_o \qquad (7.7.10)$$

where

$$\tau_o = \frac{L^2}{\mu(V_{GS} - V_T)}, \qquad \delta = 0 \qquad (7.7.11)$$

with V_{GS} being the value of the input for $t > 0$. The same numerical solution predicts that at $t = \tau_o$ the current has reached about 98 percent of the final value I_D. Note that the quantity τ_o in the above equation is the same as in (7.5.4), which was derived for dc conditions. However, the fact that the same quantity is involved in the two different types of analysis does not mean that one can casually use the dc transit time to explain directly the nonquasi-static behavior of the transistor. Care is required at this point.

If the input has a small nonzero rise time t_R, as long as t_R is much less than τ_o, the above results still hold. However, if t_R is significant (larger than τ_o), the delay time is given approximately by $\tau_d = \sqrt{t_R\tau_o}$, as found by another numerical solution.[13] If t_R is over $20\tau_o$, the numerical solution of (7.7.6) gives roughly the same results as the quasi-static model. This is the reason why the limit of validity for the latter is expressed as in (7.6.3).†

The above results have been derived for a long-channel device. If, instead, L is small, velocity saturation can occur, and electrons will be traveling at maximum speed $|v_d|_{\max}$ toward the drain. If it is assumed that this happens over the whole length of the channel, the delay time will be, for a step input,

$$\tau_d \approx \frac{L}{|v_d|_{\max}} \qquad (7.7.12)$$

which can be significantly *larger* than what long-channel theory would predict.[19, 20] On the other hand, if the rise time of the input is significantly larger than the above limit, and saturation velocity is no longer the limiting factor, the delay is found to be less than that predicted by long-channel theory. This is

---

† We remind the reader that the analysis presented assumed that the channel is in strong inversion. In the more general case, corresponding to the model of Sec. 4.3, we must allow for diffusion currents. Thus (7.7.6a) must be replaced by [see (4.3.15)]

$$q'_I(x, t) = -C'_{ox}[v_{GB}(t) - V_{FB} - \psi_s(x, t) - \gamma\sqrt{\psi_s(x, t)}]$$

where $\psi_s(x, t)$ is the surface potential at position x and at time t. Similarly, (7.7.6b) must be replaced by [see (4.3.5)]

$$i(x, t) = -\mu W q'_I(x, t) \frac{\partial \psi_s(x, t)}{\partial x} + \mu W \phi_t \frac{\partial q'_I(x, t)}{\partial x}$$

or, alternatively, (7.7.6b) can be used, with v_{CB} taken to be the quasi-Fermi potential difference (Appendix I). Equation (7.7.6c) is general and remains unchanged.

probably because in short-channel devices the drain and source act also as gates, owing to two-dimensional effects (Sec. 5.4). These "gates" have already been activated before $t = 0$ in Fig. 7.14. Hence, the main gate does not have to start building up the whole inversion layer charge "from scratch." This heuristic explanation is supported by accurate numerical calculations.[20]

REFERENCES

1. T. J. O'Reilly, "The transient response of insulated gate field-effect transistors," *Solid-State Electronics*, vol. 8, pp. 947–956, 1965.
2. Z. S. Gribnikov and Y. A. Tkhorik, "Calculation of the transient process in field triodes with an insulated gate for the saturated mode of operation," *Radio Engineering and Electronic Physics*, vol. 11, pp. 776–781, 1966.
3. A. Möschwitzer, "Zum statischen und dynamischen Grosssignalverhalten des MOS-Feldeffekt-Transistors," *NTZ*, vol. 20, pp. 150–154, 1967.
4. M. B. Das, "Switching characteristics of MOS and junction-gate field-effect transistors," *IEE Proceedings*, vol. 114, pp. 1223–1230, 1967.
5. F. A. Lindholm, R. J. Balda, and J. L. Clements, "Characterization of the four-terminal MOS transistor for digital and linear applications," *Digest of Technical Papers*, International Electronics Conference, Toronto, pp. 116–117, 1967.
6. J. R. Burns, "Large-signal transit-time effects in the MOS transistor," *RCA Review*, vol. 15, pp. 15–35, March 1969.
7. J. S. Brugler and P. G. A. Jespers, "Charge pumping in MOS devices," *IEEE Transactions on Electron Devices*, vol. ED-16, pp. 297–302, March 1969.
8. R. S. Cobbold, *Theory and Applications of Field-Effect Transistors*, Wiley-Interscience, New York, 1970.
9. K. Gocer, "Einschaltzeiten und Umladungsvorgänge bei MOS-Transistoren," *AEU*, vol. 24, pp. 21–28, 1970.
10. D. J. Hamilton, F. A. Lindholm, and A. H. Marshak, *Principles and Applications of Semiconductor Device Modeling*, Holt, Rinehart, and Winston, New York, 1971.
11. J. E. Meyer, "MOS models and circuit simulation," *RCA Review*, vol. 32, pp. 42–43, March 1971.
12. M. E. Zahn, "Calculation of the turn-on behavior of MOST," *Solid-State Electronics*, vol. 17, pp. 843–854, 1974.
13. R. M. Swanson, "Complementary MOS transistors in micropower circuits," *Technical Report 4963-1*, Integrated Circuits Laboratory, Stanford University, California, 1974.
14. F. M. Klaassen, "A MOS model for computer-aided design," *Philips Research Reports*, vol. 31, pp. 71–83, 1976.
15. J. I. Arreola, "Equivalent circuit modeling of the large signal transient response of four-terminal MOS field-effect transistors," doctoral dissertation, University of Florida, 1978.
16. D. E. Ward and R. W. Dutton, "A charge-oriented model for MOS transistor capacitances," *IEEE Journal of Solid-State Circuits*, vol. SC-13, pp. 703–707, October 1978.
17. P. E. Cottrell and E. Buturla, "Two-dimensional static and transient simulation of mobile carrier transport in a semiconductor," *Proceedings of NASECODE* I, Dublin, Ireland, June 1979.
18. J. A. Robinson, Y. A. El-Mansy, and A. R. Boothroyd, "A general four-terminal charging-current model for the insulated-gate field effect transistor," parts I and II, *Solid-State Electronics*, vol. 23, pp. 405–414, 1980.
19. S. Y. Oh, D. E. Ward, and R. W. Dutton, "Transient analysis of MOS transistors," *IEEE Journal of Solid-State Circuits*, vol. SC-15, pp. 636–643, August 1980.
20. S. Y. Oh, "A simplified two-dimensional numerical analysis of MOS devices including transient phenomena," *Technical Report G201-10*, Integrated Circuits Laboratory, Stanford University, California, June 1981.

21. D. E. Ward, "Charge-based modeling of capacitance in MOS transistors," *Technical Report G201–11*, Integrated Circuits Laboratory, Stanford University, California, June 1981.
22. M. S. Mock, "A time-dependent numerical model of the insulated-gate field-effect transistor," *Solid-State Electronics*, vol. 24, pp. 959–966, 1981.
23. Y. Ikawa, W. R. Eisenstadt, and R. W. Dutton, "Modeling of high-speed, large-signal transistor switching transients from s-parameter measurements," *IEEE Transactions on Electron Devices*, vol. ED-29, pp. 669–675, April 1982.
24. G. W. Taylor, W. Fichtner, and J. G. Simmons, "A description of MOS internodal capacitances for transient simulations," *IEEE Transactions on Computer-Aided Design of Integrated Circuits and Systems*, vol. CAD-1, pp. 150–156, October 1982.
25. R. Conilogue and E. Viswanathan, "A complete large and small signal charge model for a M.O.S. Transistor," *Technical Digest*, International Electron Devices Meeting, San Francisco, pp. 654–657, 1982.
26. K. Y. Tong, "A model for MOS transistors from transient current computations," *IEE Proceedings*, vol. 130, part I, pp. 33–36, February 1983.
27. P. Yang, B. D. Epler, and P. K. Chatterjee, "An investigation of the charge conservation problem for MOSFET circuit simulation," *IEEE Journal of Solid-State Circuits*, vol. SC-18, pp. 128–138, February 1983.
28. C. Turchetti, G. Masetti, and Y. Tsividis, "On the small-signal behavior of the MOS transistor in quasi-static operation," *Solid-State Electronics*, vol. 26, pp. 941–949, 1983.
29. B. J. Sheu, D. L. Scharfetter, C. Hu, and D. O. Pederson, "A compact IGFET charge model," *IEEE Transactions on Circuits and Systems*, vol. CAS-31, pp. 745–749, August 1984.
30. J. J. Paulos, "Measurement and modeling of small-geometry MOS transistor capacitances," Ph.D. dissertation, Department of Electrical Engineering and Computer Science, Massachusetts Institute of Technology, Cambridge, September 1984.
31. C. Turchetti, P. Prioretti, G. Masetti, E. Profumo, and M. Vanzi, "A Meyer-like approach for the transient analysis of digital MOS IC's," *IEEE Transactions on CAD*, vol. CAD-5, pp. 499–507, October 1986.
32. C. Turchetti, P. Mancini, and G. Masetti, "A CAD-oriented non quasi-static approach for the transient analysis of MOS IC's," *IEEE Journal of Solid-State Circuits*, vol. SC-21, pp. 827–836, October 1986.
33. S.M. Sze, *Physics of Semiconductor Devices*, John Wiley & Sons, Inc., New York, 1981.

PROBLEMS

7.1. Show that (7.4.4) and (7.4.5) are equivalent.

7.2. Derive in detail the expressions for the total charges Q_I, Q_B, Q_G, Q_D, and Q_S in (7.4.14), (7.4.15), (7.4.17), (7.4.19), and (7.4.20).

7.3. Consider a transistor with $N_A = 400 \ \mu m^{-3}$, $d_{ox} = 0.04 \ \mu m$, $Q'_o = 0.05 \ fC/\mu m^2$, $\phi_{MS} = 0$, $W = L = 10 \ \mu m$, with $V_{SB} = 0 \ V$. Plot the total charges Q_G, Q_B, Q_I, Q_D, and Q_S vs. V_{DS}, with V_{DS} between 0 and 5 V, for $V_{GS} = 3$ and 5 V. Use the results of Sec. 7.4.2.

7.4. Compare the empirical expressions for Q_D and Q_S in Appendix L to those corresponding to the approximate model [(7.4.19 and (7.4.20)].

7.5. Prove the expressions given for Q_B, Q_I, and Q_G corresponding to the accurate model in Appendix L.

7.6. Compare the following three expressions for the total inversion layer charge Q_I:
  (a) Empirical expression in Appendix L
  (b) Expression corresponding to the approximate model, (7.4.14)
  (c) Expression corrresponding to the accurate model in Appendix L

7.7. Prove the expressions for Q_I, Q_D, and Q_S in weak inversion given in Sec. 7.4.4.

7.8. Using the method outlined in Sec. 7.4.5, develop expressions for Q_I, Q_B, Q_G, Q_D, and Q_S in terms of ψ_{s0} and ψ_{sL} corresponding to the general model in Sec. 4.3 (this is a long problem).

7.9. Repeat Prob. 7.8 by using a first-degree polynomial approximation for Q'_B [similar to the one in (4.4.22), only in terms of ψ_s]. This problem is related to Prob. 4.12 and involves similar considerations. Lengthy computations are needed.

7.10. For the device of Prob. 7.3, plot Q_G, Q_B, Q_D, and Q_S vs. V_{GS}, with V_{GS} from -2 to $+5$ V, and for $V_{DS} = 1$ and 2 V.

7.11. Assume a fixed parasitic extrinsic capacitance C_{gde} exists between gate and drain in the device of Fig. 7.11a (such a capacitance can be caused by the physical overlap between gate and drain, as will be discussed in Sec. 8.4). Show that the effect of such a capacitance will be a downward shift of the current waveforms in Fig. 7.11d and e, between $t = 0$ and $t = t_3$.

7.12. Consider the transistor of Prob. 7.3, and assume a constant effective mobility $\mu = 70 \ \mu\text{m}^2/(\text{V} \cdot \text{ns})$. The transistor is connected as in Fig. 7.11a with $V_{DD} = 5$ V; $v_G(t)$ is as shown in Fig. 7.11b, with $t_3 = 100$ ns and $v_{G,\text{max}} = 5$ V. Plot $i_D(t)$, $i_G(t)$, $i_S(t)$, and $i_B(t)$ as functions of time.

CHAPTER
8

SMALL-SIGNAL MODELING FOR LOW AND MEDIUM FREQUENCIES

8.1 INTRODUCTION

In the previous chapter we considered the MOS transistor with terminal voltages undergoing variations with time. No restrictions were placed on the magnitude of these variations. In this chapter we will consider the case where the terminal voltage variations are sufficiently small so that the resulting small current variations can be expressed in terms of them using linear relations. We will derive such linear relations and develop linear circuits to represent them. These circuits will be called *small signal equivalent circuits*. When excited by voltages equal to the small *variations* of the actual terminal voltages, these circuits will produce currents equal to the *variations* of the actual transistor currents. Such models find wide use in analog circuit design.

In most of this chapter, we will concentrate on the *intrinsic* part of the transistor (Fig. 7.1). We will first develop a small-signal model valid when the voltage and current variations are so slow that charge storage effects can be neglected. Then we will develop a small-signal model valid at medium speeds, assuming quasi-static operation. Such models[1-45] are sufficient for many applications. (More advanced models will be presented in Chap. 9.) It is convenient to discuss modeling by assuming that the voltage and current *variations* are sinusoidal. In that case, one often talks of frequency rather than "speed," and we will adopt this convention from now on. Following the discussion of the models for the intrinsic part of the transistor, we will consider modeling for the extrinsic part. Finally, we will consider the noise generated within a MOS transistor.

As in the previous chapter, *n*-channel devices with long and wide channels on a uniform substrate and with constant mobility will be assumed unless noted otherwise.

8.2   A LOW-FREQUENCY SMALL-SIGNAL MODEL FOR THE INTRINSIC PART

8.2.1   Definitions and Small-Signal Equivalent Circuit

Let us consider an *n*-channel MOS transistor biased with V_{GS}, V_{SB}, and V_{DS} fixed at values V_{GSO}, V_{SBO}, and V_{DSO}, respectively, as shown in Fig. 8.1a. Let I_{D0} be the resulting value of I_D. We can study the effect of *very small* changes of the bias voltages on I_D by varying these voltages *one at a time*, as shown in Fig. 8.1b, c, and d. We are for now interested only in the change of the *dc steady-state* value of I_D, that is, we assume that the voltages are constant before and after each change and that I_D has reached dc steady state in both cases. We then consider the change ΔI_D between the two dc steady state values. We can relate cause and effect by using three conductance parameters, which can be measured as shown next to each figure. These parameters are:

1. The *small-signal gate transconductance* g_m, often referred to simply as "transconductance." Mathematically, it is defined by the following relation, corresponding to the measurement in Fig. 8.1b:

$$g_m = \frac{\partial I_D}{\partial V_{GS}}\bigg|_{V_{BS}, V_{DS}} \tag{8.2.1}$$

where to the right of the vertical line we show the voltages being held fixed.

2. The *small-signal substrate transconductance* g_{mb}. Corresponding to the measurement in Fig 8.1c, we have:

$$g_{mb} = \frac{\partial I_D}{\partial V_{BS}}\bigg|_{V_{GS}, V_{DS}} \tag{8.2.2}$$

Increasing V_{BS} as shown in Fig. 8.1c *decreases* V_{SB}. A consideration of the results of the body effect on I_D shows that I_D increases. Thus, ΔV_{BS} has on I_D qualitatively the same effect as ΔV_{GS} has on Fig. 8.1b. The substrate acts, in this sense, as a second gate, and is often referred to as the *back gate*.

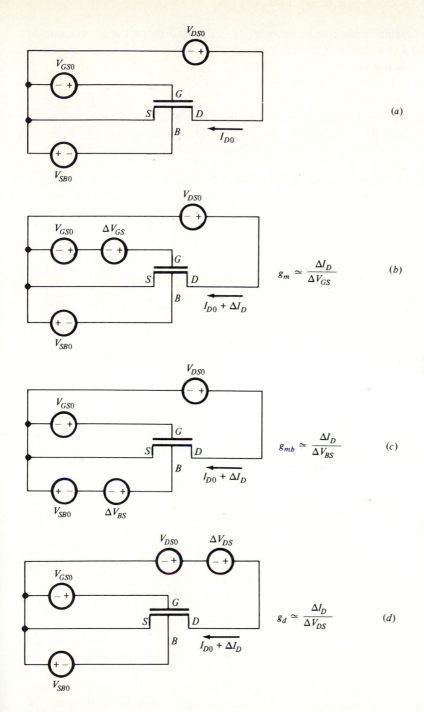

FIGURE 8.1
(a) A MOS transistor biased with dc voltages at a certain operating point. For this operating point,
(b) shows the measurement of gate small-signal transconductance, (c) the measurement of
substrate small-signal transconductance, and (d) the measurement of drain small-signal conductance. All voltage and current changes are assumed to be very small.

3. The *small-signal drain conductance* g_d. Corresponding to the measurement in Fig. 8.1*d*, we define

$$g_d = \frac{\partial I_D}{\partial V_{DS}}\bigg|_{V_{GS}, V_{BS}} \qquad (8.2.3)$$

The approximate equality signs in Fig. 8.1 become "equal" signs as ΔV_{GS}, ΔV_{BS}, and ΔV_{DS} approach zero. All three parameters have units of conductance and in this book will be expressed in μS (S stands for "Siemens"; $1\,S = 1\,\mho = 1\,A/V$).

Let us now consider the general case in which all three voltages are changed simultaneously. The corresponding total change in the drain current will be

$$\Delta I_D = \left(\frac{\partial I_D}{\partial V_{GS}}\bigg|_{V_{BS}, V_{DS}}\right)\Delta V_{GS} + \left(\frac{\partial I_D}{\partial V_{BS}}\bigg|_{V_{GS}, V_{DS}}\right)\Delta V_{BS} + \left(\frac{\partial I_D}{\partial V_{DS}}\bigg|_{V_{GS}, V_{BS}}\right)\Delta V_{DS} \qquad (8.2.4)$$

Using our above definitions, this becomes:

$$\Delta I_D = g_m\,\Delta V_{GS} + g_{mb}\,\Delta V_{BS} + g_d\,\Delta V_{DS} \qquad (8.2.5a)$$

In addition, if, as in previous chapters, the gate and substrate conductive currents are assumed to be fixed at zero (no leakage), we will have

$$\Delta I_G = 0 \qquad (8.2.5b)$$

$$\Delta I_B = 0 \qquad (8.2.5c)$$

The above three equations relate small-signal quantities and can be represented by the small-signal equivalent circuit of Fig. 8.2, where the rhombic symbols represent controlled current sources.

In the preceding model derivation, the changes ΔV_{GS}, ΔV_{BS}, and ΔV_{DS} represented differences between two dc steady-state values of the terminal voltages V_{GS}, V_{BS}, and V_{DS} respectively. However, the model derived will be valid for representing the effects of gate and substrate on the drain current, even if the changes are continuously varying with time, as long as the variations are slow enough so that capacitive effects can be neglected. This will be understood better, and will be made more quantitative, after more complete models are considered. It will then be shown that, as the frequency of variation is decreased, more complete models reduce to the one in Fig. 8.2.

In the above definitions, we followed the common convention of referring the gate, drain, and substrate potentials to the source. An alternative approach, in which all *four* terminal voltages are taken with respect to an arbitrary reference, is considered in Prob. 8.1.

We will now derive expressions for each small-signal parameter, considering each region of inversion seperately. (Models valid in all regions of inversion will be considered in Sec. 8.2.5.) For brevity, the words "small signal" may be omitted when referring to a small-signal parameter when there is no chance for confusion, e.g., g_d will be referred to as the "drain conductance."

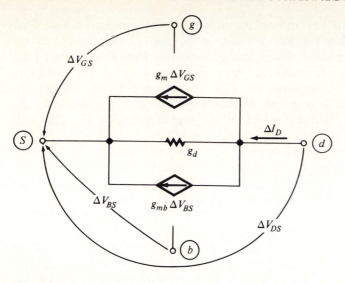

FIGURE 8.2
A low-frequency small-signal model for the MOS transistor.

8.2.2 Strong Inversion

GATE TRANSCONDUCTANCE. Consider a long-channel device with constant effective mobility. Using either the accurate or the approximate model of Sec. 4.4 in the definition for g_m (8.2.1), we find

$$g_m = \frac{W}{L} \mu C'_{ox} V_{DS}, \qquad V_{DS} \leq V'_{DS} \qquad (8.2.6a)$$

$$= \frac{W}{L} \mu C'_{ox} V'_{DS}, \qquad V_{DS} > V'_{DS} \qquad (8.2.6b)$$

which can be expressed concisely by using the parameter α, defined in (4.4.31), as follows:

$$g_m = \frac{W}{L} \mu C'_{ox} V'_{DS}(1 - \alpha), \qquad \text{all } V_{DS} \qquad (8.2.7)$$

In the saturation region, the approximate model (4.4.30b) gives for the current $I_D = \frac{1}{2}(W/L)\mu C'_{ox}(V_{GS} - V_T)^2/(1 + \delta)$. This, along with (8.2.1) produces the following equivalent forms for g_m:

$$g_m = \frac{W}{L} \frac{\mu C'_{ox}}{1 + \delta} (V_{GS} - V_T), \qquad V_{DS} > V'_{DS} \qquad (8.2.8a)$$

$$= \sqrt{2 \frac{W}{L} \frac{\mu C'_{ox}}{1 + \delta} I_D}, \qquad V_{DS} > V'_{DS} \qquad (8.2.8b)$$

$$= \frac{2I_D}{V_{GS} - V_T}, \qquad V_{DS} > V'_{DS} \qquad (8.2.8c)$$

As noted from (8.2.6a), in nonsaturation g_m is independent of V_{GS}. This is illustrated graphically in Fig. 8.3. We assume that the V_{GS} step used to obtain successive curves was fixed, so that g_m can be estimated from the spacing of the curves if the V_{GS} steps are small. As seen, for lines a and b the spacing is independent of V_{GS} but depends on V_{DS}, as expected from (8.2.6a). In saturation, the situation is reversed, as seen from (8.2.6b) and illustrated by lines c and d. Now g_m is independent of V_{DS} but depends on V_{GS} (through V'_{DS}).

Various corrections can be applied to the above equations to increase their accuracy in the presence of higher order effects. For example, if the effective mobility is not constant with V_{GS}, differentiating I_D will lead to an additional term (Prob. 8.5). An analogous correction should be applied if channel length modulation cannot be neglected. For example, a first-order correction results when obtaining g_m by differentiating (5.2.8).

Short-channel effects can strongly affect the value of all small-signal parameters. An extreme example is what happens to g_m in the presence of velocity saturation. The drain current is then roughly given by (5.3.13b). Differentiating that equation with respect to V_{GS} gives

$$g_m \approx WC'_{ox}\mu\mathscr{E}_c \quad , \qquad \text{velocity saturation} \qquad (8.2.9a)$$

$$\approx WC'_{ox}|v_d|_{max} , \qquad \text{velocity saturation} \qquad (8.2.9b)$$

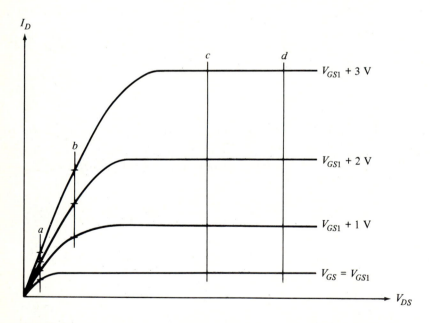

FIGURE 8.3
A family of I_D-V_{DS} curves, obtained for fixed V_{GS} increment. In nonsaturation, spacing is proportional to V_{DS} but independent of V_{GS} (lines a, b); in saturation, spacing is independent of V_{DS} but depends on V_{GS} (lines c, d).

where $\mathscr{E}_c$ and $|v_d|_{max}$ have been discussed in Sec. 5.3. As seen, in this case g_m is constant and independent of L in contrast with the long-channel case.

Approximate values of g_m in the presence of other short-channel and narrow-channel effects can be found by using expressions from Chap. 5 in the definition (8.2.1).

SURSTRATE TRANSCONDUCTANCE. Using the definition of g_{mb} of (8.2.2) with either the accurate model or the approximate model of Sec. 4.4 produces an expression that can be written in the form (Prob. 8.6)

$$g_{mb} = b g_m \qquad (8.2.10)$$

where b is different for each model. The accurate model results in the following value for b:

$$b_1 = \gamma \frac{\sqrt{V_{DS} + V_{SB} + \phi_B} - \sqrt{V_{SB} + \phi_B}}{V_{DS}}, \qquad V_{DS} \leq V'_{DS} \qquad (8.2.11a)$$

$$= \gamma \frac{\sqrt{V'_{DS} + V_{SB} + \phi_B} - \sqrt{V_{SB} + \phi_B}}{V'_{DS}}, \qquad V_{DS} > V'_{DS} \qquad (8.2.11b)$$

Care must be exercised when using (8.2.11a) because, for V_{DS} approaching zero, both the numerator and the denominator approach zero, which can cause numerical problems. To avoid such problems, we seek a better behaved approximation to this equation. If V_{DS} is small, the first square root can be approximated by the first two terms of its Taylor expansion around $V_{DS} = 0$. Then (8.2.11a) reduces to

$$b_1 \approx \frac{\gamma}{2\sqrt{\phi_B + V_{SB}}}, \qquad \text{small } V_{DS} \qquad (8.2.12)$$

For large V_{DS} this relation will be inaccurate since it does not predict the tendency of b_1 in (8.2.11a) to decrease somewhat with increasing V_{DS}. However, we can empirically modify (8.2.12) so that such tendency is predicted. A simple way to do this is shown below, where we denote the modified b by b_2:

$$b_2 = \frac{\gamma}{2\sqrt{\phi_B + V_{SB} + k_g V_{DS}}}, \qquad V_{DS} \leq V'_{DS} \qquad (8.2.13a)$$

$$= \frac{\gamma}{2\sqrt{\phi_B + V_{SB} + k_g V'_{DS}}}, \qquad V_{DS} > V'_{DS} \qquad (8.2.13b)$$

With $k_g = 0.4$, this approximates (8.2.11) very well. We can write (8.2.13) in a concise manner by using the parameter α, defined in (4.4.31) and plotted in Fig. 4.13, as follows:

$$b_2 = \frac{\gamma}{2\sqrt{\phi_B + V_{SB} + k_g V'_{DS}(1 - \alpha)}} \qquad (8.2.14)$$

We now turn to g_{mb} as it corresponds to the approximate model of (4.4.30). If δ is assumed independent of V_{SB} [see, for example, (4.4.33a) or (4.4.33e)], then the only term dependent on V_{SB} in (4.4.30) is V_T, which is given by (4.4.26a). Then the derivative $g_{mb} = \partial I_D / \partial V_{BS} = -\partial I_D / \partial V_{SB}$ gives (8.2.10), with $b = dV_T / dV_{SB} = \gamma / (2\sqrt{\phi_B + V_{SB}})$. As stated in (8.2.12), this result is satisfactory only for small V_{DS}. One is thus led to modify this quantity, ending up with (8.2.13) or (8.2.14) again. For more accurate I_D models, δ is assumed dependent on V_{BS} [see, for example, (4.4.33c) or (4.4.33d)]. In this case, dI_D / dV_{BS} will include the derivative of the semiempirical quantity δ with respect to V_{BS}. The resulting expression for g_{mb}, although satisfactory for small V_{DS}, is still unacceptable for large V_{DS} values. Such poor performance is not surprising because (4.3.30) is an *approximate* relation. It was developed to provide reasonable accuracy for I_D, with no regard to the derivative of I_D with respect to V_{BS}. "Reasonable accuracy" for a function does not necessarily imply reasonable accuracy for its derivatives. Such problems are common when differentiation of empirical or semiempirical expressions is attempted, and one must exercise caution. We will thus avoid obtaining g_{mb} by direct differentiation of the approximate drain current expression and rely only on (8.2.10) with $b = b_2$ from (8.2.14).

Let us now take a look at the value of b for $V_{DS} = 0$. Equation (8.2.12) becomes in this case exact. With the help of (4.4.26a) we observe that

$$b_1 \Big|_{V_{DS}=0} = \frac{g_{mb}}{g_m} \Big|_{V_{DS}=0} = \frac{\gamma}{2\sqrt{\phi_B + V_{SB}}} = \frac{dV_T}{dV_{SB}} \qquad (8.2.15)$$

Using the expression for γ from (3.4.11) as well as (1.5.10) and (3.4.18), it is easy to show that

$$b_1 \Big|_{V_{DS}=0} = \frac{g_{mb}}{g_m} \Big|_{V_{DS}=0} = \frac{\epsilon_s}{\epsilon_{ox}} \frac{d_{ox}}{l_{Bm}} \qquad (8.2.16)$$

where l_{Bm} is the width of the depletion region, which is uniform since $V_{DS} = 0$ ($V_{SB} = V_{DB}$). The ratio $b = g_{mb}/g_m$ can be thought of as a measure of the relative control of the "back gate" (substrate) and the "front" gate. As seen in (8.2.16), the thinner the oxide the smaller the value of b. This makes sense, since then the "front gate" is close to the channel and its control on it is strong. Thus the control of the "back gate" is smaller in a relative sense. The opposite is true if l_{Bm} is small. Then the edge of the depletion region is close to the channel and the substrate's relative influence is large. In addition, the permittivities enter the picture. Large oxide permittivity means large control of the gate on the channel through the oxide, hence a small relative influence of the "back gate" (small b). The opposite is true for large ϵ_s, which implies strong substrate control.

The quantity $(g_{mb}/g_m)|_{V_{DS}=0}$ is plotted in Fig. 8.4 as a function of V_{SB}, with the body effect coefficient as a parameter. This plot can be used to obtain rough estimates of $b = g_{mb}/g_m$ for $V_{DS} \neq 0$, since the variation of b with V_{DS} is not very strong, as seen from (8.2.13).

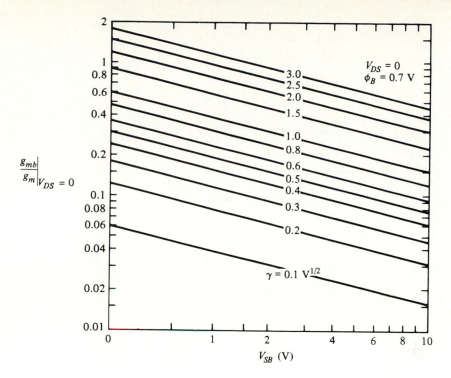

FIGURE 8.4
Ratio of substrate transconductance to gate transconductance for $V_{DS} = 0$ plotted vs. source-substrate bias for various values of the body effect coefficient. A single value of 0.7 V is assumed for ϕ_B. For very rough estimates, the plots can also be used for $V_{DS} \neq 0$.

If high-order corrections not involving V_{SB} are made on g_m [e.g., corresponding to (5.3.11)], then the corresponding corrections on g_{mb} will be taken care of automatically through (8.2.10). Corrections involving V_{SB} [such as (4.8.18)] must, of course, be considered separately. In the presence of charge-sharing effects discussed in Sec. 5.4, approximate expressions for g_{mb} can be found by using approximate equations from that section in the definition (8.2.2). As might be expected, g_{mb}/g_m can become very small in the presence of strong short-channel effects, because in such cases the trapezoidal shape of the depletion region in Fig. 5.9 becomes close to a triangle, cutting off substrate control on the channel.

DRAIN CONDUCTANCE. The small-signal drain conductance g_d[4, 10–22, 26–28, 32, 34, 35, 37, 44, 45] is the slope of the I_D-V_{DS} characteristics with V_{GS} and V_{SB} held constant. A measured set of I_D-V_{DS} characteristics and the corresponding g_d (on a logarithmic axis) are shown in Fig. 8.5.[28] Applying the definition (8.2.3) of g_d to the nonsaturation accurate model (4.4.17) gives

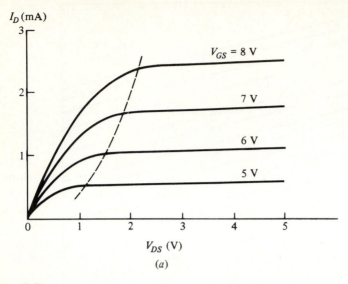

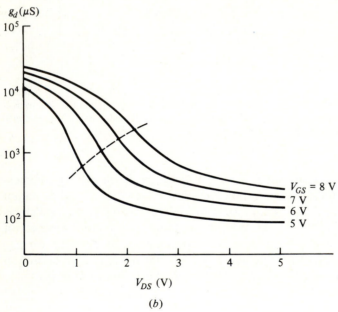

FIGURE 8.5
(a) Measured *I-V* characteristics for an *n*-channel device with $N_A = 2 \times 10^4 \ \mu\text{m}^{-3}$, $d_{ox} = 0.1 \ \mu\text{m}$, $V_{T0} = 2.59$ V, $W = 700 \ \mu\text{m}$, and $L = 6 \ \mu\text{m}$; (b) measured small-signal drain conductance corresponding to (a). The broken lines separate nonsaturation and saturation regions.[28]

$$g_d = \frac{W}{L} \mu C'_{ox}(V_{GS} - V_{DS} - V_{FB} - \phi_B - \gamma\sqrt{V_{DS} + V_{SB} + \phi_B}) \ , \qquad V_{DS} \le V'_{DS}$$
$$(8.2.17)$$

The approximate model (4.4.30a) gives

$$g_d = \frac{W}{L} \mu C'_{ox}[V_{GS} - V_T - (1 + \delta)V_{DS}] \ , \qquad V_{DS} \le V'_{DS} \qquad (8.2.18)$$

The two expressions are seen to be equivalent for $V_{DS} = 0$.

In the saturation region, simple long-channel drain current models assume that I_D is fixed at the value I'_D (the value found from nonsaturation expressions with $V_{DS} = V'_{DS}$). The quantity I_D is then predicted independent of V_{DS}, resulting in $I_D - V_{DS}$ curves parallel to the V_{DS} axis. Since g_d is the slope of these curves, its value is predicted as zero, which is unacceptable. For many applications one needs instead a model that provides an accurate slope, which implies that the plot of I_D vs. V_{DS} using such a model should track the nuances of experimentally observed behavior. This, unfortunately, represents a major problem area in MOS transistor modeling, as illustrated in Fig. 8.6.[35] In a, the solid line represents a measured characteristic. The broken line represents a model, the parameters of which have as usual been adjusted so that I_D is

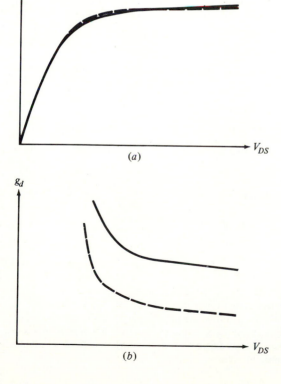

(a)

(b)

FIGURE 8.6
(a) I_D-V_{DS} characteristics; solid line: measured; broken line: model; (b) slopes obtained from (a)[35] (© 1984 by IEEE).

predicted relatively accurately. Indeed, as shown, the error in predicting I_D values is at most a few percent. In *b*, the *slopes* of the two curves are shown—the slope (g_d) error exceeds 100 percent! This can have a very serious consequence in analog circuit design. For example, the small-signal "gain" of a CMOS inverter is inversely proportional to the sum of the g_d's of two devices and can be in very large error if the above model is used to calculate it.†

If the saturation current is assumed to exhibit a first-order dependence on V_{DS} as in (5.2.8), the following g_d value results:

$$g_d \approx \frac{I'_D}{V_A} , \qquad V_{DS} > V'_{DS} \tag{8.2.19}$$

As expected from the above discussion, this formulation is too crude. One of the problems with it is that it usually does not predict accurately the variation of g_d with V_{GS} (which, in this expression, is hidden in I'_D). This variation is affected by two-dimensional effects as discussed below. An empirical modification which has been suggested to take this variation into account is[32]

$$g_d \approx \frac{I'_D}{V_A} \frac{1}{1 + B_8(V_{GS} - V_T)} , \qquad V_{DS} > V'_{DS} \tag{8.2.20}$$

where B_8 is an empirical constant.

Unfortunately, both of the above formulas predict that g_d is independent of V_{DS}. However, a closer look shows that g_d decreases with increasing V_{DS}, with V_{GS} being kept constant (assuming no breakdown or punchthrough are present). To model this effect, consider (5.2.5*b*), repeated here:[4, 12]

$$I_D = \frac{I'_D}{1 - \Delta L/L} , \qquad V_{DS} > V'_{DS} \tag{8.2.21}$$

Using this in (8.2.3) we have (in the partial derivatives below, it is understood that V_{GS} and V_{BS} are kept constant)

$$g_d = \frac{\partial I_D}{\partial V_{DS}} = \frac{\partial I_D}{\partial(\Delta L)} \frac{\partial(\Delta L)}{\partial V_{DS}}$$

$$= \frac{I'_D}{(1 - \Delta L/L)^2} \frac{1}{L} \frac{\partial(\Delta L)}{\partial V_{DS}}$$

$$= \frac{I_D^2}{I'_D} \frac{1}{L} \frac{\partial(\Delta L)}{\partial V_{DS}} , \qquad V_{DS} > V'_{DS} \tag{8.2.22}$$

---

† A similar problem can occur in the prediction of waveform distortion. If, for example, a sinusoidal variation of V_{DS} is considered in the saturation region, the shape of the corresponding variation in I_D will depend on the nuances of the I_D-V_{DS} characteristic in that region. If these nuances are lost in the modeling process, the predicted distortion (deviation from sinusoidal behavior) in the I_D variation can be seriously in error.

This, if I_D/I'_D is not very different from unity, simplifies to

$$g_d = I'_D \frac{1}{L} \frac{\partial (\Delta L)}{\partial V_{DS}}, \qquad V_{DS} > V'_{DS} \qquad (8.2.23)$$

Various expressions for g_d can be found, depending on the behavior assumed for ΔL (Sec. 5.2). For example, if (5.2.6) is used, we obtain

$$\frac{\partial (\Delta L)}{\partial V_{DS}} = \frac{B_1}{\sqrt{N_A}} \frac{1}{2\sqrt{\phi_D + V_{DS} - V'_{DS}}} \qquad (8.2.24)$$

Thus, using (8.2.23),

$$g_d = \frac{B_1 I'_D}{2L\sqrt{N_A}\sqrt{\phi_D + V_{DS} - V'_{DS}}}, \qquad V_{DS} > V'_{DS} \qquad (8.2.25)$$

To "help" this equation model the dependence of g_d on V_{GS}, one can use a multiplicative empirical factor, as was done in (8.2.20). This level of modeling is widely used in computer-aided MOS circuit analysis and design, and is often adequate for digital circuits. For certain analog circuit applications, though, it is still not satisfactory, because such applications can place heavy demands on the models of g_d in saturation, as already explained. The reason that this parameter resists attempts to model it as above is that near the drain the electric field distribution is actually *two-dimensional*. The gradual channel approximation fails in that vicinity, and the field can have a significant horizontal component. The details of the field there are influenced by the drain region details (*junction depth*, for example) and, notably, by *field lines emanating from the gate*. The result is a current flow which, at least in part, takes place in a subsurface path. The associated charge in the "pinchoff" region should be taken into account for very accurate g_d modeling. For an accurate evaluation of I_D, then (and thus g_d), one must resort to *two-dimensional* numerical simulations using a computer.[10] Pseudo-two-dimensional approaches have also been proposed.[12, 17, 18, 20, 22, 27, 28, 34] The analyses leading to reasonably accurate g_d expressions are complicated, and such expressions contain all, or most, of the quantities shown in the following relation:

$$g_d = g_d(L, N_A, d_{ox}, r, \phi_{MS}, Q_o, V_{DS}, V_{GS}, V_{FB}) \qquad (8.2.26)$$

where r is the junction depth. For simplicity, sometimes quantities such as V_T and V'_{DS} and even the inversion layer thickness are included as parameters, although, in principle, these quantities can be expressed as functions of the quantities shown in the above equation. Examples of the results of such analyses are shown in Appendix J.

In seeking an adequate solution to the problem of modeling g_d, one is faced with two conflicting requirements. On one hand, it is desirable to keep models for I_D simple for computational efficiency in the simulation of large circuits, where the equations for I_D may have to be used hundreds of thousands of times in an iterative solution of the network equations. Large-signal transient solutions are especially demanding in this regard. Simple models, though, albeit adequate for predicting I_D, will, in general, be inadequate for predicting g_d. On the other hand, models for I_D that yield very accurate predictions for g_d are likely to be extremely complicated. Their extra sophistication is not needed for I_D calculations and, in fact, can make such calculations extremely slow. A solution here may be to use a simple model for I_D and a separate, more sophisticated model for obtaining g_d.[35] This approach has often been avoided for reasons of consistency between the various types of circuit analysis (dc, transient, small-signal, etc.), but it certainly would not hurt to have it available as an extra feature in a CAD program.

What compounds the problem with modeling g_d is that in some CAD facilities, even if the model used is, in principle, capable of providing bearable accuracy for g_d, the model parameters are chosen so that this capability is not exploited. Thus, for example, in some automated "parameter extraction" systems model parameters are chosen so as to minimize the current mean-square relative error ϵ_I^2:

$$\epsilon_I^2 = \frac{1}{K} \sum_{j=1}^{K} \alpha_j \left(\frac{\hat{I}_{Dj} - I_{Dj}}{I_{Dj}} \right)^2 \tag{8.2.27}$$

where $I_{Dj}, j = 1, \ldots, K$ are measured I_D values for K different combinations of bias voltages, $\hat{I}_{Dj}$ are the corresponding calculated values, and α_j are weighting coefficients, often taken equal to 1. The above criterion would have pronounced the model in Fig. 8.6a "good," yet that model was seen in Fig. 8.6b to fail seriously in predicting g_d. In cases where accurate g_d prediction is of essence, a much better criterion for parameter extraction is the minimization of the following error:[35]

$$\epsilon^2 = \epsilon_I^2 + \epsilon_g^2 \tag{8.2.28}$$

where ϵ_I^2 is as before, and ϵ_g^2 is the mean square error in modeling g_d:

$$\epsilon_g^2 = \frac{1}{K} \sum_{j=1}^{K} \beta_j \left(\frac{\hat{g}_{dj} - g_{dj}}{g_{dj}} \right)^2 \tag{8.2.29}$$

where the weighting coefficients can be made large in saturation. With some models, use of the above criterion can provide a drastic improvement in g_d accuracy, with a negligible loss in overall current accuracy.[35, 44, 45] One must, of course, set up the appropriate facilities for measuring g_d; this measurement can be tricky.[19] Mean square errors involving g_m and g_{mb} could also be added to (8.2.28). However, these parameters can be predicted relatively accurately if the current is predicted accurately.

In addition to errors in the saturation region considered above, errors should also be expected in the "transition" from nonsaturation to saturation. As remarked in Sec. 4.4, strong-inversion models are not accurate in that region since the drain end of the channel is then moderately inverted. Thus, errors in g_d can result. Finally, the expression used for I_D as a function of V_{DS}

should provide a *continuous* g_d for all V_{DS}. If two-segment models are used, they should be designed to ensure that this is so, as discussed in Sec. 5.2.

Short channel effects can strongly affect the value of g_d. In such cases, g_d is determined by both channel length modulation and the direct influence of the drain field on a significant part of the channel charge. The situation is then very complicated and no simple model will suffice for describing it fully. Nevertheless, one can obtain some "feeling" for what happens by considering a greatly simplified situation in which the dominant effects can be modeled by the barrier-lowering or the charge-sharing pictures presented in Sec. 5.4.2. We will neglect channel length modulation for simplicity. We will assume that no velocity saturation occurs, and that the device can be described in saturation by the simple square-law equation

$$I_D = \frac{W}{L} \frac{\mu C'_{ox}}{2(1+\delta)} [V_{GS} - \hat{V}_T(V_{DS})]^2 \qquad (8.2.30)$$

where $\hat{V}_T(V_{DS})$ has been modeled as in Sec. 5.4.2. From the above equation we obtain

$$g_d = \frac{W}{L} \frac{\mu C'_{ox}}{1+\delta} [V_{GS} - \hat{V}_T(V_{DS})] \left(-\frac{\partial \hat{V}_T}{\partial V_{DS}}\right) \qquad (8.2.31)$$

which, using the material in Sec. 5.4.2, becomes (Prob. 8.9)

$$g_d = (\text{const})\frac{W}{L} \frac{\mu C'_{ox}}{1+\delta} [V_{GS} - \hat{V}_T(V_{DS})] \frac{d_{ox}}{L} \frac{\epsilon_s}{\epsilon_{ox}} \qquad (8.2.32)$$

with the constant nominally equal to 0.5. Using (8.2.30) in (8.2.1), we find that g_m is given by (8.2.8a), with V_T replaced by $\hat{V}_T(V_{DS})$. Thus we have

$$d \equiv \frac{g_d}{g_m} = 0.5 \frac{\epsilon_s}{\epsilon_{ox}} \frac{d_{ox}}{L} \qquad (8.2.33)$$

Qualitatively, the behavior predicted by this equation can be reached by using a different picture,[3] which assumes that some field lines from the drain curve down, then bend and turn up, and terminate directly on inversion layer charges throughout much of the channel. Thus, the drain acts as a "somewhat inefficient gate"; increasing the voltage on this "gate" increases the current and gives rise to a nonzero g_d. The parameter $d = g_d/g_m$ is a measure of the "competition" between this "gate" and the normal gate (just like b played a similar role as a measure of the relative competition between the substrate and the normal gate above). The smaller the L, the closer the whole of the inversion layer is to the drain region, and the stronger the influence of the latter; d can be large in this case. The smaller d_{ox}, the closer the actual gate is to the inversion layer, and the more this gate wins out in the competition; then d will be small. The relative influence of the two gates also depends on the permittivity of the media separating them from the inversion layer: Large permittivity implies a large effective capacitance and, hence, a strong influence.

All these qualitative results are consistent with (8.2.33). Finally, note that the larger the drain junction depth, the stronger will be the drain's "presence" as far as the inversion layer is concerned. Hence, g_d and d should *increase* with increasing drain junction depth. Dependence on junction depth is predicted by "charge-sharing" models such as those in Sec. 5.4.2, provided junction depth is retained as a parameter (Prob. 8.11).

According to the above results, we see that it is not only the *value* of g_d that depends on the length of the channel but also the form of the *functional dependence* of g_d on bias parameters. For example, from our discussion so far it can be deduced that g_d tends to be roughly proportional to I_D for long-channel devices and to $\sqrt{I_D}$ for short-channel devices (Prob. 8.12). Such conclusions are, of course, subject to the validity of our simplified assumptions above, which in some cases have been excessive. Such trends can, nevertheless, be seen over limited ranges in experimental results reported in the literature.[17, 26]

We remind the reader that punchthrough effects can cause extra currents which are not modeled by any of the expressions we have developed. In the punchthrough region, I_D becomes a strong function of V_{DS} (Fig. 5.18) and large g_d values can occur.

PLOT OF SMALL-SIGNAL CONDUCTANCES VS. V_{DS}. Figure 8.7 shows the three small-signal conductance parameters we discussed above plotted vs. V_{DS} for a fixed V_{GS}. The sharp corners are, of course, artificial, and are the result of the simplifications involved in the modeling process. More accurate models would provide smooth curves. For example, if one considers the transition region

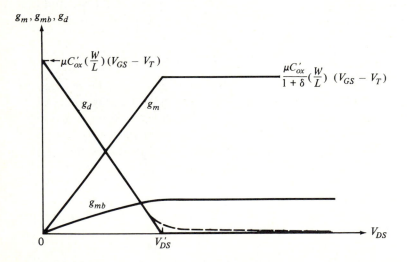

FIGURE 8.7
Small-signal gate transconductance, substrate transconductance, and drain conductance vs. V_{DS} for fixed V_{GS} and V_{SB}, as predicted by the approximate model (solid lines). The broken line represents a more accurate model for g_d.

between nonsaturation and saturation, and includes channel length modulation in saturation, the g_d plot would be of the form shown by the dashed line in the figure.

It is interesting to note that, for devices with negligible δ, we have

$$g_d|_{V_{DS}=0} \approx g_m|_{V_{DS}>V'_{DS}} , \qquad \text{if } \delta \text{ is negligible} \qquad (8.2.34)$$

assuming, of course, the same V_{GS} value.

8.2.3   Weak Inversion

Using the weak inversion current equation (4.6.17) in the definition for g_m (8.2.1), we find

$$g_m = \frac{1}{n} \frac{I_D}{\phi_t} \qquad (8.2.35)$$

where n is given by (4.6.20), assuming the effect of interface traps is negligible, a valid assumption for many modern devices (Sec. 2.6). If this effect is not negligible, n can have a larger value, best determined experimentally.

Thus, in contrast to the behavior in strong inversion, the quantity g_m/I_D is *independent of W/L*. This is a consequence of I_D being an exponential function of V_{GS} in weak inversion. In fact, the behavior here is qualitatively the same as for a bipolar transistor. For the latter, the current in the forward active region is given[46] by $I_C \approx I_o e^{V_{BE}/\phi_t}$, where V_{BE} is the base-emitter voltage and I_o is a characteristic current independent of V_{BE}. Thus, $g_m = dI_C/dV_{BE} = I_C/\phi_t$, or $g_m/I_C = 1/\phi_t$ independent of geometrical details. Note that the corresponding quantity for the MOS transistor, $g_m/I_D = 1/n\phi_t$, is always smaller since n is larger than unity. The value $1/\phi_t$, reached by the transconductance-to-current ratio for the bipolar transistor but not for the MOS transistor, is sometimes called the *Boltzmann limit*.

The substrate transductance will not be obtained from (4.6.17) since I'_X, V_X, and n depend on V_{SB} in a complicated manner. We will use instead (4.6.13) with $V_{GB} = V_{GS} - V_{BS}$ and $V_{DB} = V_{DS} - V_{BS}$. Then from the definition of g_{mb}, (8.2.2), we obtain (Prob. 8.13)

$$g_{mb} \approx \frac{n-1}{n} \frac{I_D}{\phi_t} \qquad (8.2.36)$$

Thus the ratio g_{mb}/g_m is given by:

$$b_g \equiv \frac{g_{mb}}{g_m} \approx n - 1 \qquad (8.2.37a)$$

$$\approx \frac{\gamma}{2\sqrt{V_{SB} + 1.5\phi_F}} \qquad (8.2.37b)$$

$$\approx \frac{\epsilon_s}{\epsilon_{ox}} \frac{d_{ox}}{l_B} \qquad (8.2.37c)$$

where we have assumed negligible interface trap density, and where in the last expression l_B is the approximate width of the depletion region in the middle of weak inversion. This last relation is of the same form as (8.2.16).

For g_d we find, using the definition (8.2.3) in (4.6.17),

$$g_d = \frac{e^{-V_{DS}/\phi_t}}{1 - e^{-V_{DS}/\phi_t}} \frac{I_D}{\phi_t} \qquad (8.2.38)$$

This equation predicts a g_d that rapidly goes to 0 with increasing V_{DS}. However, this neglects the direct influence of the drain field on the channel (already discussed above for the case of strong inversion). Because of this effect, one often finds that for large V_{DS} a behavior similar to that predicted for saturation by our simple strong-inversion model is exhibited. In particular, one again observes

$$g_d = (\text{const}) \frac{I_D}{L}$$

$$= \frac{I_D}{V_{AW}}, \qquad V_{DS} > 5\phi_t \qquad (8.2.39)$$

where V_{AW} plays the role of V_A in weak inversion, and $V_{DS} > 5\phi_t$ has been imposed as a condition to ensure operation in the "flat" part of the curves in Fig. 4.17. A typical value for the constant is 0.5 μm/V. For short-channel devices, g_d can be larger than the value predicted by the above equation.

8.2.4 Moderate Inversion

As has been noted in Sec. 4.5, in many models for I_D, the moderate-inversion region is neglected, and the weak- and strong-inversion regions are taken to be adjacent. This results in some error in predicting I_D, which is acceptable for several applications. Unfortunately, though, the corresponding error in the small-signal parameters is usually unacceptable, and cannot be made small no matter what empirical values are chosen for the model parameters. To illustrate this, we will choose g_m as an example, and will consider the behavior of this parameter over a wide range of V_{GS} for a fixed V_{DS}. To avoid the interference of higher order effects, such as channel length modulation or uncertainty as to the exact value of V'_{DS}, we will not choose a V_{DS} in the saturation region. In fact, we will choose a *negligibly small* V_{DS}, which corresponds to a very common condition for measuring the threshold voltage and the parameter $\mu C'_{ox}$ (see Fig. 4.20). Also, for simplicity, we will assume that the effective mobility is fixed. The results for g_m and for g_m/I_D are shown in Fig. 8.8.[33] These results were obtained by using the general charge sheet model of Sec. 4.3, which is valid in all regions of operation (see also Sec. 8.2.5). As seen, in strong inversion g_m is approximately constant. This is what one would expect from (8.2.6a) or from the slope of the dotted line in Fig. 4.20. (If the mobility were allowed to be a function of V_{GS}, g_m would reach a

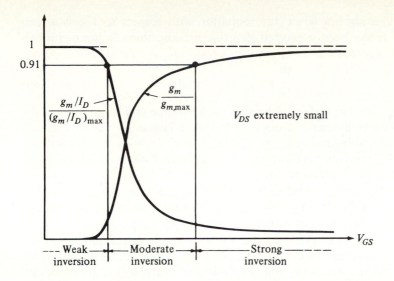

FIGURE 8.8
Transconductance and transconductance-to-current ratio, both normalized to their maximum values, as a function of V_{GS} for negligibly small, fixed V_{DS}.[33]

maximum and then decrease with increasing V_{GS}, corresponding to the slope of the solid line in Fig. 4.20.) In weak inversion, g_m/I_D is seen to be approximately constant. This is expected from (8.2.35), and is a consequence of the exponential dependence of I_D on V_{GS}. In moderate inversion, neither g_m nor g_m/I_D can be considered approximately constant, as seen in the figure. Yet, models which neglect the moderate inversion region predict that the regions of constant g_m and of constant g_m/I_D are adjacent at some point; clearly, *no* such point exists in Fig. 8.8. Thus, using such models in analog circuit applications and for V_{GS} values in the vicinity of V_T can lead to *very* wrong predictions.

Unfortunately, there are as yet no closed-form expressions for the small-signal conductances in the moderate-inversion region. Thus, one must resort to numerical evaluation, as discussed in the following subsection.

8.2.5   General Models

In Sec. 4.3 it was shown that a general expression can be developed for I_D [(4.3.8), (4.3.16), and (4.3.17)] which is valid in all regions of operation for a long-channel device (neglecting channel length modulation). Such an expression can, in principle, be used to provide expressions for the small-signal conductances, which will be valid in all regions including moderate inversion and for the transition from nonsaturation to saturation in strong inversion. The difficulty here will, of course, be complexity. The drain current contains V_{GB} explicitly in (4.3.16), and also implicitly through ψ_{s0} and ψ_{sL} [see (4.3.18)].

This leads to some algebra when differentiation with respect to V_{GS} is attempted. However, it has been suggested that one can use the following approximation to good accuracy:[25]

$$g_m = \frac{W}{L} \, \mu C'_{ox}(\psi_{sL} - \psi_{s0}) \tag{8.2.40}$$

where ψ_{s0} and ψ_{sL} are the surface potentials at the source and drain ends of the channel, which can be evaluated from (4.3.18). As a check, for the special case of strong inversion, substituting $\psi_{sL} \approx \phi_B + V_{DB}$, and $\psi_{s0} \approx \phi_B + V_{SB}$ produces (8.2.6a). In weak inversion, caution must be used if (8.2.40) is to be employed since then ψ_{sL} and ψ_{s0} are nearly equal.

Having a model for g_m valid in all regions, we can now plot that quantity over large ranges of I_D. In Fig. 8.9, $\log g_m$ is plotted vs. $\log I_D$ for various values of W/L and for operation in the flat part of the I_D-V_{DS} characteristics; a fixed V_{SB} is assumed. For each W/L value, the straight-line segment on the *right* corresponds to strong inversion, and the straight-line segment on the *left* corresponds to weak inversion. The curved part corresponds to moderate inversion. In strong inversion, for a given value of I_D, one can obtain a larger g_m by using a larger value for W/L, as expected from (8.2.6b). However, this is not true in weak inversion, as can be seen both in the figure and from (8.2.35). There, once I_D is fixed, g_m is known (remember, V_{SB} is fixed in this discussion, so that n is fixed). This behavior is compared to that of a bipolar device in Fig. 8.9 (see comments on the latter in Sec. 8.2.3). For a given I_D, g_m for the MOS

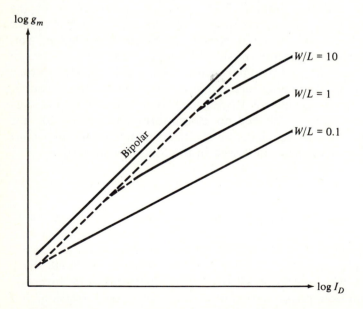

FIGURE 8.9
Comparison of $\log g_m$ vs. $\log I$ behavior for a bipolar transistor and for MOS transistors with various W/L values with a fixed V_{SB}.

transistor in weak inversion is below the corresponding value for the bipolar transistor by the factor n.

The general model of Sec. 4.3 can also be used to derive a value for g_d valid in all regions, save for channel length modulation and short-channel effects. One can show† that[25]

$$g_d = \mu \frac{W}{L} (-Q'_{I,\text{drain}}) \qquad (8.2.41)$$

Hence, using (4.3.15), we obtain

$$g_d = \frac{W}{L} \mu C'_{ox}(V_{GB} - V_{FB} - \psi_{sL} - \gamma\sqrt{\psi_{sL}}) \qquad (8.2.42)$$

As a check, consider the nonsaturation region. Substituting ψ_{sL} by $V_{DB} + \phi_B = V_{DS} + V_{SB} + \phi_B$ in the above equation produces (8.2.17). In the transition region from nonsaturation to saturation, the use of precise values for ψ_{sL} can provide accurate values for g_d in long-channel devices.

Plots of g_m, g_{mb}, and g_d vs. V_{GS} for a fixed, large V_{DS} have the form shown in Fig. 8.10. Such plots show these quantities varying continuously over all regions of inversion. The order in which the various regions are encountered as V_{GS} is increased has been discussed in Chap. 7 in conjunction with Fig. 7.8.

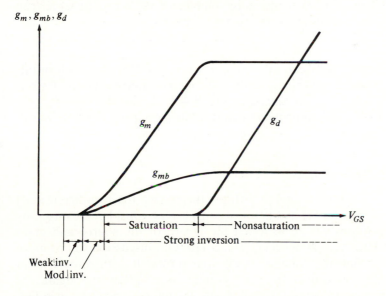

FIGURE 8.10
Small-signal gate transconductance, substrate transconductance, and drain conductance as a function of V_{GS} for fixed V_{DS} and V_{SB} as obtained from the accurate charge sheet model.

---

† The easiest way to derive this equation is through a quasi-Fermi potential formulation for the current; see (I.10) in Appendix I.

8.3   A MEDIUM FREQUENCY SMALL-SIGNAL MODEL FOR THE INTRINSIC PART

8.3.1   Introduction

When the small-signal voltages applied to an MOS transistor are varying fast, the small-signal terminal currents can be very different from those predicted by the circuit of Fig. 8.2. We now introduce a simple model that will predict such behavior as long as the frequency is not too high. The model achieves this by taking into account charge storage effects, assuming quasi-static operation. Not all such effects are included; additional charge storage effects will be considered in Chap. 9. Nevertheless, the model we are about to introduce here is important in its own right, and we present it in a self-contained manner for two reasons:

1. It is widely in use, because it achieves a reasonable balance between accuracy and complexity. Some readers might find it adequate for their purposes, so it was felt that they should not have to be subjected to the general treatment of Chap. 9 before they encountered a useful model.
2. The material in this section will be a useful foundation for the general treatment in Chap. 9. In fact, the more complete model in that chapter can be produced just by adding a few extra elements to the model we will develop here.

As before, we will only consider the *intrinsic* part of the transistor in this section. This fact will be understood without being indicated explicitly. Extrinsic device modeling will be introduced in Sec. 8.4.

In this section we will emphasize intuition. For more rigor, the reader will have to wait until Chap. 9.

8.3.2   Intrinsic Capacitances

The intrinsic part of a long-channel transistor (neglecting the two-dimensional effects very close to the source and drain regions) can be considered by itself by viewing it as a fictitious device in which the length of the source and drain regions has shrunk to zero, as shown in Fig. 8.11a. Our discussion will be more convenient if we define the voltages at the four terminals with respect to an arbitrary reference, as shown by the "ground" symbol in the figure. A subscript 0 will be used to denote the values of the voltages and charges in Fig. 8.11a. Let us consider the effects of small changes of V_S on the gate and depletion region charges (Fig. 8.11b), the effect of small changes of V_D on the gate and depletion region charges (Fig. 8.11c), and the effect of small changes of V_B on the gate charge (Fig. 8.11d). The details in these figures and the definitions next to them will be explained shortly. The three figures have been drawn by assuming that ΔV_S, ΔV_D, and ΔV_B represent increases. The voltages

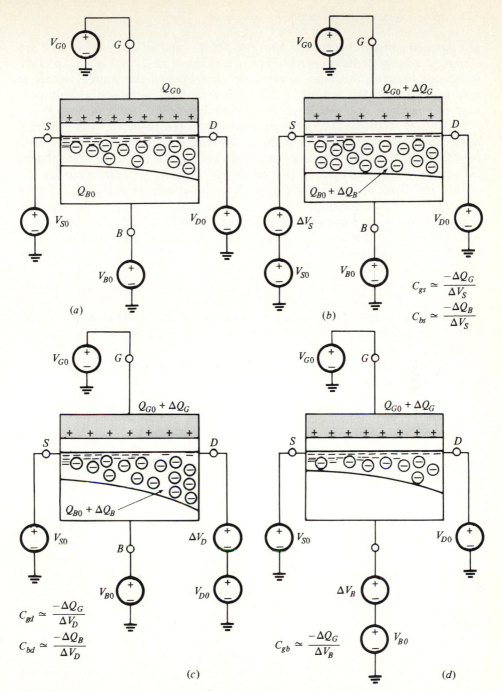

FIGURE 8.11
Measurement of intrinsic capacitances (in principle). The figure shows the intrinsic part of a transistor. (*a*) Transistor biased with four dc voltages at a certain operating point; (*b*) effect of a small increase in the source voltage; (*c*) effect of a small increase in the drain voltage; (*d*) effect of a small increase in the substrate voltage. The relations in the figures give the corresponding capacitance values.

311

are assumed constant before and after the change, and all cases in Fig. 8.11 are assumed to be in dc steady state. Thus, for example, ΔQ_G in Fig. 8.11b is the difference between the total steady-state charge when the source voltage is held fixed at $V_S + \Delta V_S$ and the steady-state charge when the source voltage is held fixed at V_S. For simplicity, the interface charge Q_o is not shown.

We now consider the experiment of Fig. 8.11b in detail. The potential across the oxide at various points decreases relative to that in Fig. 8.11a and, hence, the gate charge decreases too, and thus ΔQ_G is negative. The relation between the cause (ΔV_S) and the effect (ΔQ_G) can be represented by the small-signal equivalent circuit of Fig. 8.12. In this circuit the voltage ΔV_S places a charge $C_{gs}\Delta V_S$ on the bottom plate and a charge $-C_{gs}\Delta V_S$ on the top. For the latter charge to represent the change ΔQ_G in Fig. 8.11b, we must have $-C_{gs}\Delta V_S = \Delta Q_G$. Hence $C_{gs} = -\Delta Q_G/\Delta V_S$, as stated next to Fig. 8.11b. More formally, we have

$$C_{gs} = -\left.\frac{\partial Q_G}{\partial V_S}\right|_{V_G, V_D, V_B} \tag{8.3.1}$$

It is important *not* to associate C_{gs} with any parallel plate structure in Fig. 8.11. C_{gs} is simply the value that the fictitious capacitor in Fig. 8.12 should have in order for the charge on its top plate to be the same as the charge change ΔQ_G in Fig. 8.11b. Note that, since ΔQ_G is negative when ΔV_S is positive, the value of C_{gs} is positive.†

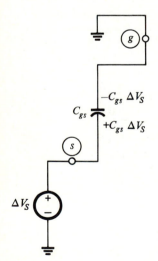

FIGURE 8.12
Meaning of C_{gs}, the small-signal intrinsic gate-source capacitance.

---

† Throughout this section, all capacitances and charges are for the intrinsic part of the device only. For example, C_{gs} is the *intrinsic* gate-source capacitance and *not* the total gate-source capacitance of the device. It will be seen in Sec. 8.4 that an extrinsic capacitance caused by the overlap of the gate with the sources must be added to C_{gs} to arrive at the total gate-source capacitance.

Figure 8.11*b* also illustrates the capacitive effect of the source on the substrate. Increasing V_S increases the width of the depletion region, thus making the total charge there more negative, and hence, ΔQ_B is negative. This is accomplished by more acceptor atoms being uncovered (in comparison to Fig. 8.11*a*), which means that holes must leave through the substrate terminal with a total charge $|\Delta Q_B|$. This is equivalent to saying that a negative charge ΔQ_B enters the device from the substrate terminal. Reasoning as before, we define

$$C_{bs} \equiv - \frac{\partial Q_B}{\partial V_S}\bigg|_{V_G, V_D, V_B} \tag{8.3.2}$$

The effects of increasing V_D are entirely analogous to that of increasing V_S, and are illustrated in Fig. 8.11*c*. We define:

$$C_{gd} \equiv - \frac{\partial Q_G}{\partial V_D}\bigg|_{V_G, V_S, V_B} \tag{8.3.3}$$

$$C_{bd} \equiv - \frac{\partial Q_B}{\partial V_D}\bigg|_{V_G, V_S, V_B} \tag{8.3.4}$$

Finally, the effect of increasing V_B is illustrated in Fig. 8.11*d*. The increasing V_B causes positive charges to flow into the substrate terminal, which are partly balanced by a decrease in Q_G. This is equivalent to a negative ΔQ_G flowing into the gate. This is easier to understand in weak inversion, where the inversion layer charge is negligible. Then practically all the positive charge change ΔQ_B must be balanced by an opposite change in the gate charge; hence ΔQ_G will be negative. We define

$$C_{gb} \equiv - \frac{\partial Q_G}{\partial V_B}\bigg|_{V_G, V_S, V_D} \tag{8.3.5}$$

All the above five effects can be modeled in a manner analogous to that of Fig. 8.12. These effects can be included in a small-signal equivalent circuit by adding to the circuit of Fig. 8.2 five capacitors, as shown in Fig. 8.13. It is important to note that the various elements in the resulting model *do not interfere with each other*. For example, keeping terminals *g*, *d*, and *b* at ground and applying ΔV_S at terminal *s* will cause a charge $-C_{gs}\,\Delta V_S$ to enter terminal *g*, thus modeling correctly the effect of the source on the gate. C_{gd} and C_{gb}, although connected to the gate, will not interfere since they will act as open circuits (the voltage across them is fixed). The reader can easily check that each of the remaining four capacitance effects are also modeled correctly by the corresponding capacitors and with no interference from other elements (Prob. 8.14). This "noninterference" is a very important property which should be carefully checked every time several elements—each meant to simulate a separate effect—are connected together to form a circuit model. Since C_{gs}, C_{gd},

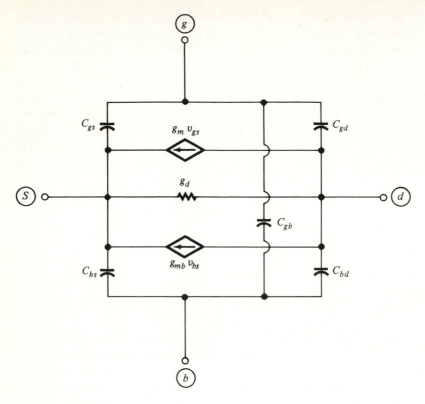

FIGURE 8.13
Simple small-signal equivalent circuit for the MOS transistor.

and C_{gb} represent the effect on the gate of each of the other three terminals, the circuit of Fig. 8.13 can model accurately the quasi-static small-signal effects one "sees looking into" the gate of a MOS transistor. Notice that for now we cannot prove a similar statement for the other terminals. (This subject will be discussed further in Chap. 9). At this point, we will only say that, as it turns out by comparison to more complete models (Chap. 9), the model topology of Fig. 8.13 is satisfactory (as far as looking into any terminal, and as far as the effect of any terminal on any other is concerned), even if the terminal voltages vary continuously with time, as long as their variation is slow enough. For sinusoidal small variations, this can be quantified by establishing an upper frequency limit of validity. The figure one comes up with depends on the accuracy desired, the region of operation, which terminals are being driven with signals, which terminal currents are of interest, whether the magnitude or the phase of those currents is of interest,† etc. Thus, it is not easy to give a

---

† As the frequency is raised, both the magnitude and the phase as predicted by the model will be increasingly in error. For many applications, the phase error becomes intolerable first.

single number. Some general indication can, nevertheless, be given by comparison to more sophisticated model topologies (Chap. 9). Thus, in strong inversion, whatever the criterion being used, the upper frequency limit of validity turns out to be proportional (but *not* equal) to the quantity:

$$\omega_o = \frac{\mu(V_{GS} - V_T)}{(1 + \delta)L^2} \tag{8.3.6}$$

where the reason for the presence of the quantities in the right-hand side can be understood after higher order models are discussed in Chap. 9. Thus, assume that satisfactory values have been obtained for all model elements at low frequencies. Then, without touching these element values, the model will continue to be valid up to about $0.1\omega_o$ (a conservative limit, for very critical applications) or even $0.5\omega_o$ (for noncritical applications). Such performance is sufficient in many cases. Note that the degradation of the model is very gradual as the frequency is increased, so no "sharp" deterioration is observed at any particular frequency. When, at high frequencies, the model eventually becomes unacceptable, it will not be because the element values are not right, but rather because the *nature* of the model (Fig. 8.13) is inadequate for such frequencies. The only way to achieve satisfactory modeling in this case is to use more sophisticated model topologies, as discussed in Chap. 9.

The five capacitances defined above are strongly dependent on the "bias values" of the terminal voltages, i.e., the values around which the small-signal voltages occur. These bias values are denoted by V_{D0}, V_{G0}, V_{B0}, and V_{S0} in Fig. 8.11a. For simplicity, from now on we will denote them simply by V_D, V_G, V_B, and V_S. We now present expressions for the capacitances in terms of the bias voltages. We will consider each region of operation separately.

STRONG INVERSION. Accurate capacitance expressions can be derived for the strong-inversion region by using the above capacitance definitions in conjunction with the charges corresponding to the accurate model of Sec. 4.4.1. Expressions for these charges are given in Appendix L. However, the resulting capacitance expressions are complicated.[13, 15] †

For simpler, approximate results, one can use the charge expressions corresponding to the approximate model of Sec. 4.4.2. In fact, most capacitance models in use are developed from such expressions, assuming that the depletion region charge per unit area Q_B' is uniform along the transistor length, i.e., that this charge is unaffected by the fact that the reverse bias V_{CB} of the channel with respect to the substrate varies from source to drain. This is an inaccurate assumption, and corresponds to setting $\delta = 0$ in (7.4.13). One can do better by allowing for $\delta \neq 0$. On the other hand, depending on the generality one allows for the value and functional dependence of δ (Sec. 4.4.2),

---

† For this reason, empirical capacitance expressions are often used in conjunction with the accurate strong-inversion model (Appendix L).

the resulting capacitance expressions can range from simple to very complicated. A good compromise between simplicity and accuracy can be obtained based on the following two assumptions: (1) the value of δ is equal to

$$\delta_1 = \frac{\gamma}{2\sqrt{\phi_B + V_{SB}}} = \frac{dV_T}{dV_{SB}} \tag{8.3.7}$$

which was one of the choices for δ in Sec. 4.4.2, and (2) the derivative of δ_1 with V_S and V_B is negligible; i.e., in our differentiation of the charge expressions, the quantity δ_1 will be treated as a *constant*. These assumptions simplify the calculations, because every time a charge containing the term V_T is differentiated with respect to V_{SB}, it will result in the term $dV_T/dV_{SB} = \delta_1$. This term can then be grouped together with other terms containing δ_1, resulting in simple expressions. From the material in Sec. 4.4.2, it is clear that the above assumptions can be justified especially for small V_{DS} and large V_{SB}. Hence, the accuracy of the resulting capacitance expressions can be expected to be good in such cases. In cases where V_{DS} is large and/or V_{SB} is small, some error can be expected. However, such error is consistent with the overall accuracy of the approximate model. Also, this error will still be smaller than that in commonly used expressions based on the assumption of uniform depletion charge per unit area. We will later show how the above error can be reduced.

Using then $\delta = \delta_1$ in (7.4.15) and (7.4.17), applying the definitions (8.3.1) to (8.3.5), and neglecting the derivative of δ_1 with V_S and V_B, we obtain, after much algebra (Prob. 8.15):

$$C_{gs} = \frac{2}{3} C_{ox} \frac{1 + 2\alpha}{(1 + \alpha)^2} \tag{8.3.8}$$

$$C_{bs} = \delta_1 \frac{2}{3} C_{ox} \frac{1 + 2\alpha}{(1 + \alpha)^2} = \delta_1 C_{gs} \tag{8.3.9}$$

$$C_{gd} = \frac{2}{3} C_{ox} \frac{\alpha^2 + 2\alpha}{(1 + \alpha)^2} \tag{8.3.10}$$

$$C_{bd} = \delta_1 \frac{2}{3} C_{ox} \frac{\alpha^2 + 2\alpha}{(1 + \alpha)^2} = \delta_1 C_{gd} \tag{8.3.11}$$

$$C_{gb} = \frac{\delta_1}{3(1 + \delta_1)} C_{ox} \left(\frac{1 - \alpha}{1 + \alpha}\right)^2 \tag{8.3.12}$$

where C_{ox} is the total *intrinsic* oxide capacitance:

$$C_{ox} = C'_{ox} WL \tag{8.3.13}$$

and α is the parameter defined in (4.4.31) and plotted in Fig. 4.13.

The above expressions give the plots shown by the dashed lines in Fig. 8.14. The solid lines show the same capacitances as are obtained from accurate calculations by using the general charge sheet model[37] (the use of the accurate strong-inversion model provides essentially the same results as the general

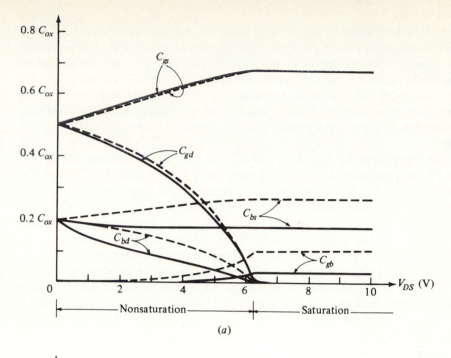

(a)

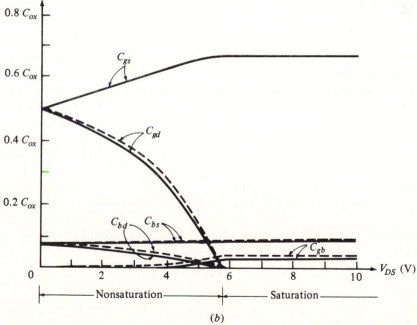

(b)

FIGURE 8.14
Small-signal capacitances vs. V_{DS} for a device with $N_A = 1700 \ \mu\mathrm{m}^{-3}$, $V_{T0} = 0.476 \ \mathrm{V}$, and $d_{ox} = 0.1 \ \mu\mathrm{m}$, with $V_{GS} = 8 \ \mathrm{V}$. Solid lines: accurate model;[37] broken lines: simple model presented in this section. (*a*) $V_{SB} = 0$; (*b*) $V_{SB} = 5 \ \mathrm{V}$.

317

model). In Fig. 8.14 the value of V'_{DS} used for the approximate model (V'_{DS} appears in the expression for α) has been chosen to agree with that predicted by the accurate results. This can be done by choosing δ in the dc equations appropriately, i.e., δ in the dc equations is assumed to be chosen *independently* of the quantity δ_1 used in the capacitance expressions; otherwise the dc drain current accuracy will suffer. For C_{gs} and C_{gd} the agreement is clearly excellent. The behavior of these capacitances will be considered intuitively later in this section.

The expressions for C_{bs}, C_{bd}, and C_{gb} are seen to be accurate at $V_{DS} = 0$. When V_{DS} is large, though, and at the same time V_{SB} is small (Fig. 8.14a), the accuracy is not good. Nevertheless, in many circuit applications the consequences of the above errors will not be serious because C_{bs}, C_{bd}, and C_{gb} are usually small and are in parallel with other capacitances (e.g., extrinsic capacitances and the capacitances of other devices in the circuit). C_{bs} in particular is often short-circuited out through a source-substrate connection. One should also point out that within the above errors the expressions for the three capacitances track satisfactorily large variations in oxide thickness and substrate doping concentration, which is a desirable property for any model parameter. If more accuracy is desired, one can use for δ_1 a modification similar to the one that led from (8.2.12) to (8.2.14). Thus, if in the capacitance expressions we substitute δ_1 by

$$\delta_5 = \frac{\gamma}{2\sqrt{\phi_B + V_{SB} + k_c V'_{DS}(1 - \alpha)}} \tag{8.3.14}$$

where k_c is a small number (e.g., 0.1 to 0.2), the accuracy of the model can be improved significantly (Prob. 8.16).

From (8.3.8) to (8.3.11), (8.3.14), (8.2.10), and (8.2.14) we obtain the following interesting approximate result, mostly valid at small V_{DS} and for large V_{SB} values:[29]

$$\frac{C_{bs}}{C_{gs}} \approx \frac{C_{bd}}{C_{gd}} \approx \frac{g_{mb}}{g_m} \approx \frac{dV_T}{dV_{SB}} \tag{8.3.15}$$

This result becomes exact for $V_{DS} = 0$.

We now consider the capacitances for two cases of interest.

Nonsaturation with $V_{DS} = 0$. With $V_{DS} = 0$ ($\alpha = 1$), the capacitance expressions give:

$$C_{gs} = C_{gd} = \tfrac{1}{2} C_{ox} \tag{8.3.16}$$

$$C_{bs} = C_{bd} = \delta_1 \tfrac{1}{2} C_{ox} \tag{8.3.17}$$

$$C_{gb} = 0 \tag{8.3.18}$$

It is easy to make these results intuitively plausible. With $V_{DS} = 0$ the channel is as shown in Fig. 8.15. Practically all the gate field lines terminate on the inversion layer, which is assumed strongly inverted throughout. If V_G and V_B are kept fixed, and both V_S and V_D are increased by the same amount ΔV, the potential across the oxide will decrease at every point by ΔV. Hence, the corresponding gate charge decrease will be $C_{ox} \Delta V$. If, instead, only V_S is increased by ΔV whereas V_D is kept fixed, the potential *change* across the oxide will vary from ΔV at the source end to 0 at the drain end. This variation will be linear for a very small ΔV. It is easy to see that now the decrease in the gate charge will only be half as much as before, i.e., $\frac{1}{2}C_{ox} \Delta V$ (Prob. 8.17). Thus, the value of C_{gs} needed to properly model this effect is $\frac{1}{2}C_{ox}$. A similar argument can be given for C_{gd}, thus verifying (8.3.16).

The values of C_{bs} and C_{bd} can be discussed in a similar manner. Here the arguments used above apply with C_{ox} replaced by C_b, where C_b is the total capacitance of the reversed-bias "field-induced junction" formed by the inversion layer and the substrate. Thus,

$$C_{bs} = C_{bd} = \tfrac{1}{2}C_b \tag{8.3.19}$$

The value of C_b is given by the area WL of the field-induced junction times a capacitance per unit area given by an expression like (1.5.20a), with V_R replaced by V_{SB} and ϕ_o by ϕ_B, the "built-in potential" of the field-induced junction. Thus,

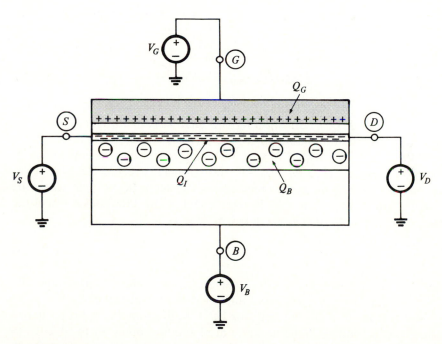

FIGURE 8.15
A MOS transistor with $V_D = V_S$.

$$C_b = WL \, \frac{F\sqrt{N_A}}{2\sqrt{V_{SB} + \phi_B}} \tag{8.3.20}$$

Recognizing now that $F\sqrt{N_A} = \gamma C'_{ox}$ from (3.4.11), and using (8.3.13), we get

$$C_b = \delta_1 C_{ox} \tag{8.3.21}$$

which, with (8.3.19), leads to (8.3.17).

We will now attempt to make the relation to transconductances, shown in (8.3.15), intuitively plausible.[29] Consider a nonzero, very small V_{DS}, so that we can have a small nonzero current I_D (we cannot talk about g_m and g_{mb} if $V_{DS} = 0$). As long as V_{DS} is very small, it will not upset appreciably the uniformity in the channel, and the picture will be practically as shown in Fig. 8.15. Keeping now V_B, V_S, and V_D fixed, let V_G change by ΔV_G. This will cause an inversion layer charge change of magnitude

$$|\Delta Q_{I1}| = C_{ox} \, \Delta V_G \tag{8.3.22}$$

and a corresponding current change

$$\Delta I_{D1} = g_m \, \Delta V_G \tag{8.3.23}$$

Repeating this experiment by using the "back gate" instead of the front gate, we obtain

$$|\Delta Q_{I2}| = C_b \, \Delta V_B \tag{8.3.24}$$

$$\Delta I_{D2} = g_{mb} \, \Delta V_B \tag{8.3.25}$$

Since the inversion layer is uniform, the current is proportional to Q_I. Thus $\Delta I_{D1}/\Delta I_{D2} = |\Delta Q_{I1}|/|\Delta Q_{I2}|$. Substituting the quantities in this relation by the corresponding right-hand sides in (8.3.22)–(8.3.25), we obtain $C_b/C_{ox} = g_{mb}/g_m$; this, with the use of (8.3.21), (8.3.9), and (8.3.11) agrees with (8.3.15).

We now consider C_{gb}. At $V_{DS} = 0$, the strongly inverted electron layer, which is "connected" to the fixed voltages $V_S = V_D$, keeps the voltage across the oxide fixed at all points, even if V_B is varied. Hence the gate does not feel the variation, and $\Delta Q_G = 0$. This is modeled by [see (8.3.5)]

$$C_{gb} = 0, \qquad V_{DS} = 0 \tag{8.3.26}$$

In other words, the strong-inversion layer acts as a "shield" throughout the channel, protecting the gate from the influence of the substrate.

It is interesting to point out that, for $V_{DS} = 0$, the complicated capacitance expressions corresponding to the accurate model reduce precisely to (8.3.16) to (8.3.18). It is easy to trace this full agreement to our choice of value for δ. Indeed, $\delta = \delta_1$ was seen in Sec. 4.4.2 to be the best choice for $V_{DS} = 0$.

Saturation. In the saturation region ($\alpha = 0$), we have from (8.3.8) to (8.3.12):

$$C_{gs} = \tfrac{2}{3} C_{ox} \tag{8.3.27}$$

$$C_{bs} = \delta_1 \tfrac{2}{3} C_{ox} \tag{8.3.28}$$

$$C_{gd} = 0 \tag{8.3.29}$$

$$C_{bd} = 0 \tag{8.3.30}$$

$$C_{gb} = \frac{\delta_1}{3(1 + \delta_1)} C_{ox} \tag{8.3.31}$$

The results for C_{gd} and C_{bd} can be easily seen to make sense as follows. In the saturation region, communication from the drain to the rest of the device is cut off owing to pinchoff (neglecting channel length modulation). Hence, when V_D is varied, the intrinsic device is not affected and all charges in it remain the same. In particular, $\Delta Q_G = 0$ and $\Delta Q_B = 0$. This, from (8.3.3) and (8.3.4) implies that $C_{gd} = 0$ and $C_{bd} = 0$, in agreement with (8.3.29) and (8.3.30).

Consider now C_{gs} in (8.3.27). This value is accurate, as found by comparisons with accurate models and measurements (see below). The fact that C_{gs} is found to be less than C_{ox} often comes as a surprise, because one tends to think of the inversion layer as the lower of two "parallel plates" of a capacitor, the other plate being the gate. If we really did have a parallel metal plate all under the oxide (neglecting the pinchoff region near the drain), and if it were attached to the source and cut off from the drain, then we would, in fact, obtain a capacitance equal to C_{ox}. This is because if the source potential were changed by ΔV_S, we would have $|\Delta \Psi_{ox}(x)| = |\Delta V_S|$ for any position x along the channel, with ψ_{ox} the oxide potential. However, this is *not* what happens in the transistor. Using the analysis in Sec. 4.4.3 and (3.2.2), one can show that we will have $|\Delta \psi_{ox}| = |\Delta V_S|$ only at the source end of the channel, and that $|\Delta \psi_{ox}(x)|$ will be smaller and smaller as one goes toward the drain (in fact, for the accurate model of Sec. 4.4.1, one can show that, in saturation, ψ_{ox} at the *drain* end remains fixed at a value corresponding to the gate-*drain* threshold voltage, which is independent of V_S). Thus, points further away from the source feel the change in the source potential less and contribute less to the change in the gate charge. This is why C_{gs} is less than C_{ox}.†

Let us now consider C_{bs} in saturation. One can obtain an intuitive feeling for the result $C_{bs} = \delta_1 \tfrac{2}{3} C_{ox} = \delta_1 C_{gs}$ for the case of large V_{SB} and small V'_{DS}

---

† In circuits literature, the value $\tfrac{2}{3} C_{ox}$ in (8.3.27) is sometimes justified by saying that the length of the pinchoff region is $\tfrac{1}{3} L$, and thus the effective channel length is $\tfrac{2}{3} L$. This explanation is not correct. The factor $\tfrac{2}{3}$ is the result of a mathematical derivation which has nothing to do with the length of the pinchoff region. This length, in fact, must be assumed zero in order to arrive at (8.3.8) and, thus, at (8.3.27). Besides, the length of the pinchoff region is not $\tfrac{1}{3} L$ in general; in fact it is predicted to be independent of L from (5.2.1). For long-channel devices, the pinchoff region occupies a very small part of the channel.

(then our choice $\delta = \delta_1$ is easy to justify). In such cases, the effective reverse bias of the channel with respect to the substrate does not vary much along the channel. Thus, the depletion region width is roughly uniform, just as was the case with $V_{DS} = 0$ above. The relative influence of the channel on the substrate and on the gate (as V_S is varied) might then be expected to be similar to that when $V_{DS} = 0$ (discussed above). Thus, the model prediction that $C_{bs} = \delta_1 C_{gs}$ is not surprising. If the above conditions on bias voltages are not satisfied, though, the above intuition does not hold and, in fact, the model is then in error, as has been seen. If V_{GS} and, thus, V'_{DS} are large, the depletion region width will increase significantly as we go toward the drain, making the influence of the channel on the substrate weaker (as V_S is varied). C_{bs} is then found to be *less* than $\delta_1 C_{gs}$, as has been seen.

Finally, we consider C_{gb}. Assume a change ΔV_B of V_B in Fig. 8.11d. Working as explained in the preceding paragraph, we find that here the resulting change in the oxide potential, $\Delta\psi_{ox}$, although zero at the source end, becomes nonzero at other points, and in fact $|\Delta\psi_{ox}(x)|$ increases toward the drain. (For example, for the accurate model of Sec. 4.4.1 in saturation, ψ_{ox} at the drain is maintained at a value corresponding to the gate-*drain* threshold, as already mentioned; when V_B is changed, this value changes due to the body effect at that point.) The nonzero changes in $\psi_{ox}(x)$ contribute to a change in the gate charge. Thus C_{gb} is nonzero in saturation, as predicted by (8.3.31).

Closing our discussion of strong-inversion capacitances, we should point out that the expressions (8.3.8) to (8.3.12), although derived by using the approximate model charges, are sometimes used in conjunction with other models. Obviously, in such cases, one should use in the expression for α a value of V'_{DS} as predicted by such models, to be consistent with the I_D-V_{DS} characteristics predicted by them.

Intrinsic cutoff frequency: Consider a transistor in the connection shown in Fig. 8.16a, where the bias is assumed such that operation is in the saturation region. The voltage $\epsilon \sin \omega t$ is a sinusoidal small signal of angular frequency ω (in rad/s). The small-signal equivalent circuit for this connection can be derived by substituting the transistor by the circuit of Fig. 8.13, and by substituting all dc voltage sources with short circuits (since for these sources $\Delta V = 0$). Removing now all elements which appear in parallel with short circuits and noting that C_{gd} is 0 in saturation, we arrive at the circuit of Fig. 8.16b. The small-signal drain and gate currents can be calculated by using this circuit, and are shown directly on the figure. Defining the current gain a_i as the ratio of the *amplitude* of the small-signal drain current to the *amplitude* of the small-signal gate current, we have

$$a_i = \frac{g_m}{\omega(C_{gs} + C_{gb})} \tag{8.3.32}$$

For $\omega \to 0$ this becomes infinite, which is to be expected since at dc there is no gate current. As ω is increased, a_i drops. The *intrinsic cutoff*

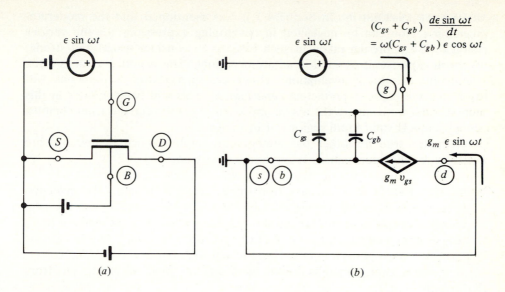

FIGURE 8.16
(a) A transistor operating in the flat part of the I_D-V_{DS} characteristics with a sinusoidal small-signal excitation; (b) the small-signal equivalent circuit for (a).

frequency or *intrinsic maximum usable frequency*, denoted by ω_T, is defined as the value of ω at which a_i drops to the value of 1. From the above equation this value is

$$\omega_T = \frac{g_m}{C_{gs} + C_{gb}} \tag{8.3.33}$$

Using (8.2.8a) and (8.3.27), and neglecting C_{gb}, we get

$$\omega_T \approx \frac{g_m}{C_{gs}} = \frac{3}{2(1+\delta)} \frac{\mu(V_{GS} - V_T)}{L^2} = \tfrac{3}{2}\omega_o \tag{8.3.34}$$

where ω_o is defined in (8.3.6). The value of ω_T is outside the region of validity of the model used, so it should initially be looked at as a suspicious result. However, calculation of ω_T using higher frequency models (Chap. 9) gives essentially the same value. The reason for this is that the above calculation involves only the *magnitude* of the currents. For these, errors using the simple model are not large at these frequencies. However, significant *phase* errors can result from using the models derived in this chapter at such high frequencies.

As an example, consider a transistor with $\mu = 60 \ \mu\text{m}^2/(\text{V}\cdot\text{ns})$, $L = 6 \ \mu\text{m}$, and $\delta = 0.2$, operating in saturation with $V_{GS} - V_T = 2 \text{ V}$. From (8.3.34) we have $\omega_T = 4167 \text{ Mrad/s}$. This corresponds to $f_T = \omega_T/2\pi = 663 \text{ MHz}$.

In practice, the current gain of a complete transistor becomes unity at some frequency less than ω_T because of the presence of extrinsic parasitic elements (Sec. 8.4).

MODERATE INVERSION. In Sec. 7.4.3 it was mentioned that the moderate-inversion region can be neglected in developing expressions for the various charges. The approach taken in such cases is to consider weak- and strong-inversion expressions as valid in adjacent regions. The resulting error is often acceptable for charge evaluation. However, such charge expressions will result in large error in predicting *capacitances*. This will be seen later in this section when we compare the above approach to results derived from complex general models valid in all regions of inversion.

As was true for other parameters, no simple explicit expressions are available for the capacitances in moderate inversion.

WEAK INVERSION. In weak inversion things are very simple. The inversion layer charge is negligible throughout the length of the channel, and the gate "sees" the depletion region directly through the oxide. A small increase in V_B will cause some holes to enter through the substrate terminal, and this will be balanced by some gate charge leaving through the gate terminal. The corresponding value of C_{gb} can be found by using the weak inversion Q_G from (7.4.34) in (8.3.5):

$$C_{gb} = C_{ox} \frac{\gamma}{2\sqrt{\gamma^2/4 + V_{GB} - V_{FB}}} \tag{8.3.35}$$

Varying V_S or V_D in weak inversion can vary the inversion layer charge drastically in a relative sense. However, this charge remains negligible compared to Q_G and Q_B, and can play no role in the charge-balancing process. Hence the gate and substrate do not "feel" the variations of V_S and V_D, and the corresponding ΔQ_G and ΔQ_B in Fig. 8.11b and c are negligible. The values for the corresponding capacitances are then†

$$C_{gd} \approx C_{gs} \approx C_{bd} \approx C_{bs} \approx 0 \tag{8.3.36}$$

An intrinsic cutoff frequency can be defined for weak inversion (with $V_{DS} > 5\phi_t$) in a similar manner as in strong inversion, and Fig. 8.16 is still valid. Using (8.3.36) in (8.3.33) we get

$$\omega_T \approx \frac{g_m}{C_{gb}} \tag{8.3.37}$$

Using the weak-inversion expressions for g_m and C_{gb}, it can be shown that (Prob. 8.22)

$$\omega_T \approx \frac{\mu\phi_t}{L^2} \frac{I_D}{I_M} \tag{8.3.38}$$

---

† This discussion only considers the effect of the source and drain through the inversion layer charge. In addition to this, one has the proximity capacitances between the gate *inside* the broken line in Fig. 7.1 and the *inside* side walls of the n^+ regions.[40] These capacitances are observed in weak inversion and depletion, but reduce to zero in strong inversion, since the inversion layer then acts as a shield between the gate and the inside side walls of the n^+ regions.

where I_D is the current at the particular operating point and I_M is the maximum achievable current in weak inversion (i.e., the current at the upper limit of the weak-inversion region).

As an example, consider a device with $\mu = 60 \ \mu\text{m}^2/(\text{V} \cdot \text{ns})$ and $L = 6 \ \mu\text{m}$, operated at room temperature with I_D equal to one-fifth the maximum weak inversion current. Then (8.3.38) gives $\omega_T = 8.7 \ \text{Mrad/s}$. This corresponds to $f_T = \omega_T/2\pi = 1.38 \ \text{MHz}$. The same device was seen earlier to have a f_T of 663 MHz in strong inversion, with $V_{GS} - V_T = 2 \ \text{V}$.

GENERAL CHARGE SHEET MODEL. In Sec. 7.4.5, we have shown how the general model of Sec. 4.3 can be used to evaluate the various charges. The resulting expressions are valid in all regions of inversion. These charges can be differentiated to produce capacitances (not an easy task). The resulting expressions are too lengthy,[37] unless an approximation is used for the bulk charge,[47] similar to the one that lead to the approximate strong inversion model in Sec. 4.4.

To show the capacitance variation over all regions of inversion, we can fix V_{DS} and plot vs. V_{GS}. This was the approach taken in the plots of Figs. 7.9 and 8.10. The resulting capacitance plots are shown in Fig. 8.17 and agree very well

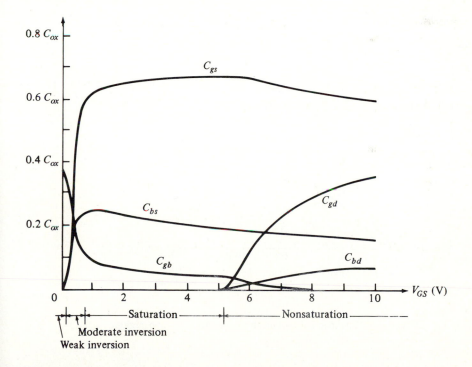

FIGURE 8.17
Small-signal capacitances vs. V_{GS}, with $V_{DS} = 4 \ \text{V}$ and $V_{SB} = 0$, for the device of Fig. 8.14, as predicted by accurate calculations.[37]

with experiment in all regions.[37] In Fig. 8.18, we show an expansion of the horizontal scale around the moderate inversion region. It is obvious that in this region both strong- and weak-inversion expressions fail completely. Yet, in many models for circuit CAD, weak and strong inversion expressions are assumed to be valid in adjacent regions.

In Fig. 8.19, we compare g_{mb}/g_m, C_{bs}/C_{gs}, and C_{bd}/C_{gd}. It is seen that (8.3.15) is approximately verified.

DEPLETION. In depletion, the only relevant capacitance is C_{gb}.† Using the corresponding gate charge (7.4.46) in the definition (8.3.5), we obtain the same expression as in weak inversion:

$$C_{gb} = C_{ox} \frac{\gamma}{2\sqrt{\gamma^2/4 + V_{GB} - V_{FB}}} \tag{8.3.39}$$

It should be noted that the above expression has been developed by assuming a perfect depletion region with a sharp edge. However, if V_{GB} gets close to V_{FB} (within a few ϕ_t), such a region cannot be defined clearly and the above expression will be somewhat in error. More exact calculations can be

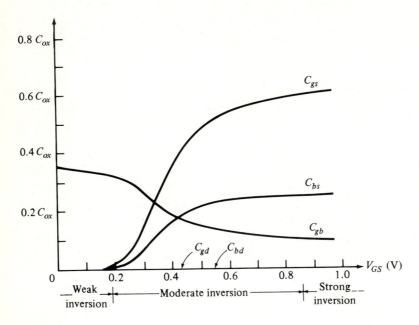

FIGURE 8.18
Part of the plot of Fig. 8.17, expanded around the moderate inversion region.[37]

_____

† See, however, the preceding footnote concerning the effect of the inside side walls.

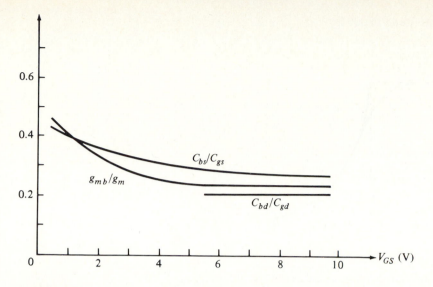

FIGURE 8.19
Comparison of capacitance ratios to transconductance ratios for the device of Fig. 8.17, with $V_{DS} = 4$ V and $V_{SB} = 0$, as they result from accurate calculations.[37]

done by taking into account the distribution of carriers below the oxide (Appendix F) in conjunction with (2.6.8).

ACCUMULATION. In developing charge expressions for the accumulation region (Sec. 7.4.7), we assumed that an abundance of holes creates a conductive sheet right under the oxide. This picture or direct use of the gate charge (7.4.47) in the definition for C_{gb} (8.3.5) results in

$$C_{gb} = C_{ox} \tag{8.3.40}$$

The above argument about the "conductive sheet" is really valid only deep in accumulation. If V_{GB} is only slightly lower than V_{FB}, the "sheet" will not have formed satisfactorily and (8.3.40) will not be very accurate. Again, C_{gb} can be calculated accurately by considering the distribution of mobile carriers with depth (Appendix F) in conjunction with (2.6.8). Figure 8.20 shows C_{gb} in the regions of accumulation and depletion. The broken line represents (8.3.39) and (8.3.40), and the solid line represents a more realistic behavior.

SHORT- AND NARROW-CHANNEL EFFECTS. The capacitances of short-channel devices are difficult to evaluate because of two-dimensional effects.[39, 42] One often relies on measurements which are difficult in themselves. Since the capacitances of such devices can be small, they are easily masked by parasitic capacitances due to extrinsic effects, packaging, and measuring circuitry. To make such measurements easier, part of the measuring instrumentation can be integrated on the same chip with the transistor under measurement.[31, 38, 40, 41]

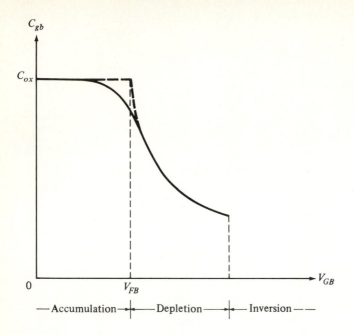

FIGURE 8.20
Gate-substrate capacitance in accumulation and depletion plotted vs. V_{GB}. Broken line: simple model; solid line: accurate model.

In general, one observes capacitance-voltage plots which are qualitatively similar to those for devices with long and wide channels. However, it is more difficult to identify particular regions of operation on such plots because the transition from region to region is very gradual. For narrow-channel devices, capacitance measurements show the dependence of the effective channel width $\hat{W}$ on the gate voltage (Sec. 5.4.3).[40, 41]

In lack of complete analytical results, the capacitances of devices with short and/or narrow channels can be roughly modeled by using expressions derived in this chapter, with V_T and W replaced by the effective quantities $\hat{V}_T$ and $\hat{W}$ discussed in Sec. 5.4.

8.4 SMALL-SIGNAL MODELING FOR THE EXTRINSIC PART

The "extrinsic" part of a transistor is everything outside the broken line in Fig. 8.21a. In this figure and in the top view in Fig. 8.21b we show some symbol definitions to be used in the following discussion.

The charge storage effects associated with the extrinsic part can be modeled by using six small-signal capacitances (one between each pair of terminals, as shown in Fig. 8.22. In the symbols used for these capacitances,

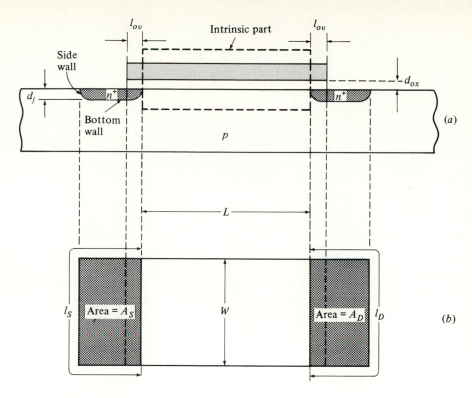

FIGURE 8.21
A MOS transistor: (*a*) Cross section; (*b*) top view.

the first two subscripts indicate the associated device terminals and the subscript *e* stands for *extrinsic*. If the transistor happens to be inside a well on a CMOS chip (Chap. 10), then one must consider also the capacitance due to the *pn* junction between the well and the common substrate on which the well has been formed. This capacitance is denoted by C'_{bb} in Fig. 8.22, with *b* corresponding to the transistor's body and *b'* corresponding to the common substrate. The dotted box represents the model of the intrinsic part, which has already been discussed in the previous two sections. We now concentrate on the seven extrinsic capacitances. Each of these can easily be associated with parts of the physical transistor structure, as discussed below.

8.4.1   Gate Overlap Capacitances

There is always some unavoidable overlap between the gate and the two n^+ regions (Chap. 10). This gives rise to the "overlap capacitances." Because of the high doping of both the gate and the n^+ regions, these can be modeled as nearly linear parallel-plate capacitors, C_{gse} and C_{gde}, with the oxide as the

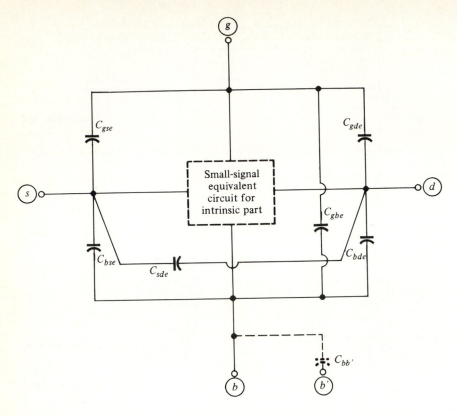

FIGURE 8.22
Extrinsic transistor capacitances added to an intrinsic small-signal model.

dielectric. If the overlap distance is l_{ov} as shown in Fig. 8.21 and the gate width is W we have, neglecting fringing effects (i.e., effects due to field lines not vertical to the surface, fringing outside the immediate overlap area)

$$C_{gse} = C_{gde} = C'_{ox} W l_{ov} \tag{8.4.1}$$

If l_{ov} is very small, then the capacitance due to the fringing field lines can add a significant percentage to the total value of the capacitances. The calculation of the fringing capacitances is involved, and empirical estimates are often used.

8.4.2 Junction Capacitances

The substrate-source and drain-source junctions give rise to small-signal capacitances C_{bse} and C_{bde}. Each of these is caused by a "bottom wall" part and a "sidewall" part. The reason one needs to make this distinction is that during fabrication the doping concentration of the p substrate near the surface outside the channel area is increased to form the "channel stop" areas (Chap. 10). Thus, the sidewall capacitance per unit area is higher than that of the bottom wall (typically by a factor of 2 to 10 near the surface). The bottom wall part of C_{bse} and C_{bde} can be expressed in terms of a capacitance per unit area (in $fF/\mu m^2$). The sidewall capacitance per unit area, on the other hand, is not constant with depth and must normally be integrated over the sidewall area for accurate calculations. A further complication arises because the sidewalls are not "plane," but are instead nearly cylindrical. For approximate calculations, one often uses an effective sidewall capacitance per unit length (in $fF/\mu m$), which only need be multiplied by the sidewall length to provide the total sidewall capacitance. In measuring sidewall length, the side contacting the channel is excluded since it is not adjacent to a channel stop area. According to the above, if A_S and C'_{js} represent the source bottom wall area and capacitance per unit area, and if l_S and C''_{js} represent the source sidewall length (Fig.8.21b) and capacitance per unit length, we will have

$$C_{bse} = A_S C'_{js} + l_S C''_{js} \tag{8.4.2}$$

Similarly, with A_D, C'_{jd}, l_D, and C''_{jd} the corresponding quantities for the drain, we will have

$$C_{bde} = A_D C'_{jd} + l_D C''_{jd} \tag{8.4.3}$$

The values for the C'_j and C''_j are usually provided for zero junction reverse bias. Under nonzero reverse bias (V_{SB} or V_{DB}), the new values of these parameters can be approximately found by assuming a functional dependence as in (1.5.22).

For devices inside a well on a CMOS chip, a third junction capacitance C'_{bb} must be considered, as already explained. For this capacitance, we have

$$C'_{bb} = A_W C'_{jw} + l_W C''_{jw} \tag{8.4.4}$$

where A_W and C'_{jw} are the well's bottom wall area and capacitance per unit area, l_W is the well's sidewall length (the total perimeter as seen from above), and C''_{jw} is the well's sidewall capacitance per unit length.

It is obvious that, if a group of more than one transistor share the same well, C'_{bb} must be included only once in the model for the group.

8.4.3 Gate-Wiring Capacitance

There exists a parasitic gate-body capacitance C_{gbe} caused by the overlap of the gate and the substrate outside the channel region (see, for example, Fig. 5.13). In parallel with C_{gbe} is another parasitic capacitance caused by the connection of the gate to other parts of the circuit through a metal or polysilicon layer. This layer is separated from the substrate by *thick* oxide (typically ten times thicker than the gate oxide). This second capacitance should be considered an external parasitic rather than being associated with the transistor.

8.4.4 Source-Drain Proximity Capacitance

As with any objects in close proximity, a capacitance exists between the source and drain n^+ regions, denoted by C_{sde} in Fig. 8.22. Because of the complicated shapes involved, the value of this capacitance is difficult to evaluate. However, it is, in general, very small and can be neglected in comparison to other capacitances, unless the channel is very short.

8.4.5 Resistances

The above capacitances are very easy to incorporate in a complete small-signal model at relatively low frequencies, since they appear in parallel with the corresponding intrinsic capacitances in the model of Fig. 8.13. However, a more complete model for the extrinsic part should include parasitic resistances as well. Such resistances are those of the source and drain regions, and of the substrate and the gate material.[13, 48] At high frequencies, the magnitude of the impedance of the capacitances drops to the point where it becomes comparable to the resistances; hence, the latter should be taken into account. This is done most simply by approximating the resistive paths by a few lumped elements. An example is shown in Fig. 8.23 where the resistance symbols with subscripts s, d, g, and b model the resistive materials of the source region, drain region, gate, and substrate, respectively. Empirical rules are used to estimate the resistance values, but they are very dependent on the construction details of a given transistor. Unfortunately, no general rules can be given for the frequency where such effects become important. This depends greatly on the resistivity of the regions, their geometry, the way they are contacted, etc.

A cutoff frequency can be defined for the complete transistor as the frequency at which the small-signal current gain becomes unity, in analogy to the intrinsic cutoff frequency defined earlier in conjunction with Fig. 8.16a. Because of the presence of the extrinsic elements, the cutoff frequency for the complete transistor is smaller than for the intrinsic part.

8.5 NOISE

8.5.1 Introduction

It has so far been assumed that the drain current of a MOS transistor varies with time only if one or more of the terminal voltages vary with time. This is not exactly true. A careful examination of the current reveals minute fluctuations, referred to as *noise*, which are present whether externally applied signals are present or not. Such fluctuations can interfere with weak signals when the transistor is part of an analog circuit,[49, 50] so ways to predict and possibly reduce noise are very important. For this reason, the subject of noise in MOS transistors has received extensive treatment in the literature.[51–134] This section is devoted to this subject. We have chosen to treat noise as part of our discussion of small-signal modeling, because noise is, in a sense, an internally

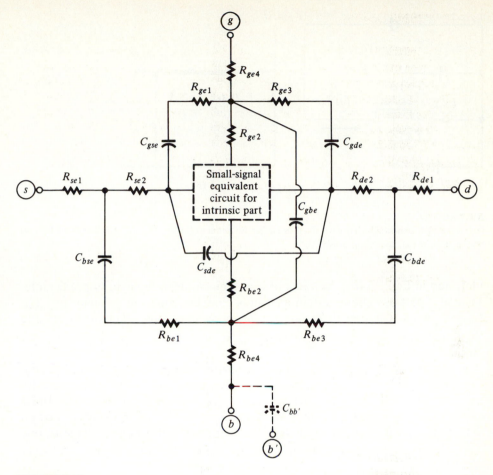

FIGURE 8.23
An example of modeling extrinsic resistances.

generated small signal in the device, and can be modeled with appropriate additions to the small-signal equivalent circuits we have already developed in this chapter.

8.5.2   Mean Square Noise and Power Spectral Density

Consider a transistor with dc bias voltages, as shown in Fig. 8.24a. The total drain current can be expressed as:

$$i_D(t) = I_D + i_n(t) \tag{8.5.1}$$

where I_D is the ideal (bias) current and $i_n(t)$ is the noise component, as

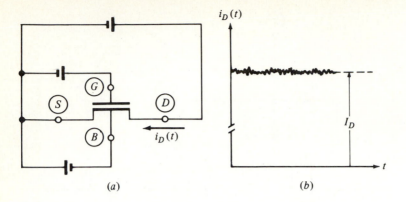

FIGURE 8.24
(a) A MOS transistor biased with fixed noiseless terminal voltages; (b) the drain current for the connection in (a), including noise.

indicated in Fig. 8.24b. The value of i_n at a given t is, of course, unpredictable. Instead, one talks about certain measures characterizing the behavior of $i_n(t)$. In noise work, such measures are the *mean square* value, denoted by $\overline{i_n^2}$, and the *root mean square* (rms) value, $\sqrt{\overline{i_n^2}}$. In measuring these quantities, the amount of noise seen depends on the bandwidth of the measuring instrument. A common measurement involves a very narrow bandwidth Δf. We will denote the mean square value of the current noise components within this bandwidth by $\Delta \overline{i_n^2}$. The ratio $\Delta \overline{i_n^2}/\Delta f$ is called the *power spectral density* of the noise current† and has units A^2/Hz. Often, the square root of the power spectral density is used instead, given in $A/\sqrt{Hz}$. Similarly, for a noise voltage v_n one uses $\Delta \overline{v_n^2}/\Delta f$ as the power spectral density (in V^2/Hz) or its square root (in $V/\sqrt{Hz}$).

A typical plot of power spectral density for the noise current of an MOS device in strong inversion is shown in Fig. 8.25 in log-log axes. Two distinct frequency regions, with different noise behavior in each can be identified. These regions can be thought of as separated by a "corner frequency" f_c. Values from several hertz to several hundred kilohertz are common for this quantity. The type of noise dominating at high frequencies is called *thermal noise* and will be considered in Sec. 8.5.3. The corresponding noise current component will be denoted by i_t. The noise dominating at low frequencies is

---

† Formally, the power spectral density is defined by letting Δf approach zero. However, this definition has little to do with practical measurements in which the bandwidth is finite. In general, in our treatment we will choose simple approaches, definitions, and notation that convey a feeling for the physical phenomena and that correspond to practical situations. This is common in device literature. More rigor is encountered in treatments on stochastic processes.

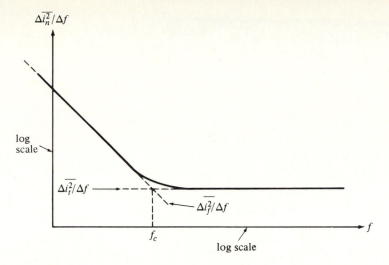

FIGURE 8.25
A typical plot of the drain-noise current power-spectral density vs. frequency in log-log axes. Subscript n refers to total noise, t to thermal noise, and f to $1/f$ noise.

called *$1/f$ noise* because the power spectral density for the current caused by this type of noise is practically proportional to $1/f$ (Sec. 8.5.4). The current component due to $1/f$ noise will be denoted by i_f. The noise components i_t and i_f are *uncorrelated*.[79, 126] For this reason, the total mean square value is the sum of the individual mean square values. Thus,

$$\frac{\overline{\Delta i_n^2}}{\Delta f} = \frac{\overline{\Delta i_t^2}}{\Delta f} + \frac{\overline{\Delta i_f^2}}{\Delta f} \qquad (8.5.2)$$

8.5.3 Thermal Noise

Thermal noise (also called *Johnson noise* or *Nyquist noise*) is certainly the type of noise best characterized for the MOS transistor. The term *thermal* is due to the origin of this noise, which can be traced to the random thermal motion of carriers in the channel. Before embarking on an evaluation of this noise, we give here two conventional relations derived for the strongly inverted MOS transistor in Sec. 4.4.1. The drain current (assumed noiseless) was shown there to be

$$I_D = - \mu W Q_I'(V_{CB}(x)) \frac{dV_{CB}(x)}{dx} \qquad (8.5.3)$$

where x is the position along the channel, $V_{CB}(x)$ is the "effective reverse bias" of the strongly inverted channel with respect to the substrate at position x (see Fig. 8.26), Q_I' is the inversion layer charge per unit area, μ is the mobility, and W is the width of the channel. Integrating this equation was seen to give, assuming a constant mobility,

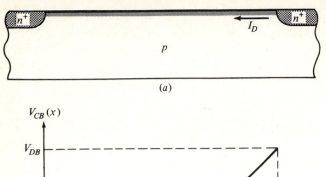

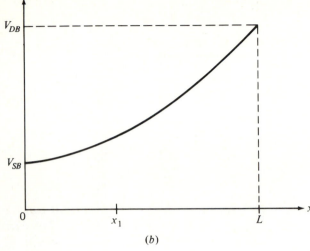

FIGURE 8.26
(a) Part of a MOS transistor in strong inversion; (b) effective reverse bias V_{CB} vs. distance along the channel.

$$I_D = -\frac{W}{L}\mu \int_{V_{SB}}^{V_{DB}} Q_I'(V_{CB}(x))\, dV_{CB}(x) \tag{8.5.4}$$

with L being the channel length. Depending on the expression for $Q_I'(V_{CB})$ we have seen that models of differing complexity and accuracy are obtained.

In the following development, we also need an expression for the resistance ΔR of a small element of the channel of length Δx† centered around a point $x = x_1$. Since $\Delta V = I_D\, \Delta R$ we have, from (8.5.3),

$$\Delta R = \frac{\Delta x}{-\mu W Q_I'(V_{CB}(x_1))} \tag{8.5.5}$$

where the right-hand side is, of course, positive, since $Q_I' < 0$.

---

† To avoid complicated notation, a single symbol Δ will be used in this section to indicate small quantities which may correspond to each other or not. For example, $\Delta \overline{i_n^2}$ is the mean square current noise corresponding to a bandwidth Δf. On the other hand, ΔR is the resistance corresponding to length Δx, with no relation to Δf. Correspondence, or the lack of it, will be clear from the context, and no confusion should arise.

Using concepts from statistical physics, it can be shown that the power spectral density of the noise voltage generated across a resistor of value R is equal to $4kTR$, where k is Boltzmann's constant and T is the absolute temperature.[79, 126] Thus, assuming that the small element of the channel acts as a resistor of resistance ΔR, we will observe across it a small noise voltage Δv_t with a mean square value of

$$\overline{(\Delta v_t)^2} = 4kT\,\Delta R\,\Delta f \qquad (8.5.6)$$

which, using (8.5.5), gives

$$\overline{(\Delta v_t)^2} = \frac{4kT\,\Delta x}{-\mu W Q_I'(V_{CB}(x_1))}\,\Delta f \qquad (8.5.7)$$

This noise will cause noise in the drain current. To study the mechanism by which this happens, we consider the following "thought" experiment. A fictitious dc voltage source of negligible length and of very small magnitude Δv is inserted at point x_1 in the channel, as shown in Fig. 8.27a. This will create a jump Δv in the potential $V_{CB}(x)$, as shown in Fig. 8.27b,[126] and will cause a

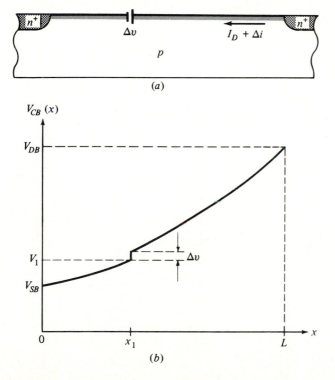

FIGURE 8.27

(a) The transistor of Fig. 8.26a, with a fictitious dc source placed at point $x = x_1$ in the channel; (b) resulting effective reverse bias V_{CB} vs. distance.

change in the drain current, compared to that in Fig. 8.26. To get a feeling for this effect, one can consider Fig. 8.28.[13] Here we have two transistors of lengths x_1 and $L - x_1$. The dimensions of the source-drain regions connected to Δv are assumed to have shrunk to zero. If $\Delta v = 0$, the connection of the two transistors is equivalent to the single transistor in Fig. 8.26. If $\Delta v \neq 0$, the drain bias of the transistor on the left and the source bias of the transistor on the right will be disturbed. A new value for the current will then be established, along with a new potential distribution. These will correspond to the situation shown in Fig. 8.27. Let the new drain current value be $I_D + \Delta i$, as noted in Figs. 8.27 and 8.28. We can write equations similar to (8.5.4) for the left and the right transistors. These will be, correspondingly,

$$I_D + \Delta i = -\frac{W}{x_1} \mu \int_{V_{SB}}^{V_1} Q_I'(V_{CB}(x)) \, dV_{CB}(x) \qquad (8.5.8)$$

$$I_D + \Delta i = -\frac{W}{L - x_1} \mu \int_{V_1 + \Delta v}^{V_{DB}} Q_I'(V_{CB}(x)) \, dV_{CB}(x) \qquad (8.5.9)$$

where V_1 is defined in Fig. 8.27b. Eliminating x_1 among these equations and using the assumption that Δv is very small easily gives (Prob. 8.23)

$$I_D + \Delta i = -\frac{W}{L} \mu \int_{V_{SB}}^{V_{DB}} Q_I'(V_{CB}(x)) \, dV_{CB}(x) + \frac{W}{L} \mu Q_I'(V_{CB}(x_1)) \, \Delta v \qquad (8.5.10)$$

As Δv goes to zero, $Q_I'(V_{CB}(x_1))$ has a well-defined value, in fact the same as in Fig. 8.26b. Recognizing in the above equation the first term on the

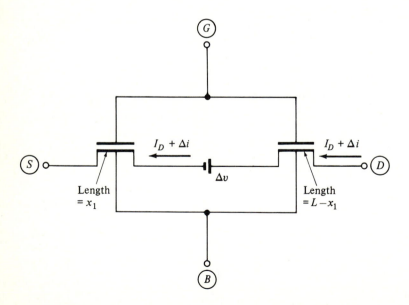

FIGURE 8.28
Schematic representation of the situation in Fig. 8.27a.

right-hand side as I_D from (8.5.4), we obtain for the change Δi:

$$\Delta i = \frac{W}{L} \mu Q'_i(V_{CB}(x_1)) \Delta v \qquad (8.5.11)$$

In the above development, we have assumed that Δv is a dc voltage. However, the result will be valid even if Δv is varying with time as long as the variation is slow enough so that quasi-static behavior is maintained (Sec. 7.2). This implies frequencies several times less than ω_o, just as was the case for the small-signal model we have already developed in Sec. 8.3. Let us now remove the battery and instead consider the thermal noise generated across the small element of the channel centered at x_1. Let Δv_t represent that part of the total thermal noise voltage which has frequency components in the above frequency range.† If Δi_t represents the corresponding drain current variation, we will have, in analogy with (8.5.11),

$$\Delta i_t(t) = \frac{W}{L} \mu Q'_i(V_{CB}(x_1)) \Delta v_t(t) \qquad (8.5.12)$$

The mean square value of Δi_t can be found by noting that, for negligibly small Δv_t, $Q'_i(V_{CB}(x_1))$ has a practically constant, well-defined value, in fact the same value as in Fig. 8.26b, as already mentioned. (We do not need the actual value, as will be seen. We only need to know that it is practically independent of Δv_t for negligibly small Δv_t.) Thus, the mean square value of Δi_t will be

$$\overline{(\Delta i_t)^2} = \left[\frac{W}{L} \mu Q'_i(V_{CB}(x_1)) \right]^2 \overline{(\Delta v_t)^2} \qquad (8.5.13)$$

Using now (8.5.7) in the above relation, we obtain

$$\overline{(\Delta i_t)^2} = -4kT \frac{\mu}{L^2} WQ'_i(V_{CB}(x_1)) \Delta x \, \Delta f \qquad (8.5.14)$$

This gives the contribution of the element at x_1 to the drain current noise. The contributions of all similar elements in the channel are assumed uncorrelated, and one can thus find the mean square value of their combined effect by adding the individual mean square values. In the limit, letting Δx become a differential and integrating over the channel length, we obtain‡

---

† This assumption will result in models sufficient for most applications. Noise of higher frequencies is difficult to treat[56, 66, 71, 78, 82, 83, 85, 86, 104] and has been the subject of controversy for some time.

‡ We assume here a "carrier temperature" equal to the lattice temperature. The so-called "hot-carrier effects" present under certain conditions in short-channel devices due to high electric fields (Sec. 5.5) are not considered. Such effects are difficult to treat.[104, 114] Short-channel devices are often found to be more noisy than what would be expected from long-channel theory. In saturation, the hot-carrier effects caused by high fields in short-channel devices can produce noise several times that predicted by long-channel theory. In addition, the substrate current caused by such effects (Sec. 5.5) contains a noise component. This produces a voltage drop across the substrate resistive material, which can be coupled to the drain current through the substrate transconductance.[133]

$$\overline{\Delta i_t^2} = -4kT \frac{\mu}{L^2} \left(\int_0^L Q_I' W \, dx \right) \Delta f \tag{8.5.15}$$

where we have used $\overline{\Delta i_t^2}$ to denote the total noise current mean square value in a bandwidth Δf, as in Sec. 8.5.2. Recognizing the integral in the above equation as the total inversion layer charge Q_I we have

$$\overline{\Delta i_t^2} = \left[4kT \frac{\mu}{L^2} (-Q_I) \right] \Delta f \tag{8.5.16}$$

This equation is valid for any model, provided the appropriate expression is used for Q_I. In particular, for the *approximate* strong inversion model, we can use Q_I from (7.4.14). This gives

$$\overline{\Delta i_t^2} = 4kT \left[\frac{W}{L} \mu C_{ox}'(V_{GS} - V_T) \frac{2}{3} \frac{1 + \alpha + \alpha^2}{1 + \alpha} \right] \Delta f \tag{8.5.17}$$

where α has been defined in (4.4.31). In saturation $\alpha = 0$, giving†

$$\overline{\Delta i_t^2} = 4kT \left[\frac{2}{3} \frac{W}{L} \mu C_{ox}'(V_{GS} - V_T) \right] \Delta f , \qquad V_{DS} > V_{DS}' \tag{8.5.18}$$

It is thus seen that for a given bias, the power spectral density $\overline{\Delta i_t^2}/\Delta f$ is *independent* of frequency, at least in the range of frequencies where the assumption of quasi-static behavior is valid.

A common representation of noise involves the so-called *equivalent input noise voltage*. This quantity is defined as the noise needed in the voltage between the gate and source of a hypothetical *noiseless* transistor, to produce the correct amount of noise current. Let us denote by $v_{in,t}$ the equivalent input noise voltage corresponding to thermal noise. Recalling the definition of transconductance, we can obtain

$$\overline{\Delta v_{in,t}^2} = \frac{\overline{\Delta i_t^2}}{g_m^2} \tag{8.5.19}$$

where, as before, Δ denotes mean square noise within a bandwidth Δf. For the approximate model, this can be easily shown to give

$$\overline{\Delta v_{in,t}^2} = 4kT \left[\frac{2}{3} \frac{(1 + \delta)^2}{(W/L) \mu C_{ox}'(V_{GS} - V_T)} \frac{1 + \alpha + \alpha^2}{(1 - \alpha^2)(1 - \alpha)} \right] \Delta f \tag{8.5.20}$$

At $V_{DS} = 0$ ($\alpha = 1$), this quantity is seen to become infinite. This is an

---

† If in (8.5.18) we use (8.2.6b) and (4.4.28), we obtain $\overline{\Delta i_t^2} = 4kT[\frac{2}{3}(1 + \delta)g_m] \Delta f$ in the saturation region. In circuits literature and circuit simulators, this formula is sometimes used indiscriminately in both saturation and nonsaturation, which can lead to very wrong results. For example, at $V_{DS} = 0$, we have $g_m = 0$, which would predict zero noise if this formula were used! This is, of course, physically impossible and clearly false, as follows from (8.5.17).

artifact caused by the fact that, at $V_{DS} = 0$, the transconductance becomes zero. The product $g_m^2 \, \Delta v_{in,t}^2$ behaves correctly in the limit as V_{DS} goes to zero, and gives the correct value of Δi_t^2.

In analog applications, an "input" signal is intentionally superimposed on the bias between gate and source. This signal can be viewed as being in series with $v_{in,t}$, and thus the two can be compared to discuss the resulting signal-to-noise ratio. As follows from (8.5.20), this ratio is worse for larger δ. The parameter δ can be traced back to (4.4.22), where it is seen to be associated with the variation of the depletion region charge along the channel. From (4.4.33b) to (4.4.33d) we see that δ, and thus the equivalent input thermal noise voltage, can be decreased by increasing V_{SB}. This has, in fact, been verified experimentally.[133]

Yet another common description of noise involves the concept of *equivalent input noise resistance*. This is a fictitious resistance of such value that its thermal noise power spectral density is $\Delta v_{in,t}^2 / \Delta f$. Since the power spectral density of the thermal noise voltage across a resistance R is $4kTR$,[79, 126] it is seen from (8.5.20) that the equivalent input noise resistance R_n for the thermal noise in a strongly inverted MOS transistor is

$$R_n = \frac{2}{3} \frac{(1+\delta)^2}{(W/L) \, \mu C_{ox}'(V_{GS} - V_T)} \frac{1 + \alpha + \alpha^2}{(1 - \alpha^2)(1 - \alpha)} \qquad (8.5.21)$$

At $V_{DS} = 0$, R_n becomes infinite, as expected from the above discussion. Some problems that can arise in relation to the equivalent input noise and the equivalent input noise resistance are considered in Prob. 8.26.

WEAK INVERSION. Transistors operating in weak inversion exhibit a "flat" part in the power spectral density for the noise current, just as devices in strong inversion do (Fig. 8.25). In some treatments, this is taken to be caused by thermal noise, just as in strong inversion[118, 123] (the alternate assumption[111] of *shot* noise is discussed later). Expressions for the power spectral density are then derived by taking (8.5.16) to be valid in weak inversion,[123] based on a proof given elsewhere.[55] Q_I can be obtained from (7.4.36), repeated here:

$$Q_I = WL \, \frac{Q_{I,\text{source}}' + Q_{I,\text{drain}}'}{2} \qquad (8.5.22)$$

Expressions for the inversion layer charge per unit area at the source and drain ends of the channel were developed in Sec. 4.6. Using these in the above equation, and using the current expression (4.6.16) in the result, we easily get (Prob. 8.27)

$$Q_I = -\frac{L^2}{2\mu\phi_t} \, I_D'(1 + e^{-V_{DS}/\phi_t}) \qquad (8.5.23)$$

where I_D' is the current in the flat part of the I_D-V_{DS} curve ($V_{DS} > 5\phi_t$). Using this in (8.5.16) (which is still considered valid[123]) and recalling that $\phi_t = kT/q$, where q is the electron charge, gives:

$$\overline{\Delta i_t^2} = [2qI_D'(1 + e^{-V_{DS}/\phi_t})]\,\Delta f \tag{8.5.24}$$

For large V_{DS} ($>5\phi_t$), this reduces to $2qI_D\,\Delta f$. Although we have assumed the presence of *thermal* noise in deriving the above result, this is precisely the same value as what one would get if a different type of noise, called *shot* noise, were assumed.[111] Shot noise is associated with dc flow produced by carriers crossing a potential barrier (such as the one from source to channel), and is due to the discreteness of the arriving charges. Shot noise can be shown to have a power spectral density of $2qI$, where I is a dc current.[79, 126] Thus, whether one assumes thermal or shot noise in weak inversion, the same result is obtained.† This has led to some controversy as to which of the two types of noise is actually present in weak inversion.[111, 118, 123]

An equivalent input noise voltage can be defined as before by using (8.5.19). Recalling from Sec. 8.2 that in weak inversion $g_m = I_D/(n\phi_t)$, one can show that (Prob. 8.27)

$$\overline{\Delta v_{in,t}^2} = \frac{2qn^2\phi_t^2}{I_D'}\,\frac{1 + e^{-V_{DS}/\phi_t}}{(1 - e^{-V_{DS}/\phi_t})^2}\,\Delta f \tag{8.5.25}$$

Equating this to $4kTR_n\,\Delta f$ shows that the equivalent input noise resistance R_n is

$$R_n = \frac{n^2}{2}\,\frac{\phi_t}{I_D'}\,\frac{1 + e^{-V_{DS}/\phi_t}}{(1 - e^{-V_{DS}/\phi_t})^2} \tag{8.5.26}$$

INDUCED GATE NOISE. The above results have been obtained based on random fluctuations of the potential in the channel. These fluctuations are coupled to the gate terminal through the oxide capacitance, and they "induce" a minute noise current in the gate terminal even if all external voltages are fixed. For frequencies up to about ω_o [see (8.3.6)], the induced gate current power spectral density (with a fixed V_{GS}) has been evaluated[53, 56] to be roughly $20kTf^2C_{ox}^2/g_{m,sat}$ in the saturation region, neglecting substrate effects. Decreas-

---

† It would appear that this equivalence does not hold as V_{DS} is reduced, since the right-hand side of (8.5.24) increases (in agreement with experiment[118, 123]) whereas the expression $2qI_D\,\Delta f$ predicts a decreasing value with decreasing V_{DS} (in fact, that value would be 0 at $V_{DS} = 0$, a physically impossible result). This would tend to favor the assumption that the noise in weak inversion is of thermal origin.[118, 123] This discrepancy between the two theories is however removed if one views I_D as the superposition of two components, one associated with the drain and one with the source[135] (a similar superposition view is encountered in bipolar transistor theory). Thus, from (4.6.10) we can write $I_D = I_1 - I_2$, where $I_1 = -(W/L)\mu\phi_t Q'_{I,source}$ and $I_2 = -(W/L)\mu\phi_t Q'_{I,drain}$. If each of I_1 and I_2 is assumed to have shot noise and the two noise components are assumed uncorrelated, their mean square values will add. Using then equations from Sec. 4.6 it is easy to show (Prob. 8.27) that the combined power spectral density of the shot noise in the two currents is given *identically* by the right-hand side of (8.5.24) for *all* values of V_{DS}. In this way, both the shot noise assumption and the thermal noise assumption are seen to produce identical results for all bias points in weak inversion. A similar observation for the noise in a zero-biased *pn* junction is well known.[126]

ing V_{DS} below V'_{DS} decreases this noise current smoothly, with a power spectral density of about 0.7 times the value of saturation at $V_{DS} = 0$. For frequencies in the region of validity of this expression, the induced gate current is very small.

An *induced substrate noise current* can also be stipulated, based on coupling of the channel random potential fluctuations to the substrate through the depletion region capacitance.

8.5.4 $1/f$ Noise

The origin of $1/f$ noise (exhibited by the varying part in the plot of Fig. 8.25) is, according to some studies, the carrier density fluctuations caused by the exchange of carriers between the channel and the interface traps (Sec. 2.6).[67] According to other studies, mobility fluctuations are instead the cause of $1/f$ noise.[99, 117] Unfortunately, the precise mechanisms involved in $1/f$ noise (also called *flicker noise*) are complicated, and have been the subject of speculation and controversy.[64, 67, 68, 70, 80, 81, 87, 107, 109, 110, 116, 117, 121, 122, 128] Other theories have also been proposed. Each theory is involved, and gives rise to a different expression for the power spectral density of the resulting noise current. Several theories are summarized and compared elsewhere.[92, 121, 122, 128] The one important point on which all theories agree, and which is verified by measurement, is that the power spectral density varies very nearly in inverse proportion to f—hence the name. The above dependence on f gives rise to a straight-line plot on log-log axes, as seen in Fig. 8.25. It appears that most devices tend to conform to a relation of the form

$$\frac{\overline{\Delta i_f^2}}{\Delta f} = \frac{M g_m^2}{C_{ox}'^a WL} \frac{1}{f} \tag{8.5.27}$$

where the exponent a is often taken equal to 1 or 2, and the quantity M has dimensions dependent on the value used for α and depends on device construction. For most devices, M shows little dependence on bias, but there are devices in which M is found to depend considerably on bias. It is usually found that "cleaner" fabrication processes result in lower values for M, other things being equal. As an example, in a common CMOS fabrication process (Chap. 10), one may find $\alpha = 2$, with M equal to 5×10^{-9} fC^2/μm^2 for n-channel devices and 2×10^{-10} fC^2/μm^2 for p-channel devices. The equivalent input noise voltage corresponding to this model has a power spectral density given by

$$\frac{\overline{\Delta v_{in,f}^2}}{\Delta f} = \frac{M}{C_{ox}'^a WL} \frac{1}{f} \tag{8.5.28}$$

8.5.5   Equivalent-circuit model

Adding a noise current source to the small-signal equivalent circuit of Fig. 8.13 produces the model in Fig. 8.29. The power spectral density of the noise source

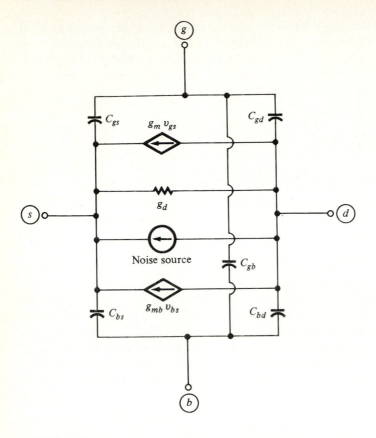

FIGURE 8.29
A small-signal equivalent circuit for the intrinsic part of a transistor, with a noise current source added; the power spectral density of this source is given by (8.5.2).

is given by (8.5.2). When using such models to calculate noise in circuits, one has to work with mean square or root mean square values of noise currents and voltages, rather than with the noise currents and voltages themselves, and this requires some care. Convenient techniques for such calculations are given in texts on circuit design.[49]

The extrinsic resistances discussed in Sec. 8.4 exhibit thermal noise. One can model this effect by placing a noise voltage source in series with each extrinsic resistor and with power spectral density $4kTR$, where R is the resistance value. For certain device structures, the polysilicon gate resistance can be a significant contributor to noise.[130] The same is true for the substrate resistance,[131,133] the noise of which is coupled to the drain current through the substrate transconductance g_{mb}. One way to reduce this effect is to decrease g_{mb} which, as follows from Sec. 8.2, can be achieved by increasing the source-substrate bias V_{SB}.[133]

REFERENCES

1. H. J. K. Ihantola and J. L. Moll, "Design theory of a surface field-effect transistor," *Solid-State Electronics*, vol. 7, pp. 423–430, June 1964.
2. C. T. Sah, "Characteristics of the metal-oxide semiconductor transistors," *IEEE Transactions on Electron Devices*, vol. ED-11, pp. 324-345, July 1964.
3. S. R. Hofstein and G. Warfield, "Carrier mobility and current saturation in the MOS transistor," *IEEE Transactions on Electron Devices*, vol. ED-12, pp. 129–138, March 1965.
4. V. K. G. Reddi and C. T. Sah, "Source to drain resistance beyond pinch-off in metal-oxide semiconductor transistors (MOST)," *IEEE Transactions on Electron Devices*, vol. ED-12, pp. 139–141, March 1965.
5. M. H. White and R. C. Gallagher, "Metal oxide semiconductor (MOS) small-signal equivalent circuits," *Proceedings of the IEEE*, vol. 53, pp. 314–315, 1965.
6. C. T. Sah and H. C. Pao, "The effects of fixed bulk charge on the characteristics of metal-oxide semiconductor transistors," *IEEE Transactions on Electron Devices*, vol. ED-13, pp. 393–409, April 1966.
7. M. B. Das, "Charge-control analysis of M.O.S. and junction-gate field-effect transistors," *IEE Proceedings*, vol. 113, pp. 1565–1570, October 1966.
8. F. A. Lindholm, R. J. Balda, and J. L. Clements, "Characterization of the four-terminal MOS transistor for digital and linear applications," *Digest of Technical Papers*, International Electronics Conference, Toronto, pp. 116–117, 1967.
9. M. B. Das, "Dependence of the characteristics of MOS transistors on the substrate resistivity," *Solid-State Electronics*, vol. 11, pp. 305–322, March 1968.
10. J. E. Schroeder and R. S. Muller, "IGFET analysis through numerical solution of Poisson's equation," *IEEE Transactions on Electron Devices*, vol. ED-15, no. 12, pp. 954–961, December 1968.
11. T. L. Chiu and C. T. Sah, "Correlation experiments with a two-section model theory of the saturation drain conductance of MOS transistors," *Solid-State Electronics*, vol. 11, pp. 1149–1163, 1968.
12. D. Frohman-Bentchkowsky and A. S. Grove, "Conductance of MOS transistors in saturation," *IEEE Transactions on Electron Devices*, vol. ED-16, pp. 108–113, January 1969.
13. R. S. C. Cobbold, *Theory and Applications of Field-Effect Transistors*, Wiley-Interscience, New York, 1970.
14. G. Baum and H. Beneking, "Drift velocity saturation in MOS transistors," *IEEE Transactions on Electron Devices*, vol. ED-17, pp. 481–482, 1970.
15. D. J. Hamilton, F. A. Lindholm, and A. H. Marshak, *Principles and Applications of Semiconductor Device Modeling*, Holt, Rinehart, and Winston, New York, 1971.
16. J. E. Meyer, "MOS models and circuit simulation," *RCA Review*, vol. 32, pp. 42–63, March 1971.
17. G. Merckel, J. Borel, and N. Z. Cupcea, "An accurate large-signal MOS transistor model for use in computer-aided design," *IEEE Transactions on Electron Devices*, vol. ED-19, pp. 681–690, May 1972.
18. A. Popa, "An injection level dependent theory of the MOS transistor in saturation," *IEEE Transactions on Electron Devices*, vol. ED-19, pp. 774–781, June 1972.
19. H. Ikeda, "An elegant method for measuring MOST drain-source conductance in the saturated current region," *IEEE Transactions on Instrumentation and Measurement*, vol. IM-21, pp. 234–236, August 1972.
20. P. Rossel, H. Martinot, and G. Vassilieff, "Accurate two-sections model for MOS transistors in saturation," *Solid-State Electronics*, vol. 19, pp. 51–56, January 1976.
21. F. M. Klaassen, "A MOS model for computer-aided design," *Philips Research Reports*, vol. 31, pp. 71–83, 1976.
22. Y. A. El-Mansy and A. R. Boothroyd, "A simple two-dimensional model for IGFET operation in the saturation region," *IEEE Transactions on Electron Devices*, vol. ED-24, pp. 254–262, March 1977.

23. E. Vittoz and J. Fellrath, "MOS analog integrated circuits based on weak inversion operation," *IEEE Journal of Solid-State Circuits*, vol. SC-12, pp. 224–231, June 1977.

24. J. Fellrath and E. Vittoz, "Small signal model of MOS transistors in weak inversion," *Proc. Journées d'Electronique 1977*, Session C4, Ecole Polytechnique Fédérale de Lausanne, Switzerland, pp. 315–324, 1977.

25. J. R. Brews, "A charge sheet model of the MOSFET," *Solid-State Electronics*, vol. 21, pp. 345–355, 1978.

26. G. W. Taylor, "The effects of two-dimensional charge sharing on the above-threshold characteristics of short-channel devices," *Solid-State Electronics*, vol. 22, pp. 701–717, 1979.

27. H. C. Poon, "V_{th} and beyond," presented at the Workshop on Device Modelling for VLSI, Burlingame, California, March 29, 1979; also L. Cong, Bell Laboratories, private communication.

28. T. Poorter and J. H. Satter, "A D.C. model for an MOS-transistor in the saturation region," *Solid-State Electronics*, vol. 23, pp. 765–772, 1980.

29. Y. P. Tsividis, "Relation between incremental intrinsic capacitances and transconductances in MOS transistors," *IEEE Transactions on Electron Devices*, vol. ED-27, pp. 946–948, May 1980.

30. D. E. Ward, "Charge-based modeling of capacitance in MOS transistors," *Technical Report G201–11*, Integrated Circuits Laboratory, Stanford University, California, June 1981.

31. J. J. Paulos, D. A. Antoniadis, and Y. P. Tsividis, "Measurement of intrinsic capacitances of MOS transistors," *Technical Digest*, IEEE International Solid-State Circuits Conference, San Francisco, pp. 238–239, February 1982.

32. G. Cardinali, S. Graffi, M. Impronta, and G. Masetti, "DC MOSFET model for analogue circuit simulation employing process-empirical parameters," *IEE Proceedings*, vol. 129, part I, pp. 61–66, April 1982.

33. Y. Tsividis, "Moderate inversion in MOS devices," *Solid-State Electronics*, vol. 25, pp. 1099–1104, 1982; see also Erratum, *ibid.*, vol. 26, p. 823, 1983.

34. S. Liu and L. W. Nagel, "Small-signal MOSFET models for analog circuit design," *IEEE Journal of Solid-State Circuits*, vol. SC-17, pp. 983–998, December 1982.

35. Y. Tsividis and G. Masetti, "Problems in precision modeling of the MOS transistor for analog applications," *IEEE Transactions on Computer-Aided Design*, vol. CAD-3, pp. 72–79, January 1983,

36. J. J. Paulos and D. A. Antoniadis,"Limitations of quasi-static capacitance models for the MOS transistor," *IEEE Electron Device Letters*, vol. EDL-4, pp. 221–224, July 1983.

37. C. Turchetti, G. Masetti, and Y. Tsividis, "On the small-signal behavior of the MOS transistor in quasi-static operation," *Solid-State Electronics*, vol. 26, pp. 941–949, 1983.

38. J. Oristian, H. Iwai, J. Walker, and R. Dutton, "Small geometry MOS transistor capacitance measurement method using simple on-chip circuits," *IEEE Electron Device Letters*, vol. EDL-5, pp. 395–397, October 1984.

39. B. J. Sheu and P. K. Ko, "An analytical model for intrinsic capacitances of short-channel MOSFETs," *Technical Digest*, International Electron Devices Meeting, pp. 300–303, San Francisco, 1984.

40. H. Iwai, J. E. Oristian, J. T. Walker, and R. W. Dutton, "A scaleable technique for the measurement of intrinsic MOS capacitance with atto-Farad resolution," *IEEE Transactions on Electron Devices*, vol. ED-32, pp. 344–356, February 1985.

41. J. J. Paulos and D. A. Antoniadis, "Measurement of minimum-geometry MOS transistor capacitances," *IEEE Transactions on Electron Devices*, vol. ED-32, pp. 357–363, February 1985.

42. H. Iwai, M. R. Pinto, C. S. Rafferty, J. E. Oristian, and R. W. Dutton, "Velocity saturation effect on short-channel MOS transistor capacitance," *IEEE Electron Device Letters*, vol. EDL-6, pp. 120–122, March 1985.

43. F. M. Klaassen, "MOS device modelling," chapter 1 in *Design of MOS VLSI Circuits for Telecommunications*, Y. Tsividis and P. Antognetti (editors), Prentice-Hall, Englewood Cliffs, N.J., 1985.

44. J. L. D'Arcy and R. C. Rennick, "MOSFET parameter optimization for accurate output conductance modeling," *Proceedings of the 1985 IEEE Custom Integrated Circuits Conference*, Portland, Oreg., pp. 512–515.

45. W. Maes, K. De Meyer, and L. Dupas, "SIMPAR: A versatile technology independent parameter extraction program using a new optimized fit strategy," *IEEE Transactions on Computer-Aided Design of Integrated Circuits and Systems*, vol. CAD-5, pp. 320–325, April 1986.

46. S. M. Sze, *Physics of Semiconductor Devices*, John Wiley, New York, 1981.

47. M. Bagheri and Y. Tsividis, "A small-signal high-frequency model for the four-terminal intrinsic MOSFET valid in all regions of operation," *IEEE Transactions on Electron Devices*, vol. ED-32, pp. 2383–2391, November 1985.

48. T. Sakurai and T. Iijuka, "Gate electrode RC delay effects in VLSI's," *IEEE Transactions on Electron Devices*, vol. ED-32, pp. 370–374, February 1985.

49. P. R. Gray and R. G. Meyer, *Analysis and Design of Analog Integrated Circuits*, Wiley, New York, 1984.

50. Y. Tsividis and P. Antognetti (editors), *Design of MOS VLSI Circuits for Telecommunications*, Prentice-Hall, Englewood Cliffs, 1985.

51. C. T. Sah, "Theory and experiments on the 1/f surface noise of MOS insulated-gate field-effect transistors," *IEEE Transactions on Electron Devices* (*Abstract*), vol. ED-11, pp. 534, November 1964.

52. A. G. Jordan and N. A. Jordan, "Theory of noise in metal oxide semiconductor devices," *IEEE Transactions on Electron Devices*, vol. ED-12, pp. 148–156, March 1965.

53. H. Johnson, "Noise in field-effect transistors," chapter 6 in *Field-Effect Transistors*, T. Wallmark and H. Johnson (editors), Prentice-Hall, Englewood Cliffs, 1966.

54. S. M. Bozic, "Noise in the metal oxide semiconductor transistor," *Electronic Engineering*, vol. 38, pp. 40–41, 1966.

55. C. T. Sah, S. Y. Wu, and F. H. Hielscher: "The effects of fixed bulk charge on the thermal noise in metal-oxide-semiconductor transistors," *IEEE Transactions on Electron Devices*, vol. ED-13, pp. 410–414, April 1966.

56. M. Shoji, "Analysis of high-frequency thermal noise of enhancement mode M.O.S. field-effect transistors," *IEEE Transactions on Electron Devices*, vol. ED-13, pp. 520–524, June 1966.

57. I. Flinn, G. Bew, and F. Berz, "Low frequency noise in M.O.S. field effect transistors," *Solid-State Electronics*, vol. 10, pp. 833–845, August 1967.

58. J. Mavor, "Noise parameters for metal-oxide-semiconductor transistors," *IEE Proceedings*, vol. 113, pp. 1463–1467, September 1967.

59. F. M. Klaassen and J. Prins, "Thermal noise of M.O.S. transistors," *Philips Research Reports*, vol. 22, pp. 505–514, October 1967.

60. G. Abowitz, E. Arnold, and E. Leventhal: "Surface states and 1/f noise in M.O.S. transistors," *IEEE Transactions on Electron Devices*, vol. ED-14, pp. 775–777, November 1967.

61. R. Paul, "Thermisches Rauschen von MOS-Transistoren," *Nachrichtentechnik*, vol. 17, pp. 458–466, December 1967.

62. S. Y. Wu, "Theory of the generation-recombination noise in MOS transistors," *Solid-State Electronics*, vol. 11, pp. 25–32, 1968.

63. I. R. M. Mansour, R. J. Hawkins, and G. G. Bloodworth, "Measurement of current noise in MOS transistors from 5.10^{-5} to 1 Hz," *The Radio and Electronic Engineer*, vol. 35, pp. 212–216, 1968.

64. E. A. Leventhal, "Derivation of 1/f noise in silicon inversion layers from carrier motion in a surface band," *Solid-State Electronics* vol. 11, pp. 621–627, June 1968.

65. A. Leupp and M. J. O. Strutt: "Noise behavior of the MOSFET at VHF and UHF," *Electronics Letters*, vol. 4, pp. 313–314, July 1968.

66. H. E. Halladay and A. van der Ziel, "Test of the thermal noise hypothesis in MOS FETS," *Electronics Letters*, vol. 4, pp. 366–367, August 23, 1968.

67. S. Christensson, I. Lundstrom, and C. Svensson, "Low frequency noise in MOS transistors—I theory," *Solid-State Electronics*, vol. 11, pp. 796–812, September 1968.

68. S. Christensson and I. Lundstrom, "Low frequency noise in MOS transistors—II experiments," *Solid-State Electronics*, vol. 11, pp. 813–820, September 1968.

69. L. D. Yau and C. T. Sah, "Theory and experiments of low-frequency generation recombination noise in MOS transistors," *IEEE Transactions on Electron Devices*, vol. ED-16, pp. 170–177, February 1969.

70. I. R. M. Mansour, R. J. Hawkins, and G. G. Bloodworth, "Physical model for the current noise spectrum of MOSTS," *British Journal of Applied Physics (Journal of Physics D: Applied Physics)* vol. 2, pp. 1063–1082, 1969.

71. H. E. Halladay and A. van der Ziel, "On the high frequency excess noise and equivalent circuit representation of the MOS-FET with n-type channel," *Solid-State Electronics*, vol. 12, pp. 161–176, March 1969.

72. P. S. Rao, "The effect of the substrate upon the gate and drain noise parameters of MOSFETs," *Solid-State Electronics*, vol. 12, pp. 549–556, 1969.

73. L. D. Yau and A. van der Ziel, "Geometrical dependences of the low-frequency generation-recombination noise in MOS transistors," *Solid-State Electronics*, vol. 12, pp. 903–905, 1969.

74. A. Takagi and A. van der Ziel, "Non-thermal noise in MOSFETs and MOS tetrodes," *Solid State Electronics*, vol. 12, p. 907, 1969.

75. N. R. Mantena and R. C. Lucas, "Experimental study of flicker noise in MIS field effect transistors," *Electronics Letters*, vol. 5, pp. 607–608, 1969.

76. F. M. Klaassen and J. Prins, "Noise of field-effect transistors at very high frequencies," *IEEE Transactions on Electron Devices*, vol. ED-16, pp. 952–957, 1969.

77. M. Nakahara, "Anomalous low-frequency noise enhancement in silicon MOS transistors," *Proceedings of the IEEE*, vol. 57, pp. 2177–2178, 1969.

78. L. D. Yau and C. T. Sah, "On the excess 'white noise' in MOS transistors," *Solid-State Electronics*, vol. 12, pp. 927–936, 1969.

79. A. van der Ziel, *Noise: Sources, Characterization, and Measurement*, Prentice-Hall, Englewood Cliffs, N.J., 1970.

80. F. Berz, "Theory of low frequency noise in Si MOSTs," *Solid-State Electronics*, vol. 13, pp. 631–647, 1970.

81. S. T. Hsu, "Surface state related 1/f noise in MOS transistors," *Solid-State Electronics*, vol. 13, pp. 1451–1459, 1970.

82. J. W. Haslett and F. N. Trofimenkoff, "Gate noise in MOSFET's at moderately high frequencies," *Solid-State Electronics*, vol. 14, pp. 239–245, 1971.

83. A. van der Ziel, "Noise resistance of FETs in the hot electron regime," *Solid-State Electronics*, vol. 14, pp 347–350, 1971.

84. J. W. Hawkins and G. G. Bloodworth, "Two components of 1/f noise in MOS transistors," *Solid-State Electronics*, vol. 14, pp. 932–939, 1971.

85. P. S. Rao and A. van der Ziel, "Noise and y parameters in MOSFETs," *Solid-State Electronics*, vol. 14, pp. 939–944, 1971.

86. E. W. Kirk, "Induced gate noise in MOSFETs," *Solid-State Electronics*, vol. 14, pp. 945–948, 1971.

87. F. M. Klaassen, "Characterization of low 1/f noise in MOS transistors," *IEEE Transactions on Electron Devices*, vol. ED-18, pp. 887–891, 1971.

88. J. W. Haslett and F. N. Trofimenkoff, "Effects of the substrate on surface state noise in silicon MOSFETS," *Solid-State Electronics*, vol. 15, pp. 117–131, 1972.

89. H. S. Fu and C. T. Sah, "Theory and experiments on surface 1/f noise," *IEEE Transactions on Electron Devices*, vol. ED-19, pp. 273–285, 1972.

90. R. S. Ronen, "Low-frequency 1/f noise in MOSFETs," *RCA Review*, vol. 34, pp. 280–307, 1973.

91. A. Hayashi and A. van der Ziel, "Correlation coefficient of gate and drain flicker noise," *Solid-State Electronics*, vol. 17, pp. 637–639, 1974.

92. M. B. Das and J. M. Moore, "Measurements and interpretation of low frequency noise in FETS," *IEEE Transactions on Electron Devices*, vol. ED-21, pp. 247–257, 1974.

93. S. T. Hsu and A. van der Ziel, "Thermal noise in ion-implanted MOSFETs," *Solid-State Electronics*, vol. 18, pp. 509–510, 1975.

94. S. T. Hsu and A. van der Ziel, "A new type of flicker noise in microwave MOSFETs," *Solid-State Electronics*, vol. 18, pp. 885–886, 1975.

95. K. Nakamura, O. Kudoh, and M. Kamoshida, "Noise characteristics of ion-implanted MOS transistors," *Journal of Applied Physics*, vol. 46, pp. 3189–3193, 1975.

96. H. Katto, Y. Kamigaki, and Y. Itoh, "MOSFETs with reduced low frequency 1/f noise," *Japanese Journal of Applied Physics*, vol. 44, pp. 243–248, 1975.

97. S. T. Hsu, "Trapping noise in SOSMOST'S. " *Fourth International Conference on Physical Aspects of Noise in Solid State Devices*, Noordwijkerhout, The Netherlands, 1975.

98. A. van der Ziel, "Limiting flicker noise in MOSFETs," *Solid-State Electronics*, vol. 18, p. 1031, 1975.

99. F. N. Hooge, "1/f noise," *Physica*, vol. 83B, pp. 14–23, 1976.

100. W. Fichtner, E. Hochmair, and D. Kranzer, "Noise measurements on SOSMOS transistors," *European Solid-State Device Research Conference*, Munich, September, 1976.

101. A. van der Ziel, "Dependence of flicker noise in MOSFET's on geometry," *Solid-State Electronics*, vol. 20, p. 267, 1977.

102. W. Fichtner and E. Hochmair, "Current-kink noise of n-channel enhancement ESFI MOS SOS transistors," *Electronics Letters*, vol. 13, pp. 675–676, 1977.

103. P. Gentil and S. Chausse, "Low-frequency measurement on silicon-on-sapphire (SOS) MOS transistors," *Solid-State Electronics*, vol. 20, pp. 935–940, 1977.

104. K. Takagi and K. Matsumoto, "Noise in silicon and FET's at high electric fields," *Solid-State Electronics*, vol. 20, pp. 1–3, 1977.

105. W. A. Baril, "High-frequency thermal noise in MOSFETs," *Solid-State Electronics*, vol. 21, pp. 589–592, 1978.

106. K. L. Wang, "Measurements of residual defects and 1/f noise in ion-implanted p-channel MOSFETs," *IEEE Transactions on Electron Devices*, vol. ED-25, pp. 478–484, 1978.

107. A. van der Ziel, "Some general relationships for flicker noise in MOSFETs," *Solid-State Electronics*, vol. 21, pp. 623–624, 1978.

108. R. P. Jindal and A. van der Ziel. "Carrier fluctuations noise in a MOSFET channel due to traps in the oxide," *Solid-State Electronics*, vol. 21, pp. 901–903, 1978.

109. P. Gentil, "Bruit bass fréquence du transistor MOS—1ere partie," *L'onde électrique*, vol. 58, pp. 565–575, August–September 1978.

110. P. Gentil, "Bruit bass fréquence du transistor MOS—2e partie," *L'onde électrique*, vol. 58, pp. 645–652, October 1978.

111. J. Fellrath, "Shot noise behavior of subthreshold MOS transistors," *Revue de Physique Appliqué*, vol. 13, pp. 719–723, December 1978.

112. P. Victorovich and P. Gentil, "Influence of the depth of interface states in the insulator on the noise properties of MOS transistors," *Solid-State Electronics*, vol. 22, pp. 21–23, 1979.

113. K. Takagi and A. van der Ziel, "Drain noise in MOSFETS at zero drain bias as a function of temperature," *Solid-State Electronics*, vol. 22, pp. 87–88, 1979.

114. K. Takagi and A. van der Ziel, "Excess high frequency noise and flicker noise in MOS-FETs," *Solid-State Electronics*, vol. 22, pp. 289–292, 1979.

115. W. V. Backensto and C. R. Viswanathan, "Bias-dependent 1/f noise model of an m.o.s. transistor," *IEE Proceedings*, vol. 127, part I, pp. 87–93, April 1980.

116. L. K. J. Vandamme and H. M. M. de Werd, "1/f noise model for MOST's biased in nonohmic region," *Solid-State Electronics*, vol. 23, pp. 325–329, 1980.

117. L. K. J. Vandamme, "Model for 1/f noise in MOS transistors biased in the linear region," *Solid-State Electronics*, vol. 23, pp. 317–323, 1980.

118. S. T. Liu and A. van der Ziel, "High-frequency noise in weakly inverted metal-oxide-semiconductor transistors," *Applied Physics Letters*, vol. 37, pp. 950–951, 1980.

119. P. Gentil and A. Mounib, "Equivalent input spectrum and drain current spectrum for $1/f$ noise in short channel MOS transistors," *Solid-State Electronics*, vol. 24, pp. 411–414, 1981.
120. R. P. Jindal and A. van der Ziel, "Effect of transverse electric field on Nyquist noise," *Solid-State Electronics*, vol. 24, pp. 905–906, 1981.
121. H. S. Park, A. van der Ziel, and S. T. Liu, "Comparison of two $1/f$ noise models in MOSFET's," *Solid-State Electronics*, vol. 23, pp. 213–217, 1982.
122. H. Mikoshiba, "1/f noise in n-channel silicon-gate MOS transistors," *IEEE Transactions on Electron Devices*, vol. ED-29, pp. 965–970, June 1982.
123. G. Reimbold and P. Gentil, "White noise of MOS transistors operating in weak inversion," *IEEE Transactions on Electron Devices*, vol. Ed-29, pp. 1722–1725, November 1982.
124. H. S. Park and A. van der Ziel, "Noise measurements in ion implanted MOSFETs," *Solid-State Electronics*, vol. 26, pp. 747–751, 1983.
125. A. van der Ziel, R. J. J. Zijstra, H. S. Park, and S. T. Liu, "Alternate explanation of $1/f$ noise in ion-implanted MOSFETs," *Solid-State Electronics*, vol. 26, pp. 927–928, 1983.
126. A. Ambrozy, *Electronic Noise*, McGraw-Hill, New York, 1982.
127. S. A. Hayat and B. K. Jones, "Thermal noise in inversion layers," *Solid-State Electronics*, vol. 27, pp. 687–688, 1984.
128. G. Reimbold, "Modified $1/f$ trapping noise theory and experiments in MOS transistors biased from weak to strong inversion—influence of interface states," *IEEE Transactions on Electron Devices*, vol. ED-31, pp. 1190–1198, September 1984.
129. J. M. Pimbley and G. Gildenblat, "Effect of hot-electron stress on low frequency MOSFET noise," *IEEE Electron Device Letters*, vol. EDL-5, pp. 345–347, September 1984.
130. R. P. Jindal, "Noise associated with distributed resistance of MOSFET gate structures in integrated circuits," *IEEE Transactions on Electron Devices*, vol. ED-31, pp. 1505–1509, October 1984.
131. R. P. Jindal, "Distributed substrate resistance noise in fine-line NMOS field-effect transistors," *IEEE Transactions on Electron Devices*, vol. ED-32, pp. 2450–2453, November 1985.
132. Z Celik and T. Y. Hsiang, "Study of $1/f$ noise in N-MOSFETs: linear region," *IEEE Transactions on Electron Devices*, vol. ED-32, pp. 2797–2802, December 1985.
133. R. P. Jindal, "High frequency noise in fine line NMOS field effect transistors," *Technical Digest*, IEEE International Electron Devices Meeting, Washington, D.C., pp. 68–71, 1985.
134. A. van der Ziel, "Integral expression for $1/f$ noise in MOSFETs at arbitrary drain bias," *Solid-State Electronics*, vol. 29, pp. 29–30, 1986.
135. E.A. Vittoz, private communication.

PROBLEMS

8.1. Restate the definitions of g_m, g_{mb}, and g_d in terms of voltages V_G, V_B, V_D, and V_S, all taken with respect to an arbitrary reference. Put these in a form as simple as possible.

8.2. Estimate g_m, g_{mb}, and g_d *graphically* from the data in Fig. P4.25, for an operating point of $V_{GS} = 6$ V, $V_{DS} = 8$ V, and $V_{SB} = 1$ V. What accuracy can be expected from such an estimation?

8.3. For an *n*-channel device in strong inversion with $V_{T0} = 1$ V, $V_{SB} = 0$ V, $(W/L)\mu C'_{ox} = 30$ μA/V^2, and $\delta = 0.5$, plot: (*a*) g_m vs. V_{GS} with V_{DS} as a parameter, (*b*) g_m vs. V_{DS} with V_{GS} as a parameter.

8.4. Prove (8.2.6) to (8.2.8).

8.5. Assume that the effective mobility varies with V_{GS} according to (4.8.18), with $\theta_B = 0$. Show how (8.2.6) should be modified to take this effect into account.

8.6. Prove (8.2.10) to (8.2.12). Verify that (8.2.13) is a good approximation to (8.2.11), and verify (8.2.14).

8.7. Choose model parameters to fit the values of g_d shown in Fig. 8.5 (saturation region only), using the model of (8.2.25). Comment on the results.

8.8. For a given I_D and V_{SB}, state qualitatively what will happen to the ratios g_{mb}/g_m and g_d/g_m if: (a) the substrate doping is increased; (b) the channel length is increased.

8.9. Prove (8.2.32) and (8.2.33).

8.10. Find g_m, g_{mb}, and g_d for the short-channel model of Example 5.4.

8.11. Show that an appropriate "charge sharing" model (Sec. 5.4) can predict an increase of g_d in saturation with increasing drain junction depth, other things being equal.

8.12. Show that the simple models in Sec. 8.2 predict a saturation g_d which varies roughly as I_D for long-channel devices, and as $\sqrt{I_D}$ for short-channel devices. (For the latter, assume no velocity saturation and neglect channel length modulation.) Note that this result is based on greatly simplified assumptions, so it should be taken with a grain of salt.

8.13. Prove (8.2.35) to (8.2.38).

8.14. Using the equivalent small-signal circuit of Fig. 8.13, perform all "measurements" illustrated in Figs. 8.1 and Fig. 8.11b, c, and d. Show that in each case the elements do not interfere with each other, i.e., the results given next to each figure are still obtained.

8.15. Prove (8.3.8) to (8.3.12) using the simplifying assumptions stated above them.

8.16. Plot C_{bs}, C_{bd}, and C_{gb} for the device of Fig. 8.14 and for the same bias conditions, using δ_s from (8.3.14) in lieu of δ_1. Choose k_c for good accuracy of C_{bs} in the saturation region. Compare to the results shown by the broken lines in Fig. 8.14.

8.17. Show that, for the device of Fig. 8.15, assuming V_D and V_S are almost equal, a very small charge ΔV of V_S only will decrease the gate charge by $\frac{1}{2} C_{ox} \Delta V$.

8.18. Derive the results in (8.3.27) to (8.3.31) by differentiating the saturation charge expressions (7.4.26) and (7.4.30), using the simplifying assumptions made in Sec. 8.3 (i.e., that $\delta = \delta_1$ and that the variation of δ_1 with V_S and V_B is negligible).

8.19. Show that (7.4.21) and (7.4.25) *cannot* be used in the capacitance definitions to derive (8.3.16) and (8.3.17). Explain the reasons for this.

8.20. For the device of Prob. 8.3 operating in strong inversion, plot all capacitances (a) vs. V_{GS}, with V_{DS} as a parameter, and (b) vs. V_{DS}, with V_{GS} as a parameter.

8.21. Prove (8.3.35).

8.22. Prove (8.3.38). [*Hint*: Use (4.6.9), (4.6.13), and the fact that, at the upper limit of weak inversion, $\psi_s \approx 2\phi_F + V_{SB}$ (Sec. 3.4.1).]

8.23. Derive (8.5.10), assuming Δv is very small.

8.24. Prove (8.5.20).

8.25. (a) For a transistor in saturation, with $\mu = 70 \ \mu m^2/(V \cdot ns)$, $C'_{ox} = 0.4 \ fF/\mu m^2$, $\delta = 0.4$, $W = L = 10 \mu m$, $V_T = 1$ V, and $V_{GS} = 3$ V, evaluate $\overline{\Delta i_t^2}/\Delta f$, $\overline{\Delta v_{in,t}^2}/\Delta f$, and R_n at $T = 200$, 300, and 400 K.
(b) Find the mean square value of the thermal noise current for the above device at 300 K, in the band from 100 to 200 kHz.

8.26. The MOS transistor is sometimes modeled by a noiseless transistor with a noise voltage source in series with its gate, representing the equivalent input noise voltage. Show that, if the device is driven by a signal source (between gate and source) with a significant internal resistance, the above model will only be adequate for calculating the noise current at low frequencies.

8.27. Prove (8.5.23) to (8.5.26) as well as the claims in the footnote following (8.5.24).

8.28. A transistor is operating in weak inversion at $T = 300$ K, with $I'_D = 10$ nA, and $n = 1.5$. Plot $\overline{\Delta i_t^2}/\Delta f$, $\overline{\Delta v_{in,t}^2}/\Delta f$, and R_n vs. V_{DS}.

8.29. The device of Prob. 8.25, operating at $T = 300$ K, exhibits a "corner frequency" f_c (see Fig. 8.25) of 4 kHZ. Assuming $a = 2$ in (8.5.27), find the value of M. Calculate the mean square value of the total current noise (flicker plus thermal) in the band of 20 Hz to 200 kHz.

8.30. Develop an expression for an equivalent input noise resistance representing both thermal and flicker noise in strong inversion.

9.1 INTRODUCTION

In this chapter we study models that are valid in a wider frequency range than the five-capacitance quasi-static model of Chap. 8.[1-39] The first model considered is what will be called the *complete quasi-static* model. This model represents an attempt to take every possible advantage of the quasi-static assumption, and gives an improved upper frequency limit of validity. Beyond that limit, though, the model becomes very inaccurate. It is then necessary to consider *nonquasi-static* models by taking into account "transmission line" effects. Such nonquasi-static models will be considered after a general discussion of y-parameter models. The chapter will conclude with a comparison of all models presented, and a justification of the limits of validity suggested for them.

All effects considered in this chapter will be understood to be for the *intrinsic* part of the transistor (see Fig. 7.1) unless stated otherwise.

9.2 A COMPLETE QUASI-STATIC MODEL

9.2.1 Complete Description of Capacitance Effects

In Sec. 8.3, we assumed quasi-static operation (defined in Sec. 7.2), and, we modeled the capacitance effect of the drain, source, and substrate on the gate, and the effects of the drain and source on the substrate. Clearly, we did not consider all possible combinations in choosing the above five effects. Nevertheless, the model was claimed to be satisfactory for many applications up to a certain frequency. We will now undertake the rigorous development of a *complete* quasi-static model. The model will be complete in the sense that the capacitance effect of *every* terminal on *every* other will be modeled.[18, 28–37, 39]

Consider an intrinsic transistor with time-varying voltages, as shown in Fig. 9.1*a*. Lowercase letters with capital subscripts denote *total* quantities (as opposed to bias or small-signal quantities). In Sec. 7.3 we showed how the transport and charging components of the drain and source currents in quasi-static operation can be evaluated. The meaning of the charging component is rather subtle, and was discussed at length. The gate and substrate currents consist only of charging components. The four charging currents satisfy (7.3.15), and are given by (7.3.16*a*)–(7.3.16*d*). We now assume that the total voltages consist of a dc bias part and a small-signal part, as shown in Fig. 9.1*b*. Bias quantities will be represented by capital symbols with capital subscripts; small-signal quantities will be represented by lowercase symbols with lowercase subscripts. If the small signals $v_d(t) = v_g(t) = v_b(t) = v_s(t) = 0$, for all t, then $dv_D/dt = dv_G/dt = dv_B/dt = dv_S/dt = 0$, and thus all currents in (7.3.16) are zero. If the small-signal voltages are nonzero but vary sufficiently

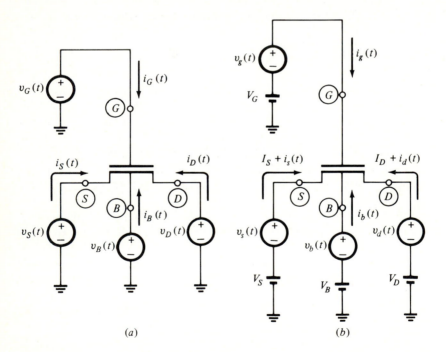

(a)   (b)

FIGURE 9.1
(*a*) A transistor with four time-varying terminal voltages; (*b*) a transistor with terminal voltages consisting of a dc bias plus a time-varying small signal.

slowly, then all charging currents in (7.3.16) will be small. They will be represented by $i_{dc}(t)$, $i_g(t)$, $i_b(t)$, and $i_{sc}(t)$. Over the small range of variation of the small-signal voltages, the slopes of the form $\partial q_X / \partial v_Y$, where q_X is any of the four charges and v_Y any of the voltages in (7.3.16), will be assumed constant and equal to their values at the bias point ($v_D = V_D$, $v_G = V_G$, $v_B = V_B$, $v_S = V_S$). Denoting evaluation at this point by "o", we define

$$C_{kk} = + \left. \frac{\partial q_K}{\partial v_K} \right|_o \tag{9.2.1a}$$

$$C_{kl} = - \left. \frac{\partial q_K}{\partial v_L} \right|_o, \qquad l \neq k \tag{9.2.1b}$$

The choice of the algebraic signs in the above definitions is common. It will prove convenient in developing small-signal equivalent circuits later in this section, and in relating these circuits to the ones in Sec. 8.3. The above choice is consistent with (8.3.1)–(8.3.5), the negative sign of which was discussed above (8.3.1) (see also Prob. 9.1).

Of the capacitances parameters defined above, five (C_{gs}, C_{bs}, C_{gd}, C_{bd}, and C_{gb}) have precisely the meaning discussed in Sec. 8.3. Ways to measure C_{kk} and C_{kl} will be considered in the next section. Using the above definitions, we have, from (7.3.16) and the above discussion, the following expressions for the small-signal charging curents:

$$i_{dc}(t) = + C_{dd} \frac{dv_d}{dt} - C_{dg} \frac{dv_g}{dt} - C_{db} \frac{dv_b}{dt} - C_{ds} \frac{dv_s}{dt} \tag{9.2.2a}$$

$$i_g(t) = - C_{gd} \frac{dv_d}{dt} + C_{gg} \frac{dv_g}{dt} - C_{gb} \frac{dv_b}{dt} - C_{gs} \frac{dv_s}{dt} \tag{9.2.2b}$$

$$i_b(t) = - C_{bd} \frac{dv_d}{dt} - C_{bg} \frac{dv_g}{dt} + C_{bb} \frac{dv_b}{dt} - C_{bs} \frac{dv_s}{dt} \tag{9.2.2c}$$

$$i_{sc}(t) = - C_{sd} \frac{dv_d}{dt} - C_{sg} \frac{dv_g}{dt} - C_{sb} \frac{dv_b}{dt} + C_{ss} \frac{dv_s}{dt} \tag{9.2.2d}$$

It will be helpful in this discussion not to associate the various capacitance parameters above with any physical capacitor-like structures in the MOS transistor. It is better to consider them for the present as simply quantities defined in the precise manner of (9.2.1). We note here that in general $C_{kl} \neq C_{lk}$. For example, consider a long-channel device in saturation. Varying the voltage at the drain will not affect the rest of the device because of pinchoff (assuming no channel-length modulation). Hence, the gate charge will not change [see (7.4.30)], and, from (9.2.1b), C_{gd} will be zero. However, varying the *gate* voltage will change the inversion layer charge. As explained in Sec. 7.3, this change will be accomplished in part by the drain current temporarily becoming different from the transport value. The difference under small-signal conditions is $i_{dc}(t)$ and (assuming all other voltages are kept constant) is equal to $-C_{dg}(dv_g/dt)$ from (9.2.2a), which can only be nonzero if $C_{dg} \neq 0$. Another way to see this is to observe that the charge "associated with the drain"† *does* depend on the gate voltage even in saturation [see (7.4.28)]. Thus, from (9.2.1b), $C_{dg} \neq 0$. Therefore, it is seen that $C_{gd} \neq C_{dg}$, and this can be verified by measurements, as will be shown. This fact may seem strange at first, because we may have a tendency to think of C_{gd} and C_{dg} as the capacitances of two-terminal capacitors between gate and drain. However, such an interpretation is *not* correct. C_{gd} represents the effect of the drain on the gate, and C_{dg} represents the effect of the gate on the drain, in terms of charging currents. There is no reason to expect that the two effects are the same in general, just as there is no reason to expect that, at dc, the effect of the drain on the gate current (which is zero assuming no leakage) is the same as the effect of the gate on the drain current (which can be large). We will expand on this point later on.

We now make some important observations about the capacitance parameters and (9.2.2). First, assume that $v_d(t) = v_g(t) = v_b(t) = v_s(t) = v(t)$ in Fig. 9.1b. This is equivalent to the situation shown in Fig. 9.2. From (9.2.2a) we will have

$$i_{dc}(t) = (C_{dd} - C_{dg} - C_{db} - C_{ds}) \frac{dv}{dt} \tag{9.2.3}$$

However, since there is no small-signal voltage across any two of the

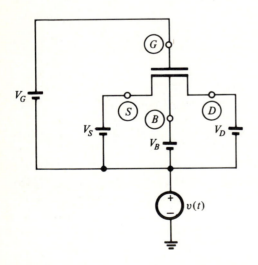

FIGURE 9.2
A transistor with all four terminal small-signal voltages equal.

---

† To appreciate the points made here requires a careful interpretation of the term "charge associated with the drain." This term can easily be misinterpreted. A related extensive discussion, which is *very* relevant to our present topic, has been given in Sec. 7.3.

terminals in Fig. 9.2, all terminal small-signal currents must be zero. Since this must be true even for nonzero dv/dt, (9.2.3) implies that

$$C_{dd} - C_{dg} - C_{db} - C_{ds} = 0 \qquad (9.2.4)$$

As follows from (7.3.15), the small-signal charging currents must add up to zero:

$$i_{dc}(t) + i_g(t) + i_b(t) + i_{sc}(t) = 0 \qquad (9.2.5)$$

Let us now assume $dv_g/dt = dv_b/dt = dv_s/dt = 0$. Using this in (9.2.2) and the results in (9.2.5), we have

$$(C_{dd} - C_{gd} - C_{bd} - C_{sd}) \frac{dv_d}{dt} = 0 \qquad (9.2.6)$$

which, since it must be valid even for nonzero dv_d/dt, implies that

$$C_{dd} - C_{gd} - C_{bd} - C_{sd} = 0 \qquad (9.2.7)$$

Equations (9.2.4) and (9.2.7) provide two expressions for C_{dd} in terms of other capacitance parameters. Similar expressions can be derived in the same manner for C_{gg}, C_{bb}, and C_{ss}. Thus, we have

$$C_{dd} = C_{dg} + C_{db} + C_{ds} = C_{gd} + C_{bd} + C_{sd} \qquad (9.2.8a)$$

$$C_{gg} = C_{gd} + C_{gb} + C_{gs} = C_{dg} + C_{bg} + C_{sg} \qquad (9.2.8b)$$

$$C_{bb} = C_{bd} + C_{bg} + C_{bs} = C_{db} + C_{gb} + C_{sb} \qquad (9.2.8c)$$

$$C_{ss} = C_{sd} + C_{sg} + C_{sb} = C_{ds} + C_{gs} + C_{bs} \qquad (9.2.8d)$$

An interesting result that can be derived from these equations is considered in Prob. 9.2.

Our next observation is simply that, if three of the small-signal charging currents are known, the fourth can be determined from (9.2.5). Thus, any one among the four equations (9.2.2) can be omitted without losing any information. We will omit the last equation from now on.

Without loss of generality, we can write (see Fig. 9.3)

$$v_D = v_{DS} + v_S \qquad (9.2.9a)$$

$$v_G = v_{GS} + v_S \qquad (9.2.9b)$$

$$v_B = v_{BS} + v_S \qquad (9.2.9c)$$

Using analogous expressions for the small-signal voltages in (9.2.2a) gives:

$$i_{dc}(t) = C_{dd} \frac{dv_{ds}}{dt} - C_{dg} \frac{dv_{gs}}{dt} - C_{db} \frac{dv_{bs}}{dt} + (C_{dd} - C_{dg} - C_{db} - C_{ds}) \frac{dv_s}{dt}$$

$$(9.2.10)$$

The quantity in parenthesis is equal to zero, as can be seen from (9.2.8a). Thus,

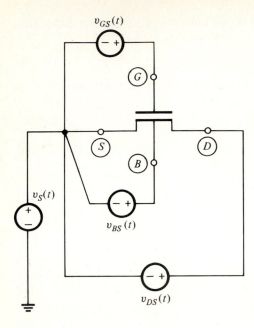

FIGURE 9.3
A transistor with terminal voltages referenced to the source.

$$i_{dc}(t) = C_{dd} \frac{dv_{ds}}{dt} - C_{dg} \frac{dv_{gs}}{dt} - C_{db} \frac{dv_{bs}}{dt} \qquad (9.2.11)$$

Similar relations can be obtained from (9.2.2b) and (9.2.2c). Equation (9.2.2d) will not be considered anymore, as explained above. Thus, we finally obtain

$$i_{dc}(t) = +C_{dd} \frac{dv_{ds}}{dt} - C_{dg} \frac{dv_{gs}}{dt} - C_{db} \frac{dv_{bs}}{dt} \qquad (9.2.12a)$$

$$i_{g}(t) = -C_{gd} \frac{dv_{ds}}{dt} + C_{gg} \frac{dv_{gs}}{dt} - C_{gb} \frac{dv_{bs}}{dt} \qquad (9.2.12b)$$

$$i_{b}(t) = -C_{bd} \frac{dv_{ds}}{dt} - C_{bg} \frac{dv_{gs}}{dt} + C_{bb} \frac{dv_{bs}}{dt} \qquad (9.2.12c)$$

It is thus clear from the above discussion that a complete small-signal description of the charging mechanisms requires no less (and no more) than *nine* independent capacitance parameters.

9.2.2 Small-Signal Equivalent Circuit Topologies

Small-signal equivalent circuits can be derived to represent (9.2.12). There is no end to the number of such circuits that can be constructed; the most straightforward one is shown in Fig. 9.4a. This circuit can be verified by writing Kirchhoff's current law for terminals g, d, and b, resulting in (9.2.12). We do not yet have a complete model for the transistor though, because the transport

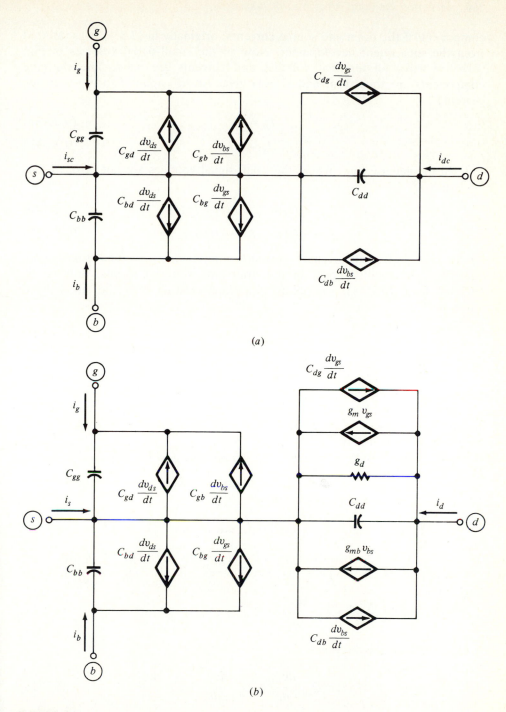

FIGURE 9.4
(a) A small-signal equivalent circuit for the charging current action; (b) a complete quasi-static model resulting from (a) by adding the transport current modeling elements of Fig. 8.2.

component of the drain and source currents, originally in (7.3.4), was omitted from the subsequent development. Now, if the small-signal voltages in Fig. 9.1*b* are zero, all terminal voltages and currents are fixed. The charging components are thus zero, and (7.3.4) gives (using capital I to represent dc current)

$$I_D = I_T \tag{9.2.13a}$$

$$I_S = -I_T \tag{9.2.13b}$$

In the general case, where the small-signal voltages are not zero, (7.3.4) leads to

$$I_D + i_d(t) = I_T + i_t(t) + i_{dc}(t) \tag{9.2.14a}$$

$$I_S + i_s(t) = -I_T - i_t(t) + i_{sc}(t) \tag{9.2.14b}$$

where now both small-signal transport components $i_t(t)$ and small-signal charging components appear in the drain and source currents. Subtracting (9.2.13) from (9.2.14), we obtain equations relating only the small-signal currents:

$$i_d(t) = i_t(t) + i_{dc}(t) \tag{9.2.15a}$$

$$i_s(t) = -i_t(t) + i_{sc}(t) \tag{9.2.15b}$$

The small-signal transport current has been modeled by the three-element combination of Fig. 8.2. Since this current *adds* to the charging currents in (9.2.15), the corresponding part of the model of Fig. 8.2 should be added in *parallel* with the rest of the elements between drain and source in Fig. 9.4*a* to arrive at the complete model of Fig. 9.4*b*.

A different small-signal equivalent circuit will now be derived. Let us use

$$v_{ds} = v_{dg} + v_{gs} = -v_{gd} + v_{gs} \tag{9.2.16a}$$

$$v_{bs} = v_{bg} + v_{gs} = -v_{gb} + v_{gs} \tag{9.2.16b}$$

Substituting these equations in (9.2.12b), we obtain

$$i_g(t) = -C_{gd}\left(-\frac{dv_{gd}}{dt} + \frac{dv_{gs}}{dt}\right) + C_{gg}\frac{dv_{gs}}{dt} - C_{gb}\left(-\frac{dv_{gb}}{dt} + \frac{dv_{gs}}{dt}\right)$$

$$= C_{gd}\frac{dv_{gd}}{dt} + C_{gb}\frac{dv_{gb}}{dt} + (C_{gg} - C_{gd} - C_{gb})\frac{dv_{gs}}{dt} \tag{9.2.17}$$

Using (9.2.8b), this becomes

$$i_g(t) = C_{gd}\frac{dv_{gd}}{dt} + C_{gb}\frac{dv_{gb}}{dt} + C_{gs}\frac{dv_{gs}}{dt} \tag{9.2.18}$$

Using similar manipulations in (9.2.12a) and (9.2.12c), (9.2.12) can be written in the form

$$i_{dc}(t) = C_{gd}\frac{dv_{dg}}{dt} + C_{sd}\frac{dv_{ds}}{dt} + C_{bd}\frac{dv_{db}}{dt} - C_m\frac{dv_{gs}}{dt} - C_{mb}\frac{dv_{bs}}{dt} \qquad (9.2.19a)$$

$$i_g(t) = C_{gd}\frac{dv_{gd}}{dt} + C_{gb}\frac{dv_{gb}}{dt} + C_{gs}\frac{dv_{gs}}{dt} \qquad (9.2.19b)$$

$$i_b(t) = C_{bd}\frac{dv_{bd}}{dt} + C_{gb}\frac{dv_{bg}}{dt} - C_{mx}\frac{dv_{gb}}{dt} + C_{bs}\frac{dv_{bs}}{dt} \qquad (9.2.19c)$$

where

$$C_m = C_{dg} - C_{gd} \qquad (9.2.20a)$$

$$C_{mb} = C_{db} - C_{bd} \qquad (9.2.20b)$$

$$C_{mx} = C_{bg} - C_{gb} \qquad (9.2.20c)$$

Equation (9.2.19b) has already been proved. To prove (9.2.19a) and (9.2.19c), simply express all voltages in these equations in terms of v_{ds}, v_{gs}, and v_{bs} and use (9.2.20) and (9.2.8); this will give (9.2.12a) and (9.2.12c).

Equations (9.2.19) are easily represented by an equivalent circuit. When the elements of Fig. 8.2 are added to it, we obtain the result shown in Fig. 9.5.[36] Five capacitors shown in this figure (C_{gs}, C_{gd}, C_{bs}, C_{bd}, and C_{gb}) are exactly the same as those in the model of Fig. 8.13. In other words, the model of Fig. 9.5 can be viewed as resulting from simply *augmenting* the model of Fig. 8.13 by four more elements, but *without* having to modify the elements already in that popular model, neither in meaning nor in value. This is an important property of the model in Fig. 9.5, in contrast to other models proposed in the literature. This point is considered further in Probs. 9.5 and 9.6. Note that at sufficiently low frequencies dv_{gs}/dt and dv_{bs}/dt will be small, and the currents proportional to these quantities can be neglected in comparison to the currents $g_m v_{gs}$ and $g_{mb} v_{bs}$, respectively. Similarly, the current through C_{sd} can then be neglected in comparison to the current through g_d. Finally, we will find below that for the approximate strong-inversion model $C_{mx} = 0$. Thus, the model of Fig. 9.5 reduces to that of Fig. 8.13 at sufficiently low frequencies. More on model comparison will be found later in this chapter.

To provide more feeling for the model in Fig. 9.5, we will consider two experiments, as illustrated in Fig. 9.6. In a, a small-signal voltage is applied only at the drain, and the resulting small-signal current entering the gate is observed; in b, the opposite is done. The small-signal equivalent circuit used in each case on the right is that of Fig. 9.5, but only elements with nonzero current through them are shown for simplicity (short-circuited capacitances or resistances, and current sources proportional to zero voltages are omitted). As seen in a, the small-signal current entering the gate is $-C_{gd}(dv_d/dt)$. Thus, C_{gd} actually represents the effect of terminal d on terminal g. However, although the capacitance C_{gd} is connected between g and d in the general case, it *does not* represent the total effect of g on d. This can be seen in b. Indeed, the current entering the drain is $g_m v_g - (C_{gd} + C_m)(dv_g/dt)$. Note that not only is there a conductive current here but also the capacitive current is *different* from

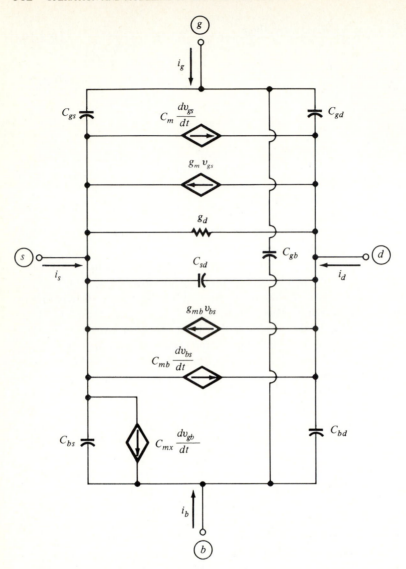

FIGURE 9.5
A complete quasi-static small-signal model. Although independently derived, the model can be viewed as resulting from the simpler model of Fig. 8.13 by adding four elements to it.

that in a. Thus, $C_{gd} + C_m$ represents the capacitive effect of g on d. From (9.2.20a), $C_{gd} + C_m = C_{dg}$, which, in general, is *different* from C_{gd}, as we have already argued, and as we will see quantitatively in the following subsection. C_m is then a *transcapacitance*, taking care of the different effect of the gate and drain on each other in terms of charging currents, just as g_m is a transconduct- ance taking care of the different effect of these two terminals on each other in terms of transport currents. Similar comments hold for C_{mb} and C_{mx}.

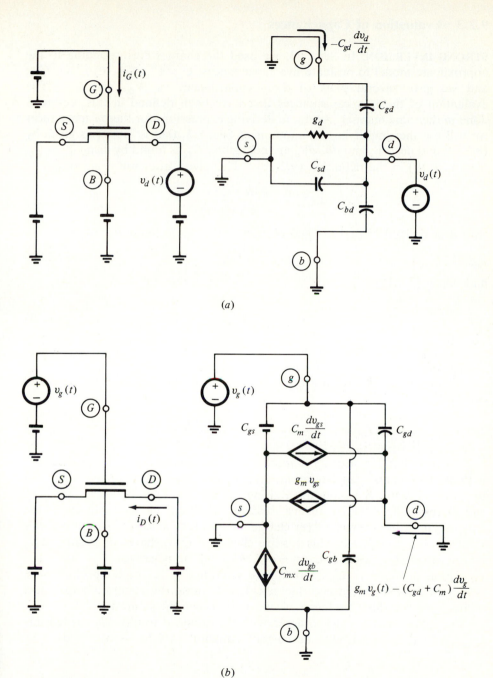

(a)

(b)

FIGURE 9.6
Illustration of the way in which the different effect of the gate and drain on each other is taken into account in the model of Fig. 9.5. (a) effect of drain voltage on gate circuit; (b) effect of gate voltage on drain current.

9.2.3   Evaluation of Capacitances

STRONG INVERSION. In Sec. 8.3, we used the charges corresponding to the approximate model to evaluate five capacitances: C_{gs}, C_{bs}, C_{gd}, C_{bd}, and C_{gb}, and we gave several plots of these capacitances vs. V_{DS} and V_{GS}. The evaluation of the new capacitances that have been defined in this section is done in the same manner. Again, in deriving expressions for these capacitances we will use the simplifying assumptions of Sec. 8.3, that is, $\delta = \delta_1$ as given by (8.3.7), and $d\delta_1/dV_S$ and $d\delta_1/dV_B$ are negligible. C_{dg} is found by using $q_D = Q_D$ from (7.4.19) in the definition (9.2.1b).† This gives, after much algebra,

$$C_{dg} = C_{ox} \frac{4 + 28\alpha + 22\alpha^2 + 6\alpha^3}{15(1+\alpha)^3} \tag{9.2.21}$$

with α as defined in (4.4.31) and plotted in Fig. 4.13. Similarly, we find:

$$C_{db} = \delta_1 C_{dg} \tag{9.2.22}$$

and, using (7.4.15),

$$C_{bg} = \frac{\delta_1}{3(1+\delta_1)} C_{ox} \left(\frac{1-\alpha}{1+\alpha}\right)^2 \tag{9.2.23}$$

Comparing the last equation to (8.3.12), we see that, for the approximate model with the simplifying assumptions we have made, $C_{bg} = C_{gb}$.

To evaluate C_{sd}, we use Q_S from (7.4.20) in the definition (9.2.1b) and obtain

$$C_{sd} = -\left[\frac{4}{15} C_{ox}(1+\delta_1) \frac{\alpha + 3\alpha^2 + \alpha^3}{(1+\alpha)^3}\right] \tag{9.2.24}$$

Notice that this quantity is *negative* in nonsaturation. This is in agreement with measurements[32] (in saturation, C_{sd} becomes zero). The negative value can be viewed intuitively as follows. Raising the drain voltage by an amount ΔV_D will increase the effective reverse bias at the drain end and will cause the magnitude of the inversion layer charge to decrease. Since Q_I is negative, this means a change $\Delta Q_I > 0$. This positive change in Q_I is shared by positive ΔQ_S and positive ΔQ_D. Hence, $C_{sd} = -\partial Q_S/\partial V_D$ will be negative.

Plots of C_{sd}, C_{dg}, C_{db}, and C_{bg} are given in Fig. 9.7 by the broken lines. The solid lines represent accurate calculations using the general charge sheet model.[36] As was done for Fig. 8.14, we have chosen the saturation voltage V'_{DS} for the approximate model to agree with the accurate results. This is feasible since δ in the approximate dc current equation (4.4.30) is assumed to be

---

† The charges and voltages in Sec. 7.4 were assumed to be dc quantities. As before, we will use the expressions developed in that section, with Q replaced by q and V replaced by v, under the assumption of quasi-static operation (Sec. 7.2).

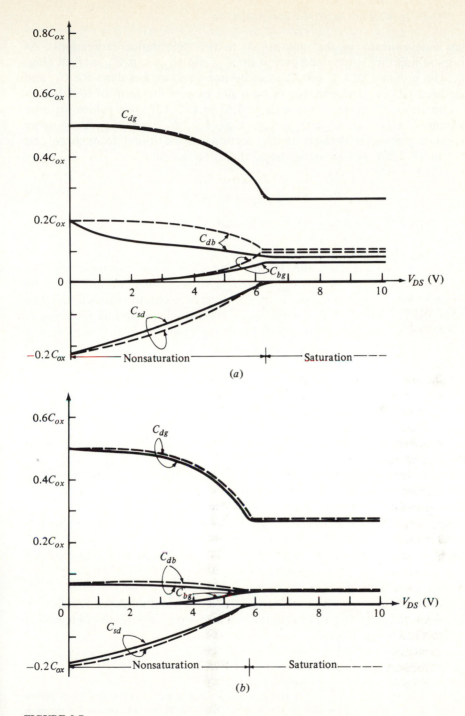

FIGURE 9.7
Drain-gate, drain-substrate, source-drain, and substrate-gate small-signal capacitances vs. V_{DS} for a device with $N_A = 1700 \ \mu m^{-3}$, $d_{ox} = 0.1 \ \mu m$, $V_{T0} = 0.476 \ V$, and $V_{GS} = 8 \ V$. Solid lines: accurate model;[36] broken lines: simple model presented in this section. (a) $V_{SB} = 0$; (b) $V_{SB} = 5 \ V$.

chosen *independently* of the quantity δ_1 in the capacitance expressions. As seen, good accuracy is obtained except for C_{db} and C_{bg} when V_{SB} is small (Fig. 9.7a). The accuracy of C_{db} and C_{bg} can be improved as was done for C_{bs} and C_{bd} in Sec. 8.3, i.e., by replacing δ_1 by a function of the form of (8.3.14).

The above relations, along with (8.3.8) to (8.3.12), give values for nine capacitances: C_{gs}, C_{bs}, C_{gd}, C_{dg}, C_{bd}, C_{db}, C_{gb}, C_{bg}, and C_{sd}. Any other capacitance parameter defined in this section can be found from these and (9.2.8) or (9.2.20). For example, using the latter we find

$$C_m = \frac{4}{15} C_{ox} \frac{1 + 2\alpha - 2\alpha^2 - \alpha^3}{(1 + \alpha)^3} \tag{9.2.25}$$

$$C_{mb} = \delta_1 C_m \tag{9.2.26}$$

$$C_{mx} = 0 \tag{9.2.27}$$

Thus, we have expressions for all nine capacitance parameters in the model of Fig. 9.5. Plots of C_m, C_{mb}, and C_{mx} vs. V_{DS} are given in Fig. 9.8 by the broken lines; again, the solid lines represent accurate calculations. The accuracy for C_{mb} for small V_{SB} is not good. It can be improved by replacing δ_1 by a function of the form of (8.3.14). However, both this parameter and C_{db} are not of prime importance for most applications. Also, note that our simple model predicts $C_{bg} = C_{gb}$ or $C_{mx} = 0$. Accurate calculations[36] give, however,

$$C_{bg} > C_{gb} \tag{9.2.28}$$

and, consequently,†

$$C_{mx} > 0 \tag{9.2.29}$$

as shown in Fig. 9.8. Nevertheless, C_{mx} is very small and will be unimportant in most practical cases.

Using results from above and (8.3.15), one obtains (if V_{DS} is small and/or V_{SB} is large)

$$\frac{C_{db}}{C_{dg}} \approx \frac{C_{sb}}{C_{sg}} \approx \frac{C_{bd}}{C_{gd}} \approx \frac{C_{bs}}{C_{gs}} \approx \frac{C_{bb}}{C_{gg}} \approx \frac{g_{mb}}{g_m} \approx \frac{dV_T}{dV_{SB}} \tag{9.2.30}$$

We consider now the values of the capacitance parameters in two special cases of interest.

Nonsaturation with $V_{DS} = 0$. Using $V_{DS} = 0$ ($\alpha = 1$) in the above results, we easily obtain the following values (below we also repeat the results obtained in Sec. 8.3 for completeness):

---

† The prediction that $C_{gb} = C_{bg}$ by our simple model is a consequence of our setting $\delta = \delta_1$ before differentiating the charge expressions, as discussed in Sec. 8.3. If we use instead $\delta < \delta_1$, as is commonly done in conjunction with drain current modeling, we find $C_{bg} < C_{gb}$ ($C_{mx} < 0$), i.e., a conclusion which is opposite from the result obtained by measurements and accurate models—a rather unexpected error.

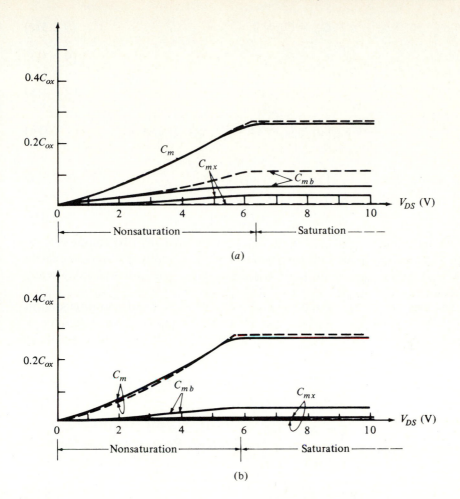

FIGURE 9.8
Small-signal transcapacitances C_m, C_{mb}, and C_{mx} vs. V_{DS} for the device of Fig. 9.7 with $V_{GS} = 8$ V. Solid lines: accurate model;[36] broken lines: simple model presented in this section. (a) $V_{SB} = 0$; (b) $V_{SB} = 5$ V.

$$C_{dg} = C_{sg} = \frac{C_{ox}}{2} \tag{9.2.31a}$$

$$C_{db} = C_{sb} = \delta_1 \frac{C_{ox}}{2} \tag{9.2.31b}$$

$$C_{gd} = C_{gs} = \frac{C_{ox}}{2} \tag{9.2.31c}$$

$$C_{bd} = C_{bs} = \delta_1 \frac{C_{ox}}{2} \tag{9.2.31d}$$

$$C_{gb} = C_{bg} = 0 \tag{9.2.31e}$$

$$C_{gg} = C_{ox} \tag{9.2.31f}$$

$$C_{bb} = \delta_1 C_{ox} \tag{9.2.31g}$$

$$C_{dd} = C_{ss} = (1 + \delta_1) \frac{C_{ox}}{3} \tag{9.2.31h}$$

$$C_{ds} = C_{sd} = -(1 + \delta_1) \frac{C_{ox}}{6} \tag{9.2.31i}$$

$$C_m = C_{mb} = C_{mx} = 0 \tag{9.2.31j}$$

We note that $C_{xy} = C_{yx}$, where x and y represent any two among s, d, g, and b. This is actually the only case where such an equality is observed exactly by all C_{xy}; with $V_{DS} \neq 0$ one finds $C_{xy} \neq C_{yx}$ in general, for reasons already discussed.

Some of the above results have already been obtained and discussed in Sec. 8.3. Here we will attempt to make plausible the rest of them. The value of the inversion layer charge per unit area, Q_I' at the source and drain ends of the channel is, from Sec. 3.4.2,

$$Q_{I,\text{source}}' = -C_{ox}'(V_{GS} - V_{TS}) \tag{9.2.32a}$$
$$Q_{I,\text{drain}}' = -C_{ox}'(V_{GD} - V_{TD}) \tag{9.2.32b}$$

where

$$V_{TS} = V_{FB} + \phi_B + \gamma\sqrt{V_{SB} + \phi_B} \tag{9.2.33a}$$
$$V_{TD} = V_{FB} + \phi_B + \gamma\sqrt{V_{DB} + \phi_B} \tag{9.2.33b}$$

Of course, here we are interested in the case $V_{DS} = 0$. However, we have allowed above for independent voltages V_D and V_S, so that we can differentiate the expressions involved in terms of one voltage while keeping the other constant in accordance with the capacitance definitions.

For $V_D \approx V_S$, one can assume a straight-line variation of Q_I' with the position x along the channel:

$$Q_I' = Q_{I,\text{source}}' + (Q_{I,\text{drain}}' - Q_{I,\text{source}}') \frac{x}{L} \tag{9.2.34}$$

One can now find Q_D and Q_S by using the above in (7.3.9). The result is

$$Q_D = -C_{ox}[\tfrac{1}{6}(V_{GS} - V_{TS}) + \tfrac{1}{3}(V_{GD} - V_{TD})] \tag{9.2.35}$$
$$Q_S = -C_{ox}[\tfrac{1}{3}(V_{GS} - V_{TS}) + \tfrac{1}{6}(V_{GD} - V_{TD})] \tag{9.2.36}$$

Various capacitance values in (9.2.31) can now be verified easily by using the above expressions. In particular, the reason for the denominators 3 and 6 in (9.2.31h) and (9.2.31i) becomes apparent.

All results in (9.2.31) agree exactly with those obtained by using the charges corresponding to the accurate strong-inversion model.

Saturation: Using the general capacitance expressions with $V_{DS} = V'_{DS}$ ($\alpha = 0$) gives the following results (some of them have already been derived in Sec. 8.3 and are repeated below for convenience).

$$C_{dg} = \tfrac{4}{15} C_{ox} \tag{9.2.37a}$$

$$C_{gd} = 0 \tag{9.2.37b}$$

$$C_{db} = \delta_1 \tfrac{4}{15} C_{ox} \tag{9.2.37c}$$

$$C_{bd} = 0 \tag{9.2.37d}$$

$$C_{sg} = \tfrac{2}{5} C_{ox} \tag{9.2.37e}$$

$$C_{gs} = \tfrac{2}{3} C_{ox} \tag{9.2.37f}$$

$$C_{sb} = \delta_1 \tfrac{2}{5} C_{ox} \tag{9.2.37g}$$

$$C_{bs} = \delta_1 \tfrac{2}{3} C_{ox} \tag{9.2.37h}$$

$$C_{gb} = C_{bg} = \frac{\delta_1}{3(1 + \delta_1)} C_{ox} \tag{9.2.37i}$$

$$C_{ds} = -(1 + \delta_1) \tfrac{4}{15} C_{ox} \tag{9.2.37j}$$

$$C_{sd} = 0 \tag{9.2.37k}$$

$$C_{gg} = \left[\frac{2}{3} + \frac{\delta_1}{3(1 + \delta_1)} \right] C_{ox} \tag{9.2.37l}$$

$$C_{bb} = \left[\frac{2}{3}\delta_1 + \frac{\delta_1}{3(1 + \delta_1)} \right] C_{ox} \tag{9.2.37m}$$

$$C_{dd} = 0 \tag{9.2.37n}$$

$$C_{ss} = (1 + \delta_1) \tfrac{2}{5} C_{ox} \tag{9.2.37o}$$

$$C_m = \tfrac{4}{15} C_{ox} \tag{9.2.37p}$$

$$C_{mb} = \delta_1 C_m \tag{9.2.37q}$$

$$C_{mx} = 0 \tag{9.2.37r}$$

Note that in saturation we have $C_{xy} \neq C_{yx}$ (for $x \neq y$), as already discussed.

WEAK INVERSION. The only important intrinsic capacitance in weak inversion, C_{gb}, has been discussed in Sec. 8.3. Deriving expressions for other intrinsic capacitances is hardly worth the effort. The effect of these capacitances will be swamped by that of extrinsic capacitances (Sec. 8.4) for all but very long devices.

GENERAL MODEL VALID IN ALL REGIONS OF INVERSION. Capacitances derived by using the accurate charge calculations suggested in Sec. 7.4.5 are shown in Fig. 9.9 vs. V_{GS}.[36] All nine capacitances used in the model of Fig. 9.5 are shown. An expansion of the horizontal axis around the moderate-inversion region results in Fig. 9.10. Finally, Fig. 9.11 compares C_{gd} to C_{dg}, C_{bd} to C_{db}, and C_{gb} to C_{bg}. As seen, the capacitances in each of these pairs are, in general, different, as predicted by the theory in this section. These predictions agree with measurements.[29, 32, 40] An example is shown in Fig. 9.12.

9.2.4 Frequency Region of Validity

The inclusion of the four capacitances C_m, C_{mb}, C_{mx}, and C_{sd} makes the complete quasi-static model better than the simple model of Fig. 8.13, as far as the frequency region of validity is concerned. The improvement depends on bias and on the terminals we are considering. For example, C_m is maximum in

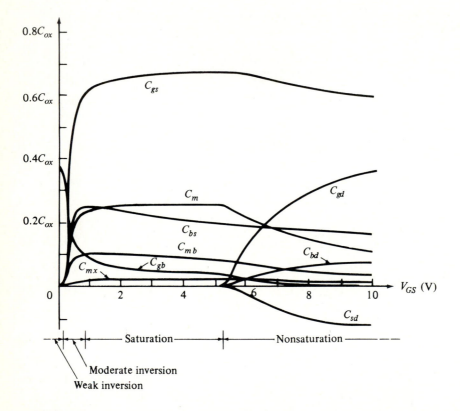

FIGURE 9.9
The nine capacitances in the small-signal model of Fig. 9.5, for the device of Fig. 9.7, plotted vs. V_{GS} for $V_{DS} = 4$ V and $V_{SB} = 0$, using accurate calculations.[36]

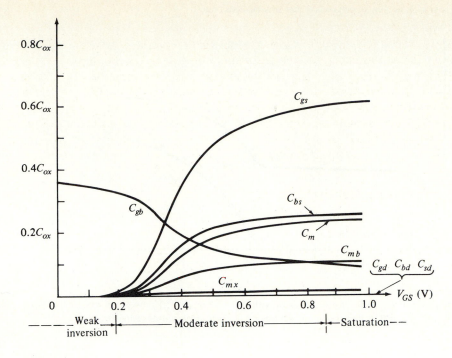

FIGURE 9.10
The plot of Fig. 9.9 expanded around the moderate-inversion region.[36]

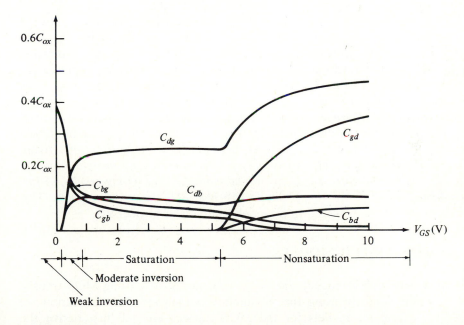

FIGURE 9.11
A comparison of C_{dg} to C_{gd}, C_{db} to C_{bd}, and C_{bg} to C_{gb} for the device of Fig. 9.7, as obtained from accurate calculations.[36]

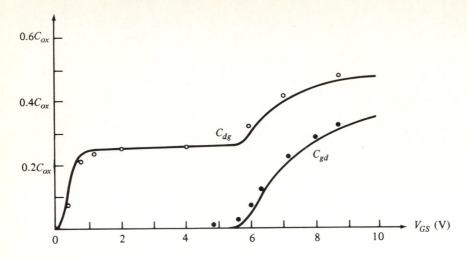

FIGURE 9.12
A comparison of C_{dg} to C_{gd} for a transistor with $N_A = 5000 \ \mu m^{-3}$, $V_{FB} = -1.18$ V, $t_{ox} = 0.088 \ \mu m$, $V_{DS} = 0$, and $V_{SB} = 0$ V. Points are measurements;[32] lines are accurate calculations.[36]

saturation, and it is there that the difference between the two models will be maximum, as far as gate-to-drain action is concerned. At $V_{DS} = 0$, $C_m = 0$ and the two models are identical in that respect. On the other hand, it is at $V_{DS} = 0$ that C_{sd} is maximum, and hence it is at this point that the difference between the two models is maximum, as far as source-to-drain action is concerned. To provide some rough indication though, consider operation in the saturation region, which is the most important region for small-signal circuit applications. Assume the element values in the model have been chosen so that, at very low frequencies, the performance is good. Then the performance will continue to be good, with practically no deterioration up to about $\omega_o/3$, where ω_o is given by (8.3.6).[39] This result follows by comparison to more sophisticated, nonquasi-static models considered in Sec. 9.4. At this point, a warning should be given. *Although the frequency region of validity for the complete quasi-static model is larger, if this region is exceeded, this model can give very wrong results, in fact worse than those of the simple model of Fig. 8.13 in some respects.* This important point is considered in a model comparison in Sec. 9.5.

9.3   *y*-PARAMETER MODELS

Design of very-high-frequency amplifiers (not necessarily using MOS transistors) is often done by using the so-called *y parameters*. In this section we develop *y*-parameter models for the MOS device. We will first derive the general form of such models. In doing so, no assumptions will be made as to the physics of the device. In fact, we do not even have to assume the device is a MOS transistor. The only restriction we will place on it is that it has four terminals. For later convenience we will denote these terminals by D, G, B, and S, but for the present we do not have to associate these symbols with particular terminals of a specific device; indeed, we might as well have used X, Y, Z, and W instead.

Let us consider the transistor driven by bias and small-signal voltages at each terminal, as shown in Fig. 9.1b. The small-signal equivalent circuit of the transistor driven by the small-signal parts of the voltage excitations is shown in Fig. 9.13a. We assume now that all small-signal voltages are sinusoidal and of the *same* angular frequency ω. Then in the *sinusoidal steady state* all small-signal currents will also be sinusoidal and of the same frequency.[41-43] The small-signal voltages and currents can be represented by cosine functions, e.g.,

$$v_g(t) = M_{vg} \cos{(\omega t + \phi_{vg})} \tag{9.3.1}$$

We will use a *phasor* representation for each small-signal voltage or current, i.e., a complex number with magnitude and angle equal to the amplitude and phase, respectively, of the corresponding cosine waveform.[41-43] Phasors will be denoted by capital letters with lowercase subscripts. For example, corresponding to $v_g(t)$ above we have a phasor V_g:

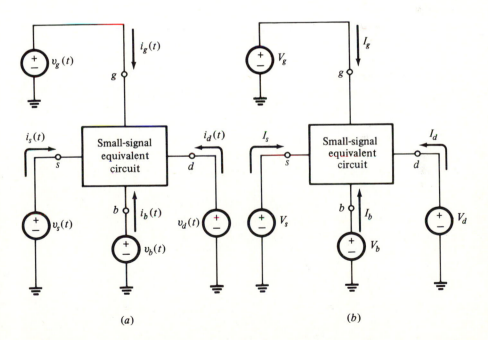

(a) $\qquad\qquad\qquad\qquad\qquad\qquad\qquad$ (b)

FIGURE 9.13
(a) The small-signal equivalent of Fig. 9.1b in the time domain; (b) corresponding representation in the frequency domain using phasors.

$$V_g = M_{vg}e^{j\phi_{vg}} \tag{9.3.2}$$

From now on we will use for brevity the terms "voltage" and "current" instead of the more complete "voltage phasor" and "current phasor." Because the context will be clear, no confusion will arise. The phasor representation for the circuit of Fig. 9.13a is shown in Fig. 9.13b.

Let us assume that we are interested in the effect of V_g, V_b, V_d, and V_s on the current I_d. We will perform four experiments. In each, we will consider only one of the four small-signal voltages by setting the other three equal to zero in Fig. 9.13b. This is equivalent to setting to zero the values of three of the small-signal voltage sources in Fig. 9.1b, but, of course, *leaving all four dc bias sources intact* in that figure. The four experiments are summarized in Fig. 9.14. In each one, the ratio of the current phasor to the voltage phasor is a complex *admittance.*[41-43] We will use the symbols shown in Fig. 9.14 for the four admittances.

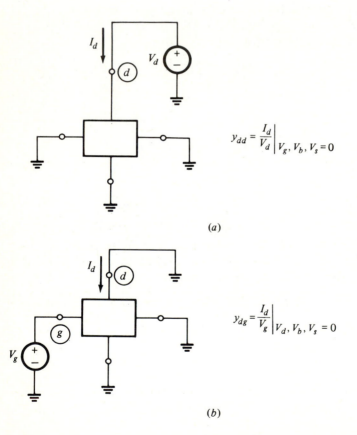

(a)

(b)

FIGURE 9.14
Definition of y parameters associated with the drain current.

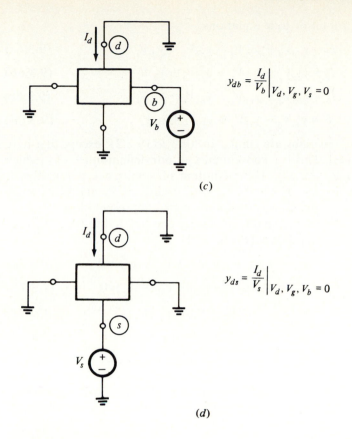

$$y_{db} = \left. \frac{I_d}{V_b} \right|_{V_d, V_g, V_s = 0}$$

(c)

$$y_{ds} = \left. \frac{I_d}{V_s} \right|_{V_d, V_g, V_b = 0}$$

(d)

FIGURE 9.14 (continued).

Small-signal equivalent circuits are *linear* circuits, representing the fact that in an actual transistor with vanishingly small signals the quantities I_d, I_g, I_b, and I_s are linear functions of V_d, V_g, V_b, and V_s. One can thus use *superposition* to find I_d when all four of the small-signal voltages are active (nonzero). This is done by considering one voltage active at a time, evaluating the resulting current, and then adding up the currents:

$$I_d = I_d\big|_{V_g, V_b, V_s=0} + I_d\big|_{V_d, V_b, V_s=0} + I_d\big|_{V_d, V_g, V_s=0} + I_d\big|_{V_d, V_g, V_b=0} \quad (9.3.3)$$

Using the definitions in Fig. 9.14, the above equation can be written as follows:

$$I_d = y_{dd}V_d + y_{dg}V_g + y_{db}V_b + y_{ds}V_s \quad (9.3.4)$$

We can perform similar experiments to determine the currents in each of the other three terminals. In each case, we define admittances as follows:

$$y_{ln} = \left. \frac{I_l}{V_n} \right|_{V_k=0, \, k \neq n} \quad (9.3.5)$$

We thus have a total of four equations:

$$I_d = y_{dd}V_d + y_{dg}V_g + y_{db}V_b + y_{ds}V_s \tag{9.3.6a}$$

$$I_g = y_{gd}V_d + y_{gg}V_g + y_{gb}V_b + y_{gs}V_s \tag{9.3.6b}$$

$$I_b = y_{bd}V_d + y_{bg}V_g + y_{bb}V_b + y_{bs}V_s \tag{9.3.6c}$$

$$I_s = y_{sd}V_d + y_{sg}V_g + y_{sb}V_b + y_{ss}V_s \tag{9.3.6d}$$

Note that these equations are similar in form to (9.2.2), except that here no minus signs are used. This is a consequence of our definition (9.3.5) [which should be compared to (9.2.1)]. This definition of admittance parameters is standard in network theory. Equation (9.3.6), expressed in matrix form, is known as a *terminal*, or *indefinite, admittance matrix* representation.[43]

We can follow a reasoning analogous to the one that led to (9.2.8) to get relations between the y parameters (Prob. 9.11):

$$y_{dd} + y_{dg} + y_{db} + y_{ds} = y_{dd} + y_{gd} + y_{bd} + y_{sd} = 0 \tag{9.3.7a}$$

$$y_{gg} + y_{gd} + y_{gb} + y_{gs} = y_{gg} + y_{dg} + y_{bg} + y_{sg} = 0 \tag{9.3.7b}$$

$$y_{bb} + y_{bd} + y_{bg} + y_{bs} = y_{bb} + y_{db} + y_{gb} + y_{sb} = 0 \tag{9.3.7c}$$

$$y_{ss} + y_{sd} + y_{sg} + y_{sb} = y_{ss} + y_{ds} + y_{gs} + y_{bs} = 0 \tag{9.3.7d}$$

Similarly, following a reasoning analogous to the one that led to (9.2.12), we conclude that the fourth equation in (9.3.6) can be omitted (in fact, any one among the four equations could have been chosen for omission) without losing information, and that the remaining three equations can be written as follows:

$$I_d = y_{dd}V_{ds} + y_{dg}V_{gs} + y_{db}V_{bs} \tag{9.3.8a}$$

$$I_g = y_{gd}V_{ds} + y_{gg}V_{gs} + y_{gb}V_{bs} \tag{9.3.8b}$$

$$I_b = y_{bd}V_{ds} + y_{bg}V_{gs} + y_{bb}V_{bs} \tag{9.3.8c}$$

with $V_{xy} = V_x - V_y$. The above set of equations can be represented by the circuit of Fig. 9.15, a fact verifiable directly by writing Kirchhoff's law for the current phasors in the circuit.

Other three-port y-parameter representations are also possible. For example, if instead of using the s terminal as a potential reference and omitting (9.3.6d) we had used the b terminal as a reference and had omitted (9.3.6c), we would have obtained the representation shown in Fig. 9.16. The appealing feature of this model for a MOS transistor is that it uses a "natural" choice as a reference—the substrate terminal. For example, in a NMOS fabrication process this is the *only* terminal that is common to *all* devices on a chip. Also, for a symmetrically laid out device, the role of source and drain is identical; thus $y_{ss} = y_{dd}$, $y_{sg} = y_{dg}$, and $y_{sd} = y_{ds}$. Using such equal values in Fig. 9.16 makes the symmetry evident. Nevertheless, small-signal models using the substrate as the reference are not in much use. This is partly owing to tradition. In the early

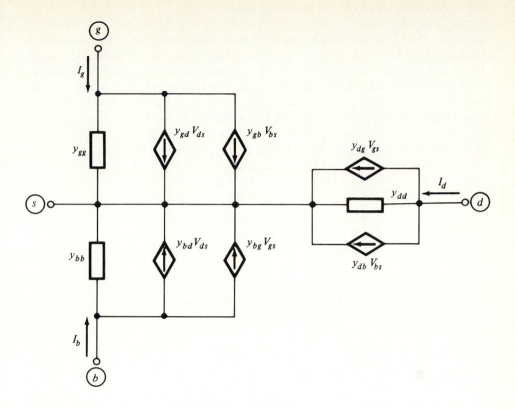

FIGURE 9.15
A general y-parameter model using the source terminal as a reference.

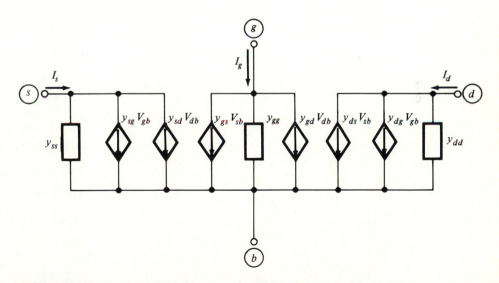

FIGURE 9.16
A general y-parameter model using the substrate terminal as a reference.

days, the MOS transistor was treated as a three-terminal device, and well-known modeling practices from vacuum tubes (using the cathode as a reference) and bipolar transistors (using the emitter as a reference) were carried over to the MOSFET (using the source as the reference). In this way, results and intuition of many years could be carried over to the new device. Also, to many engineers the gate-source part is the "natural" input. Varying v_{GS} (while keeping v_{GB} fixed), has normally a much more drastic effect on the drain current than varying v_{GB} (while keeping v_{GS} fixed), hence, the source is used as the reference point. It would be interesting, nevertheless, to see what sort of conveniences could arise from using the substrate as a reference.

We now go one step closer in relating our present models to the one in Fig. 9.5. Following an approach similar to the one that led to (9.2.19), we can rewrite (9.3.8) as follows (Prob. 9.12):

$$I_d = -y_{gd}V_{dg} - y_{sd}V_{ds} - y_{bd}V_{db} + y_mV_{gs} + y_{mb}V_{bs} \tag{9.3.9a}$$

$$I_g = -y_{gd}V_{gd} - y_{gb}V_{gb} - y_{gs}V_{gs} \tag{9.3.9b}$$

$$I_b = -y_{bd}V_{bd} - y_{gb}V_{bg} + y_{mx}V_{gb} - y_{bs}V_{bs} \tag{9.3.9c}$$

where

$$y_m = y_{dg} - y_{gd} \tag{9.3.10a}$$

$$y_{mb} = y_{db} - y_{bd} \tag{9.3.10b}$$

$$y_{mx} = y_{bg} - y_{gb} \tag{9.3.10c}$$

These equations can be represented by the circuit of Fig. 9.17. Since the development of this model was general, the model in Fig. 9.5 should simply be a special case of it. By comparing the two circuits we get,† *for this special case,*

$$-y_{gd} = j\omega C_{gd} \tag{9.3.11a}$$

$$-y_{gs} = j\omega C_{gs} \tag{9.3.11b}$$

$$-y_{bd} = j\omega C_{bd} \tag{9.3.11c}$$

$$-y_{bs} = j\omega C_{bs} \tag{9.3.11d}$$

$$-y_{gb} = j\omega C_{gb} \tag{9.3.11e}$$

$$-y_{sd} = g_d + j\omega C_{sd} \tag{9.3.11f}$$

$$y_m = g_m - j\omega C_m \tag{9.3.11g}$$

$$y_{mb} = g_{mb} - j\omega C_{mb} \tag{9.3.11h}$$

$$y_{mx} = -j\omega C_{mx} \tag{9.3.11i}$$

---

† To arrive at (9.3.11) we use the following fact:[41-43] The time-domain *i-v* equation for a capacitor, namely $i(t) = C \, dv(t)/dt$, corresponds to the phasor equation $I = j\omega CV$, where $j\omega C$ is the admittance corresponding to the capacitance C.

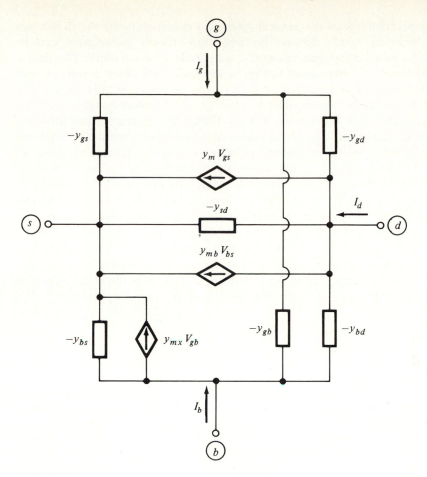

FIGURE 9.17
A general y-parameter model.

In the above equations, observe that: (1) y_m, y_{mb}, and $-y_{sd}$ have a constant, real, positive part, and (2) all y parameters have imaginary parts which are proportional to frequency. These two observations are, indeed, verified by measurements at frequencies up to about $\omega_o/3$, with ω_o as given by (8.3.6). Indeed, the capacitance values can be determined as the constant of proportionality in the imaginary part of measured admittances.[32, 38] At frequencies higher than $\omega_o/3$, however, the behavior predicted above fails. Measurements then show, for example, that both the real and the imaginary part of y_m decrease in magnitude with frequency, and that y_{gs} begins to have a nonzero real part. To explain such phenomena, the quasi-static assumption must be abandoned, and this is what will be done in the following section.

Before leaving the present section, we remark briefly on the measurement of y parameters. In the general case, all y parameters for the device are complex numbers which depend on frequency. These parameters can be measured by using signal generators and amplitude/phase meters. The device is properly biased, a small-signal voltage is applied to one of the terminals, and the resulting small-signal current at each of the terminals is observed. The y parameters can then be calculated from (9.3.5). Unfortunately, practical details can make such measurements very tricky. For example, in measuring y_{dg}, the small ac current of interest rides on top of a comparatively very large dc bias current. Special, careful circuitry is needed to separate dc from ac components without altering the phase of the latter (or, at least, without altering it in an unpredictable manner). Also, attempting to determine one component of y_{dg} (real or imaginary), when the other is much larger, is known to cause problems. Measurements of MOS transistor y parameters have been reported in the literature.[6, 14, 15, 19] However, in most cases they are performed on discrete devices and include the effect of large parasitic elements, such as those due to packaging. Estimating the latter and subtracting their effect is not always easy. Integrating part of the measuring circuitry on the same chip with the transistor under measurement can help to eliminate such problems.[40, 44–46]

9.4   NONQUASI-STATIC MODELS

9.4.1   Introduction

In this section, the quasi-static assumption will be dropped and the dynamics of the channel charge at high frequencies will be investigated in detail. Before starting a mathematical analysis, we present a short discussion as to what one might expect intuitively at frequencies where quasi-static behavior is no longer observed.

Let us consider the device in Fig. 7.3, where we will assume that only one voltage is varying at a time around its dc value and the variation is small and sinusoidal. If v_s is varying very slowly, the inversion layer charge has time to follow with practically no delay. We have seen that the resulting effect on the gate can be modeled by connecting a capacitance C_{gs} from source to gate. However, if the variation of v_s is fast, the "inertia" of the inversion layer becomes nonnegligible, and the effect (gate charge change) will lag behind the cause (source voltage change). A similar effect will be observed between drain and gate. Also, similar conclusions can be drawn for the effect of the source and of the drain on the substrate (the "back gate"). Consider now the effect of the gate voltage. If v_g is varied very fast, the inversion layer charge does not have enough time to respond fully, and thus $|y_{dg}|$, which models this response, will be small. Also, the angle of y_{dg} should be significant and negative, because of the delay between the cause (the variation in the gate voltage) and the effect (the variation in the drain current). Finally, similar observations hold for the effect of the substrate voltage on the inversion layer charge.

The above effects will be observed if the operating frequency exceeds the upper limit of validity for quasi-static modeling. From Sec. 9.2.4, this upper limit is proportional to ω_o, which in turn is proportional to $1/L^2$. One way to model the transistor at frequencies above the limit is, in principle, to split the device into sections (Fig. 7.12). The length of each section is chosen such that, for *it*, a quasi-static model *can* be used. The combination of the models of all sections will then be a valid model for the whole transistor at the frequency of interest. The higher this frequency, the shorter the length needed for each section. One is thus led to carrying the idea to the limit, i.e., considering elemental sections the lengths of which are allowed to approach zero. The following analysis corresponds mathematically to this idea. The analysis is based on well-established principles,[1, 2, 4, 17, 20, 21, 35] but is generalized to view the transistor as a four-terminal device.[39] We want to establish all steps carefully, so the procedure will be rather long; once again we ask for the reader's patience.

9.4.2 A Nonquasi-Static Model

In this section we will derive a useful high-frequency model corresponding to the approximate strong-inversion dc model. To end up with manageable expressions, we will use here the same simplifying assumptions we used in Sec. 8.3.[39] The first assumption is that, in the expressions for the charge, the quantity δ will be assumed to be given by

$$\delta = \delta_1 = \frac{\gamma}{2\sqrt{\phi_B + V_{SB}}} \tag{9.4.1}$$

The second assumption is that the derivative of δ_1 with V_S or V_B is negligible for our purposes, and thus, δ_1 will be treated as a constant during differentiation. At a later point, we will verify that the above assumptions do indeed produce a useful model by comparison to more exact models.

Many of the expressions we have developed in previous chapters will be needed here. For convenience, we will repeat these below. We will take this opportunity and present the various expressions in an organized fashion, so as to present a complete picture of, and the relation between, the following cases:

1. Dc (bias) excitation
2. Time-varying excitation
3. The special case of (2) where the time variations are small signals
4. A special case of (3), where the small signals have a form particularly useful for high-frequency model development.

DC (BIAS) EXCITATION. In our analysis we will find it convenient to express the gate, depletion region, and inversion layer charges per unit area in terms of $V_{GS} = V_{GB} - V_{SB}$ and $V_{CS}(x) = V_{CB}(x) - V_{SB}$. Recall that, in strong inversion, $V_{CB}(x)$ can be viewed as the effective reverse bias between the inversion layer at point x and the substrate. Thus, $V_{CS}(x)$ represents the potential drop across

$$q_b(t) = W \int_0^L q_b'(x, t)\, dx \qquad (9.4.38)$$

For $u_i(x, t)$, starting from (9.4.23), using (9.4.36), and proceeding as before, we easily get

$$u_i(x, t) = v_{gs}(t) + \delta_1 v_{bs}(t) - (1 + \delta_1)v_{cs}(x, t) \qquad (9.4.39a)$$

$$= [v_{gs}(t) - v_{cs}(x, t)] + \delta_1[v_{bs}(t) - v_{cs}(x, t)] \qquad (9.4.39b)$$

Since $v_{cs}(x, t)$ is zero at the source end and equal to $v_{ds}(t)$ at the drain end, we have, from the above equation,

$$u_i(0,t) = v_{gs}(t) + \delta_1 v_{bs}(t) \qquad (9.4.40)$$

$$u_i(L,t) = [v_{gs}(t) - v_{ds}(t)] + \delta_1[v_{bs}(t) - v_{ds}(t)] \qquad (9.4.41)$$

The small-signal quantity $i_i(x, t)$ can be obtained by starting from (9.4.24). Using the fact that $u_i(x, t)$ is very small, the result can be put in the form (Prob. 9.13)

$$i_i(x, t) = -\frac{\mu W C_{ox}'}{1 + \delta_1} \frac{\partial}{\partial x} [U_I(x)u_i(x, t)] \qquad (9.4.42)$$

Starting from (9.4.25) we get, using the facts that $\partial I_I(x)/\partial x = 0$ and $\partial U_I(x)/\partial t = 0$,

$$\frac{\partial i_i(x, t)}{\partial x} = -C_{ox}' W \frac{\partial u_i(x, t)}{\partial t} \qquad (9.4.43)$$

For the drain small-signal current we have, starting from (9.4.26),

$$i_d(t) = i_i(L, t) \qquad (9.4.44)$$

For the gate small-signal current, starting from (9.4.27), we obtain

$$i_g(t) = \frac{dq_g(t)}{dt} \qquad (9.4.45)$$

We can now use (9.4.34) and (9.4.32) in this equation. If in the result we substitute $v_{cs}(x, t)$ as it ensues from solving (9.4.39), we obtain

$$i_g(t) = W C_{ox}' \frac{d}{dt} \int_0^L \left\{ \frac{\delta_1}{1 + \delta_1} [v_{gs}(t) - v_{bs}(t)] + \frac{1}{1 + \delta_1} u_i(x, t) \right\} dx \qquad (9.4.46)$$

For the substrate small-signal current we have, starting from (9.4.28),

$$i_b(t) = \frac{dq_b(t)}{dt} \qquad (9.4.47)$$

Using in this equation (9.4.38) and (9.4.37), and substituting $v_{cs}(x, t)$ from (9.4.39) we obtain

$$i_b(t) = \delta_1 WC'_{ox} \frac{d}{dt} \int_0^L \left\{ \frac{1}{1 + \delta_1} [v_{bs}(t) - v_{gs}(t)] + \frac{1}{1 + \delta_1} u_i(x, t) \right\} dx$$
(9.4.48)

It is clear that to find any of the terminal currents one needs an expression for $u_i(x, t)$, and that must be found from (9.4.42) and (9.4.43). The result, of course, depends on the form of the terminal small-signal voltages through the boundary conditions (9.4.40) and (9.4.41). In what follows, we will present the solution when the terminal voltages assume a form of special interest.

COMPLEX EXPONENTIAL EXCITATION. One could assume that the small-signal voltages are sinusoids and consider the corresponding small-signal terminal currents in the sinusoidal steady state. However, the algebra turns out to be unnecessarily complicated. We will thus follow instead a standard practice and consider a fictitious complex exponential excitation[41-43] of the form

$$v_{gs}(t) = V_{gs} e^{j\omega t} \tag{9.4.49a}$$

$$v_{bs}(t) = V_{bs} e^{j\omega t} \tag{9.4.49b}$$

$$v_{ds}(t) = V_{ds} e^{j\omega t} \tag{9.4.49c}$$

where capital symbols with lower-case subscripts denote time-independent phasor quantities which can, in general, be complex, and ω is the angular frequency (in rad/s). Since the equations relating the various *small-signal* quantities (derived above) are linear, each small-signal quantity that results as an effect of the excitations in (9.4.49) in the steady state will also be equal to a complex quantity times $e^{j\omega t}$. In particular, we can write

$$u_i(x, t) = U_i(x, \omega) e^{j\omega t} \tag{9.4.50a}$$

$$i_i(x, t) = I_i(x, \omega) e^{j\omega t} \tag{9.4.50b}$$

$$i_d(t) = I_d(\omega) e^{j\omega t} \tag{9.4.50c}$$

$$i_g(t) = I_g(\omega) e^{j\omega t} \tag{9.4.50d}$$

$$i_b(t) = I_b(\omega) e^{j\omega t} \tag{9.4.50e}$$

Equations (9.4.50) are the various "responses" to the excitations (9.4.49). Although all these complex excitations and responses are fictitious, they are useful for the following reason.[41-43] If the *real* part of the above excitations is used instead to drive the device, all responses in the steady state will be given by the *real* part of the fictitious responses in (9.4.50). Now, the real part of any of the above excitations is a sinusoid. [For example, if M and ϕ are the magnitude and phase of V_{gs}, respectively, then the real part of $v_{gs}(t)$ in (9.4.49a) is simply $M \cos(\omega t + \phi)$.] Thus, working with the above fictitious exponential functions provides all useful information about sinusoidal steady state, with real excitations and real responses, only with greater mathematical ease. In addition, if the response to complex exponentials is known, the response to other types of waveforms can be determined by using transform techniques.[41-43]

The quantities in (9.4.49) and (9.4.50) can now be substituted into (9.4.42), (9.4.43), (9.4.40), (9.4.41), (9.4.44), (9.4.46), and (9.4.48). In all cases, $e^{j\omega t}$ appears as a common factor on both sides. Thus, we easily obtain (Prob.9.14)

$$I_i(x, \omega) = -\frac{\mu W C'_{ox}}{1 + \delta_1} \frac{\partial}{\partial x} [U_I(x) U_i(x, \omega)] \tag{9.4.51a}$$

$$\frac{\partial I_i(x, \omega)}{\partial x} = -j\omega C'_{ox} W U_i(x, \omega) \tag{9.4.51b}$$

$$U_i(0, \omega) = V_{gs} + \delta_1 V_{bs} \tag{9.4.52a}$$

$$U_i(L, \omega) = (V_{gs} - V_{ds}) + \delta_1 (V_{bs} - V_{ds}) \tag{9.4.52b}$$

$$I_d(\omega) = I_i(L, \omega) \tag{9.4.53a}$$

$$I_g(\omega) = j\omega C'_{ox} W \left[L \frac{\delta_1}{1 + \delta_1} (V_{gs} - V_{bs}) + \frac{1}{1 + \delta_1} \int_0^L U_i(x, \omega) \, dx \right] \tag{9.4.53b}$$

$$I_b(\omega) = j\omega \delta_1 C'_{ox} W \left[L \frac{1}{1 + \delta_1} (V_{bs} - V_{gs}) + \frac{1}{1 + \delta_1} \int_0^L U_i(x, \omega) \, dx \right] \tag{9.4.53c}$$

In the above equations, note the following: μ, W, L, and C'_{ox} are known device parameters, δ_1 is known for a given bias V_{SB} from (9.4.1), and $U_I(x)$ is a known function of x, from (9.4.13). V_{gs}, V_{bs}, and V_{ds} are known phasors representing the excitation. Thus, for a given ω, (9.4.51) is a system of two differential equations in two unknown functions, $I_i(x, \omega)$ and $U_i(x, \omega)$. This system can be solved by using Bessel functions, with the boundary conditions given in (9.4.52);[1, 7, 17, 21, 35, 39] an alternate solution uses iterative techniques.[20] Once the functions $U_i(x, \omega)$ and $I_i(x, \omega)$ have been determined, they can be substituted in (9.4.53) to give $I_d(\omega)$, $I_g(\omega)$, and $I_b(\omega)$. The mathematical details are long (Prob. 9.15) and will not be presented here. Below we summarize the form of the results. The final expressions are in the form

$$I_d(\omega) = \frac{N_{dd}(\omega)V_{ds} + N_{dg}(\omega)V_{gs} + N_{db}(\omega)V_{bs}}{D(\omega)} \tag{9.4.54}$$

$$I_g(\omega) = \frac{N_{gd}(\omega)V_{ds} + N_{gg}(\omega)V_{gs} + N_{gb}(\omega)V_{bs}}{D(\omega)} \tag{9.4.55}$$

$$I_b(\omega) = \frac{N_{bd}(\omega)V_{ds} + N_{bg}(\omega)V_{gs} + N_{bb}(\omega)V_{bs}}{D(\omega)} \tag{9.4.56}$$

where the quantities $N_{kl}(\omega)$ $(k, l = d, g, b)$ and $D(\omega)$ are infinite series in $j\omega$. For example,

$$N_{gd}(\omega) = n_{gd0} + (j\omega)n_{gd1} + (j\omega)^2 n_{gd2} + \cdots \tag{9.4.57a}$$

$$D(\omega) = d_0 + (j\omega)d_1 + (j\omega)^2 d_2 + \cdots \tag{9.4.57b}$$

The coefficients in these series up to second order as well as for all $N_{kl}(\omega)$ in (9.4.54) to (9.4.56), are given in Appendix M. One is finally able to find the y parameters, by comparing (9.4.54) to (9.4.56) with (9.3.8):

$$y_{dd} = \frac{N_{dd}(\omega)}{D(\omega)}, \qquad y_{dg} = \frac{N_{dg}(\omega)}{D(\omega)}, \qquad y_{db} = \frac{N_{db}(\omega)}{D(\omega)} \tag{9.4.58}$$

$$y_{gd} = \frac{N_{gd}(\omega)}{D(\omega)}, \qquad y_{gg} = \frac{N_{gg}(\omega)}{D(\omega)}, \qquad y_{gb} = \frac{N_{gb}(\omega)}{D(\omega)} \tag{9.4.59}$$

$$y_{bd} = \frac{N_{bd}(\omega)}{D(\omega)}, \qquad y_{bg} = \frac{N_{bg}(\omega)}{D(\omega)}, \qquad y_{bb} = \frac{N_{bb}(\omega)}{D(\omega)} \tag{9.4.60}$$

For example, using (9.4.57), we have

$$y_{gd} = \frac{n_{gd0} + (j\omega)n_{gd1} + (j\omega)^2 n_{gd2} + \cdots}{d_0 + (j\omega)d_1 + (j\omega)^2 d_2 + \cdots} \tag{9.4.61}$$

The y parameters can be computed, for a given frequency, to any desired accuracy by keeping an appropriate number of terms in the numerator and the denominator. The values thus obtained can be substituted in the small-signal equivalent circuit of Fig. 9.16.

Consider now the equivalent circuit in Fig. 9.17. In this circuit, only three of the parameters determined above appear directly: y_{gd}, y_{gb}, and y_{bd}. The rest of the parameters can be trivially found from (9.3.7) and (9.3.10):

$$y_{gs} = -y_{gg} - y_{gd} - y_{gb} \tag{9.4.62a}$$

$$y_{bs} = -y_{bb} - y_{bd} - y_{bg} \tag{9.4.62b}$$

$$y_{sd} = -y_{dd} - y_{gd} - y_{bd} \tag{9.4.62c}$$

$$y_m = y_{dg} - y_{gd} \tag{9.4.62d}$$

$$y_{mb} = y_{db} - y_{bd} \tag{9.4.62e}$$

$$y_{mx} = y_{bg} - y_{gb} \tag{9.4.62f}$$

where the quantities in the right-hand sides are given by (9.4.58) to (9.4.60).

We will write the expressions for the parameters of the model in Fig.9.17 in a way that will help relate the model to the one developed in Sec. 8.3. We start from (9.4.58) to (9.4.60). In each y-parameter expression, we factor out the first nonzero term of the numerator. For example, consider y_{gd} in (9.4.61). From Appendix M we have $n_{gd0} = 0$ and $d_0 = 1$. Thus, we can write:

$$y_{gd} = j\omega n_{gd1} \frac{1 + j\omega(n_{gd2}/n_{gd1}) + \cdots}{1 + j\omega d_1 + \cdots} \tag{9.4.63}$$

A look at Appendix M reveals that $-n_{gd1}$ has exactly the same expression as C_{gd} in (8.3.10). Thus we can write

$$y_{gd} = -j\omega C_{gd} \frac{1 + j\omega(n_{gd2}/n_{gd1}) + \cdots}{1 + j\omega d_1 + \cdots} \tag{9.4.64}$$

Proceeding in a similar manner, we can find expressions for all parameters in Fig. 9.17. As each is being developed, part of the expression can be recognized as a familiar small-signal quantity discussed in Chap. 8.† The results are summarized below (minus signs are used, corresponding to Fig. 9.17):

$$-y_{gs} = j\omega C_{gs} \frac{1 + j\omega \tau_2 + \cdots}{1 + j\omega \tau_1 + \cdots} \tag{9.4.65a}$$

$$-y_{bs} = j\omega C_{bs} \frac{1 + j\omega \tau_2 + \cdots}{1 + j\omega \tau_1 + \cdots} \tag{9.4.65b}$$

$$-y_{gd} = j\omega C_{gd} \frac{1 + j\omega \tau_3 + \cdots}{1 + j\omega \tau_1 + \cdots} \tag{9.4.65c}$$

$$-y_{bd} = j\omega C_{bd} \frac{1 + j\omega \tau_3 + \cdots}{1 + j\omega \tau_1 + \cdots} \tag{9.4.65d}$$

$$-y_{gb} = j\omega C_{gb} \frac{1 + j\omega \tau_4 + \cdots}{1 + j\omega \tau_1 + \cdots} \tag{9.4.65e}$$

$$-y_{sd} = \frac{g_d}{1 + j\omega \tau_1 + \cdots} \tag{9.4.65f}$$

$$y_m = \frac{g_m}{1 + j\omega \tau_1 + \cdots} \tag{9.4.65g}$$

$$y_{mb} = \frac{g_{mb}}{1 + j\omega \tau_1 + \cdots} \tag{9.4.65h}$$

$$y_{mx} = 0 \tag{9.4.65i}$$

where (after lengthy algebra)

---

† Some of the expressions obtained will be valid with best accuracy at low V_{DS} values because they include δ_1, which can be traced to our initial, simplifying assumption in (9.4.1). This same restriction ($\delta = \delta_1$) was encountered at various points in Sec. 8.3, and was subsequently removed. This restriction will soon be removed from the present model also.

$$\tau_1 = \frac{4}{15} \frac{1}{\omega_o} \frac{1 + 3\alpha + \alpha^2}{(1 + \alpha)^3} \tag{9.4.66a}$$

$$\tau_2 = \frac{1}{15} \frac{1}{\omega_o} \frac{2 + 8\alpha + 5\alpha^2}{(1 + \alpha)^2(1 + 2\alpha)} \tag{9.4.66b}$$

$$\tau_3 = \frac{1}{15} \frac{1}{\omega_o} \frac{5 + 8\alpha + 2\alpha^2}{(1 + \alpha)^2(2 + \alpha)} \tag{9.4.66c}$$

$$\tau_4 = \frac{2}{15} \frac{1}{\omega_o} \frac{4 + 7\alpha + 4\alpha^2}{(1 - \alpha)^2(1 + \alpha)} \tag{9.4.66d}$$

with α as given by (4.4.31), and

$$\omega_o = \frac{\mu(V_{GS} - V_T)}{(1 + \delta)L^2} \tag{9.4.67}$$

We note that the numerators in (9.4.65f) to (9.4.65h) do not contain frequency-dependent terms. This is because of cancellations which occur when (9.4.62c) to (9.4.62e) are used.

Consider now *low* frequencies, so that $\omega \ll \omega_o$. Then (9.4.65) gives $-y_{gs} \approx j\omega C_{gs}$, $-y_{bs} \approx j\omega C_{bs}$, $-y_{gd} \approx j\omega C_{gd}$, $-y_{bd} \approx j\omega C_{bd}$, $-y_{gb} \approx j\omega C_{gb}$, $-y_{sd} \approx g_d$, $y_m \approx g_m$, and $y_{mb} \approx g_{mb}$. With these, and since $y_{mx} = 0$, the model in Fig. 9.17 reduces to the model in Fig. 8.13. Thus the same model results, starting from different premises.

The quantity α as it results in the above development is given by (4.4.31), where $V'_{DS} = (V_{GS} - V_T)/(1 + \delta)$, with $\delta = \delta_1$. This value for δ is not the best one to use, as explained in Sec. 4.4.2 (unless V_{DS} is small). It simply appears here because of our initial simplifying assumption in (9.4.1), which was necessary to obtain manageable results.† It is desirable, however, that our present model be consistent with the corresponding dc model in (4.4.30), where the restriction that $\delta = \delta_1$ is not used. Thus we will remove this restriction from the present model, and we will allow V'_{DS} to have the same appropriate value as in the dc equations [see the discussion associated with (4.4.33)].

Similar comments apply to other quantities in (9.4.65) to (9.4.67) (C_{bs}, g_d, etc.). Thus, the approach we have followed leads to expressions for these quantities which are familiar from Chap. 8, only with δ_1 in place of a somewhat different quantity. [For example, we find $g_{mb} = \delta_1 g_m$, which is of the form of (8.2.10) with $b = b_1$ from (8.2.12); this is not accurate for large V_{DS}, as remarked following (8.2.12).] Also, in the saturation region, the value of g_d resulting from the above development is zero, since we have not taken channel

---

† The reader may want to try developing the model by starting from a different value of δ in order to appreciate the ensuing problems.

length modulation into account. All such limitations can be removed by adopting the following approach: *Any quantity in (9.4.65) to (9.4.67), which has already been encountered in Chap. 8, will be assumed to have the value given in that chapter.* In this way, at low frequencies, our present model will reduce to the one in Sec. 8.3, not only in topology (Fig. 8.13) but also in the values for its elements. This is a very desirable property. It makes possible the incorporation of all the refinements known for low-frequency small-signal parameters into the present model. Thus, the model will be very well behaved at low frequencies (and will, of course, also provide useful results at frequencies where low-frequency models fail).

Using (8.3.15) and (9.4.65) we obtain

$$\frac{y_{bs}}{y_{gs}} \approx \frac{y_{bd}}{y_{gd}} \approx \frac{y_{mb}}{y_m} \approx \frac{dV_T}{dV_{SB}} \tag{9.4.68}$$

These relations hold with good accuracy if V_{DS} is small and/or V_{SB} is large, in which case the depletion region is approximately uniform along the channel. In other cases, the relations hold with limited accuracy.

We now derive some very useful approximations for the relations in (9.4.65). Consider y_{gs} as an example. If the frequency of operation satisfies $\omega\tau_2 \ll 1$, we can write $1 + j\omega\tau_2 \approx 1/(1 - j\omega\tau_2)$. Using this in (9.4.65a) and neglecting high-order terms, we obtain $-y_{gs} \approx j\omega C_{gs}/[1 + j\omega(\tau_1 - \tau_2)]$; similarly for $-y_{bs}$, $-y_{gd}$, and $-y_{bd}$. The validity of these approximations will be considered shortly. Thus, we have

$$-y_{gs} \approx \frac{j\omega C_{gs}}{1 + j\omega(\tau_1 - \tau_2)}, \qquad \omega\tau_2 \ll 1 \tag{9.4.69a}$$

$$-y_{bs} \approx \frac{j\omega C_{bs}}{1 + j\omega(\tau_1 - \tau_2)}, \qquad \omega\tau_2 \ll 1 \tag{9.4.69b}$$

$$-y_{gd} \approx \frac{j\omega C_{gd}}{1 + j\omega(\tau_1 - \tau_3)}, \qquad \omega\tau_3 \ll 1 \tag{9.4.69c}$$

$$-y_{bd} \approx \frac{j\omega C_{bd}}{1 + j\omega(\tau_1 - \tau_3)}, \qquad \omega\tau_3 \ll 1 \tag{9.4.69d}$$

Unfortunately, this type of approximation cannot be used for $-y_{gb}$. The quantity $\omega\tau_4$ cannot be assumed to be $\ll 1$ for all bias voltages, since τ_4 becomes infinite for $V_{DS} = 0$ ($\alpha = 1$), as seen from (9.4.66d). [This is a rather artificial effect caused by factoring out C_{gb} in (9.4.65e); it is easily checked that the product $C_{gb}\tau_4$ *is* well behaved.] Hence, we will use

$$-y_{gb} \approx j\omega C_{gb} \frac{1 + j\omega\tau_4}{1 + j\omega\tau_1} = j\omega C_{gb} + (j\omega)^2 \frac{C_{gb}(\tau_4 - \tau_1)}{1 + j\omega\tau_1}, \qquad \omega\tau_1 \ll 1 \tag{9.4.69e}$$

In saturation, and at frequencies where the other approximations we have been making are accurate, the term containing $(j\omega)^2$ can be omitted with little penalty. In nonsaturation, and especially with very small V_{DS}, this term can be the dominant one in y_{gb}, but the magnitude of y_{gb} is then very small anyway. The small currents that can be contributed by it are almost invariably masked by other larger currents (e.g., those contributed by the extrinsic gate-substrate capacitance). Thus, the term containing $(j\omega)^2$ can be omitted for many applications (Prob. 9.17).

For the rest of the parameters in (9.4.65) we simply drop the high-order terms in the denominators:

$$-y_{sd} \approx \frac{g_d}{1 + j\omega\tau_1}, \qquad \omega\tau_1 \ll 1 \tag{9.4.69f}$$

$$y_m \approx \frac{g_m}{1 + j\omega\tau_1}, \qquad \omega\tau_1 \ll 1 \tag{9.4.69g}$$

$$y_{mb} \approx \frac{g_{mb}}{1 + j\omega\tau_1}, \qquad \omega\tau_1 \ll 1 \tag{9.4.69h}$$

$$y_{mx} = 0 \tag{9.4.69i}$$

The admittances in the right-hand side of (9.4.69a) to (9.4.69d) are of the general form $j\omega C/(1 + j\omega\tau)$. Figure 9.18a shows a simple circuit that realizes such an admittance. Figure 9.18b shows a circuit that realizes the admittance in the right-hand side of (9.4.69f). Finally, Fig. 9.18c shows a circuit that realizes the admittance in the right-hand side of (9.4.69e). R is arbitrary. The part inside the box represents the term containing $(j\omega)^2$. The three circuit representations in Fig. 9.18 can be verified through simple circuit analysis (Prob. 9.18).

With the help of Fig. 9.18, it is easy to see that using (9.4.69) the equivalent circuit of Fig. 9.17 takes the form shown in Fig. 9.19. The box shown in broken lines is as in Fig. 9.18c. In many applications this box can be omitted, for reasons already mentioned above. As follows from Fig. 9.18a and (9.4.69a) to (9.4.69d), we have

$$R_{gs}C_{gs} = R_{bs}C_{bs} = \tau_1 - \tau_2 \tag{9.4.70a}$$

$$R_{gd}C_{gd} = R_{bd}C_{bd} = \tau_1 - \tau_3 \tag{9.4.70b}$$

from which the resistance values can be calculated.† For the inductor we have,

---

† Note that since the capacitances are proportional to $C_{ox} = C'_{ox}WL$ (Sec. 8.3), whereas τ_1, τ_2, and τ_3 are inversely proportional to ω_o [see (9.4.66) and (9.4.67)], the resistances will be proportional to $(\omega_o C_{ox})^{-1} = (L/W)(1 + \delta)[\mu C'_{ox}(V_{GS} - V_T)]^{-1}$.

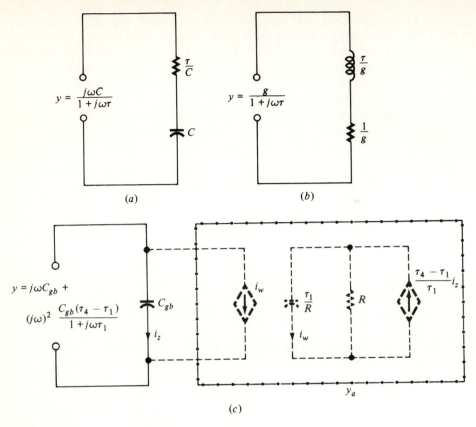

$$y = \frac{j\omega C}{1 + j\omega\tau}$$

(a)

$$y = \frac{g}{1 + j\omega\tau}$$

(b)

$$y = j\omega C_{gb} + (j\omega)^2 \frac{C_{gb}(\tau_4 - \tau_1)}{1 + j\omega\tau_1}$$

(c)

FIGURE 9.18
Simple circuits used to represent the admittances (a) in (9.4.69a) to (9.4.69d); (b) in (9.4.69f); (c) in (9.4.69e) (the value of R is arbitrary).

as follows from Fig. 9.18c and (9.4.69f)

$$L_d g_d = \tau_1 \tag{9.4.70c}$$

Plots for the resistances and the inductance are shown in Fig. 9.20.†

Despite the conditions of the form $\omega\tau_1 \ll 1$ in (9.4.69), the model just presented is found satisfactory to about $\omega = \omega_o$. A comparison of the various models will be made in Sec. 9.5.

The resistors and the inductor in Fig. 9.19 (in cooperation with the

---

† It is seen that R_{gd}, R_{bd}, and L_d become infinite in saturation, just as do the impedances of the elements in series with them (assuming no channel length modulation). When the model is implemented as part of a CAD program one should exercise care in order to avoid numerical difficulties.

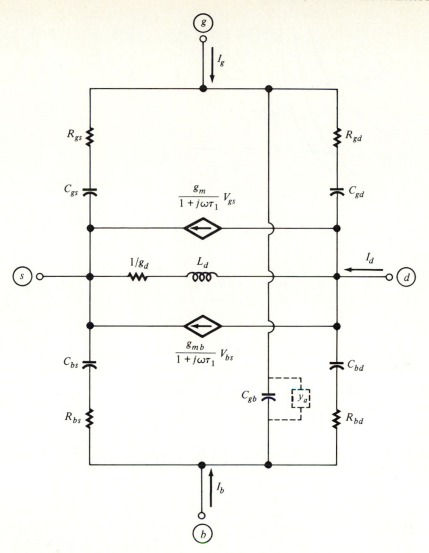

FIGURE 9.19
Small-signal equivalent circuit corresponding to (9.4.69).

elements in series with them) can be viewed as representing some of the effects of the inversion layer's inertia in responding to rapid changes. Thus, if the source voltage is changing fast, the inversion layer will "hesitate" to respond, and the corresponding changes in the gate and substrate currents will lag behind the source voltage changes; this is modeled by R_{gs}, C_{gs} and R_{bs}, C_{bs}, respectively. The combinations R_{gd}, C_{gd} and R_{bd}, C_{bd} model the corresponding effects if the drain voltage is changing fast instead (in the nonsaturation

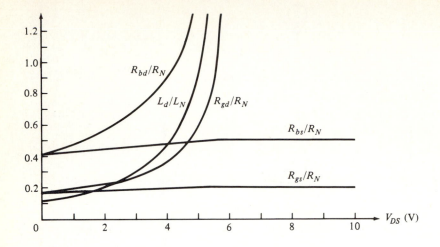

FIGURE 9.20
The quantities R_{gs}, R_{gd}, R_{bs}, R_{bd}, normalized to $R_N = (\omega_o C_{ox})^{-1}$, and L_d normalized to $L_N = (\omega_o^2 C_{ox})^{-1}$ plotted vs. V_{DS} for the device of Fig. 9.7 ($C_{ox} = C'_{ox} WL$).

region). The combination of L_d and g_d can be viewed as representing the inertia of the inversion layer in changing the source current when a fast-varying drain voltage demands such a change (in the nonsaturation region). Finally, the denominators in the values for the two current sources model the inertia of the inversion layer in changing the drain current when the gate or the substrate voltages are varying.

If the frequency of the small-signal voltages applied to the terminals becomes low enough, the inertia mentioned becomes negligible. Indeed, with decreasing frequency the magnitude of the impedances of C_{gs}, C_{bs}, C_{gd}, and C_{bd} increases. Relative to them, the series resistances become unimportant and can be omitted. Also, with decreasing frequency the impedance of the inductor decreases, and this element can be omitted in comparison to the resistance in series with it. Finally, the denominators in the current source values become approximately 1 at low frequencies. In this case, the model in Fig. 9.19 is thus seen to reduce to the model of Fig. 8.13.

The model can also be related to the complete quasi-static model of Sec. 9.2. At low frequencies, the series RC combinations in Fig. 9.19 reduce to the corresponding capacitances in Fig. 9.5, for the reasons discussed above. In addition, assuming $\omega \tau_1 \ll 1$, we can use the approximation $1/(1 + j\omega\tau_1) \approx 1 - j\omega\tau_1$, and we can write (9.4.69f) to (9.4.69h) as follows:

$$-y_{sd} \approx g_d - j\omega\tau_1 g_d \,, \qquad \omega\tau_1 \ll 1 \qquad (9.4.71a)$$

$$y_m \approx g_m - j\omega\tau_1 g_m \,, \qquad \omega\tau_1 \ll 1 \qquad (9.4.71b)$$

$$y_{mb} \approx g_{mb} - j\omega\tau_1 g_{mb} \,, \qquad \omega\tau_1 \ll 1 \qquad (9.4.71c)$$

A comparison with $-y_{sd}$, y_m, and y_{mb} for the complete quasi-static model [(9.3.11f) to (9.3.11h)] shows that the form is the same (recall that C_{sd} was a *negative* quantity). Furthermore an examination of the expressions for the various parameters in these equations reveals that (9.4.71a) to (9.4.71c) are in fact *identical* to (9.3.11f) to (9.3.11h), not only in form but even in *value* (Prob. 9.19). Thus, the model of Fig. 9.19 reduces to the complete quasi-static model of Fig. 9.5, assuming C_{mx} is negligible. Note in particular that the series resistance-inductance combination of Fig. 9.19 reduces to a parallel combination of a resistance and a *negative* capacitance. With further reduction in frequency, the terms containing ω in $-y_{sd}$, y_m, and y_{mb} become negligible, and the model reduces to the simple model of Fig. 8.13.

The coefficients of the controlled sources in Fig. 9.19 are complex. This might make it impossible to use this model *directly* in some computer analysis programs. The problem is circumvented by noting that we can write

$$\frac{g_m}{1 + j\omega\tau_1} V_{gs} = g_m V_1 \tag{9.4.72a}$$

$$\frac{g_{mb}}{1 + j\omega\tau_1} V_{bs} = g_{mb} V_2 \tag{9.4.72b}$$

where

$$V_1 = \frac{1}{1 + j\omega\tau_1} V_{gs} \tag{9.4.73a}$$

$$V_2 = \frac{1}{1 + j\omega\tau_1} V_{bs} \tag{9.4.73b}$$

and that it is very easy to develop V_1 from V_{gs} and V_2 from V_{bs} by using two simple circuits. This idea is exploited in Fig. 9.21, where it is easy to verify that (9.4.73) holds as long as $R_1 C_1 = \tau_1$ and $R_2 C_2 = \tau_1$.† However, in order not to upset the model, we have to make sure that the new elements added draw a negligible current (in comparison to the R_{gs}-C_{gs} and R_{bs}-C_{bs} combinations). This can be ensured, for example, by using

$$C_1 = 0.001 C_{gs} \tag{9.4.74a}$$

$$R_1 = \frac{\tau_1}{C_1} \tag{9.4.74b}$$

$$C_2 = 0.001 C_{bs} \tag{9.4.74c}$$

$$R_2 = \frac{\tau_1}{C_2} \tag{9.4.74d}$$

---

† Unfortunately, we could not have used the voltages across C_{gs} and C_{bs} themselves, since $R_{gs} C_{gs} = R_{bs} C_{bs} = \tau_1 - \tau_2$ rather than being equal to the desired τ_1.

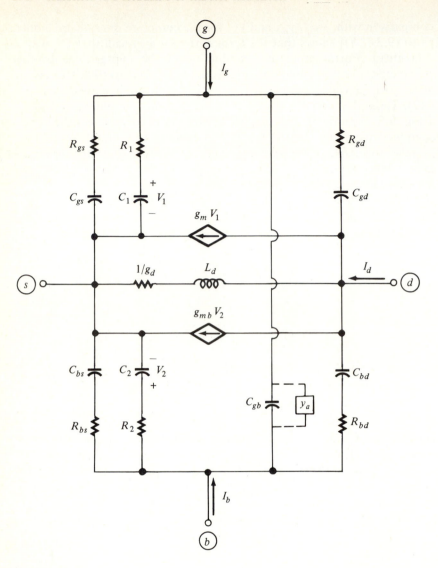

FIGURE 9.21
The model of Fig. 9.19 modified to avoid complex coefficients in the controlled-current sources.

In the saturation region, the model of Fig. 9.21 assumes a simple form, easily derived from the relations given above, and shown in Fig. 9.22. In this region g_d models channel length modulation (Sec. 5.2). This effect has largely been studied at low frequencies, and was not included in the derivations of the present model. Thus, there is no reason to assume that L_d, as given from (9.4.70c), will be the correct value to use in the saturation region. This is not likely to be a problem in practice, since in a circuit capacitances invariably exist

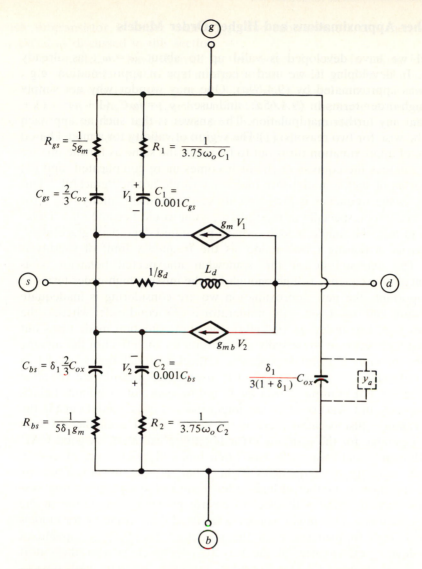

FIGURE 9.22
The model of Fig. 9.19 for the special case of operation in the saturation region.

between drain and source (e.g., because of another transistor connected to the one under consideration, or parasitics). At high frequencies, where the impedance of L_d could become comparable to $1/g_d$, the impedance of the above capacitances is low, and relatively large small-signal currents can flow in them. Compared to these, the minute small-signal current flowing through $1/g_d$ and L_d is likely to be negligible.

complete quasi-static model of Fig. 9.5, and curve c is for the model of Fig. 9.19 or 9.21. Finally, curve d is for a model resulting by keeping many terms in the numerators and denominators of (9.4.65). This model is valid even beyond $10\omega_o$.[39] It is seen in Fig. 9.23b that going from a to b produces a drastic improvement in the region of validity. The region of validity for b is limited by the fact that, at high frequencies the error in the magnitude becomes severe. This is because y_m contains a right-half-plane zero for this model (9.3.11g) in contrast to the left-half-plane pole in y_m for c (9.4.69g). The upward-going magnitude for b at high frequencies is clearly unrealistic, since it suggests an enhancement in the forward gate-to-drain action, contrary to one's expectation that, at high frequencies, control of the gate on the drain current is gradually lost due to the inversion layer's inertia. In fact, as far as magnitude is concerned, a is better than b, although it corresponds to a simpler model! Going to c eliminates the problem of b, and now both magnitude and phase are predicted satisfactorily up to about ω_o.

Similar plots can be constructed for other operating points and for other parameters in an attempt to compare the various models and determine upper frequency limits of validity.[39] It is found that the upper frequency limit of validity for a parameter of a given model depends on which parameter it is, what is the operating point, what accuracy is desired, whether magnitude or phase is of most interest, etc. Furthermore, one can always construct pathological cases where a model will fail in some way (Prob 9.17). Thus, the frequency limits of validity we have been providing should be considered in the above light. They are only rough indications of the regions within which a given model will perform satisfactorily in most cases. To summarize, the frequency limits of validity we have suggested for strong inversion models in this and the previous chapter are as follows:

1. Quasi-static model without transcapacitors (Fig. 8.13): $\dfrac{\omega_o}{10}$

2. Quasi-static model with transcapacitors (Fig. 9.5): $\dfrac{\omega_o}{3}$

3. First-order nonquasi-static model (Fig. 9.19 or 9.21): ω_o

9.6   OTHER EFFECTS

At high frequencies the extrinsic parasitics described in Sec. 8.4 can significantly affect the y parameters of a device as measured externally. Consider, for example, the model in Fig. 8.23. At high frequencies the impedances of C_{bse} and C_{bde} become negligible, and they tend to shunt the channel with the substrate resistances R_{be1} and R_{be3}. This results is an increase in the magnitude of the admittance y_{dd} seen at the drain terminal, which cannot be predicted by the intrinsic device model. Similarly, short-channel effects, effects of nonuniform substrates, etc., cannot be predicted by the models presented here. In fact, very little has been done to characterize such effects at very high frequencies other than direct measurements. If measurements can be performed accurately (which is not easy at very high frequencies), one can always use a general *y*-parameter representation such as the ones shown in Figs. 9.15 to 9.17, since these were derived for an *arbitrary* four-terminal structure *without any assumptions* as to channel length, substrate uniformity, absence of extrinsic effects, etc.

REFERENCES

1. J. A. Geurst, "Calculation of high-frequency characteristics of thin film transistors," *Solid-State Electronics*, vol. 8, pp. 88–90, 1965.
2. D. B. Candler and A. G. Jordan, "A small-signal, high-frequency analysis of the insulated-gate field-effect transistor," *International Journal of Electronics*, vol. 19, pp. 181–196, 1965.
3. M. H. White and R. C. Gallagher, "Metal oxide semiconductor (MOS) small-signal equivalent circuits," *Proceedings of the IEEE*, vol. 53, pp. 314–315, 1965.
4. J. R. Hauser, "Small-signal properties of field-effect devices," *IEEE Transactions on Electron Devices*, vol. ED-12, pp. 605–618, 1965.
5. J. A. Guerst and H. J. C. A. Nunnink, "Numerical data on the high-frequency characteristics of thin-film transistors," *Solid-State Electronics*, vol. 8, pp. 769–771, 1965.
6. W. Fischer, "Equivalent circuit and gain of MOS field-effect transistors," *Solid-State Electronics*, vol. 9, pp. 71–81, 1966.
7. R. Paul, "Hochfrequenzerhalten von Feldeffecktransistoren mit isolierter Steuer Elektrode," *AEU*, vol. 20, pp. 317–328, 1966.
8. R. Paul, "Die Ersatzschaltung von Feldeffektransistoren mit isoliertem Gate," *Nachrichtentechnik*, vol. 16, pp. 243–249, 1966.
9. R. Paul, "Einfluss einer nichtidealen Gateisolation auf die Vierpolparameter des Feldeffekttransistors," *Nachrichtentechnik*, vol. 16, pp. 278–285, 1966.
10. R. Paul, "Frequenzabhängigkeit der Vierpoleigenschaften von MOS-Transistoren," *Nachrichtentechnik*, vol. 16, pp. 401–406, 1966.
11. Z. S. Girbnikov and Yu. A. Tkhorik, "Calculation of the transient processes in field-effect triodes with an insulated gate for the saturated mode of operation," *Radio Engineering and Electronic Physics*, vol. 11, pp. 776–781, 1966.
12. H. Johnson, "A high-frequency representation of the MOS transistor," *Proceedings of the IEEE*, vol. 54, pp. 1970–1971, 1966.
13. D. H. Treleaven and F. N. Trofimenkoff, "MOSFET equivalent circuit at pinchoff," *Proceedings of the IEEE*, vol. 54, pp. 1223–1224, 1966.
14. H. C. DeGraaff, "High frequency measurements of thin-film trnasistors," *Solid-State Electronics*, vol. 10, pp. 51–56, January 1967.
15. R. Paul, "Experimentelles Hochfrequenzverhalten von MOS-Transistoren," *Nachrichtentechnik*, vol. 17, pp. 255–260, July 1967.
16. M. B. Das, "Generalized high-frequency network theory of field-effect transistors," *IEE Proceedings*, vol. 114, pp. 50–59, 1967.
17. I. R. Burns, "High-frequency characteristics of the insulated gate field-effect transistors," *RCA Review*, vol. 28, pp. 385–418, 1967.
18. F. A. Lindholm, R. J. Balda, and J. L. Clements, "Characterization of the four-terminal MOS transistor for digital and linear applications," *Digest of Technical Papers*, International Electronics Conference, Toronto, pp. 116–117, 1967.
19. M. B. Das, "High-frequency network properties of MOS transistors including the substrate resistivity effects," *IEEE Transactions on Electron Devices*, vol. ED-16, pp. 1049–1069, 1969.
20. J. A. Van Nielen, "A simple and accurate approximation to the high-frequency characteristics of IGFETs," *Solid-State Electronics*, vol. 12, pp. 826–829, 1969.

21. J. W. Haslett and F. N. Trofimenkoff, "Small-signal, high-frequency equivalent circuit for the metal-oxide semiconductor field-effect transistor," *IEE Proceedings*, vol. 116, pp. 699–702, 1969.

22. R. S. C. Cobbold, *Theory and Applications of Field-Effect Transistors*, Wiley-Interscience, New York, 1970.

23. E. M. Cherry, "Small-signal high-frequency response of the insulated gate field-effect transistor," *IEEE Transactions on Electron Devices*, vol. ED-17, pp. 569–577, 1970.

24. M. V. Balakirev and V. M. Bogachev, "Frequency and transient characteristics of metal oxide semiconductor transistors and synthesis of their equivalent circuits," *Radio Engineering and Electronics Physics*, vol. 16, pp. 1884–1897, 1971.

25. M. Reiser, "A two-dimensional numerical FET model for DC, AC and Large-Signal Analysis," *IEEE Transactions on Electron Devices*, vol. ED-20, pp. 35–45, 1976.

26. U. Kumar and S. C. Dutta Roy, "A simple small-signal two-part MOST model for the pre-pinchoff region," *Solid-State Electronics*, vol. 20, pp. 1021–1022, 1977.

27. U. Kumar, "A simple two-part model of the metal oxide semiconductor transistor," *Microelectronics Journal*, vol. 10, pp. 50–53, 1978.

28. J. I. Arreola, "Equivalent circuit modeling of the large signal transient response of four-terminal MOS field-effect transistors," doctoral dissertation, University of Florida, 1978.

29. D. E. Ward and R. W. Dutton, "A charge-oriented model for MOS transistor capacitances," *IEEE Journal of Solid-State Circuits*, vol. SC-13, pp. 703–707, October 1978.

30. J. A. Robinson, Y. A. El-Mansy, and A. R. Boothroyd, "A general four-terminal charging-current model for the insulated-gate field effect transistor," *Solid-State Electronics*, vol. 23, parts I, II, pp. 405–414, 1980.

31. S. Y. Oh, "A simplified two-dimensional numerical analysis of MOS devices including transient phenomena," *Technical Report G201–10,* Integrated Circuits Laboratory, Stanford University, California, June 1981.

32. D. E. Ward, "Charge-based modeling of capacitance in MOS transistors," *Technical Report G201–11,* Integrated Circuits Laboratory, Stanford University, California, June 1981.

33. R. Conilogue and C. Viswanathan, "A complete large and small signal charge model for a MOS transistor," *Technical Digest*, International Electron Devices Meeting, pp. 654–657, San Francisco, 1982.

34. K. Y. Tong, "AC model for MOS transistors from transient-current computations," *IEE Proceedings*, vol. 130, part I, pp. 33–36, February 1983.

35. J. J. Paulos and D. A. Antoniadis, "Limitations of quasi-static capacitance models for the MOS transistor," *IEEE Electron Device Letters*, vol. EDL-4, pp. 221–224, July 1983.

36. C. Turchetti, G. Masetti, and Y. Tsividis, "On the small-signal behavior of the MOS transistor in quasi-static operation," *Solid-State Electronics*, vol. 26, pp. 941–949, 1983.

37. Y. Tsividis and G. Masetti, "Problems in precision modeling of the MOS transistor for analog applications," *IEEE Transactions on Computer-Aided Design*, vol. CAD-3, pp. 72–79, January 1984.

38. J. J. Paulos, "Measurement and modeling of small-geometry MOS transistor capacitances," Ph.D. dissertation, Department of Electrical Engineering and Computer Science, Massachusetts Institute of Technology, Cambridge, September 1984.

39. M. Bagheri and Y. Tsividis, "A small-signal dc-to-high-frequency nonquasi-static model for the four-terminal MOSFET valid in all regions of operation," *IEEE Transactions on Electron Devices*, vol. ED-32, pp. 2383–2391, November 1985.

40. J. J. Paulos, D. A. Antoniadis, and Y. P. Tsividis, "Measurement of intrinsic capacitances of MOS transistors," *Digest of Technical Papers*, IEEE International Solid-State Circuits Conference, San Francisco, pp. 238–239, February 1982.

41. C. A. Desoer and E. S. Kuh, *Basic Circuit Theory*, McGraw-Hill, New York, 1969.

42. W. H. Hayt, Jr., and J. E. Kemmerly, *Engineering Circuit Analysis*, McGraw-Hill, New York, 1986.

43. W. H. Kim and H. E. Meadows, Jr., *Modern Network Analysis*, John Wiley, New York, 1971.

44. H. Iwai, J. E. Oristian, J. T. Walker, and R. W. Dutton, "A scaleable technique for the measurement of intrinsic MOS capacitance with atto-Farad resolution," *IEEE Transactions on Electron Devices*, vol. ED-32, pp. 344–356, February 1985.
45. J. Oristian, H. Iwai, J. Walker, and R. Dutton, "Small geometry MOS transistor capacitance measurement method using simple on-chip circuits," *IEEE Electron Device Letters*, vol. EDL-5, pp. 395–397, October 1984.
46. J. J. Paulos and D. A. Antoniadis, "Measurement of minimum-geometry MOS transistor capacitances," *IEEE Transactions on Electron Devices*, vol. ED-32, pp. 357–363, February 1985.

PROBLEMS

9.1. For the case of Fig. P9.1 (where $q_2 = -q_1$) relate the various quantities by writing equations analogous to (7.3.16) and (9.2.2). Show that in this case the signs used in the definition (9.2.1) represent a "natural" choice.

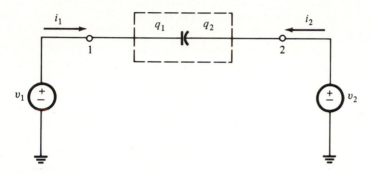

FIGURE P9.1

9.2. We define the "nonreciprocity" between two capacitance parameters C_{kl} and C_{lk} $(l \neq k)$, as the quantity $C_{kl} - C_{lk}$. Using (9.2.8), derive relations among the various nonreciprocities and comment on the result.

9.3. Using Kirchhoff's current law for all terminals, check the validity of the model in Fig. 9.4b.

9.4. Derive 9.2.19 in detail.

9.5. Consider the model of Fig. 9.5. For *all* 16 ordered pairs of terminals (k, l) perform the following experiment. Apply a voltage v_l between terminal l and ground, keeping all other terminals grounded, and determine the current i_k entering terminal k. Show that the capacitive part of this current is given by C_{kl} (dv_l/dt) if $l = k$, and by $-C_{kl}(dv_l/dt)$ if $l \neq k$. Note that six of the C_{kl} appear directly in the model, whereas others do not, in which case (9.2.8) or (9.2.20) will have to be evoked.

9.6. Show that results identical to those in Prob. 9.5 would be obtained if the model of Fig. 8.13 were used instead for five of the terminal pair combinations (those that correspond to the subscripts of the capacitors in Fig. 8.13). Show that for other terminal pairs the results will differ from those in Prob. 9.5; this points to the incompleteness of the simple model. Explain why this incompleteness does not matter at low frequencies.

9.7. Prove (9.2.21) to (9.2.27).

9.8. An intuitive argument was given following (9.2.24) concerning the fact that C_{sd} is negative in nonsaturation. Using similar arguments, explain why C_{ds} is also negative, whereas all other capacitances C_{xy} are positive.

9.9. Using the approximate strong-inversion model, $C_{mx} = 0$ was found. Allow for a nonzero C_{mx}, and show that the expressions for the capacitances would have to be modified so that (9.2.8) remains valid.

9.10. This problem continues the comparison between the simple model of Fig. 8.13 and the complete quasi-static model of Fig. 9.5, started in Prob. 9.6. Consider operation in the saturation region. Using the small-signal quantity values found for the simple model in Secs. 8.2 and 8.3, justify the upper frequency limit of validity given for the model of Fig. 8.13 following (8.3.6).

9.11. Prove (9.3.7).

9.12. Prove (9.3.9).

9.13. Provide all the details in the proofs of (9.4.36) to (9.4.48).

9.14. Prove (9.4.51) and (9.4.53) in detail.

9.15. (*Note*: This problem requires *extremely lengthy* derivations. It is not meant as a homework problem.) Solve (9.4.51) and (9.4.52) using the following iterative procedure.[20] Replace x in (9.4.51) with a dummy variable $\hat{x}$. Develop an integral form of (9.4.51a) and (9.4.51b), by integrating from x to L. Use as an initial approximation $I_i(x, \omega) = I_i(L, \omega)$ (which is actually exact for $\omega = 0$). Substitute this in the integral form of (9.4.51a) and solve for the corresponding approximation of $U_i(x, \omega)$. Use this in the integral form of (9.4.51b) to find a new approximation for $I_i(x, \omega)$. Use this in the integral form of (9.4.51a) and solve for the new approximation of $U_i(x, \omega)$, etc. Show that the procedure produces a solution from which one can obtain (9.4.58) to (9.4.60), with the values given in Appendix M.

9.16. Prove (9.4.65) to (9.4.67), using results from Appendix M (*Note*: Very lengthy derivations are involved.)

9.17. (*a*) Plot the magnitude and phase of $-y_{gb}$ vs. ω (for ω up to ω_o on a log axis) in the saturation region and at $V_{DS} = 0$, using (9.4.69e) with and without including the term containing $(j\omega)^2$. Use $\delta = 0.1$, an oxide thickness of $0.04\ \mu$m, $W = L = 10\ \mu$m, $\mu = 70\ \mu$m^2/(V·ns), and $V_{GS} - V_T = 2$ V. (*Note*: The quantity τ_4 becomes infinite as V_{DS} approaches zero, but the product $C_{gb}\tau_4$ remains finite.) Comment on the validity of approximating $-y_{gb}$ by $j\omega C_{gb}$ (which is equivalent to deleting the box shown in broken lines in Figs. 9.19, 9.21, and 9.22). Comment on currents that, in practice, are likely to mask the current due to y_{gb}.

(*b*) Assume $V_{DS} = 0$. Show instances where a terminal current being observed is only due to y_{gb} (and to extrinsic elements). Explain why such instances are unlikely to be of significance in practice and that, even then, the magnitude of the observed current is very small and likely to be dominated by extrinsic effects.

9.18. Verify the three circuit representations in Fig. 9.18.

9.19. Starting from (9.4.71), show that the model in Fig. 9.19 reduces at low frequencies to the model of Fig. 9.5, in both form and element values (y_{mx} is assumed zero), and that at even lower frequencies it further reduces to the model of Fig. 8.13.

9.20. The intrinsic cutoff frequency of a transistor was defined in Sec. 8.3, and in the strong-inversion saturation region was found to be given by (8.3.34), by using the model of Fig. 8.13. As mentioned following that equation, the model of Fig. 8.13 is not accurate at frequencies as high as $\omega = \omega_T$, and therefore the result (8.3.34) should be checked by using a more accurate model. Show that, by using the model of Fig. 9.21, one obtains practically the same value for ω_T.

9.21. Prove all the values given in the model in Fig. 9.22.

9.22. Provide plots vs. ω for normalized magnitude and phase of all parameters in Fig. 9.17 in the saturation region, for the nonquasi-static model of Sec. 9.4.

9.23. Consider a transistor with $N_A = 1000\ \mu\text{m}^{-3}$, $d_{ox} = 0.04\ \mu\text{m}$, $V_{T0} = 1\ \text{V}$, $\phi_B = 0.7\ \text{V}$, $\mu = 60\ \mu\text{m}^2/(\text{V}\cdot\text{ns})$, and $W = L = 6\ \mu\text{m}$ connected as shown in Fig. 9.1b with $V_B = 2\ \text{V}$, $V_S = 4\ \text{V}$, $V_G = 7\ \text{V}$, and $V_D = 5\ \text{V}$. Calculate all parameters for the model of Fig. 9.21.

9.24. For the device of Prob. 9.23, find the magnitude and phase of all terminal currents (Fig. 9.1b) if the small-signal voltages $v_b(t)$, $v_s(t)$, $v_g(t)$, and $v_d(t)$ are of the form $a\cos(\omega t + \phi)$, with magnitudes a of 2, 1, 4, and 3 mV, respectively, and phases of 0, 0, 40, and 50°, respectively. The frequency ω is $2\pi \times 500$ MHz.

9.25. The circuit in Fig. P9.25 has little to do with a transistor, but it will help in getting a feeling for the various levels of approximation involved in modeling.
 (*a*) Find y_{AB}, its real part y_{ABr}, and its imaginary part y_{ABi}.
 (*b*) Find the conditions under which C can be neglected in each of the above three expressions, and give a simplified model.
 (*c*) Find the conditions under which R_2 can be neglected in each of the three expressions in (*a*), and give a simplified model.
 (*d*) Show that neglecting R_2 is equivalent to assuming that the charge Q on the top plate depends quasi-statically on the voltage V defined in the figure. Show that at high frequencies this quasi-static dependence breaks down.

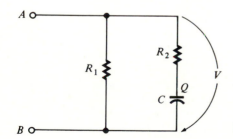

FIGURE P9.25

9.26. Shown in Fig. P9.26 is the model of Fig. 9.22 in saturation with three important extrinsic parasitics added, assuming that the substrate is short-circuited to the source and that C_{gb} and L_d are negligible. Assume $R_{de} \ll 1/g_d$, and $\omega \ll 1/(C_{bde}R_{de})$. Derive expressions for the y-parameters y_{gg}, y_{gd}, y_{dd}, and y_{dg}. Show qualitative plots for their real and imaginary parts vs. ω on log-log axes for (a) zero C_{gde}, C_{bde}, and R_{de}, and (b) nonzero C_{gde}, C_{bde}, and R_{de}. Discuss the important effects caused by the extrinsic elements.

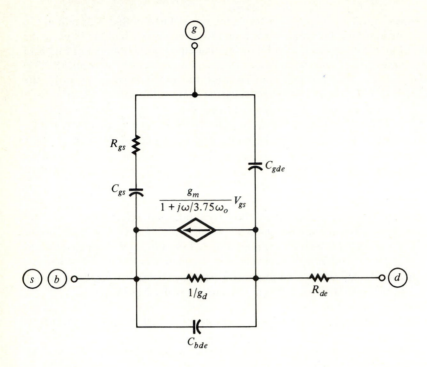

FIGURE P.9.26

9.27. Show that, if an extrinsic resistance R_{se} is added in series with the source terminal in Fig. P9.26, the real part of y_{gd} can have a nonzero positive value.

CHAPTER
10

MOS TRANSISTOR FABRICATION

BY D. A. ANTONIADIS, MASSACHUSSETS INSTITUTE OF TECHNOLOGY

10.1 INTRODUCTION

This chapter discusses how modern MOS transistors are made. The overwhelming majority of MOS transistors being fabricated at present are integral parts of complex integrated circuits (ICs). For this reason the fabrication sequence used to produce MOSFETs has to take into account that individual devices must be isolated from each other, that several device types—e.g., enhancement and depletion or n- and p-channel MOSFETs—must be realized together, that contacts must be provided for connecting the MOSFETs to the "wiring" conductors, and that space must be provided for running these interconnect wires among the active devices of the integrated circuit. Thus, to understand modern MOSFET fabrication, this chapter presents it in the context of integrated-circuit fabrication.

The processes needed to produce integrated circuits can be summarized as follows. From the circuit schematic, and assuming all relevant geometrical dimensions such as W and L values for the transistors are known, one defines the required geometrical shapes necessary to produce all required devices in the circuit. This is done by "laying out" these shapes, greatly magnified to a convenient size, on a surface such as that of paper or the screen of a computer terminal. This is called the *layout* process, and is performed by treating each physical *layer* separately. For example, all areas corresponding to polysilicon lines used for the transistor gates and interconnections constitute one layer, all areas defining metal interconnection lines constitute another layer, etc. The final drawings for each layer are then stored on computer tape, and the latter is used to drive automated systems which produce what are known as *masks*. In its simplest form, a mask is a transparent glass plate with an opaque film deposited on one surface patterned in geometrical shapes. These geometrical shapes define one layer in the final, extremely small size to be used for the actual device. The masks are used to transfer the geometrical patterns onto the surface of a silicon wafer through a series of detailed, elaborate *fabrication processing steps*. Each layout layer typically corresponds to one mask, and each mask is used for one fabrication step.

To assure that the sequence of fabrication process steps yields properly functioning circuits it is essential that the laid-out patterns for each layer obey a set of geometrical constraints called *design rules*. These rules are determined by the spatial resolution capabilities of the various processing steps as implemented in the fabrication processing line. The rules are specified as minimum permissible dimensions of geometrical patterns in each physical layer, minimum distance between such patterns, minimum distance or overlap between patterns of different layers, etc.

Two fabrication process sequences† will be considered in this chapter. The NMOS process sequence is the simpler of the two and results in *n*-channel devices (usually both enhancement mode and depletion mode devices). The second process sequence is referred to as CMOS, standing for "complementary MOS." It is used to make both *n*-channel and *p*-channel devices on the same chip, and offers more flexibility in circuit design. The simpler NMOS process will be used to illustrate most of the fabrication steps, and supplementary details will then be given for CMOS processes. Other fabrication processes can be found in several texts.[1–5]

10.2   BASIC STEPS OF MOS FABRICATION TECHNOLOGY

The starting material for silicon MOS integrated circuit fabrication is a circular wafer (slice) of monocrystalline silicon, about 500 μm in thickness and 7.5 to 15 cm (3 to 6 in) in diameter. The wafer doping is usually uniform. For typical NMOS processes, the doping is p type with resistivity in the range of 20 to 60 $\Omega \cdot$ cm ($N_A = 6 \times 10^2$ to 2×10^2 μm^{-3}). For CMOS processes, the doping is either n type or p type, with resistivity in the vicinity of 5 $\Omega \cdot$ cm ($N_A = 3 \times 10^3$ μm^{-3} or $N_D = 10^3$ μm^{-3}). The fabrication of integrated circuits con-

---

† The term *fabrication process sequence* here refers to a complete sequence of fabrication steps that result in a finished integrated circuit. The term *process* (e.g., NMOS process), or the term *technology* (e.g., CMOS technology) are also commonly used to describe the same thing.

sists of a sequence of process steps to which these wafers are subjected; some of these steps are repeated several times. The steps can be classified into the following categories: *film deposition*, *lithography*, *etching*, *ion implantation*, *diffusion*, and *epitaxy*. We now provide a brief description of each type of fabrication step.

10.2.1 Film Deposition

At several stages during fabrication the wafer is covered throughout its area by certain films of materials. These films are then selectively removed, except in certain areas where they are used to form the various layers on a chip. The films include:

1. *Silicon dioxide* (SiO_2). This insulating glassy layer is "grown" on top of the wafer surface or on top of other films already on that surface. SiO_2 is grown either by thermally oxidizing the silicon surface at high temperatures[2] (e.g., around 1000°C for one hour) or by a process called *chemical vapor deposition* (CVD),[3] at low temperatures (450 to 750°C). SiO_2 is used to separate transistor gates from the channel, to isolate connecting layers from one another, and to selectively protect silicon surface areas against ion implantation.

2. *Silicon nitride* (Si_3N_4). This layer, which is also insulating, is deposited by using the CVD process mentioned above[5, 6] at about 750°C. In the processes of interest here it is used to protect selected areas against oxidation.

3. *Polycrystalline silicon* (also called *polysilicon* or *poly*). Again, the CVD process is used to deposit this material[1, 5] at about 650°C. Doped polysilicon is used to form the transistor gates, certain interconnections, and, sometimes, resistors for special applications.

4. *Metal*. Usually aluminum (Al) or aluminum alloys are used. Metal atoms are deposited on the wafer after being emitted from a source by either evaporation in vacuum or by a process called *sputtering*.[7] Metal is used to form interconnections and, in some older processes, also the gates of the transistors.

10.2.2 Lithography

Lithography is the process by means of which geometrical patterns are transferred from a mask onto the wafer surface or onto the surface of a film covering the wafer. To achieve this, the surface is first covered by a layer of polymer called the *resist*, and the geometrical patterns are transferred onto it from a *mask*. There are several ways by which this transfer can take place, but the most dominant is currently the photographic technique. Thus, the process is called *photolithography*, and the polymer layer *photoresist*.[4] The photoresist exists initially in liquid form. It is applied uniformly on the surface and is subsequently hardened by baking at a low temperature (Fig. 10.1*a*). Geometri-

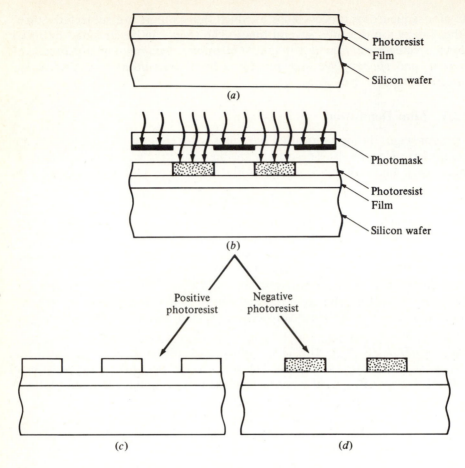

FIGURE 10.1
The basic photoresist steps in photolithography. (*a*) Application; (*b*) photoresist exposure through a mask; (*c*) positive photoresist development; (*d*) negative photoresist development.

cal patterns are then transferred onto it by using collimated ultraviolet light that casts a precise shadow of the mask, as shown in Fig. 10.1*b*. The patterns exist in the form of opaque areas on a glass plate, called the *photomask*. The photoresist is sensitive to ultraviolet light and, upon exposure as shown, its molecular structure is changed selectively below the transparent areas of the mask. Subsequently, the photoresist is "developed," much like the emulsion on a photographic plate (although the physical processes are different), by using an organic solvent. If the photoresist is *positive*, the development process will leave the unexposed areas intact, as shown in Fig. 10.1*c*, and will remove the rest. If the photoresist is *negative*, the opposite will happen, as shown in Fig. 10.1*d*. VLSI processes use almost exclusively positive photoresists since these allow better resolution.

There exist two other important processes of resist exposure, but th
use at present is limited. X-ray lithography uses X rays to transfer mas
patterns on the resist and can reproduce smaller features than ultraviolet
photolithography, and E-beam lithography uses a fine electron beam to write
patterns directly on the resist without the intermediary of a mask.

10.2.3   Etching

Etching is the process by which selected areas of a film deposited on the wafer
are removed. This process follows the lithography step described above. Thus,
let us assume that by using lithography we have arrived at the situation of Fig.
10.2a. The wafer can now be exposed to a (chemically reactive) *etching
ambient* which etches away the film areas not protected by the resist, as shown
in Fig. 10.2b. The photoresist can subsequently be removed with a photoresist
"stripper." The type of etching ambient depends on the type of film to be
etched. For example, if SiO_2 is to be etched, a solution of hydrofluoric acid is
often used to remove selectively the SiO_2 without affecting the photoresist or
the bare silicon surface once the latter is reached. For many modern etching
processes, a dry etching ambient is preferred, because it allows better control
of the film undercut visible in Fig. 10.2b. This kind of ambient consists of a
mixture of gases maintained in a plasma state by a radio frequency voltage
excitation.[1]

There are two key characteristics of the etching process that determine
which technique should be used at any particular step of the process sequence.
The first is the "etching anisotropy," which determines how accurate a
replication of the photoresist the etched pattern will be. A completely anisotropic etch replicates the photoresist pattern exactly by producing vertical etch
walls lined up with the photoresist edges. This is because the etching process

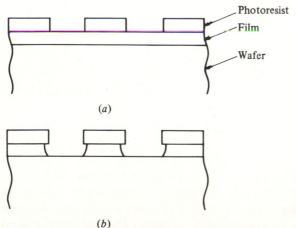

Photoresist
Film
Wafer

(a)

(b)

FIGURE 10.2
Illustration of the use of photoresist
in selective etching of films.

in the perpendicular but not in the parallel direction to the
ontrast, a completely isotropic etch attacks both directions at
wet etching processes fall in the last category; the plasma
generally partially anisotropic. Figure 10.2b shows the
...ng" that results from a typical plasma etching process.
      ...cond key characteristic of the etching process is its "selectivity,"
   ...determines the rate at which the material intended for etching is etched
compared to other materials in the same environment. For example, a high
degree of etching selectivity of the film with respect to the wafer material that
underlies it is generally desirable. Wet etching usually has very high selectivity.
The more commonly used plasma etching processes have selectivities from 2 to
1 (poor) to 20 to 1 (good) of intentional to unintentional etch rates.

10.2.4 Ion Implantation

Ion implantation is the principal process by which doping concentration is
altered. This process consists of shooting uniformly over the entire "target"
surface precise amounts of ionized atoms of the desired dopant species, such as
arsenic (As), phosphorus (P), and boron (B), using an ion-implanter ap-
paratus.[1] These ions are first accelerated in an electrostatic field, so that they
gain enough energy (10 to 300 keV) to enter the target. The ions enter the
silicon where not prevented from doing so by a protective "cover" of sufficient
thickness, as shown in Fig. 10.3a. The cover can be resist, SiO_2, Si_3N_4,
polysilicon, or a combination of the above. A typical distribution of the
implanted ions inside the target is shown in Fig. 10.3b. The implanted layer's
peak location and spread depend on the ion energy, the ion mass, and the
target material. For typical applications, they vary between 0.05 and 0.5 μm.
The total number of implanted ions per unit area, or "ion dose," illustrated in
Fig. 10.3c, can be accurately controlled, and it usually lies in the range of 10^2
to 10^8 ions/μm^2, depending on the application.
      Ion implantation is used almost exclusively as the method of doping in
modern IC processes. In MOS technologies the principal uses are:

1. Source and drain formation.
2. Adjustment of the threshold voltage (Chap. 6).
3. Formation of the proper substrate doping type and level into which the
   transistor is to be built in CMOS technologies.
4. Reduction of punchthrough effects (Sec. 5.6).

      Dopant atoms can be implanted into silicon either directly or after
passing intentionally through a thin film, usually thermally grown SiO_2.
      Ion implantation of dopant atoms is always accompanied by damage to
the silicon lattice. This damage is the result of the many collisions with the
lattice atoms that each ion undergoes until it stops. The ion implantation

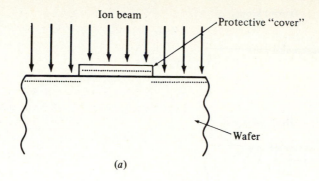

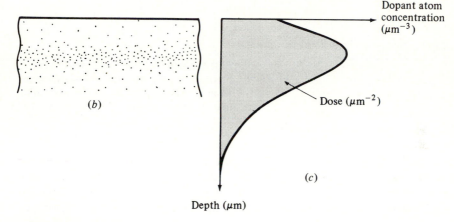

FIGURE 10.3
Illustration of the ion implantation process. (*a*) Ions are implanted in the wafer wherever it is not protected; (*b*) substrate with implanted ions; (*c*) plot of dopant atom concentration vs. depth.

damage "annealing" (i.e., repair) and dopant atom "activation" (i.e., placement of the dopant atoms on lattice sites where they can be ionized) are accomplished by exposing the wafer to an elevated temperature. This annealing step is essential and is typically combined with some other thermal treatment subsequent to ion implantation.

10.2.5 Diffusion

Dopant atoms deposited near the surface of silicon by ion implantation are driven deeper into the silicon by a process called *diffusion*. This process takes place when the wafers are inserted in a high-temperature furnace for a certain amount of time (e.g., at 1000°C for 30 min).[2] The process is illustrated in Fig. 10.4.

Dopant diffusion can be intentional or unintentional during the fabrica-

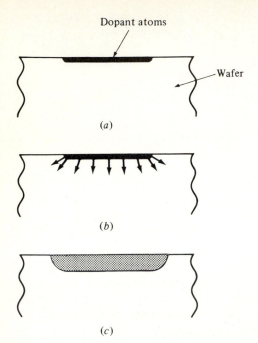

Dopant atoms

Wafer

(a)

(b)

(c)

FIGURE 10.4
Illustration of the diffusion process. (a) Deposition of dopants near the surface; (b) diffusion of dopants during high-temperature step; (c) final result.

tion process sequence. For example, when a deeply doped layer must be created, the dopant atoms are intentionally made to diffuse over relatively long distances by exposing the wafer to a high temperature for an extended period of time. However, when a thin layer of high doping near the surface is desired, the diffusion of atoms that accompanies the necessary dopant activation and ion implantation damage annealing is often undesirable because it thickens the layer. In modern processes, with the exception of deep "well" formation in CMOS (Sec. 10.4), the diffusion of dopants must be kept to a minimum. For this reason diffusion rarely appears as an independent step. It mostly occurs naturally during thermal oxidation and implant annealing because all these processes require similar temperatures and times.

10.2.6 Epitaxy

Unlike all previous fabrication steps epitaxy is a step that is used only once at the beginning of the fabrication sequence. It consists of growing a film of silicon on top of a silicon wafer. The process takes place at high temperatures on the order of 1000 to 1200°C by exposing the wafer to an ambient containing a silicon compound such as SiH_4. The silicon compound molecules decompose on the hot silicon wafer surface, and the freed-up silicon atoms are arranged according to the underlying lattice template. Thus, the epitaxially deposited silicon film is perfectly crystalline replicating the underlying crystal. The usefulness of epitaxy arises from the fact that the grown films can be doped at levels and/or type different from those of the underlying substrate. As will be seen in the CMOS technology section, this constitutes a distinct advantage over uniformly doped substrates.

10.3 AN ENHANCEMENT/DEPLETION NMOS PROCESS SEQUENCE EXAMPLE

To present the key features of the basic fabrication processes, we will describe first in general terms a typical fabrication sequence for a silicon gate NMOS technology which realizes both enhancement and depletion (E/D) MOSFETs. This is an involved process where many steps are performed in anticipation of subsequent ones. For this reason, at times, it might not be obvious why something is done. If the reader is patient, by the end of the sequence he or she will be able to put the whole picture together and every step will then make sense.

Figure 10.5 illustrates, approximately to scale, the basic features of the structures that are to be realized by the fabrication sequence. Here we show not only the transistor but also its typical environment in an integrated circuit. This is important in order to appreciate the constraints in fabricating the transistor itself, to understand the origin of parasitic resistances and capacitances external to the device, and to appreciate the techniques that allow the monolithic fabrication of a complete circuit. Shown is a cross section of an

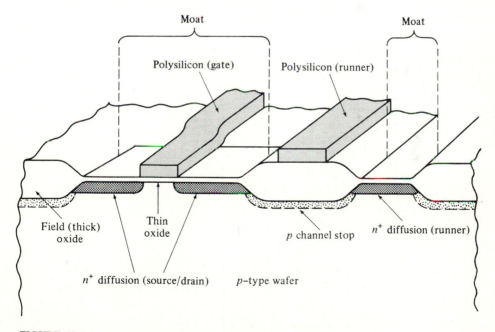

FIGURE 10.5
Illustration of basic features of modern NMOS technology.

NMOS transistor and two independent "wires" (runners) realized in polysilicon and n^+ silicon layers. These conductive paths along with the conductors (wires) fabricated by using an aluminum (metal) film, as will be shown later, provide the necessary interconnect between MOSFETs and other circuit elements (e.g., resistors, capacitors, etc.) to realize the desired circuit. For clarity at this point, the aluminum wires and some associated features discussed later on have been omitted. Transistors (only one shown in Fig. 10.5) and n^+ silicon conductors are created in *moat*† regions, which are separated by a thick SiO_2 film called *field oxide* or *thick oxide*. In addition, a p layer, so-called "channel stop," under the field oxide is used to prevent the formation there of parasitic conductive paths (e.g., parasitic inversion layers) between adjacent n^+ diffusions. Referring to Fig. 10.5, it can be seen that the NMOS transistor channel width is determined by the width of the moat formed by the field oxide that surrounds the transistor. Thus, the polysilicon that forms the gate does not have to terminate in order to define the channel width. When it climbs on the thick field oxide at the edge of the moat it can no longer control the silicon surface.

To illustrate better the NMOS fabrication process sequence, we will now describe the evolution of a cross section of a simple enhancement/depletion transistor inverter subcircuit, the topology of which is shown in Fig. 10.6. Top views of the relevant mask features will be shown where appropriate. Mask

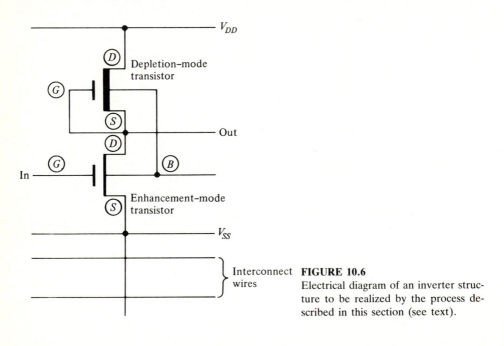

FIGURE 10.6
Electrical diagram of an inverter structure to be realized by the process described in this section (see text).

---

† Several different names are used to describe these regions. Common ones are *active region* and *thin oxide (region)*.

patterns will be identified as polygon borders, and it should always be assumed that the inside of the polygon is filled, i.e., the polygon is opaque. Thus, the polygon is a positive image of the feature it defines. Of course, depending on the requirements of the particular photoresist technology employed in fabrication, patterns of positive or negative polarity with respect to the original drawing are printed on the physical photomask. However, we do not need to concern ourselves with such details at this point.

The starting material for the NMOS technology described here is a p-type silicon wafer of 20- to 60-$\Omega \cdot$ cm resistivity ($N_A = 6 \times 10^2$ to 2×10^2 μm^{-3}). At first, an oxide (SiO$_2$) of thickness in the range of 0.05 μm is uniformly grown on the silicon wafer by direct oxidation, as described previously. Then, a silicon nitride (Si$_3$N$_4$) layer of approximately 0.1-μm thickness is formed by chemical vapor deposition (CVD) on the SiO$_2$. The so-called "strain relief" SiO$_2$ layer prevents damage of the silicon wafer that could result during subsequent process steps because of the different thermal expansion coefficients of Si and Si$_3$N$_4$. Subsequently, the Si$_3$N$_4$ is patterned as shown in Fig. 10.7 by using mask 1, which we will call *moat mask*. The Si$_3$N$_4$ film that remains

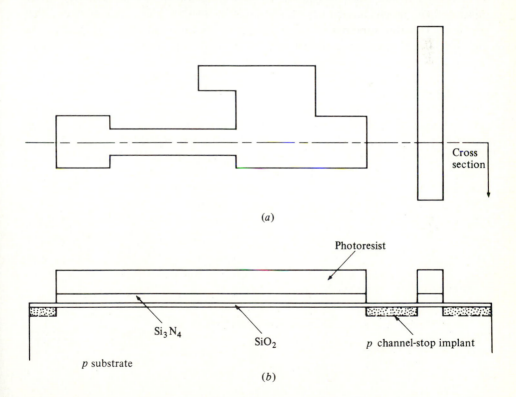

FIGURE 10.7
Mask 1 (moat mask). (*a*) Feature view, and (*b*) corresponding vertical cross section of the silicon surface after definition by means of this mask.

after patterning defines the areas where devices and n^+ conductors are to be built, i.e., the moat areas. With the photoresist that is used to pattern the Si_3N_4 acting also as an ion implantation mask, an ion implantation of boron is performed into the *field region* of the circuit to create the channel-stop p layer discussed above. Typical implantation parameters for this step are an ion dose of 10^5 μm^{-2} and energy of about 40 keV. Figure 10.7b shows the end result of the above processes. Then the photoresist is removed and the field oxidation is performed. This step selectively grows about 1 μm of oxide at the areas of silicon not covered by Si_3N_4, and thus the *field oxide* is defined. Note that this process yields *self-aligned* field oxide and channel-stop p layers. This selective or "localized" oxidation process is widely known as LOCOS. Subsequently, the oxidation-blocking Si_3N_4 and the strain relief oxide are stripped, exposing bare silicon at the moat regions, and the *gate oxide* is grown over these regions by silicon oxidation to a thickness of about 0.04 μm or less. Through the gate oxide, a new ion implantation of boron is performed (typically 10^3 to 10^4 μm^{-2}, 50 to 100 keV) to increase the threshold voltage of the enhancement mode MOSFETs to a well controlled value. The cross section of the silicon wafer at the end of this sequence is illustrated in Fig. 10.8. Note that over the field region all of the boron implant dose winds up in the thick oxide because the ions do not have enough energy to go through it; also some small fraction of the boron ion dose remains in the gate oxide. However, none of these (positive) ions contribute any charges in the oxide because they are readily neutralized by electrons supplied through the conductive substrate during the implantation process.

The next step defines the depletion mode MOSFETs, as shown in Fig. 10.9. Mask 2, often called *depletion mask*, is used to pattern the photoresist that covers all but what will become the depletion transistor channels. An ion implantation of arsenic or phosphorus is then performed, which selectively dopes with donors the areas where the channels of the depletion transistors will eventually be. The implant dose is adjusted so that it overcompensates the previous boron implant, thus making the silicon surface region n type. This then yields a negative threshold for the depletion transistors. A typical dopant is arsenic with implant parameters of 10^4 μm^{-2} dose and 100-keV energy.

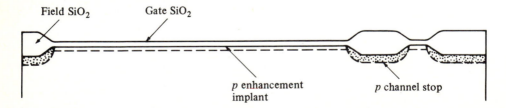

FIGURE 10.8
Surface cross section after field oxidation, removal of the silicon nitride film, gate oxide growth, and enhancement threshold-voltage-defining implant.

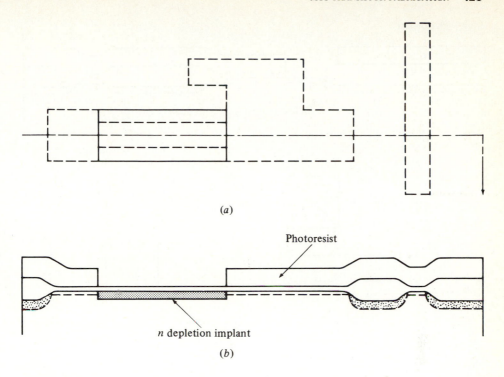

(a)

(b)

FIGURE 10.9
Definition of depletion transistor channels by means of mask 2 (depletion mask). (a) Depletion
mask pattern; (b) vertical cross section.

At this point in the fabrication, the whole wafer is covered either by thin
(gate) or thick (field) oxide. The channel-stop doping and the channel dopings
of the enhancement and depletion MOSFETs have been determined. In some
technologies, the next step is to deposit and define the gate polysilicon layer.
However, in the technology described here, which allows so-called "buried
contacts," i.e., direct contacts between the polysilicon layer and the silicon n^+
diffusion layer (still to be defined), these contact areas must be defined. This is
done by another photoresist step, as shown in Fig. 10.10. Note the different
location of the cross section in this figure. Mask 3, often called *polycon mask*,
is used to define the photoresist that covers all but the contact areas where the
gate oxide is etched to expose the underlying silicon surface. This mask is
omitted in technologies that do not allow buried contacts.

In the next step, a polysilicon layer is grown by CVD over the whole
wafer to a typical thickness of about 0.4 μm. This is usually followed by doping
of this layer n^+ by phosphorus and then by definition of the polysilicon pattern,
via mask 4, often called *poly mask*. At this point, the transistor source-drain
and n^+ silicon interconnect regions are determined by ion implantation of a
heavy dose of arsenic into the wafer, as shown in Fig. 10.11. Note that no

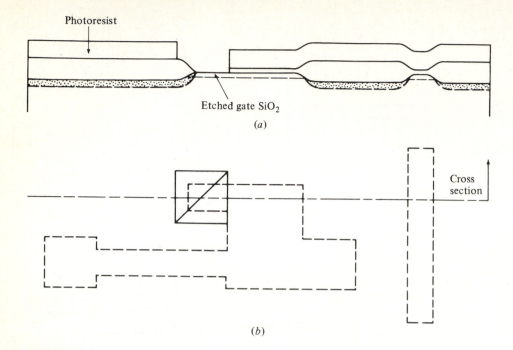

FIGURE 10.10
Definition of poly to diffusion contacts by means of mask 3 (polycon mask). (*a*) Vertical cross section; (*b*) polycon mask pattern.

additional mask is necessary for this step, since the defined polysilicon gates protect the transistor channels and the thick field oxide protects the field region against this implant. This is a particularly elegant feature of this process, since it allows self-alignment of the source and drain regions to the gate, thus minimizing parasitic overlap capacitances. The process is known as *self-aligned process*. In the polycon areas where poly comes into direct contact with silicon some outdiffusion of phosphorus takes place during the poly doping process. This phosphorus-doped n^+-type area becomes partly exposed after the poly definition and receives the heavy dose of arsenic implant as well, and thus it becomes electrically connected to the normal (arsenic only) n^+ layer, as shown in Fig. 10.11*a*. Thus, direct contact of the poly to the n^+ diffusion is achieved in the polycon regions.

Having finished now with all the dopant implantation steps, a thick layer of approximately 1 μm of CVD SiO_2 is deposited. This layer is typically doped heavily (2 to 10 percent by weight) with phosphorus and, for this reason, it is called *phosphosilicate glass* or PSG. This is the layer that insulates the diffusion and polysilicon areas from the metal to be deposited. Mask 5, called *contact mask*, is then used to define the contact cuts (or vias) in the CVD SiO_2 through which the metal layer will later be connected to diffusion regions or to

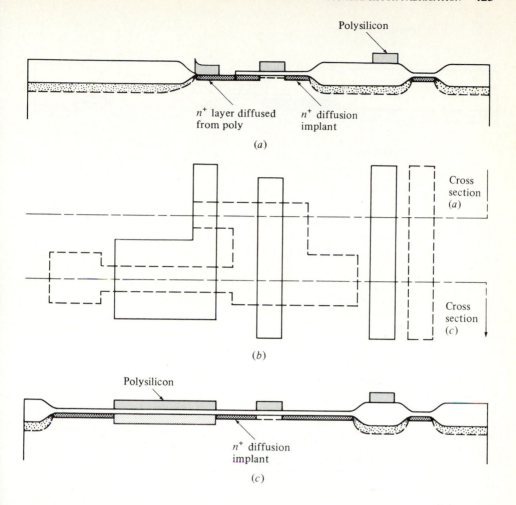

FIGURE 10.11
Definition of poly patterns by means of mask 4 (poly mask) and n^+-layer ion implantation. (*a*)
Vertical cross section along a line shown in (*b*); (*b*) polysilicon mask pattern; (*c*) vertical cross
section along a different line shown in (*b*).

polysilicon. The contact cuts are etched and the PSG is then made to *flow* at a
high temperature (around 1000°C) to reduce the sharpness of the contact hole
walls and to smooth the steps that occur at the polysilicon edges. This flow
process is facilitated by the presence of the phosphorus in the PSG, and it leads
to improved *step coverage* by the metal layer (see below). Since this flow
process takes place at a high temperature, it is commonly used to diffuse also
the n^+ implanted layer as well as all the rest of the doped layers to their
appropriate depths into the substrate. The resulting structures at the end of this
step are shown in Fig. 10.12*a* and *c*. Note that the deeper n layer under the

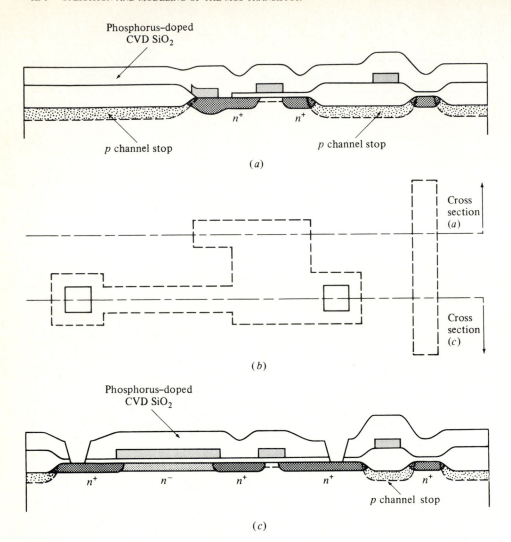

FIGURE 10.12
Surface cross section after n^+ implant, diffusion deposition of phosphorous-doped CVD SiO$_2$ (PSG), and definition of metal contact cuts by means of mask 5 (contact mask). (*a*) Vertical cross section along a line shown in (*b*); (*b*) contact mask patterns; (*c*) vertical cross section along a different line shown in (*b*).

poly in the polycon area is due to outdiffusion of phosphorus from the poly into the silicon and to the higher diffusivity of phosphorus compared to arsenic.

A few words about step coverage are in order here. Figure 10.13*a* shows a cross section of a contact hole in "as-etched" PSG, covered by a metal layer of thickness equal to that of the PSG. As can be seen, a "neck" of metal occurs with thickness significantly smaller than that in the planar region. The same

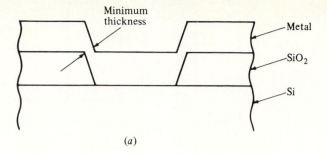

(a)

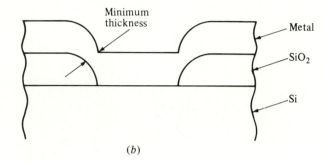

(b)

FIGURE 10.13
Illustration of step coverage by metal at contact cuts. (a) As-etched contact hole in SiO₂; (b) contact hole after PSG flow.

situation would also occur at the step created by a polysilicon conductor under unflowed PSG. Under extreme conditions of step sharpness a narrow crack appears in the metal during deposition in the neck area and the contact is open. Even if the crack is not there, during circuit operation the current density at the neck increases and the metal is likely to break by a process called *electromigration*. This is a process by which metal atoms move along the direction of electron flow at a rate which depends strongly on current density and temperature of operation. Failure by electromigration is prevented by maintaining the current density below a certain level (see also Sec. 5.8). Flow of the PSG helps to prevent this mode of failure at contacts by increasing the metal layer minimum thickness as shown in Fig. 10.13b.

In the next step, an aluminum film is deposited over the entire wafer, and is patterned by using mask 6, called *metal mask*, as shown in Fig. 10.14. Following that, the Al-Si contacts are *alloyed*, i.e., Al is made to mix up with Si to form good ohmic contacts by exposing the wafer to about 400°C. The integrated circuit is now fully operational. However, to provide protection of the circuit against the environment, the wafer is coated by a *passivation layer*, usually CVD SiO₂ or Si₃N₄. A detailed overlay of all masks and a vertical cross section through the circuit after this step are shown in Fig. 10.15. Also shown in this figure are the locations of the various circuit elements that correspond to the circuit topology of Fig. 10.6.

Electrical contact to the finished circuit is allowed by patterning the passivation layer by mask 7, called *bonding contact mask*. This patterning is

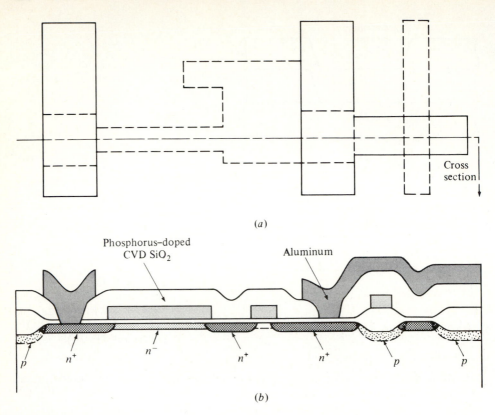

(a)

(b)

FIGURE 10.14
Surface cross section after aluminum definition by means of mask 6 (metal mask). (a) Metal mask pattern; (b) vertical cross section.

shown in Fig. 10.16. It consists of exposing the Al areas at which the circuit is to be contacted by etching the passivation layer. These Al areas are usually called *bonding pads* and they are located in the periphery of the circuit. Their typical size is about 100×100 μm, and they are separated by 50 to 100 μm. The bonding pads are used to connect the integrated circuits (after they have been cut into *chips*) to the package by a process that is often called *wire bonding*. By this process thin wires are connected between the bonding pads on the chip and the package terminals. Internal probing of the circuit, particularly during the development stage, is often necessary and it can be provided by the addition of smaller probing pads at strategic circuit nodes. One such pad is shown in Fig. 10.16; its typical size is 25×25 μm. It is, of course, desirable to make these probing pads as small as possible so that, when they are not probed, they do not load significantly the circuit node to which they are connected by excessive capacitance.

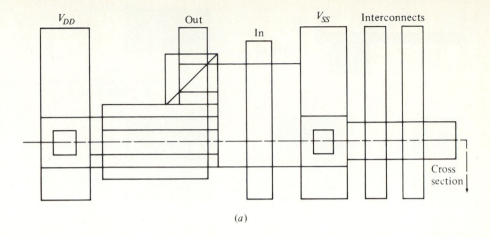

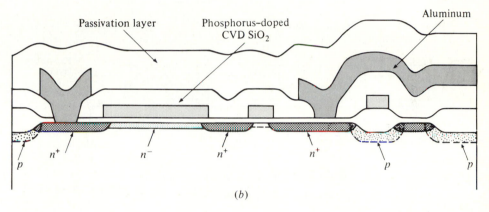

FIGURE 10.15
(*a*) Overlay of all layer patterns; (*b*) surface cross section after deposition of passivation layer.

As mentioned in Sec. 4.10, when the electric field in the gate insulator becomes excessive, a permanent short circuit through the insulator can be caused by breakdown. To avoid the buildup of externally acquired charge that can cause this phenomenon, protection circuits [so-called electrostatic discharge, (ESD) circuits] are connected to the contact pads that are attached to transistor gates. These typically consist of combinations of resistors and devices with a low breakdown voltage, such as reverse-biased *pn* junctions or short-channel transistors connected to ground potential. Since the breakdown for such devices is nondestructive, they provide a normally open path that closes only when a high voltage, due to charge-up, appears at the input terminals. The momentarily closed path discharges harmlessly the node to which it is connected.

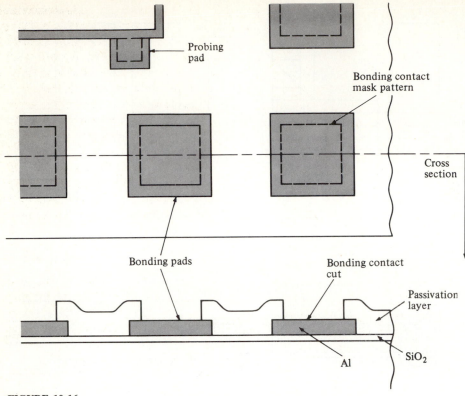

FIGURE 10.16
Passivation layer and bonding contact cuts (cross section not to scale).

10.4 CMOS TECHNOLOGY

CMOS technologies differ from NMOS (or PMOS) technologies in that both *n*- and *p*-channel transistors are fabricated on the same substrate. As we saw in the NMOS technology described in the previous section, the substrate doping type and level are selected according to the requirements of the *n*-channel devices that are to be fabricated on it. Obviously, in CMOS the starting material can satisfy the requirements of either the *n*-channel or *p*-channel device, but not of both at the same time. To accommodate the device type that cannot be built on the starting material, regions of doping type opposite to that of the starting material are formed, as shown in the two cross sections in Fig. 10.17. These regions of opposite doping type are typically called *wells* or *tubs*. We will use both terms here indiscriminately. The well areas are the first to be defined on the starting material. The well dopant is then implanted and diffused such that the proper well doping and depth are attained. The type of the well becomes the identifying characteristic of the CMOS technology. For example in Fig. 10.17*a* we are illustrating the so-called "*p*-well CMOS

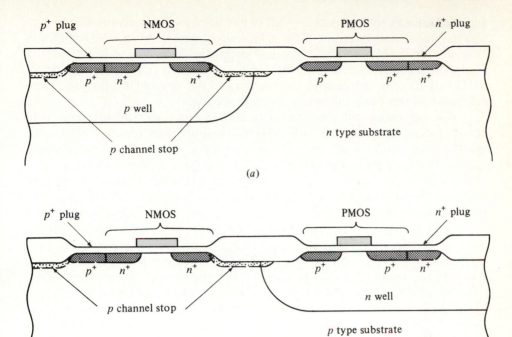

FIGURE 10.17
Basic features of vertical cross sections of (*a*) *p*-well and (*b*) *n*-well CMOS technologies. Note that PSG and metal layers are not shown.

technology," while in Fig. 10.17*b* the "*n*-well CMOS technology" is shown. Typically, the *p*- and *n*-type substrates are connected to the most negative and most positive circuit voltages, respectively, to ensure that *pn* junctions are not forward-biased during circuit operation. To achieve good ohmic contacts, the two substrates are contacted at heavily doped regions identified as *plugs* in Fig. 10.17. The plugs are most essential in the wells because the wells are totally (junction) isolated from the rest of the wafer whereas the nonwell substrate can be contacted easily at the back of the wafer.

The implementation of the *n*-well and *p*-well technologies shown in Fig. 10.17 differs from that of the NMOS technology, described in the previous section, in three major aspects. First, the well is photolithographically defined, implanted, and diffused before the definition of the moats. Second, the *p*-type channel-stop implant is blocked out (by means of photoresist) in the *n*-type regions. In fact, under some circumstances, separate channel-stop implants are performed for the main substrate and the well. Third, both n^+-type and p^+-type regions are created, which means that each of these regions must be protected (by means of photoresist) during the implantation of the opposite dopant type. Thus, CMOS technologies require at least three, and often more, additional masks with respect to NMOS technologies. It is worthwhile to note that the polysilicon layer in CMOS is typically doped n^+ even over the PMOS channels. This is because the original n^+ doping in the poly is so heavy that the p^+ doping it receives when it is blocking the p channels (i.e., self-alignment of PMOS devices) is not enough to compensate the original n^+ doping. More discussion of this issue follows in the next section.

Another major difference between NMOS and CMOS technologies is in device-spacing considerations. In NMOS, the minimum spacing of adjacent moats is determined mostly by the structural aspects of the LOCOS technique discussed in the previous section. In CMOS the same applies between devices of the same type, but the spacing consideration between devices of opposite type, i.e., p^+ to n^+ spacing is very different. This is because CMOS structures have an inherent vulnerability to a parasitic conduction mechanism, called *latchup*.[8] Latchup is a type of thyristor operating mechanism and is always possible to trigger in *npnp* structures. CMOS, of course, offers many such structures on a chip, and if any one is triggered into latchup, large currents can flow and the results are usually irreversibly catastrophic for the whole chip.

Figure 10.18a shows the cross section of a typical n-well CMOS structure and highlights its latchup potential. The n^+ region in the p-type substrate and the p^+ region in the n-type substrate may be either parts of an NMOS and PMOS transistor, respectively (typically sources when connected to the power supplies as shown), or they could be parts of n^+ or p^+ conductors. In any case, for simplicity, the rest of the structures are not shown in the figure. Note the two parasitic bipolar transistors—an *npn* device between the n^+ (emitter) and n well (collector), and a *pnp* device between the p^+ (emitter) and substrate (collector). The parasitic resistors are the result of the corresponding n-well and p-substrate bulk resistivities. Of particular importance are the resistors R_W to the n-well plug and R_S to the substrate plug. Consider now the equivalent circuit in Fig. 10.18b. Assume that a voltage disturbance could momentarily bring the emitter of T_p (or of T_n) to a voltage above (or below) the corresponding base voltage. With rapid transients on V_{DD} or V_{SS} this is quite possible, depending on the values of R_W and R_S and of the parasitic capacitances shown dashed in Fig. 10.18b. Now, depending on the current gains β_n and β_p of the transistors and on the values of the resistors, it can be easily seen from Fig. 10.18b that both transistors could turn on and very large current, limited only by R_n and R_p, would flow. Even after the disturbance is removed the circuit would remain in the latched mode and, eventually, will self-destruct.

To prevent latchup, the transistor β must be small and the resistor values, specifically R_W and R_S, must be small. For a given technology these conditions imply some specific minimum spacings:

1. The n^+ and p^+ must be sufficiently far to prevent β_n of the lateral *npn* from being very high (by making sure its base is long).
2. The well must be contacted via n^+ plugs at several points sufficiently close to each other, so that R_W can be kept low.

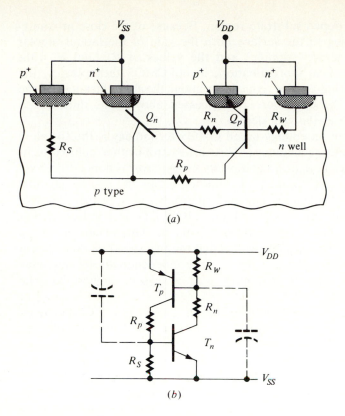

FIGURE 10.18

(*a*) An *n*-well CMOS structure showing the parasitic bipolar transistors and resistors that can lead to latchup; (*b*) equivalent network.

For simple CMOS technologies such as the ones discussed so far, the n^+ to p^+ minimum spacing may be very large, e.g., 15μm or more as compared to n^+ to n^+ and p^+ to p^+ spacings of 5 μm or less.

To address this critical problem of n^+ to p^+ spacing and latchup susceptibility, several new CMOS technologies have been introduced. The key feature of all of these technologies is that the substrate region in which the wells and the devices are built is grown epitaxially on a heavily doped silicon wafer. For example, in an *n*-well CMOS technology with final well depth of 5 μm, the starting material consists of a heavily *p*-type doped wafer with a lightly doped *p*-type epitaxial (or "epi") layer of about 10-μm thickness. The epi layer uniform doping level is chosen to be appropriate for building the NMOS transistors. The epi thickness is usually about twice the well depth because the dopants in the heavily doped substrate under the epi layer are expected to diffuse toward the surface as the well dopants are diffusing toward the bulk. The process is designed such that the bottom of the well is eventually adjacent to the heavily doped substrate region. Because of the close proximity of the heavy bulk doping to the surface both the gain of the lateral bipolar transistor (*npn* in the above example) and the values of R_S (and R_P) are drastically reduced. To first approximation, in epi-CMOS technologies, the minimum n^+ to p^+ spacing can be reduced to about the final thickness of the lightly doped part of the epi layer. As discussed above, this thickness is approximately the same as the well depth.

Another example of an epitaxy-based CMOS technology is the so-called "dual-well" or "twin tub" technology.[9] This differs from other epitaxy technologies described earlier in that the epitaxially grown layer is doped to a level significantly lower than that required for building either the *p*- or *n*-channel MOSFETs. Rather than implanting and diffusing only one well type, both of the substrate regions for *n*- and *p*-channel MOSFETs are independently implanted and diffused, hence the technology's name. The advantage of the dual well over the conventional single well is that the two substrate dopings can be optimized for their corresponding device type independently by removing the constraint that the single-well doping must always be higher than the doping of the epitaxial layer.

In terms of n^+ to p^+ minimum spacing, all epitaxy-based CMOS technologies have similar advantages with respect to nonepitaxy technologies. Further miniaturization of that distance requires more aggressive well isolation techniques, many of which are under investigation at present. The most viable of these appears to be the so-called "trench isolation" technique.[10] As can be seen in Fig. 10.19 this technique consists of literally digging a deep trench all along the well boundary and reaching down to the heavily doped substrate region. The trench is then refilled by means of a CVD film deposition technique so that the silicon surface becomes nearly planar. Typically, the film is polycrystalline silicon and is deposited conformally in the trench after a thin film of SiO_2 is grown on the trench walls and bottom. The details of this process are outside the scope of this chapter. The effect of trench isolation is to

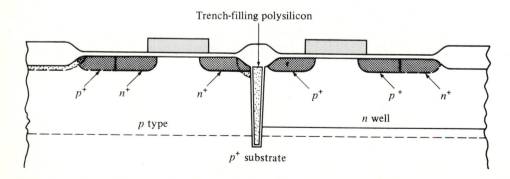

FIGURE 10.19
Cross section of a trench-isolated epitaxy-based *n*-well CMOS structure.

suppress the lateral bipolar transistor current gain so that the technology becomes latchup immune.

Even more radical CMOS technologies that are completely latchup immune are the so-called "silicon-on-insulator" (SOI) CMOS technologies. These technologies fall outside the scope of this chapter and will not be discussed herein.[11]

10.5 MINIATURIZATION (SCALING) CONSIDERATIONS

Increased circuit density and speed are made possible through continuous reduction of the device feature sizes which results from steadily improving integrated circuit fabrication processes. In Sec. 5.8 the results of miniaturization on device characteristics were presented, and scaling methodologies were discussed. In this section we will consider the fabrication issues and problems that are encountered in the quest for continuing device miniaturization. However, it is important to observe that several other problems not considered here, and which are associated more generally with overall *circuit* miniaturization, are also very significant. These are related primarily to interconnect miniaturization and, under some circumstances, can become the dominant miniaturization pacing elements.

As discussed in Sec. 5.8, proper miniaturization requires that all dimensions be scaled more or less in unison. Thus, as lateral dimensions are reduced, layer thickness (height) should be reduced accordingly. Referring back to Fig. 10.5 we can separate the key MOSFET features as follows: source, drain channel region, and isolation from adjacent circuit elements. As will be seen from the discussion that follows, there are particular miniaturization problems associated with each of these features.

10.5.1 Source

The key requirement on the source region of a MOSFET is that it should provide low resistance between the contacts to the metal and the edge of the channel. It should also be an effective emitter of carriers into the channel at that edge. With most conventional structures these two requirements go hand in hand because a highly conductive source layer is also rich in carriers of the type required in the channel. Satisfying one requirement usually satisfies the other. Thus, the two requirements can be combined into one, namely, that the source resistance should be negligible compared to the resistance of the channel, otherwise serious degradation of the device characteristics can occur (Sec. 5.7). For $L_{\text{eff}} \approx 0.5\ \mu\text{m}$ and $d_{ox} \approx 0.02\ \mu\text{m}$, a total source series resistance of 300 to $500\ \Omega \cdot \mu\text{m}$ (Ω times μm of width) is acceptable for most applications. Referring to Fig. 10.20 this number is the sum of the contact resistance between metal and n^+- or p^+-doped layer, R_{S1},

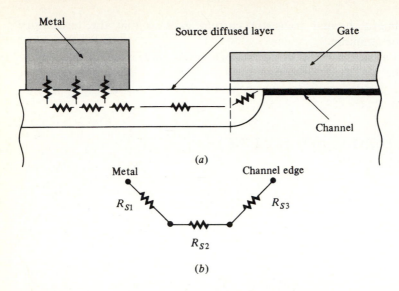

FIGURE 10.20
The components of the source series resistance in a MOSFET. (*a*) Structural correspondence; (*b*) lumped model.

the sheet resistance between the above edge and the edge of the contact to the channel, R_{S2}, and the spreading resistance between the latter edge and the edge of the channel, R_{S3}. R_{S1} is a lumped resistance including the "true" contact resistance and the resistance due to current crowding in the diffused layer. Reduction of the layer (junction) depth, as mandated by the scaling laws, increases all components of the source series resistance. This is owing to a necessary decrease in the total dopant dose. The decrease is particularly severe in PMOS devices because the characteristics of boron in silicon, which is used for the p^+ regions, are more unfavorable than those of arsenic, which is used for the n^+ regions. Specifically, boron tends to be implanted deeply into the silicon even when very low acceleration energies are used because of a phenomenon called *channeling* of ions through the silicon lattice.[12] This phenomenon is not as severe with arsenic which has a much heavier atom than boron and, thus, tends to easily destroy the lattice order and, consequently, its own channeling probability. Also, boron is a much faster diffuser than arsenic, and so it becomes difficult to keep the p^+ layer shallow during the various required high-temperature steps that follow the implantation of the source-drain regions.

For a conventionally fabricated source, such as that shown in Fig. 10.20, the implantation, annealing, and diffusion characteristics of arsenic and boron limit the junction depth to 0.15 to 0.30 μm for n^+ and 0.35 to 0.65μm for p^+, with corresponding sheet resistances of 100 to 30 Ω per square and 150 to 80 Ω per square. Although the layer sheet resistance is directly related to only one component of the total source resistance, i.e., R_{S2}, the other two components also tend to track the sheet resistance.

Considerable effort has been applied to overcome the limitations of the source resistance while maintaining shallow junctions. Perhaps the most promising approach is a combination of very shallow ion implantation with very short annealing followed by self-aligned silicide (salicide) formation on the exposed silicon surface.[13] As can be seen from Fig. 10.21, this process requires the use of an insulating *spacer* at both ends of the poly gate electrode. After the thin oxide on top of the heavily doped silicon and polysilicon has been removed, a thin layer of a refractory metal (e.g., Ti, Ta, W, etc.) is uniformly deposited, as shown in Fig. 10.21a. Then the wafer is exposed to a moderately high temperature (600 to 800°C) and the metal reacts with the silicon to form a disilicide (e.g., $TiSi_2$). However, on the spacer the metal remains unreacted since there there is no supply of silicon atoms, and it can be readily removed with a preferential metal etch resulting in self-alignment of the silicide with the exposed silicon areas, as shown in Fig. 10.21b. This process produces not only highly conductive sources (and drains) but also gate electrodes of high conductivity. Sheet resistances decrease by a factor of about 5 to 10. Also, because of the spacer, the parasitic source-to-gate and drain-to-gate capacitances are reduced.

10.5.2 Drain

As can be seen from the NMOS fabrication sequence discussed in the previous section, the typical MOSFET is a symmetrical device, i.e., the source and drain are identical and the channel is uniform along the length of the device. In principle, the source and drain structures as well as the doping in the channel could be optimized for asymmetrical operation, which is the way most devices with the exception of "pass" transistors operate in a circuit. However, the technological difficulties associated with such optimization are not at present justified by the expected benefits. Thus, in designing the source and drain

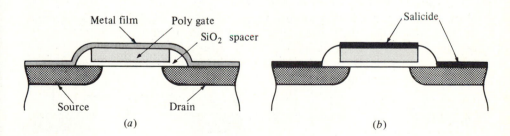

FIGURE 10.21

The process of self-aligned silicide formation on source, drain, and gate of a MOSFET. (a) Uniformly deposited refractory metal film; (b) silicide after reaction of metal with silicon and removal of unreacted metal on spacers.

structures for a given technology a compromise among the different requirements must be made.

Similar to the source side the doped layer forming the drain must be
shallow to prevent excessive drain-voltage-induced control on the channel
charge. However, at the drain side, series resistance is not as serious a problem
for most well-designed devices operating in the saturation region. This is
because the typical MOSFET slope of the I_D-V_{DS} characteristic in the saturation region is usually quite small, i.e., the drain current does not depend
strongly on the drain bias. In fact, from the device reliability standpoint, it is
advantageous for the drain to be relatively lightly doped, and thus more
resistive, because it tends to absorb some of the potential that otherwise would
exist in the channel resulting in a very high electric field there. As discussed in
Sec. 5.6, high electric fields in the channel give rise to several hot-carrier
effects that tend to reduce the useful life of the MOSFET. At this point it
could be remarked that a reduction of the circuit operating voltage would
accomplish similar improvement of reliability, but as has been discussed in
Sec. 5.8, constant-field scaling is not generally feasible for various practical
reasons.

Because of the pressure for near-constant-voltage scaling, drain structure
design has recently received a lot of attention.[14, 15] The basic principle in all
structures is the same, namely, absorption of some of the potential into the
drain. One rather typical structure, termed *lightly doped drain* or *LDD*, is
shown in Fig. 10.22.[16] Note that the source and drain regions are now formed
by means of two implants, one relatively light which is self-aligned to the gate
electrode and one heavy, which is self-aligned to the spacer. The purpose of
the light-dose region is to provide a shallow layer which, because of its light
doping, absorbs part of the potential. The heavy-dose region provides a low
resistivity access to the lightly doped region. Because this region is further
away from the channel, it can be made relatively deep without adverse effects
on the device operation. The increased junction depth not only yields lower
sheet resistance but also reduces the value of the contact resistance R_{S1} in Fig.
10.20. Another significant benefit of the increased junction depth is that the
metal-to-source or metal-to-drain contact becomes easier to fabricate. This is
because, during the alloying of such contacts, silicon tends to move into the

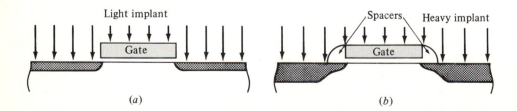

(a) *(b)*

FIGURE 10.22
Illustration of the lightly doped drain formation process. (*a*) Light source-drain implant self-aligned
with gate; (*b*) heavy source-drain implant after spacer formation.

aluminum layer and aluminum into the silicon, resulting into possible "spiking" of the metal through the junction. Spiking gives rise to leaky junctions and it is most prevalent in relatively shallow layers. It can be avoided at the expense of increased process complexity by the introduction of "barrier" layers between the aluminum and the silicon. However, deeper junctions at the contact area are always beneficial to the fabrication yield.

Other structures have been proposed where the spacer is taken advantage of to create "salicided" regions of low resistivity, as discussed in the previous section. However, as can be easily seen, the existence of the lightly doped region at the source side always results in higher source resistance.

10.5.3 Channel Region

The channel region is composed of four key parts: the substrate, the silicon-to-insulator interface, the gate insulator, and the gate electrode. Since the channel region is where all the device action takes place, it naturally attracts considerable attention in device design. The key element in the substrate is, of course, the doping since it determines both the device threshold voltage and its sensitivity (or lack thereof) to drain bias. Single or multiple implants are used in the channel to tailor the doping level and profile so that the scaling requirements, discussed in Sec. 5.8, are satisfied. These implants are made either through the gate insulator or before the latter is in place. For example, in the process sequence example discussed in Sec. 10.3, the so-called threshold tailoring implant and the depletion implant were both done through the gate SiO_2. As discussed in Sec 10.2, the subsequent high-temperature process steps are sufficient to anneal the SiO_2 and the Si-lattice damage and to activate these implants. However, the practice of implanting through the gate oxide carries some risks of compromising the gate insulator quality because of excessive handling of the wafer with that insulator exposed.

In practically all MOSFETs being fabricated today the gate insulator is silicon dioxide thermally grown on the silicon surface. Experimentation is going on with other insulators, primarily thermally grown silicon nitride or nitroxide. However, thermal SiO_2 continues to exhibit the best interface with silicon. What is meant by "best" here is that the interface has very low concentration of interface fixed charges and traps (states). Since charges at the interface can be detrimental to the surface mobility of carriers, low charge density is very valuable.[17] Considerable effort is being devoted to the development of thermal oxidation processes that would yield thin oxides of uniform thickness, with low interface charge density, low oxide bulk trap concentration, low defect density, and high breakdown voltage. As oxide thicknesses are scaled down, all these oxide properties are seriously challenged.

The predominant gate material for MOSFETs has been the n^+ doped polycrystalline silicon. Since this layer is used considerably to form interconnect conductors there is significant motivation to reduce its resistivity. Because the poly is typically degenerately doped, its bulk resistivity is usually at the minimum possible value. For typical thicknesses of around 0.4 μm the resistivity of n^+-doped poly gives rise to a sheet resistance of 20 to 30 Ω per square. Recently, refractory metal silicides are being deposited on top of the doped poly resulting into a composite gate electrode called *polycide*. Generally, polycides of equivalent thickness to n^+-doped poly have five to ten times less sheet resistance. Since it is still the polysilicon that is in contact with the gate oxide, polycide gate electrodes have the same electrical characteristics (e.g., work function) as poly. This is, of course, very advantageous because considerable manufacturing experience already exists for poly. As a result, polycides are very desirable and they are being incorporated to IC fabrication processes in an evolutionary manner. Nevertheless, experimentation, and in some isolated cases even industrial production, is under way where the gate electrode is formed by a refractory metal deposited directly on the gate oxide. The advantage here is that the gate sheet resistance is reduced by another factor of 10 with respect to polycide, but the new materials require considerable process modification.

In addition to the problems associated with the resistivity of the gate electrode material, miniaturization of devices in CMOS technologies has recently underscored the significance of the gate electrode-to-silicon contact potential. Specifically, we have seen that for constant-field scaling the device threshold voltage V_T must be scaled accordingly. Of course, practical scaling to date has proceeded more or less under constant voltage down to effective channel lengths of about 0.6 μm, but there is little doubt that further dimensional scaling will necessitate voltage reduction. As voltages are reduced, V_T will have to be scaled accordingly. With $L < 0.5$ μm the power supply voltage will have to be around 3 V to avoid instabilities due to hot-carrier injection in the oxide. Then the threshold voltage for n- and p-channel devices in CMOS should be about 0.5 V and -0.5 V respectively. Consider now how this is to be done. The two threshold voltages can be written as (2.5.29)

$$V_{TN} = \phi_{MSN} - \frac{Q'_o}{C'_{ox}} + \phi_{BN} - \frac{Q'_B}{C'_{ox}} \tag{10.1}$$

$$V_{TP} = \phi_{MSP} - \frac{Q'_o}{C'_{ox}} + \phi_{BP} - \frac{Q'_B}{C'_{ox}} \tag{10.2}$$

where all the symbols have been defined in Chap. 2 and the subscripts N and P denote n- and p-channel, respectively. Consider first the n-channel devices with n^+ poly gate electrode. Then, typical values are $\phi_{MSN} \approx -0.85$ V and $\phi_{BN} \approx 0.75$ V. Since the oxide thickness for this hypothetical scaled-down device would be very thin, say 0.015 μm, C'_{ox} is very large, and for typical Q'_o values we can neglect the Q'_o/C'_{ox} term. Then (10.1) becomes

$$V_{TN} \approx -0.1 \text{ V} - \frac{Q'_B}{C'_{ox}} \tag{10.3}$$

It was seen in Chap. 6 that the bulk charge Q'_B [given by (2.5.27)] is typically adjusted by means of ion implantation so that the desirable V_{TN} can be obtained. For typical (preimplant) substrate dopings of $N_A \approx 10^3$ μm^{-3} an increase of N_A near the Si-SiO$_2$ interface is required. This is accomplished by implanting boron atoms, as we have seen in Sec. 10.3. The result of this operation is not only to increase V_{TN} to the desirable value but also to raise the substrate doping concentration and, thus, reduce the sensitivity of V_{TN} to the drain bias (Sec. 5.4).

It is clear from the above discussion that it is desirable to use a symmetrical procedure for tailoring the threshold voltage of the p-channel device. It is easy to see how this would be done if the gate material for the PMOS devices is p^+-doped poly. Then (10.2) becomes

$$V_{TP} \approx 0.1 \text{ V} - \frac{Q'_B}{C'_{ox}} \tag{10.4}$$

where Q'_B/C'_{ox} is slightly positive. Thus making Q'_B even more positive by implanting phosphorus or arsenic in the channel achieves the desired V_{TP} value and increases the drain bias immunity. However, it has not proved practical to use both n^+- and p^+-doped poly simultaneously in CMOS technologies. The reason is that the contact areas required for connecting, via the metal, the two types of poly would be very space-consuming. On the other hand, it has also been proved impractical simply to connect (strap) the two types of poly by means of the overlying silicide in the case of polycide technologies. Although this would have required no special areas for n^+ to p^+ poly contacts, it was found that silicide strapping induces very rapid diffusion of the dopants in the poly with the result that complete inversion of the poly doping type can occur in adjacent n- and p-channel transistors.[18] This annoying phenomenon is under investigation at present and countermeasures may be discovered. However, for the time being, technology designers are forced to use either n^+ or p^+ poly. The predominant choice is still n^+, but several investigations of p^+ poly have been reported.[18, 19]

Assuming an n^+-doped poly (10.2) becomes

$$V_{TP} \approx -1 \text{ V} - \frac{Q'_B}{C'_{ox}} \tag{10.5}$$

To achieve a V_{TP} of approximately -0.5 V it is clear that Q'_B must be made negative! This means implanting the opposite dopant type into the substrate which, of course, results into a buried-channel device (Sec. 6.3). Unfortunately, this type of device has poor turnoff characteristics and poor immunity to drain bias, and thus it cannot be made as short as its surface channel counterpart.

10.5.4 Device Isolation

In integrated circuit technologies, device isolation is an integral part of device design. By far the most widely used isolation technique is the localized oxidation of silicon, or LOCOS, which was discussed in Sec. 10.3. The main problem with LOCOS is shown in Fig. 10.23. As can be seen, LOCOS produces a lateral encroachment of the oxide into the active device region (the

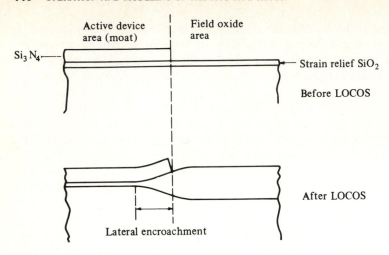

FIGURE 10.23
Lateral encroachment of field oxide into the active device area (bird's beak) after localized oxidation (LOCOS).

moat) over a distance comparable to the thickness of the grown field oxide, resulting in the so-called "bird's beak." Since the field oxide thickness cannot be decreased without increasing the poly-to-silicon and metal-to-silicon (parasitic) capacitances, the length of the encroachment cannot be decreased beyond a certain minimum value of around $0.8 \ \mu$m. Several techniques yielding reduced encroachment are at present under investigation as replacements of the standard LOCOS. Among these techniques are the so-called sidewall masked isolation (SWAMI),[20] sealed-interface local oxidation (SILO),[21] and selective epitaxial growth (SEG).[22] These techniques are more complicated than LOCOS and their description falls outside the scope of this chapter. A good review of device isolation techniques can be found elsewhere.[23]

10.6 LAYOUT AND MASK GENERATION

In this section, we discuss briefly some of the key aspects of the procedures that lead to the fabrication of the final (physical) mask set. These procedures can be separated into *layout*, *layout coding*, and *mask fabrication*. This section is mainly for the benefit of those readers who, in the course of their device-modeling work, may want to lay out a test chip containing several devices. It is hoped that the material below will help them to interact more easily with fabrication engineers (or a silicon foundry).

10.6.1 Layout

As we have mentioned in Sec. 10.1, the (layout) design rules consist of a set of geometrical constraints on the layout of circuit layers which depends on the spatial resolution of the fabrication process. The latter is limited by the distortions suffered by patterns as they are transferred to the silicon wafer. Examples of some basic distortions are shown in Fig. 10.24. Typically, design rules are expressed in absolute units of length such as micrometers. As the spatial resolution of processes improves, design rules are scaled down to permit denser layouts. In a typical manufacturing environment, this scaling is not always uniform across the whole set of the design rules, because the spatial resolution of the process is not uniform over all processes. However, by accepting the worst case resolution as the basic process resolution, it is possible to devise a very simple set of design rules that can be scaled uniformly as the process resolution improves. Such rules are widely used by universities as well as by some industries new to IC fabrication and can be found in circuit design texts.[24, 25]

Layout drafting can be done by hand, using common drafting tools, but today it is almost exclusively done by using one of the many available *computer-aided layout tools*. The latter usually consist of computer programs that interface with the designer via a video computer terminal and allow the interactive generation of artwork on the terminal screen. Such tools exist in

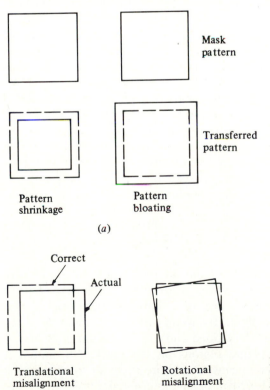

Mask pattern

Transferred pattern

Pattern shrinkage

Pattern bloating

(a)

Correct

Actual

Translational misalignment

Rotational misalignment

(b)

FIGURE 10.24
Illustration of basic pattern transfer errors. (a) Pattern distortion; (b) pattern misalignment.

many forms, from stand-alone to time-shared configurations. Several are commercially available while many others exist as proprietary or development tools within various organizations and universities.[26]

10.6.2   Layout Coding

Masks are usually produced by computer-controlled *pattern generators*. Thus, the layout must be presented to these machines in a coded form, commonly stored in a magnetic tape. The actual process of mask generation is a complicated process in itself, and depends on the particular pattern generator type and the lithography tool to be used for the circuit fabrication process. Thus, the coded form that each different type of machine wants to see varies widely. Software packages exist that allow transformation of layout codes or files from the form internal to the computer-aided layout tool to that of the specific pattern generator. If the layout was done by hand-drafting, then it must be coded by inserting the coordinates of the various patterns into a computer file in the appropriate form.

There are several disadvantages in generating layout codes directly in any of the different machine-specific forms. The most important is that other design-aid software that need to read the layout files[27] cannot be standardized. Also, layout files cannot be shared among designers in different organizations.

To circumvent these disadvantages, an intermediate layout coding form, called the *Caltech intermediate form* (CIF),[24] has been adopted as a means to describe graphic terms, i.e., mask features, by the majority of universities working with circuit layouts as well as by some new companies. Thus, CIF serves as the common denominator in the description of circuit layouts. Irrespective of the original layout generation method, the layout is translated into CIF first and, then, it is translated again to the format required by specific output devices such as plotters, video monitors, or pattern generators for mask fabrication. Various design-aid programs such as *design rule checkers* or *geometrical* (circuit) *parameter extractors* have been written which can read directly CIF format. Also, other programs exist which aid the generation of CIF files from hand-drawn layouts when sophisticated interactive graphics layout aids are not available.[28]

10.6.3   Mask Generation

As discussed above, masks are generated from the coded layout by a pattern generator. The typical basic process consists of exposing a light-sensitive or electron-beam-sensitive resist on the surface of a thin chromium (metal) film deposited on a high-quality glass plate. By using processes similar to those described in Sec. 10.2, the resist is developed and the chromium is etched to produce the desired clear and opaque regions on the mask. Chromium is preferred to photographic emulsion because it is more resistant to wear and it also gives higher contrast images. Electron beam pattern generators, which are becoming increasingly dominant, usually produce directly the mask which contains repeated images corresponding to each chip on the wafer at the final dimensions. Optical-pattern generators produce usually a mask with the image of only one chip five or ten times larger than the final size. This intermediate mask is called *reticle*. The final mask is then produced by projecting optically a precisely reduced image of the reticle on another similar photosensitive plate. This projection is repeated many times in a process which is called *step and repeat* to produce the final mask which contains the chip layer images many times.

Usually each layout layer corresponds to one mask, but there are cases where the number of masks generated is larger than the number of layout layers. These additional mask layers are created by logical operations such as NOT, AND, and OR on the layout layers. For example, if an E/D NMOS process requires that the depletion devices be protected from the enhancement implant, which was discussed in Sec. 10.3, a mask that consists of the complement (NOT) of the depletion layer is created. Similarly in CMOS, although it appears that a single layer, called the "p^+," separates the actual p^+-doped region from the n^+-doped region, it often takes two masks. One mask protects the p^+ regions from the n^+ implantation and another one containing the complement of the images in the previous one is used to protect the n^+ regions against the p^+ implantation. These extra masks are easily generated from the CIF code of the layout once the details of the actual fabrication process are determined.

REFERENCES

1. S. M. Sze (editor), *VLSI Technology*, John Wiley, New York, 1983
2. R. A. Colclaser, *Microelectronics: Processing and Device Design*, chapter 5, John Wiley , New York, 1980.
3. A. B. Glaser and G. E. Subak-Sharpe, *Integrated Circuit Engineering*, chapter 5, Addison-Wesley, Reading, 1979.
4. D. J. Elliot, *Integrated Circuit Fabrication Technology*, chapter 1, McGraw-Hill, New York, 1982.
5. S. K. Ghandi, *VLSI Fabrication Principles, Silicon and Galium Arsenide*, John Wiley, New York, 1983.
6. G. Haas and R. E. Thun, *Physics of Thin Films*, pp. 293–298, Academic Press, New York, 1969.
7. R. S. Rosler, "Low pressure CVD production processes for poly, nitride, and oxide," *Solid State Technology*, vol. 20(4), p. 63, 1977.
8. D. B. Estreich and R. W. Dutton, "Modeling latchup in CMOS integrated circuits," *IEEE Transactions on Computer-Aided Design*, vol. CAD-1, pp. 157–162, October 1982.
9. L. C. Parillo, R. S. Payne, R. E. Davis, G. W. Reutlinger, and R. L. Field, *Technical Digest*, International Electron Devices Meeting, Washington, D.C., p. 752, 1980.
10. R. D. Rung, H. Momose, and Y. Nagakubo, "Deep trench isolated CMOS devices," *Technical Digest*, International Electron Devices Meeting, San Francisco, p. 237, 1982.
11. M. P. Brassington, A. G. Lewis, and S. L. Partridge, "A comparison of fine-dimension silicon-on-sapphire and bulk-silicon complementary MOS devices and circuits," *IEEE Transactions on Electron Devices*, vol. ED-32, pp. 1858–1867, September 1985.

12. T. M. Liu and W. G. Oldham, "Channeling effect of low energy boron implant in (100) silicon," *IEEE Electron Device Letters*, vol. EDL-4, p. 59, 1983.

13. C. J. Koeneke and W. T. Lynch, "Lightly doped Schottky MOSFET," *Technical Digest*, International Electron Devices Meeting, San Francisco, p. 466, 1982.

14. S. Ogura, P. J. Tsang, W. W. Walker, D. L. Critchlow, and J. F. Shepard, "Design and characteristics of the lightly doped drain-source (LDD) insulated-gate field-effect transistor," *IEEE Transactions on Electron Devices*, vol. ED-27, pp. 1359–1367, August 1980.

15. E. Takeda, H. Kume, Y. Nakagome, T. Makino, A. Shimizu, and S. Asai, "An As-P $(n^+\text{-}n^-)$ double diffused drain MOSFET for VLSI's," *IEEE Transactions on Electron Devices*, vol. ED-30, pp. 652–657, 1983.

16. H. Mikoshiba, T. Horiuchi, and K. Hamano, "Comparison of drain structures in n-channel MOSFETs," *IEEE Transactions on Electron Devices*, vol. ED-33, pp. 140–144, January 1986.

17. S. C. Sun and J. D. Plummer, "Electron mobility in inversion and accumulation layers on thermally oxidized silicon surfaces," *IEEE Transactions on Electron Devices*, vol. ED-27, p. 1497, 1980.

18. L. C. Parillo, S. J. Hillenius, R. L. Field, E. L. Hu, W. Fichtner, and M-L. Chen, "A fine-line CMOS technology that uses p^+-polysilicon/silicide gates for NMOS and PMOS devices," *Technical Digest*, International Electron Devices Meeting, p. 418, 1984.

19. K. M. Cham, D. W. Wenocur, J. Lin, C. K. Lau, and H-S. Fu, "Submicrometer thin gate oxide p-channel transistors with p^+ polysilicon gates for VLSI applications," *IEEE Electron Device Letters*, vol. EDL-7, p. 49, 1986.

20. K. Y. Chiu, J. L. Moll, and J. Manoliu, "A bird's beak free local oxidation technology feasible for VLSI circuits fabrication," *IEEE Transactions on Electron Devices*, vol. ED-29, p. 536, 1982.

21. J. C.-H. Hui, T.-Y. Chiu, S.-W. S. Wong, and W. G. Oldham, "Sealed-interface local oxidation technology," *IEEE Transactions on Electron Devices*, vol. ED-29, p. 554, 1982.

22. N. Eudo, K. Tauo, A. Ishitani, Y. Kurogi, and H. Tsuya, "Novel device isolation technology with selective epitaxial growth," *Technical Digest*, International Electron Devices Meeting, San Francisco, CA, p. 241, 1982.

23. D. J. Bartelink and J. L. Moll, "Device Physics Perspective on Novel MOS Processes," in *VLSI Electronics, Microstructure Science No. 12, Silicon Materials*, N. Einspruch (editor), Academic Press, New York, 1985.

24. C. Mead and L. Conway, *Introduction to VLSI Systems*, Addison-Wesley, Reading, 1980.

25. L. Glasser and D. Doberpuhl, *The Design and Analysis of VLSI Circuits*, Addison-Wesley, Reading, 1985.

26. R. Armstrong, *HPEDIT, An LSI Artwork Editor for the HP2647 Graphics Terminal*, private communication, Massachusetts Institute of Technology, Cambridge, 1982.

27. P. Losleben, "Computer Aided Design for VLSI," in *VLSI Fundamentals and Applications*, D. F. Barbe (editor), Springer-Verlag, Berlin, 1980.

28. P. Penfield, Jr., *AIDS-79 User's Manual*, Massachusetts Institute of Technology, Cambridge, IC Memo 80-14, 1980.

ENERGY
BANDS
AND
RELATED
CONCEPTS

A.1   ENERGY BANDS

The energy band model is a rather involved one in solid-state physics. Here we only summarize some of its basic features for interested readers. More details can be found in the references provided in Chap. 1. The following material can be understood in the context of Sec. 1.2.

For semiconductors, the energy band model can be illustrated as shown in Fig. A.1. The horizontal axis corresponds to distance in the semiconductor, whereas the vertical axis corresponds to electron energy. In an *intrinsic* semiconductor, electrons bound to their parent atom have energy no larger than E_v; they are said to "be in the valence band." An electron with a total energy of at least E_c becomes liberated from the parent atom and is said to "be in the conduction band." Such an electron leaves "behind" a hole in the valence band. The energy of holes is measured in a direction opposite from that of electrons because of their opposite charge (i.e., hole energy increases downward in Fig. A.1). If an electron acquires a total energy $E > E_c$ (i.e., because of thermal vibration of the lattice), the difference $E - E_c$ corresponds to net kinetic energy as the electron moves in the crystal lattice. E_c itself represents the potential energy of the free electron. Energy levels between E_v

445

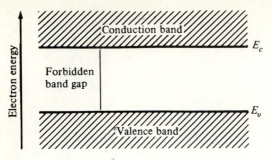

FIGURE A.1
Energy band model for a semiconductor.

and E_c are not occupied in the intrinsic semiconductor under discussion. Such energies belong to the so-called "forbidden band gap," which for silicon has a width $E_g = E_c - E_v$ of 1.12 eV at 300 K, slightly decreasing with temperature. At room temperature, few electrons acquire that much energy in an intrinsic semiconductor and, therefore, few are liberated. Thus the intrinsic carrier concentration n_i is small.

In an *extrinsic* n-type semiconductor, the "extra" electron of a donor atom (Sec. 1.2) corresponds to an energy level E_d only slightly below E_c (Fig. A.2a). Then at room temperature practically all such electrons (one per donor atom) have enough thermally acquired energy to enter the conduction band (i.e., to be set free). Similarly, in a p-type semiconductor, the vacancy in an acceptor atom corresponds to an energy level E_a only slightly above E_v (Fig. A.2.b), and thus it is easy for an electron from the valence band to fill the vacancy and leave "behind" a hole.

Although electrons and holes are governed by Fermi-Dirac statistics,

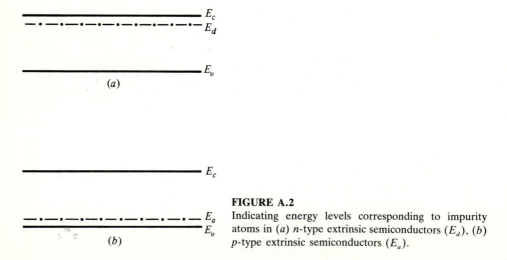

FIGURE A.2
Indicating energy levels corresponding to impurity atoms in (a) n-type extrinsic semiconductors (E_d), (b) p-type extrinsic semiconductors (E_a).

these statistics practically reduce to Maxwell-Boltzmann statistics in nondegenerate semiconductors. According to these statistics, the electron and hole concentrations at equilibrium can be expressed as follows:

$$n = n_i e^{(E_F - E_i)/(kT)} \tag{A.1}$$

$$p = n_i e^{(E_i - E_F)/(kT)} \tag{A.2}$$

where n_i is the intrinsic carrier concentration, k is Boltzmann's constant, T is the absolute temperature, E_i is the intrinsic energy level (located very close to the middle of the forbidden energy gap), and E_F is the Fermi energy. For intrinsic semiconductors $E_F = E_i$ (Fig. A.3a). For n-type extrinsic semiconductors $E_F > E_i$ (Fig. A.3b), and for p-type extrinsic semiconductors $E_F < E_i$ (Fig. A.3c). If n or p for a nondegenerate semiconductor is known, $E_F - E_i$ can be calculated from (A.1) or (A.2). For the semiconductor material to be nondegenerate, the resulting E_F must not be too close to either end of the forbidden energy gap. The relation $E_v + 3kT < E_F < E_c - 3kT$ should be satisfied for such a material.

In equilibrium, E_F is constant throughout a semiconductor. To accommodate this, the levels E_c, E_i, and E_v may have to "bend" accordingly.

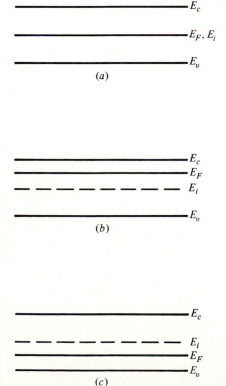

FIGURE A.3
Relative position of intrinsic energy level (E_i) and Fermi energy (E_F) for (a) intrinsic, (b) n-type, and (c) p-type semiconductors.

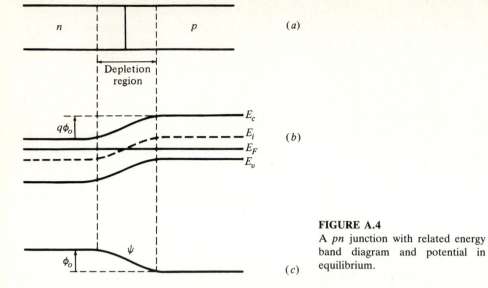

FIGURE A.4
A *pn* junction with related energy band diagram and potential in equilibrium.

This is illustrated in Fig. A.4*b*, showing the energy band diagram for a *pn* junction (Fig. A.4*a*) in equilibrium (no external bias) (Sec. 1.5). Similarly, for a junction of *p*-type silicon to intrinsic silicon (Fig. A.5*a*) in equilibrium (again, no external bias) the energy band diagram is as in Fig. A.5*b*. In both cases, the difference between any two among E_c, E_i, and E_v is kept constant with distance. For any point along the horizontal axis in Figs. A.4 and A.5, the distance between E_F and E_i, and their relative position, must be such as to give

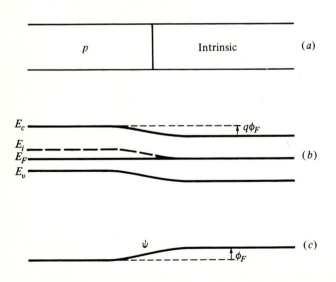

FIGURE A.5
A junction between *p*-type and intrinsic silicon with related energy band diagram and potential in equilibrium.

the correct values of n and p when (A.1) and (A.2) are used. The actual values of n and p can be found with the help of Poisson's equation (Appendix B).

Let now $\Delta E_c = \Delta E_i$ be the electron potential energy difference between two points 1 and 2 in a semiconductor at equilibrium. Then the electrostatic potential difference $\Delta\psi$ between them (potential energy difference per unit charge) will be

$$\Delta\psi = \frac{\Delta E_i}{-q} \tag{A.3}$$

Thus, electrostatic potential varies in a direction opposite from E_i, E_c, or E_v, as illustrated in Figs. A.4c and A.5c.

Using (A.1), the electron concentrations at the two points considered above will be $n_1 = n_i \exp\left[(E_F - E_{i1})/kT\right]$ and $n_2 = n_i \exp\left[(E_F - E_{i2})/kT\right]$. Dividing these and using (A.3) gives

$$\frac{n_1}{n_2} = e^{\psi_{12}/\phi_t} \tag{A.4}$$

with $\phi_t = kT/q$; (A.4) is the same as (1.2.7). Similarly, one is led to (1.2.11) starting from (A.2).

In energy band treatments, the Fermi potential ϕ_F is defined for the cases of Fig. A.3 as follows:[†]

$$\phi_F = \frac{E_F - E_i}{-q} \tag{A.5}$$

Our use of the Fermi potential in Sec. 1.4 (Fig. 1.11) is consistent with the above. This can be easily checked by relating Fig. A.5 to Fig 1.11 and using (A.3) appropriately. Also, it is easy to check directly on the energy band diagram of the pn junction in Fig. A.4b that the contact potential of the n side to the p side (built-in potential, ϕ_o) is given by (1.5.1).

If the doping concentration becomes too high, E_F becomes too close to the conduction or valence band (say, within $3kT$) and then the semiconductor is said to be degenerate. Then (A.1) and (A.2) do not hold. Thus, ϕ_F cannot be found from (1.4.2) or (1.4.3) in such cases. For a degenerate semiconductor with $E_F \approx E_c$ (n type) or $E_F \approx E_v$ (p type), we have $|E_F - E_i| \approx E_g/2$, where E_g is the band gap energy. For silicon at room temperature, this means that ϕ_F from (A.5) is approximately -0.56 V for n type and $+0.56$ V for p type.

A.2   CONTACT POTENTIALS AND WORK FUNCTIONS

In energy band treatments, contact potentials (Sec. 1.4) are handled using the so-called work functions.[‡] Consider as an example n-type and p-type materials,

---

[†] In some treatments, no minus sign is used in the denominator of the fraction in (A.5).

[‡] The treatment provided here is not rigorous. A careful treatment should be based on a foundation of thermodynamics.

initially separated as in Fig. A.6. Here E_R represents the so-called *vacuum energy level*, corresponding to the energy of an electron when it is removed from the material so that it is not influenced by it. The difference between E_R and a Fermi energy E_F is called *work function* and is denoted by W. It is a measure of "how difficult" it is for an electron to leave its host material. In Fig. A.6, we have $W_1 < W_2$, and thus electrons find it easier to leave the *n*-type material. This causes the following effect. When the two materials are brought together to form a junction as in Fig. A.4, initially electrons diffuse from the *n* side to the *p* side (and holes diffuse in the opposite direction), as discussed in Sec. 1.5. With negative charges thus increasing on the *p* side, eventually the potential of that region with respect to the *n* side becomes so negative as to inhibit a further net tendency for diffusion. This happens when the average energy of the electrons on the *p* side (relative to that on the *n* side) has increased over its value before the materials were brought together, by the amount $W_2 - W_1$. This "causes the two Fermi levels to line up," as shown in Fig. A.4, and the other energy levels to increase from left to right by the amount $W_2 - W_1$, corresponding to a drop in electrostatic potential of $(W_2 - W_1)/q$; this is the contact potential of the *n* side to the *p* side. The same idea is used to handle contact potentials between dissimilar materials, e.g., a metal and a semiconductor. In general, then, the contact potential ϕ_{J_1, J_2} of a material J_1 to a material J_2 is given by

$$\phi_{J_1, J_2} = \frac{W_{J_2} - W_{J_1}}{q} \qquad (A.6)$$

where W_{J_1} and W_{J_2} are the corresponding work functions. As noted in Sec. 1.4, work functions are not easy to measure and, in fact, have to be modified for use in MOS device modeling.

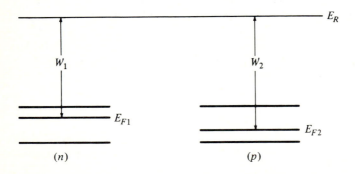

FIGURE A.6
Energy band diagrams for *n* and *p* materials separated from each other, and corresponding work functions.

A.3 QUASI-FERMI LEVELS AND CURRENTS

The discussion so far in this Appendix has been limited to equilibrium conditions (Sec. 1.2). In the absence of equilibrium (A.1) and (A.2) cannot be used, and n and p must be found from other considerations (Refs. 1–12 in Chap. 1). The system cannot be characterized by a Fermi level which is constant throughout as in equilibrium. In some treatments it is found convenient to introduce two quantities E_{Fn} and E_{Fp}, called *quasi-Fermi energy levels* (or *imrefs*) for electrons and holes, respectively. These are often defined as the quantities which satisfy the relations (see, e.g., the references in Chap. 1)[†]

$$n = n_i e^{(E_{Fn} - E_i)/(kT)} \qquad (A.7)$$

$$p = n_i e^{(E_i - E_{Fp})/(kT)} \qquad (A.8)$$

where n and p are the correct electron and hole concentration values. As is obvious by comparing the above equations to (A.1) and (A.2), in equilibrium we can set $E_{Fn} = E_{Fp} = E_F$, and thus $np = n_i^2$. Otherwise, $E_{Fn} \neq E_{Fp}$ and then $np \neq n_i^2$. This situation is encountered, for example, in the depletion region of a *pn* junction with external bias applied.

The quantities E_{Fn} and E_{Fp} can be related to electron current and hole current, respectively, in a simple manner. Thus, consider one-dimensional current flow in the x direction, uniformly distributed throughout a cross-sectional area A.[‡] Let $\psi(x)$ and $n(x)$ be the electrostatic potential and the electron concentration at x. We can express the total current due to electrons $I_n(x)$, caused by both drift and diffusion, by using (1.3.11a) and (1.3.17). If the current is defined in the *positive x* direction (*opposite* from that in Fig. 1.5 or 1.8), we will have

$$I_n(x) = qA \left[-\mu_n n(x) \frac{d\psi}{dx} + D_n \frac{dn}{dx} \right] \qquad (A.9)$$

where μ_n and D_n are the electron mobility and the diffusion constant, respectively. As follows from (A.3), if $\psi(x)$ varies with x so will $E_i(x)$. Dividing both sides of that equation by Δx and letting Δx approach zero, we obtain:

$$\frac{d\psi}{dx} = -\frac{1}{q} \frac{dE_i}{dx} \qquad (A.10)$$

From (A.7) we obtain

$$\frac{dn}{dx} = \frac{1}{kT} n(x) \left(\frac{dE_{Fn}}{dx} - \frac{dE_i}{dx} \right) \qquad (A.11)$$

[†] E_{Fn} and E_{Fp} can be introduced better in the context of thermodynamics.

[‡] If desired, one can let A shrink to zero around a point and define a *current density* at that point as dI/dA.

Using now (A.10), (A.11), and (1.3.18) in (A.9), we obtain

$$I_n(x) = A\mu_n n(x) \frac{dE_{Fn}}{dx} \tag{A.12}$$

Thus the spatial variation of the electron quasi-Fermi level depends on the *total* electron current (drift plus diffusion components). Zero total electron current implies a constant electron quasi-Fermi level, and vice versa.

In a similar manner, the total hole current can be expressed in terms of drift and diffusion components by

$$I_p(x) = qA\left[-\mu_p p(x) \frac{d\psi}{dx} - D_p \frac{dp}{dx} \right] \tag{A.13}$$

with μ_p being the hole mobility and D_p the hole diffusion constant given by $D_p = \mu\phi_t$ in analogy with (1.3.18). The algebraic signs in the above equation are easily discernible from the discussion in Secs. 1.3.2 and 1.3.3, remembering that the current direction considered there was opposite from the one here. Using (A.8) and proceeding as above, we obtain

$$I_p(x) = A\mu_p p(x) \frac{dE_{Fp}}{dx} \tag{A.14}$$

which gives the relation between the *total* hole current (drift plus diffusion components) and the hole quasi-Fermi potential. Zero hole current implies a constant E_{Fp}, and vice versa.

Since in thermal equilibrium $E_{Fn} = E_{Fp} = E_F$, it is clear from (A.12) and (A.14) that thermal equilibrium implies zero total electron current *and* zero total hole current.

Quasi-Fermi level differences in semiconductor devices are often related to externally applied voltages. As an example, consider a *pn* junction with reverse bias V_R applied (Sec. 1.5). In the regions away from the depletion region, the majority carrier concentrations remain practically at their equilibrium values. However, the electrostatic potential across the depletion region must increase by V_R, corresponding to an increase in the energy band bending by qV_R, compared to Fig. A.4. Thus the energy band diagram with reverse bias becomes as shown in Fig. A.7. Separate quasi-Fermi levels are used so that, despite the extra band bending, (A.7) and (A.8) can give majority carrier concentrations at the *n* and *p* side, respectively, which have practically the same values as for Fig. A.4. The two quasi-Fermi levels are in this case said to "split" by the amount qV_R. As shown in Fig. A.7, E_{Fn} and E_{Fp} are almost constant since I_n and I_p in (A.12) and (A.14) are very small under reverse bias, whereas n and p, correspondingly, are very large. At other places the shape of the quasi-Fermi levels can be deduced based on a number of assumptions concerning the carrier concentrations and the detailed mechanisms associated with the reverse-bias current. For the purposes of this book such considerations are not essential. It is only remarked here that assumptions commonly made lead to the conclusion that the quasi-Fermi levels continue practically horizontal over the depletion region (see, for example, Refs. 4 and 5 in Chap. 1).

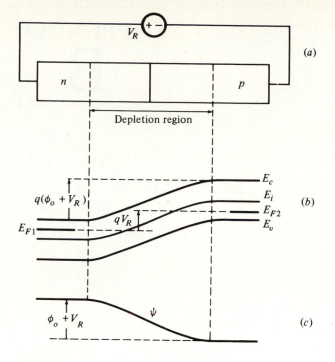

FIGURE A.7

A *pn* junction with related energy band diagram and potential under reverse bias V_R.

BASIC
LAWS OF
ELECTROSTATICS
IN ONE
DIMENSION

B.1 RELATIONS BETWEEN CHARGE DENSITY, ELECTRIC FIELD, AND POTENTIAL

The equations below are useful for one-dimensional analysis. (That is, it is assumed that all quantities involved vary only with the horizontal dimension x; they are constant over a plane perpendicular to the x dimension for any given x.) The following symbols will be used:

$\rho(x)$ = charge density per unit volume at point x (in $fC/\mu m^3$).

$\mathcal{E}(x)$ = electric field intensity at point x (in $V/\mu m$), with the field defined in the *positive* x direction.

$\psi(x)$ = electric potential at point x with respect to an arbitrary reference (in V).

ϵ = permittivity of material (in $fF/\mu m$); it is equal to $k\epsilon_0$, where k is the dielectric constant of the material and ϵ_0 the permittivity of free space ($8.854 \times 10^{-3} fF/\mu m$). The material is assumed to be characterized by a single value of ϵ everywhere, unless noted otherwise.

The above quantities are related as follows[1] (Fig. B.1):

$$\frac{d\mathcal{E}}{dx} = \frac{\rho(x)}{\epsilon} \tag{B.1}$$

$$\frac{d\psi}{dx} = -\mathcal{E}(x) \tag{B.2}$$

or, in integral form:

$$\mathcal{E}(x_2) - \mathcal{E}(x_1) = \frac{1}{\epsilon} \int_{x_1}^{x_2} \rho(x)\,dx \tag{B.1a}$$

$$\psi(x_2) - \psi(x_1) = - \int_{x_1}^{x_2} \mathcal{E}(x)\,dx \tag{B.2a}$$

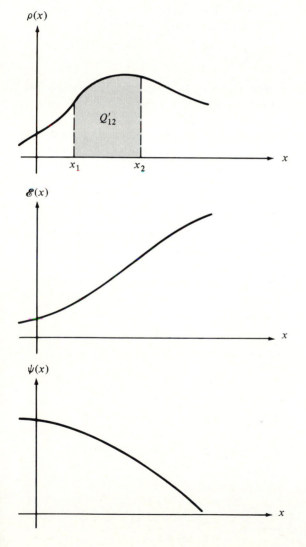

FIGURE B.1

Combining (B.1) with (B.2) we obtain Poisson's equation:

$$\frac{d^2\psi}{dx^2} = -\frac{\rho(x)}{\epsilon} \tag{B.3}$$

B.2   RELATION BETWEEN ELECTRIC FIELD AND CHARGE PER UNIT AREA

Consider a parallelepiped as shown in Fig. B.2. The charge in a vanishingly thin, vertical slice of length Δx around point x will be $\rho(x) A \Delta x$. [As stated in the beginning of this appendix, $\rho(x)$ is assumed constant over any plane perpendicular to the x axis.] The total charge Q in the parallelepiped will be the integral of $\rho(x) A \, dx$ from x_1 to x_2. Dividing this by A gives *the charge per unit area* Q' as seen from the side. Thus (B.1a) can be written

$$\mathcal{E}(x_2) - \mathcal{E}(x_1) = \frac{Q'_{12}}{\epsilon} \tag{B.4}$$

where Q'_{12} is the charge per unit area (in $fC/\mu m^2$) contained between two vertical planes at x_1 and x_2, as shown in Fig. B.1. The above equation is referred to as Gauss' law.

If points x_1 and x_2 above belong to two different materials joined at a plane perpendicular to the x dimension at a point x_0 somewhere between x_1 and x_2, and if ϵ_1 and ϵ_2 are the corresponding permittivities, we have, in lieu of (B.4),

$$\epsilon_2 \mathcal{E}(x_2) - \epsilon_1 \mathcal{E}(x_1) = Q'_{12} \tag{B.5}$$

B.3   DISCONTINUITIES IN ELECTRIC FIELD

As can be deduced from (B.5) by letting x_1 and x_2 approach the same value x_0, the electric field can be discontinuous at $x = x_0$ because of (1) change of

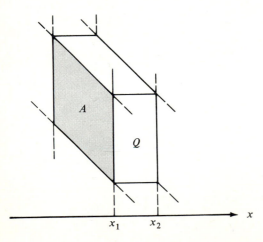

FIGURE B.2

permittivity at an interface and/or (2) a charge sheet of zero thickness located at point x_0, with a nonzero charge per unit area.

From the equations given above one can derive the following two useful results that can be applied in several cases considered in this book.

B.4 RESULT 1

Consider a region characterized by a *uniform* charge density ρ_o and permittivity ϵ enclosed between two planes F and G perpendicular to the x dimension, as shown in Fig. B.3, separated by a distance d. Assume $\mathscr{E} = \mathscr{E}_F$ at the left plane.

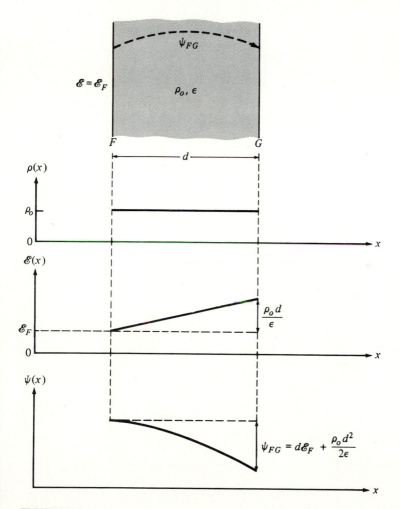

FIGURE B.3

Then the potential drop ψ_{FG} between the two planes is given by

$$\psi_{FG} = d\mathscr{E}_F + \frac{\rho_o d^2}{2\epsilon} \tag{B.6}$$

The above result is a straightforward application of (B.1) and (B.2). The plots in Fig. B.3 are shown only for points between planes F and G.

B.5   RESULT 2

Consider the situation pictured in Fig. B.4. A region with permittivity ϵ and *no* charge in it (region II) is adjacent to a region with some charge in it (region I).

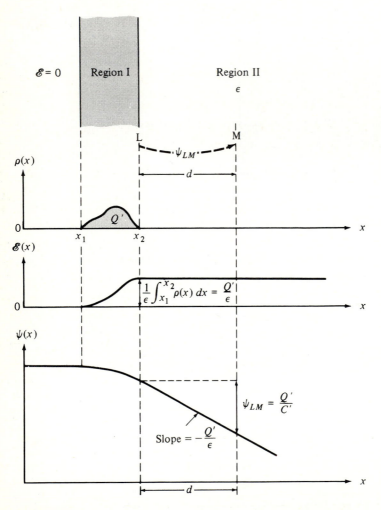

FIGURE B.4

The two regions are assumed separated by a plane perpendicular to the x dimension at point L as shown. Assume $\mathscr{E} = 0$ to the left of region I. Then the total potential drop from the boundary between the two regions to a point at a distance d inside region II will be

$$\psi_{LM} = \frac{Q'}{C'} \tag{B.7}$$

where Q' is the charge per unit area in region I as seen from the side and C' is the capacitance per unit area between the planes at L and M (in $fF/\mu m^2$), given by

$$C' = \frac{\epsilon}{d} \tag{B.8}$$

The above result is again an application of (B.1) and (B.2). Note that the result in (B.7) is *independent* of the details of the shape of $\rho(x)$ in region I. For an example of an application of the above equations, the reader is referred to Appendix C.

REFERENCE

1. J. D. Kraus, *Electromagnetics*, McGraw-Hill, New York, 1984.

CHARGE DENSITY, ELECTRIC FIELD, AND POTENTIAL IN THE *pn* JUNCTION

The equations in Appendix B can be employed in the analysis of a *pn* junction (Sec. 1.5), as shown in Fig. C.1. The external bias is assumed to be zero. The depletion approximation is used (Sec. 1.5). $\mathscr{E} = 0$ is assumed to the left of the depletion region. Note in Fig. C.1 that the contact potential *of* the *n* side *to* the *p* side is positive, as expected from the discussion in Sec. 1.5. Also, note that for $N_D \gg N_A$ we have $l_1 \ll l_2$, and practically all the potential drop ϕ_o occurs across the *p* side. If the external bias is V_R, the same analysis is valid if ϕ_o is replaced by $\phi_o + V_R$. From the relations shown on the plots one easily finds (Prob. 1.13)

$$\frac{l_1}{l_2} = \frac{N_A}{N_D} \tag{C.1}$$

$$l_1 + l_2 = \sqrt{\frac{2\epsilon_s}{q} \frac{N_A + N_D}{N_A N_D} \phi_o} \tag{C.2}$$

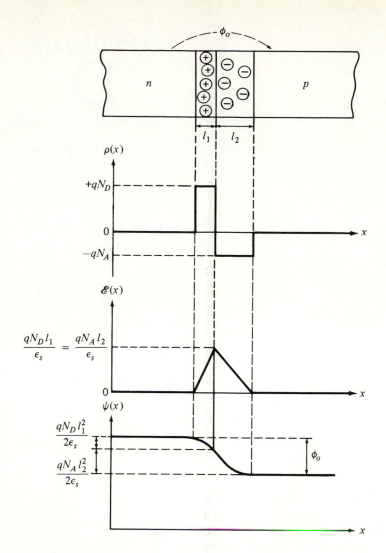

FIGURE C.1

461

ENERGY
BAND
DIAGRAMS
FOR THE
TWO-TERMINAL
MOS
STRUCTURE

The energy band model is often used in the description of MOS structures (see, for example, Refs. 1–4 in Chap. 2). The main features of such a description are summarized below. This material can best be understood by referring to Chap. 2, Secs. 2.2–2.5, and Appendix A.

Consider a two-terminal MOS structure on a p-type substrate, as shown in Fig. D.1a. Assume for the present that the effective interface charge per unit area, Q'_o, is zero. Let W_M and W_S be the work functions of the gate and substrate materials, respectively (Appendix A). As an example, assume $W_M > W_S$. If the MOS structure is short-circuited ($V_{GB} = 0$), electrons in the substrate, where the work function is lower, will find it attractive to leave and, traveling through the external wire, enter the gate. This will leave behind positive charges in the substrate, as has been shown in Fig. 2.2b, and will cause in it a potential drop. The other energy levels will thus bend until the Fermi levels in the gate and substrate can line up (like in the case of the pn junction

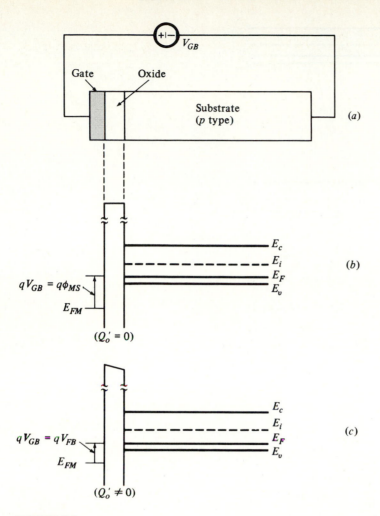

FIGURE D.1
(a) A two-terminal MOS structure with a p-type substrate (b) energy band diagram for the flat-band condition, assuming $Q_o' = 0$; (c) energy band diagram for the flat-band condition, assuming $Q_o' \neq 0$.

in Fig. A.4). If it is desired to prevent this from happening and, instead, keep the bands "flat" in the substrate region next to the oxide, no potential drop and no net charges should exist there. This can be achieved by inserting in the external circuit a battery of value $V_{GB} = (W_M - W_S)/q$. When the connection is first established the electrons in the substrate looking toward the external circuit face no longer the gate with its electrons of lower energy directly, but rather the negative terminal of the battery. The battery has increased the electron energy at that point by $W_M - W_S$. Now the environment the electrons would face if they attempted to leave the substrate is no more attractive than

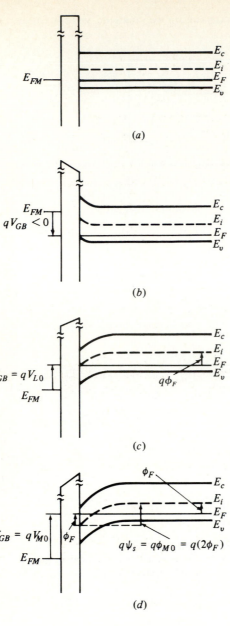

E_{FM} ───

E_c
E_i
E_F
E_v

(a)

E_{FM} ───
$qV_{GB} < 0$

E_c
E_i
E_F
E_v

(b)

$qV_{GB} = qV_{L0}$

E_{FM}

E_c
E_i
E_F
E_v

$q\phi_F$

(c)

ϕ_F

$qV_{GB} = qV_{M0}$ ϕ_F

E_{FM}

E_c
E_i
E_F
E_v

$q\psi_s = q\phi_{M0} = q(2\phi_F)$

(d)

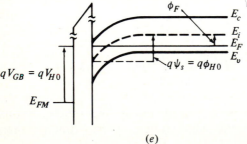

ϕ_F

$qV_{GB} = qV_{H0}$

E_{FM}

E_c
E_i
E_F
E_v

$-q\psi_s = q\phi_{H0}$

(e)

FIGURE D.2
Energy band diagrams for a two-terminal
MOS structure with a p-type substrate,
assuming $\phi_{MS} = 0$ and $Q_o' = 0$, for various
values of V_{GB} (symbols are defined in Secs.
2.2 to 2.5). (a) Flat-band condition; (b)
accumulation; (c) onset of weak inversion;
(d) onset of moderate inversion; (e) onset
of strong inversion.

their present environment (the substrate itself). Thus there is no reason for electrons to leave and for charges to pile up. The external voltage source keeps the Fermi levels of the gate (E_{FM}) and of the substrate (E_F) separated by $E_F - E_{FM} = W_M - W_S$, and achieves the so-called *flat-band* condition shown in Fig. D.1b, which corresponds to Fig. 2.2c. A conduction band can be defined for the oxide and is shown to be horizontal since there is no field in the oxide under our assumption of $Q'_o = 0$. If now $Q'_o \neq 0$, then to keep the semiconductor bands flat, one has to adjust the external voltage to the value $V_{GB} = V_{FB}$ as given by (2.2.6). Now the conduction band in the oxide will not be horizontal since there will be a nonzero oxide field (see Fig. 2.2e). The corresponding band diagram is shown in Fig. D.1c.

For simplicity in the rest of the discussion, we will assume both $\phi_{MS} = 0$ and $Q'_o = 0$. Then the flat-band condition corresponds to the band diagram shown in Fig. D.2a. Since now $V_{FB} = 0$, accumulation will be caused by $V_{GB} < 0$, and depletion or inversion by $V_{GB} > 0$. The band diagrams for various critical values of V_{GB} (defined in Secs. 2.4 and 2.5) are shown in Fig. D.2b to e. As expected from Appendix A, the surface potential ψ_s can be related to the bending of any level among E_c, E_i, E_v, as shown. The diagrams are self-explanatory.

The construction of band diagrams for MOS structures with n-type substrates follows along the same lines. As an example, at the onset of moderate inversion we will have the case illustrated in Fig. D.3.

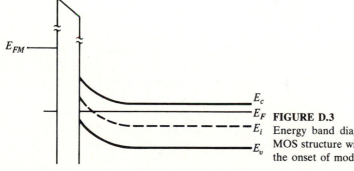

FIGURE D.3
Energy band diagram for a two-terminal MOS structure with an n-type substrate at the onset of moderate inversion.

CHARGE DENSITY, ELECTRIC FIELD, AND POTENTIAL IN THE TWO-TERMINAL MOS STRUCTURE

Figure E.1 shows the results of applying the basic laws of electrostatics given in Appendix B to the two-terminal MOS structure discussed in Chap. 2. The figure has been drawn based on three simplifying assumptions:

1. The depletion region has a uniform charge density and is assumed to contain only ionized acceptor atoms, and the region's bottom edge is sharply defined, with the semiconductor being neutral below it (depletion approximation);

2. The charges on the gate and at the interface are contained in extremely thin layers. The integral under the corresponding portions of the charge density plot (i.e., the corresponding charge per unit area) is Q'_G and Q'_o, respectively, as shown;

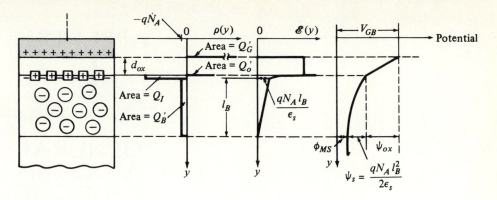

FIGURE E.1

3. The inversion layer is much thinner than the depletion region. For simplicity, we assume that the charge density $\rho(y)$ is constant in the inversion layer. The latter assumption is not valid in practice. However, it can be seen fron the material in Appendix B that, as the thickness of the inversion layer is allowed to approach zero (charge sheet model), the details of the shape of $\rho(y)$ in it become irrelevant anyway. All that counts, then, is the corresponding integral of the inversion layer charge density, which in Fig. E.1 has been denoted by Q_I'.

GENERAL ANALYSIS OF THE TWO-TERMINAL MOS STRUCTURE

In our discussion of the two-terminal MOS structure in Sec. 2.5, we have focused on inversion and have adopted the charge sheet and depletion approximations. As is mentioned in Sec. 2.5, though, it is possible to analyze the structure without making such assumptions, allowing for the presence of both electrons and holes throughout the semiconductor, with distributions dictated from semiconductor physics. Such analysis will be valid in all operating regimes (accumulation, depletion, and inversion). In inversion, it accounts for the fact that the hole concentration decreases continuously as one goes from the bulk toward the surface, and allows for the spreading of the inversion layer below the surface. Here we provide the main steps and results of this general analysis. In using relations from Appendix B, x will be replaced by y since quantities vary in the vertical direction, assuming the orientation we have adopted in drawing the MOS two-terminal structure in Chap. 2. A p-type substrate is assumed.

Let us refer to Fig. 2.4a. The charge density at depth y in the semiconductor, including holes, electrons, and ionized acceptor atoms, is given by (2.4.15) repeated here for convenience:

$$\rho(y) = q[p(y) - n(y) - N_A] \tag{F.1}$$

From (2.4.13) and (2.4.14) we have

$$n(y) = n_o e^{\psi(y)/\phi_t} \tag{F.2}$$

$$p(y) = p_o e^{-\psi(y)/\phi_t} \tag{F.3}$$

where $\psi(y)$ is the potential with respect to the bulk at y. Deep in the bulk the charge density is zero, so (F.1) gives $p_o - n_o = N_A$. Using N_A from this and also (F.2) and (F.3) in (F.1), and the result in Poisson's equation (Appendix B), we have

$$\frac{d^2\psi}{dy^2} = -\frac{q}{\epsilon_s}[p_o(e^{-\psi(y)/\phi_t} - 1) - n_o(e^{\psi(y)/\phi_t} - 1)] \tag{F.4}$$

Assuming $N_A \gg n_i$, we can use (1.2.4) and (1.2.5) in the above equation. Eliminating n_i in the result by using (1.4.2), we obtain

$$\frac{d^2\psi}{dy^2} = -\frac{qN_A}{\epsilon_s}[e^{-\psi(y)/\phi_t} - 1 - e^{-2\phi_F/\phi_t}(e^{\psi(y)/\phi_t} - 1)] \tag{F.5}$$

Multiply both sides of this equation by $2(d\psi/dy)$; the resulting left-hand side can be recognized as $(d/dy)(d\psi/dy)^2$. Replace y by a dummy variable $\hat{y}$ and integrate from a point deep in the bulk (theoretically at infinity, where $\psi = 0$ and $d\psi/dy = 0$) to a point y. Solve for $d\psi/dy$ at point y, and recall that $\mathscr{E}(y) = -d\psi/dy$ (Appendix B). We obtain

$$\mathscr{E}(y) = -\frac{d\psi}{dy} = \pm\frac{F\sqrt{N_A}}{\epsilon_s}\sqrt{\phi_t e^{-\psi/\phi_t} + \psi - \phi_t + e^{-2\phi_F/\phi_t}(\phi_t e^{\psi/\phi_t} - \psi - \phi_t)} \tag{F.6}$$

where $\psi = \psi(y)$, $F = \sqrt{2q\epsilon_s}$, and the $+$ sign in front of F is to be used with $\psi > 0$, and the $-$ sign with $\psi < 0$. This choice of signs corresponds to the fact that the signs of $\mathscr{E}$ and ψ agree, as follows from the discussion in Sec. 2.4. To find the total semiconductor charge per unit area Q_C', we can apply (B.4) of Appendix B, taking point 1 at the surface and point 2 deep in the bulk, where $\mathscr{E} = 0$. This gives $-\mathscr{E}_{\text{surface}} = Q_C'/\epsilon_s$. Evaluating $\mathscr{E}_{\text{surface}}$ from (F.6) with $\psi = \psi_s$ (the surface potential), we obtain:

$$Q_C' = \mp F\sqrt{N_A}\sqrt{\phi_t e^{-\psi_s/\phi_t} + \psi_s - \phi_t + e^{-2\phi_F/\phi_t}(\phi_t e^{\psi_s/\phi_t} - \psi_s - \phi_t)} \tag{F.7}$$

This function behaves as shown in Fig. F.1.

Using the above equation in (2.6.7) gives

$$C_c' = \pm F\sqrt{N_A}\left\{\frac{1 - e^{-\psi_s/\phi_t} + e^{-2\phi_F/\phi_t}(e^{\psi_s/\phi_t} - 1)}{2\sqrt{\phi_t e^{-\psi_s/\phi_t} + \psi_s - \phi_t + e^{-2\phi_F/\phi_t}(\phi_t e^{\psi_s/\phi_t} - \psi_s - \phi_t)}}\right\} \tag{F.8}$$

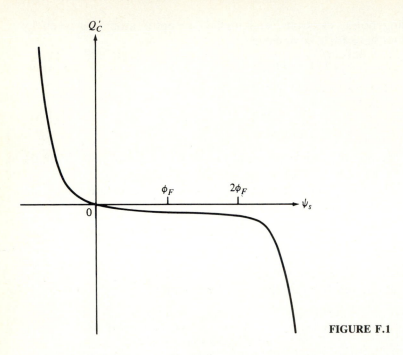

FIGURE F.1

Equations (F.7) and (F.8) are valid in all regimes (accumulation, depletion, and inversion). It is easy to see that in each regime certain terms can be neglected. When using (F.8) with very small $|\psi_s|$ one should watch out for numerical inaccuracies because both its numerator and denominator go to zero as ψ_s goes to zero.

The relation between ψ and y can be obtained from (F.6) by separating variables and integrating from a point at y to a point at the surface. This gives

$$\int_{\psi(y)}^{\psi_s} \frac{d\hat{\psi}}{\mathscr{E}[\hat{\psi}]} = y - y_{\text{surface}} \tag{F.9}$$

where $\hat{\psi}$ is a dummy variable of integration, and $\mathscr{E}[\psi]$ is given by (F.6). From this one can determine ψ for a given y (and a given ψ_s) numerically. With $\psi(y)$ obtained in this way, one can then determine $\rho(y)$, $n(y)$, $p(y)$, and $\mathscr{E}(y)$ from (F.1) to (F.3) and (F.6).

The rest of the analysis proceeds as explained in Sec. 2.4.4.

INVERSION

In inversion it is easy to see that (F.7) reduces practically to (2.5.1), and (F.8) reduces to (2.6.9). The charges and capacitances (per unit area) corresponding to the inversion region and the depletion region can be determined as follows.[†] In (2.5.4) we use $n(y)$ from (F.2) and in the result we use (1.4.1). We take y_c deep in the bulk (theoretically at infinity, where $\psi = 0$). We perform a change of variables from y to ψ. The resulting factor $(d\psi/dy)^{-1}$ in the integrand can be obtained from (F.6). This procedure gives:

$$Q_I' = -qN_A e^{-2\phi_F/\phi_t} \int_0^{\psi_s} \frac{e^{\psi/\phi_t}}{\mathscr{E}[\psi]} \, d\psi \tag{F.10}$$

A similar procedure gives the bulk charge per unit area Q_B', consisting of ionized acceptor atoms and holes:

$$Q_B' = -qN_A \int_0^{\psi_s} \frac{1 - e^{-\psi/\phi_t}}{\mathscr{E}[\psi]} \, d\psi \tag{F.11}$$

The above integrals can be evaluated numerically. However, determining the corresponding capacitances is easy. Using the above expressions in (2.6.12) and (2.6.13) and performing the differentiation results in *explicit* expressions for C_i' and C_b'. After dropping the terms that are negligible in the inversion region, we easily obtain (2.6.14) and (2.6.15).

Sometimes an intermediate level of approximation is used: the charge sheet assumption (i.e., infinitesimal thickness) for the inversion layer is taken to hold, but holes are *still* allowed to exist in the depletion region. Then $n(y)$ is taken as 0 in (F.1) at any point below the inversion layer. Thus the second term in the brackets in (F.4) will be zero as will the fourth term in the sum in (F.6). The *bulk* charge per unit area Q_B' can then be found by applying (B.4) as above, taking point 2 again in the bulk but point 1 immediately below the inversion layer. This gives

$$Q_B' \approx -F\sqrt{N_A}\sqrt{\psi_s - \phi_t} \tag{F.12}$$

Finally, if the depletion approximation is used and thus not even holes are allowed in the depletion region, the only term that will be present in the right-hand side of (F.1) (for any y below the inversion layer) is N_A. Using this directly in Poisson's equation and integrating gives (2.5.6), which is the approximation widely used in this book.

---

† Refs. 1 or 3 in Chap. 2.

ENERGY
BAND
DIAGRAMS
FOR THE
THREE-TERMINAL
MOS
STRUCTURE

Consider the three-terminal MOS structure on a p-type substrate, discussed in Chap. 3 (Fig. G.1a). Assume first that $V_{CB} = 0$. As mentioned in Sec. 3.2, this leads to the same conditions as in a two-terminal MOS structure. For a certain surface potential ψ_s of value ψ_x the energy band diagram in the semiconductor is as shown in Fig. G.1b (Appendix D). If now V_{GB} is kept unchanged and V_{CB} is made positive, the electron energy in the n^+ region will be lowered by qV_{CB} and the electrons will find this region more attractive. Their concentration in the inversion layer will be reduced. If it is desired to restore the surface to its former level of inversion, the energy at the surface must be lowered by qV_{CB} also. Thus the band bending at the surface must increase (in comparison to Fig. G.1b) by qV_{CB} (by increasing V_{GB}), resulting in the band diagram of Fig. G.1c. Now the electron concentration n at the surface has the original value. Since we now have nonequilibrium, one must use (A.7) to predict n. For this to give the same value as (A.1) gives for Fig. G.1b, the electron quasi-Fermi level E_{Fn} at the surface must maintain the same position relative to E_i as E_F has in Fig. G.1b. This is shown in Fig. G.1c. Deep in the bulk the hole quasi-Fermi level

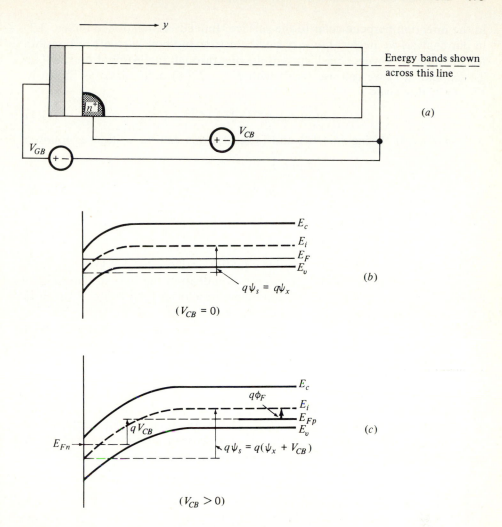

FIGURE G.1

E_{Fp} is maintained at the same position relative to E_i as E_F has in Fig. G.1b, so that (A.8) will produce the same value for p as (A.2) did in equilibrium. From the above discussion it is seen that the E_{Fn} at the surface and E_{Fp} in the bulk split by qV_{CB}.

In no charge sheet approximation is made and the electron concentration $n(y)$ is allowed to be nonzero at point y below the surface (as in the general analysis outlined in Sec. 2.4), one can extend the above arguments for point y. Thus, E_{Fn} is taken practically constant with y below the surface also (Refs. 1 and 2 in Chap. 3). This, as follows from the material on quasi-Fermi levels in Appendix A, is equivalent to assuming that there is negligible electron current in the direction perpendicular to the surface. Indeed, as mentioned in Sec. 3.2, in our analysis we neglect the very small electron and hole currents responsible for the minute "reverse-bias" current flowing through the external source V_{CB}. To express $n(y)$ we can use (A.7) with $E_{Fn} - E_i(y)$ determined as shown in Fig. G.2; this gives

$$n(y) = n_i e^{[\psi(y) - \phi_F - V_{CB}]/\phi_t} \qquad (G.1)$$

with $\phi_t = kT/q$. Using (1.4.1a) and (1.4.1b), this can be written as follows:

$$n(y) = n_o e^{[\psi(y) - V_{CB}]/\phi_t} \qquad (G.2a)$$

$$= p_o e^{[\psi(y) - 2\phi_F - V_{CB}]/\phi_t} \qquad (G.2b)$$

and, using (1.2.4),

$$n(y) \approx N_A e^{[\psi(y) - 2\phi_F - V_{CB}]/\phi_t} \qquad (G.3)$$

At the surface, where $\psi(y) = \psi_s$, this equation reduces to (3.2.1).

To claim that the electron concentration deep in the bulk in Fig. G.1c is as that shown in Fig. G.1b, one would have to allow E_{Fn} to rise eventually as one moves toward the bulk, and assume deep in the bulk the same position relative to E_i as for Fig. G.1b (from Appendix A this would imply some flow of electron current). However, at such points away from the surface, the electron concentration is extremely small, and its exact value does not make any significant difference in the analysis. For simplicity, then, the above equations for $n(y)$ are left unmodified.

The quasi-Fermi level for holes, E_{Fp}, is commonly assumed to remain constant throughout the semiconductor, because the holes do not communicate with the external source V_{CB} in the sense discussed above for electrons. A constant E_{Fp} is consistent with our assumption of zero hole current. Using

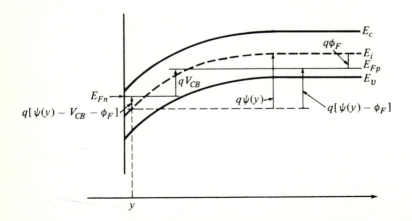

FIGURE G.2

(A.8) for Fig. G.2, we obtain

$$p(y) = n_i e^{[\phi_F - \psi(y)]/\phi_t} \tag{G.4}$$

which, using (1.4.1b), becomes

$$p(y) = p_o e^{\psi(y)/\phi_t} \tag{G.5}$$

Note that, even if E_{Fp} is not exactly constant so that $p(y)$ is not given exactly by the above equations, in inversion holes play a negligible role anyway; hence it is not worth modifying the above equations.

GENERAL ANALYSIS OF THE THREE-TERMINAL MOS STRUCTURE

For the two-terminal MOS structure on a *p*-type substrate the electron concentration at *y* was given by (2.4.13). According to the discussion in Sec. 3.2, this equation can be converted to one valid for the *p*-substrate three-terminal MOS structure of Fig. 3.1*c* by replacing $\psi(y)$ by $\psi(y) - V_{CB}$:

$$n(y) = n_o e^{[\psi(y) - V_{CB}]/\phi_t} \tag{H.1}$$

Assuming that the holes do not communicate directly with the external source in the sense discussed in Sec. 3.2 for electrons,† their concentration will depend only on $\psi(y)$, as was the case in (2.4.14) for the two-terminal structure:

$$p(y) = p_o e^{-\psi(y)/\phi_t} \tag{H.2}$$

---

† See Ref. 1 of Chap. 3. This assumption is not exactly valid because both holes and electrons are responsible for the minute reverse-bias current mentioned in Sec. 3.2.

The above two equations have also been derived and discussed by using energy band concepts in Appendix G. Proceeding now as in Appendix F, we obtain Poisson's equation as follows:

$$\frac{d^2\psi}{dy^2} = -\frac{q}{\epsilon_s}[p_o(e^{-\psi(y)/\phi_t} - 1) - n_o(e^{[\psi(y)-V_{CB}]/\phi_t} - 1)] \tag{H.3}$$

Following the procedure outlined in Appendix F, the solution of the above equation leads to the following results:

$$\mathscr{E}(y) = -\frac{d\psi}{dy}$$

$$= \pm \frac{F\sqrt{N_A}}{\epsilon_s}\sqrt{\phi_t e^{-\psi/\phi_t} + \psi - \phi_t + e^{-2\phi_F/\phi_t}(\phi_t e^{(\psi-V_{CB})/\phi_t} - \psi - \phi_t e^{-V_{CB}/\phi_t})} \tag{H.4}$$

$$Q'_C = \mp F\sqrt{N_A}\sqrt{\phi_t e^{-\psi_s/\phi_t} + \psi_s - \phi_t + e^{-2\phi_F/\phi_t}(\phi_t e^{(\psi_s-V_{CB})/\phi_t} - \psi_s - \phi_t e^{-V_{CB}/\phi_t})} \tag{H.5}$$

$$C'_c = \pm F\sqrt{N_A}\frac{1 - e^{-\psi_s/\phi_t} + e^{-2\phi_F/\phi_t}(e^{(\psi_s-V_{CB})/\phi_t} - 1)}{2\sqrt{\phi_t e^{-\psi_s/\phi_t} + \psi_s - \phi_t + e^{-2\phi_F/\phi_t}(\phi_t e^{(\psi_s-V_{CB})/\phi_t} - \psi_s - \phi_t e^{-V_{CB}/\phi_t})}} \tag{H.6}$$

$$\int_{\psi(y)}^{\psi_s} \frac{d\hat{\psi}}{\mathscr{E}[\hat{\psi}]} = y - y_{surface} \tag{H.7}$$

where $\mathscr{E}[\psi]$ is given by (H.4).

INVERSION

For the inversion region, proceeding as in Appendix F we obtain:

$$Q'_I = -qN_A e^{(-2\phi_F-V_{CB})/\phi_t}\int_0^{\psi_s} \frac{e^{\psi/\phi_t}}{\mathscr{E}[\psi]} d\psi \tag{H.8}$$

$$Q'_B = -qN_A \int_0^{\psi_s} \frac{1 - e^{-\psi/\phi_t}}{\mathscr{E}[\psi]} d\psi \tag{H.9}$$

Deleting negligible terms in (H.5) and using (2.5.2) and (3.2.5a) leads to (3.2.6). Similarly, deleting negligible terms in (H.6) leads to (3.2.11). Finally, using (H.8) in (2.6.13) and (H.9) in (2.6.12) results in explicit expressions for C'_i and C'_b. In these expressions, after deleting terms that are negligible in inversion, we obtain (3.2.12) and (3.2.13).

I

DRAIN CURRENT FORMULATION USING QUASI-FERMI POTENTIALS

In Sec. 4.3 we evaluated the drain current caused by both drift and diffusion. The current components caused by each of these two phenomena were kept separate. In this appendix we present an alternative approach, resulting in a compact formulation which combines the two effects (see Ref. 10 in Chap. 4). We consider the flow of electrons as laminar flow. That is, we assume that the total current I_D is the sum of elemental currents ΔI, each flowing horizontally in an inversion layer slice parallel to the surface, having width W and depth Δy, centered at point y, as shown in Fig. I.1. In the general case, we will have for the current in each slice, allowing Δy to become a differential,

$$dI_D = dI_{\text{drift}}(x, y) + dI_{\text{diff}}(x, y) \qquad (\text{I.1})$$

The drift component is, from (1.3.11a),

$$dI_{\text{drift}}(x, y) = (W\,dy)q\mu n(x, y)\frac{\partial\psi(x, y)}{\partial x} \qquad (\text{I.2})$$

The diffusion component is, from (1.3.17) and (1.3.18),

$$dI_{\text{diff}}(x, y) = -(W\,dy)q\mu\phi_t\,\frac{\partial n(x, y)}{\partial x} \qquad (\text{I.3})$$

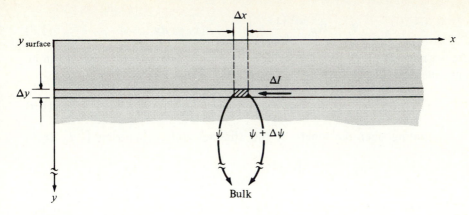

FIGURE I.1

At the source end of the channel, n will be given by (H.1), with $V_{CB} = V_{SB}$, and at the drain end of the channel, n will be given by that relation with $V_{CB} = V_{DB}$. For a position x in the channel, a similar relation can be written with V_{CB} replaced by a quantity $V(x)$:

$$n(x, y) = n_o e^{[\psi(x, y) - V(x)]/\phi_t} \tag{I.4}$$

where $V(0) = V_{SB}$ and $V(L) = V_{DB}$. At points in the channel between source and drain $V(x)$ takes the value required for (I.4) to provide the correct value of $n(x, y)$. In fact, $V(x)$ can be interpreted as the potential corresponding to the difference between the electron quasi-Fermi level in the inversion layer and the hole quasi-Fermi level in the bulk (Appendix G). This quantity is assumed independent of y in the inversion layer, as discussed in Appendix G.

Differentiating (I.4) with respect to x we obtain

$$\frac{\partial n(x, y)}{\partial x} = \frac{n(x, y)}{\phi_t} \left[\frac{\partial \psi(x, y)}{\partial x} - \frac{dV(x)}{dx} \right] \tag{I.5}$$

Using this in (I.3) gives

$$dI_{\text{diff}}(x, y) = -(W\, dy) q \mu n(x, y) \left[\frac{\partial \psi(x, y)}{\partial x} - \frac{dV(x)}{dx} \right] \tag{I.6}$$

Using this and (I.2) in (I.1) we see that the $\partial\psi/\partial x$ terms cancel out, resulting in

$$dI_D = (W\, dy) q \mu n(x, y) \frac{dV(x)}{dx} \tag{I.7}$$

The total drain current can be obtained by integrating over depth from $y = y_{\text{surface}}$ to a point $y = y_c$, below which the electron concentration is negligible:

$$I_D = W\mu \frac{dV(x)}{dx} q \int_{y_{\text{surface}}}^{y_c} n(x, y)\, dy \tag{I.8}$$

where we have assumed that μ is independent of y. The integral times q can be recognized from (2.5.4) as $-Q_I'$ at position x; thus

$$I_D = \mu W(-Q_I') \frac{dV(x)}{dx} \tag{I.9}$$

Integrating over the length of the channel and recognizing $\int_0^L I_D\, dx$ as $I_D L$, we have

$$I_D = \frac{W}{L} \int_{V_{SB}}^{V_{DB}} \mu(-Q_I')\, dV \tag{I.10}$$

Note that the above two relations are of the same form as (4.4.12) and (4.4.13), which were developed by starting from strong-inversion assumptions. However, it is clear from the above development that (I.9) and (I.10) are actually very general. They are valid in all regions of operation, since they include both drift and diffusion effects. The development of Sec. 4.4 following (4.4.13) cannot be used here, since Q_I' in (4.4.16) is only valid in strong inversion. A more general expression for Q_I' must be used. Depending on the expression used for Q_I' in conjunction with (I.10), different formulations are possible. These are shown below.

CHARGE SHEET MODEL

In the charge sheet model (Sec. 4.3), Q_I' is known as a function of the surface potential ψ_s [see (4.3.15)]. Thus a change of variables from V to ψ_s is made in (I.10):

$$I_D = \frac{W}{L} \int_{\psi_{s0}}^{\psi_{sL}} \mu(-Q_I') \frac{dV}{d\psi_s}\, d\psi_s \tag{I.11}$$

where V is related to ψ_s by an equation analogous to (4.3.18):

$$\psi = V_{GB} - V_{FB} - \gamma\sqrt{\psi_s + \phi_t e^{(\psi_s - 2\phi_F - V)/\phi_t}} \tag{I.12}$$

The quantity $dV/d\psi_s$ can be found from this and substituted in (I.11) to determine the current. This results in a rather lengthy development.† The technique we have presented in Sec. 4.3 is more straightforward.

PAO-SAH MODEL

In this model (Ref. 10 in Chap. 4) no simplifying assumptions are made, in the sense that both electrons and holes are allowed to exist in the depletion region.

---

† See Refs. 53–59 in Chap. 4.

This results, as expected from (H.8), to

$$Q'_I = -qN_A e^{(-2\phi_F - V)/\phi_t} \int_{\psi_c}^{\psi_s} \frac{e^{\psi/\phi_t}}{\mathscr{E}[\psi]} \, d\psi \tag{I.13}$$

where, consistent with our present convention, we consider the electrons between the surface and a depth beyond which the electron concentration becomes negligible. The potential at that point with respect to the substrate is denoted by ψ_c. A convenient depth is that at which $n = n_i$. From (I.4) and (1.4.1a) we easily see that the corresponding potential is $\psi_c = \phi_F + V$. The quantity $\mathscr{E}[\psi]$ in (I.13) is given in (H.4), with V_{CB} replaced by V. Using (I.13) in (I.10) we obtain

$$I_D = \frac{W}{L} \, qN_A \int_{V_{SB}}^{V_{DB}} \mu \int_{\psi_c}^{\psi_s} \frac{e^{(\psi - 2\phi_F - V)/\phi_t}}{\mathscr{E}[\psi]} \, d\psi \, dV \tag{I.14}$$

This double integral can be evaluated numerically. The resulting computation times are long, so this formulation is mainly of theoretical interest. The charge sheet model gives nearly the same results and is much simpler. A technique to reduce (I.14) to a single-integral formula (which must still be evaluated numerically) has been proposed (see Ref. 62 in Chap. 4).

APPENDIX
J

RESULTS OF DETAILED FORMULATIONS FOR THE DRAIN CURRENT AND DRAIN SMALL-SIGNAL CONDUCTANCE IN THE SATURATION REGION

The results of some detailed analyses of the saturation region are given in this appendix. These results are provided here as examples in order to demonstrate the complexity involved in such analysis. The reader should consult the references provided for the detailed derivations, discussions of the ranges of validity, etc.

It has been suggested[1] that the complex picture of the field in the pinchoff region (Sec. 5.2), including the effect on it by the gate, can be taken into account if the effective channel length reduction ΔL is modeled by the following semiempirical expression:

$$\Delta L = \left(\frac{1}{B_5\sqrt{V_{DS} - V'_{DS}}} + \frac{\epsilon_{ox}}{\epsilon_s} \frac{1}{d_{ox}} \frac{U}{V_{DS} - V'_{DS}} \right)^{-1} \tag{J.1}$$

where $B_5 = (2\epsilon_s/qN_A)^{1/2}$, ϵ_{ox} and ϵ_s are the permittivity of the oxide and of the semiconductor, respectively, d_{ox} is the oxide thickness, and

$$U = B_6(V_{DS} - V'_{GS}) + B_7(V'_{GS} - V'_{DS}) \tag{J.2}$$

with $V'_{GS} = V_{GS} + Q'_o/C'_{ox}$, and B_6, B_7 are constants independent of oxide thickness or substrate doping concentration; it has empirically been found[1] that typically $B_6 = 0.2$ and $B_7 = 0.6$. The drain current in saturation can be determined by using (J.1) in (5.2.5). From (J.1),

$$\frac{d(\Delta L)}{dV_{DS}} = \frac{(1/2B_5)(V_{DS} - V'_{DS})^{1/2} + (\epsilon_{ox}/\epsilon_s d_{ox})(B_7 - B_6)(V'_{GS} - V'_{DS})}{(1/B_5^2)(V_{DS} - V'_{DS}) + (\epsilon_{ox}/\epsilon_s d_{ox})^2 U^2 + (2\epsilon_{ox}/B_5\epsilon_s d_{ox})(V_{DS} - V'_{DS})^{1/2}U} \tag{J.3}$$

Using this, the drain small-signal conductance g_d can be determined from (8.2.22) or (8.2.23).

A variation of the above model leads to the following result[2, 3]

$$\Delta L = (B_9 L + B_{10} d_{ox}) \frac{\sqrt{(V_{DS} - V'_{DS})^2 + B_{11}} + V_{DS} - \sqrt{V'^2_{DS} + B_{11}}}{A_{DG}[V_{DS} - (V_{GS} - V_T)] + B_{GS}(V_{GS} - V_T)} \tag{J.4}$$

where B_9 and B_{10} are empirically chosen parameters, $B_{11} = 0.02\ \mathrm{V}^2$, $A_{DG} \approx 0.5$ to 2.0, $B_{GS} \approx 0.7$ to 4.0, and A_{DG} must be smaller than B_{GS}. The drain current in saturation can be determined by using the above equation in (5.2.5). From the above we obtain

$$\frac{d(\Delta L)}{dV_{DS}} = (B_9 L + B_{10} d_{ox})$$

$$\times \left\{ \frac{1 + (V_{DS} - V'_{DS})/\sqrt{(V_{DS} - V'_{DS})^2 + B_{11}}}{A_{DG}[V_{DS} - (V_{GS} - V_T)] + B_{GS}(V_{GS} - V_T)} \right.$$

$$\left. - \frac{A_{DG}(\sqrt{(V_{DS} - V'_{DS})^2 + B_{11}} + V_{DS} - \sqrt{V'^2_{DS} + B_{11}})}{\{A_{DG}[V_{DS} - (V_{GS} - V_T)] + B_{GS}(V_{GS} - V_T)\}^2} \right\} \tag{J.5}$$

which can be substituted in (8.2.22) or (8.2.23) to determine g_d.

A different formulation takes into account the drain junction depth and its influence on the inversion layer shape in the vicinity of that junction.[4] The following relation between I_D and V_{DS} in saturation is derived:

$$V_{DS} - V'_{DS} = \frac{qN_A L^2}{2\epsilon_s} \left(1 - \frac{I'_D}{I_D} \right)^2 \left[1 + \frac{2I_D}{qN_A W|v_d|_{max} r} \left(\log \frac{r}{d_i} - 1 \right) \right]$$

$$+ L\mathscr{E}_1 \left(1 - \frac{I'_D}{I_D} \right) \tag{J.6}$$

where $|v_d|_{max}$ is the magnitude of the maximum (saturated) velocity of carriers in the pinchoff region, $\mathscr{E}_1$ the approximate value of field intensity at which velocity saturation is reached (roughly $|v_d|_{max}/\mu$; see Fig. 5.4 and the associated discussion), r is the drain junction depth, and d_i is the average thickness of the inversion layer (assumed much smaller than r and taken to be typically 100 Å). Differentiation of this equation gives the following value for g_d (Sec. 8.2):

$$g_d = \left\{ \frac{qN_AL^2}{2\epsilon_s} \left(1 - \frac{I'_D}{I_D}\right)\left[2\frac{I'_D}{I_D^2} + \left(1 + \frac{I'_D}{I_D}\right)\frac{2}{qN_AWv_{max}r}\left(\log\frac{r}{di} - 1\right)\right]\right.$$

$$\left. + L\mathscr{E}_1\frac{I'_D}{I_D^2}\right\}^{-1} \tag{J.7}$$

REFERENCES

1. D. Frohman Bentchkowski and A.S. Grove, "Conductance of MOS Transistors in Saturation," *IEEE Transactions on Electron Devices*, vol. ED-16, pp. 108–113, January 1969.
2. H. C. Poon, "V_{th} and beyond," presented at the Workshop on Device Modeling for VLSI, Burlingame, Calif., March 1979; also, L. Cong, Bell Laboratories, private communication.
3. S. Liu and L. W. Nagel, "Small-signal MOSFET models for analog circuit design," *IEEE Journal of Solid-State Circuits*, vol. SC-17, pp. 983–998, December 1982.
4. G. Merckel, J. Borel, and N. Z. Cupcea, "An accurate large-signal MOS transistor model for use in computer-aided design," *IEEE Transactions on Electron Devices*, vol. ED-19, pp. 681–690, May 1972.

EVALUATION
OF THE
INTRINSIC
TRANSIENT
SOURCE
AND DRAIN
CURRENTS

We present here a proof[1] of certain statements made in Sec. 7.3 for the intrinsic part of a MOS transistor. The continuity equation is, from (7.7.5),

$$\frac{\partial i(x, t)}{\partial x} = W \frac{\partial q'_I(x, t)}{\partial t} \tag{K.1}$$

Integrating with respect to x from the source to a point x in the channel, we obtain

$$i(x, t) - i(0, t) = W \int_0^x \frac{\partial q'_I(\hat{x}, t)}{\partial t} \, d\hat{x} \tag{K.2}$$

where $\hat{x}$ is a dummy variable of integration. Recognizing $i(0, t)$ as $-i_S(t)$ (see the direction of i in Fig. 7.13), and using (7.7.6b) for $i(x, t)$ we obtain:

$$i_S(t) = \mu W q'_I(x, t) \frac{\partial v_{CB}(x, t)}{\partial x} + W \int_0^x \frac{\partial q'_I(\hat{x}, t)}{\partial t} \, d\hat{x} \tag{K.3}$$

Multiplying both sides by dx, integrating from $x = 0$ to $x = L$, and dividing both sides by L gives

485

$$i_S(t) = \frac{W}{L} \int_0^L \mu q_I'(x, t) \frac{\partial v_{CB}(x, t)}{\partial x} dx + \frac{W}{L} \int_0^L \int_0^x \frac{\partial q_I'(\hat{x}, t)}{\partial t} d\hat{x} \, dx \tag{K.4}$$

Interchanging the order of integration and differentiation in the second term, we obtain

$$i_S(t) = \frac{W}{L} \int_0^L \mu q_I'(x, t) \frac{\partial v_{CB}(x, t)}{\partial x} dx + \frac{d}{dt} \left[\frac{W}{L} \int_0^L \int_0^x q_I'(\hat{x}, t) \, d\hat{x} \, dx \right] \tag{K.5}$$

The double integral is of the form $\int_0^L G(x) \, dx$, where $G(x) = \int_0^x q_I'(\hat{x}, t) \, d\hat{x}$. Applying integration by parts to $\int_0^L G(x) \, dx$, with G and x the two variables involved, we can write (K.5) as follows:

$$i_S(t) = -\frac{W}{L} \int_0^L \mu[-q_I'(x, t)] \frac{dv_{CB}(x, t)}{dx} dx + \frac{d}{dt} \left[W \int_0^L \left(1 - \frac{x}{L}\right) q_I'(x, t) \, dx \right] \tag{K.6}$$

Comparing the first term to the right-hand side of (4.4.13), we see that, in quasi-static operation, this term will produce the same current expressions as in Sec. 4.4, only with a minus sign and with the terminal voltages as functions of time. We can then write (K.6) as

$$i_S(t) = -i_T(t) + \frac{dq_S}{dt} \tag{K.7}$$

where $i_T(t)$ will be of the form of (7.3.12), and

$$q_S = W \int_0^L \left(1 - \frac{x}{L}\right) q_I' \, dx \tag{K.8}$$

To find $i_D(t) = i(L, t)$ in quasi-static operation, we use $x = L$ in (K.2) and substitute in it (K.7) and (K.8), which gives

$$i_D(t) = i_T(t) + \frac{dq_D}{dt} \tag{K.9}$$

with
$$q_D = W \int_0^L \frac{x}{L} q_I' \, dx \tag{K.10}$$

Since quasi-static operation is assumed, (K.8) and (K.10) can be evaluated by using the dc charge per unit area Q_I' instead of q_I'. The resulting quantities have been denoted by Q_S and Q_D, respectively, in (7.3.9b) and (7.3.9a). The detailed evaluation of Q_S and Q_D is considered in Sec. 7.4.

A NOTE ON q_D and q_S

If desired, $q_D(t)$ can be defined as $\int_{-\infty}^t [i_D(\tau) - i_T(\tau)] \, d\tau = \int_{-\infty}^t i_{DC}(\tau) \, d\tau$, where τ is a dummy variable of integration and $q_S(t)$ as $\int_{-\infty}^t [i_S(\tau) + i_T(\tau)] \, d\tau = \int_{-\infty}^t i_{SC}(\tau) \, d\tau$ (i_{DC} and i_{SC} are the "charging" currents discussed in Sec. 7.3).

These definitions imply (7.3.6) and, by integrating (7.3.5), we see that they satisfy (7.3.8) (assuming that the channel was "empty" at $t = -\infty$). With these definitions, $q_D(t)$ can be interpreted as the part contributed to $q_I(t)$ by the deviation of i_D from i_T, from the "beginning of time" to the instant t. Similarly, $q_S(t)$ can be interpreted as the part contributed to $q_I(t)$ by the corresponding deviation of i_S from $- i_T(t)$. Although the above definitions may be elegant, they can confuse the issue: q_D and q_S cannot be found stored in any particular place, and neither can they be associated with specific charges that have been flowing by themselves through any terminal. This is because $i_{DC}(t)$ and $i_{SC}(t)$ are mere artifacts, each being the difference between *real* terminal currents and the values such terminal currents *would* have *if* one attempted to predict them by dc theory [see (7.3.4)]. Also, the above definitions for q_D and q_S tend to assign specific significance to the *values* of these fictitious charges, when all that matters is their *derivatives* [see (7.3.6)]. Assume q_D and q_S defined as above are given by two functions f_D and f_S, respectively, giving the correct values for i_{DC} and i_{SC} from (7.3.6). The quantities q_D and q_S satisfy (7.3.8), as already noted. Now let us redefine q_D and q_S as $f_D + K$ and $f_S + L$, respectively, where K and L are arbitrary constants. Then (7.3.6) will still predict the correct values of i_{DC} and i_{SC}. Equation (7.3.8) will, in general, not hold now, but this is of *no* consequence and does *not* mean that charge conservation is violated. This is because, since i_{DC} and i_{SC} are still predicted correctly, they still satisfy (7.3.5) and (7.3.3). Integrating (7.3.3), one sees that the total charge that entered the device through source and drain up to time t *is* equal to $q_I(t)$, and thus the charge *is* conserved.

REFERENCE

1. D. E. Ward, "Charge-based modeling of capacitance in MOS transistors," Technical Report G201-11, Integrated Circuits Laboratory, Stanford University, June 1981.

APPENDIX
L

CHARGES FOR THE ACCURATE STRONG-INVERSION MODEL

Using the charges per unit area as they correspond to the accurate strong-inversion model of Sec. 4.4.1 [(4.4.15) and (4.4.16)], and proceeding as in Sec. 7.4.2, we obtain for the nonsaturation region[1]

$$Q_B = -WLC'_{ox} \frac{\frac{2}{3}\gamma U_G(U_D^{3/2} - U_S^{3/2}) - \frac{1}{2}\gamma^2(U_D^2 - U_S^2) - \frac{2}{5}\gamma(U_D^{5/2} - U_S^{5/2})}{\hat{g}(U_G, U_D, U_S)}$$

(L.1)

$$Q_I = -WLC'_{ox}\left[\frac{U_G^2(U_D - U_S) - \frac{4}{3}\gamma U_G(U_D^{3/2} - U_S^{3/2})}{\hat{g}(U_G, U_D, U_S)} \right.$$
$$\left. - \frac{(U_G - \gamma^2/2)(U_D^2 - U_S^2) + \frac{4}{5}\gamma(U_D^{5/2} - U_S^{5/2}) + \frac{1}{3}(U_D^3 - U_S^3)}{\hat{g}(U_G, U_D, U_S)} \right]$$

(L.2)

$$Q_G = WLC'_{ox}\left[\frac{U_G^2(U_D - U_S) - \frac{2}{3}\gamma U_G(U_D^{3/2} - U_S^{3/2})}{\hat{g}(U_G, U_D, U_S)} \right.$$
$$\left. - \frac{U_G(U_D^2 - U_S^2) + \frac{2}{5}\gamma(U_D^{5/2} - U_S^{5/2}) + \frac{1}{3}(U_D^3 - U_S^3)}{\hat{g}(U_G, U_D, U_S)} \right] - Q_o$$

(L.3)

with

$$\hat{g}(U_G, U_D, U_S) = U_G(U_D - U_S) - \tfrac{2}{3}\gamma(U_D^{3/2} - U_S^{3/2}) - \tfrac{1}{2}(U_D^2 - U_S^2) \tag{L.4}$$

where

$$U_G = V_{GB} - V_{FB} \tag{L.5}$$

$$U_D = V_{DB} + \phi_B \tag{L.6}$$

$$U_S = V_{SB} + \phi_B \tag{L.7}$$

In saturation, of course, V_{DB} should be replaced by $V'_{DB} = V'_{DS} + V_{SB}$, with V'_{DS} given by (4.4.18).

The above expressions have the problem that the numerator and de- nominator become zero as $U_D - U_S$ goes to zero. This problem can be bypassed if one factors out the quantity $U_D^{1/2} - U_S^{1/2}$ from numerator and denominator.[1]

Sometimes simpler, empirical expressions are used in conjunction with this model. In choosing such expressions, one should seek to preserve the symmetry inherent in the model. Also, the expressions should be such that charge saturation is attained at the same voltage combinations as drain current saturation. For example, an empirical expression for Q_I in nonsaturation that satisfies these requirements is[2]

$$Q_I = -C'_{ox}WL \frac{2}{3}\left(V_1 + V_2 - \frac{V_1 V_2}{V_1 + V_2}\right) \tag{L.8}$$

where

$$V_1 = V_{GS} - V_T(V_{SB}) \tag{L.9}$$

$$V_2 = V_{GD} - V_T(V_{DB}) \tag{L.10}$$

and

$$V_T(V_{SB}) = V_{FB} + \phi_B + \gamma\sqrt{\phi_B + V_{SB}} \tag{L.11}$$

$$V_T(V_{DB}) = V_{FB} + \phi_B + \gamma\sqrt{\phi_B + V_{DB}} \tag{L.12}$$

By using two different thresholds as corresponding to the source and drain biases, total symmetry is ensured for Q_I with respect to V_S and V_D. In saturation at the drain, Q_I can be obtained by using $V_{GD} = V_T(V_{DB})$, i.e., $V_2 = 0$; it is easy to see that this results in (7.4.27).

The Q_D and Q_S expressions resulting from exact calculations for the accurate strong-inversion model of Sec. 4.4.1 are *extremely* complicated. Thus for these two charges the use of empirical expressions is practically a must. Two such expressions are[1]

$$Q_D \approx \tfrac{2}{5}Q_{I,\text{sat}} + \tfrac{7}{10}(Q_I - Q_{I,\text{sat}}) \tag{L.13}$$

$$Q_S \approx \tfrac{3}{5}Q_{I,\text{sat}} + \tfrac{3}{10}(Q_I - Q_{I,\text{sat}}) \tag{L.14}$$

where Q_I can be modeled empirically as discussed above. It is easy to see that, in saturation, (L.13) and (L.14) reduce to (7.4.28) and (7.4.29), respectively. Note that the above empirical expressions for Q_D and Q_S can be used in conjunction with the approximate model as well in lieu of (7.4.19) and (7.4.20).

Attempting to calculate capacitances from the charges corresponding to the accurate strong-inversion model results in very complicated expressions.[3] One thus resorts to empirical approximations. For C_{gs} and C_{gd} the following approximations have been proposed:

$$C_{gs} = \frac{2}{3} C_{ox} \left[1 - \left(\frac{V_2}{V_1 + V_2} \right)^2 \right] \tag{L.15}$$

$$C_{gd} = \frac{2}{3} C_{ox} \left[1 - \left(\frac{V_1}{V_1 + V_2} \right)^2 \right] \tag{L.16}$$

with V_1 and V_2 defined in (L.9) to (L.12). The above expressions exhibit the symmetry characteristic of the accurate strong-inversion model. In saturation at the drain, we have $V_2 = 0$; this gives $C_{gs} = \frac{2}{3} C_{ox}$ and $C_{gd} = 0$, in agreement with (8.3.27) and (8.3.29).

REFERENCES

1. D. E. Ward, " Charge-based modeling of capacitances in MOS transistors," Technical Report G201-11, Integrated Circuits Laboratory, Stanford University, June, 1981.
2. F. M. Klaassen, "A MOS model for computer-aided design," *Philips Research Reports*, vol. 31, pp. 71–83, 1976.
3. R. S. C. Cobbold, *Theory and Application of Field-Effect Transistors*, Wiley-Interscience, New York, 1970.

QUANTITIES USED IN THE DERIVATION OF THE NONQUASI-STATIC y-PARAMETER MODEL

Expressions for y-parameters, including nonquasi-static effects, have been given in (9.4.58) to (9.4.60). In these expressions, the numerators $N_{kl}(\omega)$ (where $k, l = d, g, b$) are of the form

$$N_{kl}(\omega) = n_{kl0} + (j\omega)n_{kl1} + (j\omega)^2 n_{kl2} + \cdots$$

and the denominator $D(\omega)$ is of the form

$$D(\omega) = d_0 + (j\omega)d_1 + (j\omega)^2 d_2 + \cdots$$

The coefficients in the above relations can be found as discussed in Sec. 9.4.2; the results are given below. Some of these results apply to the three-terminal transistor, with $\delta_1 = 0$;[1] all the results apply to the four-terminal transistor with $\delta_1 \neq 0$.[2]

$$n_{dd0} = \frac{W}{L} \mu C'_{ox}(V_{GS} - V_T)\alpha = g_d$$

$$n_{dg0} = \frac{W}{L} \mu C'_{ox} \frac{V_{GS} - V_T}{1 + \delta_1} (1 - \alpha) = g_m$$

$$n_{db0} = \delta_1 n_{dg0} = g_{mb}$$

$$n_{gd0} = n_{gg0} = n_{bd0} = n_{gb0} = n_{bg0} = n_{bb0} = 0$$

$$n_{dd1} = \frac{2}{3}(1 + \delta_1) C_{ox} \frac{\alpha(2 + \alpha)}{(1 + \alpha)^2}$$

$$n_{dg1} = n_{gd1} = -\frac{2}{3} C_{ox} \frac{\alpha(2 + \alpha)}{(1 + \alpha)^2}$$

$$n_{db1} = \delta_1 n_{dg1}$$

$$n_{gg1} = C_{ox} \left[\frac{2}{3(1 + \delta_1)} \frac{1 + 4\alpha + \alpha^2}{(1 + \alpha)^2} + \frac{\delta_1}{1 + \delta_1} \right]$$

$$n_{gb1} = n_{bg1} = -\frac{\delta_1}{3(1 + \delta_1)} C_{ox} \left(\frac{1 - \alpha}{1 + \alpha} \right)^2$$

$$n_{bd1} = \delta_1 n_{gd1}$$

$$n_{bb1} = C_{ox} \left[\frac{\delta_1}{1 + \delta_1} + \frac{2\delta_1^2}{3(1 + \delta_1)} \frac{1 + 4\alpha + \alpha^2}{(1 + \alpha)^2} \right]$$

$$n_{dd2} = \frac{C_{ox}}{\omega_o} \frac{2}{45}(1 + \delta_1) \frac{\alpha(5 + 8\alpha + 2\alpha^2)}{(1 + \alpha)^4}$$

$$n_{dg2} = n_{gd2} = -\frac{C_{ox}}{\omega_o} \frac{2}{45} \frac{\alpha(5 + 8\alpha + 2\alpha^2)}{(1 + \alpha)^4}$$

$$n_{db2} = \delta_1 n_{dg2}$$

$$n_{gg2} = \frac{C_{ox}}{\omega_o} \left[\frac{2}{45} \frac{1}{1 + \delta_1} \frac{2 + 11\alpha + 2\alpha^2}{(1 + \alpha)^2} + \frac{4}{15} \frac{\delta_1}{1 + \delta_1} \frac{1 + 3\alpha + \alpha^2}{(1 + \alpha)^3} \right]$$

$$n_{gb2} = n_{bg2} = -\frac{C_{ox}}{\omega_o} \frac{2}{45} \frac{\delta_1}{1 + \delta_1} \frac{4 + 7\alpha + 4\alpha^2}{(1 + \alpha)^3}$$

$$n_{bd2} = \delta_1 n_{gd2}$$

$$n_{bb2} = \frac{C_{ox}}{\omega_o} \left[\frac{4}{15} \frac{\delta_1}{1 + \delta_1} \frac{1 + 3\alpha + \alpha^2}{(1 + \alpha)^3} + \frac{2}{45} \frac{\delta_1^2}{1 + \delta_1} \frac{2 + 11\alpha + 2\alpha^2}{(1 + \alpha)^3} \right]$$

$$d_0 = 1$$

$$d_1 = \frac{4}{15} \frac{1}{\omega_o} \frac{1 + 3\alpha + \alpha^2}{(1 + \alpha)^3}$$

$$d_2 = \frac{1}{45} \frac{1}{\omega_o^2} \frac{1 + 4\alpha + \alpha^2}{(1 + \alpha)^4}$$

where

$$C_{ox} = C'_{ox} WL$$

$$\omega_o = \frac{\mu(V_{GS} - V_T)}{(1 + \delta_1)L^2}$$

$$\alpha = \begin{cases} 1 - \dfrac{V_{DS}}{V'_{DS}}, & V_{DS} \leq V'_{DS} \\ 0, & V_{DS} > V'_{DS} \end{cases}$$

and, according to the simplifying assumptions stated in the beginning of Sec. 9.4.2,

$$\delta_1 = \frac{\gamma}{2\sqrt{\phi_B + V_{SB}}}$$

As explained in Sec. 9.4, the accuracy of the expressions containing δ_1 can be improved if δ_1 is replaced by an empirical parameter which, in general, would not be the same for all expressions; a related discussion can be found in Sec. 8.3.

REFERENCES

1. J. J. Paulos and D. Antoniadis, "Limitations of quasi-static models for the MOS transistor," *IEEE Electron Device Letters*, vol. ED-4, pp. 221–224, July 1983.
2. M. Bagheri and Y. Tsividis, "A small-signal non-quasi-static model for the four-terminal MOSFET valid in all regions of operation," *IEEE Transactions on Electron Devices*, vol. ED-32, pp. 2383–2391, November 1985.

INDEX